10,000 Answers

*

The Ultimate Trivia Encyclopedia

10,000 Answers

The Ultimate **Trivia** Encyclopedia

Stanley Newman
and Hal Fittipaldi

RANDOM HOUSE REFERENCE
New York

Visit the Random House Reference Web site at
www.randomwords.com

Typeset and printed in the United States of America

Library of Congress Cataloging-in-Publication Data is available

First Edition
0 9 8 7 6 5 4 3 2 1
October 2001

ISBN: 0-375-71944-X
New York Toronto London Sydney Auckland

To my wife Marlene,
and children Amanda, Marc, and Bob,
the four most important names I've written for the book

—S.N.

In loving memory of my dad,
Dominic "The Silver Fox" Fittipaldi, whose quest
for knowledge was imparted to me throughout his lifetime

—H.F.

Contents

Foreword

As *The New York Times* crossword puzzle editor, whose desk is surrounded by 55 feet 6 inches (or thereabouts) of reference books, I know a thing or two about fact-checking.

Every clue in every puzzle needs to be accurate, and for *The Times* this means verifying or composing more than thirty thousand clues a year.

My most-used references, not surprisingly, are dictionaries, thesauruses, encyclopedias, and almanacs. But I have specialized books on geography, biography, historical events, literature, film, classical music, opera, theater, rock and roll, TV, mythology, sports, food, brand names, Shakespeare, the Bible, and virtually any other subject you can think of. God forbid there is a mistake! Solvers love to catch me making a mistake.

Over the years I've noticed that certain kinds of facts are hard to verify or find in traditional references. This is because either they don't fit in the usual broad categories (say, the names of Olympic mascots—where can you find a list of those?) or they're just too "trivial" (the name of George Washington's Arabian stallion, perhaps, or the secret identity of the cartoon hero Underdog).

Now to the rescue comes Stanley Newman, a colleague of mine who edits crosswords for *Newsday* and other newspapers, and Hal Fittipaldi, director of the Super Bowl of Trivia. They've compiled more than ten thousand entries in this encyclopedia of trivia, focusing on fun yet useful bits of information that generally can't conveniently be found anywhere else.

The result is a joy to browse through, as well as a godsend for a fact-checker like myself, for whom this volume will be positioned front and center among the 55 feet **8 inches** (or thereabouts) of reference books around my desk.

—Will Shortz

Acknowledgments

No one has all the answers. No two, either.

A great many publishing colleagues, friends, trivia comrades-in-arms, even some people that neither of us has ever met, have helped to make this book a reality.

At Random House:

Charles Levine, former publisher of Random House Reference, who immediately understood the book from our two-page proposal, and signed us up to do it. Thank you, Charles.

Sheryl Stebbins and Chad Bunning, respectively the current publishing director and associate publisher of Random House Reference, for their enthusiasm and support.

Helen Langone, who patiently guided us through the massive job of typing, coding, and indexing the manuscript.

Wendalyn Nichols, our editor, who polished our prose to a high gloss.

Beth Levy, who made sure every production step was done right and on time.

Beth Weinstein, who assisted in numerous editorial and production matters.

Martha Trachtenberg, the world's best copy editor. We were fortunate indeed to be the beneficiary of her legendary thoroughness.

Heidi North and Lynn Bennett, for the wonderful cover.

Sales execs Sid Albert and Dave Thompson, for their encouragement.

The diversity of material in the book is reflected by the wide-ranging fields of the professionals who graciously responded to our requests for information:

Marty Appel of Topps, Inc. (who kindly granted permission to use the Mark McGwire card on the cover).

April Brazill of the Floyd Memorial Library in Greenport, New York.

Stacy Gabrielle of Binney & Smith, Inc. (Crayola crayons).

Steve Gelfand (TV theme songs).

Cecilio Leonin of the U.S. Department of Transportation (Interstate highway data).

Dr. Steve Lomazow (America's preeminent expert on magazines' first issues).

Chris Lucas of the Mayor's Press Office, New York City (ticker-tape parades).

Karen Rosa of the American Humane Association (PATSY Awards).

Mary Ann Skinner of *Newsday* (cover photos).

Les Waas of the Procrastinators' Club (Procrastinator of the Year awards).

John Williams and Joe Edley of the National Scrabble Association.

And the many anonymous corporate-relations people who answered our questions by phone and e-mail. The two most memorable of these: the Baskin Robbins representative who read us the names of the thirty-one original flavors over the phone, and the McDonald's representative who confirmed via e-mail the average number of sesame seeds on a Big Mac bun.

Nine people reviewed the unfinished manuscript in various stages. They not only contributed greatly to the factual and typographical accuracy of the book, but they also helped us decide what to include and exclude. A big "thank you" to: Don Albright, Carl Cope, Jon Delfin, Mike Dupée, Mike Gessner, Ray Hamel, Douglas Lyons, Jeffrey Lyons, and Trip Payne. And a big, big "thank you" to Mike G., Ray, and Trip, who each provided many suggestions for entries.

Other friends and colleagues who offered helpful suggestions and comments: George Bredehorn, Bill Deutch, Bob Francis, Peter Gordon, Dave Guiang, Helene Hovanec, Judy-Michelle Jones, Liz Lesnick, Joel Lipman, Dave Pizzo, Hilton Rahn, Tom Reilly, Mel Rosen, Randy Ross, Jim Rudolph, L. Sabol, Nancy Schuster, Will Shortz, and Richard Silvestri. Thanks also, Will, for the thoughtful Foreword.

Finally, the person who, besides the authors, worked the longest and hardest on the book deserves special recognition: Donna Heidecker, who did all of the keyboarding of Hal's entries and much of the research and verification for them. We couldn't have done it without you.

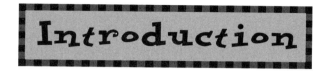
Introduction

Welcome to *10,000 Answers*, which is really two books in one:

An authoritative reference book, where you can quickly find thousands of useful facts (on hundreds of subjects) that can't easily be found elsewhere, and

A trivia book designed to reward the random browser with fun tidbits on every page.

Each of these two books had its own separate inspiration. The inspiration for the "reference" book came from my "day job" as a crossword professional—I've been Puzzle Editor for the New York newspaper *Newsday* for the past thirteen years.

It's up to me to make sure that every clue in the 365 crosswords I edit each year is accurate. And I have a pretty big library of reference books to help me. But there always seem to be facts that are either not in any of my books, or are highly inconvenient to find. For example:

- The names of the Seven Dwarfs, the one that doesn't have a beard, the one that wears glasses, etc.
- The colleges whose athletic teams have a certain nickname. (Almanacs alphabetize this information by college name rather than nickname.)
- The composer of the "Clock Symphony." (To find it in standard music references, you have to know who composed it.)

So, one reason I decided to compile this book was to be able to find the facts I couldn't find in my other books.

Inspiration for the "trivia" book came from my lifelong interest in learning new facts. I still remember the first almanac my parents bought for me when I was nine years old. I was mesmerized by the amount and variety of information it contained. World capitals, baseball records, presidential biographies—the subject didn't matter, it was all fascinating to me. From my childhood to today, I have always enjoyed discovering interesting facts I didn't know before. It has been an added pleasure to share my favorite discoveries with my friends, such as:

- What Paul Revere *really* shouted on the night of his famous ride (not "The British are coming!").
- The two towns that renamed themselves for football stars (you may have heard of Jim Thorpe, Pennsylvania, but what about Joe, Montana?).
- The only TV commercial ever done by Elvis Presley.

So the other main reason for compiling this book was to share with you my lifetime accumulation of fun facts.

Once I decided to do the book, I knew that I shouldn't do it alone. I felt certain that a collaborator with a background and knowledge base different from mine would make for a better book. That's how Hal Fittipaldi, director of the trivia competitions I've attended in Allentown, Pennsylvania, for the past ten years, came to be involved. Hal happily agreed with my "two books in one" objective, and his entries have brought all the diversity to the book that I had hoped for. (Hal's own Introduction follows this one.)

Our first job was to decide how the information in the book should be organized. Here Hal and I were of one mind. Like many trivia fans Hal and I know, our all-time favorite trivia book is Fred Worth's cult classic, *The Complete Unabridged Super Trivia Encyclopedia,* originally published in the 1970s, and long out of print. What we like most about it: the massive amount of information in all fields, the A-to-Z organization by "trivia fact" rather than subject, and the interesting lists. Open up the book at random, and you're likely to find entries on sitcoms and the Civil War on the same page. The organization of *10,000 Answers* is thus inspired by Worth's classic volume, with one major difference: the Worth book has no index (which makes it tough to find any particular fact), so this book does.

How did we decide what to include in the book? We knew we wanted to give equal importance to popular culture and more academic subjects, as the cover of the book illustrates so well. We then started outlining topics within each subject, as well as some "interdisciplinary" categories, such as nicknames of famous people.

In deciding what specific entries to include, as well as what to exclude, we were guided primarily by the "fun" and "hard to find elsewhere" objectives previously mentioned. Take film roles, for example. With thousands of roles to choose from, we decided to concentrate on two areas we felt would be the most useful and fun: Academy Award-winning roles (we believe this is the first book of any kind to include all Oscar roles), and funny names—like those of W. C. Fields and Groucho Marx. Every other topic, from sports to TV to U.S. presidents, went through a similarly thoughtful process.

Verifying the accuracy of every fact in the book was of paramount importance to us. Many entries in this book come from "pri-mary" sources, thus additional corroboration wasn't necessary. For example, I counted the number of words in Lincoln's Gettysburg Address myself. Twice. And we obtained the height of $1 million in U.S. $100 bills directly from the Bureau of Engraving and Printing.

Every entry not obtained from a primary source was verified from two reliable "secondary" sources, such as encyclopedias, almanacs, specialized reference books, and the Internet. Yes, the Internet.

The Internet is undoubtedly the largest source of information ever invented. But, as every Web user knows, the accuracy of the facts to be found on the Internet is rather less than 100 percent. Nevertheless, if one knows how and where to look, the Internet is filled with untold riches of trivia. The key to unlocking those riches is knowing how to tell "right" from "wrong." Hal and I found much useful information in "primary-source" Web sites, like those of consumer-products companies and pro-sports leagues. There were many "secondary-source" Web sites that we found we could trust, such as those of major magazines and cable networks.

Where we also found the Internet surprisingly helpful was in the accidental discovery of wonderful sources that we weren't specifically looking for. To give you just one example, while using an Internet search engine to verify the name of Sean Connery's production company, we discovered a Screen Actors Guild Web site that listed the production companies of dozens of other stars. These sorts of serendipitous discoveries helped us to cover many subjects more completely than we would have been able to otherwise. And they led us to some great new material that we were able to verify elsewhere.

There's a lot more I could say about the book and how it was put together, but I'll let the book do the rest of the talking.

Be sure to read the "How to Use This Book" section, which you should find helpful in getting the most out of the book.

Whether you use it primarily for reference or for entertainment, Hal and I hope *10,000 Answers* becomes a trusted friend that you'll keep handy and visit often.

—Stanley Newman

Trivia is about remembering. It's about being and staying a kid at heart. Like many of my baby boomer contemporaries, I have always cherished the nostalgic memories of my youth. Collaborating with Stan on this book has allowed me to share with you the best of the trivia knowledge I have collected over the years, and to bring back to mind why I love trivia in the first place.

Queens, New York, was the ideal place for a future trivia buff to grow up, and the 1950s and '60s were the ideal time. It was the Golden Age of Television, and *The Mickey Mouse Club* and *American Bandstand* were my after-school favorites. Saturday mornings were spent with my good friends Hopalong Cassidy, Sky King, Rin Tin Tin and the Lone Ranger. The old movies I watched on TV introduced me to Fred and Ginger, King Kong, Gunga Din and Errol Flynn. The Big Apple's airwaves were filled with the "platter chatter" of deejays like Murray the K and Cousin Brucie. The Giants and Dodgers left New York, but the Mets and the Jets arrived. And the late '60s left with me the indelible images of *Apollo 11* and Woodstock.

For me, trivia is remembering not only the pop icons of the past, but also the people with whom I have shared my favorite pastime. These friends have all helped to shape this book, and I am grateful to them all:

My classmates at Flushing High School, with whom I first swapped trivia questions.

My Sigma Phi fraternity brothers at Lehigh University (especially Curt Adams and C. C. Ryder), with whom many trivia games lasted far into the night.

John "Doc Zog" Hartzog, organizer of Allen-town's first Super Bowl of Trivia in 1976, and who tirelessly oversaw the event for fifteen years, after which I took over the reins.

The Trivia Bowl teams I played with and against, at the University of Colorado in the 1980s.

Scott Culpepper, Mark Dishell, Harry Hawthorne and Bob Major, trivia teammates in my early days of competition.

Andy Perkin, whose knowledge and love of rock and roll provided the cornerstone of a lifelong friendship.

Jeff Frank, station manager at Allentown's WAEB radio, who asked me to host the *Weekend World Series of Trivia* show in 1980.

John Kunda and Nick Pantages, who have been my trivia sparring partners for a quarter of a century.

George Nichols and Jim Tieser, who can recite from memory the entire script of *National Lampoon's Animal House*.

The members of the Lehigh Valley Trivia Club and the participants in our trivia competitions: Don Albright, Carl Cope, Mike Gessner, Jim Rudolph, Hilton Rahn, Joel Lipman, Dan DiNardo, Rick McKellin, Dick Green, Chris Horn, Frank Glaz, Roy DeFreitas, Tom Seddon, Brad Cohen, Joe and Tony Kurtz, Ken Young, Etta Roth, Rich and Andy Weiss, Bob Sutton, Doug Hagwood, Bruce and Arliss Paddock, Fred Tencic, and many more.

The Tuesday Night NTN Trivia Squad at the Sheraton Jetport Hotel, who play under these noms de trivia: Animal, Blax, Buffy, Dolphy, Fluffy, FX, Gemini, HTD, Josh, Magyar, Mitzva, Rufian, Samiam and Skidzz.

Anyone who has ever asked me why "Crying," "American Pie," and "Love Shack" are my favorite songs.

Stan Newman, my collaborator and close friend, who patiently instructed this newbie author in the world of book publishing. Thanks for your faith and trust, Stan.

My sons, Paul and Lee, who taught me that there is indeed music after 1980. Love ya, guys.

Finally, my wife Judy, who for more than thirty years has abided my obsession with trivia, and will be reclaiming our family room once I put away all the manuscript pages and notes I have strewn there. Thanks for your understanding and love.

—Hal Fittipaldi

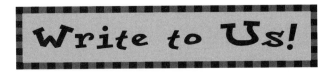

If you've got a question, comment, or quibble about the book, or if you'd like to suggest new material for future editions (either specific items, general categories, or updated facts), please write to us.

Regarding quibbles: Many hundreds of hours have gone into the verification of the 25,000+ facts that make up the book's 10,000+ entries, but it's possible that a few errors have slipped through. If you believe you've found one, please write us so we can correct it.

Before you write, please bear in mind that there are quite a few things in the book that we know look wrong, but are indisputably correct. Examples include Kelcy's Bar (Archie's hangout in *All in the Family*), Almira Gulch (Margaret Hamilton's Kansas role in *The Wizard of Oz*), and the "the" in the full name of OPEC (Organization of the Petroleum Exporting Countries). Since we will need verification for any entry we do correct, we ask that you include the source of your information with your letter.

You can reach us in two ways:

E-mail: StanAndHal@aol.com

Regular mail: Stan Newman and Hal Fittipaldi, P.O. Box 69, Massapequa Park, NY 11762. Please enclose a self-addressed stamped envelope if you'd like a reply.

We will make every effort to thank the first senders of anything that we use or correct in future editions by including their names in the Acknowledgments.

How to Use This Book

10,000 Answers is organized a bit differently from other reference books and trivia books. So, to help you find what you're looking for quickly, we offer these brief suggestions:

- Most of the time, the index, located at the back of the book, is where you should go first. Under each index item, you will find all the entries in the book that contain that item. In other words, the index is where you'll find a listing of all the "real" people, places and things that make up the topics in the book. For example:

  People: Authors, actors, comedians, composers, singers, sports stars, world leaders, etc.

  Places: Countries, cities, states, rivers, airports, etc.

  Things: Comic strips, companies, films, novels, plays, poems, products, songs, TV shows, universities, etc.

- Literary works (plays, novels, poems, etc.) are always indexed under the authors' names, and most are indexed under their own names as well.

- "Fictional" people, places, and things (like novel characters and sitcom hangouts) should be looked up in the index under their respective sources (books, TV shows, etc.). Fictional characters that have a significant number of entries (like James Bond, Sherlock Holmes and Harry Potter) are listed under their own names as well as the names of their creators.

- The main body of the book is where you should go first:

  If what you're looking for is more of a trivia fact (or trivia answer) than a topic.

  For random browsing.

  To get to know the sorts of things that the book contains.

- For easiest look-up, the numerical entries are listed together sequentially at the front of the book, rather than being alphabetized with the rest of the entries. The articles *a*, *an*, and *the*, and their equivalents in other languages, are ignored for alphabetization purposes.

- Many entries give the original names of people whose names have changed for one reason or another. For simplicity's sake, we generally describe this as the "real name" of a person, even if that person's name has been legally changed. We use "birth name" or "original name" if the person's name changed via adoption, first marriage, etc. before he or she took on his or her best-known name. Because we use "birth name" for this purpose, we use "maiden name" for a woman's original last name. If a "real first name" is given, we put parentheses around that name to show the full real name in an entry, for example: Carson: Real first name of entertainer (Carson) Wayne Newton.

- A title is called an "alternate title" if it appears after the word "or" in the title (as happens in many Gilbert and Sullivan works). Otherwise, such a title is called a "subtitle."

0

Number of irregular verbs in Esperanto.

Number of tunes on the 1974 album *Having Fun with Elvis on Stage,* which consists of Elvis Presley's between-song banter at live concerts.

Number of U.S. presidents that have been an only child. Through George W. Bush, all U.S. presidents have had at least one sibling.

Number of women in the cast of the film *Ice Station Zebra.*

Number of women in the cast of the Donald Bevan/Edmund Trzcinski play *Stalag 17.* (There are women in the film adaptation of the same name.)

Number of words spoken by the title character of the Disney animated film *Dumbo.* Dumbo is the only major character in the film that does not speak.

Winning point total in the game of darts. Players start with an initial score (such as 301 or 501), from which points are subtracted.

000

Agent number of TV cartoon character Secret Squirrel.

Emergency telephone number in Australia, comparable to 911 in the United States.

.005

Minimum proportion of alcohol in a beverage (½%) for it to be considered "intoxicating liquor," according to the Volstead Act of 1919, which provided for the enforcement of the 18th Amendment to the U.S. Constitution, aka "Prohibition."

.09 ounces

Standard weight of a Ping-Pong ball, equivalent to 2.5 grams.

⅑

Approximate fraction of an iceberg that appears above the water line, regardless of its size.

.367

Record career batting average of baseball Hall of Famer Ty Cobb.

1

Number of grooves on each side of a phonograph record.

Number of operas composed by Ludwig van Beethoven. His only opera was *Fidelio.*

Number of popes who have abdicated. Pope Celestine V was elected on July 5, 1294, and abdicated on December 13 of that year.

Number of teeth Ollie (full name Oliver J. Dragon) has, in the children's TV series *Kukla, Fran and Ollie.*

Number of time zones in China. Although China is wide enough to encompass multiple time zones, it chooses to have a single time setting for the entire country.

Social Security number that comedian Jack Benny claimed to have. According to government records, his actual Social Security Number was 561-09-5480.

1 inch

Thickness of a puck in the NHL.

1 kilogram

Weight of a woman's Olympic discus, equivalent to 2.2 pounds.

1 week

Fitting amount of time that the Barenaked Ladies tune "One Week" was #1 on the U.S. *Billboard* pop chart, in October 1998.

$1.19

Maximum amount of money in U.S. coins one can have and not be able to make change for a dollar: three quarters, four dimes, and four pennies.

1 minute, 36 seconds

Running time of the Maurice Williams and the Zodiacs tune "Stay," the shortest tune ever to reach #1 on the U.S. *Billboard* pop chart.

1.6 ounces

Standard precooked weight of a McDonald's hamburger.

1.62 ounces

Maximum weight of a ball in professional golf.

1.68 inches

Minimum circumference of a ball in professional golf.

$1.98

Price on the tag attached to the straw hat of country-music comedienne Minnie Pearl.

2

Agent number of Illya Kuryakin (David McCallum) in the TV series *The Man from U.N.C.L.E.*

Number of books in the King James Version of the Bible that do not mention the word "God": Esther and Song of Solomon.

Number of graduates in the first class of the U.S. Military Academy at West Point, in 1802.

Number of humps on a Bactrian camel. The other variety of camel, the dromedary, has one hump.

Number of domesticated insects (adapted to be beneficial to humans): the honeybee and the silkworm.

Number of scoops of raisins in each package of Kellogg's Raisin Bran, according to the TV commercials.

Number of shillings in an English florin, before the adoption of decimal coinage in 1971.

Number of talking animals in the Bible: the serpent (Genesis 3) and Balaam's ass (Numbers 22).

Number of teeth Disney cartoon character Goofy has.

Number of tickets that hockey great Wayne Gretzky will receive to every event at New York City's Madison Square Garden for the rest of his life. This is one of the terms of his final NHL player contract with the New York Rangers.

Number of Volkswagen Beetles sold in the U.S. in 1949, the year they were introduced in America.

2 to 0

Score of a forfeited game in the NFL.

2 grams

Amount of tea in an average tea bag.

2 kilograms

Weight of a man's Olympic discus, equivalent to 4.4 pounds.

2 pounds

Approximate weight of a cubic yard of air at sea level.

2¹⁄₁₆ ounces

Maximum weight of a ball in professional tennis. (Minimum is 2 ounces.)

2.20462

Number of pounds in one kilogram.

2.3 meters

Maximum length of a woman's Olympic javelin, equivalent to 7.5 feet. (Minimum is 2.2 meters, or 7.2 feet.)

2.5 miles

Width of the demilitarized zone that separates North and South Korea at the 38th parallel.

2.54

Number of centimeters in one inch.

2⅝ inches

Maximum diameter of a ball in professional tennis. (Minimum is 2½ inches.)

2.61 inches

Height of all current denominations of U.S. currency. (Width is 6.14 inches.)

2.7 meters

Maximum length of a man's Olympic javelin, equivalent to 8.9 feet. (Minimum is 2.6 meters, or 8.5 feet.)

2 pounds, 10 ounces

Maximum weight of a horseshoe, according to the official rules of the National Horseshoe Pitchers Association of America.

3

Minimum number of people necessary for a riot, according to criminal law.

Number of basketballs prepared by the referees for each NBA game, according to official rules.

Number of fillies to have won the Kentucky Derby: Regret (1915), Genuine Risk (1980) and Winning Colors (1988).

Number of heads of Cerberus, a mythical dog that guards the entrance to Hades.

Number of Interstate highways in the state of Hawaii (all on Oahu), which are designated H1,

H2, and H3. Legally speaking, any road built under the Federal Aid Highway Act is considered an Interstate, whether or not it crosses a state line.

Number of consecutive misses at one height that eliminates a high jumper in Olympic competition.

Number of plays of William Shakespeare in which Sir John Falstaff appears, more than any other Shakespearean character:
    King Henry IV, Part I
    King Henry IV, Part II
    King Henry V
Falstaff's name is mentioned (but does not appear) in *The Merry Wives of Windsor.*

Number of points scored for a ringer in horseshoes. A leaner is worth one point.

Number of U.S. presidents who did not receive *Time* magazine's Person of the Year award, since the award's inception in 1927: Calvin Coolidge, Herbert Hoover and Gerald Ford.

Number of roles played by Peter Sellers in the film *Dr. Strangelove:* the title character, Group Captain Lionel Mandrake and President Merkin Muffley.

Number of teaspoons in one tablespoon.

See also **6 seconds**

3 days
Amount of time (3 days and 3 nights, specifically) that Jonah was in the belly of the "great fish," according to Jonah 1:17 (King James Version).

3 inches
Diameter of a puck in the NHL.

3 meters
Height above water of the board in Olympic springboard diving, equivalent to 9.8 feet.

3 months
Maximum amount of time after a wedding to send thank-you cards, according to the latest (15th) edition of *Emily Post's Etiquette.*

3⅜ inches
Width of a standard credit card. (Height is 2⅛ inches.)

3½ inches
Width of a standard business card. (Height is 2 inches.)

3 pounds, 10 ounces
Maximum weight of a pin in professional bowling. (Minimum is 3 pounds, 6 ounces).

3¹⁵⁄₁₆ inches
Width of a standard audio cassette. (Height is 2½ inches.)

4
Number of acts in the Virgil Thomson/Gertrude Stein opera *Four Saints in Three Acts.* Despite the title, the cast of the opera includes more than 30 saints.

Number of balls thrown by each team per frame in the game of bocce.

Number of British Commonwealth nations that use the flag of Great Britain as part of their own national flag: Australia, Fiji, New Zealand and Tuvalu.

Number of farthings in an English penny, before the adoption of decimal coinage in 1971.

Number of players on a polo team.

Number of slave states that remained with the Union during the Civil War: Delaware, Kentucky, Maryland and Missouri.

Number of toes on each foot of a cuckoo. The two outer toes point backward.

Record number of different U.S. Cabinet positions held by Elliot Richardson:
    Health, Education and Welfare (Nixon, 1970–73)
    Defense (Nixon, 1973)
    Attorney General (Nixon, 1973–74)
    Commerce (Ford, 1975–77)

Standard number of strings on most common stringed instruments, including the cello, double bass, ukulele, viola and violin.

4 to 2
Final score of the baseball game in the Ernest L. Thayer poem "Casey at the Bat."

4 inches
Minimum depth of a hole in professional golf.

4 kilograms
Weight of the woman's shot in the Olympic shot put, equivalent to 8.8 pounds.

4¼ inches
Diameter of a hole in professional golf.

4' 33"
1952 work by composer John Cage, in which no sounds are intentionally produced by the "performers" for 4 minutes, 33 seconds, while the audience listens to whatever sounds are being made around it.

"4 C's"

The four standards by which diamonds are judged by the Gemological Institute of America.

CARATS

The larger the diamond, the more valuable, and the more valuable per carat.

CLARITY, OR LACK OF INCLUSIONS (MINUTE TRACES OF NONCRYSTALLIZED CARBON)

Fl (flawless)
IF (internally flawless)
VVS1-VVS2 (very very slightly included)
VS1-VS2 (very slightly included)
SI1-SI3 (slightly included)
I1-I3 (included)

COLOR (THE CLOSER TO COLORLESS, THE MORE VALUABLE), ON A SCALE OF D TO Z

D-F (colorless)
G-J (near colorless)
K-M (faint yellow)
N-R (very light yellow)
S-Z (light yellow)
Z+ is used to indicate a fancy color

CUT

How well the diamond has been cut to produce the maximum return of light. (This is different from the shape of the diamond, which is not in itself a determinant of value.)

4-H Club Pledge

Adopted by the delegates to the 1927 National 4-H Club Camp in Washington, D.C.

I pledge . . .
My head to clearer thinking,
My heart to greater loyalty,
My hands to larger service, and
My health for better living,
for my club, my community, my country, and
my world.

The phrase "and my world" was added to the pledge in 1973.

5

Number of dice in the game Yahtzee.

Number of holes in a White Castle hamburger.

Number of Olympics that have been cancelled due to war, listed below with their scheduled locations, and the dates when the Olympics were subsequently held in those locations:

1916 Summer Olympics (Berlin, Germany; 1936)
1940 Winter Olympics (Sapporo, Japan; 1972)
1940 Summer Olympics (Tokyo, Japan; 1964)
1944 Winter Olympics (Cortina d'Ampezzo, Italy; 1956)
1944 Summer Olympics (London, England; 1948)

Number of new pence in an English shilling.

Number of people killed by British troops at the Boston Massacre on May 5, 1770.

Number of standard foot positions in classical ballet.

Number of interlocking rings on the Olympic flag. The rings' colors (blue, yellow, black, green and red) represent the flags of the world; at least one of the colors appears on the flag of every nation.

Number of roles played by Frank Morgan in the film *The Wizard of Oz*: Professor Marvel, the title character, and a Guard, Cabby and Coachman in the Emerald City.

Number of shillings in an English crown, before the adoption of decimal coinage in 1971.

Record number of top-5 tunes of the Beatles on the U.S. *Billboard* pop chart during the week of April 4, 1964.

#1 "Can't Buy Me Love"
#2 "Twist and Shout"
#3 "She Loves You"
#4 "I Want to Hold Your Hand"
#5 "Please Please Me"

Number on Tige's collar in the logo of Buster Brown shoes.

5 feet

Diameter of the on-deck circle in major-league baseball.

5 meters

Length of the women's balance beam in Olympic gymnastics, equivalent to 16 feet, 5 inches. The beam is 10 centimeters (3.9 inches) wide.

5 minutes

Maximum time allowed for a player or caddy to search for a lost golf ball, according to USGA rules.

Recommended cooking time for Minute Rice, as indicated on the box.

5 years

Length of the mission of the starship U.S.S. *Enterprise* in the TV series *Star Trek*.

5¼ ounces

Maximum weight of a major-league baseball. (Minimum is 5 ounces.)

5 minutes, 32 seconds

Length of the climactic duel between the title character (Stewart Granger) and Noel, Marquis de Maynes (Mel Ferrer) in the film *Scaramouche*.

6

Average number of pitches that a major-league baseball is kept in play.

Minimum number of rings that a telephone caller should wait before hanging up, according to the latest (15th) edition of *Emily Post's Etiquette*.

Number of films directed by Alfred Hitchcock in which actor Leo G. Carroll appears, more than any other performer (not counting the cameo appearances of Hitchcock himself).

Rebecca (1940)
Suspicion (1941)
Spellbound (1945)
The Paradine Case (1947)
Strangers on a Train (1951)
North by Northwest (1959)

Number of fingers on each hand of the title character (Bolaji Badejo) in the film *Alien*.

Number of locks in the Panama Canal.

Number of men who signed both the Declaration of Independence and the U.S. Constitution:

George Clymer (Pennsylvania)
Benjamin Franklin (Pennsylvania)
Robert Morris (Pennsylvania)
George Read (Delaware)
Roger Sherman (Connecticut)
James Wilson (Pennsylvania)

Number of pockets on a standard pool table.

Number of soldiers raising the American flag on Iwo Jima's Mount Suribachi in the historic photograph taken by Joe Rosenthal on February 23, 1945.

Number of stars on the flag of Australia. The five stars at right represent the Southern Cross, a constellation visible throughout the country; the seven-pointed Federation Star in the lower left represents the seven states and territories of Australia.

Number of U.S. states with geographic regions called "panhandles": Alaska, Florida, Idaho, Oklahoma, Texas, and West Virginia.

See also **United Nations official languages**

6 seconds

Required time that animals must remain tied (any three feet) in the calf-roping and steer-roping rodeo events.

$6.00

Original nightly room rate at the first Motel 6, which opened in 1962 in Santa Barbara, California.

6.14 inches

Width of all current denominations of U.S. currency. (Height is 2.61 inches.)

7

Number of ages of man, as cited by Jaques in Act 2, Scene 7, of the William Shakespeare play *As You Like It*.

Number of articles in the U.S. Constitution.

Number of bones in the neck of a giraffe, which is the same as in humans.

Number of books of the Christian Protestant Bible that are divided into two parts:

OLD TESTAMENT
Samuel
Kings
Chronicles

NEW TESTAMENT
Corinthians
Thessalonians
Timothy
Peter

In addition, the New Testament book of John is divided into three parts.

Number of Emily Dickinson's poems, out of the more than 1,700 that she wrote, that were published during her lifetime.

Number of different fruits found in Hawaiian Punch.

JUICES
Pineapple
Orange
Passionfruit
Apple

PURÉES
Apricot
Papaya
Guava

Number of generations chronicled in the TV miniseries *Roots* and *Roots: The Next Generations*.

Kunta Kinte (LeVar Burton, John Amos)
Kizzy (Leslie Uggams)
Chicken George Moore (Ben Vereen, Avon Long)
Tom Harvey (Georg Stanford Brown)
Cynthia Harvey Palmer (Bever-Leigh Banfield, Beah Richards)
Bertha Palmer Haley (Irene Cara)

Alexander Murray Palmer Haley (Cristoff St. John, Damon Evans, James Earl Jones)

Number of holes in a Ritz cracker—six in a regular-hexagon shape and one in the center.

Number of perfect 10s scored by Romanian gymnast Nadia Comaneci in the 1976 Summer Olympics. These were the first 10s ever earned by an Olympic gymnast.

Number of players on a team in Olympic handball.

Number of players on a Quidditch team (the wizarding national sport), in the Harry Potter series of books by J. K. Rowling. A team consists of:
   Three Chasers (who try to put the Quaffle through a hoop)
   Two Beaters (who try to keep the attacking Bludger balls away from team members)
   One Keeper (a defensive player)
   One Seeker (who tries to catch the Golden Snitch)
   Harry Potter is a Seeker on his Quidditch team.

Number of players on a water polo team.

Number of points in the crown of the Statue of Liberty, which represent the seven continents.

Number of roles played by Eddie Murphy in the film *The Nutty Professor* (1996) (counting title character Professor Sherman Klump and his alter ego Buddy Love as two).

Number of sides on an English 20-pence coin.

Number of water jumps in an Olympic steeplechase.

Number of different ways that hashbrowns are served at the Waffle House restaurant chain:
   Chunked with ham
   Covered with cheese
   Diced with tomatoes
   Peppered with jalapeños
   Scattered on the grill
   Smothered in onions
   Topped with chili

Record number of gold medals won by swimmer Mark Spitz at the 1972 Summer Olympics at Munich.

Record number of career no-hit games pitched by baseball Hall of Famer Nolan Ryan.

Perpetual age of the title character in the comic strip *Nancy*.

Sum of any two opposite faces of a standard die.

See also **seven deadly sins; Seven Dwarfs**

7½ degrees

Minimum tilt necessary for a bowling pin to fall.

7½ Cents

Novel by Richard Bissell that was the basis for the musical *The Pajama Game*.

8

Minimum number of lanes in an Olympic-sized swimming pool.

Number of different animals that make up the puppet Flub-a-Dub in the children's TV series *Howdy Doody*:
   Head of a duck
   Ears of a cocker spaniel
   Neck of a giraffe
   Body of a dachshund
   Flippers of a seal
   Tail of a pig
   Whiskers of a cat
   Memory of an elephant

Number of digits in the serial numbers of all current denominations of U.S. currency. In the recently redesigned denominations, the digits are preceded by two letters and followed by one letter; in the older bills, the digits are preceded by one letter and followed by one letter.

Number of people who were passengers on Noah's Ark, according to the King James Version of the Bible. They included Noah and his wife, their three sons (Ham, Japheth and Shem), and their sons' wives.

Number of ribs on a standard umbrella.

Number of roles played by Sir Alec Guinness in the film *Kind Hearts and Coronets*.

Number of sections in Peter Tchaikovsky's *Nutcracker Suite*.

Number of states that border Missouri, and the number of states that border Tennessee, more than any other state.

Number of stories in the Leaning Tower of Pisa.

Number of strings on a Neapolitan mandolin, the most common type.

Number of "great tomatoes in that little bitty can" of Contadina tomato paste, as heard in TV commercials.

See also **V-8, juices in**

8 seconds

Required time for a rodeo rider to stay on his mount in the bull riding, bareback riding, and saddle-bronc riding events.

8 feet 2 inches

Height of Big Bird in the children's TV series *Sesame Street*.

8.34 pounds

Weight of one gallon of water.

8-Ball messages

See **Magic 8-Ball messages**

9

Highest score in the casino game baccarat.

Number of heads of a Hydra, a mythical serpentine creature.

Number of laps in the climactic chariot race in the film *Ben-Hur*.

Number of different letters on a standard Snellen eye chart. The bottom (11th) line of the chart includes all nine letters (in order): P E Z O L C F T D.

Number of points scored for a bull's-eye in archery.

Number of U.S. presidents who never attended college:
> George Washington
> Andrew Jackson
> Martin Van Buren
> Zachary Taylor
> Millard Fillmore
> Abraham Lincoln
> Andrew Johnson
> Grover Cleveland
> Harry S Truman

Number of rhetorical questions posed in the Bob Dylan tune "Blowin' in the Wind."

Number of rows of stars on the American flag, in a 6-5-6-5-6-5-6-5-6 pattern.

Number of times Christian Szell (Laurence Olivier) asks Thomas Levy (Dustin Hoffman) "Is it safe?" in the film *Marathon Man*.

Record number of Hart Memorial Trophies (NHL MVP awards) won by Wayne Gretzky. This is also the record for any major professional sport.

Shoe size of the title character in the tune "Clementine."

9 to 0

Score of a forfeited game in major-league baseball.

$9.00

Cost of the first TV commercial, for the Bulova Watch Company. It aired on July 1, 1941, during a Brooklyn Dodgers baseball game.

9 inches

Width of a wicket in cricket.

9¼ inches

Maximum circumference of a major-league baseball. (Minimum is 9 inches.)

9½ inches

Width of a standard #10 (business-size) envelope. (Height is 4⅛ inches.)

9.86 quarts

Amount of whole milk necessary to make one pound of butter.

10

Number of arms on a squid.

Number of hurdles in both the 110-meter and 400-meter Olympic races.

Number of legs on lobsters and crabs.

Number of marbles per player in Chinese checkers.

Number of provinces of Canada.

Number of times per minute that a telephone rings in the United States.

Record number of World Series games won by Hall of Fame pitcher Whitey Ford for the New York Yankees.

Record number of consecutive strikeouts in one game, achieved by Hall of Fame baseball pitcher Tom Seaver for the New York Mets against the San Diego Padres on April 22, 1970.

Standard number of inkblots in a Rorschach test, introduced by Swiss psychiatrist Hermann Rorschach in 1921.

10 feet

Height of a goal-post crossbar, according to NFL rules.

Height of a hoop in the NBA.

10 meters

Height above water of the platform in Olympic platform diving, equivalent to 32.8 feet.

10 years

Maximum that U.S. presidents may serve, according to the 22nd Amendment to the Constitution.

This maximum would be reached by a president completing two years of the term of his/her predecessor, then being elected to two full terms.

11

Agent number of Napoleon Solo (Robert Vaughn) in the TV series *The Man from U.N.C.L.E.*

Perpetual age of the title character in the comic strip *Little Orphan Annie*.

Record number of Academy Awards won by the films *Ben-Hur* (1959) and *Titanic* (1997).

Number of children of Earl Derr Biggers sleuth Charlie Chan.

Number of days that "never were" for England and the American colonies in 1752. September 2 was followed by September 14, due to the adoption of the Gregorian calendar in the British Empire.

Record number of consecutive PGA golf tournaments won by Byron Nelson in 1945.

Number of different herbs and spices that are advertised in the secret recipe for Kentucky Fried Chicken.

Number of European countries that first adopted the euro as their common currency on January 1, 1999:
   Austria
   Belgium
   Finland
   France
   Germany
   Iceland
   Italy
   Luxembourg
   Netherlands
   Portugal
   Spain

Number of official languages of South Africa:
   Afrikaans
   English
   Ndebele
   Northern Sotho (aka Pedi)
   Southern Sotho
   Swazi
   Tsonga
   Tswana
   Venda
   Xhosa
   Zulu

Number of members of OPEC, the Organization of the Petroleum Exporting Countries. OPEC, headquartered in Vienna, was founded in Baghdad on September 24, 1960:
   Algeria
   Iran*
   Iraq*
   Indonesia
   Kuwait*
   Libya
   Nigeria
   Qatar
   Saudi Arabia*
   United Arab Emirates
   Venezuela*
   * indicates founding member

Number of players on a cricket team.

Number of plumes on the NBC peacock when first introduced in July 1956. After a 1986 redesign, the NBC peacock now has six plumes, one for each division of NBC.

Number of sides on the recessed inner edge of a Susan B. Anthony dollar.

Number of teams that currently make up the Big Ten conference, listed below with their date of entry:
   University of Illinois (1895)
   University of Michigan (1895)
   University of Minnesota (1895)
   Northwestern University (1895)
   Purdue University (1895)
   University of Wisconsin (1895)
   Indiana University (1899)
   University of Iowa (1899)
   Ohio State University (1912)
   Michigan State University (1949)
   Penn State University (1990)
At its 1895 founding, the Big Ten was called the Intercollegiate Conference of Faculty Representatives. The University of Chicago was an original 1895 member, but withdrew in 1946.

Number of tokens currently provided in the standard version of the board game Monopoly:
   battleship
   cannon
   dog
   horse & rider
   iron
   race car
   sack of money
   shoe
   thimble
   top hat
   wheelbarrow

The sack of money was the last new token introduced, in 1999.

$11.06

Total sales on the first day of business of New York City's original Macy's in 1858.

11½ inches

Height of the first Barbie, introduced in 1959.

12

Number of astronauts (all Americans) who have walked on the moon.

Number of edges on a cube.

Number of flowers depicted on each side of Oreo cookies.

Number of hotels included in the board game Monopoly.

Number of leads in a comprehensive EKG.

Number of letters in the Hawaiian alphabet: five vowels (a, e, i, o, u) and seven consonants (h, k, l, m, n, p, w).

Number of operas composed by Giacomo Puccini, including *La Bohème, Tosca* and *Madama Butterfly.*

Number of pence in an English shilling, before the adoption of decimal coinage in 1971.

Number of consecutive strikes necessary to complete a perfect game of 300 in bowling.

Number of weight classes in Olympic boxing.

Number of words that appear on all current denominations of U.S. coins: "E pluribus unum," "United States of America," "In God We Trust," and "Liberty."

See also **Operation, playing pieces in**

$12.00

Top price for a ticket to the first Super Bowl in 1967. In contrast, the top price for a ticket to the 2001 Super Bowl was $400.

12 centimeters

Diameter of a standard CD or DVD, equivalent to 4.7 inches.

12 minutes

Length of halftime, according to NFL rules.

12 ounces

Minimum weight of a glove in professional heavyweight boxing.

13

Number of columns of beads on a standard abacus.

Number of drafts written by J. K. Rowling for *Harry Potter and the Sorcerer's Stone* (U.K. title: *Harry Potter and the Philosopher's Stone*), the first in the Harry Potter series.

Number of each of the following on the Great Seal of the United States (in honor of the original 13 colonies):
  Arrows (in the left talon of the eagle)
  Berries and leaves on the olive branch (in the right talon of the eagle)
  Stars (over the eagle's head)
  Stripes (on the shield in front of the eagle)
The eagle faces right (toward the olive branch), symbolizing the nation's preference for peace.

Number of layers in a McDonald's Big Mac.

FROM TOP TO BOTTOM:

Top bun
Onions
Meat
Pickles
Lettuce
Special sauce
Middle bun
Onions
Meat
Cheese
Lettuce
Special sauce
Bottom bun

Number of letter cubes in the game Perquackey.

Number of rounds of play in the game Yahtzee.

Number of consecutive times The Skyliners sing "you" at the end of their tune "Since I Don't Have You."

Usual number of witches in a coven.

See also **311**

14

Number of comic operas written by the team of Gilbert and Sullivan, including H.M.S. *Pinafore, The Mikado,* and *The Pirates of Penzance.*

Maximum number of golf clubs that a player may carry, according to USGA rules.

Number of hands played by Fonsia Dorsey and Weller Martin in the D. L. Coburn play *The Gin Game.*

Number of lines in a sonnet. An Italian sonnet is composed of two stanzas of eight and six lines, while an English sonnet is composed of three stanzas of four lines plus one stanza of two lines.

Number of members of the U.S. Cabinet, consisting of the heads of major departments within the Executive Branch.

Number of pounds in one stone, an English measure of weight.

Number of seasons (October 3, 1952, to September 3, 1966) that the TV sitcom *The Adventures of Ozzie and Harriet* was broadcast in prime time. This is the record for a sitcom.

Number of times the title character says "I would prefer not to," responding to various requests, in the Herman Melville short story "Bartleby, the Scrivener."

Number of times that the line "Show me the money!" is spoken in the film *Jerry Maguire*: Eight times by the title character (Tom Cruise), five times by Rod Tidwell (Cuba Gooding Jr.), and once by Dorothy Boyd (Renee Zellweger).

Record number of Academy Award nominations received by the films *All About Eve* (1950) and *Titanic* (1997).

Record number of consecutive World Series games won by the New York Yankees, from Game 3 of the 1996 World Series through Game 2 of the 2000 World Series. This is also the record for the championship round of any major professional sport.

See also **Oz book series**

14 miles
Distance from the Batcave to Gotham City, in the TV series *Batman*.

14 ounces
Size of the coffee cup served at Mel's Diner in the TV sitcom *Alice*, according to the restaurant's neon sign, seen in the opening credits.

14 AAAAAA
Shoe size of cartoon character Olive Oyl.

$14.41
Appropriate cover price of two books on the subject of palindromes (words or phrases that read the same, backward and forward) written by Jon Agee: *Go Hang a Salami! I'm a Lasagna Hog!* and *Sit on a Potato Pan, Otis!*

14 hours, 31 minutes
Gertrude Ederle's time in swimming the English Channel (from Cap Gris-Nez, France to Dover, England) on August 6, 1926. She was the first woman to do so, and beat the previous male record by 1 hour, 59 minutes.

15
Minimum age for an Olympic gymnast. Specifically, a gymnast must turn 16 within the calendar year of the Games. The age was increased by one year for the 2000 Games.

Number of books in the Book of Mormon.

Number of children in the brood of the title characters (Marjorie Main, Percy Kilbride) in the Ma and Pa Kettle series of films.

Number of people crowded into the tiny cabin in the famous "stateroom" scene of the Marx Brothers film *A Night at the Opera*:
Otis B. Driftwood (Groucho)
Fiorello (Chico)
Tomasso (Harpo)
Ricardo Baroni (Allan Jones)
Two maids
An engineer
A manicurist
The engineer's assistant
A girl looking for her Aunt Minnie
A washwoman
Four stewards

Number of puppies of Pongo and Perdita in the Disney animated film *One Hundred and One Dalmatians*.

Number of questions that a contestant must answer correctly to win the top prize in the TV game show *Who Wants to Be a Millionaire*.

Number of pieces per player in backgammon.

Number of sunflowers in the Vincent van Gogh painting *Sunflowers*, which sold for $39.9 million in a Christie's auction on March 30, 1987.

Winning point total in badminton.

See also **Skull and Bones members**

15 feet
Distance between the free-throw line and the face of the backboard in the NBA.

15 inches
Height of a pin in ten-pin bowling.

Length and width of first, second and third base in major-league baseball.

15 ounces

Maximum weight of a football, according to NFL rules. (Minimum is 14 ounces.)

15 years, 10 months, 11 days

Age of the youngest player in major-league baseball history, Joe Nuxhall. He pitched ⅔ of an inning for the Cincinnati Reds on June 10, 1944.

16

Number of initial contestants in the TV game show *Survivor*.

Number of regular-season games per team in the NFL.

Record number of consecutive weeks that the 1995 Mariah Carey/Boyz II Men tune "One Sweet Day" was #1 on the U.S. *Billboard* pop chart.

16 ounces

Maximum weight of a ball in Olympic soccer. (Minimum is 14 ounces.)

16 pounds

Maximum weight of a ball in professional bowling.

Weight of the metal sphere used in the Olympic hammer throw.

Weight of the men's shot in the Olympic shot put.

17

Number of cantos in the Lord Byron epic poem *Don Juan*.

Number of English monarchs buried at London's Westminster Abbey. They are listed below with their death dates:
Edward the Confessor (1066)
Henry III (1272)
Edward I (1307)
Edward III (1377)
Richard II (1400)
Henry V (1422)
Edward V (1483)
Henry VII (1509)
Edward VI (1553)
Mary I (1558)
Elizabeth I (1603)
James I (1625)
Charles II (1685)
Mary II (1694)

William III (1702)
Anne (1714)
George II (1760)

Since George II, British monarchs have been buried at Windsor.

Number of muscles needed to smile.

Number of questions that had to be correctly answered to win the top prize in the 1950s version of the TV game show *The $64,000 Question*.

Number of stars on the reverse of the Sacagawea dollar, which represent the number of U.S. states at the time of the Lewis and Clark expedition of 1804–06.

Number of syllables in a Japanese haiku poem, consisting of three lines of five, seven, and five syllables, respectively.

17 inches

Waist measurement of Scarlett O'Hara in the Margaret Mitchell novel *Gone With the Wind*.

17 years

Length of time that United States patents remain in effect.

17 minutes, 5 seconds

Playing time of the Iron Butterfly tune "In-A-Gadda-Da-Vida."

17 minutes, 15 seconds

Time of the "Continental" dance sequence of Fred Astaire and Ginger Rogers in the film *The Gay Divorcée*.

18

Maximum number of letters (including spaces) that can be used for the name of Thoroughbred racehorses.

Number of anvils called for in the score of the Richard Wagner opera *Das Rheingold*.

Number of applicants vying for eight available jobs, in the musical *A Chorus Line*.

Number of players on a team in Australian Rules football.

Number of precooked White Castle hamburgers to the pound.

Number on the San Francisco 49ers football jersey worn by Sally McMillan (Susan Saint James) in the TV series *McMillan and Wife*.

See also **Maher-shal-al-hash-baz; Presley, Elvis, #1 tunes of**

18 feet
Diameter of the pitcher's mound in major-league baseball.

18 inches
Inside diameter of a hoop in the NBA.

18 feet, 6 inches
Distance between goal posts, according to NFL rules.

19
Number of Emmy nominations received by Susan Lucci for playing Erica Kane on the soap opera *All My Children* before finally winning in 1999.

Typical number of hours per day that a three-toed sloth sleeps.

$19.55
Appropriate cover price of the book *Carl Erskine's Tales from the Dodger Dugout*. Erskine was a pitcher on the 1955 Brooklyn Dodgers, the only Brooklyn team that ever won a World Series.

20
Highest number on a dartboard.

Number of children fathered by composer Johann Sebastian Bach—seven by his first wife, 13 by his second.

Number of episodes in the landmark 1914 film serial *The Perils of Pauline*.

Number of possible first moves in chess.

Number of seasons (September 10, 1955, to September 1, 1975) that the TV Western series *Gunsmoke* was broadcast in prime time. This is the record for a TV dramatic series with continuing characters.

Number of shillings in an English pound, before the adoption of decimal coinage in 1971.

Record number of pass receptions in a single NFL game, achieved by Terrell Owens of the San Francisco 49ers against the Chicago Bears, on December 17, 2000.

Record number of major tournaments won by golfer Jack Nicklaus, consisting of:
   Six Masters (1963, 1965, 1966, 1972, 1975, 1986)
   Five PGAs (1963, 1971, 1973, 1975, 1980)
   Four U.S. Opens (1962, 1967, 1972, 1980)
   Three British Opens (1966, 1970, 1978)
   Two U.S. Amateurs (1959, 1961)

Record number of TV game shows hosted by Bill Cullen:
   Winner Take All (1952)
   Give and Take (1952)
   Bank on the Stars (1953–54)
   Place the Face (1954–55)
   Name That Tune (1954–55)
   Down You Go (1956)
   The Price Is Right (1956–65)
   Eye Guess (1966–69)
   Three on a Match (1971–74)
   The $25,000 Pyramid (1974–79)
   Winning Streak (1974–75)
   Blankety Blanks (1975)
   I've Got a Secret (1976)
   Pass the Buck (1978)
   The Love Experts (1978–79)
   Chain Reaction (1980)
   Blockbusters (1980–1982)
   Child's Play (1982–83)
   Hot Potato (1984)
   The Joker's Wild (1984–1986)
In addition, Cullen appeared as a substitute host on *Break the Bank* (1950s) and *Password Plus* (1980).

20 minutes
Maximum amount of time that a host should delay dinner for a late guest, according to the latest (15th) edition of *Emily Post's Etiquette*.

20 years
Length of the "nap" of the title character in the Washington Irving short story "Rip Van Winkle."

20.41 pounds
Weight of $1,000,000 in U.S. $100 bills. The same amount in $1 bills would weigh 100 times as much, or 2,041 pounds.

21
Number of letters in the Italian alphabet, consisting of all the letters in the English alphabet except j, k, w, x, and y.

Number of shillings in an English guinea, before the adoption of decimal coinage in 1971.

Total number of spots (pips) on a standard die.

21 feet
Distance from the service line to the net in tennis.

21 seconds
NHL record time in which Chicago Blackhawks right winger Bill Mosienko scored a hat trick (three goals) against the New York Rangers on March 23, 1952.

22

Number of films in which actor Sidney Toler portrayed detective Charlie Chan from 1938 to 1947. Toler's immediate predecessor, Warner Oland, portrayed Chan in 16 films from 1931 to 1937.

Number of letters in the Hebrew alphabet.

Number of operas composed by Wolfgang Amadeus Mozart, including *The Marriage of Figaro*, *Don Giovanni* and *The Magic Flute*.

Number of rare paintings in the collection of Jonathan Hemlock (Clint Eastwood) in the film *The Eiger Sanction*. The collection includes two Picassos, two Pissarros, two Matisses, an El Greco and a Klee.

Record number of heavyweight championship boxing matches refereed by Mills Lane. Lane was formerly a district court judge in Reno, Nevada.

Total number of balls used in the game of snooker.

22 EEE

Shoe size of NBA star Shaquille O'Neal.

22 ounces

Maximum weight of a basketball, according to NBA rules. (Minimum is 20 ounces.)

23

Number of different fruit flavors in Dr. Pepper, whose specific ingredients are a corporate secret.

Record number of career grand-slam home runs hit by baseball Hall of Famer Lou Gehrig.

23 degrees, 27 minutes

Latitude of the Tropic of Cancer (North Latitude) and Tropic of Capricorn (South Latitude). These imaginary lines mark the northernmost/southernmost latitudes at which the sun reaches its zenith.

24

Number of books that make up each of Homer's epic poems, *The Iliad* and *The Odyssey*.

Number of colored circles (six each of red, blue, yellow and green) on the vinyl sheet in the game Twister.

Number of letters in the Greek alphabet, consisting of 17 consonants and seven vowels.

Number of letters in Hangul, the Korean alphabet, consisting of 14 consonants and 10 vowels.

Number of numbers on a Bingo card, which are arrayed in a five-by-five pattern with the central square marked "FREE SPACE."

Number of pages in a standard U.S. passport.

Number of points on a backgammon board.

Number of stories in Geoffrey Chaucer's uncompleted Canterbury Tales:
    The Knight's Tale
    The Miller's Tale
    The Reeve's Tale
    The Cook's Tale
    The Man of Law's Tale
    The Wife of Bath's Tale
    The Friar's Tale
    The Summoner's Tale
    The Clerk's Tale
    The Merchant's Tale
    The Squire's Tale
    The Franklin's Tale
    The Physician's Tale
    The Pardoner's Tale
    The Shipman's Tale
    The Prioress' Tale
    The Tale of Sir Thopas
    The Tale of Melibee
    The Monk's Tale
    The Nun's Priest's Tale
    The Second Nun's Tale
    The Canon's Yeoman's Tale
    The Manciple's Tale
    The Parson's Tale

Number of suspects in the game Lie Detector.

Record number of consecutive games won by Hall of Fame baseball pitcher Carl Hubbell for the New York Giants in 1936-37.

Shoe size of 1930s Italian-born heavyweight boxing champ Primo Carnera.

Standard number of frames per second in which films are recorded in the U.S. In Europe, the standard is 25 frames per second.

24 years

Period of ease promised by Mephistophilis in exchange for the title character's soul, in the Christopher Marlowe play *Doctor Faustus*.

24 Years of House Work . . . and the Place Is Still a Mess

1998 autobiography of former Colorado congresswoman Pat Schroeder.

24 hours, 18 minutes

Record length of Senator Strom Thurmond's filibuster of August 28–29, 1957, in opposition to the Civil Rights Act.

25

Minimum age for a member of the House of Representatives, according to the U.S. Constitution.

Number of times heavyweight boxing champ Joe Louis successfully defended his title, from his unanimous decision against Tommy Farr on August 30, 1937, to his knockout of Jersey Joe Walcott on June 25, 1948. Louis retired as champion on March 1, 1949.

Number of brothers and sisters in the family of heavyweight boxing champ Sonny Liston (including himself).

Maximum number of characters (including spaces and punctuation) that can be used for the names of pedigreed dogs registered with the American Kennel Club.

Number of new pence in an English crown.

Number of Zener cards in a deck, which are used to test for extrasensory perception. The cards were developed at Duke University circa 1935 by Dr. Karl Zener and first used by pioneer ESP researcher Dr. J. B. Rhine. The deck contains five each of these five symbols: circle, plus sign, square, star, and wavy lines.

See also **132 years**

25 cents

Daily fee (plus expenses) charged by Encyclopedia Brown in the series of children's books by Donald J. Sobol.

25 years

Record length of time between one artist's successive #1 tunes on the U.S. *Billboard* pop chart. Cher's next #1 tune after "Dark Lady" in 1974 was "Believe" in 1999.

26

Number of consecutive albums of the Rolling Stones to reach the *Billboard* top-10 in the United States, from *12 × 5* in 1964 to *Emotional Rescue* in 1980.

Number of U.S. states' names on the back of a current U.S. $5 bill, in two rows at the top of the Lincoln Memorial:

TOP ROW (FROM LEFT TO RIGHT):

Arkansas
Michigan
Florida
Texas
Iowa
Wisconsin
California
Minnesota
Oregon
Kansas
West Virginia
Nevada
Nebraska
Colorado
North Dakota

BOTTOM ROW (FROM LEFT TO RIGHT):

Delaware
Pennsylvania
New Jersey
Georgia
Connecticut
Massachusetts
Maryland
Carolina [*sic*]
Hampshire [*sic*]
Virginia
New York

Record number of consecutive games lost by the NFL's Tampa Bay Buccaneers, from their first-ever game against the Houston Oilers on September 12, 1976, to their loss to the Chicago Bears on December 4, 1977.

Number of consecutive times Bill Withers sings "I know" in his tune "Ain't No Sunshine."

Record number of Western series that were on the prime-time TV schedule for the full 1959–60 season. (Series that were on for only a portion of the season are not counted.)

Bat Masterson
Black Saddle
Bonanza
Bronco
Cheyenne
Colt .45
The Deputy
Dick Powell's Zane Grey Theater
Gunsmoke
Have Gun Will Travel
Johnny Ringo
Laramie
Law of the Plainsman
The Lawman
The Life and Legend of Wyatt Earp
The Man From Blackhawk
Maverick
Rawhide
The Rebel
The Rifleman
Sugarfoot
Tales of Wells Fargo

The Texan
Wagon Train
Wanted: Dead or Alive
Wichita Town

Record number of consecutive years (1970 through 1995) that Elton John had at least one top-40 tune on the U.S. Billboard pop chart.

26 innings

Longest major-league baseball game ever played, a 1–1 tie between the Boston Braves and Brooklyn Dodgers on May 1, 1920.

27

Number of amendments to the U.S. Constitution.

Number of 8-by-10 glossy photos prepared as evidence against Arlo Guthrie in his trial for littering, as recounted in his tune "Alice's Restaurant."

Number of "vitamins, minerals and other essential food elements" found in Ovaltine milk supplement, according to its 1950s TV commercials.

Number of wives of Mormon leader Brigham Young. He had as many as 19 wives at one time.

27 inches

See **134 ounces**

27.002 inches

Maximum circumference of a ball in professional bowling.

27.065 megahertz

Frequency of CB radio emergency channel 9.

28

Number of dominoes in a standard set.

Number of hurdles in an Olympic steeplechase.

Number of letters in the Arabic alphabet.

Number of letters in the Spanish alphabet, consisting of 25 of the 26 letters in the English alphabet (all except w), plus ch, ll, and ñ.

Number of medals for bravery awarded to Audie Murphy during World War II, consisting of 24 from the United States (including the Medal of Honor), three from France, and one from Belgium.

Number of operas composed by Giuseppe Verdi, including Rigoletto, Aïda and La Traviata.

Number of purchasable spaces in the board game Monopoly.

See also **Howard Johnson's original flavors**

28 inches

Maximum circumference of a ball in Olympic soccer. (Minimum is 27 inches.)

28 years, 2 months, 19 days

Length of time that the title character is marooned, in the Daniel Defoe novel *Robinson Crusoe.*

29

Pennsylvania Station track from which the title train departs, in the tune "Chattanooga Choo Choo."

30

Minimum age for a member of the U.S. Senate, according to the U.S. Constitution.

Number of publishers that rejected radical Abbie Hoffman's *Steal This Book* before it was published in 1971.

The 30 Foot Bride of Candy Rock

1959 film that was Lou Costello's only starring role without Bud Abbott.

30 inches

Maximum circumference of a basketball, according to NBA rules. (Minimum is 29½ inches.)

31

Number of radio Fireside Chats broadcast by President Franklin D. Roosevelt. The first was on March 12, 1933, and the last on January 6, 1945.

Record number of lengths by which Secretariat won the Belmont Stakes in 1973.

Number of states of Mexico.

Number of travelers bound for the title destination in Geoffrey Chaucer's *Canterbury Tales,* consisting of 30 pilgrims and the author himself.

See also **Baskin Robbins original flavors**

31.5

NBA record career scoring average of Michael Jordan.

32

Number of bathrooms in the White House.

Number of disks per player in the board game Othello.

Number of drafts written by Meredith Willson of his musical *The Music Man.*

Number of houses included in the board game Monopoly.

Record number of Grammy Awards won by conductor Sir Georg Solti, more than any other recording artist in any genre. He led the Chicago Symphony from 1969 to 1991.

Number of Rhodes scholarships awarded annually to U.S. citizens, for two or three years of study at Oxford University in England.

Number of steps from Dagwood Bumstead's living-room chair to the refrigerator, in the comic strip *Blondie*.

32 days

Shortest term served by a U.S. president, that of William Henry Harrison (March 4 to April 4, 1841).

33

Age of adulthood for hobbits, in the novels of J. R. R. Tolkien.

Number of degrees of Scottish Rite freemasonry, from Entered Apprentice to Sovereign Grand Inspector General.

Number of letters in the Russian alphabet.

34

Perpetual age of cartoon character Popeye. He is 5 feet 6 inches tall and weighs 154 pounds.

Total number of Tony Awards won by the nine Broadway musicals of Rodgers and Hammerstein.

34 days

Length of the reign of Pope John Paul I (August 26, 1978, to September 28, 1978).

35

Maximum number of characters (including spaces and punctuation) that can be used for the names of pedigreed cats registered with the Cat Fanciers Association.

Minimum age for a U.S. president, according to the U.S. Constitution.

35 seconds

Performance time of the Samuel Beckett absurdist play *Breath*.

36

Number of Doric columns supporting the Lincoln Memorial in Washington, D.C., representing each state in the Union at the time of Lincoln's death.

Number of footballs made available for each game, according to NFL rules.

36 feet

Chest measurement of the title character in the film *King Kong* (1933).

36 years

Gap in the film career of comedian George Burns, between *Honolulu* in 1939 and *The Sunshine Boys* in 1975. He appeared in 13 films from 1932 to 1939, and eight films between 1975 and 1988. (He narrated the 1956 film *The Solid Gold Cadillac,* but did not appear on screen.)

37

Normal body temperature in Celsius/Centigrade degrees.

Number of Emmy nominations received by the 1977 miniseries *Roots,* the most for any program in a single year. *Roots* won "only" nine Emmys that year, in part because it was competing against itself in a number of categories.

Number of plays attributed to William Shakespeare.

37 cents

Cost of a Burger King Whopper when first introduced in 1957.

38

Numbers on a roulette wheel, including 0 and 00.

38 inches

Maximum length of a bat in cricket.

38 months

Gestation period of the Alpine black salamander, which lives in the Swiss Alps. This is the longest gestation period for any animal.

39

Age that comedian Jack Benny always claimed to be.

Number of operas composed by Gioacchino Rossini, including *The Barber of Seville* and *William Tell.*

Number of signers of the U.S. Constitution, which was signed by all on September 17, 1787.

Number of narrow wooden strips (called "boards") that make up a ten-pin bowling lane.

See also **Mouseketeers, original**

39.37008

Number of inches in one meter.

39ers

Nickname of the athletic teams of Jack Benny Middle School in Waukegan, Illinois, for Benny's perpetual claimed age. Waukegan was Benny's hometown.

40

Number of paintings on the walls depicted by Samuel Morse in his famous painting *Gallery of the Louvre,* which he completed in 1833.

Number of pieces in each player's army in the board game Stratego.

Number of seats in the Peanut Gallery in the children's TV series Howdy Doody.

Number of spaces around the board in the game Monopoly.

Record number of points scored in one NFL game (six touchdowns and four extra points), by Chicago Cardinal Ernie Nevers against the Chicago Bears on November 28, 1929.

See also **cat breeds; Jelly Belly Jelly Beans flavors**

40 feet

Standard distance between stakes in regulation horseshoes.

40.3 miles

Shore-to-shore length of the Panama Canal.

$40.55

See **$150,000**

41

Age of the title character in the Helen Reddy tune "Delta Dawn."

Number of signers of the Mayflower Compact.

42

Number of gallons of oil in one barrel.

Number of geographical territories in the board game Risk.

Number of spaces around the board (not counting the paths to the center) in the game Trivial Pursuit.

Number of stanzas in the John Keats poem "The Eve of St. Agnes."

The ultimate answer to life, the universe, and everything, according to the Douglas Adams novel The Restaurant at the Edge of the Universe.

42 inches

Maximum length of a bat in major-league baseball.

Maximum width of a lane in professionl bowling, excluding the gutters. (Minimum width is 41 inches.)

43

Number of muscles needed to frown.

43 inches

Height of a stack of $1,000,000 in U.S. $100 bills. The same amount in $1 bills would be 100 times as tall, or 358.3 feet.

45

Record number of career holes-in-one recorded by pro golfer Art Wall.

45 feet

Height of the letters in the famous Hollywood sign that overlooks Hollywood, California.

45.1 yards

NFL record career punting average of Hall of Famer Sammy Baugh.

45.52 carats

Weight of the Hope Diamond, which was donated to the Smithsonian Institution by jewelry company Harry Winston, Inc., in 1958.

45 Minutes from Harlem

Original working title of the TV sitcom *Diff'rent Strokes.*

46

Number of chromosomes in a normal human cell.

47

Number of strings on a standard orchestra harp.

Number of times its weight in stomach acid consumed by each Rolaids tablet, according to the TV commercials.

48

Number of cards in a pinochle deck, consisting of two cards each of Nine through Ace in each of the four suits.

Number of freckles on the face of the title character in the children's TV series Howdy Doody, one for each state in the Union when the series premiered.

Number of different pigs used as the title character of the film Babe. This was necessary because of the rapid growth rate of young pigs.

Number of rooms in the Carrington mansion, in the TV series Dynasty.

Number of states (out of 48) carried by presidential candidate John P. Wintergreen in the George and Ira Gershwin musical *Of Thee I Sing.*

Number of teaspoons in one cup.

49

Number of names of Russian composers rattled off in 39 seconds by Danny Kaye in the Kurt Weill/Ira Gershwin tune "Tchaikowsky (and Other Russians)" from the musical *Lady in the Dark.*

Number of professional victories (without a defeat) in the career of 1950s heavyweight boxing champ Rocky Marciano.

Number of Western Hemisphere Nobel Prize winners honored at a White House dinner hosted by President John F. Kennedy on April 29, 1962. Kennedy called this group "the most extraordinary collection of talent, of human knowledge, that has ever gathered at the White House, with the possible exception of when Thomas Jefferson dined alone."

50

Number of American flags that surround the Washington Monument in Washington, D.C., one for each state in the Union.

Number of hard-boiled eggs consumed by the title character (Paul Newman) to win a bet, in the film *Cool Hand Luke.*

Point bonus for using all seven of one's letters in Scrabble.

Record number of career steals of home by baseball Hall of Famer Ty Cobb.

"50 bells"

What the name of automaker Isuzu means in Japanese.

51

Number of churches designed by architect Sir Christopher Wren after the Great Fire of London in 1666, including St. Paul's Cathedral.

Number of languages into which the novels of Sidney Sheldon have been translated.

Number of members of the United Nations at its founding in 1945.

Total number of innovative Tucker automobiles built by Preston Tucker in 1948, before his business failed.

See also **823**

52

Highest position ever achieved by the TV series *Star Trek* in a yearly Nielsen rating, during its first (1966–67) season.

Number of "fundamental errors" found in Parker Brothers' first evaluation of Charles Darrow's board game Monopoly in 1934. Darrow began marketing the game himself, and it was bought by Parker Brothers in 1935 after it became successful.

52 feet

Length of a regulation shuffleboard court.

52 XXXXL (extra-extra-extra-extra-long)

Jersey size of NBA star Shaquille O'Neal.

53

Number painted on the side of Herbie, the title vehicle in the Disney film *The Love Bug.*

54

Number of lines in the uncompleted Samuel Taylor Coleridge poem "Kubla Khan."

Number of people saved by Bernie LaPlante (Dustin Hoffman) in the film Hero.

Number of slots in the casino game Wheel of Fortune, aka Big Six.

Number of color squares on a Rubik's Cube.

Record number of covers of Time magazine on which Richard Nixon has appeared.

55

Number of episodes of the TV miniseries *Upstairs, Downstairs* broadcast on *Masterpiece Theatre* in the U.S., from 1974 to 1977. 68 episodes were originally broadcast on British television from 1971 to 1975.

56

Number of curls that were always in the hair of child star Shirley Temple.

Number of physical characteristics listed on the Bertillon Card ID of all registered racing greyhounds.

Number of signers of the Declaration of Independence.

56 millimeters

Length of each side of a Rubik's Cube, equivalent to 2.2 inches.

57

Number of men killed by the title character (Sylvester Stallone) in the film *Rambo—First Blood Part II.*

58

Number of facets on a Round Brilliant Cut diamond.

Number of times that the comedy team Wayne and Shuster appeared on the TV variety series *The Ed Sullivan Show*, more than any other act or performer.

58 Minutes

Novel by Walter Wager that was the basis for the film *Die Hard 2*.

60

Number of baseballs prepared by the umpires for each major-league game, according to official rules.

Number of cards used in the game Rack-O.

Number of home runs hit by New York Yankee Babe Ruth in the 1927 baseball season. This was the single-season major-league record until broken by Roger Maris in 1961.

Number of spaces around the board (not counting the interior spaces) in the game Sorry!

60 feet

Distance between the foul line and the head pin in ten-pin bowling.

60 Minutes stopwatch brands

Manufacturers of the stopwatches in the opening credits of *60 Minutes*:
    Minerva: starting with the third show and for
        several shows thereafter
    Heuer: late 1968 to the late 1970s
    Aristo: late 1970s to present
No stopwatch was in the first two shows of October 8 and 15, 1968.

61

Number of bonus squares on a Scrabble board, consisting of 24 Double Letter Scores, 17 Double Word Scores, 12 Triple Letter Scores and 8 Triple Word Scores.

Number of home runs hit by New York Yankee Roger Maris in the 1961 baseball season. This was the single-season major-league record until broken by Mark McGwire in 1998.

Number of NHL records broken or tied by Wayne Gretzky in his 21-year career, consisting of 40 regular-season, 15 playoff, and six All-Star Game records.

$62.00

Weekly salary of bus driver Ralph Kramden (Jackie Gleason) in the TV sitcom *The Honeymooners*.

62.4 pounds

Weight of one cubic foot of water.

63 feet

Length of wire used to make a standard Slinky.

64

Number of Academy Award nominations received by Walt Disney, the most ever for any individual.

Number of poems in the Robert Louis Stevenson book *A Child's Garden of Verses*.

Number of squares on a checkerboard/chess board.

64 years, 258 days

Age of the oldest Olympic athlete to win a gold medal, Oscar Swahn. He won the running-deer shooting event in the 1912 Summer Olympics at Stockholm.

65 GGG

Shoe size of Snuffleupagus in the children's TV series *Sesame Street*.

66

Number of books in the Christian Protestant Bible, consisting of 39 in the Old Testament and 27 in the New Testament.

66 degrees, 32 minutes

Latitude of the Arctic and Antarctic Circles (North Latitude and South Latitude, respectively). These imaginary lines mark the southernmost/northernmost limit of the area within which the Sun does not rise for at least one day each year, and the Sun does not set for at least one day each year.

67

Number of children fathered by the King of Siam in the Rodgers and Hammerstein musical *The King and I*.

68

Number of spaces around the board (not counting the paths to the center) in the game Parcheesi.

Percentage of air (by volume) in Hostess Twinkies.

70

Record number of home runs hit by St. Louis Cardinal Mark McGwire in the 1998 baseball season.

70 minutes

Length of a game in Olympic field hockey, consisting of two 35-minute halves.

71

Number of known moons (natural satellites) in the solar system:

    Mercury: 0
    Venus: 0
    Earth: 1
    Mars: 2
    Jupiter: 16
    Saturn: 22
    Uranus: 21
    Neptune: 8
    Pluto: 1

These include four moons of Saturn whose discovery was announced in October 2000.

72

Number of people killed by John Robie (Cary Grant) while in the French Resistance, in the Alfred Hitchcock film *To Catch a Thief.*

72 days, 6 hours, 11 minutes, 14 seconds

See **Seaman, Elizabeth Cochrane**

73

Number of elevators that serve the 102-story Empire State Building in New York City.

75

IQ of the title character (Tom Hanks), as tested before entering elementary school, in the film *Forrest Gump.*

76

Number of letters in the Thai alphabet, consisting of 32 vowels and 44 consonants.

78

Fahrenheit melting point of cocoa butter, which explains why chocolate bars melt in the summer.

78.26

Exact number of revolutions per minute that 78 RPM records spin while being played.

79

Total number of episodes in the original TV series *Star Trek.*

80

Maximum Fahrenheit temperature for the water in an Olympic swimming pool. (Minimum is 78 degrees.)

Number of men who died trying to stop Baron von Richthofen, in the Royal Guardsmen tune "Snoopy vs. The Red Baron."

Number of numbers to select from in the casino game keno.

80 minutes

Length of a match in rugby, consisting of two 40-minute halves.

81

NFL record number of career interceptions by Hall of Famer Paul Krause.

Record number of PGA tour events won by golf great Sam Snead.

82

Number of regular-season games per team in the NBA.

Number of regular-season games per team in the NHL.

See also **Perry Mason book series**

82 minutes, 40 seconds

Playing time of the longest game in NFL history, an AFC divisional playoff on December 25, 1971. The Miami Dolphins defeated the Kansas City Chiefs, 27–24, after 22 minutes, 40 seconds of sudden-death overtime.

83

Number of functions of the cigarette lighter of the title character (James Coburn) in the film *Our Man Flint.*

86

Number of area codes originally assigned to all of North America by AT&T in 1947. Today, North America has over 300 area codes.

Number of symbols in the Cherokee alphabet, as developed by Sequoyah and completed in 1821.

88

Number of keys on a standard piano, consisting of 52 white keys and 36 black keys. The lowest key is an A, and the highest is a C.

Record number of consecutive games won by coach John Wooden's UCLA basketball team from 1971 to 1974.

88 miles per hour

Speed that activates the DeLorean time machine in the *Back to the Future* films.

90

Number of antique horses on Cinderella's Golden Carousel at Walt Disney World.

Number of words in the full title of the 1999 Fiona Apple album known as *When the Pawn* for short. The full title: *When the Pawn Hits the Conflicts He Thinks Like a King What He Knows Throws the Blows When He Goes to the Fight and He'll Win the Whole Thing 'Fore He Enters the Ring There's No Body to Batter When Your Mind Is Your Might So When You Go Solo, You Hold Your Own Hand and Remember That Depth Is the Greatest of Heights and If You Know Where You Stand, Then You Know Where to Land and If You Fall It Won't Matter, Cuz You'll Know That You're Right.*

90 minutes

Length of a game in Olympic soccer, consisting of two 45-minute halves.

90 *Bristol Court*

Umbrella title of the three TV sitcoms *Karen, Harris Against the World,* and *Tom, Dick and Mary,* which aired in consecutive half-hours on NBC in 1964.

91

Record number of times that Hall of Fame baseball manager Earl Weaver was ejected from a major-league game.

93

Number of secretaries hired by the title character (Candice Bergen) during the 10-year run of the TV sitcom *Murphy Brown.* The 93rd secretary, in the final episode, is portrayed by Bette Midler.

See also **823**

94

Number of Adolf Hitler clones created under the direction of Josef Mengele (Gregory Peck) in the film *The Boys from Brazil.*

94 pounds

Standard U.S. weight of a bag of cement.

96

Number of acceptable two-letter words in the Official Tournament and Club Word List of the National Scrabble Association.

96 years

Time span of the film *Things to Come,* from 1940 to 2036.

97

Number of keys on the 9½-foot long Austrian-made Bösendorfer Imperial Concert Grand piano. The extra nine keys (beyond the usual 88) are all below what is normally the lowest piano key.

97 pounds

Weight of the "weakling" in the memorable ads for the bodybuilding program of Charles Atlas.

100

NBA record number of points scored by Philadelphia Warrior Wilt Chamberlain against the New York Knicks on March 2, 1962, in Hershey, Pennsylvania.

Number of eyes of Argus, mythical giant guardian of the heifer Io.

Number of letter tiles (including the two blanks) in Scrabble.

Number of stories in Giovanni Boccaccio's *The Decameron.*

Number of zeros that follow a 1 in a googol. The term was coined in 1938 by mathematician Edward Kasner, who also coined the term "googolplex" for a 1 followed by a googol of zeroes.

$100

Fine imposed on John T. Scopes after being found guilty of teaching the theory of evolution in Dayton, Tennessee, on July 21, 1925. The conviction was later overturned on appeal.

102

Number of passengers on the *Mayflower* when it left Plymouth, England, on September 6, 1620. When the ship arrived at what is now Provincetown, Massachusetts, on November 11, there were 101 passengers aboard. (En route, two people had died and one child was born.)

103

Record number of ballots required for the 1924 Democratic National Convention to choose John W. Davis as its presidential nominee. Davis lost to Calvin Coolidge in the general election.

105

Number of Betty Boop cartoons produced by Max Fleischer, from "Silly Scandals" in 1931 to "Rhythm on the Reservation" in 1939.

108

Number of cards used in canasta, consisting of two standard decks of 52 plus four jokers.

Number of cards used in the game Uno.

Number of stitches on a major-league baseball.

Number of symphonies composed by Joseph Haydn.

109

Record number of men's pro singles tournaments won by tennis great Jimmy Connors.

110

Number of cornets in "the big parade," according to the tune "Seventy Six Trombones" from the musical *The Music Man.*

Record number of career shutouts pitched by baseball Hall of Famer Walter Johnson.

111

Emergency telephone number in New Zealand, comparable to 911 in the United States.

Number of articles in the Charter of the United Nations.

112

Number of cards used in the game Mille Bornes.

Number of sand traps on the Old Course at St. Andrews, Scotland.

114

Number of chapters (called "suras") that make up the Koran.

Number of words in the first sentence of the Charles Dickens novel *A Tale of Two Cities.*

Record number of recordings of Elvis Presley to reach the U.S. *Billboard* top-40 pop chart.

114.4

See **ice-nine**

116 years

Length of the Hundred Years' War (1337–1453).

117

Highest track number at New York City's Grand Central Station.

118

Number of islands upon which Venice, Italy is built.

Number of ridges on the edge of a United States dime.

119

Number of ridges on the edge of a United States quarter.

120 feet

Length of the world's shortest river, the D River in Oregon. It flows from Devils Lake into the Pacific.

121

Number of holes in a standard board of Chinese checkers.

Winning point total in cribbage.

124

Number of Munchkins in the cast of the film *The Wizard of Oz.*

125

Number of times the word "Duke" is sung in the Gene Chandler tune "Duke of Earl."

127 feet, 3.35 inches

Distance between home plate and second base in major-league baseball.

128

Number of cubic feet in one cord, a measure of volume for firewood.

132

Number of islands that make up the state of Hawaii.

Number of rooms in the White House.

132 years

Continuous period that the U.S. held the America's Cup yachting trophy, from the first race in 1851 (through 25 successful defenses) until losing to Australia in 1983. This is the longest winning streak (in elapsed time) in sports history.

133

Number of ridges on the edge of a Susan B. Anthony dollar (minted 1979–81). The current Sacagawea dollar has no ridges.

134 ounces

Weight of the solid-silver America's Cup yachting trophy, which is 27 inches high.

135

Number of chapters in the Herman Melville novel *Moby-Dick.* An epilogue follows the 135 chapters.

Number of words in the second presidential inaugural address of George Washington, delivered on March 4, 1793—by far the shortest inaugural address to date. The speech in full:

Fellow citizens: I am again called upon by the

voice of my country to execute the functions of its Chief Magistrate. When the occasion proper for it shall arrive, I shall endeavor to express the high sense I entertain of this distinguished honor, and of the confidence which has been reposed in me by the people of united America. Previous to the execution of any official act of the President, the Constitution requires an oath of office. This oath I am now about to take, and in your presence: That if it shall be found during my administration of the Government I have in any instance violated willingly or knowingly the injunctions thereof, I may (besides incurring constitutional punishment) be subject to the upbraidings of all who are now witnesses of the present solemn ceremony.

136

Number of marches composed by John Philip Sousa.

138

Number of career home runs hit by baseball Hall of Famer Roger Connor, which was the major-league record from 1897 until 1921, when it was broken by Babe Ruth.

142

Number of staircases at Hogwarts, in the Harry Potter series of books by J. K. Rowling.

144

Standard number of tiles in a mah-jongg set.

148

See **dog breeds**

150

Number of Psalms in the biblical book of the same name.

Number of ridges on the edge of a U.S. half dollar.

Seating capacity of the Round Table of Arthurian legend.

151

Number of spaces on the board in the Uncle Wiggily Game.

Seating capacity of New York City's Sullivan Street Playhouse, which has been the home of the musical *The Fantasticks* since its opening on May 3, 1960. The play has been performed there over 16,500 times since then.

151 feet, 1 inch

Height of the Statue of Liberty from base to torch.

153

Number of films that actor John Wayne appeared in, from *The Drop Kick* in 1927 to *The Shootist* in 1976.

154

Number of sonnets attributed to William Shakespeare.

154 pounds

See **34**

160 acres

Amount of unoccupied public land given per person under the Homestead Act of 1862, in exchange for living on the land and cultivating it.

Size of the farm of Lisa and Oliver Wendell Douglas (Eva Gabor and Eddie Albert) in the TV sitcom *Green Acres*.

160 feet

Width of a football field in the NFL.

162

Number of regular-season games per team in major-league baseball.

Number of Tom and Jerry cartoons produced by MGM, from 1940 to 1967. The characters were created by Hanna and Barbera.

167

Record number of women's pro singles tournaments won by tennis great Martina Navratilova.

168

Number of hours in one week.

Total number of spots (pips) on a standard set of dominoes.

169 pounds

Weight of one cubic foot of pure aluminum.

172

Age of Lola in the musical *Damn Yankees*.

174

Number of postgraduate scholarships awarded annually by the NCAA, to student-athletes who have excelled both academically and athletically.

178

Average number of sesame seeds on a McDonald's Big Mac bun.

180 pounds

Maximum allowable weight for Project Mercury astronauts.

184 pounds

Weight of *Sputnik 1*, first artificial satellite to orbit the Earth. It was launched by the Soviet Union on October 4, 1957.

188

Number of languages that Robby the Robot can speak, in the film *Forbidden Planet*.

188 decibels

Loudness of the whistling call of the blue whale, the loudest sound made by any animal.

190

Number of Three Stooges shorts produced by Columbia Pictures, from "Woman Haters" in 1934 to "Sappy Bullfighters" in 1959.

192

Directory-assistance telephone number (called "directory enquiries") in Great Britain, comparable to 411 in the United States.

Average number of peanut M&Ms per pound.

195

Number of Woody Woodpecker cartoons produced by Walter Lantz, from 1941 to 1972.

200

Number of laps in the Indianapolis 500, whose track is 2½ miles long.

Number of milligrams in one carat, a measure of weight for gemstones.

$200

Daily fee (plus expenses) charged by the title character (James Garner) in the TV series *The Rockford Files*.

206

Number of bones in the adult human body.

220

Number of spaceships in the caravan following the title spaceship to Earth, in the TV series *Battlestar Galactica*.

Number of different words used in the Dr. Seuss children's book *The Cat in the Hat*.

221B Baker Street

London home of Sir Arthur Conan Doyle sleuth Sherlock Holmes.

222 to 0

Score of the most lopsided game in college football history, in which Georgia Tech beat Cumberland College on October 7, 1916.

225

Number of squares on a Scrabble board.

229

Age of the title character (voiced by Paul Fusco) during the first season of the TV sitcom *ALF*.

231

Number of cubic inches in one gallon.

240

Number of bedrooms in London's Buckingham Palace, consisting of 52 for the royal family and guests, and 188 for staff.

244

Number of mythical former residents of the title town whose poems are collected in Edgar Lee Masters' *Spoon River Anthology*.

245 pounds

Weight of the title character in the Jimmy Dean tune "Big Bad John." John is 6 feet 6 inches tall.

$250

Cost of a vowel in the TV game show *Wheel of Fortune* since the show's debut on January 6, 1975. This must be one of the very few items anywhere that costs the same today as it did 25 years ago.

254

Number of counties in the state of Texas, more than any other state. Georgia, with 159, is in a distant second place. (California, the most populous state and the third-largest state in area, has only 58 counties.)

264

Number of men in the U.S. Seventh Cavalry under the command of George Armstrong Custer at the Battle of the Little Bighorn in 1876.

270

Minimum number of electoral votes required for a victory in U.S. presidential elections.

271

See **Everett, Edward**

282

Record number of consecutive NFL games in which defensive end Jim Marshall appeared, from September 25, 1960 (with the Cleveland Browns) to December 16, 1979 (with the Minnesota Vikings).

284

Number of restrooms in the Pentagon in Arlington, Virginia.

285

Number of Rules of Acquisition of the profit-hungry Ferengi in the TV series *Star Trek: Deep Space Nine*. Rule #1: Once you have their money, you never give it back.

293

Number of different combinations of current U.S. coins that add up to $1.00.

294

Number of steps to the top of the Leaning Tower of Pisa.

300

See **12**

311

Number of athletes (from 13 countries) participating in the first modern Olympics, held in Athens, Greece, in 1896. In contrast, about 10,000 athletes from over 150 countries have participated in the most recent Summer Olympics.

312

Record number of career triples hit by baseball Hall of Famer Sam Crawford.

313

Record number of career losses by Hall of Fame baseball pitcher Cy Young.

321

Area code for the region of northeast Florida that appropriately (because of the countdown allusion) includes Cape Canaveral.

322

Number of *Saturday Evening Post* covers drawn by Norman Rockwell. His first was for the May 20, 1916, issue; his last, a portrait of President John F. Kennedy, was for the December 14, 1963, issue.

324

Number of possible solutions in the standard edition of the whodunit board game Clue (6 suspects × 6 weapons × 9 rooms).

325 days

Length of the reign of King Edward VIII of Great Britain (January–December 1936), who abdicated the throne in order to marry American-born commoner Wallis Warfield Simpson.

336

Number of dimples on a regulation American golf ball.

340

Record number of NFL games in which Hall of Famer George Blanda appeared, from 1949 to 1975.

342

See **Eleanor, Beaver, and Dartmouth**

360

Number of watchtowers that guarded the ancient city of Babylon.

361

Number of points on the board in the game Go.

364

Total number of gifts given by "my true love" in the tune "The Twelve Days of Christmas."

370

Record number of total points scored in an NBA game, when the Detroit Pistons defeated the Denver Nuggets 186–184 (in triple overtime) on December 13, 1983.

375

Number of voices in the Mormon Tabernacle Choir.

400 feet

Minimum distance from home plate to the center field fence in major-league baseball. The minimum distance from home plate to each foul pole (left field and right field) is 325 feet.

406 yards

NCAA Division I-A record single-game football rushing yardage, achieved by Texas Christian University running back LaDainian Tomlinson against Texas–El Paso on November 20, 1999.

408

See **Eddie Robinson Award**

417 feet
Width of the original U.S.S. *Enterprise* in the TV series *Star Trek*.

420
NFL record career touchdown passes by Dan Marino.

423 carats
See **The Star of Rhodesia**

444 days
Length of time that the 52 American hostages were held in Iran, from November 4, 1979, to January 20, 1981.

4:50 from Paddington
Novel by Dame Agatha Christie that was the basis for the film *Murder, She Said*.

465 feet
Proportional height of the full bodies represented by the presidential heads at Mount Rushmore National Memorial in South Dakota.

478
See **Zapruder, Abraham**

480 pounds
Standard U.S. weight of one bale of cotton.

490
Number of U.S. currency notes to the pound (any denomination).

500 grams
Maximum weight of a foil or saber in Olympic fencing, equivalent to 17.6 ounces.

505
Record number of career home runs allowed by Hall of Fame baseball pitcher Robin Roberts.

508.00
Point decline of the Dow Jones Industrial Average on "Black Monday," October 19, 1987—a 22.6 percent single-day drop.

511
Record number of career wins by Hall of Fame baseball pitcher Cy Young.

512
Average number of plain M&Ms per pound.

$516.32
Prize awarded to the top-scoring performer on the original daytime version of the TV game show *The Gong Show*.

528 A.D.
Setting of the Mark Twain novel *A Connecticut Yankee in King Arthur's Court*.

532 miles
Total length of the bookshelves at the Library of Congress in Washington, D.C.

537 votes
The certified margin of victory of George W. Bush over Al Gore in Florida, in the 2000 presidential election.

555 (or KLondike 5)
Telephone exchange often used for phone numbers in films and TV, because it is reserved by phone companies nationwide for directory assistance. Thus, any phone number starting with 555 can never be the real phone number of a person or company.

555 feet, 5½ inches
Height of the Washington Monument in Washington, D.C.

580
Number of characters in the Leo Tolstoy novel *War and Peace*.

586
See **"Mighty Mouth"**

599 years, 1 month, 17 days
Age of Noah when the rains came, according to Genesis 7:11 (King James Version).

600 grams
Minimum weight of a woman's Olympic javelin, equivalent to 1.3 pounds.

624 feet
Length of the Washington, D.C. subway that connects the Rayburn House Office Building with the U.S. Capitol. It is used to transport congressmen back and forth.

635
Number of bills vetoed by President Franklin D. Roosevelt during his 12+ years in office, more than any other U.S. president. (Only nine of his vetoes

were overridden by Congress.) Second place is held by Grover Cleveland, who vetoed a total of 584 bills during his two nonconsecutive terms.

Number of tunes recorded by cowboy singer Gene Autry, which have sold a total of over 40 million copies.

639

Number of muscles in the adult human body.

640

Number of acres in one square mile.

650

Typical beats-per-minute heart rate of a mouse.

655 pounds

Weight of one cubic foot of pure silver.

660 days

Average gestation of the African elephant, the longest gestation period for any mammal.

673

Actual number of horsemen in the British Light Brigade commanded by General Lord Cardigan during the Crimean War's Battle of Balaclava on October 25, 1854. The Alfred, Lord Tennyson, poem "The Charge of the Light Brigade" commemorates the "noble six hundred" who participated in the battle.

700

Number of wives of King Solomon, according to I Kings 11:3 (King James Version).

705

See **Rostron, Arthur Henry**

708 pounds

Weight of one cubic foot of pure lead.

$712.05

Prize awarded to the top-scoring performer on the original nighttime version of the TV game show *The Gong Show*.

714

Number of career home runs hit by baseball Hall of Famer Babe Ruth. This was the major-league record from Ruth's retirement in 1935 until surpassed by Hank Aaron in 1974.

Badge number of Joe Friday (Jack Webb) in the TV series *Dragnet*. Webb selected that number as a tribute to the career home-run total of Babe Ruth.

723

Number of books written by romance novelist Dame Barbara Cartland, whose books have sold over 1 billion copies worldwide in 36 languages.

741

Record number of consecutive weeks that the 1973 Pink Floyd album *The Dark Side of the Moon* appeared on the U.S. *Billboard* top-200 album chart.

745.7

Number of watts in one horsepower.

755

Record number of career home runs hit by baseball Hall of Famer Hank Aaron.

770 grams

Maximum weight of an épée in Olympic fencing, equivalent to 27.2 ounces.

792

Number of three-digit numbers that may be used as area codes. These exclude 0 or 1 as the first digit, and numbers ending in "11," which are reserved by telephone companies.

793

Record number of career doubles hit by baseball Hall of Famer Tris Speaker.

800

Car capacity of the garage attached to the 1,788-room palace of the Sultan of Brunei.

800 grams

Minimum weight of a man's Olympic javelin, equivalent to 1.8 pounds.

813

Population of Cicely, Alaska, according to the sign in the opening sequence of the TV series *Northern Exposure*.

823

Number of words in a sentence written by Victor Hugo in the novel *Les Misérables*. The sentence contains 93 commas and 51 semicolons.

$847.63

Amount that Maggie Simpson is scanned for at the supermarket, in an opening sequence of the animated TV sitcom *The Simpsons*.

$850

Price of the first Model T Ford when introduced in 1908.

868

Record number of home runs hit by Sadaharu Oh for the Yomiuri Giants in his 22-year Japanese professional baseball career.

882 feet, 9 inches

Length of the R.M.S. *Titanic*.

894

NHL record number of career goals scored by Wayne Gretzky.

897

Number of steps to the top of the Washington Monument in Washington, D.C.

921 feet

Length of each of the five outer walls of the Pentagon in Arlington, Virginia.

947 feet

Length of the original U.S.S. *Enterprise* in the TV series *Star Trek*.

954 feet

Length of the All-American Soap Box Derby, held each August in Akron, Ohio.

958

Number of words in a single sentence written by Marcel Proust in his novel *Cities of the Plain*. This is believed to be the longest sentence in all of world literature.

962

Second-oldest recorded age in the Bible, that of Jared (grandfather of Methuselah).

969

Oldest age recorded in the Bible, that of Methuselah.

982 pounds

Weight of Hymie the robot (Dick Gautier) in the TV sitcom *Get Smart*.

984 feet

Height of the Eiffel Tower in Paris, which was the world's tallest structure from its completion in 1889 until the completion of New York City's Chrysler Building in 1930.

999

Emergency telephone number in Great Britain, comparable to 911 in the United States.

1,000 meters

Length of the course for women's Olympic rowing events, equivalent to .6 miles.

1,036 days

Length of the presidential term of John F. Kennedy.

1,037 pages

Length of the first hardcover edition of the Margaret Mitchell novel *Gone With the Wind*, published in 1936.

1,037.56 miles per hour

Speed at which the Earth rotates at the equator.

1,046

Shortage of lifeboat seating capacity on the ill-fated maiden voyage of the R.M.S. *Titanic* in 1912. There were 2,224 passengers and crew on board, and the lifeboat capacity was only 1,178.

1,050 millimeters

Maximum overall length of a saber in Olympic fencing, equivalent to 41.3 inches.

1,087

Total number of broadcasts of the TV variety series *The Ed Sullivan Show*, originally titled *Toast of the Town*. The first show aired on June 20, 1948, and the last on May 30, 1971.

1,093

Record number of patents held by Thomas Edison.

1,100 millimeters

Maximum overall length of a foil or épée in Olympic fencing, equivalent to 43.3 inches.

1,151 miles

Length of the Northern Route traveled by competitors (in even-numbered years) from Anchorage to Nome in the Iditarod Trail Sled Dog Race.

1,161 miles

Length of the Southern Route traveled by competitors (in odd-numbered years) from Anchorage to Nome in the Iditarod Trail Sled Dog Race.

1,189 pounds

Weight of one cubic foot of pure uranium (uranium-238).

1,200

Number of stamps needed to fill a book of S&H Green Stamps. One stamp was given to customers for every 10 cents spent. Circa 1962, 150 books (180,000 stamps) could be exchanged for a mink stole.

1,206 pounds

Weight of one cubic foot of pure gold.

1,220

Number of pairs of shoes found in the presidential palace closet of former Philippine first lady Imelda Marcos, after she and her husband fled the country in 1986.

1,281

Number of goals scored by Brazilian soccer star Pelé in his 22-year professional career.

1,323

Number of words in the Declaration of Independence.

1,339 pounds

Weight of one cubic foot of pure platinum.

1,343

Number of lines in the Walt Whitman poem "Song of Myself."

1,352

Number of guitar pickers in the title city, in the Lovin' Spoonful tune "Nashville Cats."

1,366

Number of seats (memberships) in the New York Stock Exchange. The number has remained fixed since 1953.

1,440

Number of minutes in one day.

1,483 feet

See **Pelli, Cesar**

1492 Pictures

Production company of director Chris Columbus.

$1,500

Amount of money given to each player at the start of the board game Monopoly.

1,520

Total number of Medals of Honor awarded for service during the Civil War, approximately 45 percent of all the Medals of Honor awarded to date.

1,569

Number of lines spoken by the title character of the William Shakespeare play *Hamlet*. This is the most lines of any Shakespearean character.

1,609.344

Number of meters in one mile.

1,611

NBA record number of career games played by Robert Parish.

1620

Inscription on Plymouth Rock in Plymouth, Massachusetts.

1,665

Number of steps to the top of the Eiffel Tower in Paris.

1,728

Number of cubic inches in one cubic yard.

1,767

NHL record number of career games played by Hall of Famer Gordie Howe.

1,788

See **800**

1815 feet, 5 inches

Height of Toronto's CN Tower, the world's tallest freestanding structure.

1,932 feet

See **Mount Mazama**

1,960

Number of listings under William Shakespeare in the current (16th) edition of *Bartlett's Familiar Quotations,* the most for any one source. The King James Bible is in second place with 1,591 listings.

1,963

NHL record number of career assists by Wayne Gretzky.

2,000 meters

Length of the course for men's Olympic rowing events, equivalent to 1.2 miles.

2,080 pounds
Weight of the Liberty Bell in Philadelphia, Pennsylvania.

2,130
Number of consecutive games played by baseball Hall of Famer Lou Gehrig for the New York Yankees, from June 1, 1925, to April 30, 1939. This was the major-league record until surpassed by Cal Ripken Jr. in 1995.

2211
Badge number of Inspector Harry Callahan (Clint Eastwood) in the *Dirty Harry* films.

2,212
Population of River City, Iowa, setting of the musical *The Music Man*.

2,224
See **1,046**

2,240
Number of pounds in one long ton, aka "ton" in Great Britain.

2,297
Record number of career runs batted in, by baseball Hall of Famer Hank Aaron.

2,343
Total number of episodes of the children's TV series *Howdy Doody*. The first show aired on December 27, 1947, and the last on September 24, 1960.

2,500
Population of Bedrock, as shown in the first-season opening credits of the animated TV sitcom *The Flintstones*.

2,520
Smallest number evenly divisible by all of the digits from 2 to 9.

2525
Large ID number painted on the roof of the bus rigged with a bomb, in the film *Speed*.

2,570
Number of steps to the top of the 1,815-foot high CN Tower in Toronto.

2,597
Record number of career strikeouts of baseball Hall of Famer Reggie Jackson.

2,632
Record number of consecutive games played by baseball star Cal Ripken Jr. for the Baltimore Orioles, from May 30, 1982, to September 19, 1998.

2,811
Number of libraries endowed worldwide by steel magnate/philanthropist Andrew Carnegie.

2,857
NHL record number of total points (goals plus assists) scored by Wayne Gretzky.

2,930
Number of different people mentioned in the King James Version of the Bible.

3,000
Number of proverbs of King Solomon, according to I Kings 4:32 (King James Version).

3,000 meters
Length of an Olympic steeplechase.

3,106 carats
Size of the Cullinan Diamond, the largest diamond ever found. It was discovered on January 26, 1905, at the Premium Mine near Pretoria, South Africa. The two largest diamonds cut from it are today part of the British Crown Jewels kept at the Tower of London.

3,108 square miles
Area of Juneau, Alaska, the largest city in the United States in terms of area.

3,215
Record number of career singles hit by baseball great Pete Rose.

3,280.84
Number of feet in one kilometer.

3,562
Record number of career games played by baseball great Pete Rose.

3,731
Record number of regular-season games won in the 53-year career of Hall of Fame baseball manager Connie Mack.

3,736 nautical miles
See **Lecomte, Benoit "Ben"**

3,933

Number of lines in *Hamlet,* the longest play of William Shakespeare.

3955 A.D.

Setting of the films *Planet of the Apes* and *Beneath the Planet of the Apes.*

3,966

NHL record number of career penalty minutes of Tiger Williams.

4,049

Number of lines in the John Keats poem *Endymion.*

4,191

Number of career hits by baseball Hall of Famer Ty Cobb. This was the major-league record from Cobb's retirement after the 1928 season until surpassed by Pete Rose in 1985.

4,256

Record number of career hits by baseball great Pete Rose.

$4,350

Cost of a first-class suite ticket on the R.M.S. *Titanic,* approximately $50,000 in today's dollars.

4,840

Number of square yards in one acre.

$5,000

Maximum prize money that can be won by a contestant in the TV game show *Win Ben Stein's Money.*

5,005

Number of rooms at the MGM Grand in Las Vegas, Nevada, America's largest hotel.

5,280

Number of feet in one mile.

5,714

Record number of career strikeouts of Hall of Fame baseball pitcher Nolan Ryan.

6,000

Number of questions included in each edition of the board game Trivial Pursuit.

6009

Next calendar year that will read the same upside-down and right-side up. The last such year was 1961.

6,076.1155

Number of feet in one nautical mile.

6,400

Approximate Fahrenheit melting point of carbon, the highest melting point for any element. The exact melting point depends on the form of carbon.

7190

Serial number of the gold ingot used by James Bond (Sean Connery) as "bait" during his golf match with the title character (Gert Frobe) in the film *Goldfinger.*

7,485

Record number of Broadway performances of the Andrew Lloyd Webber musical *Cats.* The show opened at the Winter Garden Theatre on October 7, 1982, and closed there on September 10, 2000.

8,430 miles

Maximum range of a Boeing 747.

8,829

Number of consecutive games won by the Harlem Globetrotters from 1971 to 1995, the longest winning streak in sports history.

8,833

Number of winning mounts in the 41-year career of jockey Willie Shoemaker, who won a total of $123 million in purses. This was the all-time record for wins until surpassed by Laffit Pincay Jr. in 1999.

10,000 years

Time that the Genie (voiced by Robin Williams) was inside the lamp before being released by the title character (voiced by Scott Weinger), in the Disney animated film *Aladdin.*

13,677

Number of islands in Indonesia.

14,053

Record number of career at-bats by baseball great Pete Rose.

$15,000

Amount that James Bond (Sean Connery) insists that the title character (Gert Frobe) deliberately lose at gin rummy after catching him cheating, in the film *Goldfinger.*

$15,140

Amount of play money included with the standard version of the board game Monopoly.

16,726

NFL record career rushing yardage by Hall of Famer Walter Payton.

17,447

Number of four-room Cape Cod houses built in Levittown, New York, the first planned suburban housing development, from 1947 to 1951.

21,117

Number of lines in the Robert Browning poem *The Ring and the Book.*

23,924

NBA record number of career rebounds by Hall of Famer Wilt Chamberlain.

24601

Prison number of Jean Valjean in the Victor Hugo novel *Les Misérables.*

24,901.55 miles

Equatorial circumference of the Earth.

28,000 acres

Size of the Mississippi plantation of Big Daddy Pollitt (Burl Ives) in the film *Cat on a Hot Tin Roof.*

29,066

Number of different words used in the complete works of William Shakespeare.

29,598 feet

Total distance (over 5.5 miles) traveled by the record 70 home runs hit by Mark McGwire during the 1998 baseball season.

30,000 acres

Size of the Barkley family's California ranch, in the TV series *The Big Valley.*

34,753

Number of pieces of mail carried by the Pony Express between St. Joseph, Missouri, and Sacramento, California, during its 18-month existence (April 1860 to October 1861).

36,000

Typical quantity of quills on a porcupine.

38,387

Record number of total points scored by Kareem Abdul-Jabbar in his 20-year NBA career.

38,708

Record number of participants in the Boston Marathon of 1996, which was its 100th edition.

$40,000

Amount of money embezzled by Marion Crane (Janet Leigh) from her employer, in the Alfred Hitchcock film *Psycho.*

40,000 A.D.

Setting of the film *Barbarella.*

43,306 tons

Weight of the Gateway Arch in St. Louis, Missouri, consisting of 5,199 tons of steel and 38,107 tons of concrete. It was opened to the public on July 24, 1967.

45,024.52 miles

Total length of the United States Interstate Highway System.

49,000 acres

See **Xanadu**

51,201

Population of the title town in the TV series *Twin Peaks,* as stated on its "Welcome to" sign.

52,455

Number of islands in Canada.

57,285 gallons

Maximum fuel capacity of a Boeing 747.

58,220

Number of names inscribed on the Vietnam Veterans Memorial in Washington, D.C.

61,361

NFL record career passing yardage by quarterback Dan Marino.

68,894

Number of people in the cast of the film *Around the World in 80 Days.*

£80,000

Amount of money to be inherited by Leonard Vole (Tyrone Power) from the estate of Emily French (Norma Varden), in the film *Witness for the Prosecution.*

90,854 tons

Weight of the Washington Monument in Washington, D.C.

107,501

Seating capacity of Michigan Stadium, the largest college football stadium in the U.S. It is home to the University of Michigan Wolverines.

$125,000

Price paid by the New York Yankees to obtain future baseball Hall of Famer Babe Ruth from the Boston Red Sox in 1920.

$129,000

Total prize money won by Charles Van Doren on the NBC game show *Twenty-One*. His first appearance on the program was on November 28, 1956, and his last was on March 11, 1957.

138,435

Length of a marathon, in feet.

$150,000

Fee paid to the title character (Sylvester Stallone) for fighting heavyweight champion Apollo Creed (Carl Weathers), in the film *Rocky*. In his previous professional fight, Rocky is paid $40.55 (after expenses).

151,485 miles

Length of the coastline of Canada, the longest of any country in the world.

186,282.397 miles per second

The speed of light in a vacuum.

187,888

Number of lakes in Finland.

$283,200

Theoretical maximum that a contestant can win on a single episode of the TV game show *Jeopardy!* This assumes Daily Doubles on the minimum-value questions, each selected at the end of the round, with the maximum amounts being wagered in every case.

312,000 pounds

Weight of the Statue of Liberty, consisting of 62,000 pounds of copper and 250,000 pounds of steel.

450,000

Estimated number of jokes, each carefully categorized, in the files of comedian Bob Hope, now housed at the Library of Congress.

$500,000

See **Lucky Dan**

595,000 acres

Size of Reata Ranch in the film *Giant*.

802,701 A.D.

Highest-numbered year visited by the Time Traveler in the H. G. Wells novel *The Time Machine*.

1,048,576

Number of bytes in one kilobyte, equivalent to 2 to the 20th power.

1,249,000

Number of oil barrels stacked by environmental artist Christo for his work *Houston Mastaba, Texas* in 1969.

$1,267,500

Amount paid at an October, 1999 Christie's auction for the gown worn by Marilyn Monroe when she sang "Happy Birthday to You" to President John F. Kennedy at New York City's Madison Square Garden in 1962.

$1,542,000

Amount paid by Michael Jackson for producer David O. Selznick's Best Picture Oscar for *Gone with the Wind* in a June, 1999 Sotheby's auction.

2,200,000 light-years

Distance of the Andromeda galaxy from the Earth.

2,300,000

Estimated number of blocks of stone, averaging 2.5 tons each, used to construct the Great Pyramid at Giza, Egypt.

2,598,960

Number of different five-card poker hands that can be dealt from a standard 52-card deck.

$3,005,000

Price paid by Todd McFarlane for the final (70th) home-run ball hit by Mark McGwire during the 1998 baseball season. McFarlane, creator of the comic-book character Spawn, purchased the ball at a Guernsey's auction at New York City's Madison Square Garden on January 12, 1999.

See also **Ozersky, Philip**

3,333,360

Maximum score in the video-arcade game Pac-Man. It was first reached on May 8, 1999, by Billy Mitchell of Fort Lauderdale, Florida, at the Funspot Family Fun Center in Weirs Beach, New Hampshire.

4,360,000 cubic yards

Amount of concrete used in the building of Hoover Dam and its adjacent structures. This is enough concrete to pave a 16-foot-wide highway from San Francisco to New York City. The dam is located on the Colorado River on the Nevada/Arizona border, and its construction was completed in 1935.

6,469,952

Number of black spots drawn by Disney animators for the title canines, in the film *One Hundred and One Dalmatians*.

6,750,000 gallons

Capacity of the Reflecting Pool, located between the Washington Monument and the Lincoln Memorial in Washington, D.C. It is 2,318 feet long, 160 feet wide, and 3 feet deep.

$7,200,000

Amount paid by the United States to Russia for Alaska in 1867, which was less than two cents per acre.

8,000,000

Number of stories in the *Naked City,* according to the TV series' introduction.

15,456,868

Number of Model Ts built by the Ford Motor Company from 1908 to 1927.

$20,000,000

Highest cash prize won by Beauregard Bottomley (Ronald Colman) as a contestant on the TV game show *Masquerade for Money,* in the film *Champagne for Caesar.* He loses it all on the final double-or-nothing question, when he is unable to remember his Social Security number.

$30,800,000

Price paid by Microsoft founder Bill Gates for the *Codex Hammer,* a scientific notebook of Leonardo da Vinci, auctioned by Christie's in New York City on November 11, 1994.

31,536,000

Number of seconds in a 365-day year.

53310761

Serial number of Elvis Presley while he was in the U.S. Army, from 1958 to 1960.

60,000,003 B.C.

Setting of the TV sitcom *Dinosaurs.*

$72,000,000

See **Nidetch, Jean**

$95,000,000

Value of the Clampett family fortune at the end of the run of the TV sitcom *The Beverly Hillbillies.*

$100,000,000

Amount donated by the Vito Corleone Foundation to the Roman Catholic Church for the poor of Sicily, in the film *The Godfather Part III.*

147,300,000 ounces

Quantity of gold stored at the U.S. Bullion Depository at Fort Knox, Kentucky.

$400,000,000

Cost of Yahoo!, the most expensive property in the dot-com edition of the board game Monopoly, introduced in 2000. In the standard edition of the game, the most expensive property, Boardwalk, costs $400.

$640,000,000

Value of the bearer bonds that Hans Gruber (Alan Rickman) and his gang attempt to steal from the Nakatomi company vault, in the film *Die Hard.*

$750,000,000

Amount of money to be inherited by Arthur Bach (Dudley Moore) in the film *Arthur.*

1,210,000,000 watts (1.21 gigawatts)

Amount of electricity needed to power the DeLorean time machine in the *Back to the Future* films.

$8,000,000,001.67

Amount stolen via electronic transfer from the International Clearance Bank in Kuala Lumpur by thieves Mac (Sean Connery) and Gin (Catherine Zeta-Jones) in the film *Entrapment.*

$15,000,000,000

Value of the gold at Fort Knox that the title character (Gert Frobe) intends to contaminate with nuclear radiation, in the James Bond film *Goldfinger.*

635,013,559,600

Number of different 13-card bridge hands that can be dealt from a standard 52-card deck.

5,878,639,427,505.244 (5+ trillion)

Number of miles in one light-year.

19,173,514,177,205.12 (19+ trillion)

Number of miles in one parsec.

75,000,000,000,000 (75 trillion)

Estimated number of cells in the adult human body.

43,252,003,274,489,856,000 (43+ quintillion)

Number of different color positions on a Rubik's Cube.

361,000,000,000,000,000,000 (361 quintillion) gallons

Estimated amount of seawater in the world's oceans. This is equivalent to 328,000,000 cubic miles.

6,000,000,000,000,000,000,000 (6 sextillion) metric tons

Estimated weight of the planet Earth.

A-1 Detective Agency

Crime-solving group in the radio series *I Love a Mystery*.

Abba members

This Swedish pop group was named for the first letters of the first names of its members: Agnetha Fältskog, Anni-Frid Lyngstad, Benny Andersson, and Bjorn Ulvaeus.

Abba Pater

1999 CD with lead vocalist Pope John Paul II. The Holy Father mostly speaks on the CD (in French, English, Italian, Spanish and Latin), but does sing "Pater Noster."

Abbot

Title given to the presiding officer of the Friars Club.

Abbotsford

Home of Sir Walter Scott on the bank of the Tweed River in Scotland.

Abbott and Costello films

One Night in the Tropics (1940)
Buck Privates (1941)
In the Navy (1941)
Hold That Ghost (1941)
Keep 'Em Flying (1941)
Ride 'Em Cowboy (1942)
Rio Rita (1942)
Pardon My Sarong (1942)
Who Done It? (1942)
It Ain't Hay (1943)
Hit the Ice (1943)
In Society (1944)
Lost in a Harem (1944)
The Naughty Nineties (1945)
Abbott and Costello in Hollywood (1945)
Here Come the Co-eds (1945)
Little Giant (1946)
The Time of their Lives (1946)
Buck Privates Come Home (1947)
The Wistful Widow of Wagon Gap (1947)
The Noose Hangs High (1948)
Abbott and Costello Meet Frankenstein (1948)

Mexican Hayride (1948)
Abbott and Costello Meet the Killer, Boris Karloff (1949)
Africa Screams (1949)
Abbott and Costello in the Foreign Legion (1950)
Abbott and Costello Meet the Invisible Man (1951)
Comin' Round the Mountain (1951)
Jack and the Beanstalk (1952)
Lost in Alaska (1952)
Abbott and Costello Meet Captain Kidd (1952)
Abbott and Costello Go to Mars (1953)
Abbott and Costello Meet Dr. Jekyll and Mr. Hyde (1953)
Abbott and Costello Meet the Keystone Kops (1955)
Abbott and Costello Meet the Mummy (1955)
Dance with Me, Henry (1956)

Abbott-Downing Company

See **Concord**

Abbott, Eleanor

Inventor of the board game Candy Land in 1949.

Abbott, Scott and Haney, Chris

Inventors of the board game Trivial Pursuit in 1979.

"ABC Islands"

Nickname of Aruba, Bonaire and Curaçao, located off the coast of Venezuela.

Abel, Rudolf

Jailed KGB spymaster who was exchanged by the U.S. for U-2 reconnaissance plane pilot Francis Gary Powers (who had been shot down over the Soviet Union on May 1, 1960). The exchange took place across Berlin's Glienecker Bridge on February 10, 1962.

Abercrombie and Fitch

Trash collectors in the comic strip *Hi and Lois*.

Abraham

Real last name of novelist Nelson Algren.

Abu

Pet monkey of the title character (voiced by Scott Weinger) in the Disney animated film *Aladdin*.

Abyssinia

Former name of the African nation Ethiopia.

Academia Waltz

Comic strip by cartoonist Berke Breathed while a student at the University of Texas in the 1970s. It inspired his syndicated strip *Bloom County*, which debuted in 1980.

Academy Award "animal" films

These four films whose titles contain the name of an animal have won an Academy Award for Best Picture:

One Flew Over the Cuckoo's Nest (1975)
The Deer Hunter (1978)
Dances with Wolves (1990)
The Silence of the Lambs (1991)

Academy Award songs

Winners in the Best Song category, which was instituted in 1934. The songs are listed below with the films in which they appear:

1934 "The Continental" *(The Gay Divorcée)*
1935 "Lullaby of Broadway" *(Gold Diggers of 1935)*
1936 "The Way You Look Tonight" *(Swing Time)*
1937 "Sweet Leilani" *(Waikiki Wedding)*
1938 "Thanks for the Memory" *(The Big Broadcast of 1938)*
1939 "Over the Rainbow" *(The Wizard of Oz)*
1940 "When You Wish Upon a Star" *(Pinocchio)*
1941 "The Last Time I Saw Paris" *(Lady Be Good)*
1942 "White Christmas" *(Holiday Inn)*
1943 "You'll Never Know" *(Hello Frisco, Hello)*
1944 "Swinging on a Star" *(Going My Way)*
1945 "It Might as Well Be Spring" *(State Fair)*
1946 "On the Atchison, Topeka and Santa Fe" *(The Harvey Girls)*
1947 "Zip-A-Dee-Doo-Dah" *(Song of the South)*
1948 "Buttons and Bows" *(The Paleface)*
1949 "Baby, It's Cold Outside" *(Neptune's Daughter)*
1950 "Mona Lisa" *(Captain Carey)*
1951 "In the Cool, Cool, Cool of the Evening" *(Here Comes the Groom)*
1952 "High Noon (Do Not Forsake Me, Oh My Darlin')" *(High Noon)*
1953 "Secret Love" *(Calamity Jane)*
1954 "Three Coins in the Fountain" *(Three Coins in the Fountain)*
1955 "Love Is a Many-Splendored Thing" *(Love Is a Many-Splendored Thing)*
1956 "Whatever Will Be, Will Be (Que Será, Será)" *(The Man Who Knew Too Much)*
1957 "All the Way" *(The Joker Is Wild)*

1958 "Gigi" *(Gigi)*
1959 "High Hopes" *(A Hole in the Head)*
1960 "Never on Sunday" *(Never on Sunday)*
1961 "Moon River" *(Breakfast at Tiffany's)*
1962 "Days of Wine and Roses" *(Days of Wine and Roses)*
1963 "Call Me Irresponsible" *(Papa's Delicate Condition)*
1964 "Chim Chim Cher-ee" *(Mary Poppins)*
1965 "The Shadow of Your Smile" *(The Sandpiper)*
1966 "Born Free" *(Born Free)*
1967 "Talk to the Animals" *(Doctor Dolittle)*
1968 "The Windmills of Your Mind" *(The Thomas Crown Affair)*
1969 "Raindrops Keep Fallin' on My Head" *(Butch Cassidy and the Sundance Kid)*
1970 "For All We Know" *(Lovers and Other Strangers)*
1971 "Theme from *Shaft*" *(Shaft)*
1972 "The Morning After" *(The Poseidon Adventure)*
1973 "The Way We Were" *(The Way We Were)*
1974 "We May Never Love Like This Again" *(The Towering Inferno)*
1975 "I'm Easy" *(Nashville)*
1976 "Evergreen" *(A Star Is Born)*
1977 "You Light Up My Life" *(You Light Up My Life)*
1978 "Last Dance" *(Thank God It's Friday)*
1979 "It Goes Like It Goes" *(Norma Rae)*
1980 "Fame" *(Fame)*
1981 "Arthur's Theme (Best That You Can Do)" *(Arthur)*
1982 "Up Where We Belong" *(An Officer and a Gentleman)*
1983 "Flashdance . . . What a Feeling" *(Flashdance)*
1984 "I Just Called to Say I Love You" *(The Woman in Red)*
1985 "Say You, Say Me" *(White Knights)*
1986 "Take My Breath Away" *(Top Gun)*
1987 "(I've Had) The Time of My Life" *(Dirty Dancing)*
1988 "Let the River Run" *(Working Girl)*
1989 "Under the Sea" *(The Little Mermaid)*
1990 "Sooner Or Later (I Always Get My Man)" *(Dick Tracy)*
1991 "Beauty and the Beast" *(Beauty and the Beast)*
1992 "A Whole New World" *(Aladdin)*
1993 "Streets of Philadelphia" *(Philadelphia)*
1994 "Can You Feel the Love Tonight" *(The Lion King)*
1995 "Colors of the Wind" *(Pocahontas)*

1996 "You Must Love Me" *(Evita)*
1997 "My Heart Will Go On" *(Titanic)*
1998 "When You Believe" *(The Prince of Egypt)*
1999 "You'll Be in My Heart" *(Tarzan)*
2000 "Things Have Changed" *(Wonder Boys)*

Academy Award winning actors, multiple

FOUR-TIME ACADEMY AWARDS WINNERS (1)

Katharine Hepburn: *Morning Glory* (1933), *Guess Who's Coming to Dinner* (1967), *The Lion in Winter* (1968), *On Golden Pond* (1981)

THREE-TIME WINNERS (3)

Ingrid Bergman: *Gaslight* (1944), *Anastasia* (1956), *Murder on the Orient Express* (1974*)
Walter Brennan: *Come and Get It* (1936*), *Kentucky* (1938*), *The Westerner* (1940*)
Jack Nicholson: *One Flew Over the Cuckoo's Nest* (1975), *Terms of Endearment* (1983*), *As Good As It Gets* (1997)

TWO-TIME WINNERS (29)

Marlon Brando: *On the Waterfront* (1954), *The Godfather* (1972)
Michael Caine: *Hannah and Her Sisters* (1986*), *The Cider House Rules* (1999*)
Bette Davis: *Dangerous* (1935), *Jezebel* (1938)
Olivia de Havilland: *To Each His Own* (1946), *The Heiress* (1949)
Robert De Niro: *The Godfather Part II* (1974*), *Raging Bull* (1980)
Melvyn Douglas: *Hud* (1963*), *Being There* (1979*)
Sally Field: *Norma Rae* (1979), *Places in the Heart* (1984)
Jane Fonda: *Klute* (1971), *Coming Home* (1978)
Jodie Foster: *The Accused* (1988), *The Silence of the Lambs* (1991)
Gene Hackman: *The French Connection* (1971), *Unforgiven* (1992*)
Tom Hanks: *Philadelphia* (1993), *Forrest Gump* (1994)
Helen Hayes: *The Sin of Madelon Claudet* (1931), *Airport* (1970*)
Dustin Hoffman: *Kramer vs. Kramer* (1979), *Rain Man* (1988)
Glenda Jackson: *Women in Love* (1970), *A Touch of Class* (1973)
Jessica Lange: *Tootsie* (1982*), *Blue Sky* (1994)
Vivien Leigh: *Gone with the Wind* (1939), *A Streetcar Named Desire* (1951)
Jack Lemmon: *Mister Roberts* (1955*), *Save the Tiger* (1973)
Fredric March: *Dr. Jekyll and Mr. Hyde* (1932), *The Best Years of Our Lives* (1946)

Anthony Quinn: *Viva Zapata!* (1952*), *Lust for Life* (1956*)
Luise Rainer: *The Great Ziegfeld* (1936), *The Good Earth* (1937)
Jason Robards: *All the President's Men* (1976*), *Julia* (1977*)
Maggie Smith: *The Prime of Miss Jean Brodie* (1969), *California Suite* (1978*)
Kevin Spacey: *The Usual Suspects* (1995*), *American Beauty* (1999)
Meryl Streep: *Kramer vs. Kramer* (1979*), *Sophie's Choice* (1982)
Elizabeth Taylor: *Butterfield 8* (1960), *Who's Afraid of Virginia Woolf?* (1966)
Spencer Tracy: *Captains Courageous* (1937), *Boys Town* (1938)
Peter Ustinov: *Spartacus* (1960*), *Topkapi* (1964*)
Dianne Wiest: *Hannah and Her Sisters* (1986*), *Bullets Over Broadway* (1994*)
Shelley Winters: *The Diary of Anne Frank* (1959*), *A Patch of Blue* (1965*)

CONSECUTIVE-YEAR WINNERS (4)

Tom Hanks (1993–1994)
Luise Rainer (1936–1937)
Jason Robards (1976*–1977*)
Spencer Tracy (1937–1938)

* Award was for a supporting role

Academy Award winning directors, multiple

FOUR-TIME WINNERS (1)

John Ford: *The Informer* (1935), *The Grapes of Wrath* (1940), *How Green Was My Valley* (1941), *The Quiet Man* (1952)

THREE-TIME WINNERS (2)

Frank Capra: *It Happened One Night* (1934), *Mr. Deeds Goes to Town* (1936), *You Can't Take It with You* (1938)
William Wyler: *Mrs. Miniver* (1942), *The Best Years of Our Lives* (1946), *Ben-Hur* (1959)

TWO-TIME WINNERS (14)

Frank Borzage: *7th Heaven* (1927), *Bad Girl* (1931)
Milos Forman: *One Flew Over the Cuckoo's Nest* (1975), *Amadeus* (1984)
Elia Kazan: *Gentleman's Agreement* (1947), *On the Waterfront* (1954)
David Lean: *The Bridge on the River Kwai* (1957), *Lawrence of Arabia* (1962)
Frank Lloyd: *The Divine Lady* (1929), *Cavalcade* (1933)
Joseph L. Mankiewicz: *A Letter to Three Wives* (1949), *All About Eve* (1950)
Leo McCarey: *The Awful Truth* (1937), *Going My Way* (1944)

Lewis Milestone: *Two Arabian Knights* (1927), *All Quiet on the Western Front* (1930)

Steven Spielberg: *Schindler's List* (1993), *Saving Private Ryan* (1998)

George Stevens: *A Place in the Sun* (1951), *Giant* (1956)

Oliver Stone: *Platoon* (1986), *Born on the Fourth of July* (1989)

Robert Wise: *West Side Story* (1961), *The Sound of Music* (1965)

Billy Wilder: *The Lost Weekend* (1945), *The Apartment* (1960)

Fred Zinnemann: *From Here to Eternity* (1953), *A Man for All Seasons* (1966)

CONSECUTIVE-YEAR WINNERS (2)

John Ford (1940–1941)

Joseph L. Mankiewicz (1949–1950)

Acadia

Former name of Nova Scotia.

Ace

Pet dog of Bruce Wayne in the Batman comics.

"Ace"

Nickname of photographer Ashley Covington Evans (Ted McGinley) in the TV sitcom *The Love Boat*.

The Ace

Original working title of the film *The Great Santini*.

Ace Lamont's Sensation House

New Orleans nightspot where Ruby Carter (Mae West) performs with Duke Ellington and his Orchestra in the film *Belle of the Nineties*.

acetaminophen

Chemical name of the pain reliever found in Tylenol.

acetylsalicylic acid

Chemical name of aspirin.

achromatopsia

Medical term for color blindness.

"Ack!"

Favorite exclamation of the title character in the comic strip *Cathy*.

Acme, Inc.

See **Supergrover**

Acme Thunderer

World's bestselling whistle, used most notably by sports referees. It has been manufactured by J. Hudson and Co. of Birmingham, England since 1884.

Acquatica

Shark research center in the film *Deep Blue Sea*.

Act III Productions

Production company of TV producer Norman Lear.

"Acta non verba"

Motto of the United States Merchant Marine Academy at Kings Point, New York. It is Latin for "Deeds, not words."

"The Actor"

Nickname of bank robber Willie Sutton, for the appropriate uniforms he wore when he worked.

Acushnet

Whaler on which Herman Melville served before becoming a writer.

Adams College

Setting of the film *Revenge of the Nerds*.

Adams, Samuel Hopkins

See **"Night Bus"**

Aday, Marvin Lee

Real name of rock singer Meat Loaf.

Addams, Frankie

Title character of the Carson McCullers novel *The Member of the Wedding*.

Adele D

Boat of Captain Swain (Liam Redmond) in the Disney film *The Adventures of Bullwhip Griffin*.

Adeline

Real first name of English novelist (Adeline) Virginia Woolf.

Adios Butler

See **Triple Crown races (harness-racing pacers)**

Adkins, David

Real name of actor/comedian Sinbad.

"The Admiral"

Nickname of NBA star David Robinson, who is a graduate of the U.S. Naval Academy.

Admiral Benbow Inn

Establishment owned by Jim Hawkins' father in the Robert Louis Stevenson novel *Treasure Island*.

Admiral Dewey

Pet guinea pig of President Theodore Roosevelt.

admirals

See **five-star generals and admirals**

Adolph

Pet viper of Albert (Aldo Ray) in the film *We're No Angels*.

See also **Marx Brothers' real names**

Adrift in Tahiti

School play written by the title character (Mickey Rooney) in the film *Andy Hardy Gets Spring Fever*.

Adu, Helen Folasade

Real name of Nigerian-born pop singer Sade.

Advanced Research Projects Agency

Agency of the U.S. Department of Defense that created the ARPANET computer network in 1969, which evolved into the Internet.

Adventure

See **Resolution** and **Adventure**

Adventure Galley

Best-known ship of Captain William Kidd.

"The Adventure of the Six Napoleons"

Short story by Sir Arthur Conan Doyle that was the basis of the Sherlock Holmes film *The Pearl of Death*.

Advocate-Times

Zenith newspaper in the Sinclair Lewis novel *Babbitt*.

Aeolian Concert Hall

New York City auditorium where George Gershwin's *Rhapsody in Blue* premiered on February 12, 1924. It was performed by the Palais Royal Orchestra, conducted by Paul Whiteman, with the composer at the piano.

Aerosmith members

Tom Hamilton, Joey Kramer, Joe Perry, Steve Tyler and Brad Whitford.

Affair

Last word of all episode titles of the TV series *The Man from U.N.C.L.E.*

After the Hunt

$100,000 painting by François Jacques DuBois Guilbert Beaugard, to be unveiled at the home of Mrs. Rittenhouse (Margaret Dumont) in honor of Captain Jeffrey T. Spaulding (Groucho Marx) in the Marx Brothers film *Animal Crackers*.

Agatha

First name of Dave Crabtree's (Jerry Van Dyke's) mother, who is reincarnated as the title vehicle (voiced by Ann Sothern), a 1928 Porter, in the TV sitcom *My Mother the Car*.

Agatha Awards

Presented annually since 1989 by Malice Domestic for excellence in the "mysteries of manners" typified by the works of Dame Agatha Christie.

Agca, Mehmet Ali

Native of Turkey who attempted to assassinate Pope John Paul II on May 13, 1981.

Aged in Wood

Play starring Margo Channing (Bette Davis) at the beginning of the film *All About Eve*.

Agency to Prevent Evil

See **A.P.E.**

agitrons

Wavy lines drawn in comic strips to represent movement.

aglet

Technical term for the sheath at the tip of a shoelace.

Agrabah

City that is the setting of the Disney animated film *Aladdin*.

"Agricultural and Mechanical"

What "A and M" stands for in the name of certain colleges.

Agriculture 101

Book being read by Pee-wee Herman (Paul Reubens) in the film *Big Top Pee-wee*.

Ah Chew

Pat Morita's role in the TV sitcom *Sanford and Son*.

Ahmed

Real first name of Indian-born author (Ahmed) Salman Rushdie.

"Ah, there's good news tonight"

Tag line of radio newscaster Gabriel Heatter.

Aiken, Loretta Mary

Real name of humorist Moms Mabley.

Aileen Mavoureen

Title character and narrator of the Mark Twain short story "A Dog's Life."

"Aim high"

Advertising slogan of the U.S. Air Force.

"Ain't Misbehavin' "

Theme song of comedian George Burns.

air bases, U.S. (located outside the U.S.)

Aviano (Italy)
Howard (Panama)
Incirlik (Turkey)
Kadena (Japan)
Kunsan (South Korea)
Lajes (Azores)
Lakenheath (England)
Mildenhall (England)
Misawa (Japan)
Osan (South Korea)
Ramstein (Germany)
Spangdahlem (Germany)
Yokota (Japan)

Airborne Warning and Control System

What the name of high-tech aircraft AWACS is an acronym for.

aircraft registration prefixes

These codes, seen on the sides of airplanes worldwide, are used for the first few characters of the serial number.

Afghanistan: YA
Albania: ZA
Algeria: 7T
Andorra: C3
Angola: D2
Anguilla: VPL
Antigua and Barbuda: V2
Argentina: LV
Armenia: EK
Aruba: P4
Australia: VH
Austria: OE
Azerbaijan: 4K
Bahamas: C6
Bahrain: A9C
Bangladesh: S2, S3
Barbados: 8P
Belarus: EW
Belgium: OO
Belize: V3
Benin: TY

Bermuda: VRB
Bhutan: A5
Bolivia: CP
Bosnia and Herzegovina: T9
Botswana: A2
Brazil: PP, PT
Brunei: V8
Bulgaria: LZ
Burkina Faso: XT
Burundi: 9U
Cambodia: XU
Cameroon: TJ
Canada: C
Cape Verde: D4
Cayman Islands: VRC
Central African Republic: TL
Chad: TT
Chile: CC
China: B
Colombia: HK

Comoros: D6
Congo (Democratic Republic): 9Q, 9T
Congo (People's Republic): TN
Costa Rica: TI
Croatia: 9A
Cuba: CU
Cyprus: 5B
Czech Rep: OK
Denmark: OY
Djibouti: J2
Dominica: J7
Dominican Rep: HI
Ecuador: HC
Egypt: SU
El Salvador: YS
Equatorial Guinea: 3C
Eritrea: E3
Estonia: ES
Ethiopia: ET
Falkland Islands: VPF
Fiji: DQ
Finland: OH
France: F
Gabon: TR
Gambia: C5
Georgia: 4L
Germany: D
Ghana: 9G
Gibraltar: VRG
Greece: SX
Grenada: J3
Guadeloupe: FOG
Guatemala: TG
Guinea: 3X
Guinea-Bissau: J5
Guyana: 8R
Haiti: HH
Honduras: HR
Hungary: HA
Iceland: TF
India: VT
Indonesia: PK
Iran: EP
Iraq: YI
Ireland: EI
Israel: 4X
Italy: I
Ivory Coast: TU
Jamaica: 6Y
Japan: JA
Jordan: JY
Kazakhstan: UN
Kenya: 5Y

Kiribati: T3
Korea (North): P
Korea (South): HL
Kuwait: 9K
Kyrgyzstan: EX
Laos: RDPL
Latvia: YL
Lebanon: OD
Lesotho: 7P
Liberia: EL
Libya: 5A
Liechtenstein: HB
Lithuania: LY
Luxembourg: LX
Macedonia: Z3
Madagascar: 5R
Malawi: 7Q
Malaysia: 9M
Maldives: 8Q
Mali: TZ
Malta: 9H
Marshall Islands: V7
Martinique: FOM
Mauritania: 5T
Mauritius: 3B
Mexico: XA, XB, XC
Moldova: ER
Monaco: 3A
Mongolia: BNMAU, MONGOL, MT
Montserrat: VPL
Morocco: CN
Mozambique: C9
Myanmar: XY
Namibia: V5
Nauru: C2
Nepal: 9N
Netherlands: PH
Netherlands Antilles: PJ
New Zealand: ZK, ZL
Nicaragua: YN
Niger: 5U
Nigeria: 5N
Norway: LN
Oman: A4O
Pakistan: AP
Panama: HP
Papua New Guinea: P2
Paraguay: ZP
Peru: OB
Philippines: RP
Poland: SP
Portugal: CS
Qatar: A7

Romania: YR
Russia: IS, RA, RF
Rwanda: 9XR
St. Helena: VQH
St. Kitts and Nevis: V4
St. Lucia: J6
St. Vincent and
    Grenadines: J8
Samoa: 5W
San Marino: T7
São Tomé and
    Principe: S9
Saudi Arabia: HZ
Senegal: 6V, 6W
Seychelles: S7
Sierra Leone: 9L
Singapore: 9V
Slovakia: OM
Slovenia: S5, SL
Solomon Islands: H4
Somalia: 6O
South Africa: ZS, ZT,
    ZU
Spain: EC
Sri Lanka: 4R
Sudan: ST
Suriname: PZ
Swaziland: 3D
Sweden: SE
Switzerland: HB
Syria: YK
Tajikistan: EY

Tanzania: 5H
Thailand: HS
Togo: 5V
Tonga: A3
Trinidad and Tobago:
    9Y
Tunisia: TS
Turks and Caicos Is-
    lands: VQT
Turkey: TC
Turkmenistan: EZ
Tuvalu: T2
Uganda: 5X
Ukraine: UR
United Arab Emirates:
    A6
United Kingdom: G
United Nations: 4U
United States: N
Virgin Islands (British):
    VPL
Uruguay: CX
Uzbekistan: UK
Vanuatu: YJ
Vatican City: HV
Venezuela: YV
Vietnam: VN
Yemen: 7O
Yugoslavia: YU
Zambia: 9J
Zimbabwe: Z

Airflow Records

Employer of album-cover designer Sonny Malone (Michael Beck) in the film *Xanadu*.

Air Force bases, U.S.

Altus (Altus, Oklahoma)
Andersen (Guam)
Andrews (Maryland, near Washington, D.C.)
Arnold (Tennessee, near Manchester)
Barksdale (Bossier City, Louisiana)
Beale (California, near Marysville)
Bolling (Washington, D.C.)
Brooks (San Antonio, Texas)
Cannon (New Mexico, near Clovis)
Charleston (North Charleston, South Carolina)
Columbus (Mississippi, near Columbus)
Davis-Monthan (Tucson, Arizona)
Dover (Delaware, near Dover)
Dyess (Abilene, Texas)
Edwards (California, near Rosamond)
Eglin (Florida, near Fort Walton Beach)
Eielson (Alaska, near Fairbanks)

Ellsworth (South Dakota, near Rapid City)
Elmendorf (Anchorage, Alaska)
Fairchild (Washington, near Spokane)
Falcon (Colorado, near Colorado Springs)
Goodfellow (Texas, near San Antonio)
Grand Forks (North Dakota, near Grand Forks)
Hanscom (Massachusetts, near Boston)
Hickam (Hawaii, near Honolulu)
Hill (Utah, near Ogden)
Holloman (New Mexico, near Alamogordo)
Keesler (Mississippi)
Kelly (Texas, near San Antonio)
Kirtland (New Mexico, near Albuquerque)
Lackland (Texas, near San Antonio)
Langley (Virginia, near Hampton)
Laughlin (Texas, near Del Rio)
Little Rock (Arkansas, near Little Rock)
Los Angeles (California, near Los Angeles)
Luke (Arizona, near Phoenix)
MacDill (Florida, near Tampa)
Malmstrom (Montana, near Great Falls)
Maxwell (Alabama, near Montgomery)
McChord (Washington, near Tacoma)
McClellan (California, near Sacramento)
McConnell (Kansas, near Wichita)
McGuire (New Jersey, near Trenton)
Minot (North Dakota, near Minot)
Moody (Georgia, near Valdosta)
Mountain Home (Idaho, near Mountain Home)
Nellis (Nevada, near Las Vegas)
Offutt (Nebraska, near Omaha)
Patrick (Florida, near Cocoa Beach)
Peterson (Colorado, near Colorado Springs)
Pope (North Carolina, near Fayetteville)
Randolph (San Antonio, Texas)
Robins (Georgia, near Macon)
Scott (Illinois, near Belleville)
Seymour Johnson (Goldsboro, North Carolina)
Shaw (South Carolina, near Sumter)
Sheppard (Texas, near Wichita Falls)
Tinker (Oklahoma, near Oklahoma City)
Travis (California, near Fairfield)
Tyndall (Florida, near Panama City)
Vance (Oklahoma, near Enid)
Vandenberg (California, near Lompoc)
Warren (Cheyenne, Wyoming)
Whiteman (Missouri, near Knob Noster)
Wright-Patterson (Ohio, near Dayton)

airline company abbreviations

These two-letter codes are used throughout the travel industry, and are most often seen by the public on plane tickets and reservation confirmations.

AA American Airlines   AF Air France
AC Air Canada   AI Air India

AM AeroMexico
AR Aerolineas
   Argentinas
AT Royal Air Maroc
AV Avianca
AY Finnair
AZ Alitalia
BA British Airways
BW BWIA
B6 jetBlue
CI China Airlines
CO Continental
CX Cathay Pacific
DL Delta
EI Aer Lingus
ET Ethiopian Airlines
EU Ecuatoriana
FI Icelandair
GH Ghana Airways
GY Guyana Airways
HP America West
HY Uzbekistan
   Airways
IB Iberia
JI Midway Airlines
JL Japan Airlines
JM Air Jamaica
KE Korean Air Lines
KL KLM
KU Kuwait Airways
LH Lufthansa
LO LOT Polish
LY El Al
MH Malaysia Airlines

MA Malev
MH Malaysia
MS Egyptair
MX Mexicana
NH All Nippon
   Airways
NW Northwest Airlines
NZ Air New Zealand
OA Olympic
OK Czech Airlines
OS Austrian Airlines
QF Qantas
PR Philippine Airlines
RG Varig
SA South African
   Airways
SK SAS
SN Sabena
SQ Singapore
   Airlines
SR Swissair
SU Aeroflot
SV Saudi Arabian
   Airlines
TG Thai Airways
TK Turkish Airlines
TP TAP Air Portugal
TW Trans World Air-
   lines
UA United
US U.S. Airways
VS Virgin Atlantic
WN Southwest

KLM: Flying Dutchman
Korean Air: Skypass
Lufthansa: Miles and More
Malaysia Airlines: Enrich
Northwest: WorldPerks
Olympic: Icarus
Philippine Airlines: PALsmiles
Qantas: Frequent Flyer
SAS: EuroBonus
Singapore Airlines: Krisflyer, PPS Club
South African Airways: Voyager
Southwest: Rapid Rewards
Swissair: Qualiflyer
Thai Airways: Royal Orchid Plus
TWA: Aviators
United: Mileage Plus
U.S. Airways: Dividend Miles
Varig: Smiles
Virgin Atlantic: Flying Club

airport codes, major U.S.

Albuquerque, New Mexico: ABQ
Allentown, Pennsylvania: LVI
Anchorage, Alaska: ANC
Aspen, Colorado: ASE
Atlanta, Georgia: ATL
Atlantic City, New Jersey: ACY
Baltimore, Maryland: BWI
Boston, Massachusetts: BOS
Charleston, South Carolina: CHS
Chicago, Illinois (Midway): MDW
Chicago, Illinois (O'Hare): ORD
Cincinnati, Ohio: CVG
Cleveland, Ohio: CLE
Dallas/Ft. Worth, Texas: DFW
Denver, Colorado: DEN
Des Moines, Iowa: DSM
Detroit, Michigan: DET
Fort Lauderdale, Florida: FLL
Honolulu, Hawaii: FLL
Houston, Texas (Bush Intercontinental): IAH
Houston, Texas (Hobby): HOU
Indianapolis, Indiana: IND
Kansas City, Missouri: MCI
Key West, Florida: EYW
Las Vegas, Nevada: LAS
Los Angeles, California: LAX
Memphis, Tennessee: MEM
Miami, Florida: MIA
Milwaukee, Wisconsin: MKE
Minneapolis/St. Paul, Minnesota: MSP
Nashville, Tennessee: BNA
Newark, New Jersey: EWK
New Orleans, Louisiana: MSY
New York, New York (Kennedy): JFK

airline frequent-flyer programs

Aeroflot: Aeroflot Bonus
Air Canada: Aeroplan
Air France: Frequence Plus
Air India: Flying Returns
Air New Zealand: Air Points
Alitalia: MilleMiglia Club
All Nippon Airways: ANA Mileage Club
America West: FlightFund
American Airlines: AAdvantage
Avianca: Avianca Plus
British Airways: Executive Club
Cathay Pacific: Asia Miles
China Airlines: Dynasty Flyer
Continental: OnePass
Delta: SkyMiles
El Al: Loyal, Matmid, King David Club
Finnair: Finnair Plus
Iberia: Iberia Plus
Japan Airlines: JAL Mileage Bank

New York, New York (La Guardia): LGA
Norfolk, Virginia: ORF
Oklahoma City, Oklahoma: OKC
Philadelphia, Pennsylvania: PHL
Phoenix, Arizona: PHX
Pittsburgh, Pennsylvania: PIT
Portland, Oregon: PDX
Providence, Rhode Island: PVD
Richmond, Virginia: RIC
Salt Lake City, Utah: SLC
San Diego, California: SAN
San Francisco, California: SFO
San Juan, Puerto Rico: SJU
Seattle/Tacoma, Washington: SEA
St. Croix, Virgin Islands: STX
St. Louis, Missouri: STL
Tampa, Florida: TPA
Washington, D.C. (Dulles): IAD
Washington, D.C. (Reagan/National): DCA
West Palm Beach, Florida: PBI
Zanesville, Ohio: ZZV

airport codes, major world

Acapulco, Mexico: ACA
Accra, Ghana: ACC
Addis Ababa, Ethiopia: ADD
Algiers, Algeria: ALG
Amman, Jordan: AMM
Amsterdam, Netherlands: AMS
Athens, Greece: ATH
Auckland, New Zealand: AKL
Baghdad, Iraq: SDA
Bangkok, Thailand: BKK
Barcelona, Spain: BCN
Beijing, China: PEK
Beirut, Lebanon: BEY
Belgrade, Yugoslavia: BEG
Berlin, Germany: BER
Bombay, India: BOM
Bora Bora, French Polynesia: BOB
Brasilia, Brazil: BSB
Brussels, Belgium: BRU
Bucharest, Romania: BBU
Budapest, Hungary: BUD
Cairo, Egypt: CAI
Calcutta, India: CCU
Cape Town, South Africa: CPT
Caracas, Venezuela: CCS
Casablanca, Morocco: CMN
Copenhagen, Denmark: CPH
Damascus, Syria: DAM
Edinburgh, Scotland: EDI
Frankfurt, Germany: FRA
Geneva, Switzerland: GVA
Hamilton, Bermuda: BDA

Havana, Cuba: HAV
Helsinki, Finland: HEL
Hong Kong, China: HKG
Istanbul, Turkey: IST
Johannesburg, South Africa: JNB
Karachi, Pakistan: KHI
Kuala Lumpur, Malaysia: KUL
Lagos, Nigeria: LOS
Lisbon, Portugal: LIS
London, England (Gatwick): LGW
London, England (Heathrow): LHR
Madrid, Spain: MAD
Manila, Philippines: MNL
Melbourne, Australia: MEL
Mexico City, Mexico: MEX
Monte Carlo, Monaco: MCM
Montevideo, Uruguay: MVD
Montreal, Canada: YMX
Moscow, Russia: SVO
Nairobi, Kenya: NBO
Oslo, Norway: OSL
Pago Pago, American Samoa: PPG
Paris, France (Charles de Gaulle): CDG
Paris, France (Orly): ORY
Prague, Czech Republic: PRG
Puerto Vallarta, Mexico: PVR
Rio de Janeiro, Brazil: GIG
Rome, Italy: FCO
Seoul, South Korea: SEL
Shannon, Ireland: SNN
Singapore: SIN
St. Maarten, Netherlands Antilles: SXM
Stockholm, Sweden: ARN
Sydney, Australia: SYD
Taipei, Taiwan: TPE
Teheran, Iran: THR
Tel Aviv, Israel: TLV
Tokyo, Japan: NRT
Toronto, Canada: YYZ
Vancouver, Canada: YVR
Venice, Italy: VCE
Vienna, Austria: VIE
Warsaw, Poland: WAW
Wellington, New Zealand: WLG
Zagreb, Croatia: ZAG
Zurich, Switzerland: ZRH

airports, major "named" U.S.

Atlanta, Georgia: Hartsfield International
Boston, Massachusetts: Logan International
Charleston, West Virginia: Yeager
Chicago, Illinois: Midway, O'Hare International
Cleveland, Ohio: Hopkins International
Houston, Texas: George Bush Intercontinental, Hobby

Knoxville, Tennessee: McGhee Tyson
Las Vegas, Nevada: McCarran International
Lexington, Kentucky: Blue Grass
Milwaukee, Wisconsin: Mitchell International
New York, New York: La Guardia International, John F. Kennedy International
Oklahoma City, Oklahoma: Will Rogers World Airport
Orange County, California (Santa Ana): John Wayne
Phoenix, Arizona: Sky Harbor International
San Diego, California: Lindbergh Field
San Juan, Puerto Rico: Luis Muñoz Marin International
St. Louis, Missouri: Lambert International
Washington, D.C.: Dulles, Ronald Reagan Washington National

airports, major "named" world

Amsterdam, Netherlands: Schipol
Baghdad, Iraq: Saddam International
Berlin, Germany: Tegel
Brno, Czech Republic: Tuřany
Budapest, Hungary: Ferihegi
Buenos Aires, Argentina: Ezeiza
Calcutta, India: Dum Dum
Caracas, Venezuela: Simón Bolívar International
Casablanca, Morocco: Mohammed V International
Copenhagen, Denmark: Kastrup
Florence, Italy: Amerigo Vespucci
Genoa, Italy: Christopher Columbus
Havana, Cuba: José Martí International
Hong Kong, China: Chek Lap Kok
Istanbul, Turkey: Ataturk
Lisbon, Portugal: Portela
London, England: Gatwick, Heathrow
Madrid, Spain: Barajas
Manila, Philippines: Ninoy Aquino International
Melbourne, Australia: Tullamarine International
Mexico City, Mexico: Benito Juárez International
Montreal, Canada: Mirabel
Moscow, Russia: Sheremetyevo International
Nairobi, Kenya: Jomo Kenyatta International
New Delhi, India: Indira Gandhi International
Nice, France: Côte d'Azur
Oslo, Norway: Gardermoen International
Paris, France: Charles de Gaulle, Orly
Pisa, Italy: Galileo Galilei
Prague, Czech Republic: Ruzyně
Rio de Janeiro, Brazil: Galeão International
Rome, Italy: Leonardo da Vinci
Seoul, South Korea: Kimpo International
Singapore: Changi

St. Maarten, Netherlands Antilles: Princess Juliana International
Stockholm, Sweden: Arlanda
Sydney, Australia: Kingsford Smith
Taipei, Taiwan: Chiang Kai-shek International
Tel Aviv, Israel: Ben-Gurion International
Tokyo, Japan: Narita International
Toronto, Canada: Lester B. Pearson International
Venice, Italy: Marco Polo
Vienna, Austria: Schwechat
Warsaw, Poland: Okecie

Air Quality Index (AQI)

Established by the Environmental Protection Agency (EPA) as a measure of air pollution. It measures the amount of these five pollutants in the air:
Carbon monoxide
Nitrogen dioxide
Ozone
Sulfur dioxide
Particulates

AQI VALUES RANGE FROM 0 TO 500; A VALUE OF 100 OR LESS MEETS EPA STANDARDS FOR AIR QUALITY.

0–50	Good
51–100	Moderate
101–150	Unhealthy for Sensitive Groups
201–300	Alert (very unhealthful)
301–400	Warning (hazardous)
401–500	Emergency (extremely hazardous)

Aisgill, Alice

Role for which Simone Signoret won a Best Actress Academy Award in the 1959 film *Room at the Top.*

akela

Title given to a pack leader in the Cub Scouts, named for the character in Rudyard Kipling's *The Jungle Book.*

Akeman, David

Real name of country singer Stringbean.

Akers, Floyd

Pen name used by author L. Frank Baum.

Alabama (singing group) original members

Jeff Cook, Teddy Gentry, Randy Owen, and Bennett Vartanian.

Alan Alexander

First and middle names of writer A. A. Milne.

The Alan Brady Show

Employer of comedy writer Rob Petrie (Dick Van Dyke) in the TV sitcom *The Dick Van Dyke Show.*

Alan Price Combo

Original name of rock group The Animals.

Albacore Club

Where J. J. Gittes (Jack Nicholson) meets Noah Cross (John Huston) for lunch, in the film *Chinatown.*

albatross

British golf term for a double eagle, three under par on a single hole.

Albatross

Pirate ship of Geoffrey Thorpe (Errol Flynn) in the film *The Sea Hawk.*

Albert

Middle name of singer Frank Sinatra.

Albert Fred

Real first and middle names of baseball Hall of Famer Red Schoendienst.

Albion

Literary name for Great Britain.

Albright

See **Burns and Albright**

Alceste

Title character of the Molière play *The Misanthrope.*

Aldebaran, Altair, Antares, and Rigel

The four white Arabian horses ridden by the title character (Charlton Heston) in the climactic chariot race in the film *Ben-Hur.*

Alden

Middle name of astronaut Neil Armstrong.

Alderaan

Adopted home planet of Princess Leia Organa (Carrie Fisher) in the *Star Wars* films.

Alderton, Charles

Pharmacist who in 1885 invented Dr. Pepper at Morrison's Old Corner Drug Store in Waco, Texas.

Aldrich, Charles

Real name of actor Gale Gordon.

Alert

See **Pilgrim** and *Alert*

Alexander, Flora, and Pom

Triplet children of Babar and Celeste in the series of children's books by Jean and Laurent de Brunhoff.

Alexandria Quartet

Group of four novels by Lawrence Durrell, all set in Alexandria, Egypt.
> *Justine* (1957)
> *Balthazar* (1958)
> *Mountolive* (1958)
> *Clea* (1960)

Alexandrina

Real first name of Queen (Alexandrina) Victoria of Great Britain.

Alfie

Pet sheepdog of the title character (Al Pacino) in the film *Serpico.*

Alford, Kenneth J.

See **"Colonel Bogey"**

Alfred

Real first name of English-born TV host (Alfred) Alistair Cooke.

Real first name of poet (Alfred) Joyce Kilmer.

Real first name of cowboy actor Lash La Rue.

Real first name of writer (Alfred) Damon Runyon.

Alfred Hawthorne

Real first and middle names of English comedian Benny Hill. He took his stage name as a tribute to comedian Jack Benny.

Alfred Matthew

Real first and middle names of musical parodist "Weird Al" Yankovic.

Alfredo James

Real first and middle names of actor Al Pacino.

Algonquin

Pet poodle inherited by the title character (Cassandra Peterson) in the film *Elvira, Mistress of the Dark.*

Alice

Real first name of actress Ali MacGraw.

Alicia Christian

Real first and middle names of actress Jodie Foster.

Alien Life Form

What the initials of the title character's name stands for, in the TV sitcom *ALF*.

Alighieri

Last name of Italian Renaissance poet Dante.

Alison, Joan

See Everybody Comes to Rick's

All-American Aviation

Original name of U.S. Airways.

All-American Girls' Professional Baseball League

See Rockford Peaches

Al, Lance, Lars, and Rölf

Title characters of the comic strip *The Fusco Brothers*.

"All animals are equal, but some animals are more equal than others"

Slogan adopted by the animals in the George Orwell novel *Animal Farm*.

Alleghenys

Original name of the Pittsburgh Pirates at their National League inception in 1887.

Allen, Roy

Entrepreneur who in 1919 opened his first root-beer stand in Lodi, California. In 1922, he took in a partner, Frank Wright, and renamed the company A&W Root Beer.

Allentown, Pennsylvania

Hometown of Detective Arthur Dietrich (Steve Landesberg) in the TV sitcom *Barney Miller*.

Hometown of Private Duane Doberman (Maurice Gosfield) in the TV sitcom *The Phil Silvers Show*, aka *You'll Never Get Rich*.

Allessio, Vicki

Role for which Glenda Jackson won a Best Actress Academy Award in the 1973 film *A Touch of Class*.

Alleyne, Ellen

Pen name used by poet Christina Rossetti.

"Alley Oop"

Nickname of 1950s San Francisco '49er receiver R. C. Owens, for his superb leaping ability.

All Girl Productions

Production company of singer/actress Bette Midler.

"All it takes is a little confidence!"

Slogan used to promote the film *The Sting*.

"All My Ex's Live in Texas" wives/locales

As mentioned in the George Strait tune (in order):
Rosanna (Texarkana)
Ilene (Abilene)
Allison (Galveston)
Dimples (Temple)

All My Trials and *The Bold and the Brash*

Rival soap operas of *The Sun Also Sets* in the film *Soapdish*.

Allnut, Charlie

Role for which Humphrey Bogart won a Best Actor Academy Award in the 1951 film *The African Queen*.

All's Fair

Original title of the Rodgers and Hart musical *By Jupiter*.

All-Story Weekly

See McCulley, Johnston

"All the News in the World"

See New York Sentinel

"All the news that fits"

Motto of *Rolling Stone* magazine.

"All the News That's Fit to Print"

Motto of *The New York Times*.

"All through this hour, Lord be my Guide. And by thy power, no foot shall slide."

The words to the tune by George Frideric Handel that chimes on the hour in the clock tower of the Houses of Parliament in London. Big Ben is the bell that sounds the hour.

Allure

Magazine for which Janet Walker (Joan Chandler) writes a column, in the Alfred Hitchcock film *Rope*.

"All you add is love"

Advertising slogan of Purina Dog Chow.

"All You Need Is Love"

Debut episode of the TV sitcom *Night Court*, which aired on January 4, 1984.

"All You Need Is Love," other tunes heard in

Excerpts of these other tunes are heard in this Beatles tune:

"La Marseillaise" (French national anthem)

Two-Part Invention for Piano #8 (Johann Sebastian Bach)

"In the Mood"

"Greensleeves"

"She Loves You" (earlier Beatles tune)

Almásy, Count László de

Title character (Ralph Fiennes) of the film *The English Patient.*

Alnilam

See **Mintaka, Alnilam, and Alnitak**

Alnitak

See **Mintaka, Alnilam, and Alnitak**

Alois

Middle name of actor Arnold Schwarzenegger.

Alois Maxwell

Real first and middle names of jazz trumpeter Al Hirt.

Alonzo

Real first name of actor Lon Chaney Sr.

alopecia

Medical term for baldness.

Aloysius

First name of Snuffleupagus on the children's TV series *Sesame Street.*

Real first name of the title character (Gene Wilder) in the film *Quackser Fortune Has a Cousin in the Bronx.* His nickname came from the ducklike sounds he made as an infant.

Teddy bear carried around by Oxford University student Sebastian Flyte in the Evelyn Waugh novel *Brideshead Revisited.*

Alpert, Herb and Moss, Jerry

Founders of A&M Records in 1962, which was sold to PolyGram in 1989 for $500,000,000.

Alpha 60

Supercomputer created by Professor Leonard Nosferatu (Howard Vernon) in the film *Alphaville.*

"Alphabet" Mysteries

Ongoing series of whodunits written by Sue Grafton.
  "A" Is for Alibi (1982)
  "B" Is for Burglar (1985)
  "C" Is for Corpse (1986)
  "D" Is for Deadbeat (1987)
  "E" Is for Evidence (1988)
  "F" Is for Fugitive (1989)
  "G" Is for Gumshoe (1990)
  "H" Is for Homicide (1991)
  "I" Is for Innocent (1992)
  "J" Is for Judgment (1993)
  "K" Is for Killer (1994)
  "L" Is for Lawless (1995)
  "M" Is for Malice (1996)
  "N" Is for Noose (1998)
  "O" Is for Outlaw (1999)
  "P" Is for Peril (2001)

Alpha Centauri

Intended star-system destination of the Robinson family in the TV series *Lost in Space.*

Alpha One

Spaceship of Durand Durand (Milo O'Shea) in the film *Barbarella.*

Alpha Rex Emmanuel

Real first and middle names of evangelist Rex Humbard.

Alpha Seven

Spaceship of the title character (Jane Fonda) in the film *Barbarella.*

Alquist, Paula

Role for which Ingrid Bergman won a Best Actress Academy Award in the 1944 film *Gaslight.*

Altair

See **Aldebaran, Altair, Antares, and Rigel**

Altair-IV

Planet that is the setting of the film *Forbidden Planet.*

Altamont, Catawba

Mythical town and state that is the setting of the Thomas Wolfe novel *Look Homeward, Angel.* It is modeled on Wolfe's hometown of Asheville, North Carolina.

Alton

Real first name of bandleader (Alton) Glenn Miller.

Alto Vallejo Dam

Controversial Los Angeles construction project that is the focus of the film *Chinatown.*

Alva

Middle name of TV talk host Dick Cavett.

Middle name of inventor Thomas Edison.

Alverio, Rosita Dolores
Real name of actress Rita Moreno.

Alvin Ray
Real first and middle names of former NFL commissioner Pete Rozelle.

Alvis Edgar
Real first and middle names of country singer Buck Owens.

"Always first with the news"
Motto of the *Daily Planet* in the Superman comic books.

Alyosha
See **Dmitri, Ivan, Alyosha, and Smerdyakov**

Am
See **Si and Am**

Amagiri
Japanese ship that rammed and sank *PT-109*, commanded by Lieutenant John F. Kennedy, on August 1–2, 1943.

Amanda
Mother of Mr. Spock (Leonard Nimoy) in the TV series *Star Trek,* portrayed by Jane Wyman.

"A mare usque ad mare"
National motto of Canada, which is Latin for "From sea to sea."

"Amarillo Slim"
Nickname of Thomas Preston, professional gambler and four-time winner of the World Series of Poker.

Les Ambassadeurs
See **"I admire your courage, Miss . . . ?"**

Amberjack II
Sailboat of President Franklin D. Roosevelt.

Amblin Entertainment
Steven Spielberg's first film production company, named for the first film short he directed.

"The Ambling Alp"
Nickname of 1930s heavyweight boxing champ Primo Carnera, for his height and awkwardness.

Ambrose Chapel
Church where the kidnapped Hank McKenna (Christopher Olsen) is held, in the Alfred Hitchcock film *The Man Who Knew Too Much* (1956).

Ambrose, Iowa
Setting of the film *The Puppet Masters.*

A.M. Chicago
Original name of *The Oprah Winfrey Show.*

Amelia
Real first name of actress Minnie Driver.

"The Amen Corner"
Nickname of the 11th, 12th and 13th holes at Augusta National, home of the annual Masters golf tournament. It was coined by golf journalist Herbert Warren Wind because of the holes' proximity to water—"If you hit it in the water, say Amen."

Amen Ra
Production company of actor Wesley Snipes.

American
Original working title of the film *Citizen Kane.*

"The American Cato"
Nickname of American Revolution hero Samuel Adams.

American Cereal Company
Original name of Quaker Oats.

American flag, where flown continuously
By presidential proclamation, the American flag is flown 24 hours a day at these sites:
Flag House Square, Baltimore, Maryland
Fort McHenry, Baltimore, Maryland
Valley Forge National Memorial, Valley Forge, Pennsylvania
Town Green, Lexington, Massachusetts
U.S. Marine Corps Memorial (aka Iwo Jima Memorial), Arlington, Virginia
Washington Monument, Washington, D.C.
The White House, Washington, D.C.

American Graffiti epilogue
Where it is explained what became of the main characters:
John Milner (Paul LeMat) was killed by a drunk driver in December 1964.
Terry Fields (Charles Martin Smith) was reported missing in action near An Loc in December 1965.
Steve Bolander (Ron Howard) is an insurance agent in Modesto, California.
Curt Henderson (Richard Dreyfuss) is a writer living in Canada.

American Hero
Novel by Larry Beinhart that was the basis for the film *Wag the Dog*.

American Library Association
See **Caldecott Medal; Newbery Medal**

American Messenger Company
Original name of United Parcel Service.

Americans
Original nickname of the Boston Red Sox at their American League inception in 1901. They were also known as the Puritans, Pilgrims and Somersets before adopting their present nickname in 1907.

Original nickname of the New Jersey franchise during the 1967–1968 inaugural season of the American Basketball Association.

American Theatre Wing
Organization that presents the annual Tony Awards.

American Zoetrope
Production company of director Francis Ford Coppola. A zoetrope is a type of mechanical film-viewer.

America (rock group) members
Gerry Beckley, Dewey Bunnell, and Dan Peek.

"America's foremost summer resort"
See **Sparkling Springs Lake**

"America's movable fighting man"
Advertising slogan for the G.I. Joe action figure.

"America's Sweetheart"
Nickname of actress Mary Pickford.

americium-241
Radioactive isotope used in most smoke detectors.

Amigos
Original nickname of the Anaheim franchise during the 1967–1968 inaugural season of the American Basketball Association.

Amity
New England island terrorized by the great white shark in the Steven Spielberg film *Jaws*.

Ammann, Othmar
Swiss-born engineer who designed New York City's Verrazano-Narrows Bridge, which connects the bor-

oughs of Staten Island and Brooklyn. It was the world's longest suspension bridge at the time of its opening in 1964.

Ampco Industries
See **Ranch Breakfast**

Ampipe, Pennsylvania
Setting of the film *All the Right Moves*.

A. Mutt
Original name of the comic strip *Mutt and Jeff*, when first introduced in 1907 by cartoonist Bud Fisher.

Amy
First name of the title character in the Charles Dickens novel *Little Dorrit*.

amyl acetate
Chemical name of banana oil, an organic compound that smells like bananas. It is derived from amyl alcohol, not bananas.

Anarene, Texas
Setting of the film *The Last Picture Show*.

Anastasia
Title role for which Ingrid Bergman won the 1956 Best Actress Academy Award.

Anastasia and Drizella
Stepsisters of the title character in the Disney animated film *Cinderella*.

Anatevka
Russian village that is the setting of the musical *Fiddler on the Roof*.

anchorman
Term for the United States Naval Academy midshipman who graduates at the bottom of his/her class.

Ancient and Honorable Order of Mammals, Subdivision Humans
Fraternal organization of George Antrobus, in the Thornton Wilder play *The Skin of Our Teeth*.

Ancient Arabic Order of Nobles of the Mystic Shrine
See **Imperial Potentate**

"And All Through the House"
See **"The Man Who Was Death," "And All Through the House," and "Dig That Cat . . . He's Real Gone"**

"And away go troubles down the drain"
Advertising slogan of Roto-Rooter.

"And away we go"
Inscription on the family mausoleum of comedian Jackie Gleason, who used it as his stage-exiting catchphrase.

Anderson, Roberta Joan
Real name of singer/songwriter Joni Mitchell.

"And now, from approximately coast to coast . . . "
Opening line of the public-radio broadcasts of Bob and Ray.

Andolini
Real last name of Vito Corleone (Marlon Brando, Robert De Niro) in the *Godfather* films.

Andrea Gail
Fishing boat that is the setting of the film *The Perfect Storm*.

Andrew
Real middle name of actor Michael J. Fox. He took the middle initial J in honor of character actor Michael J. Pollard.

Andrew Blythe
Real first and middle names of actress Drew Barrymore.

Andrews, Ellie
Role for which Claudette Colbert won a Best Actress Academy Award in the 1934 film *It Happened One Night*.

Andrews Sisters members
The 1940s singing trio consisted of sisters LaVerne, Maxene and Patty.

Andromeda
Pet German shepherd of Susan Evers (Hayley Mills) in the Disney film *The Parent Trap* (1961).

Andrzejewski
Maiden name of rock singer Pat Benatar. Her first husband was Dennis Benatar.

"And so it goes"
Sign-off line of telejournalist Linda Ellerbee.

"And that's the truth!"
Catchphrase (followed by a raspberry) of Lily Tomlin character Edith Ann.

"And that's the way it is"
Sign-off line of Walter Cronkite on his broadcasts of the *CBS Evening News*.

"And the angels sing"
Epitaph of lyricist Johnny Mercer, who wrote the lyrics of the tune of the same name.

"And the beat goes on"
Epitaph of Sonny Bono, who wrote and performed the song of the same name.

"And Then There's Maude"
Theme song of the TV sitcom *Maude*, performed by Donny Hathaway.

Andy
Pet St. Bernard of the title character in the comic strip *Mark Trail*.

See also **Snoopy's brothers and sisters**

Andy Hardy films
Series starring Mickey Rooney:
   A Family Affair (1937)
   You're Only Young Once (1938)
   Judge Hardy's Children (1938)
   Love Finds Andy Hardy (1938)
   Out West with the Hardys (1938)
   The Hardys Ride High (1939)
   Andy Hardy Gets Spring Fever (1939)
   Judge Hardy and Son (1939)
   Andy Hardy Meets Debutante (1940)
   Andy Hardy's Private Secretary (1941)
   Life Begins for Andy Hardy (1941)
   The Courtship of Andy Hardy (1942)
   Andy Hardy's Double Life (1942)
   Andy Hardy's Blonde Trouble (1944)
   Love Laughs at Andy Hardy (1946)
   Andy Hardy Comes Home (1958)

"Angela"
Instrumental theme of the TV sitcom *Taxi*.

Angel and the Snakes
Original name of rock group Blondie.

Angel Ark Productions
Production company of actor Jason Alexander.

Angel Beach, Florida
Setting of the film *Porky's*.

Angelglow Cosmetics

Company represented by door-to-door salesperson Stella Johnson (Barbara Eden) in the TV sitcom *Harper Valley P.T.A.*

Angelino's

Italian restaurant where Jack Tripper (John Ritter) works as a chef, in the TV sitcom *Three's Company.*

The Angel of Christian Charity

Real name of the statue commonly called *Eros,* found in London's Piccadilly Circus.

"The Angel of the Battlefield"

Nickname of American Red Cross founder Clara Barton.

Angel, Rob

Seattle waiter who invented the game Pictionary in 1986.

angels, hierarchy of

Rankings, highest to lowest, from Christian theology:
Seraphim
Cherubim
Thrones
Dominions
Virtues
Powers
Principalities
Archangels
Angels

"Angel's Serenade"

Theme song of *Amos 'n' Andy* (radio and TV versions). "The Perfect Song" was the show's radio theme before "Angel's Serenade."

Angora

Former name of Ankara, Turkey.

Angus

First name of the title character (Richard Dean Anderson) in the TV series *MacGyver.*

Anhalt-Zerbst, Sophie Friederike Auguste von

Birth name of German-born Russian empress Catherine the Great.

Anhedonia

Original working title of the Woody Allen film *Annie Hall,* which means "the inability to experience pleasure."

"Animal"

Nickname of photographer Dennis Price (Daryl Anderson) in the TV series *Lou Grant.*

"animal" adjectives

The adjectival forms for various animal names:
alligator: eusuchian
ant: formicine
anteater: myrmecophagine
antelope: bubaline
ape: simian
armadillo: tolypeutine
ass: asinine
auk: alcidine
bear: ursine
bee: apian
bird: avian
buzzard: buteonine
calf: vituline
cat: feline
cow: bovine
crow: corvine
cuckoo: cuculine
deer: cervine
dodo: didine
dog: canine
dolphin: delphine
dove: columbine
duck: anatine
eagle: aquiline
falcon: accipitrine
fish: piscine
flea: pulicine
fox: vulpine
frog: ranine
goat: caprine
goose: anserine
gull: larine
hamster: cricetine
horse: equine
kangaroo: macropodine
leopard: pardine
lion: leonine
lizard: lacertine
lobster: homarine
mongoose: herpestine
mouse: murine
ostrich: struthionine
otter: lutrine
owl: strigine
oyster: ostracine
peacock: pavonine
pig: porcine
porcupine: hystricine
rabbit: leporine

rattlesnake: crotaline
seal: phocine
sheep: ovine
shrew: soricine
silkworm: bombycine
skunk: mephitine
sparrow: passerine
squirrel: sciurine
swan: cygnine
tiger: tigrine
turkey: meleagrine
wasp: vespine
whale: cetacean
wolf: lupine
worm: vermian
zebra: zebrine

Animal House, National Lampoon's epilogue

Where it is explained what became of the main characters:

Robert Hoover (James Widdoes): Public Defender, Baltimore, Maryland

Lawrence Kroger (Thomas Hulce): Editor, *National Lampoon* Magazine

Gregory Marmalard (James Daughton): Nixon White House Aide; in prison, 1974

Eric Stratton (Tim Matheson): Gynecologist, Beverly Hills, California

Douglas C. Neidermeyer (Mark Metcalf): Killed in Vietnam by his own troops

Kent Dorfman (Stephen Furst): Sensitivity Trainer, Encounter Groups of Cleveland, Inc.

Daniel Simpson Day (Bruce McGill): Whereabouts Unknown

Boon and Katy (Peter Riegert, Karen Allen): Married 1964, Divorced 1969

Barbara Sue Jansen (Martha Smith): Tour Guide, Universal Studios

Senator & Mrs. John Blutarsky (John Belushi, Mary Louise Weller): Washington, D.C.

Animal Nature

See **Inner Urges, Human Instinct, Animal Nature, and Serrated Edge**

animals, mythical multipart

centaur: body of a horse; head and upper torso of a man

chimera: head of a lion; body of a goat; tail of a serpent

faun: upper body of a man; ears, horns, tail and legs of a goat

griffin: body of a lion; head and wings of an eagle

Harpy: head of a woman; body of a bird

manticore: body of a lion; head of a man; tail of a dragon (or scorpion)

Minotaur: body of a man; head of a bull

sphinx: body of a lion; wings of an eagle; head of a woman

Animals of the Bible

See **Caldecott Medal**

Anita

Role for which Rita Moreno won a Best Supporting Actress Academy Award in the 1961 film *West Side Story.*

Anna

Horse of Rudolph Valentino in the film *The Sheik.*

Anna and the King of Siam

Book by Margaret Landon that was the basis for the Rodgers and Hammerstein musical *The King and I.*

Anne, Princess

Role for which Audrey Hepburn won a Best Actress Academy Award in the 1953 film *Roman Holiday.*

Ann Page

House brand of A&P supermarkets.

"Annuit coeptis"

Latin phrase on the reverse of the Great Seal of the United States, which is on the back of a $1 bill. It means "He favors our undertakings."

annulary

Medical term for the ring finger.

Annunzio

First name of orchestra leader Mantovani.

Anopopei

Pacific-island setting of the Norman Mailer novel *The Naked and the Dead.*

anosmia

Medical term for the absence of a sense of smell.

Another Dawn and *Black Legion*

Films starring Norman Maine (James Mason), in the film *A Star Is Born* (1954).

Anselmo, Tony

Disney animator who succeeded Clarence "Ducky" Nash as the voice of Donald Duck after Nash's death in 1985.

Anson

Middle name of sci-fi author Robert A. Heinlein.

Antares

See **Aldebaran, Altair, Antares, and Rigel**

Antelope

Ship on which the title character serves as doctor before being shipwrecked, in the Jonathan Swift novel *Gulliver's Travels.*

Anthony

Real first name of comic-strip and film-serial hero Buck Rogers.

Anthony Armando

Real first and middle names of jazz keyboardist Chick Corea.

Anthony Awards

Presented annually since 1986 by the Bouchercon World Mystery Convention for outstanding achievement in mystery writing. They are named for mystery writer Anthony Boucher.

Anthony Jerome

Real first and middle names of diminutive NBA guard Spud Webb.

Anthony Joseph

First and middle names of auto racer A. J. Foyt.

"Anthony's Song"

Subtitle of the Billy Joel tune "Movin' Out."

Antoine

Real first name of singer Fats Domino.

Antonio

Title character of the William Shakespeare play *The Merchant of Venice.*

Anvil City

Original name of Nome, Alaska.

"Anything You Want"

Debut episode of the TV series *7th Heaven,* which aired on August 26, 1996.

"Anywhere the Bluebird Goes"

Original title of the tune "Don't Sit Under the Apple Tree (With Anyone Else but Me)."

Apana, Chang

Real-life Honolulu police detective whose career inspired the Earl Derr Biggers character Charlie Chan.

A.P.E.

Acronym for Agency to Prevent Evil, spy-organization employer of the title character in the children's TV series *Lancelot Link, Secret Chimp.*

Apollo

See **Zeus and Apollo**

Apollo mission module nicknames

Command Modules are listed first, followed by the Lunar Modules.

Apollo 9 (1969 – James McDivitt, David Scott, Russell Schweickart): Gumdrop, Spider

Apollo 10 (1969 – Thomas Stafford, John Young, Eugene Cernan): Charlie Brown, Snoopy

Apollo 11 (1969 – Neil Armstrong*, Michael Collins, Buzz Aldrin*): Columbia, Eagle

Apollo 12 (1969 – Charles Conrad*, Richard Gordon, Alan Bean*): Yankee Clipper, Intrepid

Apollo 13 (1970 – James Lovell, John Swigert, Fred Haise): Odyssey, Aquarius

Apollo 14 (1971 – Alan Shepard*, Stuart Roosa, Edgar Mitchell*): Kitty Hawk, Antares

Apollo 15 (1972 – David Scott*, Alfred Worden, James Irwin*): Endeavour, Falcon

Apollo 16 (1972 – John Young*, Thomas Mattingly, Charles Duke*): Casper, Orion

Apollo 17 (1972 – Eugene Cernan*, Ronald Evans, Harrison Schmitt*): America, Challenger

* One of the 12 astronauts to walk on the moon

"Apostle of the Indies"

Nickname of missionary St. Francis Xavier.

Apparel Arts

Original name of *Gentleman's Quarterly* magazine when first published in 1957.

Applebaum, Stanley

Real name of singer Robert Goulet.

The Apple Cup

Trophy awarded to the winning team in the annual football game between Washington State University and the University of Washington.

April, May, and June

Nieces of Daisy Duck in Disney cartoons and comics.

"Apurksody"

Theme song of the Gene Krupa orchestra. "Apurk" is "Krupa" spelled backward.

AQI

See **Air Quality Index (AQI)**

Arabella

Nanny's (Juliet Mills') antique car in the TV sitcom *Nanny and the Professor*.

Aramis, Athos, and Porthos

Title characters of the Alexandre Dumas novel *The Three Musketeers*.

Arango, Doroteo

Real name of Mexican revolutionary Pancho Villa.

Arapaho

See **Lakota Sioux, Cheyenne, and Arapaho**

Arborville

Setting of the film *The Blob* (1988).

Arbuckle, Jon

Owner of the title feline in the comic strip *Garfield*.

Arbuthnot-by-the-Sea

Maine resort hotel where Mary Bates and Win Berry have summer jobs, in the John Irving novel *The Hotel New Hampshire*.

Archbury

English village that is the setting of the film *Twelve O'Clock High*.

Archer, Isabel

Title character of the Henry James novel *The Portrait of a Lady*.

Archibald Joseph

First and middle names of novelist A. J. Cronin.

Archimedes

Pet owl of Merlin (voiced by Karl Swenson) in the Disney animated film *The Sword in the Stone*.

Arctic World

Former zoo exhibit that serves as the hideout of The Penguin (Danny DeVito) in the film *Batman Returns*.

arctophile

Technical term for a collector of teddy bears.

Arcuate

Term for the design on the back pockets of Levi's jeans.

Ardent Productions

Film production company of Prince Edward of Great Britain.

Ardmore, Maryland

Hometown of Leslie Lynnton Benedict (Elizabeth Taylor) in the film *Giant*.

area codes, North American

011 International Access
201 New Jersey (Hackensack, Morristown, Newark, Jersey City)
202 Washington, D.C.
203 Connecticut (Fairfield and New Haven Counties)
204 Manitoba
205 Alabama (Birmingham, Tuscaloosa)
206 Washington (Seattle, Bainbridge Island)
207 Maine
208 Idaho
209 California (Modesto, Stockton)
210 Texas (San Antonio)
211 Pay phone refunds
212 New York (New York City)
213 California (downtown Los Angeles)
214 Texas (Dallas)
215 Pennsylvania (Philadelphia)
216 Ohio (Cleveland)
217 Illinois (Champaign, Springfield)
218 Minnesota (Duluth)
219 Indiana (Gary, Hammond, South Bend)
224 Illinois (suburban Chicago)
225 Louisiana (Baton Rouge)
228 Mississippi (Biloxi, Gulfport, Pascagoula)
229 Georgia (Albany)
231 Michigan (Muskegon, Traverse City)
234 Ohio (Akron, Youngstown)
240 Maryland (Rockville, Silver Spring, Bethesda)
242 Bahamas
246 Barbados
248 Michigan (Hamilton County)
250 British Columbia (Victoria)
252 North Carolina (Greenville, Rocky Mount)
253 Washington (Tacoma)
254 Texas (Waco)
256 Alabama (Decatur, Gadsden, Huntsville)
262 Wisconsin (Kenosha, Racine, Waukesha)
264 Anguilla
267 Pennsylvania (Philadelphia)

268 Antigua and Barbuda
270 Kentucky (Bowling Green, Paducah)
278 Michigan (Ann Arbor, Ypsilanti)
281 Texas (Houston)
284 British Virgin Islands
301 Maryland (Rockville, Silver Spring, Bethesda)
302 Delaware
303 Colorado (Denver)
304 West Virginia
305 Florida (Miami, Key West)
306 Saskatchewan
307 Wyoming
308 Nebraska (North Platte)
309 Illinois (Bloomington, Peoria)
310 California (Beverly Hills, Gardena)
312 Illinois (Chicago)
313 Michigan (Ann Arbor, Detroit)
314 Missouri (St. Louis)
315 New York (Syracuse)
316 Kansas (Dodge City, Wichita)
317 Indiana (Indianapolis)
318 Louisiana (Alexandria, Monroe)
319 Iowa (Dubuque)
320 Minnesota (St. Cloud)
321 Florida (Cape Canaveral)
323 California (Los Angeles)
330 Ohio (Akron, Youngstown)
331 Illinois (suburban Chicago)
334 Alabama (Mobile, Montgomery, Selma)
336 North Carolina (Greensboro)
337 Louisiana (Lafayette, Lake Charles)
339 Massachusetts (Waltham)
340 U.S. Virgin Islands
341 California (Oakland)
345 Cayman Islands
347 New York (Bronx, Brooklyn, Queens, Staten Island)
351 Massachusetts (Lowell)
352 Florida (Gainesville, Ocala)
360 Washington (Bellingham, Olympia, Vancouver)
361 Texas (Corpus Christi)
385 Utah (Ogden, Provo)
401 Rhode Island
402 Nebraska (Lincoln, Omaha)
403 Alberta (Calgary)
404 Georgia (Atlanta)
405 Oklahoma (Norman, Oklahoma City, Stillwater)
406 Montana
407 Florida (Orlando)
408 California (San Jose)
409 Texas (Galveston)
410 Maryland (Baltimore)

411 Directory Services
412 Pennsylvania (Pittsburgh)
413 Massachusetts (Springfield)
414 Wisconsin (Milwaukee)
415 California (San Francisco)
416 Ontario (Toronto)
417 Missouri (Joplin, Springfield)
418 Quebec (Quebec City)
419 Ohio (Toledo)
423 Tennessee (Chattanooga)
424 California (Beverly Hills, Gardena)
425 Washington (Bothell, Everett)
435 Utah (Cedar City, St. George)
440 Ohio (Ashtabula)
441 Bermuda
443 Maryland (Baltimore)
445 Pennsylvania (Philadelphia)
450 Quebec (suburban Montreal)
464 Illinois (suburban Chicago)
469 Texas (Dallas)
473 Grenada
475 Connecticut (Fairfield, New Haven)
478 Georgia (Macon)
480 Arizona (suburban Phoenix)
484 Pennsylvania (Allentown, Bethlehem, Reading)
501 Arkansas
502 Kentucky (Louisville)
503 Oregon (Portland, Salem)
504 Louisiana (New Orleans)
505 New Mexico
506 New Brunswick
507 Minnesota (Rochester)
508 Massachusetts (Framingham, New Bedford, Plymouth)
509 Washington (Spokane)
510 California (Oakland)
512 Texas (Austin)
513 Ohio (Cincinnati, Dayton)
514 Quebec (Montreal)
515 Iowa (Des Moines)
516 New York (Long Island)
517 Michigan (Lansing)
518 New York (Albany, Schenectady)
519 Ontario (London, Windsor)
520 Arizona (Tucson, Flagstaff, Prescott, Yuma)
530 California (Chico, Redding, Yreka)
540 Virginia (Roanoke, Winchester)
541 Oregon (Eugene, Medford)
559 California (Fresno)
561 Florida (Boca Raton, Stuart, West Palm Beach)
562 California (Santa Monica, Long Beach, Whittier)

564 Washington (Bellingham, Olympia, Vancouver)
567 Ohio (Toledo)
570 Pennsylvania (Scranton, Wilkes-Barre, Williamsport)
571 Virginia (Arlington, Fairfax, Vienna)
573 Missouri (Jefferson City)
580 Oklahoma (Enid)
586 Michigan (Birmingham, Flint, Pontiac)
601 Mississippi (Hattiesburg, Jackson)
602 Arizona (Phoenix)
603 New Hampshire
604 British Columbia (Vancouver)
605 South Dakota
606 Kentucky (Ashland)
607 New York (Binghamton, Elmira)
608 Wisconsin (Madison)
609 New Jersey (Atlantic City, Princeton, Trenton)
610 Pennsylvania (Allentown, Bethlehem, Reading, West Chester)
611 Repair Service
612 Minnesota (Minneapolis)
613 Ontario (Ottawa)
614 Ohio (Columbus)
615 Tennessee (Nashville)
616 Michigan (Battle Creek, Grand Rapids, Kalamazoo)
617 Massachusetts (Boston)
618 Illinois (Collinsville, Granite City)
619 California (San Diego)
620 Kansas (Dodge City, Emporia)
623 Arizona (suburban Phoenix)
626 California (Alhambra, Pasadena)
628 California (San Francisco)
630 Illinois (suburban Chicago)
631 New York (Long Island)
636 Missouri (Chesterfield)
641 Iowa (Des Moines)
646 New York (Manhattan)
647 Ontario (Toronto)
649 Turks and Caicos
650 California (Mountain View, San Mateo)
651 Minnesota (St. Paul)
657 California (Anaheim)
660 Missouri (Kirksville)
661 California (Bakersfield)
662 Mississippi (Greenville, Oxford, Tupelo)
664 Montserrat
669 California (San Jose)
670 Mariana Islands
671 Guam
678 Georgia (Atlanta)
679 Michigan (Detroit)
682 Texas (Fort Worth)
701 North Dakota

702 Nevada (Las Vegas)
703 Virginia (Arlington, Alexandria)
704 North Carolina (Charlotte)
705 Ontario (Sault Ste. Marie)
706 Georgia (Augusta, Columbus)
707 California (Petaluma, Napa)
708 Illinois (Des Plaines, Waukegan)
709 Newfoundland
712 Iowa (Council Bluffs, Sioux City)
713 Texas (Houston)
714 California (Anaheim)
715 Wisconsin (Eau Claire)
716 New York (Buffalo, Rochester)
717 Pennsylvania (Harrisburg, York)
718 New York (Brooklyn, Queens, Staten Island)
719 Colorado (Colorado Springs)
720 Colorado (Denver)
724 Pennsylvania (Latrobe)
727 Florida (Clearwater, St. Petersburg)
731 Tennessee (Jackson)
732 New Jersey (Middlesex, Monmouth, Ocean Counties)
734 Michigan (Ann Arbor, Ypsilanti)
737 Texas (Austin)
740 Ohio (Athens, Lancaster, Marietta)
752 California (Ontario, Pomona)
757 Virginia (Newport News, Norfolk, Virginia Beach)
758 St. Lucia
760 California (Needles, Palm Springs)
763 Minnesota (Minneapolis)
764 California (San Mateo)
765 Indiana (Kokomo, Lafayette)
767 Dominica
770 Georgia (suburban Atlanta)
773 Illinois (Chicago)
774 Massachusetts (Worcester, Cape Cod)
775 Nevada (Carson City, Reno)
778 British Columbia (Vancouver area)
780 Alberta (Edmonton)
781 Massachusetts (Waltham)
784 St. Vincent/Grenadines
785 Kansas (Lawrence, Topeka)
786 Florida (Miami)
787 Puerto Rico
800 Toll-free
801 Utah (Salt Lake City, Ogden, Provo)
802 Vermont
803 South Carolina (Columbia)
804 Virginia (Norfolk, Richmond)
805 California (Bakersfield, Santa Barbara)
806 Texas (Amarillo, Lubbock)
807 Ontario (Thunder Bay)
808 Hawaii
809 Dominican Republic, Caribbean islands

810 Michigan (Birmingham, Flint, Pontiac)
812 Indiana (Bloomington, Terre Haute)
813 Florida (St. Petersburg, Tampa)
814 Pennsylvania (Altoona, Erie)
815 Illinois (Joliet, Rockford)
816 Missouri (Kansas City)
817 Texas (Arlington, Fort Worth)
818 California (Burbank, Pasadena)
819 Quebec (Sherbrooke)
828 North Carolina (Asheville)
830 Texas (New Braunfels, Uvalde)
831 California (Monterey, Salinas)
832 Texas (Houston)
835 Pennsylvania (Allentown)
843 South Carolina (Charleston)
845 New York (Hudson Valley, Catskills)
847 Illinois (suburban Chicago)
850 Florida (Panama City, Pensacola, Tallahassee)
856 New Jersey (Camden)
857 Massachusetts (Boston)
858 California (La Jolla)
859 Kentucky (Lexington)
860 Connecticut (Hartford)
863 Florida (Lakeland)
864 South Carolina (Greenville, Spartanburg)
865 Tennessee (Knoxville)
866 Toll-free
867 Yukon, Northwest Territories
868 Trinidad and Tobago
869 St. Kitts and Nevis
870 Arkansas (Pine Bluff, Texarkana)
872 Illinois (Chicago)
876 Jamaica
877 Toll-free
878 Pennsylvania (Pittsburgh)
888 Toll-free
900 "Dial-It" services
901 Tennessee (Memphis)
902 Nova Scotia, Prince Edward Island
903 Texas (Texarkana)
904 Florida (Daytona Beach, Jacksonville)
905 Ontario (Hamilton)
906 Michigan (Marquette, Sault Ste. Marie)
907 Alaska
908 New Jersey (Asbury Park, Elizabeth, New Brunswick)
909 California (Ontario, Pomona)
910 North Carolina (Fayetteville, Winston-Salem)
911 Emergency Services
912 Georgia (Savannah)
913 Kansas (Kansas City, Topeka)
914 New York (Newburgh, Poughkeepsie)
915 Texas (Abilene, El Paso)

916 California (Sacramento)
917 New York (Manhattan, Queens, Staten Island)
918 Oklahoma (Tulsa)
919 North Carolina (Durham, Raleigh)
920 Wisconsin (Green Bay, Sheboygan)
925 California (Walnut Creek)
931 Tennessee (Clarksville)
935 California (Chula Vista, El Cajon)
936 Texas (Nacogdoches)
937 Ohio (Dayton)
939 Puerto Rico
940 Texas (Wichita Falls)
941 Florida (Ft. Myers, Naples, Sarasota)
947 Michigan (Oakland County)
949 California (Costa Mesa, Irvine)
951 California (Riverside)
952 Minnesota (Minneapolis)
954 Florida (Ft. Lauderdale)
956 Texas (Brownsville, Laredo)
959 Connecticut (Hartford)
970 Colorado (Aspen, Vail)
971 Oregon (Portland, Salem)
972 Texas (Dallas)
973 New Jersey (Morris, Passaic, Essex Counties)
978 Massachusetts (Lowell)
979 Texas (College Station)
     North Carolina (Charlotte)
985 Louisiana (Hammond)
989 Michigan (Saginaw)

Arenas

Original nickname of the Toronto Maple Leafs at their NHL inception in 1917. The team became known as the St. Patricks in 1919, and took its present name in 1926.

"Aren't we devils?"

Catchphrase of host Ralph Edwards in the radio version of the game show *Truth or Consequences*.

"Are you going to finish that sandwich?"

Motto of the planet Melmac, in the TV sitcom *ALF*.

argentum

Latin name for silver, from which its chemical symbol Ag is derived.

Argo

Horse of the title character (Lucy Lawless) in the TV series *Xena: Warrior Princess*.

Argo

In Greek mythology, the ship captained by Jason in search of the Golden Fleece.

Argo City

Krypton hometown of Supergirl in the Superman comic books.

Argonaut

Allied code name for the "Big Three" (Franklin D. Roosevelt, Winston Churchill, Joseph Stalin) conference at Yalta, Russia, in February 1945.

Argonaut

Boat of Mike Nelson (Lloyd Bridges) in the TV series *Sea Hunt*.

Argus

Faithful dog of Odysseus in the Homer epic poem *The Odyssey*.

Ariel

See **film awards, national**

Aries

Shuttle between Space Station 5 and the Moon in the film *2001: A Space Odyssey*.

Aristides

Winner of the first Kentucky Derby in 1875.

Aristo

See **60 Minutes stopwatch brands**

Aristotle

Pet octopus of Pugsley Addams (Ken Weatherwax) in the TV sitcom *The Addams Family*.

"Arkansas toothpick"

Nickname of a bowie knife.

Arkham, Massachusetts

Setting of many of the works of sci-fi author H. P. Lovecraft.

Arlene

Female cat that the title character tries to impress, in the comic strip *Garfield*.

Arlen, Texas

Setting of the animated TV sitcom *King of the Hill*.

Arlington National Cemetery, famous people buried in

Constance Bennett (actress)
Hugo Black (Supreme Court justice)
Omar Bradley (World War II general)
William Jennings Bryan (statesman)
Richard E. Byrd (polar explorer)
Abner Doubleday (Civil War general)
William O. Douglas (Supreme Court justice)
Medgar Evers (civil-rights leader)
Virgil Grissom (astronaut)
William Halsey (World War II admiral)
Dashiell Hammett (novelist)
Oliver Wendell Holmes Jr. (Supreme Court justice)
John F. Kennedy (U.S. president)
Robert Kennedy (U.S. senator)
Pierre L'Enfant (designer of Washington, D.C.)
Joe Louis (boxer)
Lee Marvin (actor)
George C. Marshall (World War II general)
Thurgood Marshall (Supreme Court justice)
Audie Murphy (actor, World War II hero)
Jacqueline Kennedy Onassis (U.S. first lady)
Robert Peary (polar explorer)
John J. Pershing (World War I general)
Walter Reed (bacteriologist)
Albert Sabin (polio-vaccine developer)
William Howard Taft (U.S. president, Chief Justice)
Earl Warren (Chief Justice)

Arlo

Pet Irish setter of author Erma Bombeck.

Arluck, Hyman

Real name of songwriter Harold Arlen.

Armadillos

Texas State University football team in the film *Necessary Roughness*.

Armando

Real first name of pop singer Buddy Greco.

Armchair Sleuth

Favorite magazine of the title character (Tom Bosley) in the TV series *Father Dowling Mysteries*.

Armistice Day

Former name of Veterans Day.

Army of the Potomac trilogy

Group of books on the Civil War written by historian Bruce Catton:
   Mr. Lincoln's Army (1951)
   Glory Road (1952)
   A Stillness at Appomattox (1953)
The last of these books received a Pulitzer Prize.

Arneson, Dave and Gygax, E. Gary

Inventors of the role-playing game Dungeons & Dragons, introduced in 1973.

"Arnie's Army"
See **"Lee's Fleas"**

Arnold
Real first name of telejournalist (Arnold) Eric Sevareid.

Arnold, Elliot
See *Blood Brother*

Arnold Palmer Award
Presented annually since 1980 to the Senior PGA's leading money winner.

Arnold's
Restaurant hangout in the TV sitcom *Happy Days*.

Aron
Middle name of singer Elvis Presley, as recorded on his birth certificate. His middle name is given as Aaron on his tombstone.

Arondight
Sword of Sir Lancelot.

Arouet, François-Marie
Real name of French author/philosopher Voltaire.

Around the World in 80 Days cameo roles
THESE PERFORMERS ALL MADE BRIEF APPEARANCES IN THE FILM:

Charles Boyer	Buster Keaton
Joe E. Brown	Evelyn Keyes
John Carradine	Beatrice Lillie
Charles Coburn	Peter Lorre
Ronald Colman	Edmund Lowe
Noel Coward	Tim McCoy
Reginald Denny	Victor McLaglen
Andy Devine	John Mills
Marlene Dietrich	Alan Mowbray
Fernandel	Jack Oakie
Sir John Gielgud	George Raft
Hermione Gingold	Gilbert Roland
José Greco	Cesar Romero
Sir Cedric Hardwicke	Frank Sinatra
Trevor Howard	Red Skelton
Glynis Johns	

ARPANET
See **Advanced Research Projects Agency**

Arquillian Galaxy
See **Orion**

Arrakis
Planet that is the setting of the *Dune* series of sci-fi novels by Frank Herbert.

"Arrival"
Debut episode of the TV series *The Prisoner*, which aired on October 1, 1967.

Arrow-Flite Lines
Bus company used by Bo Decker (Don Murray) and Virgil Blessing (Arthur O'Connell) traveling to and from Phoenix, in the film *Bus Stop*.

Arrowhead
Home of author Herman Melville in Pittsfield, Massachusetts.

"Ars gratia artis"
Motto of MGM, which is Latin for "Art for art's sake."

Artemis II
Spaceship on the Moon that is destroyed by General Zod (Terence Stamp) in the film *Superman II*.

"Artes, scientia, veritas"
Motto of the University of Michigan, which is Latin for "The arts, science, truth."

Arthur
Real first name of actor Sir (Arthur) John Gielgud. Coincidentally, Gielgud won a Best Supporting Actor Academy Award for his role in the film *Arthur*.

Real first name of The Fonz (Henry Winkler) in the TV sitcom *Happy Days*.

Real first name of Bud Stamper (Warren Beatty) in the film *Splendor in the Grass*.

See also **Marx Brothers' real names**

Arthur and Louis
First names (respectively) of pianists Ferrante and Teicher.

Arthur Christopher Orme
Real first and middle names of actor Christopher Plummer.

"Artistry in Rhythm"
Theme song of bandleader Stan Kenton.

Asa
First name of labor leader A. Philip Randolph.

"As always, in parting we wish you love, peace and soul!"

Signoff line of host Don Cornelius in the TV series *Soul Train.*

ASCAP

California license plate on the Rolls-Royce of songwriter George Webber (Dudley Moore) in the film *"10."*

"As Days Go By"

See **"What a Wonderful World"**

Asher and Waller

Last names, respectively, of English pop duo Peter and Gordon.

Ashe, Stephen

Role for which Lionel Barrymore won a Best Actor Academy Award in the 1931 film *A Free Soul.*

Ashley, Maurice

The first African-American international chess grandmaster. The title was awarded in March 1999 by FIDE, the international governing body of chess. To become a grandmaster, a player must score high performance ratings in three rigorous tournaments against top-rated players within a seven-year period.

Ash, Linda

Role for which Mira Sorvino won a Best Supporting Actress Academy Award in the 1995 film *Mighty Aphrodite.*

Ashton, Lucy

Title character of the Sir Walter Scott novel *The Bride of Lammermoor.*

Asia (rock group) members

Geoff Downes, Steve Howe, Carl Palmer, and John Wetton.

"As if!"

Catchphrase of Cher Horowitz (Alicia Silverstone) in the film *Clueless.*

Asis Productions

Production company of actor Jeff Bridges.

"Ask the man who owns one"

Advertising slogan of Packard automobiles.

"As Long as We Got Each Other"

Theme song of the TV sitcom *Growing Pains,* performed by B. J. Thomas and Jennifer Warnes.

aspartame

See **L-aspartyl L-phenylalinine methyl ester**

Aspen

Presidential cabin at Camp David.

Aspercel

Title character, named for an indigestion-remedy client of adman Fred Bolton (Dean Jones), in the Disney film *The Horse in the Gray Flannel Suit.*

"As quick as a wink, you're in the pink!"

Advertising slogan of Pepto-Bismol.

"The Assassin"

Nickname of hard-hitting NFL defensive back Jack Tatum.

Astaire/Rogers films

The films in which Fred Astaire and Ginger Rogers appear together:
Flying Down to Rio (1933)
The Gay Divorcée (1934)
Roberta (1935)
Top Hat (1935)
Swing Time (1936)
Follow the Fleet (1936)
Shall We Dance (1937)
Carefree (1938)
The Story of Vernon and Irene Castle (1939)
The Barkleys of Broadway (1949)

"As the Stomach Turns"

Recurring soap-opera spoof in the TV comedy/variety series *The Carol Burnett Show.*

Aston, James

Pen name used by author T. H. White early in his career.

Aston Martin DB5

English sports car driven by James Bond (Sean Connery) in the films *Goldfinger* and *Thunderball.*

Astor, Lord

See **Patience and Fortitude**

Astrospace Industries

Employer of the title character (Diahann Carroll) in the TV sitcom *Julia.*

A.T.A.C.

Acronym for the Automatic Targeting Attack Communicator, a ballistic-missile launch system whose recovery from the sunken English spy ship *St. Georges* is the objective of James Bond (Roger Moore) in the film *For Your Eyes Only*.

"at another place"

What the word "alibi" means in Latin.

"at another time"

What the word "alias" means in Latin.

Athos

Pet dog of Leopold Bloom's father in the James Joyce novel *Ulysses*.

See also **Aramis, Athos, and Porthos**

Atisanoe, Salevaa

See **"Meat Bomb" and "Dump Truck"**

Atlantis

Spiderlike structure off the coast of Sardinia that serves as the marine-research laboratory of Karl Stromberg (Curt Jurgens), in the James Bond film *The Spy Who Loved Me*.

The Atomium

2,400 ton, 300+-foot tall sculpture designed by André Waterkeyn, built for the 1958 Universal and International Exposition at Brussels, Belgium. Still a tourist attraction today, the sculpture represents a nine-atom iron crystal magnified 160 billion times.

The Attackers

Rock band led by Ellen Aim (Diane Lane) in the film *Streets of Fire*.

Attila

Pet bloodhound of George Malley (John Travolta) in the film *Phenomenon*.

Attucks, Crispus

Merchant seaman who was the first person killed at the Boston Massacre on May 5, 1770.

At Wit's End

Syndicated newspaper column of humorist Erma Bombeck.

AU1

License plate on the Rolls-Royce Phantom 337 of the title character (Gert Frobe) in the James Bond film *Goldfinger*.

Audie Awards

Presented annually since 1996 by the Audio Publishers Association for excellence in audiobooks.

Augusta Academy

Original name of Washington and Lee University at its founding in 1749. It took its present name in 1871.

Augusta National Golf Club hole names

The home of the prestigious Masters golf tournament has named each of its 18 holes after the shrubs, trees and flowers found on the course.

1st	Tea Olive
2nd	Pink Dogwood
3rd	Flowering Peach
4th	Flowering Crab Apple
5th	Magnolia
6th	Juniper
7th	Pampas
8th	Yellow Jasmine
9th	Carolina Cherry
10th	Camellia
11th	White Dogwood
12th	Golden Bell
13th	Azalea
14th	Chinese Fir
15th	Firethorn
16th	Redbud
17th	Nandina
18th	Holly

Augustus

Middle name of aviator Charles Lindbergh.

Augustus P.

First name and middle initial of Mutt in the comic strip *Mutt and Jeff*.

Auld Lang Syne Loan Company

Business run by Alonzo Hawk (Keenan Wynn) in the Disney film *The Absent-Minded Professor*.

Aunt Julia and the Scriptwriter

Novel by Mario Vargas Llosa that was the basis for the film *Tune in Tomorrow . . . .*

"Aura Lee"

Folk ballad whose melody was used for the Elvis Presley tune "Love Me Tender."

Aurandt

Real last name of radio commentator Paul Harvey.

aurum

Latin name for gold, from which its chemical symbol Au is derived.

Austerlitz, Frederick
Real name of dancer/actor Fred Astaire.

Austin, Colonel Steve
Title character (Lee Majors) of the TV series *The Six Million Dollar Man*.

Australia II
Only sailboat from Australia to have won the America's Cup to date, having done so in 1983.

Australian English
Common Australian expressions that are not common in the U.S., including words that have different meanings in Australia and the U.S.:

apples: all right
arvo: afternoon
barbie: barbecue
beltman: lifeguard
bingle: auto accident
bingy: stomach
bitser: mongrel dog
bonzer: excellent
bosker: excellent
bowser: gas pump
brumby: wild horse
Buckley's chance: slim hope
bundy: time clock
chook: hen
choom: Englishman
cobber: friend
cossie: bathing suit
crust: livelihood
demon: police detective
dinkum: genuine
doer: eccentric person
drongo: simpleton
drum: accurate information
euchred: exhausted
fizgig: police informer
furphy: rumor
goog: egg
grouse: excellent
jumbuck: sheep
king-hit: knockout punch
lair: showoff
larrikin: hooligan
mong: mongrel dog
neddy: horse
Oz: Australia
ropable: angry
rort: rowdy party
sheila: young woman
shicer: swindler
shivoo: rowdy party
skerrick: small quantity
skite: brag
snack: easy task
snaky: irritable
spinebash: loaf (do nothing)
squib: coward
squiz: quick look
stickybeak: busybody
strides: trousers
strine: Australian English
swagman: hobo
tucker: food
willy-willy: cyclone
wipe: reject
yakka: hard work

"The Austrian Oak"
Nickname of actor Arnold Schwarzenegger.

"Aut Caesar aut nihil"
Motto of Italian cardinal/politician Cesare Borgia, which is Latin for "Either Emperor or nothing."

"The Autobiography of a Horse"
Subtitle of the Anna Sewell children's novel *Black Beauty*.

Automatic Targeting Attack Computer
See **A.T.A.C.**

auto-racing flags
Green: start
Red: stop
Yellow: caution
Black: leave the track
Blue with yellow diagonal stripe: move to the outside
White: one lap to go
Checkered: finish

Avedis Zildjian Company
World's largest manufacturer of cymbals and drumsticks, based in Norwell, Massachusetts. The Zildjian family started making cymbals in Turkey in 1673.

Avery
First name of the son of the title character (Candice Bergen) in the TV sitcom *Murphy Brown*, portrayed by Christopher Dylan, Jackson Buckley and Haley Joel Osment. He was named for the title character's mother (Colleen Dewhurst).

Avondale Dairy
Former employer of driver Hoke Colburn (Morgan Freeman) in the film *Driving Miss Daisy*.

Away We Go!

Original title of the Rodgers and Hammerstein musical *Oklahoma!*

"Axe"

Nickname of firefighter John Adcox (Scott Glenn) in the film *Backdraft.*

Axel

Pet wolverine of the title characters in the comic strip *The Fusco Brothers.*

Axelrod, George

Author of the play *The Seven Year Itch,* which was the basis for the film of the same name.

axilla

Medical term for the armpit.

Ayesha

Title character of the H. Rider Haggard novel *She.*

Azkaban

Prison where wizarding criminals are sent, in the Harry Potter series of books by J. K. Rowling.

Azrael

Pet cat of Gargamel in the children's animated TV series *The Smurfs.*

Azteca

Worker ant in the animated film *Antz,* voiced by Jennifer Lopez.

B17

Jukebox number not to play, in the Olivia Newton-John tune "Please Mr. Please."

B-52's original members

Kate Pierson, Fred Schneider, Keith Strickland, Cindy Wilson, and Ricky Wilson.

Baba Looey

Burro sidekick of cartoon sheriff Quick Draw McGraw. Both characters are voiced by Daws Butler.

"The Babbitt and the Bromide"

Tune by George and Ira Gershwin in the 1946 film *The Ziegfeld Follies* to which Fred Astaire and Gene Kelly danced together—the only time that they did so on film.

Babbitt, Raymond

Role for which Dustin Hoffman won a Best Actor Academy Award in the 1988 film *Rain Man*.

Babcock, Edward Chester

Real name of songwriter James Van Heusen. Van Heusen wrote the tunes for most of the "Road" films, including *The Road to Hong Kong*, in which Bob Hope's character was named Chester Babcock.

"Babe"

Nickname of comedian Oliver Hardy.

Babette

Middle name of author Alice B. Toklas.

Babieca

Horse of Spanish national hero El Cid.

"Babies are our business, our only business"

Former advertising slogan of Gerber baby food. The last three words of the slogan were dropped when Gerber entered the life-insurance business in 1967.

Babington

Middle name of Thomas Levy (Dustin Hoffman) in the film *Marathon Man*.

"The Baby Bull"

Nickname of baseball Hall of Famer Orlando Cepeda.

"Baby Doc"

Nickname of Jean-Claude Duvalier, son of François Duvalier, and his successor as president of Haiti.

Baby Dumpling

Original name of Alexander, son of Blondie and Dagwood Bumstead in the comic strip *Blondie*.

Baby Gee

See **Geoffrey**

"Babylon Revisited"

Short story by F. Scott Fitzgerald that was the basis for the film *The Last Time I Saw Paris*.

The Babysitter Murders

Original working title of the film *Halloween*.

Baby Steps

Self-help book written by psychiatrist Dr. Leo Marvin (Richard Dreyfuss) in the film *What About Bob?*

"Baby, you're the greatest!"

Last line of many of the episodes of the TV sitcom *The Honeymooners*, spoken by Ralph Kramden (Jackie Gleason) to his wife Alice (Audrey Meadows).

Bacall/Bogart films

The films in which Lauren Bacall and Humphrey Bogart appear together:
To Have and Have Not (1944)
Two Guys from Milwaukee (1946)*
The Big Sleep (1946)
Dark Passage (1947)
Key Largo (1948)
*Bacall and Bogart have cameo roles in this film.

Bach

Last name of the title character (Dudley Moore) in the film *Arthur*.

Bachelor-at-Large

Comic strip drawn by Paul Morgan (Tab Hunter) in the TV sitcom *The Tab Hunter Show*.

"The Bachelor's Bible"

See Marriage: A Fraud and a Failure

Bachman, Richard

Pen name used by Stephen King for these novels:
Rage (1977)
The Long Walk (1979)
Roadwork (1981)
The Running Man (1982)
Thinner (1984)
The Regulators (1996)

Bach, P. D. Q., selected works

"The last and by far the least child of the great Johann Sebastian Bach." The discovery/creation of Peter Schickele.
1712 Overture
The Art of the Ground Round
Breakfast Antiphonies
Canine Cantata
Christmas Carols: *Throw the Yule Log on, Uncle John; O Little Town of Hackensack; Good King Kong Looked Out*
Concerto for Horn and Hardart
Concerto for Two Pianos vs. Orchestra
Echo Sonata for Two Unfriendly Groups of Instruments
Fanfare for Fred
Fanfare for the Common Cold
Four Curmudgeonly Canons
Four Folk Song Upsettings
Fuga Meshuga
"Goldbrick" Variations
Grand Serenade for an Awful Lot of Winds and Percussion
Hansel & Gretel & Ted & Alice
"Howdy" Symphony
Iphegenia in Brooklyn
Last Tango in Bayreuth
Lip My Reeds
March of the Cute Little Wood Sprites
Missa Hilarious
My Bonnie Lass She Smelleth
No-No Nonette
Octoot
Oedipus Tex
The Only Piece Ever Written for Violin and Tuba
Overture to *The Abduction of Figaro*
Overture to *La Clemenza di Genghis Khan*
The Preachers of Crimetheus; Ballet in One Selfless Act
Prelude to *Einstein on the Fritz*
The Queen to Me a Royal Pain Doth Give
Rounds for Squares
Royal Firewater Musick
"Safe" Sextet
Schleptet
Shepherd on the Rocks, with a Twist
The Seasonings
The Short-Tempered Clavier
Three Teeny Preludes
"Unbegun" Symphony
Uptown Hoedown
Variations on an Unusually Simple-Minded Theme

Backbiter

Allied code name for Wake Island during World War II.

"Back in the Saddle Again"

Theme song of singing cowboy Gene Autry.

"Back Issues"

Debut episode of the TV sitcom *Just Shoot Me*, which aired on March 4, 1997.

The Back Room

Name of the Stockbridge, Massachusetts, title establishment in the film *Alice's Restaurant*.

Backstreet Boys members

Nick Carter, Howie Dorough, Brian Littrell, A. J. McLean, and Kevin Richardson.

Bacon, Henry

Architect who designed the Lincoln Memorial in Washington, D.C., dedicated in 1912.

Bacteria

Country ruled by Benzino Napaloni (Jack Oakie) in the film *The Great Dictator*.

Bada Bing!

Nightclub hangout of Tony Soprano (James Gandolfini) and his pals, in the TV series *The Sopranos*.

Bad Andy

Mischievous puppet in TV commercials for Domino's Pizza.

"Bad Boys"

Theme song of the TV documentary series *Cops*, performed by Inner Circle.

Bad Company original members

Raymond "Boz" Burrell, Simon Kirke, Mick Ralphs, and Paul Rodgers.

"Bad Finger Boogie"

Original working title of the Beatles tune "With a Little Help from My Friends."

Badge of Honor

TV police series that has Detective Jack Vincennes (Kevin Spacey) as its technical advisor, in the film *L.A. Confidential*.

Badge of Military Merit

Original name of the Purple Heart.

"Badger"

See **United States residents' nicknames**

"Badges? We ain't got no badges! We don't need no badges! I don't have to show you any stinking badges!"

Memorable (and often misquoted) line spoken by Mexican bandit Gold Hat (Alfonso Bedoya) to Fred C. Dobbs (Humphrey Bogart) in the film *The Treasure of the Sierra Madre*.

"Bad in Every Man"

Previous title of the Rodgers and Hart tune "Blue Moon." It had also been called "Prayer" and "Manhattan Melodrama" (with different lyrics in each case) prior to its best-known title.

Badwater, California

Area within Death Valley National Park that, at an elevation of 282 feet below sea level, is the lowest point in the Western Hemisphere.

Baeza, Maria Rosario Pilar Martinez Molina

Real name of entertainer Charo.

baffle ball

See **Gottlieb, David**

BAFTA

See **film awards, national**

Bagby Jr., Jim and Smith, Al

Cleveland Indian pitchers who stopped the record 56-game hitting streak of New York Yankee Joe DiMaggio on July 17, 1941, assisted by two stellar fielding plays of Indians third baseman Ken Keltner.

Bagdasarian, Ross

Real name of Chipmunks creator David Seville.

Bagel

Pet beagle of singer Barry Manilow.

Bag End

Middle-earth home of Bilbo Baggins in the J. R. R. Tolkien novel *The Hobbit*.

Baggott Employment Office

Where Passepartout (Cantinflas) finds employment with Phileas Fogg (David Niven) in the film *Around the World in 80 Days*.

Bagheera

Black panther in Rudyard Kipling's *The Jungle Book*.

Bailey

Maiden name of Lois Flagston in the comic strip *Hi and Lois*. Lois is the sister of the title character of the comic strip *Beetle Bailey*. Both strips were created by cartoonist Mort Walker.

Bailey, William

Real name of Guns N' Roses lead singer Axl Rose.

Baines

Maiden name of Edith Bunker (Jean Stapleton) in the TV sitcom *All in the Family*.

Maiden name of Lorraine McFly (Lea Thompson) in the *Back to the Future* films.

Bains, Lulu

Role for which Shirley Jones won a Best Supporting Actress Academy Award in the 1960 film *Elmer Gantry*.

Bakeman, Daniel

Last surviving veteran of the American Revolution. He died on April 5, 1869, at the age of 109.

Baker and Vanderpool

Last names (respectively) of pop singers Mickey and Sylvia.

Baker, Daisy

Real name of actress and frequent Marx Brothers foil Margaret Dumont.

Baker, Kenny

Portrayer of droid R2-D2 in the *Star Wars* films.

Baker, Mrs.

Role for which Eileen Heckart won a Best Supporting Actress Academy Award in the 1972 film *Butterflies Are Free*.

"The Bakersfield Flash"

Nickname of runner Goldine Serafin (Susan Anton) in the film *Goldengirl*.

Baker Street Irregulars

Best-known organization devoted to the study and appreciation of Sherlock Holmes, founded in 1934 by writer Christopher Morley. It is named for the group of street urchins who assist Holmes in the novels and short stories of Sir Arthur Conan Doyle.

Bala, Princess
Love interest of Z-4195 (voiced by Woody Allen) in the animated film *Antz*, voiced by Sharon Stone.

Baldwin, Jerry; Bowker, Gordon; and Siegl, Zev
Founders of the Starbucks Coffee chain. The first Starbucks opened in 1971 in Seattle's Pike Place Market.

Balios and Xanthos
Horses of Achilles.

"Ballantine Blasts"
Sportscaster Mel Allen's term for New York Yankees' home runs, while Ballantine Beer was a sponsor of the broadcasts.

Baloo
Brown-bear teacher of Mowgli in Rudyard Kipling's *The Jungle Book*.

Balthasar
Pet dog of Young Jolyon Forsyte in John Galsworthy's *The Forsyte Saga*.

Baltimore Gun Club
Group of Civil War veterans that execute a manned lunar flight, in the Jules Verne novel *From the Earth to the Moon*.

Baltimore Herald
Newspaper employer of reporter E. K. Hornbeck in the Lawrence and Lee play *Inherit the Wind*. Hornbeck is modeled on H. L. Mencken.

"Bam!"
Favorite exclamation of TV chef Emeril Lagasse.

Bambi
Pet cat of Valerie Gale (Geena Davis) in the film *Earth Girls Are Easy*.

"Bambi"
Nickname of pro football Hall of Fame wide receiver Lance Alworth, for his grace and speed.

Bambi and Thumper
Acrobatic bodyguards (Donna Garrett and Trina Parks, respectively) of kidnapped billionaire recluse Willard Whyte (Jimmy Dean) in the James Bond film *Diamonds Are Forever*.

Bambino
Original working title of the film *Breaking Away*.

Bamboo Harvester
Horse that portrays the title equine in the TV sitcom *Mister Ed*.

A Band Apart
Production company of actor/director Quentin Tarantino.

Bandaranaike, Sirimavo
First woman to serve as a head of state. She became prime minister of Ceylon (known today as Sri Lanka) in 1960.

Bandello, Cesare Enrico
Title character (Edward G. Robinson) of the film *Little Caesar*.

Bandie
Pet Pekingese of the title character (Betty White) in the TV sitcom *Life with Elizabeth*.

Bandit
Pet dog of the title character in the children's animated TV series *Jonny Quest*.

Pet collie of Laura Ingalls (Melissa Gilbert) in the TV series *Little House on the Prairie*.

Band of Renown
Band led by Les Brown.

The Band, original members
Rick Danko, Levon Helm, Garth Hudson, Richard Manuel, and Robbie Robertson.

"Bandstand Boogie"
Instrumental theme of the TV series *American Bandstand*, performed by Les Elgart and his orchestra.

Banji, Krishna
Real name of actor Ben Kingsley.

"Banjo Eyes"
Nickname of comedian Eddie Cantor.

Bank of Italy
Original name of the Bank of America, founded in San Francisco in 1904 by Amadeo Giannini, son of Italian immigrants.

Banner, Bruce/David
Alter ego of the title character in the comic and TV versions (respectively) of *The Incredible Hulk*. His

name was changed from Bruce to David in the TV series because the producers wanted a more macho-sounding name.

Banning, Texas

Hometown of the Frake family in the Rodgers and Hammerstein musical film *State Fair* (1962). The 1945 version is set in Iowa.

Bannister, Roger

First person to run the mile in less than four minutes. He accomplished this at Oxford University, England, on May 6, 1954, with a time of 3 minutes, 59.4 seconds.

Bannon, Homer

Role for which Melvyn Douglas won a Best Supporting Actor Academy Award in the 1963 film *Hud*.

Banthas

Spiral-horned animals used as beasts of burden by the Sand People of Tatooine, in the film *Star Wars*.

Bar 20 Ranch

Home of TV/film cowboy Hopalong Cassidy (William Boyd).

Barbara Anne

Presidential yacht of Dwight D. Eisenhower, which he named for his granddaughter. President John F. Kennedy renamed the yacht *Honey Fitz*, for his maternal grandfather.

See also **"Honey Fitz"**

Barbella, Thomas Rocco

Real name of 1940s middleweight boxing champ Rocky Graziano.

"The Barber"

Nickname of baseball pitcher Sal Maglie, for the "close shaves" he delivered to batters.

"The Barbers of C'ville"

Nickname of 1990s University of Virginia (at Charlottesville) twin-brother footballers Ronde and Tiki Barber.

Bar-B-Q

Original title of the James M. Cain novel *The Postman Always Rings Twice*.

"The Bard of Avon"

Nickname of English poet/playwright William Shakespeare.

"The Bard of Ayrshire"

Nickname of Scottish poet Robert Burns.

Barfy

Family dog in the comic strip *The Family Circus*.

Bargain Basement

Original working title of the Marx Brothers film *The Big Store*.

Bari, Joe

Stage name used by singer Tony Bennett early in his career.

The Bar-Kays

R&B group that lost four of its six original members in the December 10, 1967, Wisconsin plane crash that took the life of Otis Redding.

Barker, Pat

See **Union Street**

Barnard, A. M.

Pen name used by author Louisa May Alcott.

Barnard's Crossing, Massachusetts

Home of Rabbi David Small in the mystery novels of Harry Kemelman.

Barnes

Maiden name of Holly Golightly (Audrey Hepburn) in the film *Breakfast at Tiffany's*.

Barney

Horse of Corporal Randolph Agarn (Larry Storch) in the TV sitcom *F Troop*.

Pet dog of Billy Peltzer (Zach Galligan) in the film *Gremlins*.

Pet Yorkshire terrier of Margaret Pynchon (Nancy Marchand) in the TV series *Lou Grant*.

Barone

Last name of the title character (Ray Romano) in the TV sitcom *Everybody Loves Raymond*.

Baron Lamm method

Meticulous bank robbery technique followed by outlaw John Dillinger. It is named for Herman K. "Baron" Lamm, Prussian-born former army officer who planned his robberies with the precision of a military campaign.

Barr, Byron Ellsworth

Real name of actor Gig Young.

Barrett, Monte

See *Tempered Blade*

Barrie, Diana

Role (as an Academy Award loser!) for which Maggie Smith won a Best Supporting Actress Academy Award in the 1978 film *California Suite*.

Barrow, Blanche

Role for which Estelle Parsons won a Best Supporting Actress Academy Award in the 1967 film *Bonnie and Clyde*.

Barsetshire

Mythical English county that is the setting of six novels of Anthony Trollope.

Bartertown

Domain ruled by Aunty Entity (Tina Turner) in the film *Mad Max: Beyond Thunderdome*.

Bartholomew

Middle name of *Daily Planet* cub reporter Jimmy Olsen in the Superman comics and 1950s TV series.

Bartlett

Middle name of astronaut Alan Shepard.

Bartley House Hotel

New York City employer of Assistant Manager Katy O'Connor (Ann Sothern) in the TV sitcom *The Ann Sothern Show*.

Bartlow, Rosemary

Role for which Gloria Grahame won a Best Supporting Actress Academy Award in the 1952 film *The Bad and the Beautiful*.

Barton, Edmund

First prime minister of the Commonwealth of Australia, serving from 1900 to 1903.

Barton Park

Home of the Dashwood family in the Jane Austen novel *Sense and Sensibility*.

Barwood Films

Production company of Barbra Streisand.

Bascombe Cotton Mills

Employer of Julie Jordan in the Rodgers and Hammerstein musical *Carousel*.

baseball commissioners

1921–44: Kenesaw M. Landis
1945–51: Albert B. "Happy" Chandler
1951–65: Ford C. Frick
1965–69: William D. Eckert
1969–84: Bowie K. Kuhn
1984–89: Peter V. Ueberroth
1989: A. Bartlett Giamatti
1989–92: Francis T. "Fay" Vincent, Jr.
1998–present: Allan H. "Bud" Selig

baseball mascots (major leagues)

Atlanta Braves: Rally (man with a baseball head), Homer
Anaheim Angels: Clutch and Scoop (bears)
Baltimore Orioles: Oriole Bird
Boston Red Sox: Wally the Green Monster
Cleveland Indians: Slider (birdlike creature)
Colorado Rockies: Dinger (purple dinosaur)
Detroit Tigers: Paws (tiger)
Florida Marlins: Billy the Marlin
Houston Astros: Orbit (alien)
Kansas City Royals: Sluggerrr (lion)
Milwaukee Brewers: Bernie Brewer
Montreal Expos: Youppi!
New York Mets: Mr. Met (man with a baseball head)
Oakland A's: Stomper (elephant)
Philadelphia Phillies: Phillie Phanatic
Pittsburgh Pirates: Pirate Parrot
St. Louis Cardinals: Fred Bird
San Diego Padres: The Swinging Friar
San Francisco Giants: Lou Seal (aka Luigi Francisco Seal)
Seattle Mariners: Mariner Moose
Tampa Bay Devil Rays: Raymond (big blue beast)
Toronto Blue Jays: B. J. Birdy

Bases Loaded and Dark Windows

Unproduced screenplays written by Joe Gillis (William Holden) in the film *Sunset Boulevard*.

"The Bash Brothers"

Nickname of baseball sluggers Mark McGwire and Jose Canseco, while teammates for the Oakland Athletics in the late 1980s and early 1990s.

Basil

Pet rat of Manuel (Andrew Sachs) in the English TV sitcom *Fawlty Towers*.

Title character (voiced by Barrie Ingham) in the Disney animated film *The Great Mouse Detective*.

Basketball Association of America

Professional basketball league founded on June 6, 1946, whose name was changed to the National

Basketball Association (NBA) after the 1948–49 season.

basketball mascots (NBA)

Atlanta Hawks: SkyHawk and Harry the Hawk
Charlotte Hornets: Hugo the Hornet
Chicago Bulls: Da Bull and Benny the Bull
Cleveland Cavaliers: Whammer (polar bear)
Dallas Mavericks: Mavs Man (masked human basketball)
Denver Nuggets: Rocky the Mountain Lion
Golden State Warriors: ThunderBolt, aka Thunder (superhero)
Houston Rockets: Clutch (bear) and Turbo (gravity-defying dunker)
Indiana Pacers: Boomer (panther)
Miami Heat: Burnie
Milwaukee Bucks: Bango (deer)
Minnesota Timberwolves: Crunch (wolf)
New Jersey Nets: Sly (fox)
Orlando Magic: Stuff the Magic Dragon
Philadelphia 76ers: Hip-Hop (rabbit)
Phoenix Suns: Phoenix Suns Gorilla
Sacramento Kings: A lion
San Antonio Spurs: A coyote
Seattle SuperSonics: Squatch (Bigfoot)
Toronto Raptors: The Raptor (dinosaur)
Utah Jazz: A bear
Vancouver Grizzlies: Super Grizz (bear)
Washington Wizards: G. Wiz (wizard)

Baskett, James

Actor who received a special Academy Award for his portrayal of storyteller Uncle Remus in the Disney animated film *Song of the South.*

Baskin Robbins original flavors

The first 31 flavors served in the first ice cream shop opened in 1948 by Burt Baskin and Irv Robbins in Glendale, California:

Banana Nut Fudge
Black Walnut
Burgundy Cherry
Butter Pecan
Butterscotch Ribbon
Chocolate
Chocolate Almond
Chocolate Chip
Chocolate Fudge
Chocolate Ribbon
Coffee
Coffee Candy
Date Nut
Egg Nog
French Vanilla
Green Mint
Lemon Crisp
Lemon Custard
Lemon Sherbet
Maple Walnut
Orange Sherbet
Peach
Peppermint Fudge
Peppermint Stick
Pineapple Sherbet
Pistachio Nut
Raspberry Sherbet
Rocky Road
Strawberry
Vanilla
Vanilla Burnt Almond

Basoalto, Neftali Ricardo Reyes

Real name of Chilean poet Pablo Neruda.

Basutoland

Former name of the African nation Lesotho.

Batavia

Former name of Jakarta, Indonesia.

Batemans

Sussex, England home of author Rudyard Kipling from 1902 to 1936.

Bates High

School attended by the title character (Sissy Spacek) in the film *Carrie.*

Bates, Katherine Lee

See "**Materna**"

Bates, Otha Ellas

Real name of singer Bo Diddley.

Batjac

Production company of actor John Wayne.

Batman Forever riddles

The Riddles posed by The Riddler (Jim Carrey) to Batman and Robin (Val Kilmer and Chris O'Donnell, respectively) in the film. They were written by Will Shortz, crossword editor of *The New York Times:*

If you look at the numbers upon my face, you won't find 13 anyplace.
Tear off one and scratch my head. What once was red is black instead.
The eight of us go forth, not back, to protect a king from a foe's attack.
We're five little items of an everyday sort. You'll find us all in a tennis court.

Answers: A clock, a match, chess pawns, and the five vowels (a, e, i, o, u)

Batman (TV) villains

The Archer (Art Carney)
The Black Widow (Tallulah Bankhead)
The Bookworm (Roddy McDowall)
Dr. Cassandra (Ida Lupino)
Catwoman (Julie Newmar, Eartha Kitt)
Chandell (Liberace)
Nora Clavicle (Barbara Rush)
Clock King (Walter Slezak)
Egghead (Vincent Price)
Falseface (Malachi Throne)
Mr. Freeze (George Sanders, Otto Preminger, Eli Wallach)
Colonel Gumm (Roger C. Carmel)
The Joker (Cesar Romero)
King Tut (Victor Buono)
Louie the Lilac (Milton Berle)
The Mad Hatter (David Wayne)
Marsha, Queen of Diamonds (Carolyn Jones)
The Minstrel (Van Johnson)
Minerva (Zsa Zsa Gabor)
Olga, Queen of the Cossacks (Anne Baxter)
Ma Parker (Shelley Winters)
The Penguin (Burgess Meredith)
Lord Phogg (Rudy Vallee)
The Puzzler (Maurice Evans)
The Riddler (Frank Gorshin, John Astin)
The Sandman (Michael Rennie)
Shame (Cliff Robertson)
The Siren (Joan Collins)
Zelda the Great (Anne Baxter)

Batterson

Middle name of hat manufacturer John Stetson, who began his career working for his father's No Name Hat Factory. He started the John B. Stetson Hat Company in 1865.

"The Battle of the Sexes"

Nickname given to the highly publicized tennis match between Billie Jean King and Bobby Riggs at the Houston Astrodome on September 20, 1973. King defeated Riggs in straight sets, 6–4, 6–3 and 6–3, before 30,472 spectators, still the world-record attendance for a tennis match.

Baudot, Jean Maurice Émile (1845–1903)

French inventor for whom the baud (unit of telecommunications data transfer) is named.

Baumgarner

Real last name of actor James Garner.

Bavarian Brewery

Original name of Anheuser-Busch.

Baxter Beach

Setting of the TV sitcom *Clarissa Explains It All*.

Bay City

Setting of the TV soap opera *Another World*.

Bayerische Motoren Werke

What the letters of automaker BMW stand for, which is German for "Bavarian Motor Works."

Baylor, Rudy

Title character (Matt Damon) of the film *The Rainmaker* (1997).

"The Bayonne Bleeder"

Nickname of boxer Chuck Wepner, because of the frequent facial cuts he received in the ring. His unsuccessful match against Muhammad Ali for the world heavyweight title in 1975 inspired Sylvester Stallone's screenplay for *Rocky*.

The Bayou Bucket

Trophy awarded to the winning team in the annual football game between Rice University and the University of Houston.

Bayport

Hometown of the title characters in the Hardy Boys series of novels.

Bayside High

California school that is the setting of the TV sitcom *Saved by the Bell*.

"Bay Stater"

See **United States residents' nicknames**

Bea and Jay

Parents of B. J. Hunnicutt (Mike Farrell), for whom he was named, in the TV sitcom *M*A*S*H*.

Beach Boys original members

Al Jardine, Mike Love, and Brian, Carl, and Dennis Wilson.

Beacon Street Pizza

Boston restaurant that is the setting of the TV sitcom *Two Guys, a Girl and a Pizza Place*, aka *Two Guys and a Girl*.

Beale, Howard

Role for which Peter Finch won a Best Actor Academy Award in the 1976 film *Network*.

"The Beale Street Blues Boy"

Nickname of blues singer B. B. King.

Beall

Middle name of author Upton Sinclair.

"Be all that you can be"

Advertising slogan of the U.S. Army.

Beals, Dick

Voice of Speedy Alka-Seltzer in TV commercials of the 1950s and 1960s.

Beamish, Stanley

Secret identity of the crime-fighting title character (Stephen Strimpell) in the TV sitcom *Mr. Terrific*.

Beanie Babies, first

The first nine introduced in 1993:
> Brownie the Bear
> Chocolate the Moose
> Flash the Dolphin
> Legs the Frog
> Patti the Platypus
> Pinchers the Lobster
> Splash the Whale
> Spot the Dog
> Squealer the Pig

Bean, Judge Roy

Role for which Walter Brennan won a Best Supporting Actor Academy Award in the 1940 film *The Westerner*.

Bean, Normal

Pen name used by author Edgar Rice Burroughs early in his career.

Beard Jr., Matthew

Real name of Stymie, child actor in the *Our Gang* series of film shorts, aka *The Little Rascals*.

Beardsley College

Where Humbert Humbert teaches, in the Vladimir Nabokov novel *Lolita*.

Bear, Edward

Real name of Winnie-the-Pooh in the stories of A. A. Milne.

Bears Lodge

Native American name for the 1,267-foot monolith Devils Tower in Wyoming.

Beasley, Mrs.

Bespectacled rag doll of Buffy (Anissa Jones) in the TV sitcom *Family Affair*.

Beatles #1 tunes

These 20 tunes all reached #1 on the U.S. *Billboard* pop chart:
> "I Want to Hold Your Hand" (1964)
> "She Loves You" (1964)
> "Can't Buy Me Love" (1964)
> "Love Me Do" (1964)
> "A Hard Day's Night" (1964)
> "I Feel Fine" (1964)
> "Eight Days a Week" (1965)
> "Ticket to Ride" (1965)
> "Help!" (1965)
> "Yesterday" (1965)
> "We Can Work It Out" (1965)
> "Paperback Writer" (1966)
> "Penny Lane" (1967)
> "All You Need Is Love" (1967)
> "Hello Goodbye" (1967)
> "Hey Jude" (1968)
> "Get Back" (1969)
> "Come Together" (1969)
> "Let It Be" (1970)
> "The Long and Winding Road" (1970)

Beatles feature films

> *A Hard Day's Night* (1964)
> *Help!* (1965)
> *Yellow Submarine* (1968, animated)
> *Let It Be* (1970)

Beatrice

Middle name of Jessica Fletcher (Angela Lansbury) in the TV series *Murder, She Wrote*.

Beat the Time

See **Smiley, Guy**

Beaty

See **Henry**

Beau

Horse of Rooster Cogburn (John Wayne) in the film *True Grit*.

Beaufort scale

Developed in 1805 by English naval officer Sir Francis Beaufort, which measures the intensity of winds:
> 0 Calm (less than 1 mph)
> 1 Light Air (1–3 mph)
> 2 Light Breeze (4–7 mph)
> 3 Gentle Breeze (8–12 mph)
> 4 Moderate Breeze (13–18 mph)
> 5 Fresh Breeze (19–24 mph)
> 6 Strong Breeze (25–31 mph)

7 Near Gale (32–38 mph)
8 Gale (39–46 mph)
9 Strong Gale (47–54 mph)
10 Storm (55–63 mph)
11 Violent Storm (64–75 mph)
12 Hurricane (more than 75 mph)

Beaugard, François Jacques DuBois Guilbert

See *After the Hunt*

Beaulieu

Maiden name of actress Priscilla Presley.

Beaumont, Kathryn

Voice of the title character in the Disney animated film *Alice in Wonderland.*

Beauregard

See **Beulah and Beauregard**

Beauregard, Jr.

Sleepy bloodhound in the TV comedy/variety series *Hee Haw.*

Beautymist panty hose

Product endorsed (and worn) by pro footballer Joe Namath in 1970s TV commercials.

Beauty Ranch

1,400-acre home of author Jack London in Glen Ellen, California.

Beaver

See *Eleanor, Beaver,* **and** *Dartmouth*

Beaver Lodge

Fraternal lodge of George Utley (Tom Poston) and Dick Loudon (Bob Newhart) in the TV sitcom *Newhart.*

"Be careful how you use it"

Advertising slogan of Hai Karate after shave.

"Because it is there"

See **Mallory, George (1886–1924)**

"Be chewsy"

Advertising slogan of Beech-Nut gum.

Bechuanaland

Former name of the African nation Botswana.

Becker, Walter and Fagen, Donald

Founders and lead vocalists of rock group Steely Dan.

Beckett, Andrew

Role for which Tom Hanks won a Best Actor Academy Award in the 1993 film *Philadelphia.*

Beck, Helen Gould

Real name of fan dancer Sally Rand, who took her stage name from a Rand-McNally atlas.

Beckwith, Robert Todd Lincoln (1904–1985)

Last surviving descendant of Abraham Lincoln. He was a grandson of Robert Todd Lincoln, oldest son of Abraham Lincoln.

Beddoe, Philo

Clint Eastwood's role in the films *Every Which Way but Loose* and *Any Which Way You Can.*

Bedell, Grace

11-year-old girl from Westfield, New York, whose October 1860 letter to presidential candidate Abraham Lincoln suggesting that he grow a beard, resulted in him doing so.

"Be Direct"

Advertising slogan of Dell Computer Corporation.

Bedloe's Island

Former name of Liberty Island, New York Harbor home of the Statue of Liberty.

"Bedrock"

Nickname of baseball pitcher Steve Bedrosian.

Beebe, Phoebe B.

Female chimpanzee seen in the 1950s on the TV series *The Today Show.*

See also **Muggs, J. Fred**

The Beeches

Northampton, Massachusetts, home of President Calvin Coolidge from 1930 until his death in 1933.

Beeding, Francis

See *The House of Dr. Edwardes*

Beedle

Real last name of actor William Holden.

beef ratings, USDA

The ratings below, listed from highest to lowest, are based on two criteria: the age of the cattle (the younger the better) and the degree of marbling (intermixing of fat with lean, the more the better).

Prime

Choice
Select
Standard
Commercial
Utility
Cutter
Canner

Bee Gees members

Barry Gibb, Maurice Gibb, and Robin Gibb. "Bee Gees" is short for "Brothers Gibb."

beekeeper

Occupation of New Zealander Sir Edmund Hillary, who reached the top of Mount Everest on May 29, 1953.

Beelzebub

Epithet for Satan. The William Golding novel *Lord of the Flies* gets its name from the literal Hebrew meaning of the word.

"The Beer That Made Milwaukee Famous"

Advertising slogan of Schlitz beer.

"Bees Can Sting You, Watch Out"

Debut episode of the TV sitcom *Hearts Afire,* which aired on September 14, 1992.

Beethoven sonata nicknames

#8 "Pathétique"
#14 "Moonlight"
#15 "Pastoral"
#21 "Waldstein"
#23 "Appassionata"
#29 "Hammerklavier"

Beeton's Christmas Annual

English publication in which Sherlock Holmes made his 1887 debut, in the Sir Arthur Conan Doyle novel *A Study in Scarlet.*

Before This Anger

Original title of the Alex Haley book *Roots.*

Beginner's All-purpose Symbolic Instruction Code

What the letters in the name of computer language BASIC stand for.

Beheler, Ed

Jimmy Carter look-alike who portrayed Carter in several films, including *Hot Shots! Part Deux.*

Beldingsville

Setting of the Eleanor H. Porter novel *Pollyanna.*

Beldon, Carol

Role for which Teresa Wright won a Best Supporting Actress Academy Award in the 1942 film *Mrs. Miniver.*

Belgian Airhead

Breed of dog owned by David Letterman, as mentioned in his 1970s comedy routines.

Belham

English town that is the setting of the film *Mrs. Miniver.*

"Believe It or Not"

Subtitle of the tune "The Greatest American Hero" (the theme song of the TV series of the same name), performed by Joey Scarbury.

Bell

Last name of Daisy in the tune "A Bicycle Built for Two."

Bell, Acton

Pen name used by author Anne Brontë.

Bellah, James Warner

See **Cavalry Trilogy**

Bellamy, Francis

Baptist minister who wrote the Pledge of Allegiance. It was first published in the September 9, 1892, issue of *The Youth's Companion.*

Bell, Currer

Pen name used by author Charlotte Brontë.

Belle

First name of Beauty (voiced by Paige O'Hara) in the Disney animated film *Beauty and the Beast.*

See also **Matty and Belle; Snoopy's brothers and sisters**

Bellefontaine

Last name of the title character in the Henry Wadsworth Longfellow narrative poem *Evangeline.*

Bell, Ellis

Pen name used by author Emily Brontë.

Belle Reve

Ancestral home of Blanche DuBois in the Tennessee Williams play *A Streetcar Named Desire.*

Bellerophon

Antidote to the deadly Chimera virus in the film *Mission: Impossible 2.*

Bellerophon

Lost spaceship sought by Commander John Adams (Leslie Nielsen) in the film *Forbidden Planet*.

Belle Sauvage Inn

Headquarters of Tom Weller in the Charles Dickens novel *The Pickwick Papers*.

Bell, Glen

Founder of the Taco Bell fast-food chain. The first Taco Bell opened in 1962 in Downey, California.

Bellows, T. Frothingill

See **Fields, W. C., roles/pen names of**

bell players

What the word "glockenspiel" means in German.

Bellus

Fast-approaching star that is threatening Earth in the film *When Worlds Collide*.

Belmont, Dianne

Stage name used by Lucille Ball as a model, early in her career.

Belvedere

Southern California estate of the title family in the TV series *The Colbys*.

Be My Guest

1957 autobiography of hotelier Conrad Hilton.

Ben

Pet bear of the title character (Dan Haggerty) in the TV series *The Life and Times of Grizzly Adams*.

Ben & Jerry's pint flavors

As of January 1, 2001:

ORIGINAL ICE CREAM

Bovinity Divinity
Cherry Garcia
Chocolate Chip Cookie Dough
Chocolate Fudge Brownie
Chubby Hubby
Chunky Monkey
Coffee Heath Bar Crunch
Concession Obsession
DILBERT'S WORLD Totally Nuts
Mint Chocolate Cookie
New York Super Fudge Chunk
Nutty Waffle Cone
Orange & Cream
Peanut Butter Cup

Phish Food
Pistachio Pistachio
Southern Pecan Pie
Triple Caramel Chunk
Vanilla Caramel Fudge
Vanilla Heath Bar Crunch
Wavy Gravy
World's Best Chocolate
World's Best Vanilla

LOW FAT ICE CREAM

Blondies Are a Swirl's Best Friend
Coconut Cream Pie
Mocha Latte
Smore's Low Fat Ice Cream

FROZEN YOGURT

Cherry Garcia
Chocolate Chip Cookie Dough
Chocolate Fudge Brownie
Chocolate Heath Bar Crunch
Chunky Monkey
Ooey Gooey Cake
Vanilla with Heath Toffee Crunch

SORBET

Devil's Food Chocolate
Doonesberry
Lemon Swirl
Purple Passion Fruit

2-TWISTED! FLAVORS (COMBINATIONS OF TWO OR MORE OTHER FLAVORS)

Entangled Mints (Mint Chocolate Cookie + Marble Mint Chunk)
Everything but the . . . (Vanilla Heath Bar Crunch + New York Super Fudge Chunk + Peanut Butter Cup)
From Russia with Buzz (White Russian + Coffee Coffee BuzzBuzzBuzz)
Half Baked (Chocolate Fudge Brownie + Chocolate Chip Cookie Dough)
Jerry's Jubilee (Cherry Garcia + Chocolate Fudge Brownie)
Monkey Wrench (Banana + Peanut Butter Cup)
Pulp Addiction (Orange & Cream + Chocolate Orange Fudge)
Urban Jumble (Coconut Almond Fudge Chip + New York Super Fudge Chunk)

Bendini, Lambert & Locke

Memphis law-firm employer of Mitch McDeere (Tom Cruise) in the film *The Firm*.

Benevolent Order of the Bison

Fraternal lodge of Herbert T. Gillis (Frank Faylen) in the TV sitcom *The Many Loves of Dobie Gillis*.

Ben-Hur, Judah

Title role for which Charlton Heston won the 1959 Best Actor Academy Award.

Benjamin

Pet dog of the Bowden family (Jessica Lange, Nick Nolte, Juliette Lewis) in the film *Cape Fear* (1991).

First name of the title character (Andy Griffith) in the TV series *Matlock*.

Benjamin Bowring

Support ship used by Sir Ranulph Fiennes and Charles Burton in the first circumnavigation of the Earth via the Poles in 1979–82.

Benjamin Franklin

First and middle names of tire-company founder B. F. Goodrich.

Benjamin Franklin High

School where Clara Snyder (Betsy Blair) works as a chemistry teacher in the film *Marty*.

Bennett, Rheinhart and Alquist

Los Angeles law-firm employer of Martin Kazinsky (Ron Leibman) in the TV series *Kaz*.

Bensalem

Utopian setting of the Francis Bacon novel *New Atlantis*.

Benthic Petroleum

Employer of offshore drilling-rig manager Virgil "Bud" Brigman (Ed Harris) in the film *The Abyss*.

Benton, Al

Only pitcher to face both Babe Ruth and Mickey Mantle in a major-league baseball game. He faced Ruth while with the Philadelphia Athletics in 1934, and faced Mantle while with the Boston Red Sox in 1952.

benzosulfamide

Chemical name of artificial sweetener saccharin.

Beppo

Pet monkey of Superman.

Bergen, Edgar, dummies of

Charlie McCarthy, Mortimer Snerd, Effie Klinker, and Podine Puffington.

Bergh, Henry

Founder of the ASPCA, in New York City in 1866.

Bermuda

See **Pacer, Ranger, Corsair, and Citation**

Bernard

Real first name of jazz drummer Buddy Rich.

Bernardo

Role for which George Chakiris won a Best Supporting Actor Academy Award in the 1961 film *West Side Story*.

Bernhart, Larry

See **American Hero**

Bernice

Pet pigeon of Bert in the children's TV series *Sesame Street*.

Berry and Torrence

Last names (respectively) of pop duo Jan and Dean.

Berryman, Clifford

Editorial cartoonist who created the teddy bear, named for Theodore Roosevelt, after a bear-hunting trip Roosevelt made in 1902.

Berry, Marcellus Fleming

American Express agent who invented traveler's checks in 1891.

Berry, Marvin

See **Marvin Berry and the Starlighters**

Bertanzetti

Real last name of actor Billy Barty.

Bertillon Card

See **56**

Bert's Place

Diner setting of the TV sitcom *The Good Guys*.

Berwick, Ray and Renfro, Bryan

Trainers of the title canine in the TV series *Here's Boomer*.

Berwyn, Oklahoma

Town that in 1941 renamed itself Gene Autry, Oklahoma, in honor of the cowboy singer. Autry owned land in the town on which he kept livestock for his rodeo.

Besant, Norma

Role for which Mary Pickford won a Best Actress Academy Award in the 1929 film *Coquette*.

Bespin

Planet on which Lando Calrissian (Billy Dee Williams) serves as Baron Administrator of Cloud City, in the film *The Empire Strikes Back*.

Bessie

Real first name of (Bessie) Wallis Warfield Simpson, aka the Duchess of Windsor.

best boy

The first assistant to the chief electrician (gaffer) on a film set.

"Best care anywhere"

Motto of the title U.S. Army medical unit in the TV sitcom *M*A*S*H*.

"Best Friend"

Theme song of the TV sitcom *The Courtship of Eddie's Father*, performed by Harry Nilsson.

"The best is yet to come"

Epitaph of Frank Sinatra, who popularized the song of the same name.

The Best of Marcel Marceau

1970 recording consisting of 19 minutes of silence and one minute of applause on each side.

Best Performance

Original working title of the film *All About Eve*.

Best, Pete

Original drummer of the Beatles, succeeded by Ringo Starr on August 18, 1962.

"The best to you each morning"

Advertising slogan of Kellogg's cereals.

"Bet a Million"

Nickname of financier/gambler John Warne Gates.

"Betcha can't eat just one"

Advertising slogan of Lay's Potato Chips.

Betsy

Flintlock rifle of frontiersman Davy Crockett.

"Better things for better living through chemistry"

Advertising slogan of Du Pont.

Beulah

Buzzer heard on the TV game show *Truth or Consequences*.

Beulah and Beauregard

Offspring of Borden mascot Elsie the Cow.

"Beulah, peel me a grape."

Memorable line spoken by Tira (Mae West) to Beulah (Gertrude Howard) in the film *I'm No Angel*.

Bevan, Donald

See **0**

Beverly Palm Hotel

Beverly Hills hotel where Axel Foley (Eddie Murphy) stays, in the film *Beverly Hills Cop*.

Beverwyck

Original name of Albany, New York.

Bevo

Texas Longhorn steer mascot of the University of Texas.

"Bevo"

Nickname of 1950s college basketball star Clarence Francis.

Beware of the Childrun

Sign on the front fence of the home of Ma and Pa Kettle (Marjorie Main and Percy Kilbride) in the film *The Egg and I*.

BEWARE OF THE THING

Sign on the outer fence of the title family's residence in the TV sitcom *The Addams Family*.

Beyle, Marie Henri

Real name of French novelist Stendhal.

Beyond the Realm of Atomic Particles and Massless Photons

Book written by the title character (Peter Weller) in the film *The Adventures of Buckaroo Banzai Across the Eighth Dimension*.

"Beyond the Spectrum"

See **The Wreck of the Titan**

Biasone, Danny

Inventor of the NBA's 24-second shot clock, first used in 1954.

"Bibbidi bobbidi boo"

Magic words used by the title character's fairy godmother in the Disney animated film *Cinderella*.

Bibendum

Name of the Michelin Man, created in 1898. The word is Latin for "drink."

Bib-Label Lithiated Lemon-Lime Soda

See **Grigg, Charles Leiper**

Bible, expressions from the

All of these common expressions originated from the Bible, listed below with their book, chapter and verse (King James Version):

OLD TESTAMENT

Am I my brother's keeper? (Genesis 4:9)
Apple of the eye (Psalms 17:8)
Cast thy bread upon the waters (Ecclesiastes 11:1)
Eye for eye, tooth for tooth (Exodus 21:24)
Fat of the land (Genesis 45:18)
Heart's desire (Psalms 21:2)
Holier than thou (Isaiah 65:5)
How are the mighty fallen (II Samuel 1:25)
Land of the living (Job 28:13)
Let my people go (Exodus 5:1)
Love thy neighbor (Leviticus 19:18)
A man after his own heart (I Samuel 13:14)
Man doth not live by bread only (Deuteronomy 8:3)
The meek shall inherit the earth (Psalms 37:11)
My cup runneth over (Psalms 23:5)
Out of the mouths of babes (Psalms 8:2)
Reap the whirlwind (Hosea 8:7)
See eye to eye (Isaiah 52:8)
Skin of my teeth (Job 19:20)
Stranger in a strange land (Exodus 2:22)
To every thing there is a season (Ecclesiastes 3:1)
Woe is me (Isaiah 6:5)

NEW TESTAMENT

Eat, drink, and be merry (Luke 12:19)
Fallen from grace (Galatians 5:4)
Fight the good fight (I Timothy 6:12)
Filthy lucre (I Timothy 3:8)
Forgive them; for they know not what they do (Luke 23:34)
He that is not with me is against me (Matthew 12:30)
The hour is at hand (Matthew 26:45)
It is more blessed to give than to receive (Acts 20:35)
Labor of love (I Thessalonians 1:3)
The last shall be first (Matthew 19:30)
The love of money is the root of all evil (I Timothy 6:10)
Many are called, but few are chosen (Matthew 22:14)
No man can serve two masters (Matthew 6:24)
O ye of little faith (Matthew 8:26)
Patience of Job (James 5:11)
Pearl of great price (Matthew 13:46)
Pearls before swine (Matthew 7:6)
Physician, heal thyself (Luke 4:23)
Salt of the earth (Matthew 5:13)
Seek, and ye shall find (Matthew 7:7)
Signs of the times (Matthew 16:3)
The spirit is willing, but the flesh is weak (Matthew 26:41)
The truth shall make you free (John 8:32)
Strain at a gnat (Matthew 23:24)
Vengeance is mine (Romans 12:19)
What therefore God has joined together, let not man put asunder (Matthew 19:6)

Bickel, Ernest Frederick McIntyre

Real name of actor Fredric March.

BID

Appropriate stock-ticker symbol of auction company Sotheby's.

Bid Time Return

Novel by Richard Matheson that was the basis for the film *Somewhere in Time*.

"big"

What the word "Bolshoi" means in Russian.

"The Big Apricot"

Nickname of Metropolis in the Superman comic books.

The Big Book of Greek Heroes

Book being read by Kevin (Craig Warnock) in the film *Time Bandits*.

"Big Brown"

Nickname of United Parcel Service, for its fleet of brown delivery trucks.

The Big Bundle

Game show hosted by Allen Ludden, on which Ron Thurlow (Jim Antonio) wins a trip to the title vacation resort, in the film *Futureworld*.

Big Bunny

DC-9 jet once owned by magazine publisher Hugh Hefner.

"Big Cy"
Nickname of Thoroughbred racehorse Citation, winner of the Triple Crown in 1948.

"Big D"
Nickname of Dallas, Texas.

Nickname of Hall of Fame baseball pitcher Don Drysdale.

"Big Daddy"
Nickname of auto racer Don Garlits.

Nickname of NFL defensive great Eugene Lipscomb. He stood 6 feet 6 inches and weighed 284 pounds.

Big Daddy's
Where Dick Dale and the Del-Tones perform, in the film *Beach Party*.

"The Big Five"
Collective nickname of these Philadelphia-area NCAA Division I basketball teams: La Salle College, University of Pennsylvania, St. Joseph's College, Temple University and Villanova University.

The Big Giant Head
Alien superior of Dr. Dick Solomon (John Lithgow) in the TV sitcom *3rd Rock From The Sun*, portrayed by William Shatner.

Bigglesworth, Mr.
Pet cat of Dr. Evil (Mike Myers) in the *Austin Powers* films.

Biggy Rat
Gangster nemesis of the title character in the children's animated TV series *King Leonardo and His Short Subjects*. Both characters are voiced by Jackson Beck.

"Bighouse"
Nickname of basketball Hall of Fame college coach Clarence Gaines.

"The Big Hurt"
Nickname of baseball star Frank Thomas.

"The Big Island"
Nickname of the island of Hawaii, the largest in the state of Hawaii.

"The Big Mooseketeer"
See **Mouseketeers, original**

Big, Mr.
Drug-lord alter ego of Dr. Kananga (Yaphet Kotto) in the James Bond film *Live and Let Die*.

"Big Muddy"
Nickname of the Missouri River.

"The Big O"
Nickname of basketball Hall of Famer Oscar Robertson.

"Big Poison"
Nickname of baseball Hall of Famer Paul Waner.

"Big Red"
Nickname of Thoroughbred racehorse Man O' War.

"The Big Red Machine"
Nickname of the Cincinnati Reds teams that won two World Series in the early 1970s.

"The Big Red One"
Nickname of the U.S. Army's First Infantry Division.

Big Salt Lick
Original name of Nashville, Tennessee.

"Big Six"
Nickname of Hall of Fame baseball pitcher Christy Mathewson.

Big Thunder
Air Force base commanded by the title character (Dean Fredericks) in the TV series *Steve Canyon*.

"The Big Train"
Nickname of Hall of Fame baseball pitcher Walter Johnson.

The Big Valley family
The children of Victoria Barkley (Barbara Stanwyck) in this TV series:
    Jarrod (Richard Long)
    Nick (Peter Breck)
    Heath (Lee Majors)
    Eugene (Charles Briles)
    Audra (Linda Evans)

The Big W
Formation of palm trees in California's Santa Rosita State Park, under which a suitcase containing $350,000 is buried, in the film *It's a Mad Mad Mad Mad World*.

Big Whiskey, Wyoming

Town where Little Bill Daggett (Gene Hackman) is sheriff in the film *Unforgiven*.

"The Big Whistle"

Nickname of NHL referee and radio broadcaster Bill Chadwick.

Bijou

Pet dog of the title character (John Ritter) in the TV sitcom *Hooperman*.

Bill Bassler's Revenge and Hearts of Gold

Plays performed on the showboat *River Queen* in the Abbott and Costello film *The Naughty Nineties*.

billiard-ball colors

Cue ball: white
  1 ball: yellow
  2 ball: blue
  3 ball: red
  4 ball: purple
  5 ball: orange
  6 ball: green
  7 ball: plum (dark purple)
  8 ball: black
  9 ball: white with yellow stripe
 10 ball: white with blue stripe
 11 ball: white with red stripe
 12 ball: white with purple stripe
 13 ball: white with orange stripe
 14 ball: white with green stripe
 15 ball: white with plum stripe

Bill Masterton Trophy

Awarded annually since 1968 to the NHL player who "best exemplifies the qualities of perseverance, sportsmanship and dedication to hockey" of former player Bill Masterton.

Bill of Rights subjects

These first ten amendments to the U.S. Constitution took effect on December 15, 1791:
  First Amendment: Freedom of religion, freedom of speech, freedom of the press, right to assemble peaceably, right to petition the Government
  Second Amendment: Right to keep and bear arms
  Third Amendment: Quartering of soldiers
  Fourth Amendment: Unreasonable search and seizure
  Fifth Amendment: Grand juries, double jeopardy, testifying against oneself, private property taken for public use
  Sixth Amendment: Speedy trial, impartial jury, obtaining witnesses
  Seventh Amendment: Right of trial by jury
  Eighth Amendment: Excessive bail/fines, cruel and unusual punishment
  Ninth Amendment: Rights retained by the people
  Tenth Amendment: Rights retained by the States

Billy Joe

Object of the Shirelles' affection in their tune "Mama Said."

Bimbo

Pet elephant of young Corky (Mickey Braddock aka future Monkee Micky Dolenz) in the TV series *Circus Boy*.

"binary digit"

See **Tukey, John Wilder**

Binford Tools

Sponsor of the cable TV show *Tool Time* in the TV sitcom *Home Improvement*.

Bing Clawsby Music

Music publishing company of singer/pianist Michael Feinstein, named for his pet cat.

bingo

Term in Scrabble for a play that uses all seven of a player's letters.

Bingo

Dog on boxes of Cracker Jack.

Pet chimp of Lou Costello in the TV sitcom *The Abbott and Costello Show*.

Binney, Edwin and Smith, C. Harold

Paint-company owners who invented crayons in 1903, for which they created the brand name Crayola.

Biocyte Pharmaceuticals

Australian manufacturer of the deadly Chimera virus and its antidote Bellerophon, in the film *Mission: Impossible 2*.

Biograph Theatre

See **Manhattan Melodrama**

Bip

Mime character portrayed by Marcel Marceau.

Birchwood School
Elementary school attended by Charlie Brown and friends in the comic strip *Peanuts*.

Bird
Middle name of George Grinnell, editor of *Forest and Stream* magazine, who founded the Audubon Society in 1886.

"Bird"
Nickname of jazz saxophonist Charlie Parker.

"The Bird"
Nickname of 1970s baseball pitcher Mark Fidrych, for his supposed resemblance to *Sesame Street*'s Big Bird.

Birdcage Saloon
Laramie, Wyoming, establishment operated by Lily Merrill (Peggy Castle) in the TV Western series *The Lawman*.

Birds of the West Indies
Book by ornithologist James Bond that was on Ian Fleming's shelf when he was looking for a plain-sounding name for the main character of *Casino Royale*, the debut appearance of Agent 007.

Birmingham Barons
Minor-league baseball team that NBA star Michael Jordan played for in 1994.

Birnam, Don
Role for which Ray Milland won a Best Actor Academy Award in the 1945 film *The Lost Weekend*.

Birnbaum, Nathan
See **"Natty"**

Bisbee, Sam
See **Fields, W. C., roles/pen names of**

"The Biscuit"
Nickname of attorney John Cage (Peter MacNicol) in the TV series *Ally McBeal*.

Bismosal
Original name of Pepto-Bismol when first introduced in 1900.

Bissell, Richard
See **7½ Cents**

Bit of Irish
Horse of Jacqueline Kennedy when she was First Lady.

Bitsy
Pet dog of the title character in the comic strip *Marvin*.

Bitsy Big-Boy Boomeroo
Ultimate weapon developed by the Yooks in Dr. Seuss' *The Butter Battle Book*.

"bitter"
What the word "gorki" means in Russian. Writer Maxim Gorki adopted that pen name because of the bitterness of his youthful experiences.

Bitter Creek
Battle for which Jason McCord (Chuck Connors) is unjustly court-martialed and convicted of cowardice, in the TV series *Branded*.

Bixby College
Employer of caretakers Slats McCarthy and Oliver Quackenbush (Abbott and Costello) in the film *Here Come the Co-Eds*.

Black Bart
Original working title of the Mel Brooks film *Blazing Saddles*.

Black Beauty
Popular purple-skin variety of eggplant.

Automobile of the title character in the radio and TV series *The Green Hornet*.

Black Bess
Horse of English highwayman Dick Turpin.

Black Diamond
Bronx Zoo bison that was the model for the Buffalo nickel.

Horse of Western star Lash La Rue.

The Black Diamond Trophy
Awarded to the winning team in the annual football game between Virginia Tech and the University of West Virginia.

Black, Eve
See **Eve (Eve White/Eve Black/Jane)**

Black Hawk, Nebraska
Setting of the Willa Cather novel *My Ántonia*.

Blackie, Bounder, and Tiger
Pet cats of President Calvin Coolidge.

Black Jack

Riderless horse used in the funeral procession of President John F. Kennedy on November 25, 1963.

Blackjack

Rock group for which Michael Bolton served as lead singer before he embarked on a solo career.

Black Lion Inn

Establishment frequented by John and Joe Willet in the Charles Dickens novel *Barnaby Rudge*.

Black Magic

Only sailboat from New Zealand to have won the America's Cup to date, having done so in 1995.

Black Maria

World's first film studio, built by Thomas Edison in 1891 at West Orange, New Jersey.

Black Mesa, Arizona

Setting of the film *The Petrified Forest*.

"Black November"

Debut episode of the TV series *Route 66*, which aired on October 7, 1960.

"The Black Pearl"

Nickname of soccer great Pelé.

Black Pussy Cat Cafe

Bar frequented by Egbert Sousé (W. C. Fields) in the film *The Bank Dick*.

Black Rebels

See **Wrightsville**

"Black Rock"

Nickname of the Manhattan skyscraper headquarters of CBS.

"Black Sox"

Nickname of this group of eight Chicago White Sox who were permanently banned from professional baseball for their role in "fixing" the outcome of the 1919 World Series:

Eddie Cicotte (pitcher)
Oscar "Happy" Felsch (outfielder)
Arnold "Chick" Gandil (first baseman)
"Shoeless" Joe Jackson (left fielder)
Fred McMullin (pinch hitter)
Charles "Swede" Risberg (shortstop)
George "Buck" Weaver (third baseman)
Claude "Lefty" Williams (pitcher)

Black Tooth

See **White Fang and Black Tooth**

Black, Vince

Alias used by bounty hunter Reno Raines (Lorenzo Lamas) in the TV series *Renegade*.

Blackwell, Elizabeth

First woman physician in the United States, an 1849 graduate of Geneva Medical College in New York.

"The Black Widow"

Nickname of professional billiards player Jeanette Lee, for her all-black outfits.

Black Widows

Motorcycle gang that chases Philo Beddoe (Clint Eastwood) in the film *Any Which Way You Can*.

Blaiberg, Philip

South African dentist who received the world's second human heart transplant, performed by Dr. Christiaan Barnard on January 2, 1968. Blaiberg survived for more than a year after the transplant.

Blair, Eric Arthur

Real name of novelist George Orwell.

Blair General Hospital

Setting of the TV series *Dr. Kildare*.

Blake

Real last name of actor Hume Cronyn.

Blakeney, Sir Percy

Real name of the title character in the Baroness Orczy novel *The Scarlet Pimpernel*.

Blake, Nicholas

Pen name used by poet Cecil Day-Lewis for his detective novels.

Blamauer, Karoline

Real name of actress/singer Lotte Lenya.

Blanchard

Last name of the title character in the Ring Lardner book *You Know Me Al*.

Blanchette

First name of Little Red Riding Hood in the traditional fairy tale.

Blanc, Samuel

Des Moines, Iowa, inventor of the Roto-Rooter drain-cleaning machine in 1933, who founded the plumbing-service company of the same name in 1935.

Blaskó, Belá Ferenc Dezsõ
Real name of actor Bela Lugosi.

Blatt, David
See **Traynor, John "Jay"**

"The Blatt"
See **Rosenblatt Stadium**

Blau, Jeno
Real name of Hungarian-born conductor Eugene Ormandy.

bleem
Orkan time measure equivalent to 2,000 Earth years, in the TV sitcom *Mork and Mindy*.

Blefuscu
Enemy country of Lilliput in the Jonathan Swift novel *Gulliver's Travels*.

Bleriot, Louis
French aviator and aircraft designer who was the first person to fly across the English Channel, piloting his monoplane from Calais, France, to Dover, England, in 37 minutes on July 25, 1909.

Blessing, Michael
Stage name used by Michael Nesmith before joining the Monkees.

Bleuchamp, Count Balthazar de
Noble impersonated by SPECTRE leader Ernst Stavro Blofeld (Telly Savalas) in the James Bond film *On Her Majesty's Secret Service*.

Blind Date
1949–53 TV game show hosted by Arlene Francis and Jan Murray, which had a similar format to *The Dating Game*, which premiered in 1965.

Blind River, Ontario
Hometown of Mary Pilant (Kathryn Grant) in the film *Anatomy of a Murder*.

Blinky
See **Inky, Blinky, Pinky, and Clyde**

"Blipverts"
Debut episode of the TV series *Max Headroom*, which premiered on March 31, 1987.

Blitzen
Pet bee of Radar O'Reilly (Gary Burghoff) in the TV sitcom *M*A*S*H*.

Bloch, Robert
Author of the novel *Psycho*, on which the Alfred Hitchcock film of the same name was based.

Blodgett College
Minnesota alma mater of Carol Milford in the Sinclair Lewis novel *Main Street*.

Blomberg, Ron
New York Yankee who was the first designated hitter in major-league baseball history. On April 6, 1973, he drew a bases-loaded walk against Boston Red Sox pitcher Luis Tiant.

"The Blonde Bombshell"
Nickname of actress Jean Harlow.

Blondie films
Series starring Penny Singleton and Arthur Lake as Blondie and Dagwood Bumstead:
> *Blondie* (1938)
> *Blondie Meets the Boss* (1939)
> *Blondie Takes a Vacation* (1939)
> *Blondie Brings Up Baby* (1939)
> *Blondie on a Budget* (1940)
> *Blondie Has Servant Trouble* (1940)
> *Blondie Plays Cupid* (1940)
> *Blondie Goes Latin* (1941)
> *Blondie in Society* (1941)
> *Blondie Goes to College* (1942)
> *Blondie's Blessed Event* (1942)
> *Blondie for Victory* (1942)
> *It's a Great Life* (1943)
> *Footlight Glamour* (1943)
> *Leave it to Blondie* (1945)
> *Life with Blondie* (1946)
> *Blondie's Lucky Day* (1946)
> *Blondie Knows Best* (1946)
> *Blondie's Big Moment* (1947)
> *Blondie's Holiday* (1947)
> *Blondie in the Dough* (1947)
> *Blondie's Anniversary* (1947)
> *Blondie's Reward* (1948)
> *Blondie's Secret* (1948)
> *Blondie's Big Deal* (1949)
> *Blondie Hits the Jackpot* (1949)
> *Blondie's Hero* (1950)
> *Beware of Blondie* (1950)

Blood
Name of the title canine in the film *A Boy and His Dog*.

"Blood and Fire"
Motto of the Salvation Army.

Blood Brother
Novel by Elliot Arnold that was the basis for the TV Western series *Broken Arrow*.

"Bloodhounds transfused, finger prints manicured, and gin rummy"
Words on the office door of private detective Wolf J. Flywheel (Groucho Marx) in the Marx Brothers film *The Big Store*.

"Bloody Sam"
Nickname of director Sam Peckinpah, for the violence in his films.

Blount
Middle name of director Cecil B. DeMille.

Blubber, Jasper
John Houseman's role in the film *The Cheap Detective*.

Blue
Pet dog of the title character (Paul Newman) in the film *Cool Hand Luke*.

Bluebelle, Aunt
Character in 1960s–70s TV commercials for Scott paper towels, portrayed by Mae Questel.

Blue, Benjamin Buford
Real name of Bubba (Mykelti Williamson) in the film *Forrest Gump*.

Blue Blaze Irregulars
Group of children that assists the title character (Peter Weller) in the film *The Adventures of Buckaroo Banzai Across the Eighth Dimension*.

Blue Boar Inn
Coaching inn where the title character first arrives in London, in the Charles Dickens novel *David Copperfield*.

"The Blue Book of Social Usage"
Subtitle of the first etiquette book of Emily Post, published in 1922.

Blueboy
Prize hog of Abel Frake (Tom Ewell) in the Rodgers and Hammerstein musical film *State Fair* (1962).

Blue Boy
Horse of Mark McCain (Johnny Crawford) in the TV Western series *The Rifleman*.

Blue Dragon Cafe
Phoenix establishment where Cherie (Marilyn Monroe) sings "That Old Black Magic," in the film *Bus Stop*.

"Blue Flame" and "Blue Prelude"
Theme songs of bandleader Woody Herman.

Blue Justice
TV police series for which Kim Cooper (Nancy Travis) is a producer, in the TV sitcom *Almost Perfect*.

Blue Moon Detective Agency
Firm owned by Maddie Hayes (Cybill Shepherd) in the TV series *Moonlighting*.

Blue Oyster
Biker bar in the film *Police Academy*.

Blue Parrot
Nightclub owned by Ferrari (Sydney Greenstreet) in the film *Casablanca*.

blue peter
Naval flag hoisted by a ship when it is about to sail.

"Blue Prelude"
See **"Blue Flame" and "Blue Prelude"**

Blue Relief
Production company of actress Diane Keaton.

Blue Ribbon Sports
Original name of sports-shoe manufacturer Nike.

Blue Ridge Chronicle
Newspaper published by John Boy Walton (Richard Thomas) after college, in the TV series *The Waltons*.

Blue Ridge Parkway
469-mile scenic drive that links Shenandoah National Park in Virginia with Great Smoky Mountains National Park in North Carolina.

Blues
Original nickname of the Cleveland Indians at their American League inception in 1901. They were also known as the Naps before adopting their present nickname in 1915.

Blue Shamrock

Bar frequented by Jack Stein (Jay Thomas) in the TV sitcom *Love and War*.

Blue Skies

Broadway play by Joseph Sheridan (Douglas Fairbanks, Jr.) that Eva Lovelace (Katharine Hepburn) unsuccessfully tries out for, in the film *Morning Glory*.

"Blue Star"

Theme song of the TV series *Medic*.

Blue Star Airlines

Company that stockbroker Bud Fox (Charlie Sheen) obtains inside information about, in the film *Wall Street*.

Blue Velvet

1963 "theme" album by Bobby Vinton, whose song titles all contain the word "Blue":
   "Blue on Blue"
   "Am I Blue?"
   "Blue Blue Day"
   "Mr. Blue"
   "Blue Velvet"
   "St. Louis Blues"
   "Blue Skies"
   "Blue Hawaii"
   "Blue Moon"
   "Little Miss Blue"
   "Blueberry Hill"
   "My Blue Heaven"

The Blue Velvets

Original name of rock group Creedence Clearwater Revival. It was later called The Golliwogs before adopting its best-known name.

The Blue Water

Magnificent sapphire that the title character (Gary Cooper) falsely admits to having stolen, in the film *Beau Geste* (1939).

Blue Wolf Productions

Production company of actor Robin Williams.

Bluffington School

School attended by the title character (voiced by Billy West) in the animated TV series *Doug*.

Blush

Fashion magazine whose offices are the setting of the TV sitcom *Just Shoot Me*.

Blush, Fatima

SPECTRE agent (Barbara Carrera) killed by James Bond (Sean Connery) with a missile-firing fountain pen in the film *Never Say Never Again*.

Bly

English country estate that is the setting of the Henry James novel *The Turn of the Screw*.

Boar's Nest

Restaurant employer of waitress Daisy Duke (Catherine Bach) in the TV series *The Dukes of Hazzard*.

The Boat Rocker

Novel written by Terence Mann (James Earl Jones) in the film *Field of Dreams*.

Boatswain

Favorite dog of poet Lord Byron.

Dog on the whaling ship *Dolly* in the Herman Melville novel *Typee*.

Boatwright University

School attended by John Boy Walton (Richard Thomas) in the TV series *The Waltons*.

Bobbsey Twins title characters

This series of children's books by Laura Lee Hope features two sets of fraternal twins. The older pair are Nan and Bert, and the younger pair are Freddie and Flossie.

"Bobby Hockey"

Nickname of NHL Hall of Famer Bobby Orr.

Bobby Taylor and the Vancouvers

Rock band for which Tommy Chong was a guitarist and backup vocalist, before turning to comedy as half of Cheech and Chong.

Bobo

Pet cat of Doris Husselmeyer in the comic strip *The Piranha Club*.

Teddy bear of Mr. Burns (voiced by Harry Shearer) in the animated TV sitcom *The Simpsons*.

Bob's Country Bunker

Bar where the title characters (Dan Aykroyd, John Belushi), billed as The Good Ole Boys, perform in the film *The Blues Brothers*.

Bob's Pantry
See **Wian, Bob**

Bocephus

Nickname of country singer Hank Williams Jr., given to him by his father.

Bock's Car

B-29 plane that dropped a plutonium-core atomic bomb on Nagasaki, Japan on August 9, 1945. The plane, piloted by Major Charles Sweeney, was named for the usual pilot, Captain Fred Bock. Bock was flying *The Great Artiste*, the accompanying observation plane, that day.

See also **Enola Gay**

Boddy, Mr.

See **Clue suspects, weapons, and rooms**

Bodega Bay, California

Setting of the Alfred Hitchcock film *The Birds*.

Bodett, Tom

See **"We'll leave the light on for you"**

The Body

Novella by Stephen King that was the basis for the film *Stand by Me*.

body types

The three "somatypes" as identified by William H. Sheldon in his 1940 book *The Varieties of Human Physique*:
ectomorph (slender)
endomorph (roundish)
mesomorph (muscular)

Boeing passenger planes

Listed below are the numerical designations, nicknames (if any), and the years that the planes first flew.
40 (1925)
80 (1928)
247 (1933)
307 "Stratoliner" (1938)
314 "Clipper" (1938)
377 "Stratocruiser" (1947)
707 (1954)
720 (1959)
727 (1963)
737 (1967)
747 (1969)
767 (1981)
757 (1982)
777 (1994)
717 (1995)

Bogardus, Aunt Belle

Role for which Fay Bainter won a Best Supporting Actress Academy Award in the 1938 film *Jezebel*.

Bogart/Bacall films

See **Bacall/Bogart films**

Bogart/Cagney films

Films in which Humphrey Bogart and James Cagney appear together:
Angels with Dirty Faces (1938)
The Oklahoma Kid (1939)
The Roaring Twenties (1939)

Bogart/Davis films

See **Davis/Bogart films**

Bogart Slept Here

Original title of the Neil Simon play which became the screenplay for the film *The Goodbye Girl*.

Bogataj, Vinko

Yugoslav skier whose ill-fated jump symbolized "the agony of defeat" in the introduction to ABC's *Wide World of Sports*.

Bogert, Joe

Title character (Barnard Hughes) of the TV sitcom *Doc*.

Bogeymen

Invading force in the film *Babes in Toyland*.

Bogle, Charles

See **Fields, W. C., roles/pen names of**

Bogue, Merwyn

Real name of Ish Kabibble, trumpeter/comedian with Kay Kyser's orchestra.

"The Boilermaker"

Nickname of 1900s heavyweight boxing champ James J. Jeffries.

Boise

Pet cat of Ernest Hemingway.

"Bojangles"

Nickname of dancer Bill Robinson.

Bojaxhiu, Agnes Gonxha

Real name of Albanian-born Mother Teresa.

Bok, Yakov

Title character of the Bernard Malamud novel *The Fixer*.

The Bold and the Brash
*See **All My Trials** and **The Bold and the Brash***

Bollea, Terry
Real name of wrestler Hulk Hogan.

Bollywood
Nickname of the film industry of India, which is centered in Bombay.

Bolotin
Real last name of pop singer Michael Bolton.

Bomba films
Series starring Johnny Sheffield as the title character:
    Bomba, the Jungle Boy (1949)
    Bomba on Panther Island (1949)
    The Lost Volcano (1950)
    Bomba and the Hidden City (1950)
    Bomba and the Elephant Stampede (1951)
    The Lion Hunters (1951)
    African Treasure (1952)
    Bomba and the Jungle Girl (1952)
    Safari Drums (1953)
    The Golden Idol (1954)
    Killer Leopard (1954)
    Lord of the Jungle (1955)

Bombanassa, Achilles
Jerry Colonna's role in the film *Road to Singapore*.

Bombardier, Joseph-Armand
Canadian who invented the snowmobile in 1922.

"Bombshell"
Michelle Pfeiffer's role in the TV sitcom *Delta House*.

Bomont
Midwestern town that is the setting of the film *Footloose*.

Bonanza mothers
The three wives of Ben Cartwright (Lorne Greene) in this TV series:
    Elizabeth (Geraldine Brooks), mother of Adam (Pernell Roberts)
    Inger (Inga Swenson), mother of Hoss (Dan Blocker)
    Marie (Felicia Farr), mother of Little Joe (Michael Landon)

Bonaparte, Joe
Title character of the Clifford Odets play *Golden Boy*.

Bonaventure
Middle name of actor Spencer Tracy.

"Bones"
Captain Kirk's (William Shatner's) nickname for Dr. Leonard McCoy (DeForest Kelley) in the TV series *Star Trek*.

Bongo
Pet rabbit of Radar O'Reilly (Gary Burghoff) in the TV sitcom *M*A*S*H*.

Bongo Congo
Land ruled by the title character of the children's animated TV series *King Leonardo and His Short Subjects*.

Bon Jovi members
Dave Bryan, Jon Bon Jovi, Richie Sambora, Alec John Such, and Tico Torres.

Bonnie
Bakersfield Zoo orangutan that Clyde is in love with, in the film *Any Which Way You Can*.

"Bonzo"
Nickname of Led Zeppelin drummer John Bonham.

Boob, Jeremy Hillary
Real name of the Nowhere Man in the Beatles animated film *Yellow Submarine*.

Boo-Boo Kitty
Stuffed cat of Shirley Feeney (Cindy Williams) in the TV sitcom *Laverne and Shirley*.

Boogie
Pet monkey of Tira (Mae West) in the film *I'm No Angel*.

Bookbinder, Hilarius
Pen name used by Danish philosopher Sören Kierkegaard.

"Book 'em, Danno!"
Catchphrase of detective Steve McGarrett (Jack Lord), spoken to his assistant Danny Williams (James MacArthur) at the end of many episodes of the TV series *Hawaii Five-O*.

The Bookman
*See **Peck, Harry Thurston***

"Boom Boom"
Nickname of NHL Hall of Famer Bernie Geoffrion.

Nickname of boxer Ray Mancini.

Nickname of Freddie Washington (Lawrence Hilton-Jacobs) in the TV sitcom *Welcome Back, Kotter.*

See also **Picariello**

Boom Boom Room

Where singer Cha Cha O'Brien (Margarita Sierra) performs in the TV series *Surfside Six.*

Boomer

Pet golden retriever of Jasmine Dubrow (Vivica A. Fox) in the film *Independence Day.*

Boone City

Setting of the film *The Best Years of Our Lives.*

Boone, Dr. Josiah

Role for which Thomas Mitchell won a Best Supporting Actor Academy Award in the 1939 film *Stagecoach.*

Boopadoop

Maiden name of Blondie Bumstead in the comic strip *Blondie.*

Booth

Last name of the title character in the Henry Fielding novel *Amelia.*

Boothroyd, Major Algernon

Real name of gadget expert Q in the James Bond novels of Ian Fleming.

Boots

Canine mascot of Squad 51 in the TV series *Emergency.*

borborygmus

Scientific name for stomach rumbling.

Borden, Gail

Inventor of condensed milk in 1856. It became a household item during the Civil War, when troops needed milk that would not spoil.

Borglum, Gutzon

Architect who designed and carved the heads of Washington, Jefferson, Lincoln, and Theodore Roosevelt at the Mount Rushmore National Memorial in South Dakota.

born and died on the same date

JANUARY

January 3, 1945: seer Edgar Cayce (died), rock musician Stephen Stills (born)

January 11, 1928: Thomas Hardy (died), TV producer David Wolper (born)

January 16, 1935: outlaw Ma Barker (died), auto racer A. J. Foyt (born)

January 21, 1950: author George Orwell (died), singer Billy Ocean (born)

January 30, 1951: auto engineer Ferdinand Porsche (died), singer Phil Collins (born)

FEBRUARY

February 19, 1916: physicist Ernst Mach (died), jockey Eddie Arcaro (born)

MARCH

March 4, 1888: philosopher Amos Bronson Alcott (died), football coach Knute Rockne (born)

March 16, 1903: Western judge Roy Bean (died), statesman Mike Mansfield (born)

MAY

May 19, 1795: biographer James Boswell (died), philanthropist Johns Hopkins (born)

May 23, 1934: outlaws Clyde Barrow and Bonnie Parker (died), inventor Robert Moog (born)

JUNE

June 6, 1903: artist Paul Gauguin (died), composer Aram Khachaturian (born)

JULY

July 4, 1826: U.S. presidents John Adams and Thomas Jefferson (died), songwriter Stephen Foster (born)

July 7, 1901: author Johanna Spyri (died), director Vittorio De Sica (born)

July 22, 1932: producer Florenz Ziegfeld (died), designer Oscar de la Renta (born)

July 30, 1898: statesman Otto von Bismarck (died), sculptor Henry Moore (born)

AUGUST

August 3, 1924: author Joseph Conrad (died), author Leon Uris (born)

SEPTEMBER

September 26, 1947: author Hugh Lofting (died), country singer Lynn Anderson (born)

OCTOBER

October 7, 1849: author Edgar Allan Poe (died), poet James Whitcomb Riley (born)

October 15, 1917: spy Mata Hari (died), historian Arthur Schlesinger, Jr. (born)

October 26, 1902: reformer Elizabeth Cady Stanton (died), aviator Beryl Markham (born)

NOVEMBER

November 3, 1954: artist Henri Matisse (died), singer Adam Ant (born)

November 6, 1893: composer Peter Tchaikovsky (died), automaker Edsel Ford (born)

November 11, 1945: songwriter Jerome Kern (died), Nicaraguan political leader Daniel Ortega (born)

November 16, 1895: "America" lyricist Samuel Francis Smith (died), composer Paul Hindemith (born)

November 21, 1945: humorist Robert Benchley (died), actress Goldie Hawn (born)

November 22, 1943: lyricist Lorenz Hart (died), tennis pro Billie Jean King (born)

DECEMBER

December 2, 1859: abolitionist John Brown (died), artist Georges Seurat (born)

December 25, 1946: comedian W. C. Fields (died), singer Jimmy Buffett (born)

born on the same date

JANUARY

January 5, 1931: choreographer Alvin Ailey, actor Robert Duvall

January 9, 1941: singer Joan Baez, actress Susannah York

January 17, 1899: mobster Al Capone, author Nevil Shute

January 21, 1941: singers Richie Havens and Plácido Domingo

January 22, 1909: actress Ann Sothern, diplomat U Thant

January 24, 1915: artist Robert Motherwell, game-show producer Mark Goodson

January 30, 1937: actress Vanessa Redgrave, chessmaster Boris Spassky

FEBRUARY

February 9, 1909: singer Carmen Miranda, statesman Dean Rusk

February 9, 1914: stripper Gypsy Rose Lee, country singer Ernest Tubb, baseball executive Bill Veeck

February 10, 1893: comedian Jimmy Durante, tennis pro Bill Tilden

February 10, 1898: actress Dame Judith Anderson, playwright Bertolt Brecht

February 12, 1809: naturalist Charles Darwin, U.S. president Abraham Lincoln

February 14, 1913: sportscaster Mel Allen, football coach Woody Hayes, labor leader Jimmy Hoffa

February 15, 1951: singer Melissa Manchester, actress Jane Seymour

February 18, 1920: game-show host Bill Cullen, actor Jack Palance

February 18, 1931: cartoonist Johnny Hart, author Toni Morrison

February 18, 1933: actress Kim Novak, artist Yoko Ono

February 20, 1924: actor Sidney Poitier, auto racer Bobby Unser, designer Gloria Vanderbilt

MARCH

March 2, 1931: statesman Mikhail Gorbachev, author Tom Wolfe

March 21, 1962: actor Matthew Broderick, actress and talk show host Rosie O'Donnell

March 25, 1867: sculptor Gutzon Borglum, conductor Arturo Toscanini

March 31, 1935: trumpeter Herb Alpert, actor Richard Chamberlain

APRIL

April 3, 1898: entertainer George Jessel, magazine publisher Henry Luce

April 3, 1924: actor Marlon Brando, actress Doris Day

April 6, 1937: singer Merle Haggard, actor Billy Dee Williams

April 7, 1939: director Francis Ford Coppola, interviewer Sir David Frost

April 20, 1893: comedian Harold Lloyd, painter Joan Miró

April 23, 1899: author Dame Ngaio Marsh, author Vladimir Nabokov

MAY

May 6, 1856: psychoanalyst Sigmund Freud, explorer Robert Peary

May 6, 1915: actor/director Orson Welles, author T. H. White

May 8, 1940: author Peter Benchley, singer Ricky Nelson

May 10, 1899: dancer Fred Astaire, composer Dimitri Tiomkin

May 21, 1917: actor Raymond Burr, singer Dennis Day

May 27, 1911: statesman Hubert Humphrey, actor Vincent Price

JUNE

June 1, 1926: actor Andy Griffith, actress Marilyn Monroe

June 8, 1926: artist LeRoy Neiman, comedian Jerry Stiller

June 18, 1942: reviewer Roger Ebert, singer Paul McCartney

June 21, 1947: actress Meredith Baxter, actor Michael Gross (Baxter and Gross played a married couple in the TV sitcom *Family Ties*)

June 30, 1917: singer Lena Horne, drummer Buddy Rich

JULY

July 6, 1946: actor Sylvester Stallone, artist Jamie Wyeth

July 21, 1899: poet Hart Crane, author Ernest Hemingway

July 22, 1898: poet Stephen Vincent Benét, artist Alexander Calder

AUGUST

August 6, 1881: bacteriologist Sir Alexander Fleming, journalist Louella Parsons

SEPTEMBER

September 10, 1934: journalist Charles Kuralt, baseball player Roger Maris

September 18, 1905: comedian Eddie "Rochester" Anderson, actress Greta Garbo

OCTOBER

October 1, 1924: U.S. president Jimmy Carter, jurist William Rehnquist

October 15, 1959: Duchess of York Sarah Ferguson, TV chef Emeril Lagasse

NOVEMBER

November 15, 1887: poet Marianne Moore, artist Georgia O'Keeffe

November 15, 1891: statesman W. Averell Harriman, German field marshal Erwin Rommel

November 26, 1912: playwright Eugène Ionesco, journalist Eric Sevareid

DECEMBER

December 1, 1935: actor/director Woody Allen, singer Lou Rawls

Borodin, Alexander, *Kismet* melodies of

Russian composer whose works were the source of the melodies in the musical *Kismet*. Its two best-known songs and the specific sources are:

"Baubles, Bangles and Beads" (String Quartet #2)

"Stranger in Paradise" ("Polovtsian Dances" from the opera *Prince Igor*)

Borso, Bobby

Real name of Binzer (Bart Braverman), associate of detective Dan Tanna (Robert Urich) in the TV series *Vega$*.

Bosco

ATM password of George Costanza (Jason Alexander) in the TV sitcom *Seinfeld*.

"The Boss"

Nickname of rock singer Bruce Springsteen.

Nickname of baseball-team owner George Steinbrenner.

President Harry S Truman's nickname for his wife Bess.

"Boss of the Plains"

Nickname of the Stetson wide-brimmed Western hat.

Boston Blackie films

Detective series starring Chester Morris in the title role.

Meet Boston Blackie (1941)

Confessions of Boston Blackie (1941)

Alias Boston Blackie (1942)

Boston Blackie Goes Hollywood (1942)

After Midnight with Boston Blackie (1943)

The Chance of a Lifetime (1943)

One Mysterious Night (1944)

Boston Blackie Booked on Suspicion (1945)

Boston Blackie's Rendezvous (1945)

A Close Call for Boston Blackie (1946)

The Phantom Thief (1946)

Boston Blackie and the Law (1946)

Trapped by Boston Blackie (1948)

Boston Blackie's Chinese Venture (1949)

Boston Braves

Original name of the Washington Redskins at their NFL inception in 1932. The team changed its nickname to the Redskins in 1933 and moved to Washington, D.C., in 1937.

Boston (rock group) original members

Brad Delp, Barry Goudreau, Sib Hashian, Tom Scholz, and Fran Sheehan.

"The Boston Strong Boy"

Nickname of 1880s heavyweight boxing champ John L. Sullivan.

Bostrom, Swan

Role for which Walter Brennan won a Best Supporting Actor Academy Award in the 1936 film *Come and Get It*.

Bottleneck

Setting of the film *Destry Rides Again*.

Bottomley, Beauregard

See **$20,000,000**

Bottoms, Dusty; Day, Lucky; and Nederlander, Ned

Title characters of the film *¡Three Amigos!*, portrayed by Chevy Chase, Steve Martin and Martin Short, respectively.

Botts dots

Raised reflective tiles often used to mark lane boundaries on highways. They were invented by chemist Elbert D. Botts in 1953.

Bouchercon World Mystery Convention

See **Anthony Awards**

bouillabaseball

Favorite sport on the planet Melmac, in the TV sitcom *ALF*. The game is played like baseball, but instead of bats and balls, uses fish parts.

Boulle, Pierre

See **Monkey Planet**

Bounce

Pet dog of poet Alexander Pope.

Bounder

See **Blackie, Bounder, and Tiger**

Bounty Trilogy

Group of books written by Charles Nordhoff and James Hall.
  Mutiny on the Bounty (1932)
  Men Against the Sea (1934)
  Pitcairn's Island (1934)

Bouvier

Maiden name of Marge Simpson (voiced by Julie Kavner) in the TV sitcom *The Simpsons*.

Bouville, France

Setting of the Jean-Paul Sartre novel *Nausea*.

Bowdler, Thomas

English editor of *Family Shakespeare* (1818), in which, by deletions and paraphrasing, he attempted to make Shakespeare's plays suitable for a family audience. He thus gave his name to the term "bowdlerize."

Bowie, Arizona

Birthplace of John Rambo (Sylvester Stallone) in the *Rambo* films. Rambo is of Indian/German descent.

Bowker, Gordon

See **Baldwin, Jerry; Bowker, Gordon; and Siegl, Zev**

Bowles, Sally

Role for which Liza Minnelli won a Best Actress Academy Award in the 1972 film *Cabaret*.

"Bows and Strings in Teasing"

Instrumental theme of the TV sitcom *My Little Margie*.

Bowser

Pet dog of myopic cartoon character Mr. Magoo.

Box, Edgar

Pen name used by author Gore Vidal.

Boxing Cat Productions

Production company of actor Tim Allen.

boxing weight classes

The weights listed below are the maximums within each class:
  Minimumweight, aka Strawweight (105)
  Junior Flyweight, aka Light Flyweight (108)
  Flyweight (112)
  Junior Bantamweight, aka Super Flyweight (115)
  Bantamweight (118)
  Junior Featherweight, aka Super Bantamweight (122)
  Featherweight (126)
  Junior Lightweight, aka Super Featherweight (130)
  Lightweight (135)
  Junior Welterweight, aka Super Lightweight (140)
  Welterweight (147)
  Junior Middleweight, aka Super Welterweight (154)
  Middleweight (160)
  Super Middleweight (168)
  Light Heavyweight (175)
  Cruiserweight, aka Junior Heavyweight (190)
  Heavyweight (no maximum)

Boyd, Nancy

Pen name used by poet Edna St. Vincent Millay early in her career.

The Boy From Oklahoma

1954 film that was the basis for the TV Western series *Sugarfoot*.

Boyle's Thirty Acres

Jersey City, New Jersey, arena (capacity 105,000) that was the site of Jack Dempsey's defeat of Georges Carpentier, to retain the heavyweight boxing championship, on July 2, 1921. This was the first-ever boxing match with a million-dollar gate.

Boy Rangers

Scouting organization headed by the title character (James Stewart) in the film *Mr. Smith Goes to Washington*. Its official publication is *Boy Stuff*.

Boy Scout ranks

Listed below from lowest to highest.
- Tenderfoot
- Second Class
- First Class
- Star
- Life
- Eagle

Boy Scouts of America merit badges

- American Business
- American Cultures
- American Heritage
- American Labor
- Animal Science
- Archaeology
- Archery
- Architecture
- Art
- Astronomy
- Athletics
- Atomic Energy
- Auto Mechanics
- Aviation
- Backpacking
- Basketry
- Bird Study
- Bugling
- Camping
- Canoeing
- Chemistry
- Cinematography
- Citizenship in the Community
- Citizenship in the Nation
- Citizenship in the World
- Climbing
- Coin Collecting
- Collections
- Communications
- Computers
- Cooking
- Crime Prevention
- Cycling
- Dentistry
- Disabilities Awareness
- Dog Care
- Drafting
- Electricity
- Electronics
- Emergency Preparedness
- Energy
- Engineering
- Entrepreneurship
- Environmental Science
- Family Life
- Farm Mechanics
- Fingerprinting
- Fire Safety
- First Aid
- Fish and Wildlife Management
- Fishing
- Forestry
- Gardening
- Genealogy
- Geology
- Golf
- Graphic Arts
- Hiking
- Home Repairs
- Horsemanship
- Indian Lore
- Insect Study
- Journalism
- Landscape Architecture
- Law
- Leatherwork
- Lifesaving
- Mammal Study
- Medicine
- Metalwork
- Model Design and Building
- Motorboating
- Music
- Nature
- Oceanography
- Orienteering
- Painting
- Personal Fitness
- Personal Management
- Pets
- Photography
- Pioneering
- Plant Science
- Plumbing
- Pottery
- Public Health
- Public Speaking
- Pulp and Paper
- Radio
- Railroading
- Reading
- Reptile and Amphibian Study
- Rifle Shooting
- Rowing
- Safety
- Salesmanship
- Scholarship
- Sculpture
- Shotgun Shooting
- Skating

Small-Boat Sailing
Snow Sports
Soil and Water Conservation
Space Exploration
Sports
Stamp Collecting
Surveying
Swimming
Textile
Theater
Traffic Safety
Truck Transportation
Veterinary Medicine
Waterskiing
Weather
Whitewater
Wilderness Survival
Wood Carving
Woodwork

A Boy's Life
Original working title of the Steven Spielberg film *E. T. The Extra-Terrestrial*.

Boy Stuff
See **Boy Rangers**

The Boy Who Wouldn't Grow Up
Alternate title of the James M. Barrie play *Peter Pan*.

"The Boy Wonder"
Nickname of Batman sidekick Robin.

Nickname of MGM producer Irving Thalberg.

Boyz II Men members
Michael McCary, Nathan Morris, Wanya Morris, and Shawn Stockman.

Boz
Pen name used by author Charles Dickens early in his career.

Bracken, Lynn
Role for which Kim Basinger won a Best Supporting Actress Academy Award in the 1997 film *L.A. Confidential*.

Braddock, Texas
Location of Southfork Ranch in the TV series *Dallas*.

Bradham, Caleb
New Bern, North Carolina, pharmacist who invented Pepsi-Cola in 1898.

Bradlee, Ben
Role for which Jason Robards won a Best Supporting Actor Academy Award in the 1976 film *All the President's Men*.

Bradley, Damon
The man Faith Corvatch (Marisa Tomei) believes is destined to be her soulmate after it is spelled out on a Ouija board, in the film *Only You*.

Bradley Theatre
Broadway house where Janie Barlow (Joan Crawford) gets her big break, in the film *Dancing Lady*.

Bradley, Voorhees, and Day
Founders of men's underwear manufacturer BVD in 1876.

Brad's Drink
Original name of Pepsi-Cola, derived from the name of its inventor, Caleb Bradham.

Brady & Co.
New York City book-publisher employer of Richard Sherman (Tom Ewell) in the film *The Seven Year Itch*.

The Brady Bunch children
The six children of Mike and Carol Brady (Robert Reed and Florence Henderson) on this TV sitcom:
Greg (Barry Williams)
Peter (Christopher Knight)
Bobby (Mike Lookinland)
Marcia (Maureen McCormick)
Jan (Eve Plumb)
Cindy (Susan Olsen)

Brahms Baby Food
Employer of Peter Christopher (Michael Callan) in the TV sitcom *Occasional Wife*.

Braine, A.
Pen name once used by Will Shortz, current crossword editor of *The New York Times*.

"Brains and Eggs"
Debut episode of the TV sitcom *3rd Rock From The Sun*, which aired on January 9, 1996.

Brain the Wonder Dog
Pet of the title character in the children's animated TV series *Inspector Gadget*.

"The Brakeman"
Nickname of country-music pioneer Jimmie Rodgers, from his previous job as a railroad brakeman.

Bramblehurst

English setting of the H. G. Wells novel *The Invisible Man*.

The Bramford

New York City apartment building that is the setting of the film *Rosemary's Baby*.

Bram Stoker Awards

Presented annually since 1988 by the Horror Writers Association for achievement in horror publishing. They are named for the author of *Dracula*.

Brand, Max

Pen name used by Frederick Schiller Faust, author of *Destry Rides Again* and the Dr. Kildare novels.

"Brand New Life"

Theme song of the TV sitcom *Who's the Boss?*

Brandon

Pet dog of the title character (Soleil Moon Frye) in the TV sitcom *Punky Brewster*.

Brandon, Teena

See **Teena, Brandon/Brandon, Teena**

Brandy

Horse of the title character (Clint Walker) in the TV series *Cheyenne*.

"Brandy"

Original title of the Barry Manilow tune "Mandy."

Brangwen, Gudrun

Role for which Glenda Jackson won a Best Actress Academy Award in the 1970 film *Women in Love*.

Brannock Device

Metallic device used in stores to measure shoe size. It was invented by Syracuse, New York, shoe merchant Charles Brannock and patented in 1926.

"The Brass Cupcake"

Nickname of Dee Dee McCall (Stepfanie Kramer) in the TV series *Hunter*.

Braymore

Middle name of Henry Blake (McLean Stevenson) in the TV sitcom *M*A*S*H*.

Bray, Sir Hilary

Heraldry expert impersonated by James Bond (George Lazenby), to gain access to the headquarters of Ernst Stavro Blofeld (Telly Savalas), in the film *On Her Majesty's Secret Service*.

Brazil, Indiana

Birthplace of labor leader Jimmy Hoffa and popcorn manufacturer Orville Redenbacher.

"Breakaway"

Debut episode of the TV series *Space: 1999*, which aired on October 17, 1975.

The Breakfast Club title characters

John Bender (Judd Nelson)
Andrew Clark (Emilio Estevez)
Brian Johnson (Anthony Michael Hall)
Allison Reynolds (Ally Sheedy)
Claire Standish (Molly Ringwald)

"Breakfast of Champions"

Advertising slogan of Wheaties.

Breed, Allen K.

Inventor of the automobile air bag in 1968.

Breedlove, Garrett

Role for which Jack Nicholson won a Best Supporting Actor Academy Award in the 1983 film *Terms of Endearment*.

Breitenberger, Edward

Real name of actor Edd Byrnes.

Brenner, Victor David

Designer of the original Lincoln penny, minted from 1909 to 1958.

Brent Building

Location of the Los Angeles office of the title character (Raymond Burr) in the TV series *Perry Mason*.

Bret Harte High

School whose alumni are featured in the TV series *What Really Happened to the Class of '65?*

Brewster, Sir David

Scottish physicist who invented the kaleidoscope, patented in 1817.

Brewster, Tom

Real name of the title character (Will Hutchins) in the TV Western series *Sugarfoot*.

Brian

Griffin family dog in the animated TV sitcom *Family Guy*.

Brice, Fanny
Role for which Barbra Streisand won a Best Actress Academy Award in the 1968 film *Funny Girl*.

Brick, The
Tavern hangout in the TV series *Northern Exposure*.

"The Brickyard"
Nickname of the Indianapolis Motor Speedway, home of the Indianapolis 500.

"Bridal Chorus"
Tune from the Richard Wagner opera *Lohengrin* better known as "Here Comes the Bride."

Bridal Veil Mountain
Setting of the TV series *Here Come the Brides*.

Bridegrooms
Original nickname of the Brooklyn Dodgers at their National League inception in 1890. They were also known as the Superbas before adopting their present nickname.

"The Bride Possessed"
Debut episode of the TV series *One Step Beyond*, which aired on January 20, 1959.

Bridgeport, P. T.
Bear friend of the title character in the comic strip *Pogo*.

Bridger's Wells, Nevada
Setting of the Walter Van Tilburg Clark novel *The Ox-Bow Incident*.

Bridget
Pet Irish setter of the title character (David Hartman) in the TV series *Lucas Tanner*.

Bridgewood
See **Crenshaw High School**

Brigadore
Horse of Sir Guyon in the Edmund Spenser epic poem *The Faerie Queene*.

Briggs, Dan
Original leader of the IM Force in the TV series *Mission: Impossible*, portrayed by Steven Hill, who was succeeded by Jim Phelps (Peter Graves).

Brigham
Buffalo-hunting horse of Buffalo Bill Cody.

Brigid
Middle name of actress Angela Lansbury.

Brinkley
Pet dog of Joe Fox (Tom Hanks) in the film *You've Got Mail*.

Brinton
Middle name of Civil War Union general George McClellan.

Britannia
Former 400-foot royal yacht of Queen Elizabeth II, decommissioned in 1997.

British English
Common British expressions that are not common in the U.S., including words that have different meanings in Great Britain and the U.S.:
advert: advertisement
Alsatian: German shepherd
Aunt Sally: easy target
banger: sausage
barrow: pushcart
bespoke: custom-tailored
billion: 1,000,000,000,000 (U.S. trillion)
bomb: great success (the opposite of its U.S. meaning)
bonnet: car hood
boot: car trunk
braces: suspenders
brolly: umbrella
building society: savings and loan association
caravan: trailer
car park: parking lot
carriage: railroad passenger car
catapult: slingshot
chemist: pharmacist
chips: French fried potatoes
clanger: blunder
conk: nose
cornet: ice cream cone
costermonger: pushcart peddler
cotton wool: absorbent cotton
crisps: potato chips
draughts: checkers (the board game)
drawing pin: thumbtack
dual carriageway: divided highway
dummy: baby's pacifier
dustman: garbage collector
estate car: station wagon
Father Christmas: Santa Claus
first floor: second floor (the British start counting above the ground floor)
flannel: washcloth

flex: electric cord
flutter: small bet
football: soccer
Girl Guide: Girl Scout
glasshouse: greenhouse, military prison
hire-purchase: installment plan
hoarding: billboard
ironmongery: hardware store
jelly: gelatin dessert
jumble sale: rummage sale
ladder: run in a stocking
lashings: large servings of food or drink
lido: beach resort, outdoor swimming pool
lift: elevator
lorry: truck
milk float: dairy home-delivery truck
moggy: pet cat
nappy: diaper
nark: police informer
noughts-and-crosses: tic-tac-toe
nursing home: small private hospital
panda car: police patrol car
patience: solitaire (card game)
petrol: gasoline
plimsolls: sneakers
point: electrical outlet
pontoon: twenty-one (card game)
pram: baby carriage
redcap: military police officer
return ticket: round-trip ticket
roundabout: traffic circle, merry-go-round
runner beans: string beans
serviette: napkin
silencer: car muffler
singlet: undershirt
steps: stepladder
subway: underpass
torch: flashlight
tram: streetcar
trolley: cart
trunk call: long-distance call
tube: subway
turnup: trouser cuff
vest: undershirt
waistcoat: vest
warder: prison guard
wholemeal: whole-wheat
windcheater: windbreaker
windscreen: windshield
wing: fender

British Guiana

Former name of the South American nation Guyana.

British Honduras

Former name of the Central American nation Belize.

Britt, Ponsonby

Executive producer of the children's animated TV series *Rocky and His Friends*, as listed in the closing credits. This is a pseudonym of the show's creator Jay Ward.

BRLFQ

How the title character spells "Mom and Dad," in the Bobby Goldsboro tune "Watching Scotty Grow."

Broad

Real last name of pop singer Billy Idol.

Broadway

Slang term for an ace-high straight in poker.

"Broadway"

Inmates' nickname for the main cell-block corridor in Alcatraz prison.

"Broadway Joe"

Nickname of pro football Hall of Fame quarterback Joe Namath.

Brock, Alice

Owner of the Massachusetts eatery that inspired the Arlo Guthrie tune "Alice's Restaurant."

Brockert, Mary Christine

Real name of pop singer Teena Marie.

Brockovich, Erin

Title role for which Julia Roberts won the 2000 Best Actress Academy Award.

Brockway, Sylvester

Real name of Porky (Donald Keeler) in the 1950s version of the TV series *Lassie*.

Broderick and Elizabeth

Pet bulldogs of pop singing duo Captain and Tennille.

Brodie, Jean

Role for which Maggie Smith won a Best Actress Academy Award in the 1969 film *The Prime of Miss Jean Brodie*.

Brodny

Village that is the setting of the Danny Kaye film *The Inspector General*.

Broken Wheel Ranch

Setting of the children's TV series *Fury*.

Bronco's Auto Repairs and Otto's Auto Orphanage

Employers of Fonzie (Henry Winkler) before he opens his own repair shop, in the TV sitcom *Happy Days*.

Bronson

Maiden name of June Cleaver (Barbara Billingsley) in the TV sitcom *Leave It to Beaver*.

Last name of the title character (Elena Verdugo) in the TV sitcom *Meet Millie*.

Bronson/Ireland films

Films in which Charles Bronson and Jill Ireland appear together:
    Villa Rides (1968)
    Rider on the Rain (1970)
    The Family (1970)
    Cold Sweat (1970)
    Someone Behind the Door (1971)
    The Valachi Papers (1972)
    The Mechanic (1972)
    The Valdez Horses, aka *Chino* (1973)
    Hard Times (1975)
    Breakheart Pass (1975)
    Breakout (1975)
    From Noon Till Three (1976)
    Love and Bullets (1979)
    Death Wish II (1982)
    Assassination (1987)

The Bronze Boot

Trophy awarded to the winning team in the annual football game between Colorado State University and the University of Wyoming.

Brookfield

English prep school that is the setting of the James Hilton novel *Goodbye, Mr. Chips*.

Brooklyn Heights High

School attended by identical cousins Patty and Cathy Lane (Patty Duke) in the TV sitcom *The Patty Duke Show*.

Brotherhood Club

Police fraternal organization whose members include Francis Muldoon (Fred Gwynne) and Gunther Toody (Joe E. Ross) in the TV sitcom *Car 54, Where Are You?*

Brother Records

Company created by the Beach Boys to produce their recordings.

Brown, Alma

Role for which Patricia Neal won a Best Actress Academy Award in the 1963 film *Hud*.

Brown, Angeline

Real name of actress Angie Dickinson.

Brown Beauty

Horse, a Narragansett pacer, borrowed from John Larkin by Paul Revere for his famous ride of April 18, 1775.

"Brown Bess"

Nickname of the standard musket carried by redcoats during the American Revolution.

"The Brown Bomber"

Nickname of boxer Joe Louis.

Brown, Christy

Role for which Daniel Day-Lewis won a Best Actor Academy Award in the 1989 film *My Left Foot*.

Brownell

Middle name of suffragist Susan B. Anthony.

Brownhouse Productions

Film production company of singer Whitney Houston.

Brown, James, nicknames of

The popular nicknames of this soul singer:
    "The Godfather of Soul"
    "The Hardest Working Man in Show Business"
    "Mr. Dynamite"
    "Mr. Please Please"
    "Soul Brother Number One"

Brown, Linda

See **Monroe Elementary School**

Brown, Mrs.

Role for which Anne Revere won a Best Supporting Actress Academy Award in the 1945 film *National Velvet*.

Role for which Brenda Fricker won a Best Supporting Actress Academy Award in the 1989 film *My Left Foot*.

Brown, Oda Mae

Role for which Whoopi Goldberg won a Best Supporting Actress Academy Award in the 1990 film *Ghost*.

Brown, Parson

Clergyman in the tune "Winter Wonderland."

Clergyman in the George Gershwin tune "Liza."

Brown's Breakfast Sausage

Company run by Thomas Brown (Will Rogers) in the film *Doubting Thomas*.

Brown, Sneaky Pie

Cat that gets coauthor billing in the mystery novels of Rita Mae Brown.

Brown, Thornberry Bailey

First Union soldier killed in the Civil War, at Fetterman, West Virginia, on May 22, 1861.

Bruce

Pet ocelot of the title character (Anne Francis) in the TV series *Honey West*.

Affectionate name given by the crew to the mechanical shark used in the Steven Spielberg film *Jaws*.

Brugh, Spangler Arlington

Real name of actor Robert Taylor.

Bruno

Pet bear of self-styled Western lawman Judge Roy Bean.

Black bear that portrays the title character of the TV series *Gentle Ben*.

Brutus

First name of the title character of the Eugene O'Neill play *The Emperor Jones*.

Pet dog of Peter Drury (John Carradine), on which he tests his invisibility formula in the film *The Invisible Man's Revenge*.

Bryan

Real first name of pro football Hall of Fame quarterback (Bryan) Bart Starr.

Bryan, Arthur Q.

Longtime voice of Elmer Fudd, one of the very few voices in Warner Bros. cartoons not usually done by Mel Blanc.

Bryan Ray

Real first and middle names of actor Skeet Ulrich.

Bryant Park

Town that is the original (1960–1967) setting of the TV sitcom *My Three Sons*. The Douglas family lived in North Hollywood, California, for the last four years of the series.

Bryant's Gap

Where Butch Cavendish and his gang ambush and kill five of the six Texas Rangers that are pursuing them. The lone survivor, John Reid, takes the identity of the Lone Ranger soon thereafter.

Bryland

Southern town that is the setting of the TV series *I'll Fly Away*.

Bryna Productions

Production company of actor Kirk Douglas, named for his mother.

Btfsplk, Joe

Gloomy character in the comic strip *Li'l Abner*, who has a cloud hanging over his head wherever he goes.

Bubba Gump Shrimp Company

Business started by the title character (Tom Hanks) in the film *Forrest Gump*.

Bubbles

Pet chimpanzee of pop singer Michael Jackson.

"Bubbles"

Nickname of opera star Beverly Sills.

"Bubbles in the Wine"

Theme song of the Lawrence Welk orchestra.

Bubka, Sergei

Ukrainian pole vaulter who was the first to exceed 20 feet, with a vault of 20' 1¾" at an indoor meet at San Sebastian, Spain in 1991.

buccal cavity

Medical term for the mouth.

Buccaneers

Original nickname of the New Orleans franchise during the 1967–1968 inaugural season of the American Basketball Association.

Bucephalus

Horse of Alexander the Great.

Buck

Middle name of golf pro Lee Trevino.

Horse of Ben Cartwright (Lorne Greene) in the TV Western series *Bonanza*.

Canine hero of the Jack London novel *The Call of the Wild.*

Family dog in the comic strip *The Gumps.*

Pet dog of the Bundys in the TV sitcom *Married . . . with Children.*

Buck Buchanan Award

Annual trophy given to the outstanding defensive player in Division I-AA college football.

Buck Buck

Childhood street game played by Bill Cosby, as recounted in his comedy monologues.

Bucket

Last name of the title character in the Roald Dahl novel *Charlie and the Chocolate Factory.*

Buckeye

Secret Service code name for Camp David.

"Buckeye"

See **United States residents' nicknames**

Buck, Peter

See **DeLuca, Fred and Buck, Peter**

Buckshot

Horse of the title character (Guy Madison) in the TV series *Wild Bill Hickok.*

"Buckyball"

Nickname of buckminsterfullerene, a form of carbon discovered in 1985, whose structure resembles the geodesic dome invented by R. Buckminster Fuller.

Bucky Beaver

Cartoon mascot of Ipana toothpaste.

Bucky Boy

Pet bloodhound of Big Daddy Pollitt (Burl Ives) in the film *Cat on a Hot Tin Roof.*

BUD

Stock-ticker symbol of Anheuser-Busch, maker of Budweiser beer.

"Bud"

Childhood nickname of actor Marlon Brando.

Childhood nickname of astronaut John Glenn.

Buddy

Pet beagle of Sarah and Henry Turner (Annette Bening, Harrison Ford) in the film *Regarding Henry.*

Pet bulldog of the title character (Kirstie Alley) in the TV sitcom *Veronica's Closet.*

Pet dog of Alex Rieger (Judd Hirsch) in the TV sitcom *Taxi.*

Pet Labrador retriever of President Bill Clinton. The dog was named for a favorite uncle of Clinton.

Budinger, Victoria May

17-year-old who married singer Tiny Tim on *The Tonight Show*, on December 17, 1969. The couple divorced in 1977.

"Buffalo Bill"

Nickname of the serial killer (Ted Levine) in the film *The Silence of the Lambs.*

Buffalo Braves

Original name of the Los Angeles Clippers at their NBA inception in 1970.

Buffalo Pass, Scalplock, and Defiance Line

Railroad won by Ben Calhoun (Dale Robertson) in a poker game in the TV Western series *The Iron Horse.*

Buffalo Springfield original members

Richie Furay, Dewey Martin, Bruce Palmer, Stephen Stills, and Neil Young.

"Buffy"

Debut episode of the TV sitcom *Family Affair*, which aired on September 12, 1966.

Buford, Gordon

See **"Car-Boy-Girl"**

bug

Term for the transparent network logo that appears in a lower corner of television screens.

Bugleboy, Beauregard Chaulmoogra Frontenac de Montmingle

Full name of hound dog Beauregard in the comic strip *Pogo.*

Bug Tussle, Tennessee

Hometown of the Clampett family in the TV sitcom *The Beverly Hillbillies.*

"Building the World of Tomorrow"

Theme of the 1939–40 New York World's Fair.

"Build yourself a great kid"

Advertising slogan of Erector Sets.

"Bull"

Nickname of World War II admiral William Halsey.

Bull & Finch Pub

Actual Boston establishment seen in the opening credits of the TV sitcom *Cheers.*

Bulldog Cafe

Pilot hangout in the film *The Rocketeer.*

Bulldogs

See **Hill Valley, California**

Bullet

Roy Rogers' pet German shepherd.

bullfighters

Term in rodeo for the people, formerly called "rodeo clowns," who protect bull riders.

Bullitt and Company

Advertising-agency employer of the title character (Gene Tierney) in the film *Laura.*

Bullock, Anna Mae

Real name of rock singer Tina Turner.

Bull's-eye

Pet shaggy dog of Bill Sikes in the Charles Dickens novel *Oliver Twist.*

Bull Tales

Original name of the Garry Trudeau comic strip *Doonesbury.* The strip first appeared in the *Yale Daily News* on September 30, 1968 (while Trudeau was a Yale student), and was renamed *Doonesbury* when it debuted in syndication on October 26, 1970.

Bulwer-Lytton Fiction Contest

Sponsored annually since 1982 by the English Department of San Diego State University. Entrants attempt to compose the opening sentence to the worst of all possible novels. It is named for author Edward Bulwer-Lytton, whose novel *Paul Clifford* begins with the immortal line, "It was a dark and stormy night."

Bunchie

Pet terrier of Ralph Touchett in the Henry James novel *The Portrait of a Lady.*

"The Bunion Derby"

Nickname of the Great Cross-Country Marathon Race, a foot race from Los Angeles to New York City held in 1928. The winner, Oklahoman Andy Payne, won $25,000 for completing the 3,422 miles in a total running time of 573 hours, 4 minutes, 34 seconds.

Bunker Hill Academy

Military-school setting of the film *Taps.*

Bunker Hill Community College

School where Sean Maguire (Robin Williams) teaches psychology in the film *Good Will Hunting.*

Bunthorne's Bride

Alternate title of the Gilbert and Sullivan comic opera *Patience.*

Bunting, Dr. George A.

Baltimore pharmacist who developed Noxzema skin cream in 1914. It was originally marketed as a sunburn remedy.

Burbank

Pet cat of Roger Murtaugh (Danny Glover) in the *Lethal Weapon* films.

Burce, Suzanne

Real name of actress Jane Powell.

Burger Barn

Fast-food employer of Alexander Bumstead in the comic strip *Blondie.*

Burke, Sadie

Role for which Mercedes McCambridge won a Best Supporting Actress Academy Award in the 1949 film *All the King's Men.*

Burleyville, Massachusetts

Home of J. Cheever Loophole (Groucho Marx) in the film *At the Circus.*

Burnett, Chester Arthur

Real name of blues singer Howlin' Wolf.

Burnett, Murray

See **Everybody Comes to Rick's**

Burnham, Lester

Role for which Kevin Spacey won a Best Actor Academy Award in the 1999 film *American Beauty.*

The Burning of Los Angeles

Film for which Tod Hackett is a scenic artist, in the Nathanael West novel *The Day of the Locust.*

Burns and Albright

Last names of the title characters (Billy Crystal and Meg Ryan, respectively) in the film *When Harry Met Sally. . . .*

Burns, Arnold

Role for which Martin Balsam won a Best Supporting Actor Academy Award in the 1965 film *A Thousand Clowns.*

burnsides

Term for side whiskers from which the current term "sideburns" evolved. Both words are ultimately derived from the name of Civil War Union general Ambrose Everett Burnside, who wore them.

Burns, Tex

Pen name used by Western author Louis L'Amour early in his career.

Burpelson

Air Force base commanded by General Jack D. Ripper (Sterling Hayden) in the film *Dr. Strangelove.*

Burrell, Stanley Kirk

Real name of rap artist M. C. Hammer.

Burrhus Frederic

First and middle names of psychologist B. F. Skinner.

Burroughs, Daniel Benjamin

Real name of "Lifeguard" (Jim Byrnes), Organized Crime Bureau contact of undercover agent Vinnie Terranova (Ken Wahl) in the TV series *Wiseguy.*

The Burrow

Home of the Weasley family in the Harry Potter series of books by J. K. Rowling.

Burrows, Dallas Frederick

Real name of actor Orson Bean.

Burrows, Tony

Lead vocalist for many studio groups with *Billboard* top-40 hits, including The Brotherhood of Man, Edison Lighthouse, First Class, Pipkins, and White Plains.

Burt

Middle name of film producer Louis B. Mayer.

Burt, Harry

Founder of the Good Humor ice cream company, in Youngstown, Ohio, in 1920.

Burton, Charles

See **Benjamin Bowring**

Burton/Taylor films

See **Taylor/Burton films**

"The Bus"

Nickname of NFL running back Jerome Bettis, for his ability to maneuver around tackles.

"A Busher's Letters"

Subtitle of the Ring Lardner book *You Know Me Al.*

"Bushie"

Pet name of President George W. Bush and his wife Laura for each other.

Bushwood Country Club

Setting of the films *Caddyshack* and *Caddyshack II.*

business partners

Anheuser-Busch: Eberhard Anheuser, Adolphus Busch
Baskin Robbins: Burton Baskin, Irvine Robbins
Bausch and Lomb: John Jacob Bausch, Henry Lomb
Ben & Jerry's: Ben Cohen, Jerry Greenfield
Black and Decker: Samuel Black, Alonzo Decker
H&R Block: Henry and Richard Bloch
Currier and Ives: Nathaniel Currier, James Ives
Dow Jones: Charles Dow, Edward Jones
Fisher-Price: Herman Fisher, Irving Price
Funk and Wagnalls: Isaac Funk, Adam Wagnalls
Harley-Davidson: William Harley; Walter, William, and Arthur Davidson
Hewlett Packard: William Hewlett, David Packard
Johnson & Johnson: James Johnson, Edward Johnson
Merrill Lynch: Charles Merrill, Edward Lynch
Pitney Bowes: Arthur Pitney, Walter Bowes
Price Waterhouse: Samuel Price, Edwin Waterhouse
Rand McNally: William Rand, Andrew McNally
Rolls-Royce: Charles Rolls, Frederick Royce
Procter and Gamble: William Procter, James Gamble
Sears, Roebuck: Richard Sears, Alvah Roebuck
Sherwin-Williams: Henry Sherwin, Edward Williams
Smith and Wesson: Horace Smith, Daniel Wesson
Wells Fargo: Henry Wells, William Fargo

Busted Flush

Houseboat of John D. MacDonald sleuth Travis McGee.

Buster

Pet dog of character Edith Ann in the comedy routines of Lily Tomlin.

Busterkeys, Walter

Stage name used by pianist Liberace early in his career.

Butch

Pet dog of the Mertzes (William Frawley and Vivian Vance) in the TV sitcom *I Love Lucy*.

Butcher Hollow, Kentucky

Birthplace of country singer Loretta Lynn.

Butchers Run Films

Production company of actor Robert Duvall.

Butcher, Susan

Four-time winner of the Iditarod Trail Sled Dog Race, in 1986, 1987, 1988 and 1990.

Butch's Place

Bar owned by Butch Engle (Hoagy Carmichael) in the film *The Best Years of Our Lives*.

Butkus

Pet dog of Rocky Balboa (Sylvester Stallone) in the film *Rocky*.

Butler

Pet Great Dane of James T. Kirk (William Shatner) in the *Star Trek* films.

The Butler Cabin

Setting on the Augusta National course where the annual TV presentation of the green jacket is made to the winner of the Masters golf tournament.

Butler, Harold

Founder of the Denny's restaurant chain. The first Denny's, originally called "Danny's Donuts," opened in Lakewood, California, in 1953.

But Millions

Original title of the Cole Porter musical *Red, Hot and Blue*. It was later called *Wait for Baby* before taking its final name.

butterbeer

Drink served at Hogsmeade's Three Broomsticks Inn, in the Harry Potter series of books by J. K. Rowling.

Buttercup

Family cow in the Louisa May Alcott novel *Little Men*.

Butterfield, Daniel

Civil War Union general who wrote the music to "Taps."

"butterfly"

See **Charrière, Henri**

Buttermilk

Horse of Western star Dale Evans.

"Button Nose"

Ronald Reagan's nickname for his first wife, Jane Wyman.

Buttons

Pet chimpanzee of the Reynolds family in the TV sitcom *Me and the Chimp*.

Pet dog of Mindy (voiced by Nancy Cartwright) in the children's animated TV series *Animaniacs*.

Butts, Alfred

Unemployed architect who invented Scrabble in 1933.

Butts, Professor Lucifer Gorgonzola

Creator of the elaborate gadgetry in the cartoons of Rube Goldberg.

"Buy 'em by the sack"

Advertising slogan of the White Castle hamburger chain.

Buy the Book

Bookstore owned by the title character (Ellen DeGeneres) in the TV sitcom *Ellen*.

"Buzz"

See **Windrip, Berzelius "Buzz"**

Buzz Bee

Cartoon mascot of Honey Nut Cheerios.

Buzz Buzzard

Nemesis of cartoon character Woody Woodpecker.

Bwana Devil

The first 3-D feature film, which premiered in 1952.

"Bye bye baby!"

Catchphrase of New York Giants broadcaster Russ Hodges for a home-team home run.

Byerly Turk, Darley Arabian, and Godolphin Barb

The three "foundation sires" imported to England from the Mediterranean circa 1700, from which all Thoroughbred racehorses are descended. In particular, about 80 percent of today's Thoroughbreds are descended from Eclipse, a great-great-grandson of Darley Arabian.

Bypass

Southern town that is the setting of the comic strip *Kudzu*.

The Byrds, original members

Gene Clark, Mike Clarke, David Crosby, Chris Hillman, and Roger McGuinn.

Byron

Middle name of actor James Dean.

Byron Nelson Award

Presented annually since 1980 to the Senior PGA's scoring leader.

Bysshe

Middle name of English poet Percy Shelley.

Bytown

Original name of Ottawa, Canada. It took its present name in 1854.

byzanium

Fictitious radioactive element sought by Dirk Pitt in the Clive Cussler novel *Raise the Titanic!*

Byzantium

Original name of Istanbul, Turkey. It was known as Constantinople from 330 to 1930 A.D. before adopting its present name.

Cable Satellite Public Affairs Network
What the letters in C-SPAN stand for.

Cabo da Roca, Portugal
Westernmost point in continental Europe.

Cabot Cove, Maine
Home of Jessica Fletcher (Angela Lansbury) in the TV series *Murder, She Wrote*.

Cabrillo, Juan Rodríguez
Spanish explorer who discovered what is now California, landing at San Diego Bay on September 28, 1542.

Cabrini Circus
Circus blown onto Pee-wee Herman's (Paul Reubens') farm by a windstorm, in the film *Big Top Pee-wee*.

Cactus
Allied code name for Guadalcanal during World War II.

"Cactus Jack"
Nickname of John Nance Garner, Franklin D. Roosevelt's vice president during his first two terms.

Cade, Dr. Robert
University of Florida medical school professor who invented Gatorade in 1965.

caduceus
Serpent-entwined staff that is the symbol of the medical profession.

Caesar
Pet dog of the title character (James Coburn) in the film *Our Man Flint*.

Caesar and Cleo
Stage name used by Sonny and Cher early in their careers.

Café Huguette
Restaurant that Jerry Mulligan (Gene Kelly) and Adam Cook (Oscar Levant) live above, in the film *An American in Paris*.

Cafe Nervosa
Seattle coffeehouse hangout in the TV sitcom *Frasier*.

Cage/Fish & Associates
Boston law-firm employer of the title character (Calista Flockhart) in the TV series *Ally McBeal*.

Cagney/Bogart films
See **Bogart/Cagney films**

Cahulawassee River
Setting of the James Dickey novel *Deliverance* and the film adaptation of the same name.

Caidin, Martin
See **Cyborg**

Caine, Virgil
Singer of the Joan Baez tune "The Night They Drove Old Dixie Down," according to the lyrics.

Calamity Jane
Favorite putter of golf great Bobby Jones.

Caldecott Medal
Awarded annually by the American Library Association for the most distinguished new American picture book for children. Named for 19th-century English illustrator Randolph Caldecott, it was first awarded to illustrator Dorothy Lathrop in 1938 for *Animals of the Bible*.

Calder Memorial Trophy
Awarded annually since 1933 to the NHL rookie of the year, named for former NHL president Frank Calder.

Caldwell
Real last name of cab driver "Reverend" Jim Ignatowski (Christopher Lloyd) in the TV sitcom *Taxi*. He changed his name because he believed that "Ignatowski" spelled backwards was "star child."

Caledonia
Ancient Roman name for Scotland.

"The California Comet"

Nickname of tennis great Don Budge.

California Dolls

Wrestling tag team of Iris (Vicki Frederick) and Molly (Laurene Landon) in the film . . . *All the Marbles*.

California Perfume Company

Original name of Avon.

California Raisins

Quartet created by Claymation artist Will Vinton in 1986 for TV commmercials of the California Raisin Advisory Board. The Raisins' names: A.C., Beebop, Red, and Stretch.

"Californy, Here We Come"

Debut episode of the TV sitcom *The Real McCoys*, which aired on October 3, 1957.

Calling All Girls

See *Polly Pigtails*

Calogero

Real first name of actor Chazz Palminteri.

Calumet, Colorado

Setting of the film *Red Dawn*.

Calverton

Setting of the 1950s version of the TV series *Lassie*.

Calvin Coolidge High

School that is the setting of the film *Up the Down Staircase*.

Camel Lips

Rock band in the film *Serial Mom*, portrayed by rock band L7.

Camfield Place

Hertfordshire, England, estate of author Beatrix Potter, later owned by author Dame Barbara Cartland.

Campbell

Middle name of actor George C. Scott.

Campbell, Mary

Only two-time winner of the Miss America Pageant, in 1922 and 1923.

Camp Chippewa

Summer camp attended by Wednesday and Pugsley Addams (Christina Ricci and Jimmy Workman) in the film *Addams Family Values*.

Camp Crowder

Missouri army base where Rob Petrie (Dick Van Dyke) meets his future wife Laura (Mary Tyler Moore) in the TV sitcom *The Dick Van Dyke Show*.

Camp Crystal Lake

Setting of the film *Friday the 13th*.

Camp Fremont

California setting of the final season of the TV sitcom *The Phil Silvers Show* aka *You'll Never Get Rich*.

Camp Grenada

Summer camp that is the setting of the Allan Sherman tune "Hello Muddah, Hello Fadduh!"

Camp Henderson, California

Setting of the TV sitcom *Gomer Pyle, U.S.M.C.*

Camp Inch

Summer camp attended by identical twins Sharon McKendrick and Susan Evers (Hayley Mills) in the Disney film *The Parent Trap* (1961).

Camp Little Wolf

Summer-camp setting of the film *Little Darlings*.

Camp Mohawk

Snobby rival summer camp of Camp North Star in the film *Meatballs*.

Camp North Star

Setting of the film *Meatballs*.

Camp Pendleton, California

Setting of the TV series *The Lieutenant*.

Camp Rainier

Washington State setting of the film *An Officer and a Gentleman*.

Camp Singleton, California

Marine base where Major John MacGillis (Gerald McRaney) is stationed in the TV sitcom *Major Dad*.

Camp Swampy

Setting of the comic strip *Beetle Bailey*.

Camp Tamakwa

Setting of the film *Indian Summer*.

Canadian English

Common Canadian expressions that are not common in the U.S., including words that have different meanings in Canada and the U.S.:

back bacon: Canadian bacon
boomie: baby boomer
cabbagetown: urban slum
chesterbed: convertible sofa
chippy: irritable
chuck: water
dog's breakfast: hodgepodge
fuddle-duddle: depart
goaler: goalie (ice hockey)
loonie (or loony): $1 coin
moosemilk: moonshine
returned man: veteran of a foreign war
salt chuck: ocean
silly-sider: lefthander
twoonie (or toonie): $2 coin
wastelot: unkempt vacant lot

"The Canadian Kipling"

Nickname of poet Robert Service.

Canaima, California

Setting of the film *Arachnophobia*.

Canary, Martha Jane

Real name of Western frontierswoman Calamity Jane.

Candido, Candy

Comedian with whom Bud Abbott teamed in the early 1960s, after the death of Lou Costello.

"Can Do"

Motto of the U.S. Navy builders unit, the Seabees. "Seabees" is short for "construction battalion."

The Canfield Decision

1976 political novel written by former vice president Spiro Agnew.

canities

Medical term for the graying or whitening of hair.

Cannibalistic Humanoid Underground Dwellers

What the letters in the title of the film *C.H.U.D.* stand for.

Cannonball Express

Memorable train of engineer John Luther "Casey" Jones, which ran between Memphis, Tennessee, and Canton, Mississippi.

Canonsburg, Pennsylvania

Birthplace of singers Perry Como and Bobby Vinton.

"Cantstandya"

High-school nickname of George Costanza (Jason Alexander), given to him by his gym coach, in the TV sitcom *Seinfeld*.

Canty, Tom

See **Edward and Canty, Tom**

"Can we talk?"

Catchphrase of comedienne Joan Rivers.

Canyon High

School attended by the title characters in the TV series *Whiz Kids*.

"Canyon of Heroes"

See **ticker-tape parade honorees**

Cape Cod Casualty Company, Inc.

Firm that insures St. Catherine Labouré Hospital in the film *The Verdict*.

"The Caped Crusader"

Nickname of Batman.

Cape Flattery, Washington

Home of the title characters (Marjorie Main, Percy Kilbride) in the Ma and Pa Kettle series of films.

Cape Kennedy

Former name (1963–73) of Cape Canaveral, Florida, for President John F. Kennedy.

Caper One

Satellite retrieval crew in the film *The Andromeda Strain*.

Capeside High

Massachusetts school attended by the main characters in the TV series *Dawson's Creek*.

Capital General Hospital

Washington, D.C., setting of the TV sitcom *Temperature's Rising*.

"Capitalist tool"

Advertising slogan of *Forbes* magazine.

capitals of the United States

See **United States national capitals**

"Capitals" of the world

A representative sampling of the many such self-created "official" nicknames:
Blueberry: Cherryfield, Maine
Bluebird: Bickleton, Washington

Carpet: Dalton, Georgia
Chili: Hatch, New Mexico
Christmas Tree: Indiana County, Pennsylvania
Copper: Kearny, Arizona
Covered Bridge: Parke County, Indiana (home of 32 covered bridges)
Entertainment: Las Vegas, Nevada
Folk Music: Mountain View, Arkansas
Frog: Rayne, Louisiana
Furniture: High Point, North Carolina
Garlic: Gilroy, California
Halibut Fishing: Homer, Alaska
Hog: Kewanee, Illinois
Honey: Uvalde, Texas
Horse: Lexington, Kentucky
Horseradish: Collinsville, Illinois
Ice Cream: Le Mars, Iowa (home of Blue Bunny ice cream)
Killer Bee: Hidalgo, Texas (where killer bees first entered the U.S. in 1990)
Media: Burbank, California
Opal: Coober Pedy, Australia (where most of the world's opals are produced)
Pottery: Marshall, Texas
Poultry: Georgia (by legislative act)
Quartz Crystal: Mount Ida, Arkansas
Roller Coaster: Cedar Point Amusement Park, Sandusky, Ohio (home of 14 roller coasters, more than anywhere else in the world)
Soybean: Decatur, Illinois
Scarecrow: Walton, New York
Shark Tooth: Venice, Florida
Sock: Fort Payne, Alabama
Submarine: Groton, Connecticut
Watermelon: Cordele, Georgia

Caplin, Alfred Gerald
Real name of *Li'l Abner* cartoonist Al Capp.

Cappa Films
Production company of director Martin Scorsese.

Caprica
Home world of Adama (Lorne Greene) that is destroyed by the evil Cylons in the TV series *Battlestar Galactica*.

Caprice, Big Boy
Capone-like gangster in the film *Dick Tracy* (1990), portrayed by Al Pacino under heavy makeup.

Capricorn Crude
Novel written by Val Ewing (Joan Van Ark), whose characters are modeled after her in-laws, in the TV series *Knots Landing*.

capsaicin
See **Scoville units**

Captain Flint
Pet parrot of Long John Silver in the Robert Louis Stevenson novel *Treasure Island*.

Captain Howdy
Imaginary friend of Regan MacNeil (Linda Blair) that turns out to be a demon, in the film *The Exorcist*.

Captain Jack
Pet alligator of Beaver and Wally Cleaver (Jerry Mathers and Tony Dow) in the TV sitcom *Leave it to Beaver*.

Captain Trips
Name given to the killer virus in the Stephen King novel *The Stand*.

carapace
Scientific name for the upper (dorsal) shell of a turtle or tortoise.

Caravella, Johnny
Real name of Dr. Johnny Fever (Howard Hesseman) in the TV sitcom *WKRP in Cincinnati*.

"Car-Boy-Girl"
Story by Gordon Buford that was the basis for the Disney film *The Love Bug*.

Cárdenas, García López de
Associate of Francisco de Coronado who in 1540 became the first European to see the Grand Canyon.

cardinal virtues
See **virtues, cardinal**

cardiotachometer
Instrument for measuring heart rate.

Cardona, Florencia Bisenta de Casillas Martinez
Real name of singer Vikki Carr.

Cardway Corporation
Business that is the setting of the TV series *Executive Suite*.

CAREFUL / NERVOUS MOTHER DRIVING
Sign on the back of the family bus in the TV sitcom *The Partridge Family*.

"Caretaker"

Debut episode of the TV series *Star Trek: Voyager*, which aired on January 16, 1995.

Carey, Scott

Title character (Grant Williams) in the sci-fi film *The Incredible Shrinking Man*.

Carfax Abbey

English estate of the title character in the Bram Stoker novel *Dracula*.

caries

Dentists' term for tooth decay.

Carioca

Term for a native of Rio de Janeiro, Brazil, from which the dance of the same name is derived.

Carl

Real first name of trumpeter Doc Severinsen, former bandleader on *The Tonight Show*.

High-school mule mascot in the TV sitcom *Evening Shade*.

Carl and the Passions

See **The Pendletones**

Carlinsky, Dan

See **Trivia**

Carlos Ray

Real first and middle names of actor Chuck Norris.

Carlson, Chester

Inventor of the photocopier, patented in 1937.

Carlton Academy

Prep school attended by Billy Wyatt (Mark Harmon) in the film *Stealing Home*.

Carlton Arms Hotel

New York City home of the title character (Gale Storm) in the TV sitcom *My Little Margie*.

Carlton Hotel

Where John Robie (Cary Grant) stays while in Cannes, in the Alfred Hitchcock film *To Catch a Thief*.

Carmichael

Pet polar bear of Jack Benny on his radio show. Carmichael guarded Benny's basement safe.

Carney, Frank and Don

College students who founded the Pizza Hut chain. The first Pizza Hut opened in 1958 in Wichita, Kansas.

Caroline Irene

Real first and middle names of Scarlett O'Hara's sister Carreen, in the Margaret Mitchell novel *Gone With the Wind*.

Carolinum

See **The World Set Free**

Carpathia

See **Rostron, Arthur Henry**

Carpenter, John

Connecticut IRS agent who was the first person to win the top prize of $1 million on the American edition of the TV game show *Who Wants to Be a Millionaire*, on November 19, 1999.

Carpentier, Harlean

Real name of actress Jean Harlow.

car-racing flags

See **auto-racing flags**

Carr, Felicia

Role for which Lee Grant won a Best Supporting Actress Academy Award in the 1975 film *Shampoo*.

Carrie Nations

Female rock trio in the film *Beyond the Valley of the Dolls*.

Carrie Productions

Production company of actor Danny Glover.

The Cars, members of

Elliot Easton, Greg Hawkes, Ric Ocasek, Benjamin Orr, and David Robinson.

Carson

Real first name of singer (Carson) Wayne Newton.

Last name of Barbie's boyfriend Ken.

Carson, Johnny, characters of

As portrayed by Carson on *The Tonight Show*:
    Floyd R. Turbo (archconservative)
    Aunt Blabby (gossip)
    Carnac the Magnificent (psychic)
    Art Fern (huckster and host of the Tea Time Movie)

Carson, Kris
Stage name used by singer Kris Kristofferson early in his career.

Carswell, G. Harrold
See **Haynsworth Jr., Clement F. and Carswell, G. Harrold**

Carter, Garnet
Inventor of miniature golf, originally called "Tom Thumb golf." His first course was built at the Fairyland Inn resort in Lookout Mountain, Tennessee, circa 1927.

Cartwright, Nancy
Voice of Bart Simpson in the TV animated sitcom *The Simpsons*.

Caruthers
Middle name of impressionist Rich Little.

Carvel
Small-town setting of the Andy Hardy series of films.

Carver High
Los Angeles school that is the setting of the TV series *The White Shadow*.

Carver Media Group
Mega-conglomerate owned by Elliot Carver (Jonathan Pryce) in the James Bond film *Tomorrow Never Dies*.

Casa Del Gato
San Francisco nightclub owned by Pepe (Robert Carricart) that serves as the office of the title character (Robert Loggia) in the TV series *T.H.E. Cat*.

Casa Loma Orchestra
Band led by Glen Gray.

La Casa Pacifica
"Western White House" of President Richard Nixon in San Clemente, California.

Cascade, Washington
Setting of the TV series *The Sentinel*.

Caselotti, Adriana
Voice of Snow White in the Disney animated film *Snow White and the Seven Dwarfs*. She has one line in the film *The Wizard of Oz*—speaking "Wherefore art thou, Romeo?" in the Tin Man's song "If I Only Had a Heart."

"The Case of the Restless Redhead"
Debut episode of the TV series *Perry Mason*, which aired on September 21, 1957.

Case, Tiffany
Diamond smuggler (Jill St. John) who teams up with James Bond (Sean Connery) in the film *Diamonds Are Forever*.

Casey
Newt's (Carrie Henn's) doll in the film *Aliens*.

Casey, Harry Wayne
Real name of the lead singer (KC) of disco group KC and the Sunshine Band.

Casey Junior
Circus train in the Disney animated film *Dumbo*.

Casey, Katie
Girl who, according to the introductory verse, sings the refrain of the tune "Take Me Out to the Ball Game," written by Jack Norworth and Albert von Tilzer in 1908. The verse in full:
    Katie Casey was baseball mad
    Had the fever and had it bad
    Just to root for the home town crew
    Ev'ry sou Katie blew
    On a Saturday, her young beau
    Called to see if she'd like to go
    To see a show, but Miss Kate said, "No,
    I'll tell you what you can do"
    (Take me out to the ball game . . .)

Casino Gardens
Coney Island nightclub where Steve Laird (Dean Martin) performs and Seymour (Jerry Lewis) parks cars, in the film *My Friend Irma*.

Cassotto, Walden Robert
Real name of pop singer Bobby Darin.

Castelluccio, Francis
Real name of pop singer Frankie Valli.

Castevet, Minnie
Role for which Ruth Gordon won a Best Supporting Actress Academy Award in the 1968 film *Rosemary's Baby*.

Castle Adamant
Alternate title of the Gilbert and Sullivan comic opera *Princess Ida*.

Castle Rock Entertainment

Production company of director Rob Reiner, which was sold to Turner Broadcasting in 1993 and is today a subsidiary of AOL Time Warner.

Castle Rock, Maine

Home of the title canine in the Stephen King novel *Cujo*.

Castle Rock, Oregon

Setting of the film *Stand by Me*. The Stephen King story upon which the film was based is set in Castle Rock, Maine.

cast members

Term used by the Disney Corporation for its employees.

Castorini, Loretta

Role for which Cher won a Best Actress Academy Award in the 1987 film *Moonstruck*.

Castorini, Rose

Role for which Olympia Dukakis won a Best Supporting Actress Academy Award in the 1987 film *Moonstruck*.

Cat

Pet cat of Holly Golightly (Audrey Hepburn) in the film *Breakfast at Tiffany's*.

"The Cat"

Nickname of NHL Hall of Fame coach Emile Francis.

Nickname of reformed jewel thief John Robie (Cary Grant) in the Alfred Hitchcock film *To Catch a Thief*.

Catalano, Armando

Real name of actor Guy Williams.

Catbert

Evil Human Resources Director in the comic strip *Dilbert*.

cat breeds

These 40 breeds of cats are currently recognized by the Cat Fanciers' Association:

CHAMPIONSHIP CLASS (35)

Abyssinian
American Curl
American Shorthair
American Wirehair
Balinese
Birman
Bombay
British Shorthair
Burmese
Chartreux
Colorpoint Shorthair
Cornish Rex
Devon Rex
Egyptian Mau
Exotic
Havana Brown
Japanese Bobtail
Javanese
Korat
Maine Coon
Manx
Norwegian Forest Cat
Ocicat
Oriental
Persian
Russian Blue
Ragdoll
Scottish Fold
Selkirk Rex
Siamese
Singapura
Somali
Tonkinese
Turkish Angora
Turkish Van

PROVISIONAL CLASS (1)

European Burmese

MISCELLANEOUS CLASS (4)

American Bobtail
LaPerm
Siberian
Sphynx

Catch-18

Original title of the Joseph Heller novel *Catch-22*. The title was changed to avoid confusion with the Leon Uris novel *Mila 18*, which had recently been published.

"Catch a Falling Star"

1958 Perry Como tune that was the first single to be certified as a Gold Record (sales of one million) by the Recording Industry Association of America.

Catcher in the Wry

1982 autobiography of baseball broadcaster (and former catcher) Bob Uecker.

Catch You Later

1979 autobiography of Hall of Fame baseball catcher Johnny Bench.

Caterpillar Club

Organization whose members have successfully bailed out of an aircraft.

Catfish Row

Charleston, South Carolina, tenement that is the setting of the George Gershwin opera *Porgy and Bess.*

"The Cathedral of Commerce"

Nickname of the 55-story Woolworth Building in New York City, the tallest building in the world when it was completed in 1913.

Catholics

Original nickname of the athletic teams of Notre Dame. The teams were also known as the Ramblers before taking "Fighting Irish" as their official nickname in 1927.

Cat, Stimpson J.

Full name of Stimpy (voiced by Billy West) in the animated TV series *The Ren & Stimpy Show.*

Cavall

Favorite hound of legendary English monarch King Arthur.

Cavalry Trilogy

Group of Western films directed by John Ford, all based on short stories by James Warner Bellah. The titles of these short stories are listed below with the films.

Fort Apache (1948): "Massacre"
She Wore a Yellow Ribbon (1949): "War Party" and "The Big Hunt"
Rio Grande (1950): "Mission with No Record"

Cavendish

Name of the familiar variety of yellow bananas.

Cave of Wonders

Where the title character (voiced by Scott Weinger, singing by Brad Kane) finds the magic lamp, in the Disney animated film *Aladdin.*

Cavilleri

Maiden name of Jenny Barrett (Ali MacGraw) in the film *Love Story.*

Cavoukian

Last name of children's entertainer Raffi.

Cayuga Productions

Production company of Rod Serling.

Cazale, John

Actor whose brief Hollywood career consisted of five films, all of which were nominated for Best Picture Academy Awards:

The Godfather (1972)
The Conversation (1974)
The Godfather Part II (1974)
Dog Day Afternoon (1975)
The Deer Hunter (1976)

CB radio codes

These are similar to police radio codes (listed separately).

10-1	Receiving poorly
10-2	Receiving well
10-3	Stop transmitting
10-4	Message received
10-5	Relay message
10-6	Busy, stand by
10-7	Out of service, going off the air
10-8	In service
10-9	Repeat message
10-10	Transmission completed, standing by
10-11	Talking too quickly
10-12	Visitors present
10-13	Advise of weather and road conditions
10-16	Make pickup at __
10-17	Urgent business
10-18	Anything for us?
10-19	Nothing for you, return to base
10-20	My location is __
10-21	Contact by landline
10-22	Report in person to __
10-23	Stand by
10-24	Last assignment completed
10-25	Can you contact __
10-26	Disregard last information
10-27	I am moving to channel __
10-28	Identify your station
10-29	Time is up for contact
10-30	Does not conform to FCC rules
10-32	I will give you a radio check
10-33	Emergency traffic at this station
10-34	Trouble at this station, help needed
10-35	Confidential information
10-36	Correct time is __
10-37	Tow truck needed at __
10-38	Ambulance needed at __
10-39	Your message delivered
10-41	Please tune to channel __
10-42	Traffic accident at __
10-43	Traffic congestion at __
10-44	I have a message for you
10-45	All units report
10-50	Break channel __

10-60   What is the next message number?
10-62   Unable to copy, use landline
10-63   Network directed to __
10-64   Network clear
10-65   Waiting for next message
10-67   All units comply
10-70   Fire at __
10-71   Proceed with transmission in sequence
10-73   Speed trap at __
10-75   You are causing interference
10-77   Negative contact
10-81   Reserve hotel room for __
10-82   Reserve room for __
10-84   My telephone number is __
10-85   My address is __
10-89   Radio repair needed at __
10-90   I have TV interference
10-91   Talk closer to the microphone
10-92   Your transmitter is out of adjustment
10-93   Check my frequency on this channel
10-94   Please give me a long count
10-95   Transmit dead carrier for five seconds
10-99   Mission completed, all units secure
10-100 Five-minute break
10-200 Police needed at __

CBS Studio 50

See **Oscar Hammerstein Theater**

Cecil Scott

First and middle names of novelist C. S. Forester.

Cedar Creek, California

California town whose residents are infected with a deadly virus in the film *Outbreak*.

Cedar Hill

Washington, D.C., home of orator Frederick Douglass.

"Celebrate the Century" subjects

Stamps issued by the United States Postal Service from 1998 to 2000, one sheet of 15 different stamps per decade. Subjects for the 1950s through 1990s stamps were voted on by the American people.

1900s

Ash Can school painters
Crayola crayons
W. E. B. Du Bois (social activist)
First World Series
Gibson Girl
The Great Train Robbery (1903 film)
Ellis Island immigrants arrive
Kitty Hawk 1903 (the Wright brothers)
Model T Ford

John Muir (preservationist)
Pure Food and Drug Act of 1906
Robie House, Chicago (Frank Lloyd Wright design)
President Theodore Roosevelt
St. Louis World's Fair (1904)
Teddy bear created

1910s

Armory Show (historic 1913 art show)
George Washington
Charlie Chaplin's Little Tramp
Child labor reform
Construction toys
Jack Dempsey wins heavyweight boxing title (1919)
First crossword puzzle (1913)
Federal Reserve System (1913)
Grand Canyon National Park (1919)
Panama Canal opens (1914)
Jim Thorpe, star at the 1912 Summer Olympics at Stockholm
Telephone spans the nation
U.S. Boy Scouts and Girl Scouts begin
U.S. enters World War I
President Woodrow Wilson

1920s

19th Amendment (women's suffrage)
American Realism (painting style)
Art Deco
Babe Ruth
Electric toy trains
Emily Post's etiquette
Flappers do the Charleston
Four Horsemen of Notre Dame (football players)
The Gatsby style
Jazz flourishes
Charles Lindbergh flies the Atlantic
Margaret Mead (anthropologist)
Prohibition enforced
Radio entertains America
Stock market crash (1929)

1930s

America survives the depression
Empire State Building
Golden Gate Bridge
Gone With the Wind (1936 bestseller)
Household conveniences
Bobby Jones wins golf's Grand Slam (1930)
Life magazine's first issue (1936)
Monopoly (the game)
The New Deal
Jesse Owens' six world records in track
Eleanor Roosevelt

President Franklin D. Roosevelt
Snow White and the Seven Dwarfs debuts
Streamline design (locomotive)
Superman arrives (1938)

1940s

Abstract expressionism
Antibiotics save lives
Big Bands
Citizen Kane
The G.I. Bill (1944)
International style of architecture
The jitterbug sweeps the nation
Postwar Baby Boom
Jackie Robinson
A Streetcar Named Desire (1947)
President Harry S Truman
Slinky craze begins (1945)
TV entertains America
Women support war effort
World War II

1950s

3-D movies
Desegregating public schools
Drive-in movies
I Love Lucy
The Korean War
Rocky Marciano, undefeated heavyweight box-
　ing champ
Polio vaccine developed
Dr. Seuss' *The Cat in the Hat*
Rock 'n' Roll
"The Shot Heard 'Round the World" (Bobby
　Thomson's dramatic ninth-inning home run
　in the final game of the 1951 National League
　playoff)
Stock car racing
Tail fins and chrome
Teen fashions
U.S. launches satellite (*Explorer 1*)
World Series rivals (New York Yankees and
　Brooklyn Dodgers)

1960s

Barbie doll
The Beatles
Ford Mustang
Green Bay Packers
"I Have a Dream" speech of Dr. Martin Luther
　King Jr.
Integrated circuit
Lasers
Man walks on the moon
Roger Maris hits 61 home runs (1961)
The Peace Corps

Peace symbol
Star Trek
Super Bowl I
The Vietnam War
Woodstock

1970s

1970s fashions
All in the Family
Disco music
Earth Day celebrated
Smiley Face
Jumbo jets
Medical imaging
Monday Night Football
Pioneer 10 approaches Jupiter (1973)
Pittsburgh Steelers win four Super Bowls
Secretariat wins horse racing's Triple Crown
Sesame Street
U.S. celebrates 200th birthday
VCRs transform entertainment
Women's Rights movement

1980s

Cabbage Patch Kids
Cable TV
Cats
Compact disks
The Cosby Show
E. T. The Extra-Terrestrial
Fall of the Berlin Wall
Figure skating
Hip-hop culture
Hostages come home
Personal computers
San Francisco 49ers
Space Shuttle program
Video games
Vietnam Veterans Memorial

1990s

Baseball records
Cellular phones
Computer art and graphics
Extreme sports
The Gulf War
Improving education
Jurassic Park
Recovering species
Return to space
Seinfeld
Special Olympics
Sport utility vehicles
Titanic
Virtual reality
World Wide Web

Celeste

Wife of Babar in the series of children's books by Jean and Laurent de Brunhoff.

Celestial City

Destination of Christian in the John Bunyan book *Pilgrim's Progress*.

"Celluloid Heroes" stars

This tune by The Kinks mentions these film stars (in order):

Greta Garbo
Rudolph Valentino
Bela Lugosi
Bette Davis
George Sanders
Mickey Rooney
Marilyn (Monroe)

cement pond

What the Clampett family calls its swimming pool, in the TV sitcom *The Beverly Hillbillies*.

Centaur Pendragon

Pet Irish wolfhound of actor Rudolph Valentino.

centenarians, noted

Famous people who lived to be 100 or more:

George Abbott, Broadway producer (1887–1995)
Irving Berlin, songwriter (1888–1989)
Eubie Blake, songwriter (1883–1983)
Elizabeth Bowes-Lyon, Britain's Queen Mother, and mother of Queen Elizabeth II (1900–)
George Burns, comedian (1896–1996)
Irving Caesar, lyricist (1895–1996)
Madame Chiang Kai-shek (1897–)
Jimmie Davis, Louisiana governor who wrote the tune "You Are My Sunshine" (1899–2000)
Bessie and Sarah Delany, authors (1891–1995 and 1889–1999, respectively)
Mary Harris "Mother" Jones, labor organizer (1830–1930)
Joseph Nathan Kane, historian/reference-book author (1899–)
Rose Kennedy, mother of president John F. Kennedy (1890–1995)
Alf Landon, 1936 Republican presidential candidate (1887–1987)
Francis Lederer, actor (1899–2000)
Jean MacArthur, wife of General Douglas MacArthur (1898–2000)
Grandma Moses, painter (1860–1961)
Myron "Grim" Natwick, animator who created Betty Boop (1890–1990)
Irving Rapper, director (1898–1999)

Hal Roach, film producer (1892–1992)
Nellie Tayloe Ross, first woman to be a state governor (1876–1977)
Sir Thomas Sopwith, aircraft designer (1888–1989)
Amos Alonzo Stagg, college football coach (1862–1965)
Señor Wences, ventriloquist (1896–1999)
Estelle Winwood, actress (1882–1984)
Adolph Zukor, founder of Paramount Pictures (1873–1976)

CLOSE, BUT NO CIGAR

Carl Barks, Disney cartoonist who created Scrooge McDuck (1901–2000)
Dave Beck, former Teamsters president (1894–1993)
Dame Barbara Cartland, romance novelist (1901–2000)
John Nance Garner, FDR's first vice president (1868–1967)
Lillian Gish, actress (October 14, 1893–February 27, 1993)
Abel Kiviat, Olympic runner (1892–1991)
S. S. Kresge, retail-chain founder (1867–1966)
Georgia O'Keeffe, painter (1887–1986)

Centerville

Setting of the radio and TV versions of the sitcom *The Aldrich Family*.

Central City

Setting of the TV sitcom *The Many Loves of Dobie Gillis*.

Home of comics superhero The Flash.

Central Perk

Coffeehouse hangout in the TV sitcom *Friends*.

Century 21 Exposition

Official name of the Seattle World's Fair of 1962.

Century Studios

Film studio that is the setting of the TV series *Bracken's World*.

cephalgia

Medical term for a headache.

cerumen

Medical term for earwax.

César

See **film awards, national**

Cesira

Role for which Sophia Loren won a Best Actress Academy Award in the 1961 film *Two Women*.

cesta

Term for the basket used for catching and throwing the ball in jai alai.

Cetacean

Submarine of the Foundation for Oceanic Research in the TV series *The Man from Atlantis*.

C.F.&W. Railroad

Owner of the Cannonball Express in the TV sitcom *Petticoat Junction*.

"Cha Cha"

Nickname of drag racer Shirley Muldowney.

Chad Allen and the Expressions

Former name of rock group The Guess Who.

Chain Reaction and Pipe Dream

The two rock groups that joined to form the group Aerosmith.

"The Chairman of the Board"

Nickname of Hall of Fame baseball pitcher Whitey Ford.

Nickname of singer Frank Sinatra.

Challenger

Favorite horse of heiress Judith Traherne (Bette Davis), cared for by stableman Michael O'Leary (Humphrey Bogart), in the film *Dark Victory*.

Challenger astronauts

The crew of seven who perished in the explosion 73 seconds after liftoff on January 28, 1986.
  Francis R. "Dick" Scobee (commander)
  Michael J. Smith (pilot)
  Ronald E. McNair (mission specialist)
  Ellison S. Onizuka (mission specialist)
  Judith A. Resnik (mission specialist)
  Gregory B. Jarvis (payload specialist)
  S. Christa McAuliffe (payload specialist, civilian schoolteacher)

Chal Productions

Production company of actor Al Pacino.

Chamberlain, Maine

Setting of the Stephen King novel *Carrie*.

Chameleon Church

Rock group for which Chevy Chase was a drummer before he became a regular on the TV series *Saturday Night Live*.

Champagne bottle sizes

  Magnum: 2 standard-size bottles (of .75 liters each)
  Jeroboam: 4 bottles
  Rehoboam: 6 bottles
  Methuselah: 8 bottles
  Salmanazar: 10–12 bottles
  Balthazar: 16 bottles
  Nebuchadnezzar: 20 bottles

"The Champagne Lady"

Nickname of singer Norma Zimmer, a star of *The Lawrence Welk Show* from 1960 to 1982. The nickname was previously that of Alice Lon, who was on the program from 1955–1959.

"Champagne Tony"

Nickname of pro golfer Tony Lema.

"Champagne wishes and caviar dreams"

Sign-off line of host Robin Leach in the TV series *Lifestyles of the Rich and Famous*.

Chance

See **Homeward Bound: The Incredible Journey animals**

Chandler, Catherine

The "Beauty" title character (Linda Hamilton) of the TV series *Beauty and the Beast*.

Chandos

Middle name of singer Joan Baez.

"Changing Keys"

Instrumental theme of the TV game show *Wheel of Fortune*.

Chapman, John

Real name of tree-planting folk hero Johnny Appleseed.

Chapman, Ray

Cleveland Indian shortstop who was the only major-league baseball player to die as the direct result of a game-related injury. He was struck on the head by a pitch thrown by New York Yankee pitcher Carl Mays at the Polo Grounds on August 17, 1920, and died later that day.

Charalambides

Original family surname of Nick Charles in the Dashiell Hammett novel *The Thin Man*. According to the novel, his father's surname was changed by an Ellis Island official.

Charger

Horse of Heath Barkley (Lee Majors) in the TV series *The Big Valley*.

"Chariot"

French tune that (with English lyrics) became the Little Peggy March tune "I Will Follow Him."

Charity

See **Faith, Hope, and Charity**

Charlemagne the Lion and Humphrey the Hound Dog

Puppets that appeared with Walter Cronkite during his brief 1954 stint on *The Morning Show*.

Charles

First name of former U.S. surgeon general C. Everett Koop.

Real first name of actor/director (Charles) Robert Redford.

Middle name of sci-fi author Arthur C. Clarke.

Middle name of boxer Sugar Ray Leonard, who was named for singer Ray Charles.

Charles Dillon

Real first and middle names of Hall of Fame baseball manager Casey Stengel.

Charles Eugene

Real first and middle names of singer Pat Boone.

Charles, Jeannette

Queen Elizabeth II look-alike who has portrayed the Queen in several films, including *National Lampoon's European Vacation* and *The Naked Gun: From the Files of Police Squad!*

Charles Leo

Real first and middle names of Hall of Fame baseball catcher Gabby Hartnett.

Charles, Leslie Sebastian

Real name of pop singer Billy Ocean.

Charles Philip Arthur George

Full name of Prince Charles of Great Britain.

Charleston Club

Employer of Pinky Pinkham (Dorothy Provine) in the TV series *The Roaring Twenties*.

Charleston, Dick and Dora

Amateur sleuths (David Niven and Maggie Smith) in the film *Murder by Death*. Their names are inspired by the Dashiell Hammett characters Nick and Nora Charles from *The Thin Man*.

Charlestown Chiefs

Minor-league hockey team for which Reggie Dunlop (Paul Newman) is player-coach, in the film *Slap Shot*.

Charley

Title character of the Disney film *The $1,000,000 Duck*.

Charley Horse, Lamb Chop, and Hush Puppy

Sock puppets of TV ventriloquist Shari Lewis.

Charlie

Pet dog of Professor Ned Brainard (Fred MacMurray) in the Disney film *The Absent-Minded Professor*.

Pet dog of Laurel Scott (Katharine Ross) in the film *The Final Countdown*.

Charlie and the Chocolate Factory

Novel by Roald Dahl that was the basis for the film *Willy Wonka and the Chocolate Factory*.

"Charlie Hustle"

Nickname of baseballer Pete Rose, coined by Mickey Mantle.

Charlie's Angels (TV) title characters

From the 1976–81 TV series.
  Sabrina Duncan (Kate Jackson): 1976–79
  Jill Munroe (Farrah Fawcett-Majors): 1976–77
  Kelly Garrett (Jaclyn Smith)
  Kris Munroe (Cheryl Ladd): 1977–81
  Tiffany Welles (Shelley Hack): 1979–80
  Julie Rogers (Tanya Roberts): 1980–81

Charlie the Tuna

Cartoon character in TV commercials for Star-Kist tuna, voiced by Herschel Bernardi.

Charlie Wong's Ice Cream Parlor

Teen hangout in the TV sitcom *The Many Loves of Dobie Gillis*.

Charrière, Henri
Author and title character of the book *Papillon*, portrayed in the film adaptation of the same name by Steve McQueen. "Papillon" is the French word for "butterfly."

Chartwell
Kent, England, country house of Winston Churchill, which he purchased in 1922.

Chastain, Brandi
Scorer of the clinching "shootout" goal in the victory of the U.S. over China in the 1999 women's World Cup soccer finals.

Château D'If
Where Edmund Dantès is imprisoned in the Alexandre Dumas novel *The Count of Monte Cristo*.

Chauchoin, Lily
Real name of actress Claudette Colbert.

Chauncey
Cougar in 1960s TV commercials for Ford Motor Company.

Cheap Trick original members
Bun E. Carlos, Rick Nielsen, Tom Petersson, and Robin Zander.

The Cheatin' Hearts
Backup band of country singer Hank Williams Jr., named for his father's tune "Your Cheatin' Heart."

The Checkered Game of Life
The first mass-produced parlor game, developed by Milton Bradley circa 1860.

Checkers
Pet cocker spaniel of Richard Nixon in the 1950s.

"Checkpoint Charlie"
Nickname of the site at Friedrichstrasse in Berlin, Germany, that from 1961–90 was the only point at which foreigners could enter East Berlin.

Chee-Chee
Pet chimp of the title character in the Doctor Dolittle series of children's novels by Hugh Lofting.

Cheers' "*Jeopardy!*" episode
The categories played by Cliff Clavin (John Ratzenberger) on the episode of the TV sitcom *Cheers* in which he was a *Jeopardy!* contestant:
Bar Trivia

Beer
Civil Servants
Mothers and Sons
Stamps from Around the World
Celibacy

Cheese
Original family surname of actor John Cleese. It was changed to Cleese by his father Reginald.

"Cheesecake"
Childhood nickname of composer George Gershwin, whose father operated a bakery.

cheese sources
Most of the varieties of cheese that are popular in the U.S. are made from cow's milk. The varieties listed below are the notable exceptions:
chèvre: goat
feta: goat or sheep
mozzarella: water buffalo
Pecorino: sheep
Roquefort: sheep

chemical element symbols, single-letter

B	boron	O	oxygen
C	carbon	P	phosphorus
F	fluorine	S	sulfur
H	hydrogen	U	uranium
I	iodine	V	vanadium
K	potassium	W	tungsten
N	nitrogen	Y	yttrium

Cher Ami
U.S. Army Signal Corps carrier pigeon that delivered numerous messages to American troops at Verdun during World War I, and was awarded the French Croix de Guerre with Palm.

"The Cherokee Cowboy"
Nickname of country singer Ray Price.

The Cherokee Kid
Stage name used by humorist Will Rogers as a trick roper, early in his career.

Cherokee Productions
Former production company of actor James Garner.

Cherry Alley Productions
Production company of actress Goldie Hawn.

Cheryl Ann
Tugboat of Captain John Herrick (Preston Foster) in the TV series *Waterfront*.

Chesapeake

Frigate commanded by Captain James Lawrence in a battle with the H.M.S. *Shannon* on June 1, 1813, off Boston (during the War of 1812), during which he uttered the memorable words, "Don't give up the ship!"

Chessie and Peake

Feline mascots of the Chesapeake and Ohio Railway.

Chester A. Arthur Elementary School

School rigged with a fake bomb in the film *Die Hard with a Vengeance*.

Chester and Lester

Country-music album recorded by Chet Atkins and Les Paul, which won a 1976 Grammy Award for Best Country Instrumental Performance.

The Chestnuts

Surrey, England, home of author Lewis Carroll.

Cheviot Hills

Neighborhood that is the setting of the TV sitcom *The Ropers*.

Chewbacca

Wookiee sidekick of Han Solo (Harrison Ford) in the film *Star Wars*, portrayed by Peter Mayhew.

Chewing

Magazine about gum that Calvin has a subscription to, in the comic strip *Calvin and Hobbes*.

Cheyenne

See **Lakota Sioux, Cheyenne, and Arapaho**

Chez Glamour

Nightclub employer of Chuck Murray and Ferdie Jones (Abbott and Costello, respectively) in the film *Hold That Ghost*.

Chez Louisiane

New Orleans Creole restaurant operated by Frank Parrish (Tim Reid) in the TV sitcom *Frank's Place*.

Chez Luis

See **Froman, Abe**

Chicago Chronicle

Newspaper employer of Larry Appleton (Mark Linn-Baker) and Balki Bartokomous (Bronson Pinchot) in the TV sitcom *Perfect Strangers*.

Chicago nicknames

In the order mentioned in the Carl Sandburg poem "Chicago":
Hog Butcher for the World
Tool Maker
Stacker of Wheat
Player with Railroads
The Nation's Freight Handler
City of the Big Shoulders

Chicago (rock group) original members

Peter Cetera, Terry Kath, Lee Loughnane, Robert Lamm, James Pankow, Walt Parazaider, and Danny Seraphine.

Chicago Packers

Original name of the Washington Wizards at their NBA inception in 1961.

"The Chicago Seven"

Group of radicals tried by Judge Julius Hoffman in 1969–70 for conspiring to incite a riot at the 1968 Democratic National Convention in Chicago.
Rennie Davis
David Dellinger
John Froines
Tom Hayden
Abbie Hoffman
Jerry Rubin
Lee Weiner
The group was originally the Chicago Eight; Bobby Seale was severed from the case soon after the trial began, having been jailed for contempt for repeated verbal abuse of Judge Hoffman.

Chicago Weekly

Magazine whose offices are the setting for the TV sitcom *Anything but Love*.

chick-a-pen

John J. Brown (Harve Presnell's) term of endearment for his wife Molly Tobin Brown (Debbie Reynolds) in the film *The Unsinkable Molly Brown*.

Chicken Heaven

Fast-food restaurant where Jennifer Keaton (Tina Yothers) has an after-school job in the TV sitcom *Family Ties*.

"A chicken in every pot; a car in every garage"

Slogan of the Republican party in the presidential campaign of 1928.

"chickie run"

See **Millertown Bluff**

Chico's Bail Bonds

Sponsors of the title Little League team in the film *The Bad News Bears*.

"The Chicoutimi Cucumber"

Nickname of NHL Hall of Fame goalie Georges Vezina, for his "cool" style of play.

Chiffon

Pet dog of Franceska Andrassy (Roberta Shore) in the Disney film *The Shaggy Dog*.

The Children's Crusade: A Duty-Dance with Death

Alternate title of the Kurt Vonnegut novel *Slaughterhouse-Five*.

Children's Supermart

Original name of the Toys "R" Us retail chain.

Chim

Pet chimpanzee of the title character (Irish McCalla) in the TV series *Sheena, Queen of the Jungle*.

Chim Chim

Pet monkey of the title character (voiced by Peter Fernandez) in the children's animated TV series *Speed Racer*.

Chimera

Deadly virus that agent Ethan Hunt (Tom Cruise) must destroy or recover in the film *Mission: Impossible 2*.

Chingachgook

Indian chief in James Fenimore Cooper's *Leather-Stocking Tales*.

Chipper

Pet dog of Barry Lockridge (Stefan Arngrim) in the TV series *Land of the Giants*.

Chipping, Arthur "Mr. Chips"

Role for which Robert Donat won a Best Actor Academy Award in the 1939 film *Goodbye, Mr. Chips*.

chiromancer

Technical term for a palm reader.

Chlorinol

Secret ingredient in Comet cleanser.

Chlorophyll and Retsyn

Breath-freshening ingredients in Clorets breath mints.

Chocolate Shake and Chocolate Chip

Tour buses used by country group The Oak Ridge Boys.

chocolate syrup

What director Alfred Hitchcock used for blood in the shower scene of his (black-and-white) film *Psycho*.

"Chocolate Thunder"

Nickname of NBA star Darryl Dawkins, for his frequent shattering of backboards with his slam dunks.

Choc-u-lator

Solar-powered calculator that looks and smells like a Hershey chocolate bar. (No, it's not edible.)

Chopin

Pet Persian cat of author F. Scott Fitzgerald.

Chopper, Nick

Name of the Tin Woodman in the Wizard of Oz book series by L. Frank Baum.

Chow Phya

Ship that brings schoolteacher Anna Leonowens to Siam, in the Rodgers and Hammerstein musical *The King and I*.

Christa Brooke Camille

Real first and middle names of actress Brooke Shields.

Christensen, Diana

Role for which Faye Dunaway won a Best Actress Academy Award in the 1976 film *Network*.

Christian

Real first name of pro football Hall of Fame quarterback Sonny Jurgensen.

Christian Broadcasting Network

Original name of the Fox Family Channel.

Christiania

Former name of Oslo, Norway. It took its present name in 1925.

Christian Rudolf

Real first and middle names of actor Buddy Ebsen.

Christina

Yacht of Greek shipping magnate Aristotle Onassis, named for his daughter.

Private jet of singer Frank Sinatra, named for his daughter.

Christine, Virginia

Actress who portrayed Mrs. Olson in TV commercials for Folger's Coffee.

Christmas

Real first name of Chrissy Snow (Suzanne Somers) in the TV sitcom *Three's Company.*

"The Christmas Song"

Title of the tune, cowritten by Mel Tormé, that begins, "Chestnuts roasting on an open fire."

Christopher, George

Real name of "Christy" (Gary Vinson) in the TV sitcom *McHale's Navy.*

Christy, Don

Stage name used by singer Sonny Bono early in his career.

The Chronic Argonauts

Original title of the H. G. Wells novel *The Time Machine.*

The Chronicles of Narnia

Series of seven children's books by C. S. Lewis.
   The Lion, the Witch and the Wardrobe (1950)
   Prince Caspian (1951)
   The Voyage of the Dawn Treader (1952)
   The Silver Chair (1953)
   The Horse and His Boy (1954)
   The Magician's Nephew (1955)
   The Last Battle (1956)

Chronoskimmer

Time-travel device used by the title character of the video game "Where in Time Is Carmen Sandiego?"

Chub

Horse of Hoss Cartwright (Dan Blocker) in the TV Western series *Bonanza.*

The Chubby Waters Show

CBS radio series where Eugene Jerome is employed as a comedy writer in the Neil Simon play *Broadway Bound.*

Chudley Cannons

Favorite pro Quidditch team of Ron Weasley, in the Harry Potter series of books by J. K. Rowling.

C.H.U.M.P.

Acronym for Criminal Headquarters for Underworld Master Plan, evil organization intent on ruling the world, in the children's TV series *Lancelot Link, Secret Chimp.* C.H.U.M.P. is led by Baron von Butcher.

"Chump Change"

Instrumental theme of the TV game show *Now You See It,* composed by Quincy Jones.

Chun, Ellery

Hawaiian clothing merchant who created the first aloha shirt in 1931.

Chunuchi Dragons

Japanese team for which Jack Elliot (Tom Selleck) plays, in the film *Mr. Baseball.*

Church

Cat that returns from the dead in the Stephen King novel *Pet Sematary.*

Churchill, Winston

Pet lion of actress Tallulah Bankhead.

Church of the What's Happening Now

Where Flip Wilson character Reverend Leroy preaches.

Chwatt, Aaron

Real name of comedian Red Buttons.

Ciccone, Madonna Louise

Full name of pop singer Madonna.

Cicely, Alaska

Setting of the TV series *Northern Exposure.*

Cicero

Nephew of cartoon character Porky Pig.

Ciminella, Christina

Real name of country singer Wynonna Judd.

Cimmeria

Homeland of the title character in the Conan book series by Robert E. Howard.

"The Cinderella Man"

Nickname of 1930s heavyweight boxing champ James J. Braddock.

"Cindy Lou"

Original title of the Buddy Holly tune "Peggy Sue."

Cinque
See **DeFreeze, Donald**

Cipango
Name used in Marco Polo's time for Japan.

circadian dysrhythmia
Technical term for jet lag.

Circle H Ranch
Girls' dude ranch in the "Further Adventures of Spin and Marty" segment of the children's TV series *The Mickey Mouse Club*.

"Ciribiribin"
Theme song of bandleader Harry James.

Cisco
Horse of Lieutenant John Dunbar (Kevin Costner) in the film *Dances with Wolves*.

The Cisco Kid
Role for which Warner Baxter won a Best Actor Academy Award in the 1929 film *In Old Arizona*.

Citation
See **Pacer, Ranger, Corsair, and Citation**

Cities Service
Original name of CITGO gasoline, which took its present name in 1965.

"The Citizen King"
Nickname of 19th-century French king Louis Philippe.

Citizen-News
Newspaper in which Jane Hudson (Bette Davis) advertises for an accompanist, in the film *Whatever Happened to Baby Jane?*

City Lights Films
Production company of director Martin Brest.

City of Angels Investigations
Original name of Blue Moon Detective Agency in the TV series *Moonlighting*.

City of Destruction
Departure point of Christian in the John Bunyan book *Pilgrim's Progress*.

"The City of Light"
Nickname of Paris, France.

The City Slickers
Band led by Spike Jones.

Ciudad Trujillo
Former name (1936–61) of Santo Domingo, capital city of the Dominican Republic, for former president Rafael Trujillo.

"Civium in moribus rei publicae salus"
Motto of the University of Florida, which is Latin for "The welfare of the state rests in the character of its citizen."

Clairton, Pennsylvania
Setting of the film *The Deer Hunter*.

Clam, A. Pismo
Director of the film being shot in Lompoc, California, in the film *The Bank Dick*.

Clapp
Real last name of rock guitarist/singer Eric Clapton.

Clarence
Real first name of actor Larry "Buster" Crabbe.

Pet lion of the Tracy family in the TV series *Daktari*.

Real first name of Lumpy Rutherford (Frank Bank), friend of Wally Cleaver (Tony Dow) in the TV sitcom *Leave It to Beaver*.

Clarence Eugene
Real first and middle names of country singer Hank Snow.

Clarissa
First name of the title character in the Virginia Woolf novel *Mrs. Dalloway*.

Clark, Barney
Retired dentist who became the world's first recipient of an artificial heart, at the University of Utah in 1982. Clark lived for 112 days after the operation.

Clarksdale Register
Local newspaper in the Tennessee Williams play *Cat on a Hot Tin Roof*.

Clark Street Hospital
Chicago setting of the TV sitcom *E/R* (1984–85).

clasp-locker
See **Judson, Whitcomb**

"The Class" artists

This Chubby Checker tune mentions these musical artists (in order):

Fats (Domino)	Ricky (Nelson)
The Coasters	Frankie (Avalon)
Elvis (Presley)	Fabian
Cozy (Cole)	

"Class of Beverly Hills"

Debut episode of the TV series *Beverly Hills 90210*, which aired on October 4, 1990.

Claude

Pet poodle of Margaret Drysdale (Harriet MacGibbon) in the TV sitcom *The Beverly Hillbillies*.

Claudet, Madelon

Role for which Helen Hayes won a Best Actress Academy Award in the 1931 film *The Sin of Madelon Claudet*.

Claudia Alta

Real first and middle names of former First Lady Lady Bird Johnson.

clavicle

Medical term for the collarbone.

Clavileño

Wooden horse of Sancho Panza in the Miguel de Cervantes novel *Don Quixote de la Mancha*.

claw hold

Submission tactic of 1960s pro wrestler Killer Kowalski.

Claymoore

Psychiatric hospital that is the setting of the film *Girl, Interrupted*.

Clayton, John

Father of Tarzan, aka Lord Greystoke, in the stories of Edgar Rice Burroughs.

Clayton, Patti

First singer of the familiar jingle for Chiquita bananas, which began airing on radio in 1944.

"cleaning woman"

Phrase that causes detective Rigby Reardon (Steve Martin) to lose control, in the film *Dead Men Don't Wear Plaid*.

Cleansweep 7

Type of broomstick used by Fred and George Weasley, in the Harry Potter series of books by J. K. Rowling.

Clearwater, Texas

Setting of the film *The Sons of Katie Elder*.

Cleary, John

Role for which Jack Albertson won a Best Supporting Actor Academy Award in the 1968 film *The Subject Was Roses*.

Cleaves Mills, Maine

Setting of the Stephen King novel *The Dead Zone*.

Cleishbotham, Jedediah

Pen name used by Scottish author Sir Walter Scott.

Clematis

Pet dog of Genesis, the family handyman, in the Booth Tarkington novel *Seventeen*.

Clementine

Spelding family cat in the film *Visit to a Small Planet*.

Clements

Maiden name of Val Ewing (Joan Van Ark) in the TV series *Knots Landing*.

Cleo

Pet goldfish of Geppetto in the Disney animated film *Pinocchio*.

Pet basset hound of Sock Miller (Jackie Cooper) in the TV sitcom *The People's Choice*, voiced by Mary Jane Croft.

See also **Caesar and Cleo**

Cleopatra

Pet African Strangler plant of Morticia Addams (Carolyn Jones) in the TV sitcom *The Addams Family*.

Sow of Betty and Bob (Claudette Colbert and Fred MacMurray) in the film *The Egg and I*.

Clerow

Real first name of comedian Flip Wilson.

Clifford

Middle name of Gregory Montgomery (Thomas Gibson) in the TV sitcom *Dharma and Greg*.

The Clinkers

Bumbling robot couple portrayed by the title mimes in the TV comedy/variety series *Shields and Yarnell*.

Clinton Corners, Georgia

Setting of the TV sitcom *Carter Country*.

"Clipper"

See **Boeing passenger planes**

Clive Staples

First and middle names of author C. S. Lewis.

clo

Unit of measurement for the thermal insulation value of clothing. A wool business suit has an insulation value of about one clo.

Clockwork Wizards

Life-size wind-up band created by the title character (Vincent Price) in the film *The Abominable Dr. Phibes*.

Clokey, Art

Creator of the clay animation character Gumby. The character first appeared in five-minute segments of the children's TV series *Howdy Doody*.

Clongoweswood College

School attended by Stephen Dedalus in the James Joyce novel *A Portrait of the Artist as a Young Man*.

Clortho, Vinz

Spirit who possesses the body of accountant Louis Tully (Rick Moranis) in the film *Ghostbusters*.

close encounters

As publicized for the Steven Spielberg film *Close Encounters of the Third Kind*.
   close encounter of the first kind: sighting of
      a UFO
   close encounter of the second kind: physical evidence
   close encounter of the third kind: contact

"Closer to Free"

Theme song of the TV series *Party of Five*, performed by The Bodeans.

Cloud City

See **Bespin**

Clowers, Clifton

Mountain man in the Claude King tune "Wolverton Mountain."

"The Clown Prince of Baseball"

Nickname of baseball comic Al Schacht, and his de-facto successor Max Patkin.

"The Clown Prince of Basketball"

Nickname of Harlem Globetrotters star Meadowlark Lemon.

Cloyd

See **Gidney and Cloyd**

Club Intime

New York City employer of hostess Mary Dwight (Bette Davis) in the film *Marked Woman*.

Club Obi Wan

Shanghai setting of the opening scene of the Steven Spielberg film *Indiana Jones and the Temple of Doom*, where Willie Scott (Kate Capshaw) sings "Anything Goes" in Chinese. The club is presumably named for the character Obi-Wan Kenobi in *Star Wars*, whose director, George Lucas, was an executive producer of this film.

Clue suspects, weapons, and rooms

As featured in the standard edition of the whodunit board game.

SUSPECTS (6)

Mr. Green (green token)
Colonel Mustard (yellow token)
Mrs. Peacock (blue token)
Professor Plum (purple token)
Miss Scarlet (red token)
Mrs. White (white token)
(the victim's name is Mr. Boddy)

WEAPONS (6)

Candlestick
Knife
Lead pipe
Revolver
Rope
Wrench

ROOMS (9)

Ballroom
Billiard room
Conservatory
Dining Room
Hall
Kitchen
Library
Lounge
Study

Clutterbuck, Captain Cuthbert

Pen name used by author Sir Walter Scott.

Clybourne Park

Chicago neighborhood that the Younger family is moving to, in the Lorraine Hansberry play *A Raisin in the Sun*.

Clyde

Camel of the title character in the Ray Stevens tune "Ahab the Arab."

Orangutan sidekick of Philo Beddoe (Clint Eastwood) in the films *Every Which Way but Loose* and *Any Which Way You Can*.

See also **Inky, Blinky, Pinky, and Clyde; Stuart and Clyde**

"Coach"

Nickname of bartender Ernie Pantusso (Nicholas Colasanto) in the TV sitcom *Cheers*.

Coach and Horses

Inn where the title character is a lodger, in the H. G. Wells novel *The Invisible Man*.

The Coasters, original members

Carl Gardner, Billy Guy, Leon Hughes, and Bobby Nunn.

"The Coast is Toast"

Slogan used to promote the film *Volcano*.

Cobblepot, Oswald

Real name of Batman adversary The Penguin.

Cobb's

Employer of supermarket manager Howard Bannister (Don Adams) in the TV sitcom *Check It Out*.

Cochise

Horse of Little Joe Cartwright (Michael Landon) in the TV series *Bonanza*.

"Cockroach"

Sergeant Schultz's (John Banner's) nickname for Corporal Louis LeBeau (Robert Clary), in the TV sitcom *Hogan's Heroes*.

Cocktails & Dreams

Bar opened by Brian Flanagan (Tom Cruise) in the film *Cocktail*.

coco butt

Head-to-head smashing move popularized in the 1960s by pro wrestler Bobo Brazil.

Coconino County

Setting of the comic strip *Krazy Kat*.

Cocozza, Alfredo

Real name of opera singer Mario Lanza.

Code 7

Boat of Roger Murtaugh (Danny Glover) in the film *Lethal Weapon 4*.

Cody College of Mines and Agriculture

Western setting of the film *Girl Crazy* (1943).

Cody's Speedrome

Demolition-derby arena owned by Michelle "Mike" Cody (Jamie Lee Curtis) in the film *Grandview, U.S.A.*

"Coffee Cantata"

Nickname of Johann Sebastian Bach's Cantata #211.

Cogburn, Reuben J. "Rooster"

Role for which John Wayne won a Best Actor Academy Award in the 1969 film *True Grit*.

Cogswell Cogs

Business rival of Spacely's Space Sprockets in the children's animated TV sitcom *The Jetsons*.

Cohan, George M.

Role for which James Cagney won a Best Actor Academy Award in the 1942 film *Yankee Doodle Dandy*.

Cohen, Ellen Naomi

Real name of singer "Mama" Cass Elliot, of The Mamas & the Papas.

Cohen, Jacob

Real name of comedian Rodney Dangerfield.

Cohn, Nik

See **"Tribal Rites of the New Saturday Night"**

coins, diameter of U.S.

 Penny: .75 inches (19.05 millimeters)
 Nickel: .835 inches (21.21 millimeters)
 Dime: .705 inches (17.91 millimeters)
 Quarter: .955 inches (24.26 millimeters)
 Half Dollar: 1.205 inches (30.61 millimeters)
 Sacagawea Dollar: 1.043 inches (26.5 millimeters)

coins, one foot of U.S.

The number of coins in a one-foot stack.
Pennies: 197
Nickels: 156
Dimes: 226
Quarters: 174
Half Dollars: 142
Sacagawea Dollars: 152

coins, one pound of U.S.

The number of coins per pound.
Pennies: 181
Nickels: 91
Dimes: 200
Quarters: 80
Half Dollars: 40
Sacagawea Dollars: 56

coins, thickness of U.S.

Penny: .061 inches (1.55 millimeters)
Nickel: .077 inches (1.95 millimeters)
Dime: .053 inches (1.35 millimeters)
Quarter: .069 inches (1.75 millimeters)
Half Dollar: .085 inches (2.15 millimeters)
Sacagawea Dollar: .079 inches (2 millimeters)

coins, weight of U.S.

Penny: .088 ounces (2.5 grams)
Nickel: .176 ounces (5 grams)
Dime: .08 ounces (2.268 grams)
Quarter: .2 ounces (5.67 grams)
Half Dollar: .4 ounces (11.34 grams)
Sacagawea Dollar: .286 ounces (8.1 grams)

Colada

Sword of Spanish national hero El Cid.

Colbert

See **Dorsey and Colbert**

Colder, Ben

Stage name used by country singer Sheb Wooley for humorous songs.

Cold Mountain Correctional Facility

Setting of the film *The Green Mile*, and the Stephen King novel of the same name on which it was based.

Coles, Nathaniel Adams

Real name of singer Nat "King" Cole.

Collazo, Oscar and Torresola, Griselio

Puerto Rican nationalists who attempted to assassinate President Harry S Truman at Washington, D.C.'s Blair House, on November 1, 1950. Torresola was killed in the attempt. Collazo was sentenced to death, but his sentence was later commuted by Truman to life imprisonment.

College of New Jersey

Original name of Princeton University, from its founding in 1746 until 1896.

college team nicknames

LISTED ALPHABETICALLY BY NICKNAME:

Aces: Evansville
Aggies: New Mexico State, North Carolina A&T, Texas A&M, Utah State
Anteaters: California-Irvine
Aztecs: San Diego State
Badgers: Wisconsin
Bearcats: Cincinnati
Bearkats: Sam Houston State
Bears: Baylor, Brown, Mercer, Morgan State, Southwest Missouri State
Beavers: Oregon State
Bengals: Idaho State
Big Green: Dartmouth
Big Red: Cornell
Billikens: St. Louis
Bison: Bucknell, Howard
Black Bears: Maine
Blackbirds: Long Island-Brooklyn
Blazers: Alabama-Birmingham
Blue Demons: DePaul
Blue Devils: Central Connecticut State, Duke
Blue Raiders: Middle Tennessee State
Bluejays: Creighton
Bobcats: Montana State, Ohio, Southwest Texas State
Boilermakers: Purdue
Bonnies: St. Bonaventure
Braves: Alcorn State, Bradley, Quinnipiac
Broncos: Boise State, Santa Clara, Western Michigan
Broncs: Rider, Texas-Pan American
Bruins: California-Los Angeles
Buccaneers: Charleston Southern, East Tennessee State
Buckeyes: Ohio State
Buffaloes: Colorado
Bulldogs: Butler, The Citadel, Drake, Fresno State, Georgia, Gonzaga, Louisiana Tech, Mississippi State, North Carolina-Asheville, Samford, South Carolina State, Yale
Bulls: Buffalo, South Florida
Cadets: Army
Cardinal: Stanford

Cardinals: Ball State, Lamar, Louisville
Catamounts: Vermont, Western Carolina
Cavaliers: Virginia
Chanticleers: Coastal Carolina
Chippewas: Central Michigan
Colonials: George Washington, Robert Morris
Colonels: Eastern Kentucky, Nicholls State
Commodores: Vanderbilt
Cornhuskers: Nebraska
Cougars: Brigham Young, Chicago State, College of Charleston, Houston, Washington State
Cowboys: McNeese State, Oklahoma State, Wyoming
Crimson: Harvard
Crimson Tide: Alabama
Crusaders: Holy Cross, Valparaiso
Cyclones: Iowa State
Delta Devils: Mississippi Valley State
Demon Deacons: Wake Forest
Demons: Northwestern State
Dolphins: Jacksonville
Dons: San Francisco
Dragons: Drexel
Ducks: Oregon
Dukes: Duquesne, James Madison
Eagles: American, Boston College, Coppin State, Eastern Michigan, Eastern Washington, Georgia Southern, Morehead State, Winthrop
Elis: Yale
Explorers: La Salle
Falcons: Air Force, Bowling Green
Fightin' Blue Hens: Delaware
Fighting Camels: Campbell
Fighting Illini: Illinois
Fighting Irish: Notre Dame
Fighting Tigers: Louisiana State
Flames: Liberty, Illinois-Chicago
Flyers: Dayton
49ers: Long Beach State, North Carolina-Charlotte
Friars: Providence
Gaels: Iona, St. Mary's-California
Gamecocks: Jacksonville State, South Carolina
Gators: Florida
Gauchos: California-Santa Barbara
Gentlemen: Centenary
Golden Bears: California
Golden Eagles: Marquette, Oral Roberts, Southern Mississippi, Tennessee Tech
Golden Flashes: Kent
Golden Gophers: Minnesota
Golden Griffins: Canisius
Golden Hurricane: Tulsa
Golden Knights: Central Florida
Golden Lions: Arkansas-Pine Bluff

Golden Panthers: Florida International
Governors: Austin Peay State
Green Wave: Tulane
Greyhounds: Loyola-Maryland
Grizzlies: Montana
Hatters: Stetson
Hawkeyes: Iowa
Hawks: Hartford, Maryland-Eastern Shore, Monmouth
Highlanders: Radford
Hilltoppers: Western Kentucky
Hokies: Virginia Tech
Hoosiers: Indiana
Horned Frogs: Texas Christian
Hornets: Alabama State, California-Sacramento, Delaware State
Hoyas: Georgetown
Hurricanes: Miami-Florida
Huskies: Connecticut, Northeastern, Northern Illinois, Washington
Indians: Arkansas State, Northeast Louisiana, Southeast Missouri State
Jaguars: South Alabama, Southern-Baton Rouge
Jaspers: Manhattan
Jayhawks: Kansas
Kangaroos: Missouri-Kansas City
Keydets: Virginia Military
Knights: Fairleigh Dickinson
Leathernecks: Western Illinois
Leopards: Lafayette
Lions: Columbia, Loyola Marymount, Southeast Louisiana
Lobos: New Mexico
Longhorns: Texas
Lumberjacks: Northern Arizona, Stephen F. Austin State
Matadors: California-Northridge
Mavericks: Texas-Arlington
Mean Green: North Texas
Metros: Indiana/Purdue
Midshipmen: Navy
Miners: Texas-El Paso
Minutemen: Massachusetts
Mocs: Tennessee-Chattanooga
Monarchs: Old Dominion
Mountain Hawks: Lehigh
Mountaineers: Appalachian State, Mount St. Mary's, West Virginia
Musketeers: Xavier
Mustangs: Cal Poly-San Luis Obispo, Southern Methodist
Nittany Lions: Penn State
Orangemen: Syracuse
Owls: Florida Atlantic, Rice, Temple

Paladins: Furman

Panthers: Eastern Illinois, Georgia State, Northern Iowa, Pittsburgh, Prairie View A&M, Wisconsin-Milwaukee

Patriots: George Mason

Peacocks: St. Peter's

Penguins: Youngstown State

Phoenix: Wisconsin-Green Bay

Pilots: Portland

Pirates: East Carolina, Hampton, Seton Hall

Pioneers: Oakland

Pride: Hofstra

Privateers: New Orleans

Purple Eagles: Niagara

Quakers: Pennsylvania

Racers: Murray State

Ragin' Cajuns: Southwest Louisiana

Raiders: Wright State

Rainbows: Hawaii

Ramblers: Loyola-Illinois

Rams: Colorado State, Fordham, Rhode Island, Virginia Commonwealth

Rattlers: Florida A&M

Razorbacks: Arkansas

Rebels: Mississippi

Red Flash: St. Francis-Pennsylvania

Red Foxes: Marist

Red Hawks: Miami-Ohio

Red Raiders: Colgate, Texas Tech

Red Storm: St. John's

Redbirds: Illinois State

Retrievers: Maryland-Baltimore

Roadrunners: Texas-San Antonio

Rockets: Toledo

Runnin' Rebels: Nevada-Las Vegas

Saints: Siena

Salukis: Southern Illinois

Scarlet Knights: Rutgers

Seahawks: North Carolina-Wilmington, Wagner

Seminoles: Florida State

Shockers: Wichita State

Skyhawks: Tennessee-Martin

Sooners: Oklahoma

Spartans: Michigan State, Norfolk State, North Carolina-Greensboro, San Jose State

Spiders: Richmond

Stags: Fairfield

Sun Devils: Arizona State

Sycamores: Indiana State

Tar Heels: North Carolina

Terrapins (or Terps): Maryland

Terriers: Boston, St. Francis-New York, Wofford

Thunderbirds: Southern Utah

Thundering Herd: Marshall

Tigers: Auburn, Clemson, Grambling, Jackson State, Memphis, Missouri, Pacific, Princeton, Tennessee State, Texas Southern, Towson

Titans: California-Fullerton, Detroit Mercy

Toreros: San Diego

Tribe: William and Mary

Trojans: Arkansas-Little Rock, Troy State, Southern California

Utes: Utah

Vandals: Idaho

Vikings: Cleveland State, Portland State

Volunteers (or Vols): Tennessee

Waves: Pepperdine

Wildcats: Arizona, Bethune-Cookman, Davidson, Kansas State, Kentucky, New Hampshire, Northwestern, Villanova, Weber State

Wolf Pack: Nevada

Wolfpack: North Carolina State

Wolverines: Michigan

Yellow Jackets: Georgia Tech

Zips: Akron

Collegiate Church of St. Peter, Westminster

Formal name of Westminster Abbey in London. It has technically not been an abbey since the 16th century, when monks last resided there.

Collett, Lorraine

Fresno, California, native who in 1915 became the original model for Sun Maid raisins.

Collins, Eileen

First woman to command a space shuttle mission, heading the *Columbia* flight of July 22–27, 1999.

Collins, Mary Cathleen

Real name of actress Bo Derek.

Collinsport, Maine

Setting of the TV series *Dark Shadows*.

Collinwood

Haunted mansion in the TV series *Dark Shadows*.

"Colonel Bogey"

March by English composer Kenneth J. Alford that is used as the theme music for the film *The Bridge on the River Kwai*.

Colonel Puff-Puff

Childhood soldier doll of Ramon Vega (George Hamilton), in the film *Zorro, The Gay Blade*.

Colonel Warden

Allied code name for Winston Churchill during World War II.

The Colours

Original name of pop group The Bangles.

Colt .45s

Original nickname of the Houston Astros at their National League inception in 1962. The team adopted its present nickname when it moved into the Astrodome for the 1965 season.

Colu

Home planet of Brainiac, comic-book foe of Superman.

Columbia Airlines Flight 109

Setting of the film *Airport 1975*.

Columbiad

Rocket-launching cannon in the Jules Verne novel *From the Earth to the Moon*.

The Columbine

Presidential plane of Dwight D. Eisenhower.

columbium

Original name of the chemical element niobium.

Comanche

Horse, ridden by Captain Miles Keogh, that was the only survivor of the Battle of the Little Bighorn on June 25-26, 1876.

"A Comedy and a Philosophy"

Subtitle of the George Bernard Shaw play *Man and Superman*.

"A Comedy Romance in Pantomime"

Subtitle of the Charlie Chaplin film *City Lights*.

"Come, Friends, Who Plough the Sea"

1879 Gilbert and Sullivan tune from *The Pirates of Penzance* whose melody was used by Theodore Morse for the 1917 tune "Hail! Hail! The Gang's All Here."

"Come on down!"

Phrase that announces new contestants on the TV game show *The Price Is Right*, spoken by announcer Johnny Olson and his successor Rod Roddy.

"Come On, Get Happy"

See **"When We're Singin'"**

Comet

Family dog in the TV sitcom *Full House*.

Horse of Superman.

Comfort

Middle name of stained-glass artist Louis Tiffany.

Coming Attractions

Film-review show hosted by Jay Sherman (voiced by Jon Lovitz) in the animated TV series *The Critic*.

Commencement City

Original name of Tacoma, Washington.

Commerce Bank of Beverly Hills

Where Jed Clampett (Buddy Ebsen) keeps his fortune, in the TV sitcom *The Beverly Hillbillies*.

"The Commerce Comet"

Early nickname of baseball Hall of Famer Mickey Mantle, derived from Commerce, Oklahoma, Mantle's hometown.

Commerce High

School attended by Deanie (Natalie Wood) and Bud (Warren Beatty) in the film *Splendor in the Grass*.

Committee for State Security

See **Komitet Gosudarstvennoi Bezopasnosti**

Commodores original members

William King, Ronald LaPread, Thomas McClary, Walter "Clyde" Orange, Lionel Richie, and Milan Williams.

commonwealths, U.S.

Four of the 50 states call themselves "commonwealths": Kentucky, Massachusetts, Pennsylvania, and Virginia.

Communiqué

New York City magazine whose offices are the setting of the TV series *Central Park West*.

Community Chests and Councils of America

Original name (1918–65) of the United Way. It was known as United Community Funds and Councils of America from 1965 to 1970, when it took its present name.

compact disk, read-only memory

What the letters in CD-ROM stand for.

"The company you keep"

Advertising slogan of New York Life.

composer biopics (classical)

Listed below by composer, portrayer of the title character, film title and year:

Ludwig van Beethoven (Gary Oldman): *Immortal Beloved* (1994)

Frédéric Chopin (Cornel Wilde): *A Song to Remember* (1945)

Edvard Grieg (Toralv Maurstad): *Song of Norway* (1970)

George Frideric Handel (Wilfrid Lawson): *The Great Mr. Handel* (1942)

Franz Liszt (Dirk Bogarde): *Song Without End* (1960)

Franz Liszt (Roger Daltrey): *Lisztomania* (1975)

Gustav Mahler (Robert Powell): *Mahler* (1974)

Wolfgang Amadeus Mozart (Tom Hulce): *Amadeus* (1984)

Nikolai Rimsky-Korsakov (Jean-Pierre Aumont): *Song of Scheherazade* (1947)

Franz Schubert (Alan Curtis): *New Wine* (1941)

Johann Strauss Jr. (Fernand Gravet): *The Great Waltz* (1938)

Johann Strauss Jr. (Horst Buchholz): *The Great Waltz* (1972)

Peter Tchaikovsky (Richard Chamberlain): *The Music Lovers* (1971)

Richard Wagner (Alan Badel): *Magic Fire* (1956)

Richard Wagner (Richard Burton): *Wagner* (1983)

composer biopics (popular)

Listed below by composer, portrayer of the title character, film title and year:

Ernest R. Ball (Dick Haymes): *Irish Eyes Are Smiling* (1944)

George M. Cohan (James Cagney): *Yankee Doodle Dandy* (1942)

Paul Dresser (Victor Mature): *My Gal Sal* (1942)

Daniel Decatur Emmett (Bing Crosby): *Dixie* (1943)

Stephen Foster (Douglass Montgomery): *Harmony Lane* (1935)

Stephen Foster (Don Ameche): *Swanee River* (1939)

Stephen Foster (Bill Shirley): *I Dream of Jeannie* (1952)

George Gershwin (Robert Alda): *Rhapsody in Blue* (1945)

Gilbert and Sullivan (Robert Morley and Maurice Evans, respectively): *The Great Gilbert and Sullivan* (1953)

Gilbert and Sullivan (Jim Broadbest and Allan Corduner, respectively): *Topsy-Turvy* (1999)

Woody Guthrie (David Carradine): *Bound for Glory* (1976)

W. C. Handy (Nat "King" Cole): *St. Louis Blues* (1958)

Victor Herbert (Walter Connolly): *The Great Victor Herbert* (1939)

Joseph E. Howard (Mark Stevens): *I Wonder Who's Kissing Her Now* (1947)

Scott Joplin (Billy Dee Williams): *Scott Joplin* (1977)

Gus Kahn (Danny Thomas): *I'll See You in My Dreams* (1951)

Bert Kalmar and Harry Ruby (Fred Astaire and Red Skelton, respectively): *Three Little Words* (1950)

Jerome Kern (Robert Walker): *Till the Clouds Roll By* (1946)

Cole Porter (Cary Grant): *Night and Day* (1946)

Rodgers and Hart (Tom Drake and Mickey Rooney, respectively): *Words and Music* (1946)

Sigmund Romberg (José Ferrer): *Deep in My Heart* (1954)

John Philip Sousa (Clifton Webb): *Stars and Stripes Forever* (1952)

Compost

Allied code name for English foreign secretary (later prime minister) Anthony Eden during World War II.

computerized axial tomography

What the "CAT" in "CAT scan" stands for. Tomography is the x-raying of cross-sections of the body.

Computing-Tabulating-Recording Company

Original name of IBM.

Concepción

See *Victoria*

The Concert Feature

Original working title of the Disney animated film *Fantasia*.

conchologist

Technical term for an expert in or collector of seashells.

Concord

Elegantly appointed "mail coach" that was the leading model of stagecoach in the Old West during the second half of the 19th century. It was named for the Concord, New Hampshire home of its manufacturer, the Abbott-Downing Company.

The Concord School

Setting of the TV series *The Headmaster*, starring Andy Griffith as the title character.

The Cone of Silence

Anti-eavesdropping device lowered from the ceiling, used for secret conversations by CONTROL agents in the TV sitcom *Get Smart*.

Conger, Darva and Rockwell, Rick

Couple who married on the short-lived TV series *Who Wants to Marry a Multi-Millionaire*. Their marriage was annulled shortly thereafter.

Congress of Racial Equality

What name of civil-rights organization CORE is an acronym for. CORE was founded in Chicago by James Farmer in 1942.

Conklin, Ethel

Full name of Mrs. C. (Peg Murray) in the TV sitcom *Me & Mrs. C.*

Conn, Catharine

Real name of actress Kitty Carlisle.

Connecticut Leather Company

Original name of Coleco, the toy company best known for its Cabbage Patch Kids, which went into bankruptcy in the 1980s.

Connecticut Yankees

Band led by Rudy Vallee.

Connelly, Carol

Role for which Helen Hunt won a Best Actress Academy Award in the 1997 film *As Good As It Gets*.

Connemara

Flat Rock, North Carolina, home of author/poet Carl Sandburg.

Connor, Macauley "Mike"

Role for which James Stewart won a Best Actor Academy Award in the 1940 film *The Philadelphia Story*.

Connor, Roger

See 138

Connors and Davenport

Advertising-agency employer of Ann Romano (Bonnie Franklin) in the TV sitcom *One Day at a Time*.

Conn Smythe Trophy

Awarded annually since 1965 to the most valuable player of the Stanley Cup playoffs. It is named for the former owner of the Toronto Maple Leafs.

Conrad

First name of the title character in the musical *Bye Bye Birdie*.

Conrad, Robert Arnold

Real name of playwright Moss Hart.

Consolidated Companies, Inc.

Employer of Judy Bernly (Jane Fonda), Doralee Rhodes (Dolly Parton) and Violet Newstead (Lily Tomlin) in the film *9 to 5*.

Consolidated Kitchenware Company

Employer of bookkeeper Vic Gook (Art Van Harvey) in the radio sitcom *Vic and Sade*.

Consolidated Life of New York

Employer of C. C. Baxter (Jack Lemmon) in the film *The Apartment*.

Constant c Productions

Production company of author Michael Crichton, named for the symbol for the speed of light.

Constantine

Middle name of pro football quarterback Dan Marino.

Middle name of pro football Hall of Fame quarterback Johnny Unitas.

Constantinople

See **Byzantium**

Constant, Marius

Romanian-born composer who created the instrumental theme of the TV series *The Twilight Zone*.

construction battalion

See **"Can Do"**

Consumer News and Business Channel

What the letters in the name of cable network CNBC stand for.

The Contemplative Man's Recreation

Alternate title of the Izaak Walton book *The Compleat Angler*.

Contento

Mule of Father Latour in the Willa Cather novel *Death Comes for the Archbishop*.

Continental Flange Company

Employer of Arnie Nuvo (Herschel Bernardi) in the TV sitcom *Arnie*.

Continental Sports Channel

Cable network whose New York City studios are the setting of the TV sitcom *Sports Night*.

"Contrasts"

Theme song of the Jimmy Dorsey orchestra.

control of electromagnetic radiation

What the name of one-time U.S. civil-defense system Conelrad was an acronym for.

contusion

Medical term for a bruise.

Convent San Tanco

Puerto Rican setting of the TV sitcom *The Flying Nun*.

Conway and Twitty

Pet goldfish of Loretta Haggers (Mary Kay Place) in the TV sitcom *Mary Hartman, Mary Hartman*.

Cook, Ann Turner

Mystery novelist and English teacher whose baby portrait has been used by Gerber baby food since 1928.

Cook County General Hospital

Chicago setting of the TV series *ER* (1994–).

Cook Data Services

Original name of Blockbuster Video.

Cookie, Alistair

Host (aka Cookie Monster) of *Monsterpiece Theatre* in the children's TV series *Sesame Street*.

Cook, Natalie; Sanders, Dylan; and Munday, Alex

Title characters in the film *Charlie's Angels*, portrayed by Cameron Diaz, Drew Barrymore and Lucy Liu, respectively.

Cool, Gomar

See **Mount Idy**

Coombs, Harry

Role for which Art Carney won a Best Actor Academy Award in the 1974 film *Harry and Tonto*.

Cooper, Pat

Role for which Wendy Hiller won a Best Supporting Actress Academy Award in the 1958 film *Separate Tables*.

Copa Club

New York City nightclub where Danny Williams (Danny Thomas) entertains, in the TV sitcom *Make Room for Daddy*.

Copenhagen

Horse of the Duke of Wellington at the Battle of Waterloo on June 18, 1815.

Copernicus

Pet dog of 1955's Dr. Emmett L. Brown (Christopher Lloyd) in the *Back to the Future* films.

"Cophouse"

Debut episode of the TV series *Lou Grant*, which aired on September 20, 1977.

copoclephilist

Technical term for a collector of key rings.

Coppertin

Submarine commanded by Captain Cassidy (Cary Grant) in the film *Destination Tokyo*.

Cora

Shopkeeper in TV commercials for Maxwell House coffee, portrayed by Margaret Hamilton.

"The Corduroy Killer"

Nickname of former world chess champion Bobby Fischer, for the pants he wore during his matches.

Corinne

Real first name of broadcast journalist Cokie Roberts.

Corinth Coffee Shop

Where Susan Parrish (Claire Forlani) first meets the title character (Brad Pitt) in the film *Meet Joe Black*.

"Corkhead"

Family nickname of the title character (Jerry Lewis) in the film *Cinderfella*.

Corleone, Vito

Only role for which two performers have won Academy Awards:
> Marlon Brando (Best Actor): *The Godfather* (1972)
> Robert De Niro (Best Supporting Actor): *The Godfather Part II* (1974)

Corley

Middle name of former Alabama governor George Wallace.

"Cormac Mac Carthy *fortis me fieri fecit*, A.D. 1446"

Inscription on the Blarney Stone, located at Blarney Castle near Cork, Ireland. The inscription translates as "Built in 1446 A.D. by Cormac Mac Carthy."

Corman, Avery

Author of the novel *Kramer vs. Kramer*, upon which the film of the same name was based.

Cornelius

Green rooster on boxes of Kellogg's Corn Flakes.

Cornelius Coot

Ancestor of Donald Duck and founder of his hometown of Duckburg, in the Disney comic books.

Cornelius Crane

Real first and middle names of comedian Chevy Chase.

"Cornhusker"

See **United States residents' nicknames**

Cornpone, Jubilation T.

Founder of Dogpatch in the comic strip *Li'l Abner*.

Cornwell, David

Real name of novelist John Le Carré.

The Corpse Danced at Midnight

Whodunit novel written by Jessica Fletcher (Angela Lansbury) in the TV series *Murder, She Wrote*.

"Correctamundo!"

Acknowledgment often used by Fonzie (Henry Winkler) in the TV sitcom *Happy Days*.

Corsair

See **Pacer, Ranger, Corsair, and Citation**

Cortés, Gulf of

Former name of the Gulf of California, named for Spanish explorer Hernando Cortés, who explored it in 1536.

Coryell, John Russell

Creator of fictional detective Nick Carter. The character first appeared in "The Old Detective's Pupil," published in the *New York Weekly* in 1886.

coryza

Medical term for the common cold.

Cosmic Cow

Comic strip drawn by Henry Rush (Ted Knight) in the TV sitcom *Too Close for Comfort*.

Cosmic Creepers

Pet cat of Eglantine Price (Angela Lansbury) in the Disney film *Bedknobs and Broomsticks*.

Cosmo

First name of Kramer (Michael Richards) in the TV sitcom *Seinfeld*.

"Cosmo"

Nickname of Creedence Clearwater Revival drummer Doug Clifford.

Cotchford Farm

Sussex, England, estate of author A. A. Milne, later owned by Brian Jones of the Rolling Stones.

Cotter

Real last name of actresses Audrey and Jayne Meadows.

Cotter City, Illinois

Hometown of Merritt Andrews (Dolores Hart) in the film *Where the Boys Are*.

Cottle, Josephine

Real name of actress Gale Storm.

Cotton Blossom

Riverboat in the Jerome Kern/Oscar Hammerstein II musical *Show Boat*.

Cottonwoods, Utah

Setting of the Zane Grey novel *Riders of the Purple Sage*.

Cougars

Original nickname of the Detroit Red Wings at their NHL inception in 1926. The team was known as the Falcons from 1929 until 1932, when it took its present nickname.

Coulter, Ernest

Children's court clerk who founded the first Big Brothers agency in New York City in 1904.

counties of major U.S. cities and state capitals

Akron, Ohio: Summit
Albany, New York: Albany
Albuquerque, New Mexico: Bernalillo
Anaheim, California: Orange
Annapolis, Maryland: Anne Arundel
Atlanta, Georgia: Fulton
Augusta, Maine: Kennebec
Austin, Texas: Travis
Baltimore, Maryland (independent city)
Baton Rouge, Louisiana: East Baton Rouge (parish)
Birmingham, Alabama: Jefferson
Bismarck, North Dakota: Burleigh

Boise, Idaho: Ada
Boston, Massachusetts: Suffolk
Buffalo, New York: Erie
Carson City, Nevada (independent city)
Charleston, West Virginia: Kanawha
Charlotte, North Carolina: Mecklenburg
Cheyenne, Wyoming: Laramie
Chicago, Illinois: Cook
Cincinnati, Ohio: Hamilton
Cleveland, Ohio: Cuyahoga
Colorado Springs, Colorado: El Paso
Columbia, South Carolina: Richland
Columbus, Ohio: Franklin
Concord, New Hampshire: Merrimack
Corpus Christi, Texas: Nueces
Dallas, Texas: Dallas
Denver, Colorado: Denver
Des Moines, Iowa: Humboldt
Detroit, Michigan: Wayne
Dover, Delaware: Kent
El Paso, Texas: El Paso
Fort Wayne, Indiana: Allen
Fort Worth, Texas: Tarrant
Frankfort, Kentucky: Franklin
Fresno, California: Fresno
Grand Rapids, Michigan: Kent
Harrisburg, Pennsylvania: Dauphin
Hartford, Connecticut: Hartford
Helena, Montana: Lewis and Clark
Honolulu, Hawaii: Honolulu
Houston, Texas: Harris
Indianapolis, Indiana: Marion
Jackson, Mississippi: Hinds
Jacksonville, Florida: Duval
Jefferson City, Missouri: Cole
Kansas City, Missouri: Clay, Jackson, Platte
Lansing, Michigan: Clinton, Eaton, Ingham
Las Vegas, Nevada: Clark
Lexington, Kentucky: Fayette
Little Rock, Arkansas: Pulaski
Lincoln, Nebraska: Lancaster
Los Angeles, California: Los Angeles
Long Beach, California: Los Angeles
Louisville, Kentucky: Jefferson
Madison, Wisconsin: Dane
Memphis, Tennessee: Shelby
Mesa, Arizona: Maricopa
Miami, Florida: Miami-Dade
Milwaukee, Wisconsin: Milwaukee
Minneapolis, Minnesota: Hennepin
Mobile, Alabama: Mobile
Montgomery, Alabama: Montgomery
Montpelier, Vermont: Washington
Nashville, Tennessee: Davidson
Newark, New Jersey: Essex

New Orleans, Louisiana: Orleans (parish)
New York City, New York: Bronx, Kings, New York, Queens, Richmond
Oakland, California: Alameda
Oklahoma City, Oklahoma: Oklahoma
Olympia, Washington: Thurston
Omaha, Nebraska: Douglas
Philadelphia, Pennsylvania: Philadelphia
Phoenix, Arizona: Maricopa
Pierre, South Dakota: Hughes
Pittsburgh, Pennsylvania: Allegheny
Portland, Oregon: Multnomah
Providence, Rhode Island: Providence
Raleigh, North Carolina: Wake
Richmond, Virginia: Henrico
Rochester, New York: Monroe
Sacramento, California: Sacramento
Salem, Oregon: Marion
Salt Lake City, Utah: Salt Lake
San Antonio, Texas: Bexar
San Diego, California: San Diego
San Francisco, California: San Francisco
San Jose, California: Santa Clara
Santa Ana, California: Orange
Santa Fe, New Mexico: Santa Fe
Seattle, Washington: King
Shreveport, Louisiana: Caddo (parish)
Springfield, Illinois: Sangamon
St. Paul, Minnesota: Ramsey
St. Petersburg, Florida: Pinellas
Tallahassee, Florida: Leon
Tampa, Florida: Hillsborough
Toledo, Ohio: Lucas
Topeka, Kansas: Shawnee
Trenton, New Jersey: Mercer
Tucson, Arizona: Pima
Tulsa, Oklahoma: Tulsa
Wichita, Kansas: Sedgwick

"The country cannot stand Pat"

Slogan used by comedian Pat Paulsen for his tongue-in-cheek presidential campaigns.

The Country Cut-Ups

Original name of country group The Oak Ridge Boys.

A Country Made of Ice Cream

First novel written by Hubbell Gardner (Robert Redford) in the film *The Way We Were*.

"The Country's Best Yogurt"

See **Hickingbotham, Frank D.**

County General Hospital

Setting of the TV series *Ben Casey*.

county names, most popular

The county names (including parish names in Louisiana) used by the most states.

Washington (31 states)
Jefferson (26)
Franklin (24)
Jackson (24)
Lincoln (24)
Madison (20)
Montgomery (18)
Union (18)
Clay (17)
Marion (17)
Monroe (17)

Courage, Alexander

Composer of the theme music for the TV series *Star Trek*.

Cousin Bessie

Pet chimpanzee of Elly May Clampett (Donna Douglas) in the TV sitcom *The Beverly Hillbillies*.

Covenant

America-bound ship to which David Balfour is forcibly taken in the Robert Louis Stevenson novel *Kidnapped*.

"Cover the Earth"

Advertising slogan of Sherwin-Williams paints. The company's logo features the Earth covered by paint.

Cowboy Bill's

California fast-food restaurant owned by Frank De Fazio (Phil Foster) in the TV sitcom *Laverne and Shirley*.

The Cowboy Code

As created by Gene Autry.

1. The Cowboy must never shoot first, hit a smaller man, or take unfair advantage.
2. He must never go back on his word, or a trust confided in him.
3. He must always tell the truth.
4. He must be gentle with children, the elderly, and animals.
5. He must not advocate or possess racially or religiously intolerant ideas.
6. He must help people in distress.
7. He must be a good worker.
8. He must keep himself clean in thought, speech, action, and personal habits.
9. He must respect women, parents, and his nation's laws.
10. A Cowboy is a patriot.

Cowen, Joshua

Inventor of the toy electric train, circa 1900. The name of his company came from his middle name, Lionel.

Cowperwood trilogy

Group of novels written by Theodore Dreiser:
The Financier (1912)
The Titan (1914)
The Stoic (1947)

Cowtown, Texas

Hometown of Flo Castleberry (Polly Holliday) in the TV sitcom *Alice*.

Cox, Edwin W.

Cookware salesman who invented S.O.S. soap pads in 1917.

Coyoteville, New Mexico

See **Dead Man's Fang, Arizona; Oat Meal, Nebraska; and Coyoteville, New Mexico**

CQD

International distress signal used before the adoption of SOS circa 1910.

Crab

Pet dog of Launce in the William Shakespeare play *Two Gentlemen of Verona*. This is the only dog's name mentioned in Shakespeare's plays.

Crabapple Cove, Maine

Hometown of Benjamin Franklin "Hawkeye" Pierce (Alan Alda) in the TV sitcom *M*A*S*H*.

crabapple preserves

Concoction created by Mrs. Emily Hardy (Fay Holden) in massive quantities in the Andy Hardy series of films.

Crabb, Jack

Title character of the Thomas Berger novel *Little Big Man*, portrayed in the film adaptation of the same name by Dustin Hoffman.

Crab Key

Island off the coast of Jamaica that is the headquarters of the title character (Joseph Wiseman) in the James Bond film *Dr. No*.

Cracked Ice

Original working title of the Marx Brothers film *Duck Soup*. It was later titled *Grasshoppers* before taking its final name.

Crackle!

See **Snap!, Crackle!, and Pop!**

"The Cradle of Aviation"

Nickname of Dayton, Ohio, the home of the Wright brothers.

"The Cradle of Liberty"

Nickname of Faneuil Hall in Boston, Massachusetts.

Craig Theater

Where Richard Sherman (Tom Ewell) and "The Girl" (Marilyn Monroe) see *Creature from the Black Lagoon,* in the film *The Seven Year Itch.*

Cramton, Raymond

Real name of actor Chad Everett.

Crane, Clarence

Inventor of Life Savers candies in 1912. He was the father of author Hart Crane.

Cranston, Lamont

Secret identity of the title character in the radio series *The Shadow.* Orson Welles was one of the portrayers of the character.

Crawford, John

Real name of Plato (Sal Mineo) in the film *Rebel Without a Cause.*

Crawford, Thomas

See **Statue of Freedom**

Crayola Crayon color history

CRAYOLA COLORS AVAILABLE BEGINNING 1903 (8)

Black	Orange
Blue	Red
Brown	Violet
Green	Yellow

COLORS AVAILABLE 1949–1957 (48)

Apricot	Flesh (name changed
Bittersweet	to "Peach" in 1962)
Black	Gold
Blue	Gray
Blue Green	Green
Blue Violet	Green Blue
Brick Red	Green Yellow
Brown	Lemon Yellow
Burnt Sienna	Magenta
Carnation Pink	Mahogany
Cornflower	Maize

Maroon	Salmon
Melon	Sea Green
Olive Green	Silver
Orange	Spring Green
Orange Red	Tan
Orange Yellow	Thistle
Orchid	Turquoise Blue
Periwinkle	Violet (Purple)
Pine Green	Violet Blue
Prussian Blue (name	Violet Red
changed to "Mid-	White
night Blue" in 1958)	Yellow
Red	Yellow Green
Red Orange	Yellow Orange
Red Violet	

COLORS AVAILABLE 1958–1971 (64). ALL COLORS
LISTED ABOVE, PLUS:

Aquamarine	Lavender
Blue Gray	Mulberry
Burnt Orange	Navy Blue
Cadet Blue	Plum
Copper	Raw Sienna
Forest Green	Raw Umber
Goldenrod	Sepia
Indian Red (name	Sky Blue
changed to "Chest-	
nut" in 1999)	

COLORS AVAILABLE 1972–1989 (72). ALL COLORS
LISTED ABOVE, PLUS THESE FLUORESCENT COLORS:

Atomic Tangerine	Outrageous Orange
Blizzard Blue	Screamin' Green
Hot Magenta	Shocking Pink
Laser Lemon	Wild Watermelon

COLORS AVAILABLE 1990–1992 (80). ALL COLORS
LISTED ABOVE, PLUS THESE FLUORESCENT COLORS:

Electric Lime	Razzle Dazzle Rose
Magic Mint	Sunglow
Purple Pizzazz	Unmellow Yellow
Radical Red	Neon Carrot

IN 1990, EIGHT COLORS WERE RETIRED (GREEN BLUE, ORANGE RED, ORANGE YELLOW, VIOLET BLUE, MAIZE, LEMON YELLOW, BLUE GRAY, RAW UMBER) AND WERE REPLACED BY EIGHT NEW SHADES:

Cerulean	Dandelion
Vivid Tangerine	Teal Blue
Jungle Green	Royal Purple
Fuchsia	Wild Strawberry

COLORS AVAILABLE 1993–1997 (96). THESE 16
NEW COLORS WERE ALL NAMED BY CONSUMERS:

Asparagus	Denim
Cerise	Granny Smith Apple

Macaroni and Cheese
Mauvelous
Pacific Blue
Purple Mountain's
    Majesty
Razzmatazz
Robin's Egg Blue

Shamrock
Tickle Me Pink
Timber Wolf
Tropical Rain Forest
Tumbleweed
Wisteria

Colors available 1998 to present (120). These 24 new colors were added:

Almond
Antique Brass
Banana Mania
Beaver
Blue Bell
Brink Pink
Canary
Caribbean Green
Cotton Candy
Cranberry
Desert Sand
Eggplant

Fern
Fuzzy Wuzzy Brown
Manatee
Mountain Meadow
Outer Space
Pig Pink
Pink Flamingo
Purple Heart
Shadow
Sunset Orange
Torch Red
Vivid Violet

Crayon, Geoffrey
Pen name used by author Washington Irving.

"Crazy Legs"
Nickname of football great Elroy Hirsch, because his legs seemed to be out of control as he ran.

Cream, Arnold Raymond
Real name of boxer Jersey Joe Walcott.

Cream (rock group) members
Ginger Baker, Eric Clapton, and Jack Bruce.

Creedence Clearwater Revival members
Doug "Cosmo" Clifford, Stu Cook, John Fogerty, and Tom Fogerty.

Cregg III, Hugh Anthony
Real name of rock singer Huey Lewis.

Creighton
Real first name of actor Lon Chaney Jr.

Middle name of comedienne Carol Burnett.

Crenshaw High School
Los Angeles public school attended by the title character (Brandy) before attending Bridgewood, a private prep school, in the TV sitcom *Moesha*.

"Crescat scientia, vita excolatur"
Motto of the University of Chicago, which is Latin for "Let knowledge grow, let life be enriched."

"The Crescent City"
Nickname of New Orleans, Louisiana.

Crestridge High
School attended by the title character (Peter Barton) in the TV series *The Powers of Matthew Star*.

Criblecoblis, Otis
See **Fields, W. C., roles/pen names of**

The Crickets
Backup band for singer Buddy Holly.

"The Crime Dog"
Nickname of baseball player Fred McGriff, because of the similarity of his name to cartoon canine McGruff in TV commercials for crime prevention.

Crime Magazine
Employer of senior editor Dan Farrell (Robert Stack) in the TV series *The Name of the Game*.

Crimeways
See **Januth Publications**

Criminal Headquarters for Underworld Master Plan
See **C.H.U.M.P.**

Crimson Jihad
Terrorist group in the film *True Lies*.

Criss-crosswords
See **Lexiko**

Cristillo
Real last name of comedian Lou Costello.

Cristofori, Bartolomeo
Italian harpsichord maker who invented the piano circa 1700.

Crocea Mors
Sword of Julius Caesar. The name is Latin for "yellow death."

Crocetti, Dino
See **Kid Crochet**

The Crock of Gold
Novel by Irish author James Stephens that was the basis for the musical *Finian's Rainbow*.

"Le Crocodile"
Nickname of tennis pro Rene Lacoste, who founded the Izod sportswear label.

Croftangry, Chrystal
Pen name used by author Sir Walter Scott.

Crookshanks
Pet cat of Hermione Granger in the Harry Potter series of books by J. K. Rowling.

Crooper, Illinois
Setting of the radio sitcom *Vic and Sade*.

Cross Corners, New Hampshire
Home of Jabez Stone in the Stephen Vincent Benét short story "The Devil and Daniel Webster."

"Crossed Swords"
Debut episode of the TV sitcom *Sanford and Son*, which aired on September 14, 1972.

Cross Keys Inn
Coaching inn where Pip first arrives in London, in the Charles Dickens novel *Great Expectations*.

The Crossroads
St. Louis bus terminal where John Hemingway (John Larroquette) works as night manager in the TV sitcom *The John Larroquette Show*.

Crowell, Luther
Inventor of the square-bottom grocery bag and the machine to manufacture it, circa 1872.

Crowninshield
Middle name of journalist Ben Bradlee.

Crozet, Virginia
Setting of the mystery novels of Rita Mae Brown.

Crump, Diane
First woman jockey to ride in the Kentucky Derby, in 1970. Her horse Fathom finished 15th in a field of 17.

Crum, Simon
Stage name used by country singer Ferlin Husky as a comic.

Crushito
One-time cartoon mascot of Orange Crush soft drinks.

C.S.S. *Virginia*
Name of the Confederate ironclad vessel at the time of its encounter with the Union ironclad vessel U.S.S. *Monitor* at the Battle of Hampton Roads on March 9, 1862. The *Virginia* had been a Union frigate named U.S.S. *Merrimack*, before being abandoned by the Union and rebuilt as an ironclad by the Confederacy.

"Cubby"
Nickname of James Bond film producer Albert R. Broccoli.

Cub Scout ranks
Listed below from lowest to highest:
　　Bobcat
　　Wolf
　　Bear
　　Webelos
　　Arrow of Light

"Cucumber"
Nickname of mobster Frank de Marco (Alec Baldwin) in the film *Married to the Mob*.

cucumber split
Favorite dessert of Dennis Day in Jack Benny's radio show.

"Cuddles"
Nickname of comic character actor S. Z. Sakall.

La Cuesta Encantada
Home of publisher William Randolph Hearst at San Simeon, California. Its name is Spanish for "the enchanted hill."

Cuff and Link
Pet turtles of Rocky Balboa (Sylvester Stallone) in the film *Rocky*.

Culliford, Pierre "Peyo"
Belgian cartoonist who created the Smurfs. They first appeared in the weekly *Le Journal de Spirou* on October 23, 1958.

"A cultivated mind is the guardian genius of democracy"
Motto of the University of Texas.

"Cump"
Nickname of Civil War Union general William Tecumseh Sherman.

Cunningham Aircraft
See **Stevenson Aircraft**

Cunningham, John W.
See **"The Tin Star"**

Cunningham, Zamah
See **Manicotti, Mrs.**

cuprum

Latin name for copper, from which its chemical symbol Cu is derived.

Curl Up & Dye

Beauty-parlor employer of Valerie Gale (Geena Davis) in the film *Earth Girls Are Easy*.

Curly

Role for which Jack Palance won a Best Supporting Actor Academy Award in the 1991 film *City Slickers*.

Dancing caterpillar in the Norman Corwin radio play *Once Upon a Time*.

Curran

Middle name of actor/dancer Gene Kelly.

"Current of Love"

See **"Save Me"**

Curry, Izola Ware

Attempted assassin of Martin Luther King Jr. on September 20, 1958. While King was doing a book signing in a Manhattan bookstore, Curry stabbed him with a letter opener.

The Curse of Capistrano

See **McCulley, Johnston**

Curtana

Blunted sword of 11th-century English king Edward the Confessor, used as a symbol of mercy in the coronation ceremonies of English monarchs.

Curtin, Hoyt

Music director for Hanna-Barbera who wrote the theme songs for *The Flintstones*, *The Jetsons* and *Yogi Bear*.

Curtis Wells, Montana

Setting of TV's *Lonesome Dove: The Series*.

Custer College

School where Ray Blant (Anthony Perkins) is a star basketball player in the film *Tall Story*.

Custerville, Arizona

Setting of the George and Ira Gershwin musical *Girl Crazy*.

Cuthbert

Middle name of author William Faulkner.

Cutler, Abner

Buffalo, New York, furniture maker who invented the roll-top desk, patented in 1850.

Cutting, Dick

See **Manners**

Cyborg

Novel by Martin Caidin that was the basis for the TV series *The Six Million Dollar Man* and *The Bionic Woman*.

cyclamates

Artificial sweeteners banned by the FDA in 1969 as a possible carcinogen.

Cyclops

Electronic device used in pro tennis to determine whether or not a tennis serve is in bounds.

Cylons

See **Caprica**

Cynthia

Pet basset hound of Mr. Haney (Pat Buttram) in the TV sitcom *Green Acres*.

Cyrano

Ferret that Carl Jenkins (Neil Patrick Harris) communicates with telepathically, in the film *Starship Troopers*.

Czolgosz, Leon

Anarchist who assassinated President William McKinley at the Pan-American Exposition in Buffalo, New York, in 1901. McKinley was shot on September 6 and died on September 14.

DAA
Advertising-agency employer of Michael Steadman (Ken Olin) and Elliot Weston (Timothy Busfield) in the TV series *thirtysomething*.

Dab-Dab
Pet duck of the title character in the Doctor Dolittle series of children's novels by Hugh Lofting.

D'Abruzzo, Alphonso
Real name of actor Alan Alda.

Daddy Long Legs
Novel by Jean Webster that was the basis for the Shirley Temple film *Curly Top*.

Daddy's Home
Original working title of the film *Look Who's Talking*.

Dafoe, Allan
See **Dionne quintuplets**

Daggett, Little Bill
Role for which Gene Hackman won a Best Supporting Actor Academy Award in the 1992 film *Unforgiven*.

Dagobah
Planet that is the home and hiding place of Yoda (voiced by Frank Oz) in the film *The Empire Strikes Back*.

Dahl, Gary
California advertising man who invented the Pet Rock in 1975.

Dahomey
Former name of the African nation Benin.

The Daily Beacon
Southern newspaper run by Billy Bob Davis (Billy Bob Thornton) and his daughter Carson Lee Davis (Doren Fein) in the TV sitcom *Hearts Afire*.

Daily Bugle
Newspaper published by J. Jonah Jameson, nemesis of the title character in Spider-Man comics.

"The Daily Diary of the American Dream"
Advertising slogan of *The Wall Street Journal*.

Daily Faberian
Faber College's campus newspaper in the film *National Lampoon's Animal House*.

The Daily Prophet
National wizarding newspaper in the Harry Potter series of books by J. K. Rowling.

Daily Sentinel
Newspaper published by Britt Reid in the radio and TV series *The Green Hornet*.

Daisy
Pet dog of the Bumsteads in the comic strip *Blondie*.

Pet mouse of Radar O'Reilly (Gary Burghoff) in the TV sitcom *M*A*S*H*.

"Daisy Hawkins"
Original title of the Beatles tune "Eleanor Rigby."

Daisy Hill Puppy Farm
Birthplace of Snoopy in the comic strip *Peanuts*.

Daleks
Evil mutant race in the British TV series *Dr. Who*.

Dallas
Golden palomino horse of Barbie, introduced in 1981.

Dallas Texans
Original name of the Kansas City Chiefs team at their AFL inception in 1960. The team adopted its present name when it moved to Kansas City for the 1963 season.

Daly
Maiden name of Olivia Walton (Michael Learned) in the TV series *The Waltons*.

Damariscotta, Maine
Small town whose Lincoln Theater was the site of the world premiere of the Disney animated film

Bambi in 1942. This was the hometown of Disney animator Maurice Day, who brought the novel upon which the film was based to the attention of Walt Disney.

Damita

Middle name of pop singer Janet Jackson.

"Dance of the Cuckoos"

Theme song of Laurel and Hardy, aka "Ku-ku."

"Dance of the Hours"

Piece from the Amilcare Ponchielli opera *La Gioconda* adapted by Allan Sherman for his tune "Hello Muddah, Hello Fadduh!"

Dancer

Secret Service code name for Rosalynn Carter.

Dancer, April

Title character of the TV series *The Girl from U.N.C.L.E.*, portrayed by Stefanie Powers.

The Dancing Cavalier

First talkie made by Monumental Pictures, in the film *Singin' in the Rain*.

"Dancing in the Street" locales

This Martha and the Vandellas tune mentions these cities (in order):
    Chicago
    New Orleans
    New York City
    Philadelphia, Pa.
    The Motor City
    Baltimore
    D.C.
    L.A.

D&D Advertising

Employer of Alison Parker (Courtney Thorne-Smith) in the TV series *Melrose Place*. She begins as a receptionist and eventually becomes its president.

Danfield, Connecticut

Setting of the TV sitcom *The Lucy Show*.

Danger Man

British TV series that was the basis for the TV series *Secret Agent*.

"Dangerous Business"

Song written by Lyle Rogers (Warren Beatty) and Chuck Clarke (Dustin Hoffman) in the film *Ishtar*.

"Dangerous Games"

Debut episode of the TV series *Police Story*, which aired on October 2, 1973.

Daniel, Eliot

Composer of the theme song of the TV sitcom *I Love Lucy*.

Daniels, Anthony

Portrayer of droid C-3PO in the *Star Wars* films.

Daniels, Bree

Role for which Jane Fonda won a Best Actress Academy Award in the 1971 film *Klute*.

Danish West Indies

Former name of the U.S. Virgin Islands.

Dan'l Webster

Title amphibian of the Mark Twain short story "The Celebrated Jumping Frog of Calaveras County."

Dann

Middle name of novelist John D. MacDonald.

"Danny Dreamer"

Childhood nickname of McDonald's founder Ray Kroc.

"Danny's Donuts"

See **Butler, Harold**

Dante, Ron

Lead vocalist for these studio groups that had top-40 *Billboard* pop tunes in the U.S.:
    The Detergents ("Leader of the Laundromat" in 1964)
    The Archies ("Sugar, Sugar" in 1969)
    The Cuff Links ("Tracy" in 1969)

Dantès, Edmond

Pen name used by John Hughes for his screenwriter's credit in the film *Beethoven*, which is the title character of the Alexandre Dumas novel *The Count of Monte Cristo*.

The Danube Waves

Instrumental work by Romanian composer Iosif Ivanovici used for the melody of "Anniversary Song," introduced in the film *The Jolson Story*.

Danzig, Allison

Tennis writer who in 1938 coined the term "Grand Slam" for wins in the four major championships: Wimbledon, Australian Open, French Open, and

U.S. Open. It was coined for Don Budge, who in that year became the first to accomplish the feat.

Daphne Productions

Production company of TV talk host Dick Cavett.

Dapple

Donkey of Sancho Panza in the Miguel de Cervantes novel *Don Quixote de la Mancha.*

D'Arcy, Rose-Ann

Role for which Shelley Winters won a Best Supporting Actress Academy Award in the 1965 film *A Patch of Blue.*

Dare, Virginia

First English child born in the Americas, on August 18, 1587, on Roanoke Island, Virginia.

Darkbloom, Vivian

Minor character in the Vladimir Nabokov novel *Lolita,* whose name is an anagram of the author's.

Dark Helmet

Darth Vader-like character (Rick Moranis) in the Mel Brooks film *Spaceballs.*

Dark Horse Records

Company created by former Beatle George Harrison to produce his recordings.

dark seven

Term used by hip-talking Gerald Lloyd "Kookie" Kookson III (Edd Byrnes) to describe a depressing week, in the TV series *77 Sunset Strip.*

Dark Windows

See **Bases Loaded** and *Dark Windows*

Darley Arabian

See **Byerly Turk, Darley Arabian, and Godolphin Barb**

Darling

Last name of the title character (Melissa Joan Hart) in the TV sitcom *Clarissa Explains It All.*

Darrow, Charles

See **52**

Dartmouth

See **Eleanor, Beaver,** and *Dartmouth*

Dartmouth Medal

Presented annually since 1975 by the Reference and User Services Association (RUSA) for the creation of a reference work of outstanding quality and significance.

Darwin

Talking dolphin in the TV series *seaQuest DSV.*

Darwish

Last name of pop singer Tiffany.

Dash

See **Jim and Dash**

Dassler, Adolf "Adi"

Creator of Adidas athletic shoes, circa 1920. His brother Rudolf founded the company that manufactures Puma shoes in 1948.

Data Analyzing Robot Youth Lifeform

Full name of the cyborg title character (Barret Oliver) in the film *D.A.R.Y.L.*

La Dauphine

Ship commanded by explorer Giovanni da Verrazano on his voyage to the east coast of North America in 1524.

Dave

See **Sol-leks and Dave**

Dave and Ken

First names of the title characters (Paul Michael Glaser and David Soul, respectively) in the TV series *Starsky and Hutch.*

Dave Clark Five members

Dave Clark, Lenny Davidson, Rick Huxley, Denis Payton, and Mike Smith.

Davenport, Andrew

See **Wood, Anne and Davenport, Andrew**

David

Real first name of director Sam Peckinpah.

First name of Dr. Zorba (Sam Jaffe), mentor of the title character (Vince Edwards) in the TV series *Ben Casey.*

Real first name of the title character in the Mark Twain novel *The Tragedy of Pudd'nhead Wilson.*

David di Donatello

See **film awards, national**

David Herbert

First and middle names of English writer D. H. Lawrence.

David Jacob

First and middle names of D. J. Conner (Michael Fishman) in the TV sitcom *Roseanne*.

Davies, Valentine

Author of the novel *Miracle on 34th Street*, upon which the films of the same name were based.

Davis/Bogart films

The films in which Bette Davis and Humphrey Bogart appear together. (Davis appears in more Bogart films than any other actress.)
  Bad Sister (1931)
  Three on a Match (1932)
  The Petrified Forest (1936)
  Marked Woman (1937)
  Kid Galahad (1937)
  Dark Victory (1939)
  In This Our Life (1942)*
  Thank Your Lucky Stars (1943)
  * Bogart and the rest of the principal cast of *The Maltese Falcon* make a cameo appearance in this film.

Dawes Tomes Mousley Grubbs Fidelity Fiduciary Bank

Employer of George Banks (David Tomlinson) in the Disney film *Mary Poppins*.

Dawg

Family dog in the comic strip *Hi and Lois*.

Dawkins, John

Real name of the Artful Dodger in the Charles Dickens novel *Oliver Twist*.

Dawn

Backup singers for Tony Orlando: Telma Hopkins and Joyce Vincent.

Dawn, Billie

Role for which Judy Holliday won a Best Actress Academy Award in the 1950 film *Born Yesterday*.

Dawn, Gaye

Role for which Claire Trevor won a Best Supporting Actress Academy Award in the 1948 film *Key Largo*.

"Dawn of a New Day"

Theme song of the 1939–40 New York World's Fair, written by George and Ira Gershwin. Ira wrote the lyrics to an unused melody of George's (George had died in 1937).

Dawson High

School attended by Jim Stark (James Dean), Plato (Sal Mineo) and Judy (Natalie Wood) in the film *Rebel Without a Cause*.

Dawson, Velma

Hollywood dollmaker who created the title character of the children's TV series *Howdy Doody*.

"day"

What "D" stands for in "D-Day."

Day, Cecil B.

Real-estate developer who founded the Days Inn motel chain. The first Days Inn opened in April, 1970, in Tybee Island, Georgia.

Day/Hudson films

The films in which Doris Day and Rock Hudson appear together:
  Pillow Talk (1959)
  Lover Come Back (1961)
  Send Me No Flowers (1964)

daylight savings time

Currently observed annually from the first Sunday in April until the last Sunday in October everywhere in the United States except Hawaii, Arizona and 87 of the 92 counties of Indiana. The southeastern Indiana counties of Clark, Dearborn, Floyd, Harrison and Ohio "unofficially" observe daylight savings time.

Day, Lucky

See **Bottoms, Dusty; Day, Lucky; and Nederlander, Ned**

Day, Maurice

See **Damariscotta, Maine**

Day, Otis

See **Dexter Lake Club**

days of the week, ancient Roman

  Sunday: *dies Solis* (sun's day)
  Monday: *dies Lunae* (moon's day)
  Tuesday: *dies Martis* (Mars' day)
  Wednesday: *dies Mercurii* (Mercury's day)
  Thursday: *dies Jovis* (Jove's day)
  Friday: *dies Veneris* (Venus' day)
  Saturday: *dies Saturni* (Saturn's day)

Day with the Giants

1952 autobiography of actress Laraine Day, who was married to New York Giants manager Leo Durocher at the time.

Dazzledent

Toothpaste for which "The Girl" (Marilyn Monroe) does TV commercials, in the film *The Seven Year Itch*.

D.C.

Title character of the Disney film *That Darn Cat!*

D-Day beaches

The five beaches along the Normandy coast on which Allied forces landed on June 6, 1944. Code names (from west to east): Utah, Omaha, Gold, Juno, and Sword.

Deacon

Secret Service code name for Jimmy Carter.

Dead Dog Records

Company run by undercover agent Vinnie Terranova (Ken Wahl) in the TV series *Wiseguy*.

Deadheads

What fanatical followers of rock group the Grateful Dead call themselves.

deadly sins

See **sins, seven deadly**

"The Dead Man" and "The Housekeeper"

Debut episodes of the TV series *Night Gallery*, which aired on December 16, 1970.

Dead Man's Fang, Arizona; Oat Meal, Nebraska; and Coyoteville, New Mexico

Vaudeville stops for Don Lockwood (Gene Kelly) and Cosmo Brown (Donald O'Connor) in the film *Singin' in the Rain*.

dead man's hand

A holding of two pairs, aces and eights, in the game of poker. This was the hand held by Wild Bill Hickok when he was killed by Jack McCall on August 2, 1876, in Deadwood, South Dakota.

Deadrock, Arkansas

Setting of the musical *Crazy for You*.

Dean & DeLuca

Restaurant employer of the title character (Keri Russell) in the TV series *Felicity*.

Dearborn

Middle name of Western author Louis L'Amour.

"Dear John"

See **"Hi There!" and "Dear John"**

"Dear Libby"

Debut episode of the TV sitcom *The Brady Bunch*, which aired on October 3, 1969.

Deason, Ellen Muriel

Real name of country singer Kitty Wells.

The Death and Life of Dith Pran

Book by Sydney Schanberg that was the basis for the film *The Killing Fields*.

Death in the Fast Lane

Mystery novel written by Ben Coleman (Matthew Laurance) in the TV series *Duet*.

Deathmobile

Souped-up Lincoln Continental used by Delta House to ruin the Faber College homecoming parade, in the film *National Lampoon's Animal House*.

***Death Valley Days* hosts**

This syndicated Western anthology was one of television's longest-running series.

    Stanley Andrews aka "The Old Ranger"
       (1952–65)
    Ronald Reagan (1965–66)
    Robert Taylor (1966–68)
    Dale Robertson (1968–72)
    Merle Haggard (1975)

Debby

Childhood horse of President Franklin D. Roosevelt.

de Bergerac, Cyrano

Title role for which José Ferrer won the 1950 Best Actor Academy Award.

decathlon events

As held for men at each Summer Olympics, over two days.

    FIRST DAY

100-meter run
Long jump
Shot put
High jump
400-meter run

    SECOND DAY

110-meter hurdles
Discus throw
Pole vault
Javelin throw
1500-meter run

Decatur Staleys

Original name of the Chicago Bears at their NFL inception in 1920. The team moved from Decatur, Illinois, to Chicago in 1921 and took its present name in 1922.

Deckers, Jeanine

Real name of The Singing Nun, whose "Dominique" was a #1 *Billboard* tune in 1963.

"The Decline of a Family"

Subtitle of the Thomas Mann novel *Buddenbrooks*.

Dedalus, Stephen

Title character of the James Joyce novel *A Portrait of the Artist as a Young Man*.

Deep Blue

IBM RS/6000 chess computer that defeated world champion Garry Kasparov in a six-game match in May 1997.

deepies

1950s slang term for 3-D movies.

Deep Quest

Ship that locates the title vessel in the film *Raise the Titanic*.

Deep Thought

Supercomputer in the Douglas Adams novel *The Hitchhiker's Guide to the Galaxy*.

Deep Wells Ranger Station

Setting of the TV Western sitcom *Rango*, starring Tim Conway in the title role as a Texas Ranger.

"The Defense of Fort McHenry"

Francis Scott Key's original title of "The Star-Spangled Banner."

Def Leppard original members

Rick Allen, Steve Clark, Joe Elliott, Rick Savage, and Pete Willis.

DeForest

Middle name of actor Humphrey Bogart.

DeFreeze, Donald

Real name of Cinque, leader of the Symbionese Liberation Army, radical group that kidnapped Patricia Hearst on February 5, 1974.

deglutition

Medical term for swallowing.

de Havilland/Flynn films

The films in which Olivia de Havilland and Errol Flynn appear together:
Captain Blood (1935)
The Charge of the Light Brigade (1936)
The Adventures of Robin Hood (1938)
Four's a Crowd (1938)
Dodge City (1939)
The Private Lives of Elizabeth and Essex (1939)
Santa Fe Trail (1940)
They Died with Their Boots On (1941)
Thank Your Lucky Stars (1943)

"Dei sub numine viget"

Motto of Princeton University, which is Latin for "Under God's power she flourishes."

"Deke"

Nickname of Donald Slayton, the only one of the seven original Mercury astronauts not to be part of a Mercury mission, because of a heart ailment. Slayton finally went into space as part of the Apollo-Soyuz mission of 1975.

Delahanty, Thomas

Washington, D.C., police officer who was wounded in the assassination attempt on President Ronald Reagan outside the Washington Hilton hotel on March 30, 1981. Reagan press secretary James Brady and Secret Service agent Timothy McCarthy were also wounded in the attempt.

Delaney, Lola

Role for which Shirley Booth won a Best Actress Academy Award in the 1952 film *Come Back, Little Sheba*.

De Lesseps, Viola

Role for which Gwyneth Paltrow won a Best Actress Academy Award in the 1998 film *Shakespeare in Love*.

Del Floria's

New York City tailor shop that fronts U.N.C.L.E. headquarters in the TV series *The Man from U.N.C.L.E.*

Delight

Middle name of composer Quincy Jones.

Delle Rose, Serafina

Role for which Anna Magnani won a Best Actress Academy Award in the 1956 film *The Rose Tattoo*.

Delos

Island site of the $1000/day amusement parks Medievalworld, Romanworld and Westworld in the film *Westworld*. Slogan: "The vacation of the future today!"

The Del-Phis

Original name of the pop group Martha and the Vandellas.

The Del Satins

Vocal group that backs up Dion on his tunes "Runaround Sue" and "The Wanderer."

Delta City

See **Omni Consumer Products**

Delta Tau Chi

Fraternity pledged by Larry Kroger (Tom Hulce) and Kent Dorfman (Stephen Furst) in the film *National Lampoon's Animal House*.

deltiologist

Technical term for a collector of postcards.

DeLuca, Fred and Buck, Peter

Founders of the Subway restaurant chain. The first Subway, originally called "Pete's Super Submarines", opened on August 28, 1965, in Bridgeport, Connecticut.

Deluxe International Orange

Color of paint on San Francisco's Golden Gate Bridge.

Demara, Ferdinand

See **"The Great Impostor"**

Democracity

Model of a futuristic metropolis of 2039, displayed within the Perisphere at the 1939–40 New York World's Fair.

"The Demon Barber of Fleet Street"

Nickname of the title character in the Stephen Sondheim musical *Sweeney Todd*.

Demsky, Issur Danielovitch

Real name of actor Kirk Douglas.

Denial of Death

Book bought by Alvy Singer (Woody Allen) for the title character (Diane Keaton) in the film *Annie Hall*.

Denison University

Alma mater of the title character in the comic strip *Mary Worth*.

dentifrice

Technical term for a toothpaste or other preparation used to clean teeth.

Denton, Brady

Buick salesman from Saginaw, Michigan, who became the one-millionth shareholder of AT&T in 1951—the first company with that many shareholders. The company presented Denton and his family with a trip to AT&T headquarters in New York City.

Denton, Ohio

Setting of the film *The Rocky Horror Picture Show*.

Denton True

Real first and middle names of Hall of Fame baseball pitcher Cy Young.

"Deo ac veritati"

Motto of Colgate University, which is Latin for "For God and truth."

"Deo vindice"

Motto of the Confederate States of America, which is Latin for "God will vindicate."

"Der Alte"

Nickname of German chancellor Konrad Adenauer, which is German for "The Old One."

Derek, John, wives of

Pati Behrs (married 1951, divorced 1957)
Ursula Andress (married 1957, divorced 1966)
Linda Evans (married 1968, divorced 1974)
Bo Derek (married 1974)

dermatherm

Instrument for measuring skin temperature.

Derry Church

Original name of Hershey, Pennsylvania.

Derry, Maine

Setting of the Stephen King novels *It* and *Insomnia*.

Derval, Dominique

Real name of Domino (Claudine Auger), girlfriend of Emilio Largo (Adolfo Celi) in the James Bond film *Thunderball*.

Deseret

Original name given to Utah by the first Mormon settlers.

"desert"

What the word "Sahara" means in Arabic.

Desert Bar

Hershey chocolate bar provided to American soldiers during the Gulf War, which could withstand temperatures of up to 140 degrees.

"The Desert Fox"

Nickname of World War II German field marshal Erwin Rommel.

Desilu

Production company of Desi Arnaz and Lucille Ball, which was sold to Paramount Pictures in 1968.

DeSoto

See **Roscoe and DeSoto**

"Details at Eleven"

Debut episode of the TV series *Simon and Simon*, which aired on November 24, 1981.

"Detroit Red"

Nickname of civil-rights leader Malcolm X.

Dettrey, Anne

Role for which Celeste Holm won a Best Supporting Actress Academy Award in the 1947 film *Gentleman's Agreement*.

Deutschendorf, John Henry

Real name of pop singer John Denver.

Deutschmann, Theodore

Founder of the Radio Shack retail chain. The first Radio Shack opened in 1921 in Boston, Massachusetts.

Deveraux, Lionel Q.

See **Marx, Groucho, roles of**

DeVito, Tommy

Role for which Joe Pesci won a Best Supporting Actor Academy Award in the 1990 film *Goodfellas*.

Devlin, Linkman and O'Brien

Law-firm employer of the title character (Vincent Baggetta) in the TV series *The Eddie Capra Mysteries*.

De Vore Department Store

Employer of Harold Lloyd (portraying himself) in the film *Safety Last*.

Devotions Upon Emergent Occasions

Work by John Donne from which Ernest Hemingway derived the title of his novel *For Whom the Bell Tolls*.

Dewar, James

See **Little Shortcake Fingers**

de Weldon, Felix

Austrian-born sculptor of the U.S. Marine Corps War Memorial, aka the Iwo Jima Memorial, at Arlington National Cemetery.

Dewey

See **Huey, Dewey, and Louie**

Dewey Decimal System major categories

As conceived by Melvil Dewey and first published in 1876:

   000   Generalities
   100   Philosophy
   200   Religion
   300   Social Sciences
   400   Languages
   500   Pure Sciences
   600   Applied Sciences and Technology
   700   Arts
   800   Literature
   900   History and Geography

Dewey High

School attended by Mike and Carol Seaver (Kirk Cameron and Tracey Gold) in the sitcom *Growing Pains*. The school's athletic teams are the Hooters.

Dewey, Stone & Company

Investment-firm employer of Jack Trainer (Harrison Ford) in the film *Working Girl*.

De Witt, Addison

Role for which George Sanders won a Best Supporting Actor Academy Award in the 1950 film *All About Eve*.

Dexter Lake Club

Nightspot where Otis Day and the Knights perform, in the film *National Lampoon's Animal House*.

Dezire, Jezebel

Ann-Margret's role in the film *The Cheap Detective*.

Diablo

Setting of the TV Western series *Annie Oakley*.

Horse of Western hero The Cisco Kid.

Pet raven of Maleficent (voiced by Eleanor Audley) in the Disney animated film *Sleeping Beauty*.

"diabolical order"

How the names of the stars are claimed to be listed (actually alphabetical order) in the opening credits of the film *Murder by Death*.

Diagon Alley

Magically concealed London street filled with wizarding shops, in the Harry Potter series of books by J. K. Rowling.

Diamond

Pet Pomeranian dog of Sir Isaac Newton.

"A diamond is forever"

Advertising slogan of De Beers.

Diamond Rio members

Gene Johnson, Jimmy Olander, Brian Prout, Marty Roe, Dan Truman, and Dana Williams.

Diamonds in the Sidewalk

Original working title of the Marx Brothers film *Love Happy*.

Diana

Real first name of country singer Naomi Judd.

Diane

Role for which Janet Gaynor won a Best Actress Academy Award in the 1927 film *7th Heaven*.

diaphoresis

Medical term for sweating or perspiration.

diastema

Medical term for a natural gap between two teeth.

Diat, Louis

Chef at New York City's Ritz-Carlton Hotel who invented vichyssoise in 1917.

Díaz de Vivar, Rodrigo

Real name of Spanish national hero El Cid.

diazepam

Chemical name of the drug Valium.

Di Bassetto, Corno

Pen name used by playwright George Bernard Shaw as a music critic. The name is an Italian term for a tenor clarinet.

Dibble, Officer

Nemesis of the title character in the children's animated TV sitcom *Top Cat*, voiced by Allen Jenkins.

dichlorodiphenyltrichloroethane

Full chemical name of banned insecticide DDT.

Dick

Pet mockingbird of President Thomas Jefferson.

Dickens, Charles

Author of *A Tale of Two Cities*, as listed in the closing credits of the film *Airplane!*, for no discernable reason.

Dickson, Earl

Johnson & Johnson employee who invented Band-Aids, circa 1920.

Dickson, J. T. and Winfield, John R.

English inventors of the synthetic fiber Dacron in 1940. It was originally called "terylene," and is still known by that name in Great Britain.

Dick, Tim Allen

Real name of comedian Tim Allen.

"Did you ever dance with the devil in the pale moonlight?"

Question asked by The Joker (Jack Nicholson) to his potential victims in the film *Batman*.

died on their birthday

January 22: actor Telly Savalas (born 1922, died 1994)

April 23: playwright William Shakespeare (born 1564, died 1616)

August 29: actress Ingrid Bergman (born 1915, died 1982)

died on the same date

JANUARY

January 13, 1958: movie executive Jesse Lasky, actress Edna Purviance

January 21, 1959: director Cecil B. DeMille, actor Carl "Alfalfa" Switzer

January 30, 1948: reformer Mahatma Gandhi, inventor Orville Wright

FEBRUARY

February 1, 1966: columnist Hedda Hopper, actor Buster Keaton

February 7, 2001: actress Dale Evans, author Anne Morrow Lindbergh

February 14, 1884: the mother (Martha Bulloch Roosevelt) and wife (Alice Lee Roosevelt) of future president Theodore Roosevelt (of different causes)

February 17, 1982: acting teacher Lee Strasberg, jazz musician Thelonious Monk

February 20, 1980: presidential daughter Alice Roosevelt Longworth, parapsychology pioneer Dr. J. B. Rhine

MARCH

March 5, 1953: Soviet leader Joseph Stalin, composer Sergei Prokofiev

March 8, 1999: comedienne Peggy Cass, baseball player Joe DiMaggio

March 17, 1956: comedian Fred Allen, physicist Irene Joliot-Curie

APRIL

April 23, 1986: songwriter Harold Arlen, director Otto Preminger

April 25, 1995: game-show host Art Fleming, actress Ginger Rogers

April 30, 1983: blues singer Muddy Waters, choreographer George Balanchine

MAY

May 16, 1984: author Irwin Shaw, comedian Andy Kaufman

May 21, 2000: author Dame Barbara Cartland, actor Sir John Gielgud

JUNE

June 14, 1896: lyricist Alan Jay Lerner, TV host Marlin Perkins

June 29, 1967: boxer Primo Carnera, actress Jayne Mansfield

JULY

July 21, 1998: astronaut Alan Shepard, actor Robert Young

July 29, 1983: actor Raymond Massey, director Luis Buñuel

AUGUST

August 27, 1971: photographer Margaret Bourke-White, publisher Bennett Cerf

SEPTEMBER

September 5, 1997: Mother Teresa, conductor Sir Georg Solti

September 28, 1970: author John Dos Passos, Egyptian president Gamal Abdel Nasser

OCTOBER

October 14, 1977: singer Bing Crosby, diarist Anaïs Nin

NOVEMBER

November 5, 1960: actor Ward Bond, director Mack Sennett

November 9, 1953: Saudi king Ibn Saud, poet Dylan Thomas

November 22, 1963: author Aldous Huxley, author C. S. Lewis, U.S. president John F. Kennedy

DECEMBER

December 10, 1946: baseball pitcher Walter Johnson, author Damon Runyon

RELATED ODDITIES

Author Miguel de Cervantes and playwright/poet William Shakespeare both died on April 23, 1616, but Shakespeare actually died 11 days after Cervantes. Spain had already adopted the Gregorian calendar by 1616, but Great Britain remained on the Julian calendar until 1752.

Songwriter Cole Porter died on October 15, 1964, the same day that an "American Music" U.S. stamp was issued (honoring the 50th anniversary of the founding of ASCAP, the American music-licensing organization).

Actor William Demarest and pro golfer Jimmy Demaret, whose last names differ by only one letter, died on successive days (December 27th and 28th, 1983, respectively).

Actor McLean Stevenson, who portrayed Colonel Henry Blake in the TV sitcom *M*A*S*H*, and actor Roger Bowen, who had the same role in the film *M*A*S*H*, died on successive days (February 15th and 16th, 1996, respectively).

Diemer, Walter E.

Accountant for the Fleer chewing gum company who invented bubble gum in 1928.

"The Diesel"

Nickname of pro football Hall of Fame running back John Riggins.

Dietrich, Dena

Actress who portrayed Mother Nature in TV commercials for Parkay margarine.

"Different bites for different likes"

Advertising slogan of Peter Paul candy bars, including Mounds and Almond Joy.

"Different Worlds"

Theme song of the TV sitcom *Angie*, performed by Maureen McGovern.

"Difficulties are things that show what men are"

Translation of the Greek motto of Rice University.

Dig'em

Cartoon frog in TV commercials for Kellogg's Sugar Smacks cereal.

"Digger's Daughter"
Premiere episode of the TV series *Dallas*, which aired on April 2, 1978.

Diggs, Oscar Zoroaster Phadrig Isaac Norman Henkle Emmanuel Ambroise
Full name of the title character in the Wizard of Oz book series by L. Frank Baum.

"Dig That Cat . . . He's Real Gone"
See **"The Man Who Was Death," "And All Through the House,"** and **"Dig That Cat . . . He's Real Gone"**

dilithium crystals
Power source of the starship U.S.S. *Enterprise* in the TV series *Star Trek*.

"The Diminutive Dancing Duse from Duluth"
Childhood nickname of Baby Jane Hudson (Bette Davis, Julie Allred as a child) in the film *Whatever Happened to Baby Jane?*

Dimitri
Toy sheep of Balki Bartokomous (Bronson Pinchot) in the TV sitcom *Perfect Strangers*.

DiMucci
Last name of pop singer Dion.

Dinah
Pet cat of the title character in the Lewis Carroll novel *Alice in Wonderland*.

diner slang, numerical
The numbers below were used as "verbal shorthand" by diner employees circa the 1930s.
  2½: small glass of milk
   5: large glass of milk
  41: lemonade
  42: two lemonades (etc.)
  51: hot chocolate
  52: two hot chocolates (etc.)
  55: root beer
  81: glass of water
  82: two glasses of water (etc.)
  86: all out of an item, disregard previous order, person not to be served
  95: customer leaving without paying
  99: report to the manager

"Dingbat"
Archie Bunker's (Carroll O'Connor's) nickname for his wife Edith (Jean Stapleton) in the TV sitcom *All in the Family*.

Dingle, Benjamin
Role for which Charles Coburn won a Best Supporting Actor Academy Award in the 1943 film *The More the Merrier*.

Dinky
Talking Chihuahua in TV commercials for Taco Bell.

Dinny
Pet dinosaur of the title character in the comic strip *Alley Oop*.

Dino
Cartoon dinosaur in TV commercials for Sinclair gasoline.

Pet snorkasaurus (voiced by Mel Blanc) of the title family in the animated TV sitcom *The Flintstones*.

Dino's
Restaurant adjacent to the detective agency in the TV series *77 Sunset Strip*, where Gerald Lloyd "Kookie" Kookson III (Edd Byrnes) is the parking lot attendant. When Kookie becomes a full-fledged detective, J. R. Hale (Robert Logan) replaces him at Dino's.

Dinty Moore's
Favorite bar of Jiggs in the comic strip *Bringing Up Father*.

Dinwiddie, Sebastian
Lou Costello's role in the film *The Naughty Nineties*.

Diogenes
Pet dog of Florence Dombey in the Charles Dickens novel *Dombey and Son*.

Diogenes Club
Private London men's club whose members include Mycroft Holmes, brother of Sherlock Holmes.

Dionne quintuplets
The first known quintuplets to survive past infancy, born to Olivia and Elzire Dionne near Callender, Ontario on May 28, 1934, and delivered by physician Allan Dafoe. Their names: Annette, Cécile, Émilie, Marie, and Yvonne.

Dip
Mixture of turpentine, acetone, and benzene that can kill toons, developed by Judge Doom (Christopher Lloyd) in the film *Who Framed Roger Rabbit*.

diplopia
Medical term for double vision.

Dippy Dawg
Original name of Disney cartoon character Goofy.

Dipsy
See **Tinky Winky, Dipsy, Laa-Laa, and Po**

"The Dipsy Doodle Dandy From Delisle"
Nickname of NHL Hall of Fame center Max Bentley.

directors' first feature films
Woody Allen: *Take the Money and Run* (1969)
Robert Altman: *The Delinquents* (1957)
Peter Bogdanovich: *Targets* (1968)
Mel Brooks: *The Producers* (1968)
Tim Burton: *Pee-wee's Big Adventure* (1985)
James Cameron: *Piranha Part Two: The Spawning* (1981)
Frank Capra: *The Strong Man* (1926)
Francis Ford Coppola: *Dementia 13* (1963)
Wes Craven: *Last House on the Left* (1972)
George Cukor: *Grumpy* (1930)
Cecil B. DeMille: *The Squaw Man* (1914)
Jonathan Demme: *Caged Heat* (1974)
John Frankenheimer: *The Young Stranger* (1957)
Alfred Hitchcock: *The Pleasure Garden* (1925)
John Huston: *The Maltese Falcon* (1941)
Elia Kazan: *A Tree Grows in Brooklyn* (1945)
Stanley Kramer: *Not as a Stranger* (1955)
Stanley Kubrick: *Fear and Desire* (1953)
John Landis: *Schlock* (1971)
David Lean: *In Which We Serve* (1942)
Spike Lee: *She's Gotta Have It* (1986)
Barry Levinson: *Diner* (1982)
David Lynch: *Eraserhead* (1978)
Joseph L. Mankiewicz: *Dragonwyck* (1946)
Vincente Minnelli: *Cabin in the Sky* (1943)
Mike Nichols: *Who's Afraid of Virginia Woolf?* (1966)
Roman Polanski: *Knife in the Water* (1962)
Sydney Pollack: *The Slender Thread* (1965)
Martin Scorsese: *Who's That Knocking at My Door* (1968)
Ridley Scott: *The Duellists* (1977)
Steven Spielberg: *The Sugarland Express* (1974)
Oliver Stone: *Seizure* (1974)
Orson Welles: *Citizen Kane* (1941)
Billy Wilder: *The Major and the Minor* (1942)*
Robert Wise: *The Curse of the Cat People* (1944)
William Wyler: *Crook Buster* (1925)
Robert Zemeckis: *I Wanna Hold Your Hand* (1978)
* First English-language film

directors' last feature films
Frank Capra: *Pocketful of Miracles* (1961)
George Cukor: *Rich and Famous* (1981)
Cecil B. DeMille: *The Ten Commandments* (1956)
Alfred Hitchcock: *Family Plot* (1976)
John Huston: *The Dead* (1987)
Elia Kazan: *The Last Tycoon* (1976)
Stanley Kramer: *The Runner Stumbles* (1979)
Stanley Kubrick: *Eyes Wide Shut* (1999)
David Lean: *A Passage to India* (1984)
Joseph L. Mankiewicz: *Sleuth* (1972)
Vincente Minnelli: *A Matter of Time* (1976)
Orson Welles: *F for Fake* (1974)
Billy Wilder: *Buddy Buddy* (1981)
Robert Wise: *Rooftops* (1989)
William Wyler: *The Liberation of L. B. Jones* (1970)

Dire Straits original members
John Illsley, Dave Knopfler, Mark Knopfler, and Pick Withers.

The Dirty Dozen title characters
Tassos Bravos (Al Mancini)
Victor Franko (John Cassavetes)
Glenn Gilpin (Ben Carruthers)
Robert Jefferson (Jim Brown)
Pedro Jiminez (Trini Lopez)
Roscoe Lever (Stuart Cooper)
Archer Maggott (Telly Savalas)
Vernon Pinkley (Donald Sutherland)
Samson Posey (Clint Walker)
Seth Sawyer (Colin Maitland)
Milo Vladek (Tom Busby)
Joseph Wladislaw (Charles Bronson)
Bronson is the only actor to also portray one of the title characters of *The Magnificent Seven*.

Dirty Harry Burger
See **Hog's Breath Inn**

"Dirty Linen"
Recurring segment in the TV comedy/variety series *The Sonny and Cher Comedy Hour*, set at a coin laundry.

"Disciplina praesidium civitatis"
Motto of the University of Texas, which is Latin for "Education, the defense of the state."

"Disco Lady"
1976 Johnnie Taylor tune that was the first single to be certified as a Platinum Record (sales of two million) by the Recording Industry Association of America.

discophile
Technical term for a collector of phonograph records.

Discovery
See Sarah Constant, Goodspeed, and Discovery

Disco Volante
Yacht of Emilio Largo (Adolfo Celi) in the James Bond film Thunderball.

Disneyland, original areas of
These were the five original areas at Disneyland's opening on July 17, 1955.
>   Main Street, U.S.A. (at the entrance)
>   Adventureland
>   Fantasyland
>   Frontierland
>   Tomorrowland

Disraeli, Benjamin
Role for which George Arliss won a Best Actor Academy Award in the 1929 film Disraeli.

dissected maps
Original name given to jigsaw puzzles, first created in the 18th century to teach geography to children.

"The Divine Miss M"
Nickname of singer/actress Bette Midler.

"divine wind"
What the word "kamikaze" means in Japanese.

Divot, Min
Role for which Marie Dressler won a Best Actress Academy Award in the 1930 film Min and Bill.

Dixie
See "I hate meeces to pieces!"

Dixie Boy Truck Stop
Where vehicles come to life in the film Maximum Overdrive, the directing debut of author Stephen King.

Dixie Chicks original members
Emily Erwin, Martie Erwin, Laura Lynch, and Robin Lynn Macy.

The Dixie Hummingbirds
Gospel quartet that backs up Paul Simon on his Grammy Award-winning tune "Love Me Like a Rock."

Dixieland Bob Cats
Band led by Bob Crosby.

Dixon
Real last name of singer Gene Chandler.

Last name of the title character in the Kingsley Amis novel Lucky Jim.

Dixon, Mason
David Miller's role in the film Attack of the Killer Tomatoes!

Dixon Mills
Small-town setting of the TV series Dr. Simon Locke.

Dixon, Richard M.
Richard Nixon look-alike who portrayed Nixon in several 1970s films, including The Faking of the President.

Dixville Notch, New Hampshire
Town that is traditionally the first to report its presidential election results. All of the town's 30-or-so residents vote right after midnight on Election Day; federal law permits a polling place to close once all eligible votes have been cast.

Djali
Pet goat of Esmeralda (voiced by Demi Moore) in the Disney animated film The Hunchback of Notre Dame.

Djinn Djinn
Pet dog of Jeannie (Barbara Eden) in the TV sitcom I Dream of Jeannie.

Dmitri, Ivan, Alyosha, and Smerdyakov
Title characters of the Fyodor Dostoevsky novel The Brothers Karamazov.

DNA
Stock-ticker symbol of biotech company Genentech.

Do Androids Dream of Electric Sheep?
Novel by Philip K. Dick that was the basis for the film Blade Runner.

Dobson
Maiden name of Samantha Stephens (Elizabeth Montgomery) in the TV sitcom Bewitched.

Dobson and Kelley
Law-firm employer of David Nelson in the TV sitcom The Adventures of Ozzie and Harriet.

Doc Hopper's French Fried Frog Legs
Fast-food establishment whose eponymous owner (Charles Durning) unsuccessfully tries to hire Kermit the Frog as a spokesman, in The Muppet Movie.

Doctor of Bovinity

Honorary degree awarded to Borden mascot Elsie the Cow. Elsie has also received the honorary degrees Doctor of Human Kindness and Doctor of Ecownomics.

"The Doctor Will See You Now"

Vaudeville comedy sketch that Al Lewis and Willie Clark reunite to perform, in the Neil Simon play *The Sunshine Boys*.

"Does she . . . or doesn't she?"

Advertising slogan of Miss Clairol hair color.

Dog

Pet basset hound of the title character (Peter Falk) in the TV series *Columbo*.

dog breeds

These 148 breeds of dogs are currently eligible for registration by the American Kennel Club (AKC):

SPORTING DOGS (25)

Brittany
Pointer
German Shorthaired Pointer
German Wirehaired Pointer
Chesapeake Bay Retriever
Curly-Coated Retriever
Flat-Coated Retriever
Golden Retriever
Labrador Retriever
English Setter
Gordon Setter
Irish Setter
American Water Spaniel
Clumber Spaniel
Cocker Spaniel
English Cocker Spaniel
English Springer Spaniel
Field Spaniel
Irish Water Spaniel
Spinone Italiano
Sussex Spaniel
Welsh Springer Spaniel
Vizsla
Weimaraner
Wirehaired Pointing Griffon

HOUNDS (22)

Afghan Hound
Basenji
Basset Hound
Beagle
Black and Tan Coonhound
Bloodhound

Borzoi
Dachshund
Foxhound (American)
Foxhound (English)
Greyhound
Harrier
Ibizan Hound
Irish Wolfhound
Norwegian Elkhound
Otterhound
Petit Basset Griffon Vendeen
Pharaoh Hound
Rhodesian Ridgeback
Saluki
Scottish Deerhound
Whippet

WORKING DOGS (21)

Akita
Alaskan Malamute
Anatolian Shepherd
Bernese Mountain Dog
Boxer
Bullmastiff
Doberman Pinscher
Giant Schnauzer
Great Dane
Great Pyrenees
Greater Swiss Mountain Dog
Komondor
Kuvasz
Mastiff
Newfoundland
Portuguese Water Dog
Rottweiler
Saint Bernard
Samoyed
Siberian Husky
Standard Schnauzer

TERRIERS (26)

Airedale Terrier
American Staffordshire Terrier
Australian Terrier
Bedlington Terrier
Border Terrier
Bull Terrier
Cairn Terrier
Dandie Dinmont Terrier
Fox Terrier (Smooth)
Fox Terrier (Wire)
Irish Terrier
Jack Russell Terrier
Kerry Blue Terrier
Lakeland Terrier
Manchester Terrier (Standard)

Miniature Bull Terrier
Miniature Schnauzer
Norfolk Terrier
Norwich Terrier
Scottish Terrier
Sealyham Terrier
Skye Terrier
Soft Coated Wheaten Terrier
Staffordshire Bull Terrier
Welsh Terrier
West Highland White Terrier

Toy Dogs (20)

Affenpinscher
Brussels Griffon
Cavalier King Charles Spaniel
Chihuahua
Chinese Crested
English Toy Spaniel
Havanese
Italian Greyhound
Japanese Chin
Maltese
Manchester Terrier
Miniature Pinscher
Papillon
Pekingese
Pomeranian
Poodle
Pug
Shih Tzu
Silky Terrier
Yorkshire Terrier

Non-Sporting Dogs (17)

American Eskimo Dog
Bichon Frise
Boston Terrier
Bulldog
Chinese Shar-pei
Chow Chow
Dalmatian
Finnish Spitz
French Bulldog
Keeshond
Lhasa Apso
Löwchen
Poodle
Schipperke
Shiba Inu
Tibetan Spaniel
Tibetan Terrier

Herding Dogs (17)

Australian Cattle Dog
Australian Shepherd

Bearded Collie
Belgian Malinois
Belgian Sheepdog
Belgian Tervuren
Border Collie
Bouvier des Flandres
Briard
Canaan Dog
Collie
German Shepherd Dog
Old English Sheepdog
Puli
Shetland Sheepdog
Welsh Corgi (Cardigan)
Welsh Corgi (Pembroke)

THESE NEW BREEDS, BEING CONSIDERED FOR EVEN-
TUAL AKC REGISTRATION, ARE CURRENTLY IN A
"MISCELLANEOUS" CLASS:

Polish Lowland Sheepdog
Plott Hound
German Pinscher
Toy Fox Terrier

"The Dog-Gone Affair"

Debut episode of the TV series *The Girl from
U.N.C.L.E.*, which aired on September 13, 1966.

"The dogs kids love to bite"

Advertising slogan of Armour hot dogs.

Dogsled Delight

See **Frosty Palace**

"D'oh!"

All-purpose exclamation of Homer Simpson (voiced
by Dan Castellaneta) in the animated TV sitcom
The Simpsons.

"Doing what we do best"

Advertising slogan of American Airlines.

"Doin' It the Best I Can"

Theme song of the TV sitcom *Just the Ten of Us*, performed by Bill Medley.

Dollar

Pet dog of the title character in the *Richie Rich* comic
books.

"Dollar Bill"

Nickname of basketball Hall of Famer Bill Bradley,
for his frugality.

Dolly
See **Boatswain**

Dollywood
Pigeon Forge, Tennessee, theme park of country singer Dolly Parton, which opened in 1986.

Dolores
Real first name of the title character (last name Haze) in the Vladimir Nabokov novel *Lolita*.

Dolphin
Abandoned ship where Garrity (Tommy Lee Jones) makes his home in the film *Blown Away*.

Domination
3-D video game played by James Bond (Sean Connery) and Maximilian Largo (Klaus Maria Brandauer) in the film *Never Say Never Again*.

"Domine dirige nos"
Motto of London, England, which is Latin for "Lord, direct us."

The Domingoes
Original name of pop group The Spinners.

"The Dominican Dandy"
Nickname of Hall of Fame baseball pitcher Juan Marichal.

Dominion Day
Former name of Canada Day (July 1), which celebrates the formation of the Dominion of Canada on that date in 1867.

Domino
Horse of Jeff Miller (Tommy Rettig) in the 1950s version of the TV series *Lassie*.

"Dominus illuminatio mea"
Motto of Oxford University, which is Latin for "The Lord is my light."

Don
Broken-down racehorse (voiced by John Candy) that wins the El Segundo Stakes by an incisor in the climactic scene of the film *Hot to Trot*.

Don Juan Triumphant
See **Hannibal, Il Muto, and Don Juan Triumphant**

"Donna Diana Overture"
Instrumental theme of the children's TV series *Sergeant Preston of the Yukon*.

Donnell and Associates
Original name of the law firm in the TV series *The Practice*, which was later called Donnell, Young, Dole, and Frutt.

Donovan, Marion
Inventor of disposable diapers in 1951.

Don Quixote de la Mancha, expressions from
All of these common expressions originated from this Miguel de Cervantes book:
  A finger in every pie
  Born with a silver spoon in one's mouth
  Forewarned is forearmed
  Give the devil his due
  Honesty is the best policy
  Mum's the word
  No love lost
  The pot calling the kettle black
  The proof of the pudding is in the eating
  Raise a hue and cry
  The sky's the limit
  A stone's throw
  Smell a rat
  Thank you for nothing
  Time out of mind
  Turn over a new leaf
  Too much of a good thing
  Wild-goose chase
  A word to the wise is sufficient

Don's Diner
Where Clark Kent (Christopher Reeve) is beaten up by Rocky (Pepper Martin) after losing his superpowers, in the film *Superman II*.

"Don't be ridikalus!"
Catchphrase of Balki Bartokomous (Bronson Pinchot) in the TV sitcom *Perfect Strangers*.

"Don't Eat the Snow in Hawaii"
Debut episode of the TV series *Magnum, p.i.*, which aired on December 11, 1980.

"Don't get mad. Get everything."
Slogan used to promote the film *The First Wives Club*. The line was spoken in the film by Ivana Trump, portraying herself in a cameo.

"Don't get me started!"
Catchphrase of comedian Buddy Young Jr. (Billy Crystal) in the film *Mr. Saturday Night*.

"Don't give up the ship"
See **Chesapeake**

"Don't leave home without it"
Advertising slogan of the American Express credit card.

"Don't put a cold in your pocket"
Advertising slogan of Kleenex tissues.

"Don't You Worry 'Bout Me"
Subtitle of the tune "Opus 17," performed by The Four Seasons.

Doodyville
Setting of the children's TV series *Howdy Doody*.

Dookie
Childhood pet Corgi of Queen Elizabeth II.

Dooley
Boy who wears crazy clothes in the Dodie Stevens tune "Pink Shoelaces."

Doolin, Elmer
San Antonio native who created Fritos corn chips in 1932.

"The Doomsday Defense"
Nickname of the defensive unit of the Dallas Cowboys from the mid-1960s to the early 1970s, led by Bob Lilly, Jethro Pugh, and Mel Renfro.

Doom, Thulsa
Enemy of the title character (Arnold Schwarzenegger) in the film *Conan the Barbarian*, portrayed by James Earl Jones.

The Doors (rock group) members
John Densmore, Robby Krieger, Ray Manzarek, and Jim Morrison.

Dorgan, Tad
New York sports cartoonist credited with coining the term "hot dogs" for frankfurters in 1901.

The Do-Rights
Backup band of country singer Barbara Mandrell.

Dorothy
Real first name of actress (Dorothy) Faye Dunaway.

Instrument pack built by Jo Harding (Helen Hunt) for studying tornadoes from the inside, in the film *Twister*, named for the character in *The Wizard of Oz*.

Dorsett
Last name of the title character in the Flora Rheta Schreiber book *Sybil*.

Dorsey and Colbert
Last names of the title characters (Thomas Haden Church and Debra Messing, respectively) in the TV sitcom *Ned and Stacey*.

Dorsey, Arnold George
Real name of pop singer Engelbert Humperdinck.

"Do the Bop"
Original name of the Danny and the Juniors tune "At the Hop."

Dotheboys Hall
School where the title character is assistant master, in the Charles Dickens novel *The Life and Adventures of Nicholas Nickleby*.

Dot Matrix
Robot portrayed by Lorene Yarnell (voiced by Joan Rivers) in the film *Spaceballs*.

Dottie
Name given to the asteroid on a collision course with Earth in the film *Armageddon*.

Dottie's Squat 'n' Gobble
Restaurant where Butch Haynes (Kevin Costner) and his young hostage Phillip Perry (T. J. Lowther) stop for hamburgers in the film *A Perfect World*.

Double Crunch
Favorite cereal of the title character in the TV sitcom *Seinfeld*.

Double Doody
Stand-in for the title character in the children's TV series *Howdy Doody*.

Double Eagle II
The first balloon to make a successful transatlantic crossing, August 11–17, 1978. Passengers Ben Abruzzo, Maxie Anderson, and Larry Newman traveled from Presque Isle, Maine, to a farm field in France.

"Double No Hit"
Nickname of Cincinnati Reds pitcher Johnny Vander Meer, the only hurler to toss consecutive no-hitters. The first was against the Boston Bees on June 11, 1938, and second versus the Brooklyn Dodgers on June 15 (the first night game ever played at Ebbets Field).

Double R Bar Ranch

Home of TV Western stars Roy Rogers and Dale Evans.

"Double Showdown"

Debut episode of the TV Western series *Bat Masterson*, which aired on September 8, 1958.

Douglas

Real first name of the title character (Neil Patrick Harris) in the TV sitcom *Doogie Howser, M.D.*

Douglas Commercial

What "DC" stands for in the names of McDonnell Douglas aircraft such as the DC-10.

Douglas, Sir John Sholto

Real name of the 8th Marquis of Queensberry, who in 1857 formulated the modern rules of boxing. Its main elements:

Three-minute rounds
One-minute rest between rounds
Wearing of boxing gloves
Returning to a neutral corner in case of a knock-down
Ten-second count for a knockout

Dove Cottage

Home of poet William Wordsworth, located in the Lake District of northern England.

Dover

Horse that Eliza Doolittle bets on at Ascot, in the Lerner and Loewe musical *My Fair Lady*.

Dow Jones Industrial Average numerical milestones

November 14, 1972: First close over 1,000
January 8, 1987: First close over 2,000
April 17, 1991: First close over 3,000
February 23, 1995: First close over 4,000
November 21, 1995: First close over 5,000
October 14, 1996: First close over 6,000
February 13, 1997: First close over 7,000
July 16, 1997: First close over 8,000
April 6, 1998: First close over 9,000
March 28, 1999: First close over 10,000

Dow Jones Industrial Average original stocks

Now consisting of 30 stocks, the Dow Jones Industrial Average was created by Charles Dow in May 1896, with these 12 stocks:

American Cotton Oil
American Sugar Refining Co.
American Tobacco
Chicago Gas
Distilling & Cattle Feeding Co.
General Electric Co.
Laclede Gas Light Co.
National Lead
North American Co.
Tennessee Coal, Iron & Railroad Co.
U.S. Leather
U.S. Rubber Co.

"down-easter"

See **United States residents' nicknames**

The Down Homers

Original name of rock group Bill Haley and the Comets. It was later called The Saddlemen before adopting its best-known name. (The group originally specialized in country music.)

Downingtown Diner

Establishment attacked by the title character in the film *The Blob* (1958).

"Down with common sense"

See **Surprise Party**

Doyle, Edie

Role for which Eva Marie Saint won a Best Supporting Actress Academy Award in the 1954 film *On the Waterfront*.

Doyle, James "Popeye"

Role for which Gene Hackman won a Best Actor Academy Award in the 1971 film *The French Connection*.

"Do you believe in miracles?"

Memorable words spoken by sportscaster Al Michaels as the underdog U.S. hockey team defeated the Soviet Union at the 1980 Winter Olympics at Lake Placid, New York.

"Do You Know What It Means to Miss New Orleans?"

Theme song of the TV sitcom *Frank's Place*, performed by Louis Armstrong.

"Do you mind? Do . . . you . . . mind?"

Catchphrase of Officer Gunther Toody (Joe E. Ross) in the TV sitcom *Car 54, Where Are You?*

Dozier, William

Executive producer of the TV series *Batman*, who served as the show's narrator.

"Draco dormiens nunquam titillandus"

Motto of Hogwarts (Latin for "Never tickle a sleeping dragon") in the Harry Potter series of books by J. K. Rowling.

Draconians

Enemy aliens in the TV series *Buck Rogers in the 25th Century.*

Draco, Tracy

Diana Rigg's role in the James Bond film *On Her Majesty's Secret Service.* Briefly married to James Bond (George Lazenby), she is murdered on her wedding day.

Dracula

Maiden name of Lily Munster (Yvonne DeCarlo) in the TV sitcom *The Munsters.*

Dragline

Role for which George Kennedy won a Best Supporting Actor Academy Award in the 1967 film *Cool Hand Luke.*

Dragon, Daryl

Real name of The Captain, of the pop duo the Captain and Tennille. His father was bandleader/composer Carmen Dragon.

Dragonfly Ripple

Ice-cream flavor enjoyed by Kermit the Frog in *The Muppet Movie.*

Dragon, Oliver J.

See 1

Drake

Last name of Eve (Ida Lupino) in the TV sitcom *Mr. Adams and Eve.*

Drake, Edwin

Driller of the world's first oil well, at Titusville, Pennsylvania, which struck oil on August 17, 1859.

Dravot, Daniel

Title character of the Rudyard Kipling short story "The Man Who Would Be King," portrayed in the film adaptation of the same name by Sean Connery.

Drayton, Christina

Role for which Katharine Hepburn won a Best Actress Academy Award in the 1967 film *Guess Who's Coming to Dinner.*

Dream

Allied code name for Pearl Harbor during World War II.

"Dream Butcher"

Nickname coined by the press for the murderer of Colonel MacFay (C. Aubrey Smith) in the film *Another Thin Man.*

Dreamchaser

Tour bus of country-music duo The Judds.

The Dreamlovers

Vocal group that backs up Chubby Checker on his tune "The Twist."

"The Dream Team"

Nickname of the victorious U.S. basketball team at the 1992 Summer Olympics, coached by Chuck Daly.

    Charles Barkley
    Larry Bird
    Clyde Drexler
    Patrick Ewing
    Magic Johnson
    Michael Jordan
    Christian Laettner
    Karl Malone
    Chris Mullin
    Scottie Pippen
    David Robinson
    John Stockton

This was the first time that NBA players were allowed to be on an Olympic team. Duke University senior Christian Laettner was the only non-NBA player on the team.

"Dreamy Blues"

Original title of the Duke Ellington tune "Mood Indigo."

Drew, Richard

3M employee who invented masking tape in 1925 and transparent tape in 1930.

Dreyfus, Alfred

Role for which Joseph Schildkraut won a Best Supporting Actor Academy Award in the 1937 film *The Life of Emile Zola.*

Dreyfuss

Family dog in the TV sitcom *Empty Nest.*

"Dr. Hug"

Nickname of self-help author Leo Buscaglia.

The Drifting Cowboys
Backup band of country singer Hank Williams.

Driftwood, Otis B.
See **Marx, Groucho, roles of**

"Drink it and sleep"
Advertising slogan of Sanka decaffeinated coffee.

"drive on the left" countries

Anguilla	Mauritania
Antigua and Barbuda	Mozambique
Australia	Namibia
Bangladesh	Nepal
Barbados	New Zealand
Bhutan	Pakistan
Brunei	Papua New Guinea
Bahamas	Seychelles
Bermuda	Singapore
Botswana	Solomon Islands
Cyprus	South Africa
Dominica	Sri Lanka
Falkland Islands	St. Lucia
Fiji	St. Vincent and
Grenada	Grenadines
Guyana	Suriname
Hong Kong	Swaziland
India	Tanzania
Indonesia	Thailand
Jamaica	Tonga
Japan	Trinidad and Tobago
Kenya	Uganda
Lesotho	United Kingdom
Macau	Virgin Islands (U.S.
Malta	and British)
Malawi	Zambia
Malaysia	Zimbabwe

Driver
Real last name of comedienne Phyllis Diller.

"Drivers wanted"
Advertising slogan of Volkswagen.

Driver, William
Salem, Massachusetts, sea captain who coined the nickname "Old Glory" for the American flag in 1831.

"driving delight"
See **"Fahrvergnügen"**

Drizella
See **Anastasia and Drizella**

"Dr. J"
Nickname of pro basketball player Julius Erving.

Dr. Kildare films

Joel McCrea as Dr. Kildare
Internes Can't Take Money (1937)

Lew Ayres as Dr. Kildare
Young Dr. Kildare (1938)
Calling Dr. Kildare (1939)
The Secret of Dr. Kildare (1939)
Dr. Kildare's Strange Case (1940)
Dr. Kildare Goes Home (1940)
Dr. Kildare's Crisis (1940)
The People vs. Dr. Kildare (1941)
Dr. Kildare's Victory (1941)

Droogs
Gang led by Alex (Malcolm McDowell) in the film *A Clockwork Orange*.

Droopalong
Coyote sidekick of TV cartoon character Ricochet Rabbit, voiced by Mel Blanc.

drosometer
Instrument for measuring the amount of dew on a surface.

Drowsy Venus Chapter
See **Sacred Stars of the Milky Way**

Dr. Who portrayers
Actors who have played the title role of this British TV series:
William Hartnell (1963–66)
Patrick Troughton (1966–69)
John Pertwee (1969–73)
Tom Baker (1974–80)
Peter Davison (1980–84)
Colin Baker (1984–86)
Sylvester McCoy (1986–96)
Paul McGann (1996)

DuBois
Last name of the title character (Robert Guillaume) in the TV sitcom *Benson*.

DuBois, Blanche
Role for which Vivien Leigh won a Best Actress Academy Award in the 1951 film *A Streetcar Named Desire*.

Dubonnet
Horse owned by Caroline Whipple (Binnie Barnes) in the film *Broadway Melody of 1938*.

Duc de Duras

French merchant ship that was renamed the *Bonhomme Richard* when placed under the command of Revolutionary War naval hero John Paul Jones. Jones renamed the vessel for Richard Saunders, pen name of Benjamin Franklin.

The Duchess of Brighton

Role for which Margaret Rutherford won a Best Supporting Actress Academy Award in the 1963 film *The V.I.P.s*.

Duckburg, Calisota

Home of Disney cartoon character Donald Duck.

Duckpin

Allied code name for General Dwight D. Eisenhower during World War II.

duckwalk

Distinctive guitar-playing crouch step invented by rock singer Chuck Berry.

Dudevant, Amandine-Aurore-Lucile (née Dupin)

Real name of French author George Sand.

Duff

Favorite beer brand of Homer Simpson (voiced by Dan Castellaneta) in the animated TV sitcom *The Simpsons*.

Dugan's Detective Training

School (DDT for short) from which Bud Alexander (Bud Abbott) and Louis Francis (Lou Costello) graduate in the film *Abbott and Costello Meet the Invisible Man*.

Duke

Childhood pet dog of John Wayne, which was the source of his nickname.

Pet bloodhound of Jed Clampett (Buddy Ebsen) in the TV sitcom *The Beverly Hillbillies*.

Pet dog of Groucho Marx, circa 1940.

See also **Turk and Duke**

Dukenfield, William Claude

Real name of actor W. C. Fields.

The Duke of Death

Book written by W. W. Beauchamp (Saul Rubinek) about gunfighter English Bob (Richard Harris) in the film *Unforgiven*.

Duke of Edinburgh

Title held by Prince Philip of Great Britain, husband of Queen Elizabeth II.

Dumbella

Sister of Disney cartoon character Donald Duck. She is the mother of Donald's nephews Huey, Dewey, and Louie.

Dumble-Smith

Real last name of English stage actor/singer Michael Crawford.

Dummar, Lynda

Role for which Mary Steenburgen won a Best Supporting Actress Academy Award in the 1980 film *Melvin and Howard*.

du Motier, Marie Joseph Paul Yves Roch Gilbert

Real name of Revolutionary War hero, the Marquis de Lafayette.

"Dump Truck"

See **"Meat Bomb" and "Dump Truck"**

Duncan, Lee

Trainer of the title character in the children's TV series *The Adventures of Rin Tin Tin*.

Dunker

Allied code name for Russian foreign minister Vyacheslav Molotov during World War II.

Dunkie

1950s cartoon mascot of Dunkin' Donuts. He had a donut for a head, and crullers for arms and legs.

"The Dunking Dutchman"

Nickname of NBA player Rik Smits, who was born in the Netherlands.

Dunk-U-Very-Much University

Alma mater of ThunderBolt, aka Thunder, superhero mascot of the NBA's Golden State Warriors.

Dunn's River, Connecticut

Setting of the TV sitcom *Soap*.

Duran Duran original members

Simon Le Bon, Nick Rhodes, Andy Taylor, John Taylor, and Roger Taylor. (None of the Taylors are related.)

Durante, Sal

Brooklyn, New York, delivery driver who caught the record 61st home-run ball of 1961 hit by New York Yankee Roger Maris, on October 1st at Yankee Stadium.

"dusty"

What the word "khaki" means in Hindi.

Dutch East Indies

Former name of the Asian nation Indonesia.

Dutch Guiana

Former name of the South American nation Suriname.

Dutch West Indies

Former name of the Netherlands Antilles.

"Duty, Honor, Country"

Motto of the U.S. Military Academy at West Point, New York.

Dymaxion 4D

11-seat garageable aluminum vehicle built by R. Buckminster Fuller in 1933, the precursor of the minivan.

The Dynamics of an Asteroid

Book published by Professor James Moriarty, as mentioned by Sherlock Holmes in the Sir Arthur Conan Doyle novel *The Valley of Fear*.

dynamic tension

Bodybuilding technique of Charles Atlas.

Dynamite

Wild white stallion in the "Further Adventures of Spin and Marty" segment of the children's TV series *The Mickey Mouse Club*.

Dynamo

Allied code name for the evacuation of Dunkirk in May/June 1940.

Secret Service code name for Amy Carter.

"Dy-no-mite!"

Favorite exclamation of James Evans Jr. (Jimmie Walker) in the TV sitcom *Good Times*.

dyspepsia

Medical term for indigestion.

Dzugashvili

Real last name of Russian leader Joseph Stalin. "Stalin" means "man of steel" in Russian.

Eagan, Eddie
Only athlete to have won a gold medal in both the Summer Olympics (boxing, 1920) and Winter Olympics (bobsled team, 1932).

Eagle
Code name of fighter pilot Steven Hiller (Will Smith) in the film *Independence Day*.

Secret Service code name for Bill Clinton.

Eagle, Jack
Actor who portrayed Brother Dominic in TV commercials for Xerox.

Eagle Nation Films
Production company of actor LeVar Burton.

Eagle of Saladin
Bird depicted on the flag of Egypt.

Eagle Rock, Iowa
Town that attempts to give up smoking for one month to win $25,000,000, in the film *Cold Turkey*.

Earl
Real first name of Green Bay Packers founder/player/coach Curly Lambeau.

Earle, Diane
Real name of pop singer Diana Ross.

Earl of Wessex
Title bestowed on Great Britain's Prince Edward by his mother, Queen Elizabeth II, upon his marriage to Sophie Rhys-Jones in June 1999.

Earlybird
The first commercial communications satellite, launched by the U.S. in 1965.

Early, Delloreese Patricia
Real name of singer/actress Della Reese.

"earth pig"
What the word "aardvark" means in Afrikaans.

Earwicker, Humphrey Chimpden
Man whose night of dreams is the focus of the James Joyce novel *Finnegans Wake*.

East Egg, New York
Long Island home of Tom and Daisy Buchanan in the F. Scott Fitzgerald novel *The Great Gatsby*.

Eastland School for Girls
Setting of the TV sitcom *The Facts of Life*.

East London Christian Mission
Original name of the organization that would become the Salvation Army.

Eastman, Kevin
See **Teenage Mutant Ninja Turtles**

Eastman Medical Center
Los Angeles employer of the title character (Neil Patrick Harris) in the TV sitcom *Doogie Howser, M.D.*

"The Easton Assassin"
Nickname of 1980s heavyweight boxing champ Larry Holmes.

East Pakistan
Former name of the Asian nation Bangladesh.

Eastport, Massachusetts
Setting of the film *Mermaids*.

East Side Story
Original working title of the Broadway musical *West Side Story*.

Eastwood, Clint
Pseudonym used by Marty McFly (Michael J. Fox) in 1885's Hill Valley, California, in the film *Back to the Future Part III*.

Eastwood/Locke films
Films in which Clint Eastwood and Sondra Locke appear together:
  The Outlaw Josey Wales (1976)
  The Gauntlet (1977)

Every Which Way but Loose (1978)
Bronco Billy (1980)
Any Which Way You Can (1980)
Sudden Impact (1983)

"Easy Ed"

Nickname of basketball Hall of Fame center Ed Macauley.

Easy Valley, California

Setting of the TV sitcom *The Jimmy Stewart Show*, where Professor James Howard (Stewart) teaches anthropology at Josiah Kessel College.

Eatanswill Gazette and *Eatanswill Independent*

Rival publications in the Charles Dickens novel *The Pickwick Papers*.

Eaton, Shirley

English actress who portrays Jill Masterson in the 1964 James Bond film *Goldfinger*, in which her character is murdered by being painted gold from head to toe.

eBay, prohibited items on

eBay is the Internet's most popular auction site.
Advertisements
Alcohol
Animals and wildlife products
Cable TV descramblers
Catalogs (current issues)
Counterfeit items
Drugs and drug paraphernalia
Embargoed goods
Firearms
Fireworks
Government IDs and licenses
Human body parts
Lock-picking devices
Lottery tickets
Postage meters
Prescription drugs and materials
Recalled items
Stocks and other securities
Stolen property
Surveillance equipment
Tobacco

Ebenezer

Pet donkey of President Calvin Coolidge.

E. Buzz

Family dog in the film *Poltergeist*.

ecchymosis

Medical term for a bruise.

Eclipse

See **Byerly Turk, Darley Arabian, and Godolphin Barb**

Eclipse

Original title of the Pink Floyd album *The Dark Side of the Moon*.

"The Ecology"

Subtitle of the Marvin Gaye tune "Mercy Mercy Me."

Ecomcon

Secret military group stationed near El Paso, formed to help General James Matoon Scott (Burt Lancaster) overthrow the U.S. government, in the film *Seven Days in May*.

Ecstasy

Pet cat of Ernest Hemingway.

ECTO-1

License plate of the converted ambulance of the title characters in the film *Ghostbusters*.

Edda Gunnar

First and middle names of actor E. G. Marshall.

Eddie

Dog that regularly chases bikers Marcus and David Sommers (Kevin Costner and David Grant) in the film *American Flyers*.

Pet Jack Russell terrier of Martin Crane (John Mahoney) in the TV sitcom *Frasier*.

Eddie Gottlieb Trophy

Awarded annually since 1953 to the NBA rookie of the year, named for the former owner-coach of the Philadelphia Warriors.

Eddie Robinson Award

Annual trophy given to the outstanding head coach in Division I-AA college football, named for the all-time winningest college coach (408 wins at Grambling State).

Eddy/MacDonald films

See **MacDonald/Eddy films**

Eddy, Mary Baker

Founder of Christian Science in 1879.

"Edelweiss"

Last song lyric written by Oscar Hammerstein II, for *The Sound of Music*.

Edgar

Real first name of Zonker Harris in the comic strip *Doonesbury*.

Middle name of Captain Jeffrey T. Spaulding (Groucho Marx) in the Marx Brothers film *Animal Crackers*.

Edgar Allan Poe Awards

Presented annually since 1954 by the Mystery Writers of America for excellence in fiction and nonfiction mystery writing. The awards are familiarly known as the "Edgars."

Edgar Lawrence

First and middle names of novelist E. L. Doctorow.

Edgar Montillion

Real first and middle names of actor Monty Woolley.

Edgerton, David

See **McLamore, James and Edgerton, David**

Edie

Ex-wife of Lou Grant (Edward Asner) in the TV sitcom *The Mary Tyler Moore Show*, portrayed by Priscilla Morrill.

Edison

Potts family sheepdog in the film *Chitty Chitty Bang Bang*.

Last name of the title character in the Beatles tune "Maxwell's Silver Hammer."

Edith

Real first name of actress (Edith) Norma Shearer.

Edmont Hotel

New York City residence of Holden Caulfield in the J. D. Salinger novel *The Catcher in the Rye*.

Edmund

Real first name of cowboy actor Hoot Gibson, who got his nickname because he hunted owls as a boy.

Edna, Colorado

Hometown of the title character (Charles Bronson) in the film *Mr. Majestyk*.

Edna Mae

Real first and middle names of actress Deanna Durbin.

Edward

Real first name of actor (Edward) Montgomery Clift.

Pet Welsh corgi of Macon Leary (William Hurt) in the film *The Accidental Tourist*.

Edward Albert Christian George Andrew Patrick David

Full name of King Edward VIII of Great Britain, later the Duke of Windsor. His friends and family called him David.

Edward and Canty, Tom

Title characters of the Mark Twain novel *The Prince and the Pauper*.

Edward Charles

Real first and middle names of Hall of Fame baseball pitcher Whitey Ford.

Edward Estlin

First and middle names of poet e. e. cummings.

Edward Fairfax

First and middle names of Captain Vere in the Herman Melville novel *Billy Budd*.

Edward Kennedy

Real first and middle names of composer/bandleader Duke Ellington.

Edward Morgan

First and middle names of novelist E. M. Forster.

Edwards and Peabody

Last names of the title characters (Chester Lauck and Norris Goff, respectively) in the radio sitcom *Lum and Abner*.

Edwards, Eileen Regina

Birth name of country singer Shania Twain.

Edwards, Elwood

Professional voice-over artist heard by America Online users saying, "You've got mail," "Welcome," "File's done," and "Goodbye."

Edwin

Middle name of author Stephen King.

Edwin Donald

Real first and middle names of baseball Hall of Famer Duke Snider.

Edwin Eugene

Real first and middle names of astronaut Buzz Aldrin.

Edwinton

Original name of Bismarck, North Dakota, before being renamed in 1873 (in honor of German chancellor Otto von Bismarck) to encourage German immigrants to settle there.

"Effendi"

Nickname of publisher Frank N. Doubleday (1862–1934), derived from his initials. The nickname (the Turkish word for "master") was given to Doubleday by author Rudyard Kipling.

Efthimios

Middle name of diver Greg Louganis.

Egdon Heath

English setting of the Thomas Hardy novel *The Return of the Native*.

Eggleston, Estelle

Real name of actress Stella Stevens.

Egg Pictures

Production company of actress Jodie Foster.

egg sizes

As regulated by the U.S. Department of Agriculture, listed below with the minimum net weight (in ounces) per dozen.

Peewee (15)
Small (18)
Medium (21)
Large (24)
Extra Large (27)
Jumbo (30)

Egingwah, Ooqueah, Ootah, and Seegloo

The four Greenland Eskimos who, together with Matthew Henson and Robert Peary, were the first to reach the North Pole, on April 6, 1909.

Egstrom, Norma

Real name of singer Peggy Lee.

Eight Arms to Hold You

Original working title of the Beatles film *Help!*

Eight Ball messages

See **Magic 8-Ball messages**

Eight Is Enough children

The children of Tom Bradford (Dick Van Patten) in this TV series (from oldest to youngest):

David (Grant Goodeve)
Mary (Lani O'Grady)
Joannie (Laurie Walters)
Susan (Susan Richardson)
Nancy (Dianne Kay)
Elizabeth (Connie Needham)
Tommy (Willie Aames)
Nicholas (Adam Rich)

Einstein

Pet dog of Dr. Emmett L. Brown (Christopher Lloyd) in the *Back to the Future* films.

Einstein, Albert

See **Parkyakarkis**

El Dorado

Manhattan apartment building that is the home of the title character in the Herman Wouk novel *Marjorie Morningstar*.

El Dorado Pictures

Production company of actor Alec Baldwin.

Eldred

Real first name of actor (Eldred) Gregory Peck.

Eldrick

Real first name of pro golfer Tiger Woods.

ELE

Abbreviation for Extinction Level Event, military term applied to the impending collision of a comet with Earth, in the film *Deep Impact*.

Eleanor

Real first name of former First Lady (Eleanor) Rosalynn Carter.

Douglas family cow in the TV sitcom *Green Acres*.

Eleanor, Beaver, and Dartmouth

The three English ships from which a total of 342 chests of tea were thrown overboard during the Boston Tea Party on December 16, 1773.

Eleanor of Aquitaine

Role for which Katharine Hepburn won a Best Actress Academy Award in the 1968 film *The Lion in Winter*.

Electra

Pet dog of the title character in the comic strip *Cathy*.

Electric & Musical Industries

What the letters of English recording label EMI stand for.

"The Electric Company"

Nickname of the 1970s offensive line of the NFL Buffalo Bills, led by Reggie McKenzie.

electric hand torch

Original name of the flashlight.

Electric Lady Studios

First recording studio owned and operated by a major artist, built by Jimi Hendrix and opened in New York City on August 27, 1970, less than a month before his death. The studio, named for Hendrix's album *Electric Ladyland*, is still in operation today, with scores of well-known artists having recorded there.

The Electric Mayhem

Backup band of Dr. Teeth (voiced by Jim Henson) in the children's TV series *The Muppet Show*.

Electro-Alkaline Company

Original name of Clorox.

Electronicam

Filming technique (replacing the kinescope process) used for the 39 original 1955 episodes of the TV sitcom *The Honeymooners*.

"electronic bay"

What the name of Internet auction service eBay, headquartered in the San Francisco Bay area, stands for.

Electronic Cafe International

The first cybercafe, which opened in Santa Monica, California, in 1988.

Electronic Numerical Integrator and Calculator

Full name of ENIAC, the world's first large-scale general-purpose electronic computer, which was activated at the University of Pennsylvania in 1946.

Electro Steel Corporation

Employer of the main character (Charlie Chaplin) in the film *Modern Times*.

"elephant's trunk"

What the name of Khartoum, capital city of the Sudan, means in Arabic.

"Eleven Days to Zero"

Debut episode of the TV series *Voyage to the Bottom of the Sea*, which aired on September 14, 1964.

Elgin, Georgie

Role for which Grace Kelly won a Best Actress Academy Award in the 1954 film *The Country Girl*.

The Elgins

Original name of the pop group The Temptations.

Elia

Pen name of English essayist/author Charles Lamb.

Elias

Middle name of Walt Disney.

Elijah's Manna

Original name of the corn-flake cereal known today as Post Toasties.

The Eliminator

Overpowering pitch developed by Cleveland Indian pitcher Ricky Vaughn (Charlie Sheen) in the film *Major League II*.

Elinor and Marianne

Original working title of the Jane Austen novel *Sense and Sensibility*.

The Elixir of Egypt

Secret-formula potion bought by Laurey from Ali Hakim in the Rodgers and Hammerstein musical *Oklahoma!*

Eli Yale

Pet macaw of President Theodore Roosevelt.

Elizabeth

See **Broderick and Elizabeth**

Elizabeth I, Queen

Role for which Dame Judi Dench won a Best Supporting Actress Academy Award in the 1998 film *Shakespeare in Love*.

Elizabeth Barrett Browning

Pet cat of Diane Chambers (Shelley Long) in the TV sitcom *Cheers*.

Elkins

Last name of the title character (Michael Caine) in the film *Alfie*.

Elk Mills, Winnemac

Mythical hometown and home state of the title character in the Sinclair Lewis novel *Arrowsmith*.

Elkridge, Indiana

Hometown of Sam Beckett (Scott Bakula) in the TV series *Quantum Leap*.

Elle

Code name of Dr. Laurel Weaver (Linda Fiorentino) in the film *Men in Black*.

Ellice Islands

Former name of the Pacific island nation of Tuvalu.

Elliot

Role for which Michael Caine won a Best Supporting Actor Academy Award in the 1986 film *Hannah and Her Sisters*.

Elliott

Title character of the Disney animated film *Pete's Dragon*, voiced by Charlie Callas.

Elliott and Goulding

Respective last names of the radio comedy team Bob and Ray.

Elmer

Original name of Howdy Doody.

Puppy of Daisy, family dog in the comic strip *Blondie*.

Sailor doll of Ethel Thayer (Katharine Hepburn) in the film *On Golden Pond*.

Pet hunting dog of folklore lumberjack Paul Bunyan.

Elmore

Real first name of actor Rip Torn.

Eloi

Future race of peaceful humans who are preyed upon by the Morlocks in the H. G. Wells novel *The Time Machine*.

Elrose Fashions

Garment-manufacturing business owned by Eli Sternberg (Jerry Lewis) in the TV series *Wiseguy*.

Elsener, Karl

Inventor of the Swiss army knife in 1891.

Elsinore Brewery

Employer of Bob and Doug McKenzie (Rick Moranis and Dave Thomas) in the film *Strange Brew*.

El Sleezo Cafe

Nightclub visited by Kermit the Frog in *The Muppet Movie*.

El Squeako

Mouse in the children's TV series *Rootie Kazootie*.

El Toro Club

Nightclub run by James Frazier (Humphrey Bogart) in the film *Angels with Dirty Faces*.

Elvis

Pet alligator of Sonny Crockett (Don Johnson) in the TV series *Miami Vice*.

Elvis and Jesse

Twins born to Carla Tortelli (Rhea Perlman) and Eddie LeBec (Jay Thomas) in the TV sitcom *Cheers*.

"Elvis has left the building"

Phrase used by P.A. announcers at the conclusion of Elvis Presley concerts, to encourage attendees to exit.

Elwyn Brooks

First and middle names of novelist E. B. White.

Elysian Fields

New Orleans street that is the setting of the Tennessee Williams play *A Streetcar Named Desire*.

EM-50

Code name of the secret "urban assault vehicle" (a heavily armed, high-tech motor home) in the film *Stripes*.

Emanuel, David and Elizabeth

Designers of the silk dress worn by Princess Diana for her wedding to Prince Charles on July 29, 1981.

Emerson

Last name of the title character (Charles S. Dutton) in the TV sitcom *Roc*.

Emily Dickinson College

Women's school near Faber College in the film *National Lampoon's Animal House*.

Emily Marie

Doll of the title character in the comic strip *Little Orphan Annie*.

"Emissary"

Debut episode of the TV series *Star Trek: Deep Space Nine*, which aired in January, 1993.

"Emitte spiritum tuum"

Motto of the University of San Diego, which is Latin for "Send forth thy spirit."

Emma

First name of the title character in the Gustave Flaubert novel *Madame Bovary*.

Emmett, Daniel Decatur

Composer of the 1859 tune "Dixie" (original title "Dixie's Land").

Emmett Evan

Real first and middle names of actor Van Heflin.

"Emollit mores nec sinit esse feros"

Motto of the University of South Carolina, which is Latin for "Learning humanizes character and does not permit it to be cruel."

emoticons

Illustrations created from standard computer-keyboard characters, that, when turned on their sides, represent faces displaying certain emotions. A representative sampling of commonly used emoticons:

:)	smiling	:(	frowning
;)	winking	:/	frustration
:D	grinning	:O	surprise
:'(	crying	:|	not talking

"Emotions in Motion"

Debut episode of the TV series *Dawson's Creek*, which aired on January 20, 1998.

"Emperor Concerto"

Nickname of Ludwig van Beethoven's Piano Concerto #5.

Empire Hotel

San Francisco residence of Judy Barton (Kim Novak) in the Alfred Hitchcock film *Vertigo*.

Empire State University

School attended by Peter Parker in Spider-Man comics.

"The Empty Chair"

Debut episode of the TV series *The Untouchables*, which aired on October 15, 1959.

"empty hand"

What the word "karate" means in Japanese.

"empty orchestra"

What the word "karaoke" means in Japanese.

The Enchanted Hour

Film for which Vicki Lester (Janet Gaynor) wins an Academy Award, in the film *A Star Is Born* (1937).

Enchantment Under the Sea Dance

Where Marty McFly's future parents (Crispin Glover and Lea Thompson) have their first date in the film *Back to the Future*.

Encom

Communications conglomerate in the Disney film *Tron*.

"Encounter at Farpoint"

Debut episode of the TV series *Star Trek: The Next Generation*, which aired in September, 1987.

Endeavor Airlines

Company run by Tom Mullen (Mel Gibson) in the film *Ransom*.

Endeavour

Ship commanded by Captain James Cook on his first circumnavigation of the globe from 1768 to 1771.

"The End Game"

Debut episode of the TV series *Police Woman*, which aired on September 13, 1974.

Endicott Building

Building that Maynard G. Krebs (Bob Denver) often asks Dobie Gillis (Dwayne Hickman) to watch being torn down with him, in the TV sitcom *The Many Loves of Dobie Gillis*.

Endor

Forest-moon home of the furry Ewoks in the Star Wars series film *Return of the Jedi*.

"Energy Turns the World"

Theme of the Knoxville World's Fair of 1982.

Engelbart, Douglas

Inventor of the computer mouse circa 1968.

ENIAC

See **Electronic Numerical Integrator and Calculator**

Enke, Elizabeth Edith

Real name of singer Edie Adams.

Enoch

Pet goose of President Calvin Coolidge.

Enola Gay

B-29 plane that dropped a uranium-core atomic bomb on Hiroshima, Japan on August 6, 1945. The plane was piloted by Lieutenant Colonel Paul Tibbets, who named the plane for his mother.
See also **Bock's Car; The Great Artiste**

Enos, William Berkeley

Real name of director Busby Berkeley.

Enrico Fermi Presidential Award

Presented annually since 1956 to recognize scientists for lifetime achievement in atomic energy, named for the Italian-born physicist.

Enrico Salvatore

Real first and middle names of "Ratso" Rizzo (Dustin Hoffman) in the film *Midnight Cowboy*.

"An Ensign for McHale"

Debut episode of the TV sitcom *McHale's Navy*, which aired on October 11, 1962.

Entered Apprentice

See **33**

Enterprise

Sternwheeler that is the setting of the TV series *Riverboat*.

Enterprise, Alabama

Town that erected a monument to the boll weevil in December 1919. The insect destroyed its cotton crop, which led to the town's successful diversification into other crops.

Entertainment and Sports Programming Network

What the letters ESPN stand for.

"Enter to learn, go forth to serve"

Motto of Tennessee State University.

"Entry of the Gladiators"

Instrumental march by Czech composer Julius Fučík that is the most frequently played piece of circus music.

Ents

Ancient race of treelike beings in J. R. R. Tolkien's *The Lord of the Rings* trilogy.

En Vogue members

Terry Ellis, Cindy Herron, Maxine Jones, and Dawn Robinson.

Enzio

Middle name of actor Sylvester Stallone.

Epic

Horse of the title character in the comic strip *Tumbleweeds*.

epistaxis

Medical term for a nosebleed.

Epitaph

See **Paul Revere, Valentine, and Epitaph**

Epperson, Frank

11-year-old California boy who invented the Popsicle in 1905. It was originally called the "Epsicle" in his honor.

"Eppie"

Nickname of advice columnist Ann Landers.

Epsilon 3

Planet around which the title space station revolves, in the TV series *Babylon 5*.

Epstein

Birth surname of TV talk host Kathie Lee Gifford.

"Equality"

Motto of the University of Wyoming.

"Equal Justice Under Law"

Inscription over the entrance to the Supreme Court building in Washington, D.C.

Eric

World War II code name of fictional sleuth Matt Helm.

Eriksen, Edvard

Danish sculptor who created the "Little Mermaid" statue inspired by the Hans Christian Andersen story of the same name. The statue, at the entrance to Copenhagen harbor, was unveiled in 1913.

Ernest feature films

Starring Jim Varney as Ernest P. Worrell:
　Ernest Goes to Camp (1987)
　Ernest Saves Christmas (1988)
　Ernest Goes to Jail (1990)
　Ernest Scared Stupid (1991)
　Ernest Rides Again (1993)
　Ernest Goes to School (1994)
　Slam Dunk Ernest (1995)*
　Ernest Goes to Africa (1997)
　Ernest in the Army (1997)
　* Direct-to-video release

Ernestine

Real first name of actress Jane Russell.

Ernesto

Real first name of Argentine-born revolutionary Che Guevara.

Ernie

Former name of the comic strip *The Piranha Club*.

Ernie and India

Pet cats of president George W. Bush. India's nickname is "Willie."

Ernie's

San Francisco restaurant where John Ferguson (James Stewart) first sees Madeleine Elster (Kim Novak) in the Alfred Hitchcock film *Vertigo*.

Ernst

Real first name of Swedish director (Ernst) Ingmar Bergman.

Middle name of novelist John Steinbeck.

Eroica

Middle name of pianist Robert Dupeau (Jack Nicholson) in the film *Five Easy Pieces*.

Errol

Weasley family owl in the Harry Potter series of books by J. K. Rowling.

Errol, Cedric

Real name of the title character in the Frances Hodgson Burnett novel *Little Lord Fauntleroy*.

eructation

Medical term for belching.

"Eruditio et religio"

Motto of Duke University, which is Latin for "Knowledge and religion."

erythrocytes

Medical term for red blood cells.

Escovedo

Last name of rock singer/drummer Sheila E.

Esmeralda

Seal in the film *20,000 Leagues Under the Sea*.

Esmerelda

Middle name of Lucy Ricardo (Lucille Ball) in the TV sitcom *I Love Lucy*.

Esmie

Pet boa constrictor of Mr. Hennessey (Burgess Meredith) in the film *Foul Play*.

Esperanto, Doktoro

Pen name used by Russian-born physician Ludwig Lejzer Zamenhof for his 1887 book *Lingvo Interna-cia*, which introduced his self-created "international language." It would eventually be called Esperanto in his honor, which means "one who hopes" in that language.

Estrada

Real last name of labor leader Cesar Chavez.

Estrovia

Homeland of exiled King Shahdov (Charlie Chaplin) in the film *A King in New York*.

" . . . etcetera, etcetera, etcetera"

Sentence-ending catchphrase of the King of Siam in the Rodgers and Hammerstein musical *The King and I*.

"The Eternal City"

Nickname of Rome, Italy.

Ethel

Woman who is repeatedly told "Don't look," in the Ray Stevens tune "The Streak."

Ethel Hilda

Real first and middle names of actress Ruby Keeler.

Etherington, John

London haberdasher who invented the top hat in 1797.

Ethrington, Elsie

Real name of Sister Bertrille (Sally Field) in the TV sitcom *The Flying Nun*.

"Et Maintenant"

Original French title of the tune "What Now, My Love," which means "And Now."

"Et one, Bruté?"

Advertising slogan in 1960s ads for Lay's potato chips, which featured comedian Bert Lahr dressed as Julius Caesar.

Eufemio

Role for which Anthony Quinn won a Best Supporting Actor Academy Award in the 1952 film *Viva Zapata!*

Eugene

Middle name of actor Jim Carrey.

Eugene Luther

Real first and middle names of author Gore Vidal.

Eugenia

Real first name of model/radio personality Jinx Falkenburg.

Eunice, Arizona

Setting of the film *Murphy's Romance.*

Euphegenia

First name (pronounced "you-fa-jen-EYE-a") of the title character (Robin Williams) in the film *Mrs. Doubtfire.*

Euphoria II

50-foot ketch of country singer Jimmy Buffett.

Eureka

Allied code name for the "Big Three" (Franklin D. Roosevelt, Winston Churchill, and Joseph Stalin) conference at Teheran in 1943.

Eustace

First name of Mr. Haney (Pat Buttram) in the TV sitcom *Green Acres.*

Eustis, Dorothy Harrison

Founder of Seeing Eye, Inc., provider of guide dogs for the blind, in Morristown, New Jersey, in 1929.

Evans City, Pennsylvania

Setting of the film *Night of the Living Dead* (1968).

Evans, Ernest

Real name of singer Chubby Checker. He took the name as a tribute to singer Fats Domino.

Evans, Rudolph

Sculptor who created the 19-foot statue of Thomas Jefferson that stands within the Jefferson Memorial in Washington, D.C.

Eve (Eve White/Eve Black/Jane)

Role(s) for which Joanne Woodward won a Best Actress Academy Award in the 1957 film *The Three Faces of Eve.*

Evelyn

Middle name of polar explorer Richard E. Byrd.

Middle name of June Cleaver (Barbara Billingsley) in the TV sitcom *Leave It to Beaver.*

Real first name of Angel Martin (Stuart Margolin) in the TV series *The Rockford Files.*

"Even a policeman can get stuck in traffic"

Advertising slogan of Talon zippers.

"Eventually . . . why not now?"

Advertising slogan of Gold Medal flour.

Everest, Sir George

See **Peak XV**

Everett, Edward

Orator who gave a 28,000-word speech at Gettysburg, Pennsylvania, on November 19, 1863, immediately before President Abraham Lincoln's 271-word Gettysburg Address. Everett wrote Lincoln shortly thereafter, "I should be glad that, if I could flatter myself that I came as near to the central idea of the occasion, in two hours, as you did in two minutes."

Evergreen

Secret Service code name for Hillary Clinton.

Everlasting Gobstopper

Sucking candy that never gets smaller, developed by the title character (Gene Wilder) in the film *Willy Wonka and the Chocolate Factory.*

Everwrite Fountain Pen Co.

Legend on the train car broken into by Rocky Sullivan (Frankie Burke) and Jerry Connolly (William Tracy) in the film *Angels with Dirty Faces.*

Everybody Comes to Rick's

Play by Murray Burnett and Joan Alison that was the basis for the film *Casablanca.*

Everybody's Welcome
See **Hupfeld, Herman**

"Everybody wants to get into the act!"
Catchphrase of comedian Jimmy Durante.

"Every man a king"
Slogan of Louisiana senator Huey Long for his proposed "Share Our Wealth" program.

"Everyone needs more space"
Slogan used to promote the film *Star Trek: Generations*.

Everytown
Setting of the futuristic H. G. Wells novel *Things to Come* and the film adaptation of the same name, for which Wells wrote the screenplay.

Ewart
Middle name of English statesman William Gladstone.

Excalibur
Sword of King Arthur.

Excelsior, New Jersey
Setting of the Thornton Wilder play *The Skin of Our Teeth*.

The Executioners
Novel by John D. MacDonald that was the basis for both versions of the film *Cape Fear*.

The Execution of Charles Horman
Book by Thomas Hauser that was the basis for the film *Missing*.

El Exigente
See **Montalbán, Carlos**

"Exit, pursued by a bear"
Called "perhaps the most famous stage direction in English" by *Bartlett's Familiar Quotations*, it appears in Act 3, Scene 3, of the William Shakespeare play *The Winter's Tale*.

"Exit, stage left"
Catchphrase of cartoon lion Snagglepuss.

"Exitus acta probat"
Family motto of George Washington, which is Latin for "The end justifies the means."

"Ex luna, scientia"
Motto of the ill-fated *Apollo 13* lunar mission. It is Latin for "From the moon, knowledge."

Exorcist films
> *The Exorcist* (1973)
> *Exorcist II: The Heretic* (1977)
> *The Exorcist III* (1990)

"Exordium & Terminus"
Subtitle of the Zager and Evans tune "In the Year 2525." The word "exordium" means "beginning."

Experimental Prototype Community of Tomorrow
What the letters in the name of Disney's Florida complex EPCOT Center stand for.

Explorer
Ship that brings the title character to New York, in the film *King Kong* (1976).

"Ex scientia tridens"
Motto of the United States Naval Academy at Annapolis, Maryland. It is Latin for "From knowledge, sea power."

Extinction Level Event
See **ELE**

eyeblack
Dark paste that athletes in baseball and football smear under their eyes, to minimize the glare of the sun or stadium lighting.

The Eye of the Daughter of the Moon
Gem with an ancient curse smuggled into the U.S. from China by Brandon Edwards (Morgan Wallace), whose murder is solved by the title character (Boris Karloff) in the film *The Mystery of Mr. Wong*.

"eye of the dawn"
What the name of Dutch-born World War I spy Mata Hari means in Malay.

"Eye of the Tiger"
Theme song of the film *Rocky III*, performed by Survivor.

Fabbrica Italiana Automobili Torino
What the letters in the name of Italian automaker Fiat stand for, which is Italian for "Italian automobile factory of Turin."

Faber College
Setting of the film *National Lampoon's Animal House*.

"The Fab Four"
Nickname of British rock group the Beatles.

The Fabulous Baseball Diamond
Stolen jewel in the film *The Great Muppet Caper*.

Face Productions
Production company of comedian Billy Crystal.

"Face the Music with Me"
Original title of the Vernon Duke/Ira Gershwin tune "I Can't Get Started," introduced by Bob Hope and Eve Arden in the film *Ziegfeld Follies of 1936*.

Facha
Dog in the Arlo Guthrie tune "Alice's Restaurant."

Factor, Max
Russian-born creator of the first makeup designed specifically for films, in 1914. His cosmetics company is today a subsidiary of Procter and Gamble.

Fagan, Eleanora
Real name of blues singer Billie Holiday.

Fagen, Donald
See **Becker, Walter and Fagen, Donald**

Faget, Maxime
Aeronautical engineer who designed the Project Mercury space capsule.

Fahrid
First name of actor F. Murray Abraham.

"Fahrvergnügen"
Advertising slogan of Volkswagen. The word is German for "driving delight."

Fair, A. A.
Pen name used by author Erle Stanley Gardner.

Fairfield, Cicily
Real name of author Dame Rebecca West.

Fairfield, Flora
Pen name used by author Louisa May Alcott.

Fairlane
Estate of automaker Henry Ford in Dearborn, Michigan.

Fairvale
Town where Marion Crane (Janet Leigh) is to meet her boyfriend Sam Loomis (John Gavin) after stopping at the nearby Bates Motel, in the Alfred Hitchcock film *Psycho*.

Fairview, Connecticut
Setting of the Richard Bachman (Stephen King) novel *Thinner*.

"Fairy Floss"
See **Morrison, William and Wharton, John**

Faith, Hope, and Charity
The three hatchets used by anti-alcohol activist Carry Nation to destroy saloons.

Fajardo
Maiden name of pop singer Gloria Estefan.

Fala
See **Murray of Fala Hill**

***The Falcon* films**

GEORGE SANDERS IN THE TITLE ROLE
The Gay Falcon (1941)
A Date with the Falcon (1941)
The Falcon Takes Over (1942)
The Falcon's Brother (1942)

TOM CONWAY (REAL-LIFE BROTHER OF GEORGE SANDERS) IN THE TITLE ROLE
The Falcon Strikes Back (1943)
The Falcon and the Co-eds (1943)

The Falcon in Danger (1943)
The Falcon in Hollywood (1944)
The Falcon in Mexico (1944)
The Falcon Out West (1944)
The Falcon in San Francisco (1945)
The Falcon's Alibi (1946)
The Falcon's Adventure (1946)

JOHN CALVERT IN THE TITLE ROLE

The Devil's Cargo (1948)
Appointment with Murder (1948)
Search for Danger (1949)

Falcons

See **Cougars**

Falcon's Lair

Los Angeles home of actor Rudolph Valentino.

Faline

Mate of the title character in the Disney animated film *Bambi*.

Falk, Conrad Robert

Real name of actor Robert Conrad.

"The Fallen Woman"

English translation of the title of the Giuseppe Verdi opera *La Traviata*.

"Falling"

Instrumental theme of the TV series *Twin Peaks*.

Fallingwater

Best-known home designed by architect Frank Lloyd Wright, noted for its integration of waterfalls and rock formations. Located in Mill Run, Pennsylvania, it was designed in 1936 for Pittsburgh department-store owner Edgar J. Kaufmann and opened to the public in 1964.

Fallwell, Massachusetts

Setting of the film *Elvira: Mistress of the Dark*.

Fame, Happiness, and Money

The three areas in which points are accumulated in the board game Careers.

Family Channel

See **Christian Broadcasting Network**

"A family comedy without the family"

Slogan used to promote the film *Home Alone*.

Fan-Dango Ballroom

Manhattan establishment where the title character is employed as a "social consultant" in the musical *Sweet Charity*.

Fanning, Shawn and Parker, Sean

Founders of the music-community Web site Napster in May 1999.

Fantasia

Mythical land that is the setting of the film *The Never-Ending Story*.

Fantasia/2000 sections

Every section after the first has a celebrity introduction.
   Symphony #5 (first movement): Ludwig van Beethoven
   Pines of Rome: Ottorino Respighi (Steve Martin, Itzhak Perlman)
   Rhapsody in Blue: George Gershwin (Quincy Jones)
   Piano Concerto #2 (Allegro): Dmitri Shostakovich (Bette Midler)
   Carnival of the Animals: Camille Saint-Saëns (James Earl Jones)
   The Sorcerer's Apprentice: Paul Dukas (Penn and Teller)
   Pomp and Circumstance: Sir Edward Elgar (James Levine, conductor of the orchestra)
   Firebird Suite: Igor Stravinsky (Angela Lansbury)

"A Fantasia in the Russian Manner on English Themes"

Subtitle of the George Bernard Shaw play *Heartbreak House*.

Fantasia sections

The musical selections heard in the original (1940) Disney film:
   Toccata and Fugue in D minor: Johann Sebastian Bach
   Nutcracker Suite ("Dance of the Sugarplum Fairy," "Chinese Dance," "Dance of the Flutes," "Russian Dance," "Waltz of the Flowers"): Peter Tchaikovsky
   "The Sorcerer's Apprentice": Paul Dukas
   The Rite of Spring: Igor Stravinsky
   Symphony #6 (Pastoral Symphony): Ludwig van Beethoven
   "Dance of the Hours": Amilcare Ponchielli
   "A Night on Bald Mountain": Modeste Mussorgsky
   "Ave Maria": Franz Schubert

Fantastic Four members

Superhero team featured in Marvel Comics and cartoons, originally consisting of Reed Richards, Sue Richards, Johnny Storm, and Ben Grimm. With their superpowers they become Mr. Fantastic, Invisible Girl, The Human Torch, and The Thing, respectively.

Farber High

School attended by Gary Wallace (John Mallory Asher) and Wyatt Donnelly (Michael Manasseri) in the TV sitcom *Weird Science*.

Farfel

Hound-dog puppet in 1950s–60s TV commercials for Nestle's chocolate. The character was created by puppeteer Danny O'Day and ventriloquist Jimmy Nelson.

Farinola, Vito

Real name of singer Vic Damone.

Farmer, Frank

Title character of the film *The Bodyguard*, portrayed by Kevin Costner.

Farmer, James

See **Congress of Racial Equality**

Farmers State Bank

Failed bank that the title characters (Faye Dunaway and Warren Beatty) unsuccessfully attempt to rob, in the film *Bonnie and Clyde*.

The Farriss Brothers

Original name of rock group INXS.

Faske, Donna Ivy

Real name of fashion designer Donna Karan.

"Fast and Furry-ous"

1949 Warner Bros. cartoon that features the debut appearance of Road Runner and Wile E. Coyote.

Fast Asleep

Horse at 40-to-1 odds that Pete (Buddy Ebsen) and Sonny (George Murphy) are supposed to bet on, but fail to, in the film *Broadway Melody of 1938*.

Fast Cars

Novel written by Paul Sheldon in the Stephen King novel *Misery*.

"Fasten your seat belts. It's going to be a bumpy night."

Memorable line spoken by Margo Channing (Bette Davis) in the film *All About Eve*.

Fates

In Greek mythology, the three goddesses who determine human destiny.
Clotho (spins the thread of life)
Lachesis (determines its length)
Atropos (cuts the thread)

"Father of American Football"

Nickname of Walter Camp, who cofounded the Ivy League and developed the rules for modern-day football.

"The Father of History"

Nickname of Greek historian Herodotus, whose history of the Greco-Persian Wars is the earliest known narrative history.

"The Father of Medicine"

Nickname of Greek physician Hippocrates.

"The Father of Television"

Nickname of inventor Vladimir Zworykin.

"Father of the Atomic Submarine"

Nickname of Admiral Hyman Rickover.

"Father of the Blues"

Nickname of composer W. C. Handy.

"Father of the Hydrogen Bomb"

Nickname of physicist Edward Teller.

"Father of the Skyscraper"

Nickname of William Jenney, architect who designed the world's first skyscraper (tall building supported by an internal steel frame rather than by walls), the Home Insurance Company Building in Chicago. It was completed in 1885.

Fatso

See **The Ghostly Trio**

"fat Tuesday"

What the words "Mardi Gras" mean in French.

Fauna

See **Flora, Fauna, and Merryweather**

Fauntleroy

Middle name of Donald Duck.

Fawkes

Pet phoenix of Hogwarts headmaster Albus Dumbledore, in the Harry Potter series of books by J. K. Rowling.

Fawkes, Guy

Pen name used by author Robert Benchley.

Fawley

Last name of the title character in the Thomas Hardy novel *Jude the Obscure*.

"Fear in a Desert City"

Debut episode of the original TV series *The Fugitive*, which aired on September 17, 1963.

"The Fearsome Foursome"

Nickname of the Los Angeles Rams defensive line of the late 1960s and early 1970s: Rosey Grier, Deacon Jones, Lamar Lundy, and Merlin Olsen.

federal agencies and bureaus

Major governmental services that are part of a Cabinet department.

AGRICULTURE

Food and Nutrition Service
Food Safety Inspection Service
Forest Service

COMMERCE

Bureau of the Census
National Oceanic and Atmospheric Administration (NOAA)

HEALTH AND HUMAN SERVICES

Centers for Disease Control and Prevention (CDC)
Food and Drug Administration (FDA)
Health Care Financing Administration (Medicare/Medicaid)
National Institutes of Health (NIH)

HOUSING AND URBAN DEVELOPMENT

Government National Mortgage Association (GNMA or Ginnie Mae)

INTERIOR

Bureau of Indian Affairs
Bureau of Land Management
National Park Service
U.S. Fish and Wildlife Service
U.S. Geological Survey

JUSTICE

Drug Enforcement Administration (DEA)
Federal Bureau of Investigation (FBI)
Federal Bureau of Prisons
Immigration and Naturalization Service (INS)

LABOR

Bureau of Labor Statistics
Mine Safety and Health Administration
Occupational Safety and Health Administration (OSHA)

TRANSPORTATION

Federal Aviation Administration (FAA)
Federal Highway Administration
Federal Railroad Administration
Maritime Administration (including U.S. Merchant Marine Academy)
National Highway Traffic Safety Administration
U.S. Coast Guard

TREASURY

Bureau of Alcohol, Tobacco and Firearms (ATF)
Bureau of Engraving and Printing
Federal Law Enforcement Training Center (at Brunswick, Georgia)
Internal Revenue Service (IRS)
Office of Thrift Supervision
U.S. Customs Service
U.S. Mint
U.S. Secret Service

Federal Insurance Contributions Act

What the pay-stub abbreviation "FICA" stands for. The Federal Insurance Contributions Act is the federal law under which Social Security deductions are taken from an employee's salary.

Federation of Interstate Truckers

Labor union headed by Johnny Kovak (Sylvester Stallone) in the film *F.I.S.T.*

Federation Star

See **6**

Federkiewicz, Stefania Zofia

Real name of actress Stefanie Powers.

Feder, Richard

Fort Lee, New Jersey, resident whose letters are often read by Roseanne Roseannadanna (Gilda Radner) in the TV series *Saturday Night Live*.

Feinberg, Louis

See **Three Stooges' real names**

"Felgercarb!"

Expletive used by the crew of the title vessel in the TV series *Battlestar Galactica*.

Felice

Real first name of self-help author Dr. Leo Buscaglia.

Fellini

Pet cat of Dave (Dennis Christopher) in the film *Breaking Away*.

Fellows, Alvin J.
New Haven, Connecticut, inventor of the tape measure, patented in 1868.

Fells Point Diner
Baltimore setting of the film *Diner*.

Felson, "Fast Eddie"
Role for which Paul Newman won a Best Actor Academy Award in the 1986 film *The Color of Money*.

Felton, Rebecca
Republican of Georgia who was the first woman to serve in the United States Senate. She served for only one day, November 22, 1922.

"feminisim"
How the word "feminism" is misspelled on the cover of the May/June 1996 issue of *Ms.* magazine.

Feminum
Metal from which the belt and bracelets worn by Wonder Woman are made, which are the source of her superpowers.

femur
Medical term for the thighbone.

Fenwick, Nell
Girlfriend of cartoon character Mountie Dudley Do-Right, voiced by June Foray.

Ferdinand
Real first name of basketball great (Ferdinand) Lewis Alcindor, today known as Kareem Abdul-Jabbar.

Fernwood, Ohio
Setting of the TV sitcom *Mary Hartman, Mary Hartman*.

Ferrari, Vic
Smooth-talking alter ego of Latka Gravas (Andy Kaufman) who speaks perfect, unaccented English, in the TV sitcom *Taxi*.

"Ferret Face"
Nickname of Major Frank Burns (Larry Linville) in the TV sitcom *M*A*S*H*.

Ferruccio
First name of Italian sports-car manufacturer Lamborghini, who built his first prototype vehicle in 1963.

ferrule
Technical term for the metal band that attaches an eraser to a pencil.

ferrum
Latin name for iron, from which its chemical symbol Fe is derived.

Festivus
Holiday on December 23 created by Frank Costanza (Jerry Stiller) in the TV sitcom *Seinfeld*.

Fey, Charles
Berkeley, California, machinist who invented the three-wheel, pull-handle slot machine in 1895.

"Fiat lux"
Motto of the University of California, which is Latin for "Let there be light."

Fickelgruber's
Rival chocolate brand of the title character (Gene Wilder) in the film *Willy Wonka and the Chocolate Factory*.

Fickling, Forrest E.
Creator of fictional detective Honey West.

"Fidelity, Bravery, Integrity"
Motto of the FBI.

Fido
Pet watchdog of folklore lumberjack Paul Bunyan.

Fields, W. C., roles/pen names of
Fields' humorous-sounding film-role names and screenwriting pen names:

FILM ROLES
Elmer Prettywillie: *It's the Old Army Game* (1926)
Augustus Winterbottom: *Tillie and Gus* (1933)
Sam Bisbee: *You're Telling Me* (1934)
The Great McGonigle: *The Old-Fashioned Way* (1934)
Harold Bissonette: *It's a Gift* (1934)
Ambrose Wolfinger: *The Man on the Flying Trapeze* (1935)
Professor Eustace McGargle: *Poppy* (1936)
T. Frothingill Bellows: *The Big Broadcast of 1938* (1938)
Larson E. Whipsnade: *You Can't Cheat an Honest Man* (1939)
Cuthbert J. Twillie: *My Little Chickadee* (1940)
Egbert Sousé: *The Bank Dick* (1940)

SCREENWRITING PEN NAMES

Charles Bogle: *The Old-Fashioned Way* (and others)
Mahatma Kane Jeeves: *The Bank Dick*
Otis Criblecoblis: *Never Give a Sucker an Even Break* (1941)

"Fiel pero desdichado"

Family motto of Winston Churchill, which is Spanish for "Faithful but unfortunate."

Fiennes, Sir Ranulph

See **Benjamin Bowring**

Fiersohn, Reba

Real name of opera star Alma Gluck.

Fiesta

Original title of the Ernest Hemingway novel *The Sun Also Rises*.

Fifi

Pet dog of Maggie in the comic strip *Bringing Up Father*.

Pet dog of Disney cartoon character Minnie Mouse.

The Fifteenth Pelican

Novel by Tere Rios that was the basis for the TV sitcom *The Flying Nun*.

The 5th Dimension members

Billy Davis Jr., Florence LaRue, Marilyn McCoo, Lamonte McLemore, and Ron Townson.

Fifth Northumberland Fusiliers

English Army regiment that Dr. John Watson joins in Afghanistan, in the Sir Arthur Conan Doyle novel *A Study in Scarlet*. After being wounded there, he returns to London, becoming the roommate and chronicler of Sherlock Holmes.

Figalilly, Phoebe

Real name of Nanny (Juliet Mills) in the TV sitcom *Nanny and the Professor*.

Figaro

Geppetto's pet cat in the Disney animated film *Pinocchio*.

Figgy Fizz

Brand of bottle caps collected by Ernie in the children's TV series *Sesame Street*.

"Fightertown, USA"

Nickname of Miramar, California, site of the Fighter Weapons School where pilot Pete Mitchell (Tom Cruise) trains in the film *Top Gun*.

"The Fighting Blue Devils"

Nickname of the 101st Cavalry, the unit that adopts Rusty (Lee Aaker) in the children's TV series *The Adventures of Rin Tin Tin*.

"Fighting Ignorance Since 1973. [It's taking longer than we thought]"

Slogan of syndicated column *The Straight Dope*.

"Fighting Joe"

Nickname of Civil War Union general Joseph Hooker.

Figrin D'an and the Modal Nodes

Cantina band in the film *Star Wars*.

figure-four leglock

Hold popularized in the 1940s by pro wrestler Buddy Rogers.

Fillet of Soul

Restaurant chain that Mr. Big (Yaphet Kotto) uses as a front to distribute illegal drugs, in the James Bond film *Live and Let Die*.

Fillmore

Bear sidekick of cartoon frog Hoppity Hooper, voiced by Bill Scott.

Fillmore Junior High

School attended by the children in the TV sitcom *The Brady Bunch*.

Fillmore, North Dakota

Hometown of Esther Blodgett (Janet Gaynor) in the film *A Star Is Born* (1937).

film awards, national

The awards in other countries that are comparable to the Academy Award:
Australia: Lovely
Canada: Genie
France: César
Great Britain: British Academy Film Award (formerly called BAFTA)
Italy: David di Donatello
Mexico: Ariel
Spain: Goya
Sweden: Guldbagge (golden ram)
Taiwan: Golden Horse

film ratings

The Motion Picture Association of America introduced voluntary ratings for films on November 1, 1968, superseding the Hays Production Code previously in effect.

ORIGINAL 1968 RATINGS

G General Audiences (all ages admitted)

M Mature Audiences (all ages admitted, but parental guidance suggested)

R Restricted (children under 16 not admitted without a parent or guardian, later raised to 17)

X no one under 17 admitted

NAME CHANGES/ADDITIONS

1969 M changed to GP

1970 GP changed to PG

1984 PG split into PG and PG-13 ("Parents strongly cautioned. Some material may be inappropriate for pre-teenagers.")

1990 X changed to NC-17

"The Final Round"

Debut episode of the TV series *The Incredible Hulk*, which aired on March 10, 1978.

Finca Vigia

Farm home of author Ernest Hemingway, located near Havana, Cuba.

Finch, Atticus

Role for which Gregory Peck won a Best Actor Academy Award in the 1962 film *To Kill a Mockingbird*.

Finder's Keepers

Thrift shop located around the corner in the children's TV series *Sesame Street*.

Findlay's Friendly Appliances

Store owned by Walter Findlay (Bill Macy) in the TV sitcom *Maude*.

Fine, Fran

Title character (Fran Drescher) of the TV sitcom *The Nanny*.

"Finger lickin' good"

Advertising slogan of Kentucky Fried Chicken.

Finis

Middle name of Confederate States of America president Jefferson Davis.

"Finis origine pendet"

Motto of Phillips Exeter Academy, a prestigious prep school in Exeter, New Hampshire, founded in 1781. It is Latin for "The end depends on the beginning."

Finkelstein

Maiden name of Dharma Montgomery (Jenna Elfman) in the TV sitcom *Dharma and Greg*.

Fink, Janis Eddy

Real name of pop singer Janis Ian.

Finklea, Tula

Real name of actress/dancer Cyd Charisse.

Finley Breese

Middle names of artist/inventor Samuel Morse.

Finley, Tom "Boss"

Role for which Ed Begley won a Best Supporting Actor Academy Award in the 1962 film *Sweet Bird of Youth*.

Fiona

Real first name of Pickles, seldom seen wife of Buddy Sorrell (Morey Amsterdam) in the TV sitcom *The Dick Van Dyke Show*.

Middle name of actress Julia Roberts.

Fireball

Technologically advanced broomstick for playing Quidditch, in the Harry Potter series of books by J. K. Rowling.

Firefly

Home of author/songwriter Noel Coward in Port Maria, Jamaica.

Horse of Rudolph Valentino in the film *The Son of the Sheik*.

Firefly, Rufus T.

See **Marx, Groucho, roles of**

"First Call"

Bugle fanfare that is played before the start of a horse race.

First Community Church of Philadelphia

Where Ernest Frye (Sherman Hemsley) serves as deacon in the TV sitcom *Amen*.

"first fruits"

What the name of the annual festival Kwanzaa (December 26 to January 1) means in Swahili.

First Impressions

Original working title of the Jane Austen novel *Pride and Prejudice*.

First in the Hearts

Original working title of the Cole Porter musical *Leave It to Me*.

"First in war, first in peace, and first in the hearts of his countrymen"

Memorable eulogy to George Washington, written by Henry Lee in December 1799.

First Kiss Productions

Production company of actress Alicia Silverstone.

"First Lady of Song"

Nickname of singer Ella Fitzgerald.

"First Lady of the American Theater"

Nickname of actress Ethel Barrymore.

Nickname of actress Helen Hayes.

"First Lady of the Screen"

Nickname of actress Norma Shearer.

"First Lady of the World"

Nickname of Eleanor Roosevelt.

first lines of famous works

THE ADVENTURES OF HUCKLEBERRY FINN (Mark Twain)

"You don't know about me without you have read a book by the name of The Adventures of Tom Sawyer; but that ain't no matter."

AIRPORT (Arthur Hailey)

"At half-past six on a Friday evening in January, Lincoln International Airport, Illinois, was functioning, though with difficulty."

ALICE'S ADVENTURES IN WONDERLAND (Lewis Carroll)

"Alice was beginning to get very tired of sitting by her sister on the bank, and of having nothing to do: once or twice she had peeped into the book her sister was reading, but it had no pictures or conversations in it, 'and what is the use of a book,' thought Alice, 'without pictures or conversations?'"

ANNA KARENINA (Leo Tolstoy)

"Happy families are all alike; every unhappy family is unhappy in its own way."

AROUND THE WORLD IN EIGHTY DAYS (Jules Verne)

"Mr. Phileas Fogg lived, in 1872, at No. 7. Saville Row, Burlington Gardens, the house in which Sheridan died in 1814."

ATLAS SHRUGGED (Ayn Rand)

"Who is John Galt?"

BELOVED (Toni Morrison)

"124 was spiteful."

BRAVE NEW WORLD (Aldous Huxley)

"A squat gray building of only thirty-four stories."

BREAKFAST AT TIFFANY'S (Truman Capote)

"I am always drawn back to the places where I have lived, the houses and their neighborhoods."

BREAKFAST OF CHAMPIONS (Kurt Vonnegut)

"This is a tale of a meeting of two lonesome, skinny, fairly old white men on a planet which was dying fast."

THE BRIDGE OF SAN LUIS REY (Thornton Wilder)

"On Friday noon, July the twentieth, 1714, the finest bridge in all Peru broke and precipitated five travelers into the gulf below."

THE BRIDGES OF MADISON COUNTY (Robert Waller)

"On the morning of August 8, 1965, Robert Kincaid locked the door to his small two-room apartment on the third floor of a rambling house in Bellingham, Washington."

THE CALL OF THE WILD (Jack London)

"Buck did not read the newspapers, or he would have known that trouble was brewing, not alone for himself, but for every tide-water dog, strong of muscle and with warm, long hair, from Puget Sound to San Diego."

CANDIDE (Voltaire)

"In the country of Westphalia, in the castle of the most noble Baron of Thunder-ten-tronckh, lived a youth whom Nature had endowed with a most sweet disposition."

CANNERY ROW (John Steinbeck)

"Cannery Row in Monterey in California is a poem, a stink, a grating noise, a quality of light, a tone, a habit, a nostalgia, a dream."

CARRIE (Stephen King)

"Nobody was really surprised when it happened, not really, not on the subconscious level where savage things grow."

"THE CASK OF AMONTILLADO" (EDGAR ALLAN POE)

"The thousand injuries of Fortunato I had borne as I best could, but when he ventured upon insult, I vowed revenge."

THE CATCHER IN THE RYE (J. D. Salinger)

"If you really want to hear about it, the first thing you'll probably want to know is where I was born, and what my lousy childhood was like, and how my parents were occupied and all before they had me, and all that David Copperfield kind of crap, but I don't feel like going into it, if you want to know the truth."

CAT'S CRADLE (Kurt Vonnegut)

"Call me Jonah."

CHARLOTTE'S WEB (E. B. White)

" 'Where's Papa going with that ax?' said Fern to her mother as they were setting the table for breakfast."

A CHRISTMAS CAROL (Charles Dickens)

"Marley was dead, to begin with."

THE COLOR PURPLE (Alice Walker)

"You better not never tell nobody but God."

THE COUNT OF MONTE CRISTO (Alexandre Dumas)

"On the 24th of February, 1810, the look-out at Notre-Dame de La Garde signalled the three-master, the Pharaon from Smyrna, Trieste, and Naples."

CRIME AND PUNISHMENT (Fyodor Dostoevsky)

"On an exceptionally hot evening early in July a young man came out of the garret in which he lodged in S. Place and walked slowly, as though in hesitation, towards K. bridge."

DAVID COPPERFIELD (Charles Dickens)

"Whether I shall turn out to be the hero of my own life, or whether that station will be held by anybody else, these pages must show."

DOCTOR ZHIVAGO (Boris Pasternak)

"On they went, singing 'Rest Eternal,' and whenever they stopped, their feet, the horses, and the gusts of wind seemed to carry on their singing."

DRACULA (Bram Stoker)

"3 May. Bistritz. Left Munich at 8:35 P.M., on 1st May, arriving at Vienna early next morning; should have arrived at 6:46, but train was an hour late."

DUNE (Frank Herbert)

"In the week before their departure to Arrakis, when all the final scurrying about had reached a nearly unbearable frenzy, an old crone came to visit the mother of the boy, Paul."

EMMA (Jane Austen)

"Emma Woodhouse, handsome, clever, and rich, with a comfortable home and happy disposition, seemed to unite some of the best blessings of existence; and had lived nearly twenty-one years in the world with very little to distress or vex her."

ETHAN FROME (Edith Wharton)

"I had the story, bit by bit, from various people, and, as generally happens in such cases, each time it was a different story."

THE EXORCIST (William Peter Blatty)

"Like the brief doomed flare of exploding suns that registers dimly on blind men's eyes, the beginning of the horror passed almost unnoticed; in the shriek of what followed, in fact, was forgotten and perhaps not connected to the horror at all."

FAHRENHEIT 451 (Ray Bradbury)

"It was a pleasure to burn."

FEAR OF FLYING (Erica Jong)

"There were 117 psychoanalysts on the Pan Am flight to Vienna and I'd been treated by at least six of them."

FOUNDATION (Isaac Asimov)

"His name was Gaal Dornick and he was just a country boy who had never seen Trantor before."

FRANKENSTEIN (Mary Shelley)

"You will rejoice to hear that no disaster has accompanied the commencement of an enterprise which you have regarded with such evil forebodings."

THE FRENCH LIEUTENANT'S WOMAN (John Fowles)

"An easterly is the most disagreeable wind in Lyme Bay—Lyme Bay being that largest byte from the underside of England's outstretched southwestern leg—and a person of curiosity could at once have deduced several strong probabilities about the pair who began to walk down the quay at Lyme Regis, the small but ancient eponym of the inbite, one incisively sharp and blustery morning in the late March of 1867."

THE GODFATHER (Mario Puzo)

"Amerigo Bonasera sat in New York Criminal Court Number 3 and waited for justice; vengeance on the men who had so cruelly hurt his daughter, who had tried to dishonor her."

GONE WITH THE WIND (Margaret Mitchell)

"Scarlett O'Hara was not beautiful, but men seldom realized it when caught by her charm as the Tarleton twins were."

THE GOOD EARTH (Pearl S. Buck)

"It was Wang Lung's marriage day."

THE GRAPES OF WRATH (John Steinbeck)

"To the red country and part of the gray country of Oklahoma, the last rains came gently, and they did not cut the scarred earth."

GRAVITY'S RAINBOW (Thomas Pynchon)

"A screaming comes across the sky."

GREAT EXPECTATIONS (Charles Dickens)

"My father's family name being Pirrip, and my Christian name Philip, my infant tongue could make of both names nothing longer or more explicit than Pip."

THE GREAT GATSBY (F. Scott Fitzgerald)

"In my younger and more vulnerable years my father gave me some advice that I've been turning over in my mind ever since."

THE HEART IS A LONELY HUNTER (Carson McCullers)

"In the town there were two mutes, and they were always together."

HEART OF DARKNESS (Joseph Conrad)

"The Nellie, a cruising yawl, swung to her anchor without a flutter of the sails, and was at rest."

HUMBOLDT'S GIFT (Saul Bellow)

"The book of ballads published by Von Humboldt Fleisher in Thirties was an immediate hit."

THE HUNCHBACK OF NOTRE DAME (Victor Hugo)

"It was three hundred forty-eight years, six months, and nineteen days ago today that the citizens of Paris were awakened by the pealing of all the bells in the triple precincts of the City, the University, and the Town."

IN COLD BLOOD (Truman Capote)

"The village of Holcomb stands on the high wheat plains of western Kansas, a lonesome area that other Kansans call 'out there.'"

THE INVISIBLE MAN (H. G. Wells)

"The stranger came early in February one wintry day, through a biting wind and a driving snow, the last snowfall of the year, over the down, walking as it seemed from Bramblehurst railway station and carrying a little black portmanteau in his thickly gloved hand."

JANE EYRE (Charlotte Brontë)

"There was no possibility of taking a walk that day."

JAWS (Peter Benchley)

"The great fish moved silently through the night water, propelled by short sweeps of its crescent tail."

THE JUNGLE BOOK (Rudyard Kipling)

"It was seven o'clock of a very warm evening in the Seeonee hills when Father Wolf woke up from his day's rest, scratched himself, yawned, and spread out his paws one after the other to get rid of the sleepy feeling in their tips."

KIDNAPPED (Robert Louis Stevenson)

"I will begin the story of my adventures with a certain morning early in the month of June, the year of grace 1751, when I took the key for the last time out of the door of my father's house."

THE LAST OF THE MOHICANS (James Fenimore Cooper)

"It was a feature peculiar to the colonial wars of North America, that the toils and dangers of the wilderness were to be encountered before the adverse hosts could meet."

LITTLE WOMEN (Louisa May Alcott)

"'Christmas won't be Christmas without any presents,' grumbled Jo, lying on the rug."

LORD JIM (Joseph Conrad)

"He was an inch, perhaps two, under six feet, powerfully built, and he advanced straight at you with a slight stoop of the shoulders, head forward, and a fixed from-under stare which made you think of a charging bull."

LORD OF THE FLIES (William Golding)

"The boy with fair hair lowered himself down the last few feet of rock and began to pick his way towards the lagoon."

MAIN STREET (Sinclair Lewis)

"This is America—a town of a few thousand, in a region of wheat and corn and dairies and little groves."

MARY POPPINS (P. L. Travers)

"If you want to find Cherry Tree Lane all you have to do is ask a policeman at the crossroads."

METAMORPHOSIS (Franz Kafka)

"As Gregor Samsa awoke one morning from uneasy dreams he found himself transformed into a giant insect."

MIDDLEMARCH (George Eliot)

"Miss Brooke had that kind of beauty which seems to be thrown into relief by poor dress."

Moby-Dick (Herman Melville)

"Call me Ishmael."

1984 (George Orwell)

"It was a bright cold day in April, and the clocks were striking thirteen."

Of Mice and Men (John Steinbeck)

"A few miles south of Soledad, the Salinas River drops in close to the hill-side bank and runs deep and green."

The Old Man and the Sea (Ernest Hemingway)

"He was an old man who fished alone in a skiff in the Gulf Stream and he had gone eighty-four days now without taking a fish."

101 Dalmatians (Dodie Smith)

"Not long ago, there lived in London a young married couple of Dalmatian dogs named Pongo and Misses Pongo."

O Pioneers! (Willa Cather)

"One January day, thirty years ago, the little town of Hanover, anchored on a windy Nebraska tableland, was trying not to be blown away."

A Passage to India (E. M. Forster)

"Except for the Marabar Caves—and they are twenty miles off—the city of Chandrapore presents nothing extraordinary."

Peter Pan (James M. Barrie)

"All children, except one, grow up."

Peyton Place (Grace Metalious)

"Indian summer is like a woman."

Pride and Prejudice (Jane Austen)

"It is a truth universally acknowledged, that a single man in possession of a good fortune, must be in want of a wife."

The Princess Bride (William Goldman)

"This is my favorite book in all the world, though I have never read it."

Ragtime (E. L. Doctorow)

"In 1902 Father built a house at the crest of the Broadview Avenue hill in New Rochelle, New York."

Rebecca (Daphne du Maurier)

"Last night I dreamt I went to Manderly again."

Rebecca of Sunnybrook Farm (Kate Douglas Wiggin)

"The old stage coach was rumbling along the dusty road that runs from Maplewood to Riverboro."

The Red Badge of Courage (Stephen Crane)

"The cold passed reluctantly from the earth, and the retiring fogs revealed an army stretched out on the hills, resting."

Rich Man, Poor Man (Irwin Shaw)

"Mr. Donnelly, the track coach, ended the day's practice early because Henry Fuller's father came down to the high-school field to tell Henry that they had just got a telegram from Washington announcing that Henry's brother had been killed in action in Germany."

"Rip Van Winkle" (Washington Irving)

"Whoever has made a voyage up the Hudson must remember the Kaatskill mountains."

Robinson Crusoe (Daniel Defoe)

"I was born in the year 1632, in the city of York, of a good family, though not of that country, my father being a foreigner of Bremen, who settled first at Hull."

Roots (Alex Haley)

"Early in the spring of 1750, in the village of Juffure, four days upriver from the coast of Gambia, West Africa, a manchild was born to Omoro and Binta Kinte."

Rosemary's Baby (Ira Levin)

"Rosemary and Guy Woodhouse had signed a lease on a five-room apartment in a geometric white house on First Avenue when they received word, from a woman named Mrs. Cortez, that a four-room apartment in Bramford had become available."

Sanctuary (William Faulkner)

"From behind the screen of bushes which surrounded the spring, Popeye watched the man drinking."

The Satanic Verses (Salman Rushdie)

"'To be born again' sang Gibreel Farishta tumbling from the heavens, 'first you have to die.'"

The Scarlet Letter (Nathaniel Hawthorne)

"A throng of bearded men, in sad-colored garments and gray, steeple-crowned hats, intermixed with women, some wearing hoods, and others bareheaded, was assembled in front of a wooden edifice, the door of which was heavily timbered with oak, and studded with iron spikes."

The Sea-Wolf (Jack London)

"I scarcely know where to begin, though I sometimes facetiously place the cause of it all to Charley Furuseth's credit."

THE SECRET GARDEN (Frances Hodgson Burnett)

"When Mary Lennox was sent to Misselthwaite Manor to live with her uncle everybody said she was the most disagreeable-looking child ever seen."

SHIP OF FOOLS (Katherine Anne Porter)

"August, 1931—The port town of Veracruz is a little purgatory between land and sea for the traveler, but the people who live there are very fond of themselves and the town they have helped to make."

SILAS MARNER (George Eliot)

"In the days when the spinning-wheels hummed busily in the farmhouses—and even great ladies, clothed in silk and thread-lace, had their toy spinning-wheels of polished oak—there might be seen, in districts far away among the lanes, or deep in the bosom of the hills, certain pallid undersized men, who, by the side of the brawny country-folk, looked like the remnants of a disinherited race."

SLAUGHTERHOUSE-FIVE (Kurt Vonnegut)

"All this happened, more or less."

THE STRANGER (Albert Camus)

"Mother died today."

STUART LITTLE (E. B. White)

"When Mrs. Frederick C. Little's second son arrived, everybody noticed that he was not much bigger than a mouse."

THE SUN ALSO RISES (Ernest Hemingway)

"Robert Cohn was once middleweight boxing champion of Princeton."

THE SWISS FAMILY ROBINSON (Johann Wyss)

"For many days we had been tempest-tossed."

A TALE OF TWO CITIES (Charles Dickens)

"It was the best of times, it was the worst of times, it was the age of wisdom, it was the age of foolishness, it was the epoch of belief, it was the epoch of incredulity, it was the season of Light, it was the season of Darkness, it was the spring of hope, it was the winter of despair, we had everything before us, we were all going direct to Heaven, we were all going direct the other way—in short, the period was so far like the present period, that some of its noisiest authorities insisted on its being received, for good or for evil, in the superlative degree of comparison only."

"THE TELL-TALE HEART" (Edgar Allan Poe)

"True! nervous, very, very dreadfully nervous I had been and am; but why will you say that I am mad?"

TERMS OF ENDEARMENT (Larry McMurtry)

"'The success of a marriage invariably depends on the woman,' Mrs. Greenway said."

TESS OF THE D'URBERVILLES (Thomas Hardy)

"On an evening in the latter part of May a middle-aged man was walking homeward from Shaston to the village of Marlott, in the adjoining Vale of Blakemore, or Blackmoor."

THE THORN BIRDS (Colleen McCullough)

"On December 8th, 1915, Meggie Cleary had her fourth birthday."

THE THREE MUSKETEERS (Alexandre Dumas)

"On the first Monday of the month of April, 1625, the market town of Meung, in which the author of *Romance of the Rose* was born, appeared to be in as perfect a state of revolution as if the Huguenots had just made a second La Rochelle of it."

THROUGH THE LOOKING-GLASS (Lewis Carroll)

"One thing was certain, that the white kitten had had nothing to do with it:—it was the black kitten's fault entirely."

THE TIME MACHINE (H. G. Wells)

"The Time Traveller (for so it will be convenient to speak of him) was expounding a recondite matter to us."

TO KILL A MOCKINGBIRD (Harper Lee)

"When he was nearly thirteen, my brother Jem got his arm badly broken at the elbow."

A TREE GROWS IN BROOKLYN (Betty Smith)

"Serene was a word you could put to Brooklyn, New York."

2001: A SPACE ODYSSEY (Arthur C. Clarke)

"The drought had lasted now for ten million years, and the reign of the terrible lizards had long since ended."

VANITY FAIR (William Makepeace Thackeray)

"While the present century was in its teens, and on one sunshiny morning in June, there drove up to the great iron gate of Miss Pinkerton's academy for young ladies, on Chiswick Mall, a large family coach, with two fat horses in blazing harness, driven by a fat coachman in a three-cornered hat and wig, at the rate of four miles an hour."

WAITING TO EXHALE (Terry McMillan)

"Right now I'm supposed to be all geeked up because I'm getting ready for a New Year's Eve party that some guy named Lionel invited me to."

WALDEN (Henry David Thoreau)

"When I wrote the following pages, or rather the bulk of them, I lived alone, in the woods, a mile from any neighbor, in a house which I had built myself, on the shore of Walden Pond, in Concord, Massachusetts, and earned my living by the labor of my hands only."

WAR AND PEACE (Leo Tolstoy)

"'Well, Prince, so Genoa and Lucca are now just family estates of the Buonapartes . . .'"

THE WAR OF THE WORLDS (H. G. Wells)

"No one would have believed in the last years of the nineteenth century that this world was being watched keenly and closely by intelligences greater than man's and yet as mortal as his own; that as men busied themselves about their various concerns they were scrutinised and studied, perhaps almost as narrowly as a man with a microscope might scrutinise the transient creatures that swarm and multiply in a drop of water."

WHITE FANG (Jack London)

"Dark spruce forest frowned on either side the frozen waterway."

THE WIND IN THE WILLOWS (Kenneth Grahame)

"The Mole had been working very hard all the morning, spring-cleaning his little home."

THE WIZARD OF OZ (L. Frank Baum)

"Dorothy lived in the midst of the great Kansas prairies, with Uncle Henry, who was a farmer, and Aunt Em, who was the farmer's wife."

THE WORLD ACCORDING TO GARP (John Irving)

"Garp's mother, Jenny Fields, was arrested in Boston in 1942 for wounding a man in a movie theater."

WUTHERING HEIGHTS (Emily Brontë)

"1801—I have just returned from a visit to my landlord—the solitary neighbour that I shall be troubled with."

YOU CAN'T GO HOME AGAIN (Thomas Wolfe)

"It was the hour of twilight on a soft spring day toward the end of April in the year of Our Lord 1929, and George Webber leaned his elbows on the sill of his back window and looked out at what he could see of New York."

"First Mama"

CB radio "handle" used by former First Lady Betty Ford when in the White House.

"The First Meeting"

Debut episode of the TV sitcom *Mister Ed*, which aired on October 1, 1961.

"The First Time"

Debut episode of the TV series *Scarecrow and Mrs. King*, which aired on October 3, 1983.

First United States Volunteer Cavalry

Official name of Theodore Roosevelt's Rough Riders.

Fischbacher and Horn

Last names (respectively) of magicians Siegfried and Roy.

Fisher-Price original toys

The first 16 toys introduced by Fisher-Price at the 1931 Toy Fair in New York City.

Barky Puppy
Bunny Scoot
Dizzy Dino (dinosaur)
Doctor Doodle (duck)
Drummer Bear
Go 'n' Back Bruno (bear)
Go 'n' Back Jumbo (elephant)
Go 'n' Back Mule
Granny Doodle (duck)
Lofty Lizzy (giraffe)
Lookee Monk
Stoopy Storky (stork)
Tailspin Tabby (cat)
Woodsy-Wee Circus (clown, bear, camel, dog, mother/baby elephant, giraffe, horse, lion, monkey)
Woodsy-Wee Pets (cow, donkey, goat, pig)
Woodsy-Wee Zoo (bear, camel, elephant, giraffe)

"Fishhead"

Charlotte Flax's (Winona Ryder's) nickname for her sister Kate (Christina Ricci) in the film *Mermaids*.

Fitch

See **Abercrombie and Fitch**

Fitch, Clarke

Pen name used by author Upton Sinclair early in his career.

Fittipaldi

Speedboat of Dale McKussic (Mel Gibson) in the film *Tequila Sunrise*.

Fitzgerald Theater

St. Paul site of the Minnesota Public Radio broadcasts of Garrison Keillor's *Prairie Home Companion, A.* Formerly called the World Theater, it was renamed for F. Scott Fitzgerald in 1994.

Fitzgibbon, Father

Role for which Barry Fitzgerald won a Best Supporting Actor Academy Award in the 1944 film *Going My Way.*

FitzRoy, Robert

Captain of the H.M.S. *Beagle,* on which Charles Darwin served as naturalist from 1831 to 1836.

Fitzsimmons

Real last name of actress Maureen O'Hara.

Five Continent Imports, Inc.

Front used by the CIA in the film *Three Days of the Condor.*

The Five Pennies

Band led by Red Nichols.

Five Points

Small-town setting of the radio soap opera *The Guiding Light* from its 1937 debut until 1947. From 1947 until the last radio episode in 1956, the show was set in Selby Flats, California.

five-star generals and admirals

U.S. military officers who have held the five-star rank. They are listed below with the effective dates.

FIVE-STAR GENERAL (GENERAL OF THE ARMY)

George C. Marshall (December 16, 1944)
Douglas MacArthur (December 18, 1944)
Dwight D. Eisenhower (December 20, 1944)
Henry H. Arnold (December 21, 1944)
Omar Bradley (September 20, 1950)

FIVE-STAR ADMIRAL (FLEET ADMIRAL)

William Leahy (December 15, 1944)
Ernest King (December 17, 1944)
Chester Nimitz (December 19, 1944)
William Halsey (December 11, 1945)

The rank General of the Armies of the United States, higher than five-star but with no specific insignia, was held by John J. Pershing (from December 3, 1919), and was awarded posthumously to George Washington in 1976.

Flag

Fawn of Jody Baxter in the Marjorie Kinnan Rawlings novel *The Yearling.*

Flagston

Last name of the family in the comic strip *Hi and Lois.*

Flamingo, Placido

Opera-singer Muppet in the children's TV series *Sesame Street.*

Flanagan, Father Edward

Role for which Spencer Tracy won a Best Actor Academy Award in the 1938 film *Boys Town.*

Flannagan, John

Designer of the Washington quarter, minted since 1932.

Flash

Pet basset hound of Roscoe P. Coltrane (James Best) in the TV series *The Dukes of Hazzard.*

The Flash

Newspaper employer of the title character in the comic strip *Brenda Starr.*

Flashmatic

The first wireless TV remote control, invented by Zenith engineer Eugene Polley and introduced in 1955.

See also **Lazy Bones**

Flashy Sir Award

Presented annually to the nation's top "distance" greyhound by the National Greyhound Association. It is named for a star greyhound of the 1940s.

"flat-footed"

What the word "platypus" means in Greek.

Flavor

Magazine employer of editor Khadijah James (Queen Latifah) in the TV sitcom *Living Single.*

flavorific

Adjective describing Beech-Nut gum in TV commercials.

Flegenheimer, Arthur

Real name of gangster Dutch Schultz.

Fleisher, Von Humboldt

Full name of the title character in the Saul Bellow novel *Humboldt's Gift.*

Flem Building

Location of the WKRP studios in the TV sitcom *WKRP in Cincinnati.*

"The Flesh Failures"

Subtitle of the Galt MacDermot/James Rado/Gerome Ragni tune "Let the Sunshine In," written for the musical *Hair*.

Fletcher

See **Irwin**

Fletcher Rabbit

Puppet mailman in the children's TV series *Kukla, Fran & Ollie*.

fletching

Term in archery for the feathers attached to an arrow.

Fleugelheim Museum

Where Vicki Vale (Kim Basinger) first meets The Joker (Jack Nicholson) in the film *Batman*.

Fleur-de-Lis

Escort-service employer of Lynn Bracken (Kim Basinger) in the film *L.A. Confidential*. Its motto is "Whatever you desire."

Flick, Vic

Guitarist on the first recording of the James Bond theme, in the film *Dr. No*.

"Flight of the Bumble Bee"

Instrumental theme of the radio and TV versions of *The Green Hornet*, composed by Nikolai Rimsky-Korsakov. The theme for the 1966 to 1967 TV version was performed by trumpeter Al Hirt.

Flit

Hummingbird (voiced by Frank Welker) in the Disney animated film *Pocahontas*.

Flopit

Pet dog of Miss Pratt in the Booth Tarkington novel *Seventeen*.

Flora

See **Alexander, Flora, and Pom**

Flora, Fauna, and Merryweather

The three good fairies in the Disney animated film *Sleeping Beauty*.

Floral Heights

Fashionable neighborhood in Zenith that is home to the title character of the Sinclair Lewis novel *Babbitt*.

Florence Nightingale Pledge

Oath taken by new registered nurses:

I solemnly pledge myself before God and presence of this assembly to pass my life in purity and to practice my profession faithfully. I will abstain from whatever is deleterious and mischievous and will not take or knowingly administer any harmful drug. I will do all in my power to maintain and elevate the standard of my profession and will hold in confidence all personal matters committed to my keeping and all family affairs coming to my knowledge in the practice of my calling. With loyalty will I endeavor to aid the physician in his work, and devote myself to the welfare of those committed to my care.

Florists' Telegraph Delivery

What the letters in "FTD" originally stood for. It now stands for "Florists' Transworld Delivery."

Flo's Yellow Rose

Roadhouse restaurant owned by the title character (Polly Holliday) in the TV sitcom *Flo*.

Flotsam and Jetsam

Names given to the miniature aliens by Faye Riley (Jessica Tandy) in the film **batteries not included*.

The Flotsam Family

Original working title of the radio series *The Life of Riley*. The show was originally written for Groucho Marx.

Flourish and Blotts

Wizardry bookshop on Diagon Alley, in the Harry Potter series of books by J. K. Rowling.

Flower

Skunk friend of the title character in the Disney animated film *Bambi*.

Flower Films

Production company of actress Drew Barrymore.

"Flowers for Algernon"

Short story by Daniel Keyes that was the basis for the film *Charly*.

The Flowers of Progress

Alternate title of the Gilbert and Sullivan comic opera *Utopia Unlimited*.

Floyd Bennett

Ford Trimotor airplane in which Richard E. Byrd became the first to fly over the South Pole on November 29, 1929.

Floyd of Rosedale

Bronze hog trophy awarded to the winning team in the annual football game between the University of Iowa and the University of Minnesota.

Flub-a-Dub

See **8**

"Fluctuat nec mergitur"

Motto of Paris, France, which is Latin for "It tosses, but does not sink."

Fluffy

Pet rabbit of Radar O'Reilly (Gary Burghoff) in the TV series *M*A*S*H*.

Flush

Pet cocker spaniel of English poets Elizabeth Barrett and Robert Browning.

flux capacitor

Invention of Dr. Emmett L. Brown (Christopher Lloyd) that makes time travel possible, in the *Back to the Future* films.

Flyer

Biplane of the Wright brothers, first successfully flown at Kitty Hawk, North Carolina, on December 17, 1903.

The Fly films

The Fly (1958)
The Return of the Fly (1959)
The Curse of the Fly (1965)
The Fly (1986)
The Fly II (1989)

The Fly Girls

Five-person dance group in the TV comedy/variety series *In Living Color*, one of whom was future star Jennifer Lopez.

Flying A Productions

Production company of Western actor Gene Autry.

flying carpet

Favorite mode of transportation of cartoon character Felix the Cat.

Flying Crown Ranch

Setting of the children's TV series *Sky King*.

Flying Eagle

Indian name awarded to the title character (voiced by Bobby Driscoll) in the Disney animated film *Peter Pan*.

"The Flying Finn"

Nickname of Finnish distance runner Paavo Nurmi, who won a total of six individual gold medals at the 1920, 1924, and 1928 Summer Olympics.

Flying Freehold Productions

Production company of actor Patrick Stewart.

"Flying Home"

Theme song of vibraphonist Lionel Hampton.

"The Flying Policeman"

Nickname of Kenyan distance runner Hezekiah Kipchoge "Kip" Keino.

Flying Saucer

300-foot yacht of Maximilian Largo (Klaus Maria Brandauer) in the James Bond film *Never Say Never Again*. The yacht was actually owned by arms merchant Adnan Khashoggi.

"flying teapot"

Nickname of the early 1900s steam-powered automobile, the Stanley Steamer.

Flying Wasp

Sailboat of Judge Smails (Ted Knight) in the film *Caddyshack*.

"Fly Me to the Moon"

Doorbell tune of Jennifer Marlowe (Loni Anderson) in the TV sitcom *WKRP in Cincinnati*.

Flynn/de Havilland films

See **de Havilland/Flynn films**

"Fly the Unfriendly Skies"

Debut episode of the TV sitcom *The Bob Newhart Show*, which aired on September 16, 1972.

Flywheel, Wolf J.

See **Marx, Groucho, roles of**

Fogel, Millie

Real name of actress Barbara Bain.

"Foggy Mountain Breakdown"

Instrumental theme of the film *Bonnie and Clyde*, performed by Flatt and Scruggs.

Foghorn

Middle name coined by actor Walter Matthau in 1937 for his Social Security card, still listed as such in U.S. government records.

Foley

Movie-industry term for the post-production addition of sound effects.

Foley, Sergeant Emil

Role for which Louis Gossett Jr. won a Best Supporting Actor Academy Award in the 1982 film *An Officer and a Gentleman*.

Foley's Fire-Eaters

Words on the sweatshirts worn by the soldiers during the final obstacle course, in the film *An Officer and a Gentleman*.

Follet

Pet dog of novelist Jules Verne.

FON

Appropriate stock-ticker symbol of telephone company Sprint.

Fontenoy Hall

Margaret Mitchell's original name for Tara in her novel *Gone With the Wind*.

Foofram Enterprises

Hi's employer in the comic strip *Hi and Lois*.

football mascots (NFL)

Arizona Cardinals: Big Red (cardinal)
Atlanta Falcons: Freddie the Falcon
Baltimore Ravens: Edgar, Allan, and Poe (ravens)
Carolina Panthers: Sir Purr
Chicago Bears: Grizz (bear)
Dallas Cowboys: Rowdy (cowboy)
Denver Broncos: Thunder (Arabian stallion)
Detroit Lions: Roary the Lion
Jacksonville Jaguars: Jaxson de Ville (jaguar)
Kansas City Chiefs: K. C. Wolf
Miami Dolphins: T. D. (dolphin)
Minnesota Vikings: Vikadontis Rex (dinosaur)
New England Patriots: Pat Patriot
New Orleans Saints: Fetch Monster (dog)

Philadelphia Eagles: Swoop (eagle)
San Francisco 49ers: Sourdough Sam
Tampa Bay Buccaneers: Skully (parrot)

Footlight Frenzy

Film seen by Bruce Wayne's parents (David Baxt and Sharon Holm) at the Monarch Theater before being murdered, in the film *Batman*.

"For breakfast it's dandy, for snacks it's quite handy, or eat it like candy"

Advertising slogan of Post Sugar Crisp cereal.

Ford, Chris

Boston Celtic who scored the first three-point field goal in NBA history on October 12, 1979.

"The Fordham Flash"

Nickname of baseball Hall of Famer Frank Frisch, who graduated from Fordham University.

Ford, Mistress and Page, Mistress

Title characters of the William Shakespeare play *The Merry Wives of Windsor*.

Ford, Thelma Booth

Real name of actress Shirley Booth.

Foreigner original members

Dennis Elliott, Ed Gagliardi, Lou Gramm, Al Greenwood, Mick Jones, and Ian McDonald.

Forest

Horse of Deputy Sheriff Lofty Craig (Brad Johnson) in the TV Western series *Annie Oakley*.

Forman, Sir Denis

See **Son of Adam**

Forrest Claire

Real first and middle names of basketball Hall of Fame coach Phog Allen, whose nickname was short for "foghorn."

Forrester, Paul

Earth identity assumed by the alien title character (Robert Hays) in the TV series *Starman*.

Forrester's Club

Tavern inherited by Chuck Murray and Ferdie Jones (Abbott and Costello, respectively) in the film *Hold That Ghost*.

The Forsyte Saga

Series of three novels and two connecting short-story "interludes" written by John Galsworthy.
The Man of Property (1906)
"Indian Summer of a Forsyte" (1918)
In Chancery (1920)
"Awakening" (1920)
To Let (1921)

Forsythe Pendleton

Real first and middle names of Jughead Jones in Archie comics.

Fort Arnold

Where army recruits John Winger (Bill Murray) and Russell Ziskey (Harold Ramis) receive basic training in the film *Stripes*.

Fort Baxter

Setting of the first three seasons of the TV sitcom *The Phil Silvers Show* aka *You'll Never Get Rich*.

Fort Courage, Kansas

Setting of the TV sitcom *F Troop*.

Fort Daly, Alabama

Setting of the film *Body Snatchers*.

Fort Hercules

Ancient name of Monaco.

"For Those Who Are Young"

Theme song of the TV series *Peyton Place*, which has the same melody as "Wonderful Season of Love," the theme song of the earlier film version of *Peyton Place*.

"Fortis et liber"

Motto of Alberta, Canada, which is Latin for "Strong and free."

Fortis Films

Production company of actress Sandra Bullock.

"Fortiter et suaviter"

Motto of Fairleigh Dickinson University, which is Latin for "Bravely and pleasurably."

Fortitude

See **Patience and Fortitude**

"Fort Lauderdale or I'll kill myself"

Sign worn by hitchhiking Michigan State student T. V. Thompson (Jim Hutton) in the film *Where the Boys Are*.

Fortress of Solitude

Arctic hideaway of Superman.

Fort Severn, Maryland

Annapolis site on which the United States Naval Academy is built.

Fortuna

Gambling yacht of the title character (John Vivyan) in the TV series *Mr. Lucky*.

Fortunate Islands

Ancient name of the Canary Islands.

Fortune

Parrot inherited by Ralph Kramden (Jackie Gleason) in the TV sitcom *The Honeymooners*.

Fortune

Fishing boat sunk by the title monster in the film *The Beast From 20,000 Fathoms*.

Fort William Henry

New York setting of the James Fenimore Cooper novel *The Last of the Mohicans*.

Forty Acres & a Mule Filmworks

Production company of director Spike Lee.

Fort Zinderneuf

Setting of the film *Beau Geste* (1939).

"Fosbury flop"

Headfirst-and-backward technique for the high jump devised by Dick Fosbury, with which he won a gold medal at the 1968 Summer Olympics.

Foster's Temporary Employment Service

Employer of the title character (Imogene Coca) in the TV sitcom *Grindl*.

The Foundation Trilogy

Group of science-fiction novels written by Isaac Asimov.
Foundation (1951)
Foundation and Empire (1952)
Second Foundation (1953)

"The Foundling"

Debut episode of the TV series *The Waltons*, which aired on September 14, 1972.

Fountainbridge Films

Production company of actor Sean Connery.

The Four Aims

Original name of the pop group the Four Tops. The name was changed to avoid confusion with the Ames Brothers.

Four Boys and a Guitar

Original name of singing group the Mills Brothers.

"Four corners" countries

The only point in the world where the borders of four countries meet is at the boundary of Botswana, Namibia, Zambia, and Zimbabwe.

"Four Corners" states

The only point in the United States where the borders of four states meet is at the boundary of Colorado, New Mexico, Arizona, and Utah.

Fourfold

Allied code name for General George C. Marshall during World War II.

Four Freedoms

As presented in a speech delivered to a joint session of Congress by President Franklin D. Roosevelt on January 6, 1941.
> Freedom of speech and expression
> Freedom of worship
> Freedom from want
> Freedom from fear

"The Four Horsemen"

Nickname coined by sportswriter Grantland Rice in 1924 for the backfield of the Notre Dame football team:
> Jim Crowley (halfback)
> Elmer Layden (fullback)
> Don Miller (halfback)
> Harry Stuhldreher (quarterback)

See also **"The Seven Mules"**

Four Horsemen of the Apocalypse

From Revelation 6:2-8 (King James Version)
> Pestilence (on a white horse)
> War (on a red horse)
> Famine (on a black horse)
> Death (on a pale horse)

The Four Lovers

See **The Variatones**

"Four Quartets"

Series of poems written by T. S. Eliot:
> "Burnt Norton" (1936)

> "East Coker" (1940)
> "The Dry Salvages" (1941)
> "Little Gidding" (1942)

Four Star Productions

Production company formed in the early 1950s by the four stars Charles Boyer, Joel McCrea, Dick Powell, and Rosalind Russell.

Four Tops members

Levi Stubbs (lead singer), Renaldo "Obie" Benson, Abdul "Duke" Fakir, and Lawrence Payton.

The Four Winds

Staten Island, New York, Albanian restaurant visited by Corie and Paul Bratter in the Neil Simon play *Barefoot in the Park*.

Fowler

Real last name of actor Kevin Spacey.

Fowler, Clara Ann

See **Page Milk Company**

Fowl Tips

Title of a book of chicken recipes written by baseball great Wade Boggs, who ate a chicken meal before every game he played.

"fox"

What the word "Zorro" means in Spanish.

Foxridge, New York

Setting of the TV sitcom *Gloria*.

Fox River, Illinois

Home of Father Roger Dowling in the mystery novels of Ralph M. McInerny.

Foyle, Kitty

Title role for which Ginger Rogers won the 1940 Best Actress Academy Award.

"fragrant harbor"

What "Hong Kong" means in Chinese.

Frahm, Herbert

Real name of German statesman Willy Brandt.

Francis

First name of attorney F. Lee Bailey.

First name of novelist F. Scott Fitzgerald, who was a descendant of Francis Scott Key, the writer of the lyrics of "The Star-Spangled Banner."

Francis, Arthur

Pen name used by lyricist Ira Gershwin prior to his collaboration with his brother George. The name was derived from the first names of his brother Arthur and sister Frances.

Francis Asbury

Real first and middle names of pro football Hall of Fame quarterback Fran Tarkenton.

Francis Brett

Real first and middle names of novelist Bret Harte.

Francisco

First name of Scaramanga (Christopher Lee) in the James Bond film *The Man with the Golden Gun*.

Francis D. Ouimet Memorial Trophy

Presented annually since 1980 to the winner of the U.S. Senior Open golf tournament. It is named for the Hall of Fame golfer who won the 1913 U.S. Open champion.

Francis films

Series featuring a talking mule as the title character (voiced by Chill Wills) and starring Donald O'Connor:

Francis (1949)
Francis Goes to the Races (1951)
Francis Goes to West Point (1952)
Francis Covers the Big Town (1953)
Francis Joins the WACS (1954)
Francis in the Navy (1955)
Francis in the Haunted House (1956)*

* Mickey Rooney replaced O'Connor, and Paul Frees replaced Wills as the voice of Francis.

François Henri

Real first and middle names of fitness guru Jack La Lanne.

Franconero, Concetta Rosa Maria

Real name of singer Connie Francis.

Frank

See **Johnny and Frank**

Frank Edwin

Real first and middle names of baseball pitcher Tug McGraw, father of country singer Tim McGraw.

Frankel, Bernice

Real name of actress Bea Arthur.

Frankenberg, Joyce Penelope Wilhelmina

Real name of actress Jane Seymour.

Frankie

See **Louie and Frankie**

Frank James

Real first and middle names of actor Gary Cooper.

Franklin, Vermont

Hometown of Eva Lovelace (Katharine Hepburn) in the film *Morning Glory*.

Frank Morrison

Real first and middle names of novelist Mickey Spillane.

Frank-N-Furter, Dr.

Mad scientist in the film *The Rocky Horror Picture Show*, portrayed by Tim Curry.

Frank Urban

Real first and middle names of golf pro Fuzzy Zoeller, whose nickname comes from his monogram.

Frank Winfield

First and middle names of retail magnate F. W. Woolworth.

Fraser-Smith, Charles

World War II English gadget inventor who was the basis for Q in the James Bond novels of Ian Fleming.

Fraze, Ermal Cleon

Inventor of the pull-tab can, patented in 1963.

"The Freak"

Nickname of NFL defensive lineman Jevon Kearse, for his huge hands and unusually wide arm span.

Fred

Pet cockatoo of the title character (Robert Blake) in the TV series *Baretta*.

Pet dog of Little Ricky Ricardo (Richard Keith) in the TV sitcom *I Love Lucy*.

Pet dog of Cledus Snow (Jerry Reed) in the film *Smokey and the Bandit*.

Frederic

Real first name of poet (Frederic) Ogden Nash.

Frederick

Real first name of Olympic track star Carl Lewis.

Frederick August Otto

First and middle names of upscale toy retailer F. A. O. Schwarz, who opened his first store in New York City in 1870.

Frederick Tyrone Edmond

Real first and middle names of actor Tyrone Power.

Fredi, Pierre de

Real name of Baron de Coubertin, French educator who was primarily responsible for the revival of the Olympic Games in 1896.

Freedom

Middle name of Dharma Montgomery (Jenna Elfman) in the TV sitcom *Dharma and Greg*.

Freedomland, U.S.A.

Bronx, New York, 205-acre U.S.-history theme park, which opened on June 19, 1960, and closed in 1964. Shaped like a map of the continental United States, Freedomland's seven sections were: Little Old New York, New England, New Orleans, Great Plains, Old Southwest, San Francisco, and the futuristic Satellite City. Freedomland was America's largest theme park at that time.

Freedonia

Country headed by Rufus T. Firefly (Groucho Marx) in the Marx Brothers film *Duck Soup*.

"Freely have you received; freely give."

Translation of the Greek motto of Drew University.

Freemason

Middle name of Sergeant Phil Esterhaus (Michael Conrad) in the TV series *Hill Street Blues*.

"The Freep"

Nickname of the *Detroit Free Press* newspaper.

Freeway

Family dog in the TV series *Hart to Hart*.

Freisen, Samille Diane

Real name of actress Dyan Cannon.

Fremont

Pet dog of George Wilson (Joseph Kearns) in the children's TV series *Dennis the Menace*.

French, Daniel Chester

Sculptor who created the marble statue of Abraham Lincoln found within the Lincoln Memorial in Washington, D.C. The Lincoln Memorial was dedicated on May 30, 1922.

French Harmless Hair Dye Company

Original name of L'Oréal.

"The French Mistake"

Musical number interrupted on its film set by the free-for-all at the end of the Mel Brooks film *Blazing Saddles*.

French, Paul

Pen name used by author Isaac Asimov.

French Somaliland

Former name of the African nation Djibouti.

French Sudan

Former name of the African nation of Mali.

Fresh-Air Taxi Company

Company owned by Amos Brown and Andy Jones on *Amos 'n' Andy*, so named because their taxi had no roof.

Fresh-Up Freddie

1950s bird mascot of 7 UP.

Freund

Real last name of actor John Forsythe.

Friday the 13th films

Listed below with the portrayers of serial killer Jason:

Friday the 13th (1980): Ari Lehman
Friday the 13th Part 2 (1981): Warrington Gillette
Friday the 13th Part 3 (1982): Richard Brooker
Friday the 13th: The Final Chapter (1984): Ted White
Friday the 13th Part V: A New Beginning (1985): Dick Wieand
Friday the 13th Part VI: Jason Lives (1986): C. J. Graham
Friday the 13th Part VII: The New Blood (1988): Kane Hodder
Friday the 13th Part VIII: Jason Takes Manhattan (1989): Kane Hodder
Jason Goes to Hell: The Final Friday (1993): Kane Hodder

Friedman

Real last name of bandleader Ted Lewis.

Friedman, Esther Pauline

Real name of advice columnist Ann Landers.

Friedman, Pauline Esther

Real name of advice columnist Abigail Van Buren, aka Dear Abby.

"A Friend in Need"

Debut episode of the TV sitcom *The Jeffersons*, which aired on January 18, 1975.

Friendship

See **Grand Turk** and **Friendship**

Fritz, Michael, Pierre, and José

Parrot hosts of the Enchanted Tiki Room attraction at Disneyland.

From Among the Dead

Original title of the Alfred Hitchcock film *Vertigo*. This is the English translation of the title of the French novel upon which the film was based.

Froman, Abe

"Sausage King of Chicago," whom the title character (Matthew Broderick) impersonates to secure a table at ritzy restaurant Chez Luis, in the film *Ferris Bueller's Day Off*.

"From A to G"

Inscription on the cigarette lighter that seemingly implicates Guy Haines (Farley Granger) in a murder, in the Alfred Hitchcock film *Strangers on a Train*.

"From contented cows"

Advertising slogan of Carnation evaporated milk.

Fromme, Lynette

See **"Squeaky"**

"From Me to You"

First tune written by John Lennon and Paul McCartney (recorded by Del Shannon) to appear on the U.S. *Billboard* top-100 pop charts, in June 1963. This was six months before the Beatles' "I Want to Hold Your Hand" became their first U.S. top-100 *Billboard* tune, in January 1964.

fronton

Term for the building in which jai alai is played.

Frost, C. F.

Name on the sample cards in ads for the American Express card. Mr. Frost was an employee of the ad agency that formerly represented American Express.

Frosty Palace

Ice-cream parlor hangout in the film *Grease*. Menu items include the Dogsled Delight and the Polar Burger.

Frowick, Roy Halston

Real name of fashion designer Halston.

frozen concentrated orange juice

Commodity that the Duke brothers (Don Ameche and Ralph Bellamy) attempt to corner the market in, in the film *Trading Places*.

Fruit Garden and Home

Original name of *Better Homes and Gardens* magazine when first published in 1922. It took its present name in 1923.

Frump

Maiden name of Morticia Addams (Carolyn Jones) in the TV sitcom *The Addams Family*.

Fry, Arthur

3M scientist who invented Post-It Notes in 1980.

Fryburg

California town where gangster Vincent Antonelli (Steve Martin) is relocated by the FBI, in the film *My Blue Heaven*.

Fučik, Julius

See **"Entry of the Gladiators"**

The Fugitive (original TV series) introduction

(Spoken by actor William Conrad.)

The Fugitive. A QM Production. Starring David Janssen as Doctor Richard Kimble. An innocent victim of blind justice. Falsely convicted for the murder of his wife. Reprieved by fate when a train wreck freed him en route to the death house. Freed him to hide in lonely desperation. To change his identity. To toil at many jobs. Freed him to search for a one-armed man he saw leave the scene of the crime. Freed him to run, before the relentless pursuit of the police lieutenant obsessed with his capture.

Fujita scale

Scale used to measure the intensity of tornadoes.

Category F0: Gale tornado (40–72 mph). Some damage to chimneys, broken tree branches, shallow-rooted trees pushed over.

Category F1: Moderate tornado (73–112 mph). Roof surfaces peel, mobile homes pushed off foundations or overturned, moving autos pushed off the road.

Category F2: Significant tornado (113–157 mph). Roofs torn off frame houses, mobile homes demolished, boxcars pushed over, large trees snapped or uprooted.

Category F3: Severe tornado (158–206 mph). Roofs and walls torn off well-constructed houses, trains overturned, heavy cars lifted off the ground.

Category F4: Devastating tornado (207–260 mph). Well-constructed houses leveled, structures with weak foundation moved some distance, cars thrown, large missiles generated.

Category F5: Incredible tornado (261–318 mph). Strong frame houses lifted off foundations and carried considerable distance, car-sized missiles fly through the air more than 100 yards.

Fuld, Isaac and William

Inventors of the Ouija board, patented in 1892 and first sold through their Southern Novelty Company of Baltimore, Maryland.

Fuller, Ida (1874–1975)

Retired legal secretary from Vermont who received the first Social Security check in 1940. She had invested about $22 in the program, and received over $20,000 in benefits over the following 35 years.

Fuller, Paul

Swiss-born designer of 17 models of Wurlitzer jukeboxes in the 1930s and 1940s. These included the all-time bestseller introduced in 1946, the Model 1015, memorable for its revolving color columns and bubble tubes.

"Full Fathom Five"

Debut episode of the TV series *Hawaii Five-O*, which aired on September 26, 1968.

FUN

Stock-ticker symbol of theme-park operator Cedar Point LP. The company's properties include Cedar Point in Ohio, Dorney Park and Wildwater Kingdom in Allentown, Pennsylvania, and Knott's Berry Farm in California.

funambulist

Technical term for a tightrope walker.

"Funeral March of a Marionette"

Theme of the TV series *Alfred Hitchcock Presents*, composed by Charles Gounod.

Funk, Casimir

Polish biochemist who coined the word "vitamin" in 1911.

"Fun with a Purpose"

Slogan of *Highlights for Children* magazine.

furcula

Scientific name for a bird's wishbone.

Furies

In Greek mythology, the three sister goddesses who avenge crimes: Alecto, Megaera, and Tisiphone.

Furnier, Vincent

Real name of rock singer Alice Cooper.

Further Films

Production company of actor Michael Douglas.

Fuss, Martin

Real name of film producer Ross Hunter.

Futility

See *The Wreck of the Titan*

Futurama

Name of the General Motors exhibits at the New York World's Fairs of 1939–40 and 1964–65.

"The future belongs to those who prepare for it"

Advertising slogan of Prudential Insurance.

Future Enterprisers

High-school business group that Joel Goodson (Tom Cruise) belongs to, in the film *Risky Business*.

Fuzz

Pet dog of the title character in the comic strip *Ziggy*.

F.Y.I.

CBS newsmagazine for which the title character (Candice Bergen) works as an investigative reporter in the TV series *Murphy Brown*.

Fyrine IV

Planet that is the setting of the film *Enemy Mine*.

G7

Group of seven industrialized nations that meet regularly to discuss global financial policies: Canada, France, Germany, Great Britain, Italy, Japan, and the United States. Russia is sometimes included in this group, which is then called G8.

Gabilan Mountains

Name of the title equine in the John Steinbeck short story "The Red Pony."

"GABLE's back! and GARSON's got him!"

Slogan used to promote the 1945 Clark Gable/Greer Garson film *Adventure*. This was Gable's first film after his service in World War II.

Gabriele

Middle name of auto racer Mario Andretti.

Gabrielle Bonheur

Real first and middle names of French fashion designer Coco Chanel.

"Gadge"

Nickname of director Elia Kazan.

Gad's Hill Place

Kent, England, home of novelist Charles Dickens.

Gaetano Albert

Real first and middle names of bandleader Guy Lombardo.

gaffer

Chief electrician on a film set.

Gail

Middle name of talk-show host Oprah Winfrey.

Gaines, Adrian Donna

Real name of pop singer Donna Summer.

Galahad Glen

Home of the title character (voiced by Lucille Bliss and Ge Ge Pearson) in the children's animated TV series *Crusader Rabbit*.

Gala Poochie Pup

Pet dog of the title character in the children's TV series *Rootie Kazootie*.

Galaxy

Evil organization in the film *Our Man Flint*.

Galaxy

Spaceship of the title character (Richard Coogan, Al Hodge) in the children's TV series *Captain Video and His Video Rangers*.

"The Galaxy Being"

Debut episode of the TV series *The Outer Limits*, which aired on September 16, 1963.

Gale, Cathy

Original partner of John Steed (Patrick Macnee) in the British TV series *The Avengers*, portrayed by Honor Blackman.

Gallifrey

Home planet of the title character in the British TV series *Dr. Who*.

"The Galloping Ghost"

Nickname of football great Harold "Red" Grange.

Galt's Gulch

Utopian community in the Ayn Rand novel *Atlas Shrugged*.

Galvin, Paul

Inventor of the car radio in 1929, which was the basis for his founding of the Motorola company.

Gamaliel

Middle name of President Warren G. Harding, which is from the Hebrew for "the recompense of God."

Gambol and Japes

Wizardry joke shop on Diagon Alley, in the Harry Potter series of books by J. K. Rowling.

The Game of Life

See **Life, The Game of, currency portraits**

Gandhi, Mohandas

Role for which Ben Kingsley won a Best Actor Academy Award in the 1982 film *Gandhi*.

Gang of Four

Group of radical members of China's Communist Party who were imprisoned after the death of Mao Zedong in 1976: Jiang Qing (widow of Mao), Wang Hongwen, Yao Wenyuan, and Zhang Chunqiao.

Gantry, Elmer

Title role for which Burt Lancaster won the 1960 Best Actor Academy Award.

"Garbo laughs!"

Slogan used to promote the 1939 film *Ninotchka*, which featured Greta Garbo's first comedic role.

"Garbo talks!"

Slogan used to promote the 1930 film *Anna Christie*, Greta Garbo's first talkie.

"The Garden Weasel"

Debut episode of the TV sitcom *The Larry Sanders Show*, which aired on August 15, 1992.

Gardiners Island

Largest privately owned island in the United States, located in New York off the coast of eastern Long Island. It is reputed to be the burial site of some of the pirate loot of Captain William Kidd.

Gardol

Ingredient in Colgate Dental Cream. The word is Colgate's trademark for sodium n-lauroyl sarcosinate.

Garfield, Elliott

Role for which Richard Dreyfuss won a Best Actor Academy Award in the 1977 film *the Goodbye Girl*.

Garfinkle, Jacob Julius

Real name of actor John Garfield.

Garland/Rooney films

The films in which Judy Garland and Mickey Rooney appear together:
Thoroughbreds Don't Cry (1937)
Love Finds Andy Hardy (1938)
Babes in Arms (1939)
Strike Up the Band (1940)
Andy Hardy Meets Debutante (1940)
Babes on Broadway (1941)
Life Begins for Andy Hardy (1941)
Girl Crazy (1943)
Thousands Cheer (1943)
Words and Music (1948)

Garretson Beekman

Real first and middle names of cartoonist Garry Trudeau.

Garrison, New Jersey

Setting of the film *Copland*.

Garrity

Last name of the lead singer of the rock group Freddie and the Dreamers.

Garter Inn

Setting of several scenes of the William Shakespeare play *The Merry Wives of Windsor*.

Gary's Shoe Emporium

Employer of Al Bundy (Ed O'Neill) in the TV sitcom *Married . . . with Children*.

Gasparro, Frank

Designer of the Kennedy half dollar (minted since 1964), Eisenhower dollar (minted 1971–78) and Susan B. Anthony dollar (minted 1979–81). He also designed the current reverse ("tails") of the Lincoln penny (minted since 1959).

Gassion

Real last name of of French cabaret singer Edith Piaf. Her stage surname is the French word for "sparrow."

The Gas Station

Comedy club that is the setting of the film *Punchline*.

Gaston

Man-eating shark that escapes from the Paris Aquarium into the Seine River in the Laurel and Hardy film *The Flying Deuces*.

gastroesophageal reflux

Medical term for the digestive disorder that causes heartburn, aka acid indigestion.

Gasworks

Nightclub where Wayne Campbell (Mike Myers) meets Cassandra (Tia Carrere) in the film *Wayne's World*.

The Gate

Magazine employer of columnist Susan Keane (Brooke Shields) in the TV sitcom *Suddenly Susan*.

Gateman, Goodbury, and Graves

Funeral-home employer of Herman Munster (Fred Gwynne) in the TV sitcom *The Munsters*.

Gateshead Hall

Childhood home of the title character in the Charlotte Brontë novel *Jane Eyre*.

Gatlin Brothers members

Brothers Larry, Rudy, and Steve Gatlin.

Gatlin, Nebraska

Setting of the Stephen King short story "Children of the Corn."

Gatz, James

Real name of the title character in the F. Scott Fitzgerald novel *The Great Gatsby*.

Gauguin, Paul

Role for which Anthony Quinn won a Best Supporting Actor Academy Award in the 1956 film *Lust for Life*.

Gayetty, Joseph C.

Inventor of the first packaged bathroom tissue, introduced in 1857.

Gearloose, Gyro

Cartoon inventor in Disney comic books.

Geisman, Ella

Real name of actress June Allyson.

Gekko, Gordon

Role for which Michael Douglas won a Best Actor Academy Award in the 1987 film *Wall Street*.

Gemini XII

Original name of the *Jupiter II* spacecraft in the TV series *Lost in Space*. The name was changed to avoid confusion with NASA's Gemini program.

Genco Importing Company

Business owned by Vito Corleone (Marlon Brando) in the film *The Godfather*.

Gene-Gene the Dancing Machine

Stagehand often seen dancing frenetically in the TV series *The Gong Show*.

The General

Horse of President John Tyler.

"The General"

Nickname of Piet Wetjoen in the Eugene O'Neill play *The Iceman Cometh*.

General Equipment Corporation

Employer of product tester Fielding Mellish (Woody Allen) in the film *Bananas*.

General Insurance Company

Employer of Jim Anderson (Robert Young) in the TV series *Father Knows Best*.

General Lee

Dodge Charger automobile driven by Luke and Bo Duke (Tom Wopat and John Schneider) in the TV series *The Dukes of Hazzard*.

General Pershing Veterans Administration Hospital

River Bend, Missouri, setting of the TV sitcom *Aftermash*.

generals

See **five-star generals and admirals**

General Sherman

World's largest tree (by volume), located in Sequoia National Park, California. It has an estimated volume of 52,500 cubic feet, stands 261 feet tall and has a girth of 1,024 inches.

"Genesis"

Debut episode of the TV series *Nash Bridges*, which aired on March 29, 1996.

"Genesis—September 13, 1956"

Debut episode of the TV series *Quantum Leap*, which aired on March 26, 1989.

"Gene the Machine"

Nickname of golf great Gene Littler, for his picture-perfect swing.

Genevieve

Uncle Fester's (Jackie Coogan's) rifle in the TV sitcom *The Addams Family*.

Genie

See **film awards, national**

Genoa City, Wisconsin

Setting of the TV soap opera *The Young and the Restless*.

Gentile, Antonio

Virginia schoolboy who designed the Mr. Peanut logo for Planters Peanuts in 1916, as the winning entry in a contest run by the company.

"The Gentleman from Virginia"

Nickname of actor Randolph Scott, for his courtliness.

"Gentleman Rankers"

Rudyard Kipling poem from which James Jones derived the title of his novel *From Here to Eternity*.

Geoffrey

Cartoon giraffe mascot of the Toys "R" Us retail chain. GiGi is Geoffrey's female partner, and Baby Gee is their child.

Geophysical Service Inc.

Original name of Texas Instruments.

George

Real first name of jockey Eddie Arcaro.

Real first name of actor (George) Richard Chamberlain.

Real first name of Western actor Gabby Hayes.

Real first name of Hall of Fame baseball pitcher Tom Seaver.

Real first name of actor/director (George) Orson Welles.

First name of the title character in the Sinclair Lewis novel *Babbitt*.

George and Gracie

Humpback whales brought from the 20th century to the 23rd century in the film *Star Trek IV: The Voyage Home*.

George and Vulture Inn

Where the title character stays while in London, in the Charles Dickens novel *The Pickwick Papers*.

George Emmett

Real first and middle names of Spanky McFarland of the *Our Gang* series of film shorts, aka *The Little Rascals*.

George Lee

Real first and middle names of Hall of Fame baseball manager Sparky Anderson.

George, Peter

See Two Hours to Doom

George, Robert

Designer of the original alligator logo on Lacoste shirts.

George S. Halas Trophy

Awarded annually to the National Football Conference champion. George Halas was the original owner and longtime coach of the Chicago Bears.

George S. Patton Vocational High

School where Fonzie (Henry Winkler) serves as Dean of Students late in the run of the TV sitcom *Happy Days*.

George Street Pictures

Production company of actor Chris O'Donnell.

Geraldo

Stuffed armadillo of Max Schreck (Christopher Walken) in the film *Batman Returns*. "Geraldo" is also his computer password.

Gerard, Sam

Role for which Tommy Lee Jones won a Best Supporting Actor Academy Award in the 1993 film *The Fugitive*.

German Ocean

Former name of the North Sea.

German Southwest Africa

Former name of Namibia.

Germany, Reichs of

First Reich: Holy Roman Empire (9th century–1806)
Second Reich: German Empire (1871–1918)
Third Reich (1933–1945)

Germ, D. K.

Enemy of Bucky Beaver in TV commercials for Ipana toothpaste.

Gertrude

Duck that accompanies Professor Oliver Lindenbrook (James Mason) and his expedition in the film *Journey to the Center of the Earth*.

Gervis Jr., Bert John

Real name of actor Burt Ward.

Gessner, Mike

Farmer on whose land the pods are first found, in the film *Invasion of the Body Snatchers* (1956).

Gesundheit Institute

Clinic run by the title character (Robin Williams) in the film *Patch Adams*.

"Getting Up the Rent"

Debut episode of the TV sitcom *Good Times*, which aired on February 1, 1974.

Geza

Middle name of actor Ben Affleck.

Ghost

Schooner of Wolf Larsen in the Jack London novel *The Sea Wolf*.

Ghostbusters title characters

Peter Venkman (Bill Murray)
Egon Spengler (Harold Ramis)
Ray Stantz (Dan Aykroyd)
Winston Zeddemore (Ernie Hudson)

The Ghostly Trio

The three people-hating uncles of Casper the Friendly Ghost: Stretch, Fatso, and Stinkie.

Giacobe

Real first name of 1950s middleweight boxing champ Jake LaMotta.

"the giant's shoulder"

What the name of the star Betelgeuse means in Arabic. The star is located on the eastern shoulder of the constellation Orion.

Gibbet Island

See **Oyster Island**

Gibbons, Cedric

MGM executive art director who designed the Academy Awards statuette in 1927, which was then sculpted by George Stanley.

Gibbons, Euell

Naturalist who extolled the virtues of Post Grape-Nuts cereal in TV commercials.

Gibbsville, Pennsylvania

Setting of many of the works of writer John O'Hara. It was based on his hometown of Pottsville, Pennsylvania.

Gibson

Maiden name of Alice Kramden (Audrey Meadows) in the TV sitcom *The Honeymooners*.

Gidget feature films

Listed below with the portrayer of the title character.
Gidget (1959): Sandra Dee
Gidget Goes Hawaiian (1961): Deborah Walley
Gidget Goes to Rome (1963): Cindy Carol

Gidney and Cloyd

Noseless moon men in the children's animated TV series *Rocky and His Friends*.

"The Gift Outright"

Poem read by Robert Frost at the inauguration of President John F. Kennedy on January 20, 1961, written by Frost for the occasion.

"the gift that starts the home"

1950s advertising slogan for Lane cedar chests.

GiGi

See **Geoffrey**

Gignilliat

Middle name of actress Joanne Woodward.

Gilbert

Nephew of the Disney cartoon character Goofy, who wears a mortarboard on his head.

Gilbert, Cass

Architect who designed the Woolworth Building in New York City (completed in 1913) and the U.S. Supreme Court building in Washington, D.C. (completed in 1935).

Gilbert Keith

First and middle names of writer G. K. Chesterton.

Gilbert, Sir Alfred

Sculptor of the statue *The Angel of Christian Charity*, aka *Eros*, standing in London's Piccadilly Circus. It was unveiled in 1893.

Gilchrist, John

Boy who portrayed Mikey in the memorable commercial for Life cereal, which first aired in 1977.

The Gilded Truffle

Posh Springfield restaurant in the TV sitcom *The Simpsons*.

Gildersleeve, Throckmorton P.

Water commissioner in the radio sitcom *Fibber McGee and Molly*, portrayed by Harold Peary.

Gilead

Futuristic society that is the setting of the Margaret Atwood novel *The Handmaid's Tale*.

Gilhooley, Edna Rae

Real name of actress Ellen Burstyn.

Gillars, Mildred Elizabeth

See **Midge**

Gillespie, Bill

Role for which Rod Steiger won a Best Actor Academy Award in the 1967 film *In the Heat of the Night*.

Gillis, Davey

Seldom-seen older brother of the title character (Dwayne Hickman) in the TV sitcom *The Many Loves of Dobie Gillis*, portrayed by Darryl Hickman, Dwayne's real-life older brother.

Gillis Jr., Willie

Soldier character created by artist Norman Rockwell, which he used on eight of his *Saturday Evening Post* covers between 1941 and 1944.

Gillis, Lester

Real name of bank robber Baby Face Nelson.

Gilman, George

See **Hartford, George Huntington and Gilman, George**

"Gimme a whiskey, ginger ale on the side. And don't be stingy, baby."

Memorable line spoken by the title character (Greta Garbo) in the film *Anna Christie*.

Ginger

Pet dog of Barbie.

gingivae

Dentists' term for the gums.

Gingrich, William H. "Whiplash Willie"

Role for which Walter Matthau won a Best Supporting Actor Academy Award in the 1966 film *The Fortune Cookie*.

Gipson, Fred

Author of the novel *Old Yeller*, upon which the Disney film of the same name was based.

Girl Crazy opening-night orchestra

The October 14, 1930, Broadway opening of this George and Ira Gershwin musical included this remarkable assemblage of greats:
Jimmy Dorsey
Benny Goodman
Gene Krupa
Glenn Miller
Red Nichols (leader)
Jack Teagarden

"Girl on the Run"

Debut episode of the TV series *77 Sunset Strip*, which aired on October 10, 1958.

Girl Scout Cookie varieties

Apple Cinnamon
Do-Si-Dos (oatmeal peanut-butter cremes)
Lemon Drops
Samoas (vanilla with caramel/coconut/cocoa covering)
Striped Chocolate Chip
Tagalongs (chocolate-covered peanut butter patties)
Thin Mints
Trefoils (shortbread)

Girl Scout levels

Based on school grade or age.
Daisy (grades K–1 or age 5–6)
Brownie (grades 1–3 or age 6–8)
Junior (grades 3–6 or age 8–11)
Cadette (grades 6–9 or age 11–14)
Senior (grades 9–12 or age 14–17)

Girl Scouts of the U.S.A. Interest Patches

LIFE SKILLS (16)
Car Sense
Child Care
Conflict Resolution
Cookies and Dough
Dollars and Sense
Family Living
From Fitness to Fashion
From Stress to Success
Generations Hand in Hand
Home Improvement
Law and Order
Leadership
Travel
Understanding Yourself and Others
Your Best Defense
Your Own Business

NATURE, SCIENCE, AND HEALTH (17)

All About Birds
Build a Better Future
Creative Cooking
Digging Through the Past
Eco-Action
The Food Connection
From Shore to Sea
Inventions and Inquiry
It's About Time
Math, Maps, and More
Pets
Planet Power
Plant Life
Space Exploration
Why in the World?
Wildlife
Women's Health

COMMUNICATIONS (13)

Computers in Everyday Life
Desktop Publishing
Do You Get the Message?
Exploring the Net
From A to V: Audiovisual Production
Graphic Communications
The Lure of Language
Media Savvy
Once Upon a Story
Public Relations
Reading
A World of Understanding
Writing for Real

THE ARTS AND HISTORY (17)

Architecture and Environmental Design
Artistic Crafts
Collecting
Fashion Design
Folk Arts
Heritage Hunt
Invitation to the Dance
Just Jewelry
Museum Discovery
On a High Note
Paper Works
The Performing Arts
Photography
The Play's the Thing
Textile Arts
Visual Arts
Women Through Time

SPORTS AND RECREATION (15)

Backpacking
Camping
Emergency Preparedness
Games for Life
High Adventure
Horse Sense
On the Court
On the Playing Field
Orienteering
Outdoor Survival
Paddle, Pole, and Roll
Rolling Along
Smooth Sailing
Sports for Life
Water Sports

The Girls Upstairs

Original working title of the Stephen Sondheim musical *Follies*.

"The Girls Want to Go to a Nightclub"

Debut episode of the TV sitcom *I Love Lucy*, which aired on September 15, 1951.

"Gitmo"

Military nickname of the U.S. naval base at Guantánamo, Cuba.

"Give a hoot, don't pollute!"

See **Woodsy Owl**

"Give Me a Ring Sometime"

Debut episode of the TV sitcom *Cheers,* which aired on September 30, 1982.

Gizmo

Name of the cuddly Mogwai creature (voiced by Howie Mandel) brought home by Rand Peltzer (Hoyt Axton) in the film *Gremlins*.

GL-70

Secret ingredient in Gleem toothpaste.

Gladstone

Middle name of playwright Eugene O'Neill.

Gladstone, Mr.

Phony name used by Benjamin Braddock (Dustin Hoffman) when he registers at the Taft Hotel, in the film *The Graduate*.

"Glad we could get together"

Sign-off line of longtime newscaster John Cameron Swayze, who became the first TV news anchorman in 1949. The line is currently used by his son, CBS radio newscaster Cameron Swayze.

Glamorous Glennis

Bell X-1 airplane in which Chuck Yeager became the first person to break the sound barrier on October 14, 1947. Yaeger named the plane for his wife; since then, he has given the same name to each of his planes.

Glassboro State College

New Jersey school that was the site of an impromptu summit meeting between President Lyndon Johnson and Soviet prime minister Aleksei Kosygin on June 23 and 25, 1967. The site was chosen because of its location—exactly halfway between New York City (where Kosygin had just addressed the United Nations) and Washington, D.C. The school is known today as Rowan University.

The Glass Inferno

See *The Tower* and *The Glass Inferno*

Glass, Louis

Inventor of the jukebox, introduced in San Francisco in 1889.

Glass, Zachary

Real name of Zooey in the J. D. Salinger novel *Franny and Zooey.*

Gleason, Jackie

Girlfriend of Lenny Markowitz (Adam Arkin) in the TV sitcom *Busting Loose,* portrayed by Louise Williams.

Gleason, Jackie, characters of

As portrayed by Gleason on his various TV variety series:

   Charlie Bratton aka "The Loudmouth" (boorish know-it-all)
   Reginald Van Gleason III (wealth-flaunting millionaire)
   The Poor Soul (nonspeaking, downcast character)
   Joe the Bartender
   Fenwick Babbitt (klutzy bachelor)
   Rudy the Repairman

Glen Brook Grill

Diner owned by Libby and Drew Thatcher (Patti LuPone and Bill Smitrovich) in the TV series *Life Goes On.*

Glenlawn, California

Setting of the TV sitcom *Gimme a Break.*

Glenmont

Home of inventor Thomas Edison in West Orange, New Jersey.

Glenn Scobey

Real first and middle names of college football Hall of Fame coach Pop Warner.

Glennville, Georgia

Setting of the film *Rambling Rose.*

Glen Ridge, California

Setting of the children's TV series *The New Lassie.*

GLH Formula Number 9

Spray-on hair invented by infomercial king Ron Popeil. GLH stands for "great looking hair."

Glick

Last name of the title character in the Budd Schulberg novel *What Makes Sammy Run?*

Glienecker Bridge

See **Abel, Rudolf**

Glimmerglass

New York lake that is the setting of the James Fenimore Cooper novel *The Deerslayer.*

Global Thermonuclear War

Computer game played by David Lightman (Matthew Broderick) in the film *WarGames.*

Gloriana

Title character of the Edmund Spenser epic poem *The Faerie Queene.*

Gloribee, California

Setting of the TV Western series *Tales of Wells Fargo.*

"Glorifying the American Girl"

Slogan of the Ziegfeld Follies.

Glorious Hill, Mississippi

Setting of the Tennessee Williams play *Summer and Smoke.*

"Gloryosky!"

Favorite exclamation of the title character in the comic strip *Little Annie Rooney.*

Glubdubdrib

Land of sorcerers and magicians visited by the title character of the Jonathan Swift novel *Gulliver's Travels.*

"Glue Fingers"

Nickname of sure-handed pro football Hall of Fame wide receiver Dante Lavelli.

Glyptic

Allied code name for Russian leader Joseph Stalin during World War II.

Gnasher

See **Wolf and Gnasher**

gnomon

The raised part of a sundial that casts the shadow.

Gnorm Gnat

1970s comic strip drawn by cartoonist Jim Davis for an Indiana newspaper, before the premiere of *Garfield* in 1978.

"Go ahead, make my day"

Memorable line spoken by Harry Callahan (Clint Eastwood) in the film *Sudden Impact.*

Goat Cay Productions

Production company of actress Sigourney Weaver.

Gobbler's Knob

Hilltop spot in Punxsutawney, Pennsylvania, that is the center of the ceremonies every Groundhog Day (February 2).

"God Bless the Child"

Theme song of the TV sitcom *Roc,* performed by En Vogue.

Goddard, Stuart Leslie

Real name of rock singer Adam Ant.

Goddess of Democracy

33-foot high styrofoam-and-plaster statue, modeled after the Statue of Liberty, that was unveiled by protestors in Beijing's Tiananmen Square on May 30, 1989. The statue was toppled by a tank on June 4.

"The Godfather of Soul"

See **Brown, James, nicknames of**

"Godfrey Daniels!"

Euphemistic oath used by W. C. Fields in his films.

"God'll get you for that!"

Catchphrase of the title character (Bea Arthur) in the TV sitcom *Maude.*

Godolphin Barb

See **Byerly Turk, Darley Arabian, and Godolphin Barb**

Godse, Nathuram

Hindu who assassinated Mahatma Gandhi on January 30, 1948.

The Gods Grown Old

Alternate title of the Gilbert and Sullivan comic opera *Thespis.*

Godspeed

See **Sarah Constant, Goodspeed, and *Discovery***

"Go Fight City Hall . . . to the Death!"

Debut episode of the TV series *Quincy, M.E.,* which aired on October 3, 1976.

Go for Broke

TV game show on which Greta Hanson (Lori Nelson) is a hostess, in the TV sitcom *How to Marry a Millionaire.*

"Go forth to serve"

Motto of Brigham Young University.

Gogo

Boat owned by Steve McCaffrey (Kurt Russell) in the film *Backdraft.*

"Go home!"

Parting words of the title star to the audience, in the TV comedy/variety series *The Tracey Ullman Show.*

Going My Own Way

1982 autobiography of actor Gary Crosby. The title is a reference to the film *Going My Way,* which starred his father, Bing Crosby.

Goldberg, Dora

Real name of vaudevillian Nora Bayes.

Goldbogen, Avrom Hirsch

Real name of film producer Michael Todd.

Gold Coast

Former name of the African nation Ghana.

Gold Coast Flyer

San Francisco-to-San Diego train hijacked by Harry Doyle (Burt Lancaster) and Archie Long (Kirk Douglas) in the film *Tough Guys*.

Gold Dust No. 5

Perfume used by Lovey Howell (Natalie Schafer) in the TV sitcom *Gilligan's Island*.

"The Golden Bear"

Nickname of pro golfer Jack Nicklaus.

The Golden Boot

Trophy awarded to the winning team in the annual football game between Louisiana State University and the University of Arkansas. The trophy is shaped like a map of Louisiana and Arkansas.

The Golden Bough

Broadway play by Joseph Sheridan (Douglas Fairbanks Jr.) in which Eva Lovelace (Katharine Hepburn) gets her first starring role, in the film *Morning Glory*.

"The Golden Boy"

Nickname of pro football Hall of Fame running back Paul Hornung.

Golden Buckle

Award (given to the world champion saddle-bronco rider) that is sought by the title character (Jack Lord) in the TV Western series *Stoney Burke*.

Golden Cloud

Original name of Trigger, Roy Rogers' golden palomino.

The Golden Egg

Trophy awarded to the winning team in the annual football game between Mississippi State University and the University of Mississippi.

Goldeneye

Jamaica home of Ian Fleming, where he wrote his first James Bond novel, *Casino Royale,* in 1952.

Golden Fluffo

Procter and Gamble shortening of the 1950s for which telejournalist Mike Wallace did a TV commercial (without laughing!).

Golden Gate Casino

San Francisco setting of the TV series *The Barbary Coast*.

The Golden Hat

Trophy awarded to the winning team in the annual football game between the University of Oklahoma and the University of Texas, aka "The Red River Shootout."

Golden Horse

See **film awards, national**

"The Golden Jet"

Nickname of NHL Hall of Famer Bobby Hull.

The Golden Knights

Precision parachuting team of the U.S. Army.

Golden Rule Stores

Original name of the J. C. Penney retail chain.

Golden Spikes Award

Presented annually since 1978 by USA Baseball to the top amateur baseball player.

Goldfish Club

Organization of World War II airmen who have been rescued from the sea after being shot down.

Gold Hill School

Orphanage run by the title character (Merlin Olsen) in the TV series *Father Murphy*.

Goldie

Pet goldfish of the title character in the comic strip *Ziggy*.

Goldilocks

Code name for Colonel Hogan (Bob Crane) in the TV sitcom *Hogan's Heroes*.

Goldman, Emma

Role for which Maureen Stapleton won a Best Supporting Actress Academy Award in the 1981 film *Reds*.

Goldman, Sylvan

Oklahoma grocer who invented the shopping cart, circa 1937.

Gold Medal Wheat Flakes

Original name of Wheaties cereal when first introduced in 1924.

The Golliwogs

See **The Blue Velvets**

"Gomer Overcomes the Obstacle Course"

Debut episode of the TV sitcom *Gomer Pyle, U.S.M.C.*, which aired on September 25, 1964.

Goodacre, Glenna

Creator of the Vietnam Women's Memorial, a bronze sculpture depicting three women, one of whom is tending to a wounded soldier. The sculpture, part of Washington, D.C.'s Vietnam Veterans Memorial, was dedicated in 1993. Goodacre also designed the obverse ("heads") of the Sacagawea dollar.

Goodbye Blue Monday

Alternate title of the Kurt Vonnegut novel *Breakfast of Champions*.

"Goodbye, Farewell, and Amen"

Final episode of the TV sitcom *M*A*S*H*, which aired on February 28, 1983.

"Goodbye, kids"

See **Hornblow**

Goodbye to Berlin

Novel by Christopher Isherwood that was the basis for the play *I Am a Camera* and the musical *Cabaret*.

The Good Conduct Medal

Award won by Herbert T. Gillis (Frank Faylen) for World War II service, which he speaks about proudly and often in the TV sitcom *The Many Loves of Dobie Gillis*.

"Good evening, Mr. and Mrs. North and South America and all the ships at sea. Let's go to press!"

Opening line of the radio broadcasts of Walter Winchell.

Goodgold, Edwin

See **Trivia**

"Good grief!"

Favorite exclamation of Charlie Brown in the comic strip *Peanuts*.

Good Guys

Brand of doll that the evil Chucky is, in the film *Child's Play*.

Goodhead, Dr. Holly

Scientist/CIA agent (Lois Chiles) who assists James Bond (Roger Moore) in the film *Moonraker*.

Good Luck Margarine

Product for which former First Lady Eleanor Roosevelt did a TV commercial in 1959.

Goodman, Dr. Reason A.

Lexicographer (Editor-in-Chief of *The World Book Dictionary*) who served as judge on the original version of the TV game show *Password*.

"Good Morning to All"

Original title of the tune "Happy Birthday to You."

"Good night and good luck"

Sign-off line of CBS newscaster Edward R. Murrow.

"Good night and good news"

Sign-off line of WJM-TV anchorman Ted Baxter (Ted Knight) in the TV sitcom *The Mary Tyler Moore Show*.

"Good night, and have a pleasant tomorrow"

Sign-off line of Jane Curtin in the "Weekend Update" segment of the TV series *Saturday Night Live*.

Goodnight, Eula

Katharine Hepburn's role in the film *Rooster Cogburn*.

"Good night, Mrs. Calabash, wherever you are!"

Sign-off line of comedian Jimmy Durante.

"Goodnight, My Someone"

Love song in the musical *The Music Man* that uses a melody that is nearly identical to the march "Seventy Six Trombones."

"Good Old Days"

Instrumental theme of the *Our Gang* series of film shorts, aka *The Little Rascals*.

The Good Ole Boys

See **Bob's Country Bunker**

"The Good Son"

Debut episode of the TV sitcom *Frasier*, which aired on September 16, 1993.

Goodspeed

See **Sarah Constant, Goodspeed, and Discovery**

Goodthighs, Giovanna

First film role of Jacqueline Bisset, in the James Bond spoof film *Casino Royale*.

Good Times, Bad Times

1983 autobiography of former *London Times* editor Harold Evans.

"Good to the last drop"

Advertising slogan of Maxwell House coffee, reputedly coined by President Theodore Roosevelt.

Goodwin, Peter

Role for which Walter Brennan won a Best Supporting Actor Academy Award in the 1938 film *Kentucky*.

Goodyear blimps

The first Goodyear blimp was the *Pilgrim*, built in 1925. There are currently seven blimps in the Goodyear corporate fleet, based on four continents.
Spirit of Goodyear (Akron, Ohio)
Eagle (Carson, California)
Stars and Stripes (Pompano Beach, Florida)
Spirit of the Americas (São Paulo, Brazil)
Spirit of Europe I (Europe)
Spirit of Europe II (Europe)
Spirit of the South Pacific (Sydney, Australia)

"Googie"

George Burns' nickname for his wife and partner, Gracie Allen.

Goose Bar Ranch

Montana setting of the children's TV series *My Friend Flicka*. "Flicka" is the Swedish word for "girl."

"Gootch"

Nickname of Hollywood producer Jesse Kiplinger (because of his custom-made Gucci shoes) in the Neil Simon play *Plaza Suite*.

Gopher Prairie, Minnesota

Setting of the Sinclair Lewis novel *Main Street*. It is based on Lewis' hometown of Sauk Centre, Minnesota.

Gordon

Real first name of jazz saxophonist Tex Beneke.

Gordon, Charly

Role for which Cliff Robertson won a Best Actor Academy Award in the 1968 film *Charly*.

Gordon Stanley

Real first and middle names of Hall of Fame baseball catcher Mickey Cochrane.

Gordy, Kennedy

Real name of pop singer Rockwell. He is the son of Motown Records founder Berry Gordy.

Gorelick

Last name of saxophonist Kenny G.

Gorgan, Sirak

Pen name used by novelist William Saroyan early in his career.

Gorman Elementary School

Employer of third-grade teacher Emily Hartley (Suzanne Pleshette) in the TV sitcom *The Bob Newhart Show*.

Gorman, Margaret

First winner of the Miss America Pageant, in 1921.

Gort

See **"Klaatu barada nikto"**

Gossamer Condor

The first human-powered airplane, built by Paul MacCready in 1977. In 1979, his *Gossamer Albatross* became the first human-powered plane to cross the English Channel.

"Gotcha"

Instrumental theme of the TV series *Starsky & Hutch*.

Gotham Bus Company

Employer of Ralph Kramden (Jackie Gleason) in the TV sitcom *The Honeymooners*.

Gotham Conservatory of Music

Where Ravelli (Chico Marx) is employed as a piano teacher in the Marx Brothers film *The Big Store*.

Gotham Globe

Newspaper employer of Alexander Knox (Robert Wuhl) in the film *Batman*.

"Got milk?"

See **"milk mustache" celebrities**

Gottlieb, David

Creator of the first commercially successful coin-operated pinball machine, circa 1931. He called his new game "baffle ball."

Gottlieb, Joseph Abraham

Real name of comedian Joey Bishop.

Goulding

See **Elliott and Goulding**

Gourdine

Last name of pop singer Little Anthony.

Gow, Eleanor

Real name of model Elle Macpherson.

Gower Gulch, Arizona

Setting of the Abbott and Costello film *Ride 'Em Cowboy*.

Goya

See **film awards, national**

"Grab the whole team, then throw them out one by one until you find the guy with the ball."

Pro football Hall of Famer Bubba Smith's way to tackle a quarterback, in TV commercials for Miller Lite beer.

Graces

In Greek mythology, the three sister goddesses of beauty, brightness, and joy, listed below with their specialties:
    Aglaia (brightness)
    Euphrosyne (joy)
    Thalia (bloom of life)

Gracie

See **George and Gracie**

Grady, South Carolina

"Squash Capital of the South" that is the setting of the film *Doc Hollywood*.

Graham, Barbara

Role for which Susan Hayward won a Best Actress Academy Award in the 1958 film *I Want to Live*.

Graham, Bette Nesmith

Inventor of Liquid Paper circa 1951. She was the mother of Michael Nesmith of the Monkees.

Graham, Florence Nightingale

Real name of cosmetics executive Elizabeth Arden.

Graham, Tom

Pen name used by Sinclair Lewis for his first novel, *Hike and the Aeroplane*.

Grainbelt University

Setting of the film *The Affairs of Dobie Gillis*. The school's motto is "Learn, learn, learn; work, work, work."

grain weight per bushel

The standard U.S. weight (in pounds) of one bushel of each of these grains:
    Barley: 48
    Corn (shelled): 56
    Corn (husked ears): 70
    Oats: 32
    Rye: 56
    Wheat: 60

Gram, Anna

Pen name used by Margaret Farrar, first crossword editor of *The New York Times*, from 1942 to 1969.

"The Granddaddy of Them All"

Nickname of the Rose Bowl college football game, held in Pasadena, California, each January. The first Rose Bowl game was played in 1902.

Grand Exalted Big Dipper

See **Sacred Stars of the Milky Way**

Grand Exalted Ruler

Title given to the presiding officer of an Elks lodge.

Grand Fenwick

Duchy that declares war on the United States in the film *The Mouse That Roared*.

Grand Funk Railroad original members

Don Brewer, Mark Farner, and Mel Schacher.

Grand Lakes College

Setting of the film *Back to School*.

Grandmaster B

Bud Bundy's (David Faustino's) rap-star alter ego in the TV sitcom *Married . . . with Children*.

"Le Grand Orange"

Nickname of red-haired baseball player Rusty Staub, coined while he was with the Montreal Expos.

Grand Republic, Minnesota

Setting of the Sinclair Lewis novel *Cass Timberlane*.

Grand Slam (men's golf)

Currently these four PGA events: The Masters, U.S. Open, British Open, and PGA Championship. No one has yet won all four events in the same year.

Grand Slam (tennis)

Comprises these tournaments: Australian Open, French Open, Wimbledon, and U.S. Open. Winners of all four events in a single year:

MEN

Don Budge (1938)
Rod Laver (1962, 1969)

WOMEN

Maureen Connolly (1953)
Margaret Court (1970)
Steffi Graf (1988)

Grand Slam (women's golf)

Currently comprises these four LPGA events: the U.S. Women's Open, the LPGA Championship, the Nabisco Dinah Shore, and the du Maurier Classic. No one has yet won all four events in the same year.

Grand Turk and Friendship

Sailing ships featured on bottles of Old Spice men's toiletries.

"The Grand Twins of the Twin Grands"

Nickname of pianists Ferrante and Teicher.

Granite

Lead dog of Susan Butcher for her first three wins in the Iditarod Trail Sled Dog Race (1986–88).

Granjean, Arthur

Frenchman who invented the Etch-a-Sketch circa 1959.

Grant College

School attended by Mallory Keaton (Justine Bateman) in the TV sitcom *Family Ties*.

Grant, Gene

Artist who created the paintings used in the film *An American in Paris*.

Grant, George

Inventor of the golf tee, patented in 1899. Before the tee, golfers elevated the ball on a small mound of sand for their drives.

Grant/Hepburn films

See **Hepburn/Grant films**

Grant High

School attended by Bailey Salinger (Scott Wolf) in the TV series *Party of Five*.

See also **John F. Kennedy High**

Grant/Hitchcock films

See **Hitchcock/Grant films**

Grant Memorial Hospital

New York City setting of the TV series *Nurse*.

Gran Turismo Omologato

What the letters of sports-car designation GTO stand for, which is Italian for "certified (for) grand touring."

Granville

Real first name of evangelist (Granville) Oral Roberts.

Grapes of Roth

Favorite Manhattan bar of Chuck Baxter in the musical *Promises, Promises*.

graphospasm

Medical term for writer's cramp.

"Grasshopper"

Nickname given to Kwai Chang Caine (David Carradine) by his mentor Master Po (Keye Luke) in the TV series *Kung Fu*.

Grasshoppers

See **Cracked Ice**

Grattan

Middle name of actor Leo G. Carroll.

"The Graveyard of the Atlantic"

Nickname of the waters off Cape Hatteras, North Carolina, because of the many sailing ships that have sunk there.

gravidity

Medical term for pregnancy.

"Gravity, schmavity"

Advertising slogan of Wonderbra.

Gravy, Ham

Boyfriend of Olive Oyl before Popeye.

Gray Ghost

Horse ridden by Sitting Bull in Buffalo Bill's Wild West Show.

"The Gray Ghost"

Nickname of 1950s racehorse Native Dancer.

Gray, Pete

Outfielder who played in 77 games for the 1945 St. Louis Browns, batting .218. A beneficiary of the World War II player shortage, he is in this book because he had no right arm.

Gray, William

Inventor of the pay phone, first installed at a bank in Hartford, Connecticut, in 1889. Gray had previously invented the inflatable chest protector used by baseball catchers and umpires.

Grazer One

Earthquake-inducing satellite in the film *Under Siege 2: Dark Territory.*

"Grease for peace!"

Signoff line of Jon "Bowzer" Bauman in the TV musical/variety series *Sha Na Na.*

Greasewood City

Western town that appoints Cuthbert J. Twillie (W. C. Fields) sheriff, in the film *My Little Chickadee.*

"greasy kid stuff"

Undesirable alternative to Vitalis hair-grooming aid, according to its TV commercials.

The Great Artiste

B-29 observation plane that accompanied *Enola Gay* on its August 6, 1945, atomic bomb mission to Hiroshima, Japan, and *Bock's Car* on its August 9, 1945, atomic-bomb mission to Nagasaki, Japan.

"The Great Atlantic and Pacific Tea Company"

See **Hartford, George Huntington and Gilman, George**

Great Bend

Hometown of Harold Lloyd (portraying himself) in the film *Safety Last.*

"Great Bird of the Galaxy"

Nickname of *Star Trek* creator Gene Roddenberry.

"Great Caesar's ghost!"

Favorite exclamation of *Daily Planet* editor Perry White in the Superman comic books and 1950s TV series.

"The Great Collaborator"

Nickname of playwright George S. Kaufman, because most of his plays were written with coauthors, most notably Moss Hart.

"The Great Commoner"

Nickname of orator/politician William Jennings Bryan.

"The Great Compromiser"

Nickname of statesman Henry Clay.

"The Great Debate"

Debut episode of the TV sitcom *Welcome Back, Kotter,* which aired on September 9, 1975.

"The Great Dissenter"

Nickname of Supreme Court justice Oliver Wendell Holmes Jr.

The Greatest Gift

Original working title of the Frank Capra film *It's a Wonderful Life.*

"The Greatest Show on Earth"

Advertising slogan of Ringling Brothers and Barnum & Bailey circus.

"The Great Five Cent Store"

The first retail establishment of F. W. Woolworth, which opened on February 22, 1879, in Utica, New York.

Great Guns

Original title of the Cole Porter musical film *Born to Dance.*

"great hill"

What the name of Pennsylvania college Bryn Mawr means in Welsh.

"The Great Impostor"

Nickname of Ferdinand Demara, who successfully masqueraded as a monk, prison warden, surgeon, etc. His life was the basis for the film of the same name, starring Tony Curtis in the title role.

Great Northern Hotel

Where FBI agent Dale Cooper (Kyle MacLachlan) resides while investigating the murder of Laura Palmer, in the TV series *Twin Peaks.*

"The Great One"

Nickname of comedian Jackie Gleason.

Nickname of hockey great Wayne Gretzky.

The Great Society

Rock group fronted by former fashion model Grace Slick (and her husband Jerry Slick) prior to becoming lead singer for Jefferson Airplane.

"The Great Stone Face"

Nickname of comic actor Buster Keaton.

"The Great Triumvirate"
Nickname of statesmen Henry Clay, John C. Calhoun, and Daniel Webster.

The Great Unknown
Pen name used by Sir Walter Scott for the initial publication of his novel *Waverly*.

Great Value
"Bargain" house brand of the Wal-Mart retail chain.

"The Great White Shark"
Nickname of pro golfer Greg Norman.

Grecco, Cyndi
See **"Making Our Dreams Come True"**

"Greed, for lack of a better word, is good. Greed is right. Greed works."
Memorable (and often misquoted) line spoken by financier Gordon Gekko (Michael Douglas) in the film *Wall Street*.

Greeley's
Billiard parlor/saloon owned by Skinny Dubois (Anthony James) in the film *Unforgiven*.

Green
Birth surname of David Ben-Gurion, first prime minister of Israel.

Greenacres
Beverly Hills estate of comic actor Harold Lloyd.

Green, Andy
Royal Air Force pilot who became first person to break the sound barrier on land, on October 13, 1997. Driving a Thrust SuperSonic automobile, he reached a top speed of 764.168 mph at Nevada's Black Rock Desert.

Greenblatt's
Neighborhood grocery store in the Neil Simon play *Brighton Beach Memoirs*.

Greenbow, Alabama
Hometown of the title character (Tom Hanks) in the film *Forrest Gump*.

Green Destiny
Sword that is stolen in the film *Crouching Tiger, Hidden Dragon*.

Green Grow the Lilacs
Play by Lynn Riggs that was the basis for the Rodgers and Hammerstein musical *Oklahoma!*

Green Lane Country Club
Where Neil Klugman first meets Brenda Patimkin, in the Philip Roth novel *Goodbye, Columbus*.

Greenleaf, Indiana
Setting of the film *In & Out*.

Green Moon Productions
Production company of actors Antonio Banderas and Melanie Griffith.

Greenpoint
Setting of the *Our Gang* series of film shorts, aka *The Little Rascals*.

Green, Robert
Philadelphian who invented the ice cream soda in 1874.

Greenspan
Real last name of actor Jason Alexander.

Green Town, Illinois
Setting of the Ray Bradbury novels *Dandelion Wine* and *Something Wicked This Way Comes*.

Greenway, Aurora
Role for which Shirley MacLaine won a Best Actress Academy Award in the 1983 film *Terms of Endearment*.

Greenwood, Chester
15-year-old resident of Farmington, Maine, who invented earmuffs in 1873. Farmington celebrates Chester Greenwood Day in his honor each year on the first Saturday in December.

"Greetings, Gate!"
Jerry Colonna's greeting for Bob Hope on Hope's radio show.

Gregory, Hanson
Inventor of the donut hole in 1847.

Grendel
Pet dog of Hope and Michael Steadman (Mel Harris and Ken Olin) in the TV series *thirtysomething*.

Grey Cup
Awarded annually since 1954 to the champion of the Canadian Football League. From 1909 to 1953, it was awarded annually to the champion of the Canada Rugby Union. The cup is named for its donor, former Governor-General of Canada Earl Grey.

"The Grey Eagle"

Nickname of baseball Hall of Famer Tris Speaker.

Griffin, Jack

Title character (Claude Rains) in the film version of the H. G. Wells novel *The Invisible Man*. In Wells' novel, he is identified only as "Griffin."

Griffin's Wharf

Site of the Boston Tea Party of December 16, 1773.

Grigg, Charles Leiper

Missourian who invented 7 UP in 1929. Its original name was "Bib-Label Lithiated Lemon-Lime Soda."

Grile, Dod

Pen name used by journalist/author Ambrose Bierce.

Grimaldi

Last name of the family that has ruled Monaco since 1297. (From 1793 to 1814, Monaco was annexed to France.)

Grimalkin

Pet cat of Heathcliff in the Emily Brontë novel *Wuthering Heights*.

Grimes, Burleigh

Hall of Fame baseball pitcher who threw the last legal spitball in 1934. The pitch was outlawed in 1920, but those already throwing it were permitted to continue.

Grimley's Rug Cleaners

Employer of deliveryman Bernie LaPlante (Dustin Hoffman) in the film *Hero*.

Grimy Gulch

Setting of the comic strip *Tumbleweeds*.

Grinders Switch, Tennessee

Mythical hometown of country comic Minnie Pearl.

Grinding It Out

1977 autobiography of McDonald's founder Ray Kroc.

Gringotts

Wizard bank in London, in the Harry Potter series of books by J. K. Rowling.

Grip

Talking raven in the Charles Dickens novel *Barnaby Rudge*. Dickens owned a talking raven with the same name.

Grits

Pet dog of Amy Carter while living in the White House.

Grossel, Ira

Real name of actor Jeff Chandler.

Grossman

Real last name of lyricist/MGM musical producer Arthur Freed.

Grouseland

Home of President William Henry Harrison in Vincennes, Indiana, when he was Governor of Indiana Territory.

Grouse-Moor Hotel

Where Inspector Clouseau (Peter Sellers) stays while in London, in the film *Trail of the Pink Panther*.

Grover

Middle name of author James Thurber.

Grover's Corners, New Hampshire

Setting of the Thornton Wilder play *Our Town*.

Grovers Mill, New Jersey

Rural setting of the radio adaptation of H. G. Wells' *The War of the Worlds* that was broadcast by CBS on October 30, 1938. The location was selected at random from a map of New Jersey by Howard Koch, who adapted Wells' novel for Mercury Theatre producers Orson Welles and John Houseman.

Grover, Utah

Hometown of Jack Holman (Steve McQueen) in the film *The Sand Pebbles*.

Growth of a Poet's Mind

Alternate title of the William Wordsworth epic poem *The Prelude*.

Gruelle, John B.

Creator of the Raggedy Ann doll, patented in 1915. His Raggedy Andy was introduced in 1920.

Grumby, Jonas

Real name of the Skipper (Alan Hale) in the TV sitcom *Gilligan's Island*.

Grungetta

Girlfriend of Oscar the Grouch in the children's TV series *Sesame Street*.

Grunion, Sam

See **Marx, Groucho, roles of**

Gruoch

First name of the 11th-century Queen of Scotland upon which William Shakespeare based Lady Macbeth in his play *Macbeth*. (No first name is mentioned for Lady Macbeth in the play.)

Gryffindor House

School home of the title character in the Harry Potter series of books by J. K. Rowling. The other three houses at Hogwarts are Hufflepuff, Ravenclaw, and Slytherin.

Gryphon

Yacht of industrialist John Gage (Robert Redford) in the film *Indecent Proposal*.

Guano, Colonel Bat

Keenan Wynn's role in the film *Dr. Strangelove*.

Guapo

Pet parrot of Jack McFarland (Sean Hayes) in the TV sitcom *Will & Grace*.

Guapo, El

Mexican adversary of the title characters (Chevy Chase, Steve Martin, Martin Short) in the film *¡Three Amigos!*, portrayed by Alfonso Arau.

Guaragna, Salvatore

Real name of songwriter Harry Warren, perhaps the least-known of America's most important songwriters. Among the dozens of song standards he wrote: "I Only Have Eyes for You," "Lullaby of Broadway," and "That's Amore."

Guardian

Russian computer that joins with the American computer Colossus in an attempt to rule the world, in the film *Colossus: The Forbin Project*.

Gubbins, Ernest Sidney

Real name of Norman Maine (James Mason) in the film *A Star Is Born* (1954).

Gub-Gub

Pet pig of the title character in the Doctor Dolittle series of children's novels by Hugh Lofting.

Gubitosi, Michael

Real name of actor Robert Blake.

Guess Who original members

Chad Allan, Bob Ashley, Randy Bachman, Jim Kale, and Garry Peterson.

Guglielmi di Valentina d'Antonguolla, Rodolfo Alfonso Raffaelo Pierre Filibert

Real name of silent-screen actor Rudolph Valentino.

Guiteau, Charles J.

Disappointed office seeker who shot President James A. Garfield in Washington, D.C., on July 2, 1881. Garfield died from his wounds on September 19.

Gulch, Almira

Margaret Hamilton's "Kansas" role in the film *The Wizard of Oz*.

Guldbagge

See **film awards, national**

Gulick, Luther and Charlotte

Founders of the Camp Fire Girls, the first nonsectarian organization for girls in the United States, in 1910.

Gulliver

Pet dog of Opie Taylor (Ronny Howard) in the TV sitcom *The Andy Griffith Show*.

Gumba and Gumbo

Mother and father (respectively) of clay animated character Gumby.

Gumlegs

Horse of Beau Maverick (Roger Moore) in the TV Western series *Maverick*.

Gump, Forrest

Title role for which Tom Hanks won the 1994 Best Actor Academy Award.

Gunderson, Marge

Role for which Frances McDormand won a Best Actress Academy Award in the 1996 film *Fargo*.

Gunn, Elston

Stage name used by Bob Dylan early in his career.

Gunpowder

Horse of Ichabod Crane in the Washington Irving tale *The Legend of Sleepy Hollow*.

Guns N' Roses original members

Steve Adler, Mike McKagan, Axl Rose, Slash, and Izzy Stradlin.

Gurevich, Mikhail
See **Mikoyan, Artem and Gurevich, Mikhail**

Gus and Jaq
Mice who befriend the title character in the Disney animated film *Cinderella*.

Guthrie, Janet
First woman to compete in the Indianapolis 500, in 1977.

Guynes, Demetria
Real name of actress Demi Moore.

"Gwine to Run All Night"
Original title of the Stephen Foster tune "De Camptown Races."

Gwyllyn Samuel Newton
Real first and middle names of actor Glenn Ford.

Gygax, E. Gary
See **Arneson, Dave and Gygax, E. Gary**

Gypsy Lovers* and *The King's Musketeer
Plays starring Anna and Frederick Bronski (Anne Bancroft and Mel Brooks) in the film *To Be or Not to Be*.

H.

Full first name of retired Desert Storm general H. Norman Schwarzkopf. His father, Herbert Norman Schwarzkopf, disliked his first name. The elder Schwarzkopf, as Superintendent of the New Jersey State Police, led the state's investigation of the kidnapping and murder of the son of aviator Charles Lindbergh in 1932.

Haag, Ruth

Stage name used by actress Betty Grable when singing with the orchestra of Harry James, her husband at the time.

Haas III, Eduard

Austrian inventor of PEZ candies in 1927. The name comes from the first, middle, and last letters of the German word for peppermint, *pfefferminz*.

"Habs"

Nickname of the NHL's Montreal Canadiens, which is short for the French word *habitants*.

Hackenbush, Dr. Hugo Z.

See **Marx, Groucho, roles of**

Hackensack Bulls

Team for which Montgomery Brewster (Richard Pryor) is a pitcher in the film *Brewster's Millions*.

Hacker, Leonard

Real name of comedian Buddy Hackett.

Hacklemore Prize

Fellowship won by pianist/composer Adam Cook (Oscar Levant) in the film *An American in Paris*.

Haddonfield, Illinois

Setting of the film *Halloween*.

Hadley Cove, Texas

Setting of the TV sitcom *Down Home*.

Hadley, Marylee

Role for which Dorothy Malone won a Best Supporting Actress Academy Award in the 1956 film *Written on the Wind*.

Hadleyville

Western setting of the film *High Noon*.

Hadleyville, Pennsylvania

Setting of the film *Gung Ho*.

"Hail Columbia"

Tune played for the entrance of the Vice President of the United States when unaccompanied by the President, as "Hail to the Chief" is played for the President.

Hailey, Royce

See **The Pig Stand**

Hail to the Chef!

Cookbook written by former president Russell Kramer (Jack Lemmon) in the film *My Fellow Americans*.

Haines, Joseph

Real name of "Happy" (Gavin MacLeod) in the TV sitcom *McHale's Navy*.

Hairi, Mata

Chimpanzee spy and girlfriend of the title character in the children's TV series *Lancelot Link, Secret Chimp*.

HAL

See **Heuristically Programmed Algorithmic Computer 9000**

Hale, Chris

Wagonmaster who succeeds Major Seth Adams (Ward Bond) in the TV Western series *Wagon Train*, portrayed by John McIntire.

Hale, Maryland

Hometown of Maggie Carpenter (Julia Roberts) in the film *Runaway Bride*.

Hale, Sarah Josepha (1788–1879)

Author/poet who wrote the poem "Mary's Lamb," aka "Mary Had a Little Lamb."

Half Moon

Ship captained by explorer Henry Hudson on his voyage to the eastern coast of North America in 1609.

"Half Pint"

Charles Ingalls' (Michael Landon's) nickname for his daughter Laura (Melissa Gilbert) in the TV series *Little House on the Prairie*.

halitosis

Medical term for bad breath, popularized in ads for Listerine.

Hall

Real last name of actress Diane Keaton.

Hall, Annie

Title role for which Diane Keaton won the 1977 Best Actress Academy Award.

Hall, Charles Prior

California furniture designer who invented the waterbed circa 1968.

Hall, Kevin Peter

Tall actor who portrayed the title alien in the films *Predator* and *Predator 2*, and the Bigfoot in the film *Harry and the Hendersons*.

"Hall of Flame"

Nickname of the Museum of Firefighting in Phoenix, Arizona.

"Hall of Fumes"

See **Halls of Fame, nonathletic**

Hall, Sir Benjamin

Man for whom Big Ben, the bell in the clock tower of the Houses of Parliament in London, is named. He was London's commissioner of works at the time of Big Ben's installation in 1859.

Halls of Fame, major athletic

Many of these have Internet Web sites where you can find additional information, such as a list of their members.

- Baseball: Cooperstown, New York
  (www.baseballhalloffame.org)
- Basketball: Springfield, Massachusetts
  (www.hoophall.org)
- Bowling: St. Louis, Missouri
  (www.bowlingmuseum.com)
- Boxing: Canastota, New York (www.ibhof.com)
- Football (college): South Bend, Indiana
  (www.collegefootball.org)
- Football (NFL): Canton, Ohio
  (www.profootballhof.com)
- Golf: St. Augustine, Florida
- Hockey (NHL): Toronto, Canada
  (www.hhof.com)
- Horse Racing: Saratoga Springs, New York
- Motorsports: Talladega, Alabama
  (www.mshf.org)
- Olympics (U.S.): Colorado Springs, Colorado
  (www.olympic-usa.org)
- Soccer: Disneyland Paris
- Swimming: Fort Lauderdale, Florida
  (www.ishof.org)
- Tennis: Newport, Rhode Island
  (www.tennisfame.com)
- Track and Field: Indianapolis, Indiana
- Volleyball: Holyoke, Massachusetts
  (www.volleyhall.com)

Halls of Fame, nonathletic

Many of these have Internet Web sites where you can find additional information, such as a list of their members.

- Accounting: Columbus, Ohio
  (fisher.osu.edu/acctmis/hof/hall.html)
- Advertising: Washington, D.C.
  (www.aaf.org/awards/ahof.html)
- Afro-Americans: Louisville, Kentucky
- Agriculture: Banner Springs, Kansas
  (www.aghalloffame.com)
- Astronauts: Titusville, Florida
- (Great) Americans: Bronx, New York
- Automotive: Dearborn, Michigan
  (www.automuseum.com/HallFame.html)
- Aviation: Dayton, Ohio
  (www.nationalaviation.org)
- Business: Macomb, Illinois
  (mccoy.lib.siu.edu/projects/advert/abhf.htm)
- Burlesque: Helendale, California
- Car Collectors: Nashville, Tennessee
- Checkers: Petal, Mississippi
- Chess: Washington, D.C.
  (www.chesslinks.org/hof)
- Circus: Peru, Indiana
- Classical Music: Cincinnati, Ohio
  (www.classicalhall.org)
- Clowns: Milwaukee, Wisconsin
  (www.clownmuseum.org)
- Comedy: St. Petersburg, Florida
  (www.comedyhall.com)
- Country Music: Nashville, Tennessee
- Cowgirls: Hereford, Texas (www.cowgirl.net)

Ecology: Santa Cruz, California
  (www.ecotopia.org)
(Oldtime) Fiddlers: Weiser, Idaho
Hamburgers: Seymour, Wisconsin
Hot Dogs: Fairfield, California
Inventors: Akron, OH (www.invent.org)
Jewish-Americans: Berkeley, California
  (amuseum.org/jahf)
Nurses: Washington, D.C.
  (www.nursingworld.org/hof)
Photography: Oklahoma City, Oklahoma
Police: Miami, Florida (www.aphf.org)
Quilters: Marion, Indiana
  (www.quiltershalloffame.org)
Rivers: Dubuque, Iowa
Rock and Roll: Cleveland, Ohio
  (www.rockhall.com)
RVs/Motor Homes: Elkhart, Indiana
(Rotten) Sneakers "Hall of Fumes": Montpelier,
  Vermont
(Nashville) Songwriters: Nashville, Tennessee
  (www.nashvillesongwritersfoundation.com)
Songwriters: New York, New York
  (www.popularsongs.org/shof)
Space: Alamogordo, New Mexico
(Hollywood) Stuntmen: Moab, Utah
(National) Teachers: Emporia, Kansas
  (www.nthf.org)
(National) Women: Seneca Falls, New York
  (www.greatwomen.org)

hallux
Scientific name for the big toe.

Hallward, Basil
Painter of the title work of art in the Oscar Wilde novel *The Picture of Dorian Gray*.

Halo
See **Rocks and Halo**

Haloid Company
Original name of Xerox.

The Halos
Vocal group that backs up Curtis Lee on his tune "Pretty Little Angel Eyes."

Halparin, Monte
Real name of game-show host Monty Hall.

Halpern, Renata
Pen name used by Susannah Wingo in the Pat Conroy novel *The Prince of Tides*.

Halprin, Lawrence
Designer of the FDR Memorial in Washington, D.C., which opened in May 1997.

Hamilton High
School where the title character serves as principal, in the TV sitcom *The Stu Erwin Show*.

Hamilton, Sarah Jane
Real name of Aunt Pittypat in the Margaret Mitchell novel *Gone With the Wind*.

Hamlet
Title role for which Laurence Olivier won the 1948 Best Actor Academy Award.

Hammelburg
Bavarian town near Stalag 13 in the TV sitcom *Hogan's Heroes*.

"The Hammer"
Nickname of 1970s NHL player Dave Schultz, for his intimidating style of play.

Hammes, John W.
Inventor of the kitchen garbage disposer in 1927.

Hammett, Dashiell
Role for which Jason Robards won a Best Supporting Actor Academy Award in the 1977 film *Julia*.

Hamster Huey and the Gooey Kablooie
Calvin's favorite bedtime story in the comic strip *Calvin and Hobbes*.

Hana
Role for which Juliette Binoche won a Best Supporting Actress Academy Award in the 1996 film *The English Patient*.

Handler, Ruth and Elliot
Founders of Mattel, and creators of Barbie, first sold in 1959. Barbie was named for their daughter Barbara.

Handley, Mark
See **Idioglossia**

"Hands of Stone"
Nickname of boxer Roberto Duran.

Handsome Dan
Bulldog mascot of Yale University since 1889. Yale was the first university in the U.S. to adopt a mascot.

Haney, Chris
See **Abbott, Scott and Haney, Chris**

"Hang by your thumbs"
Sign-off line of Bob Elliott of Bob and Ray radio fame.

See also **"Write if you get work"**

Hangul
See **24**

The Hank McCune Show
1950 sitcom that was the first TV series to use a laugh track.

Hanks
Maiden name of Clair Huxtable (Phylicia Rashad) in the TV sitcom *The Cosby Show*, which is also the maiden name of Bill Cosby's wife Camille.

Maiden name of Mammy Yokum in the comic strip *Li'l Abner*.

Hannah
Schooner that was the first ship of the U.S. Navy. It was built in Beverly, Massachusetts, and commissioned by George Washington on September 2, 1775.

Hannah, Miss
Character (Fran Ryan) who took over the Long Branch Saloon when Miss Kitty (Amanda Blake) departed the TV Western series *Gunsmoke*.

Hannassey, Rufus
Role for which Burl Ives won a Best Supporting Actor Academy Award in the 1958 film *The Big Country*.

Hannibal
Pet goose of Israel Boone (Darby Hinton), son of the title character (Fess Parker) in the TV series *Daniel Boone*.

Hannibal, Il Muto, and Don Juan Triumphant
Fictional operas within the plot of the Andrew Lloyd Webber musical *The Phantom of the Opera*.

"The Hanoi Hilton"
Infamous nickname of Hua Lo prison, which housed many American POWs during the Vietnam War.

Hanover, Indiana
Hometown of Woody Boyd (Woody Harrelson) in the TV sitcom *Cheers*.

Hans
First name of Dr. Zarkov, scientist colleague of Flash Gordon.

Hansburg, George B.
Inventor of the pogo stick in 1919.

Hansel
Pet dachshund of Hall Ebbing (Conrad Veidt) in the film *All Through The Night*.

Hansen, Annika
Birth name of Seven of Nine (Jeri Ryan) in the TV series *Star Trek: Voyager*.

Hansen, Barrett
Real name of novelty-record deejay Dr. Demento.

"Hap"
Nickname of General Henry H. Arnold, the first commander of the U.S. Air Force.

Happiness
See **Fame, Happiness, and Money**

Happiness Ahead and It's a New World
Films starring Vicki Lester (Judy Garland) in the film *A Star Is Born* (1954).

"The Happiness Boys"
Nickname of Billy Jones and Ernie Hare, who were among the first stars of network radio in the 1920s.

"Happy"
See **baseball commissioners**

Happydale Sanitarium
Where the aunts and uncle of Mortimer Brewster (Cary Grant) are relocated to, at the end of the film *Arsenic and Old Lace*.

"Happy Days"
Instrumental theme of the TV sitcom *The Donna Reed Show*.

"Happy Days Are Here Again"
Debut episode of the TV series *Jake and the Fatman*, which aired on September 26, 1987.

Happy Endings
Musical film starring Francine Evans (Liza Minnelli) in the film *New York, New York*.

Happy-Go-Lucky Toy Company

Employer of product inspector Peter Griffin (voiced by Seth MacFarlane) in the animated TV sitcom *Family Guy*.

The Happy Hobo

Silent-film character created by comedian-turned-studio head Alfie Alperin (Malcolm McDowell), in the film *Sunset*.

The Happy Homemaker

WJM-TV show hosted by Sue Ann Nivens (Betty White) in the TV sitcom *The Mary Tyler Moore Show*.

Happy Hotpoint

Dancing pixie character portrayed in 1950s TV appliance commercials by Mary Tyler Moore early in her career.

"Happy motoring!"

Advertising slogan of Esso (Standard Oil of New Jersey).

Happy, Texas

Where escaped convict Butch Haynes (Kevin Costner) is finally stopped in the film *A Perfect World*.

"Happy Trails"

Theme song of Western stars Roy Rogers and Dale Evans, written by Evans.

Happy, Walter, and Smiley

Pet white German shepherds of fitness guru Jack La Lanne, often seen on his TV programs of the 1960s.

"The Hardest Working Man in Show Business"

See **Brown, James, nicknames of**

Hardy, Carroll

Only man ever to pinch-hit for baseball Hall of Famer Ted Williams, on September 20, 1960. Williams was forced to leave the game that day after fouling a ball off his ankle.

Harger, Rolla N.

Indiana University biochemistry professor who invented the first blood-alcohol breath analyzer in 1931.

Harkless, John

Title character of the Booth Tarkington novel *The Gentleman from Indiana*.

"Harlem Nocturne"

Instrumental theme of the TV series *Mickey Spillane's Mike Hammer (1984–87)*.

Harmon, California

Setting of the film *Phenomenon*.

Harmon, John

Title character of the Charles Dickens novel *Our Mutual Friend*.

Harold

Real first name of poet (Harold) Hart Crane.

Harold Henry

Real first and middle names of baseball Hall of Famer Pee Wee Reese.

Harold Joseph

Real first and middle names of baseball Hall of Famer Pie Traynor.

Harpo

Production company of Oprah Winfrey. ("Harpo" is "Oprah" spelled backward.) Harpo is also the name of the husband of Winfrey's character in the Steven Spielberg film *The Color Purple*.

Middle name of Dr. Richard H. Thorndyke (Mel Brooks) in the film *High Anxiety*. (His mother loved the Marx Brothers.)

Harpo Speaks!

1961 autobiography of nonspeaking comedian Harpo Marx.

Harrington

Town that is the setting of the Disney film *Pollyanna*.

Harris, Houston

Real name of pro wrestler Bobo Brazil.

Harrison

Maiden name of Emily Hartley (Suzanne Pleshette) in the TV sitcom *The Bob Newhart Show*.

First name of the title character in the Max Brand novel *Destry Rides Again*. The same character in the film version, portrayed by James Stewart, is named Thomas Jefferson Destry.

Real first name of "Tinker" Bell (Billy Sands) in the TV sitcom *McHale's Navy*.

Harrisongs

Music publishing company of former Beatle George Harrison.

Harrison, Harry

See **Make Room! Make Room!**

Harrison High

Where Neil Hendry (Dick Clark) teaches, in the film *Because They're Young*.

Harrison, John

Inventor of the marine chronometer in 1736, which made it possible for sailors to calculate their longitude while at sea. (Only latitude could be calculated before, using solar/stellar observation and a sextant.)

Harris, Paul Percy

Chicago attorney who founded the Rotary Club in 1905.

Harroun, Ray

Winner of the first Indianapolis 500 in 1911, with an average speed of 74.6 mph.

Harry

Real first name of novelist (Harry) Sinclair Lewis.

Family dog of humorist Erma Bombeck.

"Harry"

See **Murphy, Mrs.**

Harry Potter series

The first four of the seven planned books by J. K. Rowling:

> *Harry Potter and the Sorcerer's Stone* (1998) (U.K. title: *Harry Potter and the Philosopher's Stone*)
> *Harry Potter and the Chamber of Secrets* (1999)
> *Harry Potter and the Prisoner of Azkaban* (1999)
> *Harry Potter and the Goblet of Fire* (2000)

Harshman

Middle name of comedian Jonathan Winters.

Hartford, George Huntington and Gilman, George

Founders of the A&P grocery chain, whose full corporate name is "The Great Atlantic and Pacific Tea Company." They opened their first store on Manhattan's Vesey Street in 1859.

Hart, Frederick

See **Statue of the Three Servicemen**

Hartley, Vivian

Birth name of actress Vivien Leigh.

Hart Memorial Trophy

Awarded annually since 1924 to the NHL's most valuable player, named for former Montreal Canadiens coach Cecil Hart.

Hartnell, Sir Norman

Designer of the dress worn by Queen Elizabeth II of Great Britain (then Princess Elizabeth) at her wedding to Prince Philip on November 20, 1947.

Hartnett, Jeff

Role for which Van Heflin won a Best Supporting Actor Academy Award in the 1942 film *Johnny Eager*.

Hartwell County

Setting of the Alice Walker novel *The Color Purple*.

Harum

Real last name of TV host Mary Hart.

Harvard University, notable honorary degree recipients

1753 Benjamin Franklin
1776 George Washington
1781 John Adams
1787 Thomas Jefferson
1792 Samuel Adams
1822 John Quincy Adams
1832 Washington Irving
1833 Andrew Jackson
1859 Henry Wadsworth Longfellow
1866 Ralph Waldo Emerson
1872 Ulysses S. Grant
1896 Booker T. Washington
1905 William Howard Taft
1907 Woodrow Wilson
1917 Herbert Hoover
1919 Theodore Roosevelt
1929 Franklin D. Roosevelt
1935 Albert Einstein
1937 Robert Frost
1938 Walt Disney
1940 Carl Sandburg
1943 Winston Churchill
1946 Dwight D. Eisenhower
1951 Thornton Wilder
1956 John F. Kennedy
1961 Aaron Copland
1963 U Thant
1965 Adlai Stevenson
1966 Martha Graham
1967 Leonard Bernstein
1968 Shah of Iran
1972 Saul Bellow
1973 Georgia O'Keeffe
1973 Robert Penn Warren
1974 Ralph Ellison
1974 Beverly Sills
1976 Arthur Fiedler

1977 Eudora Welty
1978 Alexander Solzhenitsyn
1979 Desmond Tutu
1981 Ansel Adams
1981 Leontyne Price
1982 Mother Teresa
1982 Tennessee Williams
1984 King Juan Carlos I
1984 Benny Goodman
1986 Itzhak Perlman
1987 Tip O'Neill
1989 Toni Morrison
1990 Ella Fitzgerald
1990 Stephen Hawking
1990 Helmut Kohl
1991 Yo-Yo Ma
1992 Isaac Stern
1993 Colin Powell
1993 Ravi Shankar
1994 Al Gore
1995 Václav Havel
1997 Madeleine Albright
1997 Quincy Jones
1999 Alan Greenspan

Harvey

Pet boxer of actor Humphrey Bogart.

Pet dog of Elliott (Henry Thomas) in the Steven Spielberg film *E. T. The Extra-Terrestrial.*

Harvey Lavan

Real first and middle names of pianist Van Cliburn.

"Hasn't scratched yet"

Advertising slogan of Bon Ami cleanser.

Hastings, Captain Arthur

Frequent sidekick of Hercule Poirot in the novels and short stories of Dame Agatha Christie.

Hasty Pudding Man/Woman of the Year

Awarded by Hasty Pudding Theatricals, the theater company of Harvard University.
1951 Gertrude Lawrence
1952 Barbara Bel Geddes
1953 Mamie Eisenhower
1954 Shirley Booth
1955 Debbie Reynolds
1956 Peggy Ann Garner
1957 Carroll Baker
1958 Katharine Hepburn
1959 Joanne Woodward
1960 Carol Lawrence
1961 Jane Fonda
1962 Piper Laurie

1963 Shirley MacLaine
1964 Rosalind Russell
1965 Lee Remick
1966 Ethel Merman
1967 Lauren Bacall and Bob Hope
1968 Angela Lansbury and Paul Newman
1969 Carol Burnett and Bill Cosby
1970 Dionne Warwick and Robert Redford
1971 Carol Channing and James Stewart
1972 Ruby Keeler and Dustin Hoffman
1973 Liza Minnelli and Jack Lemmon
1974 Faye Dunaway and Peter Falk
1975 Valerie Harper and Warren Beatty
1976 Bette Midler and Robert Blake
1977 Elizabeth Taylor and Johnny Carson
1978 Beverly Sills and Richard Dreyfuss
1979 Candice Bergen and Robert De Niro
1980 Meryl Streep and Alan Alda
1981 Mary Tyler Moore and John Travolta
1982 Ella Fitzgerald and James Cagney
1983 Julie Andrews and Steven Spielberg
1984 Joan Rivers and Sean Connery
1985 Cher and Bill Murray
1986 Sally Field and Sylvester Stallone
1987 Bernadette Peters and Mikhail Baryshnikov
1988 Lucille Ball and Steve Martin
1989 Kathleen Turner and Robin Williams
1990 Glenn Close and Kevin Costner
1991 Diane Keaton and Clint Eastwood
1992 Jodie Foster and Michael Douglas
1993 Whoopi Goldberg and Chevy Chase
1994 Meg Ryan and Tom Cruise
1995 Michelle Pfeiffer and Tom Hanks
1996 Susan Sarandon and Harrison Ford
1997 Julia Roberts and Mel Gibson
1998 Sigourney Weaver and Kevin Kline
1999 Goldie Hawn and Samuel L. Jackson
2000 Jamie Lee Curtis and Billy Crystal
2001 Drew Barrymore and Anthony Hopkins

The Hatchet, The Home Defender, and *The Smasher's Mail*

Newsletters published by anti-alcohol activist Carry Nation, noted for her hatchet-wielding destruction of saloons.

Hathi

Elephant in Rudyard Kipling's *The Jungle Book.*

Hauser, Thomas

See The Execution of Charles Horman

"Have it your way"

Advertising slogan of Burger King.

Haven, Maine

Setting of the Stephen King novel *The Tommyknockers*.

"haven of peace"

What the name of Tanzanian city Dar es Salaam means in Arabic.

"Have you figured it out? Do you know who the murderer is?"

Questions posed to viewers by the title character at the end of each episode of the various incarnations of the TV series *The Adventures of Ellery Queen*.

Having Fun with Elvis on Stage

See **0**

Havoc Inc.

Production company of actor Tim Robbins.

Hawaiian Village Hotel

Setting of the TV series *Hawaiian Eye*.

"Hawk"

Nickname of deputy Tommy Hill (Michael Horse) in the TV series *Twin Peaks*.

"The Hawk"

Nickname of golf great Ben Hogan, for the way he studied golf courses.

"Hawkeye"

Nickname of Dr. Benjamin Franklin Pierce (Alan Alda) in the TV sitcom *M*A*S*H*.

See also **United States residents' nicknames**

Hawkins

Real last name of actor Christian Slater.

Hawkins, Jamesetta

Real name of soul singer Etta James.

Haworth Parsonage

West Yorkshire, England, home of the Brontë sisters.

Haycox, Ernest

See **"Stage to Lordsburg"**

Hayden-Guest, Lady

English title held by actress Jamie Lee Curtis, whose husband, actor Christopher Guest, was made a Lord by Queen Elizabeth II.

Haynsworth Jr., Clement F. and Carswell, G. Harrold

Supreme Court nominees of Richard Nixon who were rejected by the Senate in 1969 and 1970, respectively.

Hayslope

English village that is the setting of the George Eliot novel *Adam Bede*.

Haze

See **Dolores**

Hazel

Pet Labrador retriever of actor Jim Carrey.

HDL

See **high-density lipoprotein**

Headlong

Novel by Emlyn Williams that was the basis for the film *King Ralph*.

Head of the Family

Original title of the TV sitcom *The Dick Van Dyke Show*.

Hearsay

Pet dog of Mitch McDeere (Tom Cruise) in the film *The Firm*.

The Heartbeats

Original name of rock group Herman's Hermits.

Heart of Darkness

Novel by Joseph Conrad that was the basis for the film *Apocalypse Now*.

Heart of Gold

Spaceship stolen by Zaphod Beeblebrox in the Douglas Adams novel *The Hitchhiker's Guide to the Galaxy*.

The Heart of the Ocean

Sapphire and diamond necklace given to Rose DeWitt Bukater (Kate Winslet) by her fiancé Cal Hockley (Billy Zane) in the film *Titanic* (1997).

Hearts Insurgent

Original title of the Thomas Hardy novel *Jude the Obscure*.

Hearts of Gold

See ***Bill Bassler's Revenge*** and ***Hearts of Gold***

Heath, Joyce
Role for which Bette Davis won a Best Actress Academy Award in the 1935 film *Dangerous*.

"Heavens to Murgatroyd!"
All-purpose exclamation of cartoon lion Snagglepuss.

"He best serves himself who serves others"
Motto of the Screen Actors Guild.

Hector
Pet dog of Natty Bumppo in the stories of James Fenimore Cooper.

Hector Hugh
First and middle names of writer H. H. Munro, aka Saki.

Hedwig
Pet owl of the title character in the Harry Potter series of books by J. K. Rowling.

Hee, T.
Real person (full name Thornton Hee) whose name is seen in the credits of many Disney cartoons, as director or animator.

Hefty Hideaway, the House of Fashion for the Ample Woman
Employer of model Tracy Turnblad (Ricki Lake) in the film *Hairspray*.

Heggen, Thomas
Author of the play *Mister Roberts*, upon which the film of the same name was based.

Heidi
Pet Weimaraner of President Dwight D. Eisenhower.

Heidi Doody
Sister of the title character in the children's TV series *Howdy Doody*.

Heimberger, Edward
Real name of actor Eddie Albert.

Heineman, Arthur
See **Milestone Mo-Tel**

Hekawi Indians
Friendly tribe in the TV sitcom *F Troop*. Sergeant Morgan O'Rourke (Forrest Tucker) negotiates a secret treaty with the Hekawis to sell their souvenirs to tourists.

Held, Anna
Role for which Luise Rainer won a Best Actress Academy Award in the 1936 film *The Great Ziegfeld*.

Helen
Real first name of children's book author/illustrator (Helen) Beatrix Potter.

Helfgott, David
Role for which Geoffrey Rush won a Best Actor Academy Award in the 1996 film *Shine*.

"Helga pictures"
See **Testorf, Helga**

Helix
Sci-film starring Anna Scott (Julia Roberts) in the film *Notting Hill*.

"He'll Never See Daylight Again"
Debut episode of the TV series *Baretta*, which aired on January 17, 1975.

"Hello, ball!"
Ed Norton's (Art Carney's) definitive way of "addressing" a golf ball, in the TV sitcom *The Honeymooners*.

***Hello, Dolly!* title-role portrayers**
The portrayers of the title role during the original (1964–70) run of this Broadway play (in order):
  Carol Channing
  Ginger Rogers
  Martha Raye
  Betty Grable
  Bibi Osterwald
  Pearl Bailey
  Phyllis Diller
  Ethel Merman
Hello, Dolly! was the longest-running Broadway musical at the time of its 1970 closing.

"Hello, Goodbye, Hello"
Debut episode of the TV series *Marcus Welby, M.D.*, which aired on September 23, 1969.

Hello Gorgeous
Beauty-salon employer of Angela de Marco (Michelle Pfeiffer) in the film *Married to the Mob*.

"Hello, gorgeous!"
Memorable line spoken by Fanny Brice (Barbra Streisand) to herself (looking into a mirror), in the film *Funny Girl*.

"Hell Ride"

Debut episode of the TV series *Charlie's Angels*, which aired on September 22, 1976.

"Helps build strong bodies 12 ways"

Advertising slogan of Wonder Bread.

Helvetia

Ancient Roman name for Switzerland.

He-Man Woman Haters Club

Group formed by Spanky and Alfalfa that does not associate with girls, in the *Our Gang* series of film shorts, aka *The Little Rascals*.

Hemery High

School attended by the title character (Kristy Swanson) in the film *Buffy the Vampire Slayer*.

Hempel's

Minneapolis department store where Rhoda Morgenstern (Valerie Harper) is employed as a window dresser, in the TV sitcom *The Mary Tyler Moore Show*.

Henchard, Michael

Title character of the Thomas Hardy novel *The Mayor of Casterbridge*.

Henderson

Setting of the TV soap opera *Search for Tomorrow*.

Henderson, Mr.

Pet cat of Sally Rogers (Rose Marie) in the TV sitcom *The Dick Van Dyke Show*.

Henery Hawk

Chicken-hawk foil of cartoon rooster Foghorn Leghorn.

Henkel, Alfred

Real name of Norman Maine (Fredric March) in the film *A Star Is Born* (1937).

Henleyville, Alabama

Setting of the film *Norma Rae*.

Henrietta

Middle name of actress Joan Collins.

Henrietta

Ship that takes Passepartout (Cantinflas) and Phileas Fogg (David Niven) from New York to England in the film *Around the World in 80 Days*.

Henry

Real first name of actor Warren Beatty. His real last name is Beaty.

First name of computer-industry magnate H. Ross Perot.

Real first name of sportswriter (Henry) Grantland Rice.

Middle name of comedian Bill (William) Cosby.

See also **Indiana**

Henry VIII, King

Role for which Charles Laughton won a Best Actor Academy Award in the 1933 film *The Private Life of Henry VIII*.

Henry VIII, six wives of

Catherine of Aragon: daughter of Ferdinand and Isabella, mother of Mary I (married 1509, marriage annulled 1533)
Anne Boleyn: mother of Elizabeth I (married 1533, beheaded 1536)
Jane Seymour: mother of Edward VI (married 1536, died 1537)
Anne of Cleaves (married 1540, marriage annulled 1540)
Catherine Howard (married 1540, beheaded 1542)
Catherine Parr (married 1543, survived him)

Henry Charles Albert David

Full name of Prince Harry of Great Britain, younger son of Prince Charles and Princess Diana.

Henry Louis

First and middle names of writer H. L. Mencken.

Henry the Horse

Waltz-dancing beast in the Beatles tune "Being for the Benefit of Mr. Kite."

Hensley, Virginia Patterson

Real name of country singer Patsy Cline.

Heorot

Mead hall built by order of Hrothgar in the epic poem *Beowulf*.

Hepburn/Grant films

The films in which Cary Grant and Katharine Hepburn appear together:
Sylvia Scarlett (1936)
Bringing Up Baby (1938)

Holiday (1938)
The Philadelphia Story (1940)

Hepburn-Ruston, Edda Kathleen van Heemstra
Real name of actress Audrey Hepburn.

Hepburn/Tracy films
The films in which Katharine Hepburn and Spencer Tracy appear together:
Keeper of the Flame (1942)
Woman of the Year (1942)
Without Love (1945)
The Sea of Grass (1947)
State of the Union (1948)
Adam's Rib (1949)
Pat and Mike (1952)
Desk Set (1957)
Guess Who's Coming to Dinner (1967)

heptathlon events
As held for women at each Summer Olympics, over two days.

FIRST DAY
100-meter hurdles
High jump
Shot put
200-meter run

SECOND DAY
Long jump
Javelin throw
800-meter run

Her
See **Him and Her**

Herbert
Real first name of comedian Jackie Gleason.

Real first name of Canadian communications theorist (Herbert) Marshall McLuhan.

See also **Marx Brothers' real names**

Herbert George
First and middle names of novelist H. G. Wells.

Herbie and the Heartbeats
Rock group in the film *American Graffiti*, portrayed by Flash Cadillac and the Continental Kids.

Herbie films
See ***The Love Bug* (Herbie) films**

herbs/spices sources
Most popular herbs and spices come from plants of the same name (such as allspice, dill and ginger).

The varieties listed below are the notable exceptions:
    mace: nutmeg
    oregano: marjoram
    paprika: chili pepper
    saffron: crocus
    vanilla: orchid

Hercules
Self-selected middle name of pop singer Elton John.

Hercules Vacuum Cleaner Company
Employer of sales manager John Morrison and salesman Benny Miller (Abbott and Costello) in the film *Little Giant*.

"Here men from the planet Earth first set foot upon the moon. July 1969 a.d. We came in peace for all mankind."
Inscription on the plaque left on the moon by *Apollo 11* astronauts Neil Armstrong and Buzz Aldrin.

"Here rests in honored glory an American soldier known but to God"
Inscription on the Tomb of the Unknowns at Arlington National Cemetery. The Tomb was opened to the public on April 9, 1932, and has been guarded 24 hours a day by the U.S. Army since 1936.

Heritage Club
Posh Philadelphia establishment whose members include the Duke brothers (Don Ameche and Ralph Bellamy) and Louis Winthorpe III (Dan Aykroyd), in the film *Trading Places*.

Heritage U.S.A.
Theme park in Fort Mill, South Carolina, formerly run by Jim and Tammy Faye Bakker.

Herman Goelitz Company
See **Jelly Belly Jelly Beans flavors**

The Hermitage
Home of President Andrew Jackson near Nashville, Tennessee.

Hernando, Lolita Rodriguez
Full name of Lola in the musical *Damn Yankees*.

"Her Nibs"
Nickname of singer Georgia Gibbs.

Herschel
Middle name of astronaut John Glenn.

Heth, Joice

First successful exhibition of P. T. Barnum in 1835. Heth claimed to be 161 years old and to have been George Washington's nurse. When Heth died in 1836, the postmortem revealed that she could not have been much more than half her claimed age.

Heuer

See *60 Minutes* **stopwatch brands**

Heuristically Programmed Algorithmic Computer 9000

Full name of HAL, onboard computer in the film *2001: A Space Odyssey.*

"He used to be a bigshot"

Memorable line spoken by Panama Smith (Gladys George), referring to gunned-down racketeer Eddie Bartlett (James Cagney), in the film *The Roaring Twenties.*

"He who enlightens"

What the name of Vietnamese leader Ho Chi Minh means in Vietnamese.

Hewson, Paul

Real name of U2 lead singer Bono.

hexachlorophene

Antibacterial agent used in many toothpastes and soaps.

Hezekiah Kipchoge

See **"The Flying Policeman"**

Hezikiah

Middle name of cowboy actor Tom Mix.

Hibbard, Susan

Inventor of the feather duster, patented in 1876.

Hibernia

Ancient Roman name for Ireland.

Hickingbotham, Frank D.

Founder of the TCBY retail chain, originally named "This Can't Be Yogurt!!" The first store opened in 1981 in Little Rock, Arkansas. TCBY now stands for "The Country's Best Yogurt."

Hickory Hill

Home of the Robert Kennedy family in McLean, Virginia.

Hickory, Indiana

Setting of the Disney film *Follow Me, Boys!*

Town whose high school basketball team, coached by Norman Dale (Gene Hackman), reaches the state championships in the film *Hoosiers.*

"Hi Diddle Riddle"

Debut episode of the TV series *Batman,* which aired on January 12, 1966.

Higgins

Last name of the title character of the radio sitcom *Baby Snooks,* portrayed by Fanny Brice.

Higgins, Henry

Role for which Rex Harrison won a Best Actor Academy Award in the 1964 film *My Fair Lady.*

Higgins' Universal Alphabet

Phonetics book written by Henry Higgins in the Lerner and Loewe musical *My Fair Lady.*

High Adventure

1955 book by Sir Edmund Hillary, which recounts his conquest of Mount Everest in May 1953.

Highbury

English setting of the Jane Austen novel *Emma.*

high-density lipoprotein

What "HDL," medical term for "good" cholesterol, stands for.

High Hat

Horse ridden by Stuffy (Harpo Marx) in the Marx Brothers film *A Day at the Races.*

Highland Dale

Horse that portrayed the title character in the children's TV series *Fury.*

Highlanders

Original nickname of the New York Yankees at their American League inception in 1903. (In 1901 and 1902, the team was based in Baltimore and was known as the Orioles.)

Highland Farms

Doylestown, Pennsylvania, estate of lyricist Oscar Hammerstein II, which is a bed-and-breakfast inn today.

Highland Lake Community Church

Headquarters near Washington, D.C.'s Dulles Airport commandeered by terrorists, in the film *Die Hard 2*.

The High Numbers

Original name of rock group The Who.

High Sky

Horse of Civil War Confederate general J. E. B. Stuart.

Highwater, Vermont

Setting of the Alfred Hitchcock film *The Trouble with Harry*.

The Highwaymen

Country-music quartet formed in 1985, consisting of superstars Johnny Cash, Waylon Jennings, Kris Kristofferson, and Willie Nelson.

"Higitus Figitus"

Words that start the spells of Merlin (voiced by Karl Swenson) in the Disney animated film *The Sword in the Stone*.

Hilaire Germain

Real first and second names of French artist (Hilaire Germain) Edgar Degas.

Hilary

Real first name of Norm Peterson (George Wendt) in the TV sitcom *Cheers*.

Hilda

Middle name of former English prime minister Lady Margaret Thatcher.

Hildebrand

Real first name of Hildy Johnson (Pat O'Brien) in the film *The Front Page* (1931).

"The Hillbilly Shakespeare"

Nickname of country singer Hank Williams.

Hilldale

Neighborhood of Hill Valley, California, that is home to the Marty McFly (Michael J. Fox) of 2015 in the film *Back to the Future Part II*.

Setting of the TV sitcom *Dennis the Menace*.

Setting of the TV sitcom *The Donna Reed Show*.

Hill, Dixon

Fictional 1940s San Francisco private detective that is a favorite of Captain Jean-Luc Picard (Patrick Stewart) in the TV series *Star Trek: The Next Generation*.

Hillegass, Clifton

Nebraska book salesman who originated CliffNotes study guides in 1958.

Hill, Julia Butterfly

Environmental activist who lived atop a 1,000-year-old redwood tree in Stafford, California, from December 10, 1997, until December 18, 1999, succeeding in her attempt to prevent a lumber company from cutting it down.

Hillman College

Alma mater of Cliff Huxtable (Bill Cosby) in the TV sitcom *The Cosby Show*.

Hill, Mildred and Patty

Louisville schoolteachers who wrote "Happy Birthday to You" in 1893, today one of the most frequently performed songs in the English language.

"hill of spring"

What "Tel Aviv" means in Hebrew.

Hill, Professor Harold

Title character of the musical *The Music Man*, portrayed by Robert Preston in the film version.

Hill, Samuel E; Knights, William J.; and Nicholson, John H.

Founders of the Gideons International, at Janesville, Wisconsin, on July 1, 1899. The organization distributes Christian bibles to hotels, prisons, hospitals and to the military.

Hillsboro, Tennessee

Setting of the Broadway and film versions of *Inherit the Wind*, a dramatization of the Scopes trial of 1925. The town is based on the real-life trial venue of Dayton, Tennessee.

Hill Valley, California

Setting of the *Back to the Future* films. The city's newspaper is the *Hill Valley Telegraph*, and its high school's football team is the Bulldogs.

Him and Her

Pet beagles of President Lyndon Johnson.

Hinckley Jr., John

Attempted assassin of Ronald Reagan on March 30, 1981. He was acquitted by reason of insanity in 1982.

Hindu trinity

In Hinduism, the three Gods of the universe:
    Brahma (the creator)

Vishnu (the preserver)
Shiva (the destroyer)

Hinkley, Roy

Real name of the Professor (Russell Johnson) in the TV sitcom *Gilligan's Island*.

hinny

Offspring of a male horse and a female donkey. (A mule is the offspring of a male donkey and a female horse.)

Hippie

Hippopotamus puppet in the children's TV series *The Soupy Sales Show*.

Hiram

Real first name of country singer Hank Williams.

Real first name of the title character in the comic strip *Hi and Lois*.

Hiram Ulysses

Real first and middle names of President Ulysses S. Grant.

Hires, Charles

Philadelphia druggist who invented root beer, circa 1873.

Hirshfield, Leo

Austrian immigrant who created the Tootsie Roll in 1896. It was named for his five-year-old daughter Clara, whose nickname was "Tootsie."

Hispaniola

Schooner that travels to the title locale in the Robert Louis Stevenson novel *Treasure Island*.

Hi-Spot

Teen restaurant hangout in the film *Footloose*.

"History as a Novel, the Novel as History"

Subtitle of the Norman Mailer novel *The Armies of the Night*.

Hitchcock/Grant films

The films directed by Alfred Hitchcock in which Cary Grant appears:
Suspicion (1941)
Notorious (1946)
To Catch a Thief (1955)
North by Northwest (1959)

Hitchcock/Stewart films

The films directed by Alfred Hitchcock in which James Stewart appears:

Rope (1948)
Rear Window (1954)
The Man Who Knew Too Much (1956)
Vertigo (1958)

The Hitchhiker's Guide to the Galaxy series

Series of five novels by Douglas Adams:
The Hitchhiker's Guide to the Galaxy (1979)
The Restaurant at the End of the Universe (1980)
Life, the Universe and Everything (1982)
So Long, and Thanks for All the Fish (1984)
Mostly Harmless (1992)

"Hi There!" and "Dear John"

Phrases painted on the hydrogen bombs aboard Major T. J. "King" Kong's (Slim Pickens') bomber in the film *Dr. Strangelove*.

"The Hitless Wonders"

Nickname of the 1906 Chicago White Sox, who, despite a meager .230 team batting average, won the American League pennant and World Series that year.

"Hit sign, win suit"

Memorable phrase on a billboard painted on the center-field wall of Ebbets Field (home of the Brooklyn Dodgers) circa 1950, which advertised Abe Stark's clothing store. Stark later served as borough president of Brooklyn.

"Hitsville, U.S.A."

Nickname of Motown Records.

H.M.S. *Ark Royal*

Flagship of the English fleet, under Lord High Admiral Charles Howard, that defeated the Spanish Armada in 1588.

H.M.S. *Beagle*

See **FitzRoy, Robert**

H.M.S. *Bellerophon*

English ship on which Napoleon formally surrendered after the Battle of Waterloo, on July 15, 1815.

H.M.S. *Director*

English ship captained by William Bligh in 1797, eight years after the 1789 mutiny aboard his H.M.S. *Bounty* in the South Pacific. The crew of the *Director* also mutinied, in England on the River Thames, and Bligh was put ashore.

H.M.S. *Fury*

English destroyer on which the former King Edward VIII left England for France after abdicating the throne, on December 12, 1936.

H.M.S. *Indomitable*
English warship commanded by Captain Vere in the Herman Melville novel *Billy Budd*.

H.M.S. *Lydia*
Frigate commanded by the title character of the C. S. Forester novel *Captain Horatio Hornblower*.

H.M.S. *Sutherland*
Battleship commanded by the title character of the C. S. Forester novel *Captain Horatio Hornblower*.

H.M.S. *Victory*
Flagship of English admiral Horatio Nelson.

Hoagland Howard
Real first and middle names of songwriter Hoagy Carmichael.

Hoban, James
Irish-born architect who designed the White House, completed in 1801.

Hobart
Middle name of Fred Mertz (William Frawley) in the TV sitcom *I Love Lucy*.

The Hoboken Four
Singing group (Frank Sinatra, Patty Prince, Jimmy Petro, and Fred Tamburro) that won the September 8, 1935, radio broadcast of *Major Bowes' Amateur Hour*.

Hobson
Role for which Sir John Gielgud won a Best Supporting Actor Academy Award in the 1981 film *Arthur*.

hockey mascots (NHL)
Mighty Ducks of Anaheim: Wild Wing (duck)
Atlanta Thrashers: Thrash (brown thrasher, Georgia state bird)
Buffalo Sabres: Sabretooth (tiger)
Calgary Flames: Harvey the Hound
Carolina Hurricanes: Stormy (pig)
Colorado Avalanche: Howler (Abominable Snowman)
Columbus Blue Jackets: Stinger (wasp)
Florida Panthers: Stanley C. Panther
New Jersey Devils: N. J. Devil
Ottawa Senators: Spartacat
Pittsburgh Penguins: Iceburgh (penguin)
Quebec Nordiques: Badaboum
San Jose Sharks: S. J. Sharkie
Tampa Bay Lightning: ThunderBug and LadyBug

Toronto Maple Leafs: Carlton (polar bear)
Washington Capitals: Slapshot (eagle)

Hodge
Pet cat of lexicographer Samuel Johnson.

Höek
Last name of Ren (voiced by John Kricfalusi and Billy West) in the animated TV series *The Ren & Stimpy Show*.

Hoffman, Judge Julius
See "The Chicago Seven"

Hog's Breath Inn
Carmel, California, restaurant owned by actor Clint Eastwood, noted for its Dirty Harry Burger.

Hogthrob, Captain Link
Commander (voiced by Jim Henson) of the starship *Swinetrek* in the "Pigs in Space" segment of the children's TV series *The Muppet Show*.

Hogwarts required reading
From the Harry Potter series of books by J. K. Rowling.

FIRST YEAR
The Standard Book of Spells, Grade 1 by Miranda Goshawk
A History of Magic by Bathilda Bagshot
Magical Theory by Adalbert Waffling
A Beginner's Guide to Transfiguration by Emeric Switch
One Thousand Magical Herbs and Fungi by Phyllida Spore
Magical Drafts and Potions by Arsenius Jigger
Fantastic Beasts and Where to Find Them by Newt Scamander
The Dark Forces: A Guide to Self-Protection by Quentin Trimble

SECOND YEAR
The Standard Book of Spells, Grade 2 by Miranda Goshawk
Break with a Banshee by Gilderoy Lockhart
Gadding with Ghouls by Gilderoy Lockhart
Holidays with Hags by Gilderoy Lockhart
Travels with Trolls by Gilderoy Lockhart
Voyages with Vampires by Gilderoy Lockhart
Wanderings with Werewolves by Gilderoy Lockhart
Year with the Yeti by Gilderoy Lockhart

"The Ho-Ho Song"
See "Strange Things Are Happening"

"Hokey smokes!"

Favorite exclamation of Rocket J. Squirrel (voiced by June Foray) in the children's animated TV series *Rocky and His Friends*.

"Holiday for Strings"

Theme song of the TV comedy/variety series *The Red Skelton Show*, composed by David Rose.

Holland

Last name of the title character in the Wendy Wasserstein play *The Heidi Chronicles*.

Hollen, Andrea

Rhodes scholar who was the first woman to graduate from the U.S. Military Academy at West Point, New York, in 1980.

Hollenbeck, Webb Parmalee

Real name of actor Clifton Webb.

Holley, Charles Hardin

Real name of singer Buddy Holly.

Hollies original members

Allan Clarke, Eric Haydock, Tony Hicks, Graham Nash, and Don Rathbone.

Hollingshead Jr., Richard

Inventor of the drive-in theater. His first drive-in opened on June 3, 1933, in Camden, New Jersey.

Hollisport, Louisiana

Setting of the film *Hush . . . Hush, Sweet Charlotte*.

Holloman, Alva "Bobo"

Only pitcher to hurl a no-hitter in his first major-league start, when his St. Louis Browns handcuffed the Philadelphia Athletics on May 6, 1953. He never pitched another complete game in his brief career in the majors.

Hollow Valley, New York

Setting of the film *The Money Pit*.

Holly

Role for which Dianne Wiest won a Best Supporting Actress Academy Award in the 1986 film *Hannah and Her Sisters*.

Hollywood Foreign Press Association

Group that bestows the annual Golden Globe Awards.

HOLLYWOODLAND

The original Hollywood sign, when first built in 1923 to promote a nearby housing development of the same name. When the sign was remodeled in the 1940s, it became the familiar "HOLLYWOOD."

"The Hollywood Ten"

Group of nine screenwriters and one director who were blacklisted for refusing to testify before the House Un-American Activities Committee in 1947.
Alvah Bessie
Herbert Biberman
Lester Cole
Edward Dmytryk (director)
Ring Lardner Jr.
John Howard Lawson
Albert Maltz
Samuel Ornitz
Adrian Scott
Dalton Trumbo

Holstrom, Katrin

Role for which Loretta Young won a Best Actress Academy Award in the 1947 film *The Farmer's Daughter*.

Holtom, Gerald

English commercial artist who created the peace symbol (resembling an inverted Y in a circle), for the Campaign for Nuclear Disarmament in 1958.

Holt, Patricia Louise

Real name of singer Patti LaBelle.

"Holy cow!"

Favorite exclamation of baseball broadcasters Harry Caray and Phil Rizzuto.

The Holy Spirit Association for the Unification of World Christianity

Full name of the Unification Church, founded on May 1, 1954, by Korean evangelist Sun Myung Moon.

HOLYWOOD

How the famous Hollywood sign was temporarily altered in honor of the visit of Pope John Paul II to southern California in September 1987.

The Home Defender

*See **The Hatchet, The Home Defender,** and **The Smasher's Mail***

Homer

Pet spider of Wednesday Addams (Lisa Loring) in the TV sitcom *The Addams Family*.

Homer Louis

Real first and middle names of country-music saxophonist Boots Randolph.

Home Sweet Home

See **Midge**

"Home to Emily"

Theme song of the TV sitcom *The Bob Newhart Show.*

Homeward Bound: The Incredible Journey animals

The main characters of this Disney film:
    Shadow (golden retriever): voiced by Don
      Ameche
    Chance (bulldog): voiced by Michael J. Fox
    Sassy (Himalayan cat): voiced by Sally Field

"Homo minister et interpres naturae"

Motto of Lehigh University, which is Latin for "Man, the servant and interpreter of nature."

Honalee

Home of the title character in the Peter, Paul, and Mary tune "Puff the Magic Dragon."

"Hondo"

Nickname of basketball Hall of Famer John Havlicek.

Nickname of baseball player Frank Howard.

Honey

Role for which Sandy Dennis won a Best Supporting Actress Academy Award in the 1966 film *Who's Afraid of Virginia Woolf?*

Honey Fitz

See **Barbara Anne**

"Honey Fitz"

Nickname of John F. Fitzgerald (1863–1950), two-term mayor of Boston and maternal grandfather of President John F. Kennedy.

"Honey, I forgot to duck"

Memorable line spoken by heavyweight boxer Jack Dempsey to his wife Estelle, after he was knocked out by Gene Tunney at Philadelphia's Sesquicentennial Stadium on September 23, 1926.

Honeywell and Todd

Investment-firm employer of Vern Albright (Charles Farrell) in the TV sitcom *My Little Margie.*

Hong Kong Cavaliers

Rock band of the title character (Peter Weller) in the film *The Adventures of Buckaroo Banzai Across the Eighth Dimension.*

Hong Kong Gardens

Chinese restaurant frequented by the Kramdens and Nortons in the TV sitcom *The Honeymooners.*

Hong Kong Noodle Company

See **Jung, George**

honorary citizens of the United States

    Sir Winston Churchill (1963)
    Raoul Wallenberg (1981)
    William and Hannah Penn (1984)
    Mother Teresa (1996)
The Marquis de Lafayette was made an honorary citizen of several states, but not of the U.S. as a whole.

"Honor Before Honesty"

Motto of the larcenous Fleming and St. Clair families in the TV series *The Rogues.*

Honoria

Sister of Major Charles Emerson Winchester (David Ogden Stiers) in the TV sitcom *M*A*S*H.* (Her name is pronounced "on-OR-ee-uh.")

Hookham, Margaret

Real name of ballet star Dame Margot Fonteyn.

"Hooray for Captain Spaulding"

Instrumental theme of the TV game show *You Bet Your Life,* hosted by Groucho Marx. It was originally composed by Bert Kalmar and Harry Ruby for the Marx Brothers film *Animal Crackers.*

"Hoosier"

See **United States residents' nicknames**

"The Hoosier Poet"

Nickname of poet James Whitcomb Riley.

Hooters

See **Dewey High**

Hooterville

Setting of the TV sitcom *Petticoat Junction.*

Hooterville World Guardian

Newspaper published by Sam Drucker (Frank Cady) in the TV sitcoms *Petticoat Junction* and *Green Acres.*

Hootin' Holler Mountain
Setting of the comic strip *Barney Google and Snuffy Smith*.

Hope
Family cat in the comic strip *The Gumps*.

See also **Faith, Hope, and Charity**

"The Hope"
What *"Hatikvah,"* the title of the national anthem of Israel, means in Hebrew.

Hopewell
Ship commanded by explorer Henry Hudson on his first two voyages (1607, 1608) in search of a northern sea route to Asia.

Hopkins, Samuel
Holder of the first U.S. patent, issued in 1790 for his method of producing potash and pearlash.

Horatio
First name of the title character in TV commercials for Cap'n Crunch cereal.

Horn
See **Fischbacher and Horn**

Hornberger, Dr. H. Richard
Surgeon who wrote the novel *M*A*S*H* under the pen name Richard Hooker.

Hornblow
Last name of nonspeaking clown Clarabell in the children's TV series *Howdy Doody*. He was portrayed by Bob Keeshan, Bob Nicholson and Lou Anderson. On the final show, Clarabell broke his silence with a tearful "Goodbye, kids" to the Peanut Gallery.

Horn, Bob
Original host of the TV series *American Bandstand* from 1952 to 1956, when he was succeeded by Dick Clark.

Hornby, Leslie
Real name of 1960s fashion model Twiggy.

The Horndogs
High-school band of the title character in the TV sitcom *The Drew Carey Show*.

"The Hornet's Nest"
Nickname of Charlotte, North Carolina. It was coined by English general Cornwallis during his troops' 1780 occupation of the city, because of the residents' vigorous opposition to the English.

Horowitz
Real last name of actress Winona Ryder.

horripilation
Technical term for goose bumps.

Horror Writers Association
See **Bram Stoker Awards**

"The Horse"
Nickname of Heisman Trophy winner and college football Hall of Famer Alan Ameche.

Horseman, Pass By
Novel by McMurtry that was the basis for the film *Hud*.

Hortense, Madame
Role for which Lila Kedrova won a Best Supporting Actress Academy Award in the 1964 film *Zorba the Greek*.

Horwich, Dr. Frances
Full name of Miss Frances, host of the children's TV series *Ding Dong School*. She had been the head of the education department of a Chicago college.

Horwitz
See **Three Stooges' real names**

Hosehead
Pet dog of Bob and Doug McKenzie (Rick Moranis and Dave Thomas) in the film *Strange Brew*.

"Host of the Highways"
Advertising slogan of Howard Johnson's restaurants and motor lodges.

Hot Dog
Pet dog of Jughead Jones in Archie comics.

Pet cat of the title character in the comic strip *Dennis the Menace*.

hot dog tree
Invention of the title character (Paul Reubens) in the film *Big Top Pee-wee*. When eaten, the hot dogs from the tree turn senior citizens into children.

Hotel Belvedere
San Francisco establishment where Joel Cairo (Peter Lorre) is staying, in the film *The Maltese Falcon*.

Hotel Carlton

San Francisco home of Paladin (Richard Boone) in the TV Western series *Have Gun Will Travel*.

Hotel Costa Plente

Ritzy home of the Three Stooges in the film short "Healthy, Wealthy and Dumb."

Hotel Marquis

Fort de France, Martinique home of Harry Morgan (Humphrey Bogart) and Marie Browning (Lauren Bacall), in the film *To Have and Have Not*.

Hotel Park Plaza

New York City setting of the first scene of the Mercury Theatre radio adaptation of H. G. Wells' *The War of the Worlds*, where Ramón Raquello and his Orchestra are performing "La Cumparsita" in the Meridian Room before being interrupted.

Hotel Sedgewick

Where the title characters perform their first job in the film *Ghostbusters*.

Hotel Vista del Rio

Setting of the Abbott and Costello film *Rio Rita*.

Hot Foot Teddy

Original name of Smokey Bear.

Hot Metal

Stage name of the dancing group of unemployed steelworkers in the film *The Full Monty*.

"Hot pups!"

Favorite exclamation of the title character in the comic strip *Harold Teen*.

"Hot Snow"

U.S. debut episode of the TV series *The Avengers*, which aired on January 7, 1961.

Hot Springs, New Mexico

Town that renamed itself Truth or Consequences in 1950, in response to a contest on the TV game show of the same name.

"Hot Toddy"

Nickname of actress Thelma Todd.

"Hot Voodoo"

Tune performed by Helen Faraday (Marlene Dietrich) while wearing a gorilla suit, in the film *Blonde Venus*.

"Houdini of the Hardwood"

Nickname of basketball Hall of Famer Bob Cousy.

Houghton

Middle name of actress Katharine Hepburn.

Hour of Charm All-Girl Orchestra

Band led by Phil Spitalny.

"The Housekeeper"

See **"The Dead Man" and "The Housekeeper"**

The House of Dr. Edwardes

Novel by Francis Beeding that was the basis for the Alfred Hitchcock film *Spellbound*.

The House of Earth

Trilogy of novels by Pearl S. Buck:
   The Good Earth (1931)
   Sons (1932)
   A House Divided (1935)

House of Toast

Restaurant chain featured in the comedy routines of Bob and Ray.

House, Tom

Atlanta Braves relief pitcher who caught Hank Aaron's record-breaking 715th career home run in the Braves bullpen, in Atlanta on April 8, 1974.

Hover Board

Mattel antigravity skateboard of the future used by Marty McFly (Michael J. Fox) in the film *Back to the Future Part II*.

Hovick, Rose Louise

Real name of stripper Gypsy Rose Lee.

Howard

Real first name of singer Andy Williams.

Role for which Walter Huston won a Best Supporting Actor in the 1948 film *The Treasure of the Sierra Madre*.

First name of Mr. Adams (Howard Duff) in the TV sitcom *Mr. Adams and Eve*.

Teddy bear of Jonah Baldwin (Ross Malinger) in the film *Sleepless in Seattle*.

Howard, Charles

See **H.M.S. *Ark Royal***

Howard J. Lamade Stadium

Williamsport, Pennsylvania, site of the Little League World Series since 1959.

Howard Johnson's original flavors

The 28 ice cream flavors Johnson developed circa 1925 for his first drugstore soda fountain in Wollaston, Massachusetts:

Banana	Lemon Stick
Black Raspberry	Macaroon
Burgundy Cherry	Maple Walnut
Butter Pecan	Mocha Chip
Buttercrunch	Orange Pineapple
Butterscotch	Peach
Caramel Fudge	Peanut Brittle
Chocolate	Pecan Brittle
Chocolate Chip	Peppermint Stick
Cocoanut	Pineapple
Coffee	Pistachio
Frozen Pudding	Strawberry
Fruit Salad	Strawberry Ripple
Fudge Ripple	Vanilla

Howard Phillips

First and middle names of writer H. P. Lovecraft.

"How are you? You have been in Afghanistan, I perceive."

First words spoken by Sherlock Holmes to Dr. John Watson, in the Sir Arthur Conan Doyle novel *A Study in Scarlet*.

HOW DADDY IS DOING

Riddle posed to Harris K. Telemacher (Steve Martin) by a magic freeway sign in the film *L.A. Story*. The answer to the riddle is "Sing Doo Wah Diddy," which is an anagram of "How Daddy is doing."

"How do you spell relief?"

Advertising slogan of Rolaids.

How I Got Here

Autobiography written by gangster Vincent Antonelli (Steve Martin) in the film *My Blue Heaven*.

How I Learned to Stop Worrying and Love the Bomb

Alternate title of the film *Dr. Strangelove*.

Howitzer

Yearbook of the U.S. Military Academy at West Point.

"How kind of you to let me come"

Diction-practice phrase for Eliza Doolittle in the Lerner and Loewe musical *My Fair Lady*.

The Howling films

The Howling (1981)
Howling II: Your Sister Is a Werewolf (1985)
Howling III (1987)
Howling IV: The Original Nightmare (1988)
Howling V: The Rebirth (1989)
Howling VI: The Freaks (1991)
The Howling: New Moon Rising (1995)

"How sweet it is!"

Catchphrase used by comedian Jackie Gleason to acknowledge applause.

"How to Stay Young"

List popularized by "ageless" Hall of Fame baseball pitcher Satchel Paige, and inscribed in its entirety on his tombstone.

1. Avoid fried meats which angry up the blood.
2. If your stomach disputes you, lie down and pacify it with cool thoughts.
3. Keep the juices flowing by jangling around gently as you move.
4. Go very light in the vices, such as carrying on in society. The social ramble ain't restful.
5. Avoid running at all times.
6. Don't look back. Something might be gaining on you.

Hoyt-Clagwell

Make of the tractor sold by Mr. Haney (Pat Buttram) to Oliver Wendell Douglas (Eddie Albert) in the TV sitcom *Green Acres*.

Hsing-Hsing

See **Ling-Ling and Hsing-Hsing**

Hua Lo Prison

See **"The Hanoi Hilton"**

Hubbard, Cal

Only person to be elected to both the Baseball Hall of Fame (as an umpire) and pro football Hall of Fame (as a player).

Hubbell, Carl, consecutive strikeouts by

In the 1934 All-Star Game, this New York Giant future Hall of Fame pitcher struck out these five future Hall of Fame American Leaguers consecutively: Babe Ruth, Lou Gehrig, Jimmie Foxx, Al Simmons, and Joe Cronin.

Hubble Length

Longest unit of distance in astronomy, named for astronomer Edwin Hubble. It is equivalent to the radius of the observable universe, about 10 billion light-years.

Hubert

First name of French fashion designer Givenchy.

Hubert, Conrad

Inventor of the flashlight in 1898, which was the basis for his founding of the company that would eventually become Eveready.

Hubert Prior

Real first and middle names of singer Rudy Vallee.

Hudson/Day films

See **Day/Hudson films**

Hudson High

School attended by the title character in the radio series *Jack Armstrong, the All-American Boy.*

Hudson, Jeffrey

Pen name used by Michael Crichton for the mystery *A Case of Need*, which won a 1969 Edgar Award for Best Novel.

Hudson, Saul

Real name of "Slash," lead guitarist of rock group Guns N' Roses.

Huerta, Baldemar

Real name of singer Freddy Fender.

Huey, Dewey, and Louie

Nephews of Disney cartoon character Donald Duck.

See also **Dumbella; Junior Woodchucks**

Huff-Daland Dusters

Original name of Delta Air Lines.

Hufflepuff

See **Gryffindor House**

Huffman

Real last name of actress Barbara Eden.

Hugh

Real first name of the title character (George Coulouris, Santos Ortega, Ned Wever) in the radio series *Bulldog Drummond.*

Hughes, Sarah T.

Texas District Court judge who administered the presidential oath of office to Lyndon Johnson in Dallas, aboard *Air Force One*, on November 22, 1963.

Hugo Award

Presented annually since 1953 by the World Science Fiction Convention for outstanding writing. It is named for sci-fi author Hugo Gernsback.

Human Beings

TV show that Isaac Davis (Woody Allen) writes for, in the film *Manhattan.*

"The Human Highlight Film"

Nickname of NBA star Dominique Wilkins.

Human Instinct

See **Inner Urges, Human Instinct, Animal Nature, and Serrated Edge**

"The Human Locomotive"

Nickname of former boxer Harry Knowles (Frank McRae) in the film **batteries not included.*

"The Human Vacuum Cleaner"

Nickname of baseball Hall of Fame third baseman Brooks Robinson, for his fielding ability.

"Humor in a Jugular Vein"

Slogan once used by *Mad* magazine.

Humphrey the Hound Dog

See **Charlemagne the Lion and Humphrey the Hound Dog**

Hundred Acre Wood

Home of Winnie-the-Pooh and friends in the stories of A. A. Milne.

Hungerdunger, Hungerdunger, Hungerdunger, Hungerdunger and McCormick

Law firm retained by Captain Jeffrey T. Spaulding (Groucho Marx) in the Marx Brothers film *Animal Crackers.*

Hungry Brain

Beatnik joint visited by Kreton (Jerry Lewis) and Ellen Spelding (Joan Blackman) in the film *Visit to a Small Planet.*

The Hungry Heifer

Favorite restaurant of Norm Peterson (George Wendt) in the TV sitcom *Cheers.*

Hunt

Last name of the title character (Gene Tierney) in the film *Laura.*

Hunter's *Civic Biology*

Textbook from which Bertram Cates teaches the theory of evolution to his sophomore science class, in the Lawrence and Lee play *Inherit the Wind*.

Hunt, Walter

Inventor of the safety pin in 1849.

Hupfeld, Herman

Composer of the tune "As Time Goes By," in the 1941 film *Casablanca*. The tune was first heard in the 1931 Broadway play *Everybody's Welcome*.

Hurricane IV

Speedboat owned by Bob Merrick (Rock Hudson) in the film *Magnificent Obsession*.

Hurricanes

Bowling team of Ralph Kramden (Jackie Gleason) and Ed Norton (Art Carney) in the TV sitcom *The Honeymooners*.

"Hurry Up"

Nickname of college football Hall of Fame coach Fielding Harris Yost.

Hurwitz, Lieutenant

Hospitalized soldier in the film *Airplane!* who thinks he's Ethel Merman, and gives an energetic rendition of "Everything's Coming Up Roses" before being sedated. The character is portrayed by Ethel Merman.

Hush Hush Magazine

Tabloid publication edited by Sid Hudgens (Danny DeVito) in the film *L.A. Confidential*.

Hush Puppy

See **Charley Horse, Lamb Chop, and Hush Puppy**

Hutchins, Robert

Real name of Wheezer, child actor in the *Our Gang* series of film shorts, aka *The Little Rascals*.

Hutton, Nedenia

Real name of actress Dina Merrill. Merrill's mother was cereal heiress Marjorie Merriweather Post; her father was stockbroker E. F. Hutton.

Hyatt, Alice

Role for which Ellen Burstyn won a Best Actress Academy Award in the 1974 film *Alice Doesn't Live Here Anymore*.

Hyborian Age

Time period that is the setting of the Conan book series by Robert E. Howard.

Hyde, Jacqueline

See **Romanoff, Noodles and Hyde, Jacqueline**

Hyde, Sally

Role for which Jane Fonda won a Best Actress Academy Award in the 1978 film *Coming Home*.

hydrargyrum

Latin name for mercury (literally "silver water"), from which its chemical symbol Hg is derived.

Hymie

CONTROL robot colleague of Maxwell Smart (Don Adams) in the TV sitcom *Get Smart*, portrayed by Dick Gautier.

Hynkel, Adenoid

Charlie Chaplin's role in the film *The Great Dictator*, which is a spoof of Adolf Hitler.

hyperopia

Medical term for farsightedness.

Hypertext Markup Language

What the letters in "HTML," the Internet programming language, stand for.

"I admire your courage, Miss . . . ?"

First line spoken on screen by James Bond (Sean Connery), to Sylvia Trench (Eunice Gayson) while playing chemin de fer at the English gambling club Les Ambassadeurs in the film *Dr. No*.

Iago

Parrot of Jafar in the Disney animated film *Aladdin*, voiced by Gilbert Gottfried.

I Am Legend

Novel by Richard Matheson that was the basis for the film *The Omega Man*.

"I bid you peace"

Sign-off line of Jeff Smith in the TV series *The Frugal Gourmet*.

IBM RS/6000

See **Deep Blue**

ibuprofen

Chemical name of the pain reliever found in Advil and Nuprin.

"I can't believe I ate the whole thing!"

Memorable complaint in a 1970s TV commercial for Alka-Seltzer.

I Can't Wait Until Tomorrow . . . 'Cause I Get Better Looking Every Day

1969 autobiography of pro football Hall of Fame quarterback Joe Namath.

Icarus

Spaceship that brings George Taylor (Charlton Heston) and his crewmates to the title location in the film *Planet of the Apes*.

ICE

See **Intelligence Coordination and Exploitation**

"The Ice Maiden"

Nickname of tennis great Chris Evert, for her unflappable style of play.

"The Ice Man"

Nickname of pop singer Jerry Butler.

ice-nine

Ice with a melting point of 114.4 degrees Fahrenheit that freezes any liquid it touches, in the Kurt Vonnegut novel *Cat's Cradle*.

"Ich dien"

Motto of the Prince of Wales, which is German for "I serve."

Icon Productions

Production company of actor Mel Gibson.

Idaho Springs, Colorado

Hometown of David Chappellet (Robert Redford) in the film *Downhill Racer*.

"Ida Red"

Original working title of the Chuck Berry tune "Maybellene."

"I Darrin, Take This Witch Samantha"

Debut episode of the TV sitcom *Bewitched*, which aired on September 17, 1964.

Idaville

Hometown of the title character in the Encyclopedia Brown series of children's books by Donald J. Sobol.

Idioglossia

Play by Mark Handley that was the basis for the film *Nell*.

Idlewild

Former name of John F. Kennedy International Airport in New York City.

"I'd like to kiss you, but I just washed my hair."

Memorable line spoken by Madge (Bette Davis) in the film *The Cabin in the Cotton*.

"I don't get no respect!"

Catchphrase of comedian Rodney Dangerfield.

"I don't mess around, boy!"
Catchphrase of Ricky Nelson in the TV sitcom *The Adventures of Ozzie and Harriet.*

"I dood it!"
Favorite expression of the Red Skelton character The Mean Widdle Kid.

Ieoh Ming
First and middle names of Chinese-born architect I. M. Pei.

"I forbid"
What the word "veto" means in Latin.

"If you build it, he will come"
Phrase spoken repeatedly to Ray Kinsella (Kevin Costner) by a mysterious voice, in the film *Field of Dreams.*

"If you don't look good, we don't look good."
Advertising slogan of Vidal Sassoon hair products.

"If You Knew Susie"
Theme song of comedian Eddie Cantor.

Igloo
Pet fox terrier of Admiral Richard E. Byrd. Igloo traveled with Byrd on his Arctic and Antarctic expeditions.

Ignatz Mouse
Nemesis of the title character in the comic strip *Krazy Kat.*

"I had a lover's quarrel with the world"
Epitaph of poet Robert Frost.

"I hate meeces to pieces!"
All-purpose exclamation of cartoon feline Mr. Jinks, nemesis of mice Pixie and Dixie in the children's TV series *The Huckleberry Hound Show.*

"I have sworn upon the altar of God eternal hostility against every form of tyranny over the mind of man"
Inscription around the rotunda of the Jefferson Memorial in Washington, D.C.

"I kid you not"
Catchphrase of Jack Paar, former host of *The Tonight Show.*

"I know nothing!"
Catchphrase of Sergeant Hans Schultz (John Banner) in the TV sitcom *Hogan's Heroes.*

Ilderim, Sheik
Role for which Hugh Griffith won a Best Supporting Actor Academy Award in the 1959 film *Ben-Hur.*

Île de France
Former name of the Indian Ocean island nation of Mauritius.

"I'll Be There for You"
Theme song of the TV sitcom *Friends,* performed by the Rembrandts.

"I'll Cherish You"
Original title of the Shirelles tune "Baby It's You."

"I'll do all the thinnin' around here, and don't you forget it!"
Catchphrase of cartoon sheriff Quick Draw McGraw.

Illium, New York
Hometown of Billy Pilgrim in the Kurt Vonnegut novel *Slaughterhouse-Five.*

"I'll Love You in My Dreams"
Theme song of bandleader Horace Heidt.

Illusion Entertainment
Production company of director Oliver Stone.

Il Muto
See ***Hannibal,* *Il Muto,* and *Don Juan Triumphant***

"I Love Trash"
Anthem of Oscar the Grouch in the children's TV series *Sesame Street.*

"I-M-4-U"
Instrumental theme of *The Tonight Show* while Jack Paar was the host.

"I'm a bad boy!"
Catchphrase of comedian Lou Costello.

ImageMovers
Production company of director Robert Zemeckis.

Imagine Entertainment
Production company of director Ron Howard.

"I'm Always Here"
See **"Save Me"**

"I'm a man who likes talking to a man who likes to talk"
Memorable line spoken by Casper Gutman (Sydney Greenstreet) to Sam Spade (Humphrey Bogart) in the film *The Maltese Falcon.*

"I'm Chevy Chase, and you're not"
Opening line of Chevy Chase as host of the "Weekend Update" segment of the TV series *Saturday Night Live.*

"I'm Getting Sentimental Over You"
Theme song of bandleader Tommy Dorsey.

Imgwee Gwee Valley
African home of the title character (voiced by Bill Scott) in the children's animated TV series *George of the Jungle.*

"The Immaculate Reception"
Nickname of the miraculous shoestring catch made by Pittsburgh Steeler Franco Harris of a Terry Bradshaw pass, against the Oakland Raiders in an AFC playoff game on December 23, 1972. Harris scored on the play with five seconds left in the game, giving Pittsburgh a 13–7 win.

"I'm mad as hell, and I'm not going to take this anymore!"
Memorable line spoken by TV news anchorman Howard Beale (Peter Finch) in the film *Network.*

"the immortal four of Italy"
Term coined by Henry Wadsworth Longfellow in his poem "The Wayside Inn" for the poets Dante, Petrarch, Ariosto, and Tasso.

"I'm not bad. I'm just drawn that way."
Memorable line spoken by toon Jessica Rabbit (voiced by Kathleen Turner) to Eddie Valiant (Bob Hoskins) in the film *Who Framed Roger Rabbit.*

Imperial Potentate
Title given to the presiding officer of the Shriners, aka Ancient Arabic Order of Nobles of the Mystic Shrine.

"The Impossible Mission"
Debut episode of the TV series *Adam 12*, which aired on September 21, 1968.

The Imposter
Alternate title of the Molière play *Tartuffe.*

". . . I must say"
Sentence-ending catchphrase of nerdy Ed Grimley (Martin Short) in the TV series *Saturday Night Live.*

"I'm worth it"
Advertising slogan of L'Oréal hair coloring.

"I'm Your School Bell"
Theme song of the children's TV series *Ding Dong School.*

In & Out Academy Award nominees
Cameron Drake (Matt Dillon) wins a Best Actor Academy Award in this film, for his role in the film *To Serve and Protect.* The other nominees, all real-life performers, were nominated for these mythical films:
    Paul Newman for *Coot*
    Clint Eastwood for *Codger*
    Michael Douglas for *Primary Urges*
    Steven Seagal for *Snowball in Hell*

"In brightest day, in blackest night, no evil shall escape my sight. Let those who worship evil's might beware my power . . . Green Lantern's Light."
Oath spoken by comics superhero the Green Lantern (aka Hal Jordan) when recharging his power ring by touching it to his lantern.

"In canis corpore transmuto"
Inscription on the ring that transforms Wilby Daniels (Tommy Kirk) into the title character in the Disney film *The Shaggy Dog.*

Incident at West Egg
Original working title of the F. Scott Fitzgerald novel *The Great Gatsby.*

"Incident of the Tumbleweed Wagon"
Debut episode of the TV Western series *Rawhide*, which aired on January 9, 1959.

Incitatus
Horse of Roman emperor Caligula.

"In Deep"
Debut episode of the TV series *Baywatch*, which aired on September 22, 1989.

"In Deo speramus"
Motto of Brown University, which is Latin for "In God we trust."

Independence
Presidential plane of Harry S Truman.

Independent News Service
Chicago employer of investigative reporter Carl Kolchak (Darren McGavin) in the TV series *Kolchak: The Night Stalker.*

"Indescribably delicious"
Advertising slogan of Peter Paul candy bars, including Mounds and Almond Joy.

India
See **Ernie and India**

Indiana
Childhood pet dog of Henry Jones Jr. (Harrison Ford), from which he got his nickname, as revealed in the Steven Spielberg film *Indiana Jones and the Last Crusade.*

Indiana Jones trilogy
Group of films directed by Steven Spielberg, starring Harrison Ford.
     Raiders of the Lost Ark (1981)
     Indiana Jones and the Temple of Doom (1984)
     Indiana Jones and the Last Crusade (1989)

The Indian War Drum
Trophy awarded to the winning team in the annual football game between the University of Kansas and the University of Missouri.

infanticipating
Term for "pregnant" coined by columnist Walter Winchell.

Inflato
Money-changing machine that a con man sells to Laurel and Hardy (playing themselves) in the film *A-Haunting We Will Go.*

"The Informer"
Debut episode of the TV sitcom *Hogan's Heroes,* which aired on September 17, 1965.

Ingram, E. W. "Billy"
Founder of the White Castle fast-food chain. The first White Castle opened in 1921 in Wichita, Kansas.

"In Hartford, Hereford, and Hampshire, hurricanes hardly ever happen"
Diction-practice phrase for Eliza Doolittle in the Lerner and Loewe musical *My Fair Lady.*

"In His Father's House"
Debut episode of the TV series *Falcon Crest,* which aired on December 4, 1981.

"In hoc signo vinces"
Motto of Roman emperor Constantine the Great, which is Latin for "By this sign you will conquer."

Initech
Company whose offices are the setting of the film *Office Space.*

"Inka Dinka Doo"
Theme song of comedian Jimmy Durante.

Inky, Blinky, Pinky, and Clyde
The four menacing ghosts in the video game Pac-Man.

The Inland Sea
Alternate title of the James Fenimore Cooper novel *The Pathfinder.*

"In lumine Tuo videbimus lumen"
Motto of Columbia University, which is Latin for "In Thy light, shall we see light."

In My Own Fashion
1987 autobiography of fashion designer Oleg Cassini.

Inner Urges, Human Instinct, Animal Nature, and *Serrated Edge*
Films starring Elise Eliot (Goldie Hawn) in the film *The First Wives Club.*

Innisfail
Literary name for Ireland.

Innisfree
Irish village that is the setting of the film *The Quiet Man.*

"Inquiring minds want to know"
Advertising slogan of *The National Enquirer.*

"In Search of America"
Subtitle of the John Steinbeck travel memoir *Travels with Charley.*

Inside View

Supermarket tabloid that offers Johnny Smith a job as a psychic in the Stephen King novel *The Dead Zone*.

"In space no one can hear you scream"

Slogan used to promote the sci-fi film *Alien*.

Inspiration Point

Local lovers' lane in the TV sitcom *Happy Days*.

Institute of Muscular Harmony

Establishment run by Clara Pelf (Lotte Lenya) in the film *Semi-Tough*.

Intelligence Coordination and Exploitation

Full name of ICE, employer of the title character (Dean Martin) in the Matt Helm series of films.

"In tempore"

Motto of the University of Houston, which is Latin for "In time."

Inter-Agency Defense Command

Employer of Diana Prince (Lynda Carter) in the TV series *The New Adventures of Wonder Woman*.

Inter-City Beauty Contest

Original name of the Miss America Pageant when it began in 1921.

Intercollegiate Conference of Faculty Representatives

See **11**

International Bank for Reconstruction and Development

Official name of the World Bank, an agency of the United Nations.

International Clearance Bank

See **$8,000,000,001.67**

International Lawn Tennis Challenge Trophy

Official name of the Davis Cup, donated by Dwight F. Davis in 1900.

International Olympic Committee presidents

Listed below with their terms of office and native countries:

1894–96: Dimítrios Vikélas (Greece)
1896–1925: Pierre, baron de Coubertin (France)
1925–42: Henri, comte de Baillet-Latour (Belgium)
1946–52: J. Sigfrid Edström (Sweden)
1952–72: Avery Brundage (United States)
1972–80: Michael Morris, Lord Killanin (Ireland)
1980–present: Juan António Samaranch (Spain)

Internet country suffixes

ad	Andorra	cn	China
ae	United Arab Emirates	co	Colombia
		cr	Costa Rica
af	Afghanistan	cu	Cuba
ag	Antigua and Barbuda	cv	Cape Verde
		cx	Christmas Island
ai	Anguilla	cy	Cyprus
al	Albania	cz	Czech Republic
am	Armenia	de	Germany
an	Netherlands Antilles	dj	Djibouti
		dk	Denmark
ao	Angola	dm	Dominica
aq	Antarctica	do	Dominican Republic
ar	Argentina		
as	American Samoa	dz	Algeria
		ec	Ecuador
at	Austria	ee	Estonia
au	Australia	eg	Egypt
aw	Aruba	eh	Western Sahara
az	Azerbaijan	er	Eritrea
ba	Bosnia and Herzegovina	es	Spain
		et	Ethiopia
bb	Barbados	fi	Finland
bd	Bangladesh	fj	Fiji
be	Belgium	fk	Falkland Islands
bf	Burkina Faso	fm	Micronesia
bg	Bulgaria	fo	Faroe Islands
bh	Bahrain	fr	France
bi	Burundi	ga	Gabon
bj	Benin	gb	Great Britain
bm	Bermuda	gd	Grenada
bn	Brunei	ge	Georgia
bo	Bolivia	gf	French Guiana
br	Brazil	gh	Ghana
bs	Bahamas	gi	Gibraltar
bt	Bhutan	gl	Greenland
bv	Bouvet Island	gm	Gambia
bw	Botswana	gn	Guinea
by	Belarus	gp	Guadeloupe
bz	Belize	gq	Equatorial Guinea
ca	Canada		
cc	Cocos Islands	gr	Greece
cf	Central African Republic	gs	South Georgia and South Sandwich Islands
cg	Congo		
ch	Switzerland		
ci	Ivory Coast	gt	Guatemala
ck	Cook Islands	gu	Guam
cl	Chile	gw	Guinea-Bissau
cm	Cameroon	gy	Guyana

hk	Hong Kong	mp	Northern	sj	Svalbard and	tw	Taiwan
hm	Heard and		Mariana Islands		Jan Mayen	tz	Tanzania
	McDonald	mq	Martinique		Islands	ua	Ukraine
	Islands	mr	Mauritania	sk	Slovakia	ug	Uganda
hn	Honduras	ms	Montserrat	sl	Sierra Leone	uk	United Kingdom
hr	Croatia	mt	Malta	sm	San Marino	um	U.S. Minor
ht	Haiti	mu	Mauritius	sn	Senegal		Outlying Islands
hu	Hungary	mv	Maldives	so	Somalia	us	United States
id	Indonesia	mw	Malawi	sr	Suriname	uy	Uruguay
ie	Ireland	mx	Mexico	st	São Tomé and	uz	Uzbekistan
il	Israel	my	Malaysia		Principe	va	Vatican City
in	India	mz	Mozambique	sv	El Salvador	vc	Saint Vincent
io	British Indian	na	Namibia	sy	Syria		and the
	Ocean Territory	nc	New Caledonia	sz	Swaziland		Grenadines
iq	Iraq	ne	Niger	tc	Turks and Caicos	ve	Venezuela
ir	Iran	nf	Norfolk Island		Islands	vg	British Virgin
is	Iceland	ng	Nigeria	td	Chad		Islands
it	Italy	ni	Nicaragua	tf	French Southern	vi	U.S. Virgin
jm	Jamaica	nl	Netherlands		Territories		Islands
jo	Jordan	no	Norway	tg	Togo	vn	Vietnam
jp	Japan	np	Nepal	th	Thailand	vu	Vanuatu
ke	Kenya	nr	Nauru	tj	Tajikistan	wf	Wallis and
kg	Kyrgyzstan	nu	Niue	tk	Tokelau		Futuna Islands
kh	Cambodia	nz	New Zealand	tm	Turkmenistan	ws	Samoa
ki	Kiribati	om	Oman	tn	Tunisia	ye	Yemen
km	Comoros	pa	Panama	to	Tonga	yt	Mayotte
kn	Saint Kitts and	pe	Peru	tp	East Timor	yu	Yugoslavia
	Nevis	pf	French Polynesia	tr	Turkey	za	South Africa
kp	North Korea	pg	Papua New	tt	Trinidad and	zm	Zambia
kr	South Korea		Guinea		Tobago	zr	Zaire
kw	Kuwait	ph	Philippines	tv	Tuvalu	zw	Zimbabwe
ky	Cayman Islands	pk	Pakistan				
kz	Kazakhstan	pl	Poland				
la	Laos	pm	St. Pierre and				
lb	Lebanon		Miquelon				
lc	Saint Lucia	pn	Pitcairn Island				
li	Liechtenstein	pr	Puerto Rico				
lk	Sri Lanka	pt	Portugal				
lr	Liberia	pw	Palau				
ls	Lesotho	py	Paraguay				
lt	Lithuania	qa	Qatar				
lu	Luxembourg	re	Réunion				
lv	Latvia	ro	Romania				
ly	Libya	ru	Russian				
ma	Morocco		Federation				
mc	Monaco	rw	Rwanda				
md	Moldova	sa	Saudi Arabia				
mg	Madagascar	sb	Solomon				
mh	Marshall		Islands				
	Islands	sc	Seychelles				
mk	Macedonia	sd	Sudan				
ml	Mali	se	Sweden				
mm	Myanmar	sg	Singapore				
mn	Mongolia	sh	St. Helena				
mo	Macau	si	Slovenia				

interrobang

Punctuation mark created by Martin K. Speckter in 1962, which is a question mark superimposed on an exclamation point: ‽

Interstate highways, major cities served by

Also listed below are the total mileage and the states covered by each of the major (one- and two-digit) Interstates. Odd-numbered routes run north-south, even-numbered routes run east-west:

I-4 (132 MILES; FLORIDA)

Daytona Beach, Florida
Orlando, Florida
Tampa, Florida

I-5 (1,382 MILES; WASHINGTON, OREGON, CALIFORNIA)

Seattle, Washington
Portland, Oregon
Sacramento, California
Los Angeles, California
San Diego, California

I-8 (348 MILES; ARIZONA, CALIFORNIA)

Yuma, Arizona
San Diego, California

I-10 (2,460 MILES; FLORIDA, ALABAMA, MISSISSIPPI, LOUISIANA, TEXAS, NEW MEXICO, ARIZONA, CALIFORNIA)

Jacksonville, Florida
Pensacola, Florida
Mobile, Alabama
Biloxi, Mississippi
New Orleans, Louisiana
Baton Rouge, Louisiana
Houston, Texas
El Paso, Texas
Las Cruces, New Mexico
Tucson, Arizona
Phoenix, Arizona
Los Angeles, California

I-12 (86 MILES; LOUISIANA)

Baton Rouge, Louisiana

I-15 (1,437 MILES; MONTANA, IDAHO, UTAH, ARIZONA, NEVADA, CALIFORNIA)

Butte, Montana
Great Falls, Montana
Pocatello, Idaho
Ogden, Utah
Salt Lake City, Utah
Provo, Utah
Las Vegas, Nevada
San Diego, California

I-16 (165 MILES; GEORGIA)

Savannah, Georgia
Macon, Georgia

I-17 (145 MILES; ARIZONA)

Flagstaff, Arizona
Phoenix, Arizona

I-19 (63 MILES; ARIZONA)

Tucson, Arizona
Nogales, Arizona

I-20 (1,538 MILES; SOUTH CAROLINA, GEORGIA, ALABAMA, MISSISSIPPI, LOUISIANA, TEXAS)

Columbia, South Carolina
Augusta, Georgia
Atlanta, Georgia
Birmingham, Alabama
Tuscaloosa, Alabama
Vicksburg, Mississippi
Shreveport, Louisiana
Dallas/Ft. Worth, Texas

I-24 (317 MILES; ILLINOIS, KENTUCKY, TENNESSEE, GEORGIA)

Paducah, Kentucky
Nashville, Tennessee
Chattanooga, Tennessee

I-25 (1,062 MILES; WYOMING, COLORADO, NEW MEXICO)

Casper, Wyoming
Cheyenne, Wyoming
Denver, Colorado
Colorado Springs, Colorado
Albuquerque, New Mexico

I-26 (261 MILES; NORTH CAROLINA, SOUTH CAROLINA)

Asheville, North Carolina
Spartanburg, South Carolina
Charleston, South Carolina

I-27 (124 MILES; TEXAS)

Amarillo, Texas

I-29 (752 MILES; NORTH DAKOTA, SOUTH DAKOTA, IOWA, MISSOURI)

Fargo, North Dakota
Sioux Falls, South Dakota
Sioux City, Iowa
Kansas City, Missouri

I-30 (367 MILES; ARKANSAS, TEXAS)

Little Rock, Arkansas
Dallas/Ft. Worth, Texas
Texarkana, Texas

I-35 (1,568 MILES; MINNESOTA, IOWA, MISSOURI, KANSAS, OKLAHOMA, TEXAS)

Duluth, Minnesota
St. Paul, Minnesota
Des Moines, Iowa
Kansas City, Missouri
Wichita, Kansas
Oklahoma City, Oklahoma
Dallas, Texas
Waco, Texas
Austin, Texas
San Antonio, Texas
Laredo, Texas

I-37 (143 MILES; TEXAS)

Corpus Christi, Texas

I-39 (64 MILES; ILLINOIS)

Rockford, Illinois

I-40 (2,554 MILES; NORTH CAROLINA, TENNESSEE, ARKANSAS, OKLAHOMA, TEXAS, NEW MEXICO, ARIZONA, CALIFORNIA)

Raleigh, North Carolina
Winston-Salem, North Carolina

Asheville, North Carolina
Knoxville, Tennessee
Nashville, Tennessee
Memphis, Tennessee
Little Rock, Arkansas
Oklahoma City, Oklahoma
Amarillo, Texas
Albuquerque, New Mexico
Flagstaff, Arizona
Barstow, California

I-43 (183 miles; Wisconsin)

Green Bay, Wisconsin
Milwaukee, Wisconsin

I-44 (634 miles; Missouri, Oklahoma, Texas)

St. Louis, Missouri
Springfield, Missouri
Tulsa, Oklahoma
Oklahoma City, Oklahoma
Wichita Falls, Texas

I-45 (285 miles; Texas)

Dallas, Texas
Houston, Texas
Galveston, Texas

I-49 (207 miles; Louisiana)

Shreveport, Louisiana

I-55 (944 miles; Illinois, Missouri, Arkansas, Tennessee, Mississippi, Louisiana)

Chicago, Illinois
Springfield, Illinois
St. Louis, Missouri
Memphis, Tennessee

I-57 (381 miles; Illinois, Missouri)

Chicago, Illinois
Champaign-Urbana, Illinois

I-59 (444 miles; Georgia, Alabama, Mississippi, Louisiana)

Birmingham, Alabama
Tuscaloosa, Alabama
Meridian, Mississippi

I-64 (944 miles; Virginia, West Virginia, Kentucky, Indiana, Illinois, Missouri)

Norfolk, Virginia
Richmond, Virginia
Charleston, West Virginia
Lexington, Kentucky
Louisville, Kentucky
Evansville, Indiana
St. Louis, Missouri

I-65 (888 miles; Indiana, Kentucky, Tennessee, Alabama)

Gary, Indiana

Indianapolis, Indiana
Louisville, Kentucky
Nashville, Tennessee
Birmingham, Alabama
Montgomery, Alabama
Mobile, Alabama

I-66 (76 miles; District of Columbia, Virginia)

Washington, D.C.
Arlington, Virginia

I-68 (112 miles; Maryland, West Virginia)

Morgantown, West Virginia

I-69 (356 miles; Michigan, Indiana)

Flint, Michigan
Battle Creek, Michigan
Fort Wayne, Indiana
Indianapolis, Indiana

I-70 (2,175 miles; Maryland, Pennsylvania, West Virginia, Ohio, Indiana, Illinois, Missouri, Kansas, Colorado, Utah)

Baltimore, Maryland
Wheeling, West Virginia
Columbus, Ohio
Indianapolis, Indiana
Terre Haute, Indiana
St. Louis, Missouri
Kansas City, Missouri
Abilene, Kansas
Denver, Colorado

I-71 (346 miles; Ohio, Kentucky)

Cleveland, Ohio
Columbus, Ohio
Cincinnati, Ohio
Louisville, Kentucky

I-72 (79 miles; Illinois)

Springfield, Illinois

I-74 (417 miles; Ohio, Indiana, Illinois, Iowa)

Cincinnati, Ohio
Indianapolis, Indiana
Champaign-Urbana, Illinois
Peoria, Illinois
Davenport, Iowa

I-75 (1,787 miles; Michigan, Ohio, Kentucky, Tennessee, Georgia, Florida)

Sault Ste. Marie, Michigan
Detroit, Michigan
Toledo, Ohio
Dayton, Ohio
Cincinnati, Ohio
Lexington, Kentucky
Knoxville, Tennessee
Chattanooga, Tennessee

Atlanta, Georgia
Macon, Georgia
Tampa, Florida
Sarasota, Florida
Miami, Florida

I-76 (432 MILES; NEW JERSEY, PENNSYLVANIA, OHIO)

Camden, New Jersey
Philadelphia, Pennsylvania
Pittsburgh, Pennsylvania
Akron, Ohio

I-76 (187 MILES; NEBRASKA, COLORADO)

Denver, Colorado

I-77 (598 MILES; OHIO, WEST VIRGINIA, VIRGINIA, NORTH CAROLINA, SOUTH CAROLINA)

Cleveland, Ohio
Akron, Ohio
Charleston, West Virginia
Charlotte, North Carolina
Columbia, South Carolina

I-78 (145 MILES; NEW YORK, NEW JERSEY, PENNSYLVANIA)

New York, New York
Newark, New Jersey
Easton, Pennsylvania
Allentown, Pennsylvania

I-79 (344 MILES; PENNSYLVANIA, WEST VIRGINIA)

Erie, Pennsylvania
Pittsburgh, Pennsylvania
Charleston, West Virginia

I-80 (2,907 MILES; NEW JERSEY, PENNSYLVANIA, OHIO, INDIANA, ILLINOIS, IOWA, NEBRASKA, WYOMING, UTAH, NEVADA, CALIFORNIA)

Teaneck, New Jersey
Cleveland, Ohio
Toledo, Ohio
South Bend, Indiana
Gary, Indiana
Chicago, Illinois
Moline, Illinois
Davenport, Iowa
Des Moines, Iowa
Omaha, Nebraska
Cheyenne, Wyoming
Salt Lake City, Utah
Reno, Nevada
Oakland, California
San Francisco, California

I-81 (855 MILES; NEW YORK, PENNSYLVANIA, MARYLAND, WEST VIRGINIA, VIRGINIA, TENNESSEE)

Syracuse, New York
Scranton, Pennsylvania

Hagerstown, Maryland
Roanoke, Virginia

I-82 (143 MILES; WASHINGTON, OREGON)

Yakima, Washington

I-83 (84 MILES; PENNSYLVANIA, MARYLAND)

Harrisburg, Pennsylvania
Baltimore, Maryland

I-84 (228 MILES; MASSACHUSETTS, CONNECTICUT, NEW YORK, PENNSYLVANIA)

Hartford, Connecticut
Scranton, Pennsylvania

I-84 (768 MILES; UTAH, IDAHO, OREGON)

Ogden, Utah
Portland, Oregon
Boise, Idaho

I-85 (667 MILES; VIRGINIA, NORTH CAROLINA, SOUTH CAROLINA, GEORGIA, ALABAMA)

Charlotte, North Carolina
Spartanburg, South Carolina
Atlanta, Georgia
Montgomery, Alabama

I-86 (63 MILES; IDAHO)

Pocatello, Idaho

I-87 (333 MILES; NEW YORK)

Albany, New York
New York, New York

I-88 (118 MILES; NEW YORK)

Schenectady, New York

I-88 (141 MILES; ILLINOIS)

Chicago, Illinois

I-89 (191 MILES; VERMONT, NEW HAMPSHIRE)

Burlington, Vermont
Concord, New Hampshire

I-90 (3,085 MILES; MASSACHUSETTS, NEW YORK, PENNSYLVANIA, OHIO, INDIANA, ILLINOIS, WISCONSIN, MINNESOTA, SOUTH DAKOTA, WYOMING, MONTANA, IDAHO, WASHINGTON)

Boston, Massachusetts
Springfield, Massachusetts
Syracuse, New York
Rochester, New York
Buffalo, New York
Erie, Pennsylvania
Cleveland, Ohio
Toledo, Ohio
South Bend, Indiana
Gary, Indiana
Chicago, Illinois
Madison, Wisconsin

Rochester, Minnesota
Sioux Falls, South Dakota
Billings, Montana
Spokane, Washington

I-91 (291 MILES; VERMONT, MASSACHUSETTS, CONNECTICUT)

Brattleboro, Vermont
Springfield, Massachusetts
Hartford, Connecticut
New Haven, Connecticut

I-93 (189 MILES; VERMONT, NEW HAMPSHIRE, MASSACHUSETTS)

Concord, New Hampshire
Boston, Massachusetts

I-94 (1,607 MILES; MICHIGAN, INDIANA, ILLINOIS, WISCONSIN, MINNESOTA, NORTH DAKOTA, MONTANA)

Detroit, Michigan
Gary, Indiana
Chicago, Illinois
Milwaukee, Wisconsin
Minneapolis/St. Paul, Minnesota
Fargo, North Dakota
Billings, Montana

I-95 (1,894 MILES; MAINE, NEW HAMPSHIRE, MASSACHUSETTS, RHODE ISLAND, CONNECTICUT, NEW YORK, NEW JERSEY, PENNSYLVANIA, DELAWARE, MARYLAND, DISTRICT OF COLUMBIA, VIRGINIA, NORTH CAROLINA, SOUTH CAROLINA, GEORGIA, FLORIDA)

Portland, Maine
Portsmouth, New Hampshire
Boston, Massachusetts
Providence, Rhode Island
New Haven, Connecticut
New York, New York
Newark, New Jersey
Philadelphia, Pennsylvania
Wilmington, Delaware
Baltimore, Maryland
Washington, D.C.
Richmond, Virginia
Fayetteville, North Carolina
Savannah, Georgia
Jacksonville, Florida
Daytona Beach, Florida
West Palm Beach, Florida
Fort Lauderdale, Florida
Miami, Florida

I-96 (193 MILES; MICHIGAN)

Detroit, Michigan
Grand Rapids, Michigan

I-97 (18 MILES; MARYLAND)

Baltimore, Maryland
Annapolis, Maryland

There are also three Interstate highways in Hawaii.

See also **3**

Intertect

Detective-agency employer of the title character (Mike Connors) in the TV series *Mannix*.

"In the Beginning"

Debut episode of the TV sitcom *Newhart*, which aired on October 25, 1982.

"In the Best of Families"

Debut episode of the TV series *The Commish*, which aired on September 28, 1991.

"In the Year 2525" years

This Zager and Evans tune mentions these future years (in order):
2525
3535
4545
5555
6565
7510
8510
9595

"In this temple, as in the hearts of the people for whom he saved the Union, the memory of Abraham Lincoln is enshrined forever"

Inscription on the wall above the marble statue of Abraham Lincoln at the Lincoln Memorial in Washington, D.C.

"The Intimidator"

Nickname of auto racer Dale Earnhardt Sr.

Inverness, Earl of

Title held by Prince Andrew of Great Britain.

INXS original members

Garry Beers, Andy Farriss, Jon Farriss, Tim Farriss, Michael Hutchence, and Kirk Pengilly.

"In your heart you know he's right"

Slogan of Republican candidate Barry Goldwater in the 1964 presidential campaign.

IPS

Delivery-service employer of truck driver Doug Heffernan (Kevin James) in the TV sitcom *The King of Queens*.

Iranistan

Bridgeport, Connecticut, mansion of showman P. T. Barnum, where he lived from 1848 until it was destroyed by fire in 1857.

I READ

Texas license plate of former first lady Barbara Bush's SUV. Mrs. Bush is an active supporter of literacy programs.

Ireland/Bronson films

See **Bronson/Ireland films**

Ireland Trophy

Trophy awarded to the winning team in the annual football game between Boston College and Notre Dame.

I Remember It Well

1970 autobiography of director Vincente Minnelli. It is also the title of a Lerner and Loewe song in the film *Gigi*, which was directed by Minnelli.

Irish Nip

Horse ridden by jockey Laffit Pincay Jr. for his record-breaking 8,834th win at Hollywood Park, Inglewood, California, on December 10, 1999. Pincay's win broke the record held since 1970 by Willie Shoemaker.

Irium

Tooth-decay fighting ingredient in Pepsodent toothpaste, as touted in 1950s TV commercials.

"I roll"

What the word "Volvo" means in Latin.

"The Iron Butterfly"

Nickname of former Philippine first lady Imelda Marcos.

"The Iron Chancellor"

Nickname of German chancellor Otto von Bismarck.

Iron City

Setting of the film *Anatomy of a Murder*.

"The Iron Horse"

Nickname of baseball Hall of Famer Lou Gehrig.

"The Iron Lady"

Nickname of former English prime minister Lady Margaret Thatcher.

Ironman Triathlon

A 2.4-mile swim, followed by a 112-mile bike race, followed by a 26.2-mile run. The World Championships have been held annually in Hawaii since 1978. The top competitors usually complete the Triathlon in 8 to 9 hours.

Ironville

Setting of the opening scene of the Abbott and Costello film *The Naughty Nineties*.

Iroquois League

Confederation of Indian tribes who lived in what is today New York State, formed circa 1570 with these members:
Cayuga
Mohawk
Oneida
Onondaga
Seneca
The Tuscarora joined the League in 1722.

"irrational exuberance"

Phrase coined by Federal Reserve chairman Alan Greenspan to describe speculative excesses on Wall Street, first used in a December 1996 speech.

Irwin

First name of the title character (Chevy Chase) in the film *Fletch*. The character's real last name is Fletcher.

Isaac

Real first name of comedian Sid Caesar.

Real first name of pop singer Don Everly.

Isadore

Real first name of pioneer animator Friz Freleng. His nickname was derived from the first two letters in his last and first names, respectively.

Isaly, Samuel

Native of Pittsburgh who created the Klondike Bar in 1929.

Isère

French frigate that brought the disassembled Statue of Liberty to the United States in 1885.

"Is ev'rybody happy?"

Catchphrase of vaudevillian Ted Lewis.

Isham

Horse ridden by Buffalo Bill Cody in his Wild West Show.

Ishihara test

Standard test for color blindness, introduced by Japanese ophthalmologist Shinobu Ishihara in 1917. It consists of a series of colored-dot patterns that have a different appearance to normal-vision and color-blind people.

I Should Care

1974 autobiography of lyricist Sammy Cahn, named for one of his songs.

"Is it safe?"

See **9**

Islam, Yusuf

Muslim name adopted by singer Cat Stevens.

Island Manor

Retirement home that Sid and Muriel (Tom Aldredge and Jane Hoffman) move to, in the film *batteries not included*.

Island Princess

Charter fishing boat operated by Sam Bailey (Paul Ford) in the TV sitcom *The Baileys of Balboa*.

Isla Nublar

Island west of Costa Rica that is the setting of the Steven Spielberg film *Jurassic Park*.

Isley, Phylis Lee

Real name of actress Jennifer Jones.

Ismay, Montana

Town (population 22) that in 1993 renamed itself Joe, Montana, in honor of the NFL quarterback.

"Isn't that special?"

Catchphrase of the Church Lady (Dana Carvey) in the TV series *Saturday Night Live*.

Isola, New York

Setting of the *87th Precinct* series of novels by Ed McBain.

"Is that your final answer?"

Catchphrase of host Regis Philbin in the TV game show *Who Wants to Be a Millionaire*.

"Is this the party to whom I am speaking?"

Catchphrase used by Lily Tomlin in her comedy routines as telephone operator Ernestine.

"Is this trip really necessary?"

World War II-era slogan to persuade Americans to reduce their consumption of gasoline.

"I stick my neck out for nobody"

Memorable line spoken by Rick Blaine (Humphrey Bogart) in the film *Casablanca*.

Isuzu, Joe

Pathological-liar spokesperson in TV commercials for Izusu automobiles, portrayed by David Leisure.

Italiano, Anna Maria Louisa

Real name of actress Anne Bancroft.

Itasca

Coast Guard cutter that had the last communication with aviator Amelia Earhart, whose plane vanished on July 2, 1937.

"It fulfills your deepest desires"

See **Ravish**

"The It Girl"

Nickname of silent-screen actress Clara Bow, for her starring role in the 1927 film *It*.

Ithaca, California

Setting of the William Saroyan novel *The Human Comedy*.

"It is a far, far better thing that I do, than I have ever done; it is a far, far better rest that I go to than I have ever known."

Last line of the Charles Dickens novel *A Tale of Two Cities*, spoken by Sydney Carton.

It Pays to Steal

1963 autobiography of baseball player and noted base-stealer Maury Wills.

It's A New World

See **Happiness Ahead** and **It's a New World**

"It's downright upright"

Advertising slogan of Harvey's Bristol Cream sherry.

"It's everywhere you want to be"

Advertising slogan of Visa credit cards.

"It's good to be the king!"

Catchphrase of King Louis XIV (Mel Brooks) in the film *History of the World Part I*.

"It shines for all"

See **New York Sun**

"It's Howdy Doody time!"
See **"Say kids! What time is it?"**

"It's Time to Say So Long"
Theme song of the TV comedy/variety series *The Carol Burnett Show*, composed by Joe Hamilton, Burnett's former husband.

"It takes a licking and keeps on ticking"
Advertising slogan of Timex watches, spoken in TV commercials by John Cameron Swayze.

"It was a dark and stormy night"
See **Bulwer-Lytton Fiction Contest**

Ivan
See **Dmitri, Ivan, Alyosha, and Smerdyakov**

Ivanhoe
Real last name of actor/singer Burl Ives.

"I've Written a Letter to Daddy"
Signature song of child vaudevillian Baby Jane Hudson (Bette Davis, Julie Allred as a child) in the film *Whatever Happened to Baby Jane?* The tune was written especially for the film by Frank DeVol.

Ivy House
London home of ballet star Anna Pavlova.

Ivy League schools
Listed below with their founding dates:
    Brown University (1764)
    Columbia University (1754)
    Cornell University (1865)
    Dartmouth University (1769)
    Harvard University (1636)
    University of Pennsylvania (1740)
    Princeton University (1746)
    Yale University (1701)

"I want to be alone"
Memorable line spoken by Grusinskaya (Greta Garbo) to Baron Felix von Geigern (John Barrymore) in the film *Grand Hotel*.

"I Want to Love You"
Instrumental theme of the TV series *The Asphalt Jungle*, composed by Duke Ellington.

I Was a Teenage Teenager
Original working title of the film *Clueless*.

"I was touched"
English translation of the French fencing term "touché."

Iwatani, Toru
Japanese programmer who invented the video game Pac-Man in 1979. The game was originally called Puck-Man.

"I would found an institution where any person can find instruction in any study"
Motto of Cornell University, from the words of founder Ezra Cornell.

Ixcatlan, Mexico
Village that is the setting of the film *The Magnificent Seven*.

Jack

Boy dressed in a sailor suit on boxes of Cracker Jack.

Jack Adams Award

Presented annually since 1974 to the NHL coach "adjudged to have contributed the most to his team's success," named for the former Detroit Red Wings coach and general manager.

Jackie Robinson Sports Institute

Employer of Marcus Sommers (Kevin Costner) and Dennis Conrad (John Amos) in the film *American Flyers*.

"Jack of All Trades"

Self-styled nickname of the serial killer (Dennis Christopher) in the TV series *Profiler*.

Jack's Bistro

Restaurant owned by Jack Tripper (John Ritter) in the TV sitcoms *Three's Company* and *Three's a Crowd*.

Jackson

Middle name of golf great Sam Snead.

Middle name of Sheriff Andy Taylor (Andy Griffith) in the TV sitcom *The Andy Griffith Show*.

Jackson 5 members

Members of the pop group, from oldest to youngest: Jackie (real first name Sigmund), Tito (real first name Toriano), Jermaine, Marlon, and Michael.

Jackson City

Capital of the unnamed state represented in the U.S. Senate by the title character (James Stewart) in the Frank Capra film *Mr. Smith Goes to Washington*. The local newspaper is the *Jackson City Star*.

Jackson, O'Shea

Real name of rap singer/actor Ice Cube.

Jackson Steinem & Co.

Employer of Bud Fox (Charlie Sheen) in the film *Wall Street*.

"Jack the Dripper"

Nickname of artist Jackson Pollock, for his splashing technique.

Jacob

Real first name of baseball Hall of Famer Nellie Fox.

Jacob and Wilhelm

First names of the Brothers Grimm, German folklorists best-known for their collection of fairy tales.

Jacobson

Real last name of TV host Bert Parks.

Jahan, Marine

Uncredited performer who does the dancing for actress Jennifer Beals in the film *Flashdance*.

"Jailhouse Rock" band

As mentioned in this Elvis Presley tune:
Spider Murphy: tenor saxophone
Little Joe: slide trombone
"The drummer boy from Illinois"
The Purple Gang: rhythm section

Jake

Title feline of the Disney film *The Cat from Outer Space*.

"Jake the Snake"

Nickname of NHL Hall of Fame goalie Jacques Plante.

Jalna

Ontario estate of the Whiteoak family in novels of Mazo de la Roche.

James

Real first name of Sonny Crockett (Don Johnson) in the TV series *Miami Vice*.

James Bond films/actors

SEAN CONNERY
Dr. No (1962)
From Russia with Love (1963)
Goldfinger (1964)

Thunderball (1965)
You Only Live Twice (1967)
Diamonds Are Forever (1971)
Never Say Never Again (1983)

GEORGE LAZENBY

On Her Majesty's Secret Service (1969)

ROGER MOORE

Live and Let Die (1973)
The Man with the Golden Gun (1974)
The Spy Who Loved Me (1977)
Moonraker (1979)
For Your Eyes Only (1981)
Octopussy (1983)
A View to a Kill (1985)

TIMOTHY DALTON

The Living Daylights (1987)
Licence to Kill (1989)

PIERCE BROSNAN

GoldenEye (1995)
Tomorrow Never Dies (1997)
The World Is Not Enough (1999)

David Niven portrayed James Bond in the spoof film *Casino Royale* (1967).

James Bond film songs/singers

Where no song title is listed below, the title is the same as the film's title. (Only the instrumental "James Bond Theme" was performed in the first Bond film, *Dr. No* [1962].)

From Russia With Love (1963): Matt Monro
Goldfinger (1964): Shirley Bassey
Thunderball (1965): Tom Jones
You Only Live Twice (1967): Nancy Sinatra
Casino Royale (1967): Herb Alpert and the Tijuana Brass
On Her Majesty's Secret Service (1969), "We Have All the Time in the World": Louis Armstrong
Diamonds Are Forever (1971): Shirley Bassey
Live and Let Die (1973): Paul McCartney and Wings
The Man with the Golden Gun (1974): Lulu
The Spy Who Loved Me (1977), "Nobody Does It Better": Carly Simon
Moonraker (1979): Shirley Bassey
For Your Eyes Only (1981): Sheena Easton
Octopussy (1983), "All Time High": Rita Coolidge
Never Say Never Again (1983): Lani Hall
A View to a Kill (1985): Duran Duran
The Living Daylights (1987): a-ha
Licence to Kill (1989): Gladys Knight
GoldenEye (1995): Tina Turner
Tomorrow Never Dies (1997): Sheryl Crow
The World Is Not Enough (1999): Garbage

Shirley Bassey (*Goldfinger, Diamonds Are Forever* and *Moonraker*) is the only artist to perform the opening song in more than one James Bond film.

James Buchanan High

Brooklyn, New York, school that is the setting of the TV sitcom *Welcome Back, Kotter.*

James Butler

Real first and middle names of frontiersman Wild Bill Hickok.

"The James Caan Con"

Debut episode of the TV series *Switch*, which aired on September 9, 1975.

James Cash

First and middle names of retail-chain founder J. C. Penney.

James Cleveland

Real first and middle names of track star Jesse Owens.

James David Graham

Real first and middle names of actor David Niven.

James Douglas Muir

Real first and middle names of comedian/talk-show host Jay Leno.

James Ewell Brown

First and middle names of Civil War Confederate general J. E. B. Stuart.

James, Freddy

See **"The World's Worst Juggler"**

James Hubert

Real first and middle names of songwriter Eubie Blake.

James Joseph

Real first and middle names of boxer Gene Tunney.

James King Kern

Real first and middle names of comedic bandleader Kay Kyser.

James K. Polk High

Alma mater of Peg and Al Bundy (Katey Sagal and Ed O'Neill) in the TV sitcom *Married . . . with Children.*

James Marshall

Real first and middle names of rock guitarist Jimi Hendrix.

James Mercer Langston

Real first and middle names of writer Langston Hughes.

James Norris Memorial Trophy

Presented annually since 1954 to the NHL's most outstanding defenseman, named for the former Detroit Red Wings owner.

James, Ralph

Voice of Orson, Orkan superior of Mork (Robin Williams) in the TV sitcom *Mork and Mindy*.

James, Richard

Mechanical engineer who invented Slinky, introduced in 1946.

Jamestown, North Dakota

Birthplace of author Louis L'Amour and singer Peggy Lee.

Janairo, Althea

Real name of actress Tia Carrere.

Jane

See **Eve (Eve White/Eve Black/Jane)**

Janet

Real first name of author (Janet) Taylor Caldwell.

Janos, James George

Real name of wrestler/politician Jesse Ventura.

Januth Publications

Company that publishes *Crimeways* magazine in the film *The Big Clock*.

Jaq

See **Gus and Jaq**

Jarrett, Conrad

Role for which Timothy Hutton won a Best Supporting Actor Academy Award in the 1980 film *Ordinary People*.

Jarvis, Anna

West Virginia schoolteacher who originated the idea of Mother's Day, first celebrated nationwide by presidential proclamation in 1914.

Jasper

Gregg family dog in the TV sitcom *Bachelor Father*.

Pet raccoon of Laura Ingalls (Melissa Gilbert) in the TV series *Little House on the Prairie*.

Original name of Tom (the cat) in Tom and Jerry cartoons.

Javacheff

Last name of Bulgarian-born environmental artist Christo, noted for his giant "wrappings" of large objects such as buildings and bridges.

Javal, Camille

Real name of actress Brigitte Bardot.

Jawas

Diminutive hooded desert people that capture C-3PO and R2-D2 in the film *Star Wars*.

Jaws 19

See **"This time, it's REALLY REALLY personal"**

Jaws films

Jaws (1975)	*Jaws the Revenge*
Jaws 2 (1978)	(1987)
Jaws 3-D (1983)	

Jay

Code name of James Darrel Edwards III (Will Smith) in the film *Men in Black*.

Middle name of Homer Simpson (voiced by Dan Castellaneta) in the animated TV sitcom *The Simpsons*.

See also **Bea and Jay**

Jay Billington

First and middle names of the title character (Warren Beatty) in the film *Bulworth*.

"Jayhawker"

See **United States residents' nicknames**

Jaynes

Middle name of actor Henry Fonda.

J. C. Forest and Son

Law-firm employer of Rachel Flax (Cher) in the film *Mermaids*.

Jean

First name of oil magnate J. Paul Getty.

Jeanneret, Charles-Édouard

Real name of Swiss architect Le Corbusier.

Jeeves, Mahatma Kane

See **Fields, W. C., roles/pen names of**

Jefferson

First name of the title character (James Stewart) in the film *Mr. Smith Goes to Washington.*

Jefferson Davis

Real first and middle names of "Boss" Hogg (Sorrell Booke) in the TV series *The Dukes of Hazzard.*

Jefferson High

Los Angeles setting of the TV series *Mr. Novak.*

Milwaukee school attended by Richie Cunningham (Ron Howard) in the TV sitcom *Happy Days.*

Jefferson Junior High

School that is the setting of the TV sitcom *Mr. Peepers.*

Jefferson, Mississippi

Seat of Yoknapatawpha County, setting of the most of the novels of William Faulkner. It is modeled on Faulkner's hometown of Oxford.

See also **Yoknapatawpha County, Mississippi**

Jefferson National Expansion Monument

Official name of the Gateway Arch in St. Louis, Missouri. The arch was designed by Finnish-born architect Eero Saarinen and dedicated in 1966.

Jekyll, Dr. Henry

Role for which Fredric March won a Best Actor Academy Award in the 1932 film *Dr. Jekyll and Mr. Hyde.*

Jelly Belly Jelly Beans flavors

Manufactured by the Herman Goelitz Company of Fairfield, California, since 1976. They were a favorite snack of President Ronald Reagan.

THE 40 OFFICIAL FLAVORS:

Blueberry	Juicy Pear
Bubble Gum	Lemon
Buttered Popcorn	Lemon Lime
Cantaloupe	Licorice
Cappuccino	Margarita
Champagne Punch	Orange Juice
Chocolate Pudding	Orange Sherbet
Cinnamon	Peach
Coconut	Peanut Butter
Cotton Candy	Peppermint Stick
A&W Cream Soda	Piña Colada
Crushed Pineapple	Pink Grapefruit
Grape Jelly	Raspberry
Green Apple	A&W Root Beer
Hawaiian Punch	Sizzling Cinnamon
Island Punch	Strawberry Cheesecake
Jalapeño	Strawberry Daiquiri
Tangerine	Tutti-Frutti
Toasted Marshmallow	Very Cherry
Top Banana	Watermelon

Jellystone Park

Home of TV cartoon character Yogi Bear.

"Je me souviens"

Motto of the province of Quebec, Canada, which is French for "I remember."

Jenkins

Real last name of actor Richard Burton.

"Jenkins' Band"

See **Newman, Stan**

Jenkins, Harold Lloyd

Real name of country singer Conway Twitty.

Jenkins Hill

Washington, D.C., site on which the U.S. Capitol was built, which is known as Capitol Hill today.

Jennings

Maiden name of Krystle Carrington (Linda Evans) in the TV series *Dynasty.*

Jennings, Ohio

Birthplace of the title character in the comic strip *Mary Worth.*

Jerome David

First and middle names of novelist J. D. Salinger.

Jerome, Eugene

The "Neil Simon" character in Simon's autobiographical plays *Brighton Beach Memoirs, Biloxi Blues,* and *Broadway Bound.*

Jerome Jeremiah

First and middle names of the title character (Dale Robertson) in the TV series *J. J. Starbuck.*

Jerry

Role for which Norma Shearer won a Best Actress Academy Award in the 1930 film *The Divorcée.*

Jerry and Pamela

First names of the title characters in the radio and TV series *Mr. & Mrs. North.*

Jersey Films

Production company of actor/director Danny DeVito.

"The Jersey Lily"
Nickname of English actress Lillie Langtry.

Jesse
See **Elvis and Jesse**

Jessy Dixon Singers
Vocal group that backs up Paul Simon and Phoebe Snow on their tune "Gone At Last."

"Jesus wept."
Shortest verse in the King James Bible, found at John 11:35.

"The Jet"
Nickname of speedy pro football Hall of Fame running back Joe Perry.

"Je T'Appartiens"
Original French title of the tune "Let It Be Me," which means "I Belong to You."

Jetexas
See **Little Reata**

Jetman
Comic strip drawn by Dick Hollister (Richard Benjamin) in the TV sitcom *He & She*.

Jetsam
See **Flotsam and Jetsam**

Jets and Sharks
Rival gangs in the musical *West Side Story*.

The Jet Set
Original name of rock group The Byrds.

Jettison Scrap and Salvage Company
Firm operated by Harry Broderick (Andy Griffith) in the TV series *Salvage 1*.

The Jeweled Shillelagh
Trophy awarded to the winning team in the annual football game between Notre Dame and U.S.C.

J. Geils Band original members
Stephen Jo Bladd, Jerome Geils, Seth Justman, Danny Klein, Dick Salwitz, and Peter Wolf.

Jill
Childhood pony of author John Steinbeck, which was the inspiration for his short story "The Red Pony."

Jim
See **Kenny and Jim**

Jim and Dash
First names (respectively) of singers Seals and Crofts.

"Jimmy Tomorrow"
Nickname of James Cameron in the Eugene O'Neill play *The Iceman Cometh*.

Jim Thorpe, Pennsylvania
See **Mauch Chunk**

Jingles, Mr.
Pet mouse of Paul Edgecomb (Tom Hanks, Dabbs Greer) in the film *The Green Mile*.

Jip
Pet dog of Dora Spenlow in the Charles Dickens novel *David Copperfield*.

Pet dog of the title character in the Doctor Dolittle novels of Hugh Lofting.

Joad, Ma
Role for which Jane Darwell won a Best Supporting Actress Academy Award in the 1940 film *The Grapes of Wrath*.

Joanne Kathleen
First and middle names of J. K. Rowling, author of the Harry Potter series.

Joe
Middle name of basketball Hall of Famer Larry Bird.

Pet parrot of Guffy McGovern (Paul Douglas) in the film *Angels in the Outfield* (1951).

What they call "fire" in the Lerner and Loewe tune "They Call the Wind Maria."

See also **Willie and Joe**

John
Real first name of golf great (John) Byron Nelson.

First name of the title character (James Franciscus) in the TV series *Mr. Novak*.

John, Anthony
Role for which Ronald Colman won a Best Actor Academy Award in the 1947 film *A Double Life*.

John Bertrand
Real first and middle names of Hall of Fame baseball umpire Jocko Conlan.

John Birks

Real first and middle names of jazz trumpeter Dizzy Gillespie.

John F. Kennedy High

School that is the setting of the film *Mr. Holland's Opus*. The school is called Grant High at the beginning of the film, and renamed after Kennedy's assassination.

John Huffam

Middle names of author Charles Dickens.

Johnnie

Real first name of baseball player/manager Dusty Baker.

Johnny

"Hand" puppet of ventriloquist Señor Wences, which was drawn on his hand. His "head-in-a-box" puppet, whose favorite word was "S'awright," was named Pedro.

Johnny and Frank

First names (respectively) of comedy team Wayne and Shuster.

Johnny and the Moondogs

See **The Quarrymen**

Johnny Casino and the Gamblers

Rock group portrayed by Sha Na Na in the film *Grease*.

Johnny Corkscrew

Smee's name for his cutlass in the James M. Barrie novel *Peter Pan*.

Johnny Hays and the Bluecats

See **The Rattlesnakes**

John Peter

Real first and middle names of baseball Hall of Famer Honus Wagner.

John Pierpont

First and middle names of financier J. P. Morgan.

John Ronald Reuel

First and middle names of novelist J. R. R. Tolkien.

Johnson, Benjamin F.

Pen name used by poet James Whitcomb Riley.

Johnson, Bob

Voice on the tape played by Jim Phelps (Peter Graves) at the beginning of each episode of the TV series *Mission: Impossible*. Johnson also provided the voice of many of the monsters on the TV series *The Outer Limits*.

Johnson, Caryn Elaine

Real name of actress Whoopi Goldberg.

Johnson, Fred

One-armed man, portrayed by Bill Raisch, who is the real murderer of Helen Kimble in the original TV series *The Fugitive*.

Johnson, Lorraine

See **My Posse Don't Do Homework**

Johnson, Merle

Real name of actor Troy Donahue. It is also the name of the character he portrays, the fiancé of Connie Corleone (Talia Shire), in the film *The Godfather Part II*.

Johnson, Sherwood "Shakey" and Plummer, Ed

Founders of the Shakey's Pizza chain. The first Shakey's opened in 1954 in Sacramento, California.

Johnson, Willie

Inventor of the mechanical eggbeater, patented in 1884.

"Join the Army and See the Navy"

Freedonian recruiting sign carried by Pinky (Harpo Marx) in the Marx Brothers film *Duck Soup*.

"Join up . . . join in"

Advertising slogan of the American Red Cross.

Jo-Jo

Middle name of Bart Simpson (voiced by Nancy Cartwright) in the animated TV sitcom *The Simpsons*.

Jolly Roger

Ship of Captain Hook in the James M. Barrie novel *Peter Pan*.

Jonathan Southworth

Real first and middle names of actor John Ritter.

Jones

Real last name of actress Vivian Vance.

Jones, Arthur
Inventor of the Nautilus exercise machine, first sold in 1970.

Jones, Christopher
Captain of the *Mayflower* on its voyage to Massachusetts in 1620.

Jones, David Robert
Real name of rock singer David Bowie. He changed his name to avoid confusion with Davy Jones of the Monkees.

Jones, Desmond and Molly
Couple in the Beatles tune "Ob-La-Di, Ob-La-Da."

Jones, Dick
Voice of the title character in the Disney animated film *Pinocchio*.

Jones, George
See **Raymond, Henry J. and Jones, George**

Jones, Kenney
Drummer who succeeded Keith Moon in rock group The Who after Moon's death in 1978.

Jones, Mr.
Thanksgiving turkey in the film *Holiday Inn*.

Jones, Ruth Lee
Real name of pop singer Dinah Washington.

Jones, Stinky
Obnoxious boy (Joe Besser) in a Little Lord Fauntleroy outfit in the TV sitcom *The Abbott and Costello Show*.

The Jordanaires
The most successful backup singing group in recording history, having performed with over 2,000 different artists on over 30,000 tunes since the 1950s. The group's most notable recordings include:
"Hound Dog" and "Don't Be Cruel" (Elvis Presley)
"The Battle of New Orleans" (Johnny Horton)
"Travelin' Man" (Ricky Nelson)
"Big Bad John" (Jimmy Dean)
"Crazy" (Patsy Cline)
"Coal Miner's Daughter" (Loretta Lynn)

Jordan, Will
Impressionist who has portrayed TV host Ed Sullivan in several films, including *The Doors* and *Mr. Saturday Night*.

Jorden, Rebecca
Real name of Newt (Carrie Henn) in the film *Aliens*.

José
See **Fritz, Michael, Pierre, and José**

Joseph
Real first name of author (Joseph) Rudyard Kipling.

Real first name of actor Nathan Lane.

Real first name of "Rocky" Rockford (Noah Beery Jr.) in the TV series *The Rockford Files*.

Joseph and His Brothers series
Group of four novels by Thomas Mann based on the biblical book of Genesis:
Joseph and His Brothers (1933)
Young Joseph (1934)
Joseph in Egypt (1936)
Joseph the Provider (1943)

Joseph Francis
Real first and middle names of actor Buster Keaton.

Josephine
Plumber in TV commercials for Comet cleanser, portrayed by former child actress Jane Withers.

Josephine Ford
Fokker Trimotor airplane in which Richard E. Byrd and Floyd Bennett became the first to fly over the North Pole on May 9, 1926.

Josh
Pet parrot of the title character in the comic strip *Ziggy*.

Joshua
Middle name of composer Stephen Sondheim.

Josiah
Pet badger of President Theodore Roosevelt.

Josiah Kessel College
See **Easy Valley, California**

Journey Beyond the Stars
Original working title of the film *2001: A Space Odyssey*.

Joy Comes to Dead Horse
Cowboy musical by Harvey Schmidt and Tom Jones that was reworked into *The Fantasticks*.

JT Lancer

TV police series for which Sam Weber (Tom Berenger) portrays the title character, in the film *The Big Chill.*

J. T. Marlin

Fly-by-night brokerage firm that is the setting of the film *Boiler Room.*

"The Judgment"

Final two-part episode of the original TV series *The Fugitive*, which aired on August 22 and 29, 1967.

Judson, Whitcomb

Inventor of the zipper, patented in 1893 as the "clasp-locker."

Judy

Pet chimpanzee of the Tracy family in the TV series *Daktari.*

Judy Kay

Real first and middle names of pop singer Juice Newton.

Jules and Verne

Children of Dr. Emmett L. Brown (Christopher Lloyd) and his wife Clara Clayton (Mary Steenburgen), named for his favorite author, in the film *Back to the Future Part III.*

Jules Rimet Trophy

Official name of the former World Cup soccer trophy, named for the first president of the International Federation of Association Football. It was retired by Brazil in 1970, as the first three-time winner.

Julia

Title role for which Vanessa Redgrave won the 1977 Best Actress Academy Award.

Julia

English whaler that rescues sailor Herman Melville in the Melville novel *Omoo.* (The author himself is the main character in the novel.)

Julia Jean Mildred Frances

Real first and middle names of actress Lana Turner.

Julian Edwin

Real first and middle names of jazz saxophonist Cannonball Adderley.

Julie

Middle name of pop singer Paula Abdul.

Julius

First name of physicist J. Robert Oppenheimer.

First name of the title character (Joseph Wiseman) in the James Bond film *Dr. No.*

Pet cat of Vincent Benedict (Danny DeVito) in the film *Twins.*

Julius Caesar

First and middle names of J. C. Dithers, boss of Dagwood Bumstead in the comic strip *Blondie.*

Julius Henry

See **Marx Brothers' real names**

JULY IV MDCCLXXVI

Inscription on the tablet held in the left hand of the Statue of Liberty.

Jumper

Coates family mule in the Disney film *Old Yeller.*

Jump, Gordon

See **White, Jesse**

"jumping flea"

What the word "ukulele" means in Hawaiian.

Jumpman

Original name of Mario, hero of video game Donkey Kong.

Junction Cafe

Popular Mayberry restaurant in the TV sitcom *The Andy Griffith Show.*

June

See **April, May, and June**

Junger, Sebastian

Author of the book *The Perfect Storm*, upon which the film of the same name was based.

Jung, George

Los Angeles owner of the Hong Kong Noodle Company who invented fortune cookies in 1916.

Jungle Jim films

Series starring Johnny Weissmuller in the title role:
> *Jungle Jim* (1948)
> *The Lost Tribe* (1949)
> *Captive Girl* (1950)
> *Mark of the Gorilla* (1950)
> *Pygmy Island* (1950)

Fury of the Congo (1951)
Jungle Manhunt (1951)
Jungle Jim in the Forbidden Land (1952)
Voodoo Tiger (1952)
Savage Mutiny (1953)
Killer Ape (1953)
Valley of Head Hunters (1953)
Jungle Man-Eaters (1954)
Cannibal Attack (1954)*
Jungle Moon Men (1955)*
Devil Goddess (1955)*
* Weissmuller portrays himself in the last three films of the series

Junior Woodchucks

Scouting organization that Donald Duck's nephews Huey, Dewey, and Louie belong to.

Jupiter II

See **Gemini XII**

"Just a little bit better"

Advertising slogan of Post cereals.

"Just do it"

Advertising slogan of Nike shoes.

Justerini and Brooks

What the letters in J&B Scotch stand for. Londoner Alfred Brooks purchased the business of liquor merchant Giacomo Justerini in 1831.

Justice, Archie

Original name of Archie Bunker (Carroll O'Connor) in the TV sitcom *All in the Family*, which was used in the first pilot episode.

Justice for All

Original working title of the TV sitcom *All in the Family*.

"Justice is founded in the rights bestowed by nature upon man. Liberty is maintained in security of justice."

Inscription on the Department of Justice building in Washington, D.C.

"Justitia omnibus"

Motto of Washington, D.C., which is Latin for "Justice for all."

"Just Over the Brooklyn Bridge"

Theme song of the TV series *Brooklyn Bridge*, performed by Art Garfunkel.

"Just slightly ahead of our time"

Advertising slogan of Panasonic.

Justus Amusement Company

Baltimore "front" of the bookmaker employer of Lilly Dillon (Anjelica Huston) in the film *The Grifters*.

"Just when you thought it was safe to go back in the water . . ."

Slogan used to promote the film *Jaws 2*.

Kaa

Python in Rudyard Kipling's *The Jungle Book*.

Kabibble, Ish

See **Bogue, Merwyn**

Kabong, El

Masked crimefighting alter ego of cartoon sheriff Quick Draw McGraw.

KACL

Seattle radio station where the psychiatrist title character (Kelsey Grammer) works as an advice-show host, in the TV sitcom *Frasier*.

Kafiristan

Setting of the Rudyard Kipling story *The Man Who Would Be King*, and the film adaptation of the same name.

Kalimantan

Indonesian name for the island of Borneo.

kalium

Former name for potassium, from which its chemical symbol K is derived.

Kalogeropoulos

Real last name of Greek-born opera star Maria Callas.

Kaminker

Real last name of actress Simone Signoret.

Kaminsky

Real last name of actor/director Mel Brooks.

Kampuchea, People's Republic of

Former name (circa 1976–89) of Cambodia.

The Kandy Bar

Where Lisa (Kelly LeBrock) takes Wyatt (Ilan Mitchell-Smith) and Gary (Anthony Michael Hall) on their first date, in the film *Weird Science*.

Kandy Kake

Original name of the Baby Ruth candy bar.

Kane, Francis

Real name of novelist Harold Robbins.

Kane, Will

Role for which Gary Cooper won a Best Actor Academy Award in the 1952 film *High Noon*.

"The Kangaroo Kid"

Nickname of basketball Hall of Famer Jim Pollard, for his leaping ability.

Kansas Star

Speeding train that teenage Clark Kent (Jeff East) outruns, in *Superman: The Movie*.

Kantner, Dee and Palmer, Violet

First two women to referee an NBA regular-season game, during the 1997–98 season.

Kapell, Dave

Inventor of Magnetic Poetry (individual words printed on magnetized metal) in 1993.

Kaplan

Original family name of composer Aaron Copland. It was changed to Copland by his father Harris.

Kaplan, George

Government agent that Roger Thornhill (Cary Grant) is mistaken for, in the Alfred Hitchcock film *North by Northwest*.

Karnicar, Davo

Slovenian ski instructor who became the first person to ski down Mount Everest, accomplishing the feat in five hours on October 7, 2000.

Karolinska Institute

Swedish medical college that selects the winners of the Nobel Prize in physiology or medicine.

KARTEL

Nemesis organization of the title character Robert Conrad in the TV series *A Man Called Sloane*.

Karuna

Middle name of actress Uma Thurman.

Kasbec
Pet Afghan hound of artist Pablo Picasso.

Kasner, Edward
See **100**

Kassir, John
Voice of The Crypt Keeper, skeletal host of the TV series *Tales from the Crypt*.

Katherine Dawn
First and middle names of singer k. d. lang.

Katie
Real first name of (Katie) Scarlett O'Hara in the Margaret Mitchell novel *Gone With the Wind*.

Katsumi
Role for which Miyoshi Umeki won a Best Supporting Actress Academy Award in the 1957 film *Sayonara*.

Kaufman, Seymour
Real name of songwriter Cy Coleman.

Kaumeyer
Real last name of actress Dorothy Lamour.

Kay
Code name of the alien fighter portrayed by Tommy Lee Jones in the film *Men in Black*.

"Kaye's Theme"
Theme song of bandleader Sammy Kaye.

Kay Toinette
First and middle names of country singer K. T. Oslin.

Kazak
Space-traveling dog of Winston Niles Runfoord in the Kurt Vonnegut novel *The Sirens of Titan*.

KBHR
Employer of deejay Chris Stevens (John Corbett) in the TV series *Northern Exposure*.

Keck, Emile J.
See **Marx, Groucho, roles of**

Keeney's Oriental Garden
New York theater where Fanny Brice (Barbra Streisand) gets her first break, in the film *Funny Girl*.

keeper
Loop on a belt adjacent to the buckle that holds the tip of the belt in place.

Keep It in the Family
English TV series that was the basis for the sitcom *Too Close for Comfort*.

"Keep Your Eye on the Sparrow"
Theme song of the TV series *Baretta*, performed by Sammy Davis Jr.

"Keep your feet on the ground, and keep reaching for the stars"
Sign-off line of syndicated deejay Casey Kasem.

The Keg of Nails
Trophy awarded to the winning team in the annual football game between the University of Cincinnati and the University of Louisville.

Keith
Real first name of Australian-born media mogul (Keith) Rupert Murdoch.

Kelcy's Bar
Favorite hangout of Archie Bunker (Carroll O'Connor) in the TV sitcom *All in the Family*.

Kell
Maiden name of Marion Cunningham (Marion Ross) in the TV sitcom *Happy Days*.

Keller, Helen
Role for which Patty Duke won a Best Supporting Actress Academy Award in the 1962 film *The Miracle Worker*.

Kellerman's Mountain House
Catskill Mountains resort that is the setting of the film *Dirty Dancing*.

Kelly, Joe
Role for which Red Buttons won a Best Supporting Actor Academy Award in the 1957 film *Sayonara*.

Kelly School Klarion
Newspaper in the comic strip *Miss Peach*.

Kelm, Andrew Arthur
Birth name of actor Tab Hunter.

Keltish
Ship led by Brock Lovett (Bill Paxton) that explores the wreck of the title vessel in the film *Titanic* (1997).

Keltner, Ken
See **Bagby Jr., Jim and Smith, Al**

Kemal Amin
Real first and middle names of syndicated deejay Casey Kasem.

Kemmerer, Wyoming
Site of J. C. Penney's first retail store, which he opened in 1902.

Kemo Sabe
See **"Trusty Scout"**

Ken
See **Dave and Ken**

Kenmore University
School attended by Merritt Andrews (Dolores Hart), Melanie Coleman (Yvette Mimieux), Tuggle Carpenter (Paula Prentiss), and Angie (Connie Francis) in the film *Where the Boys Are*.

Kennedy Biscuit Company
See **Mitchell, James Henry**

Kennedy Center Honors recipients
Honorees are recognized for their lifetime contributions to American culture through the performing arts.
- 1978 Marian Anderson, Fred Astaire, George Balanchine, Richard Rodgers, Arthur Rubenstein
- 1979 Aaron Copland, Ella Fitzgerald, Henry Fonda, Martha Graham, Tennessee Williams
- 1980 Leonard Bernstein, James Cagney, Agnes de Mille, Lynn Fontanne, Leontyne Price
- 1981 Count Basie, Cary Grant, Helen Hayes, Jerome Robbins, Rudolf Serkin
- 1982 George Abbott, Lillian Gish, Benny Goodman, Gene Kelly, Eugene Ormandy
- 1983 Katherine Dunham, Elia Kazan, Frank Sinatra, James Stewart, Virgil Thomson
- 1984 Lena Horne, Danny Kaye, Gian Carlo Menotti, Arthur Miller, Isaac Stern
- 1985 Merce Cunningham, Irene Dunne, Bob Hope, Alan Jay Lerner, Frederick Loewe, Beverly Sills
- 1986 Lucille Ball, Ray Charles, Hume Cronyn, Jessica Tandy, Yehudi Menuhin, Antony Tudor
- 1987 Perry Como, Bette Davis, Sammy Davis Jr., Nathan Milstein, Alwin Nikolais
- 1988 Alvin Ailey, George Burns, Myrna Loy, Alexander Schneider, Roger L. Stevens
- 1989 Harry Belafonte, Claudette Colbert, Alexandra Danilova, Mary Martin, William Schuman
- 1990 Dizzy Gillespie, Katharine Hepburn, Risë Stevens, Jule Styne, Billy Wilder
- 1991 Roy Acuff, Betty Comden, Adolph Green, Fayard Nichols, Harold Nicholas, Gregory Peck, Robert Shaw
- 1992 Lionel Hampton, Paul Newman, Ginger Rogers, Mstislav Rostropovich, Paul Taylor, Joanne Woodward
- 1993 Johnny Carson, Arthur Mitchell, Georg Solti, Stephen Sondheim, Marion Williams
- 1994 Kirk Douglas, Aretha Franklin, Morton Gould, Harold Prince, Pete Seeger
- 1995 Jacques d'Amboise, Marilyn Horne, B. B. King, Sidney Poitier, Neil Simon
- 1996 Edward Albee, Benny Carter, Johnny Cash, Jack Lemmon, Maria Tallchief
- 1997 Lauren Bacall, Bob Dylan, Charlton Heston, Jessye Norman, Edward Villella
- 1998 Bill Cosby, Fred Ebb, John Kander, Willie Nelson, André Previn, Shirley Temple Black
- 1999 Victor Borge, Sean Connery, Judith Jamison, Jason Robards, Stevie Wonder
- 2000 Mikhail Baryshnikov, Chuck Berry, Plácido Domingo, Clint Eastwood, Angela Lansbury

Kennedy, Willard
Announcer of the introduction to the TV series *The Adventures of Superman*.

Kenneth
Real first name of college football Hall of Fame coach (Kenneth) Knute Rockne.

Kenneth Yarborough
First and middle names of the veterinarian title character (Dennis Weaver) in the TV series *Kentucky Jones*. His nickname is derived from the initials of his first and middle names.

Kenny and Jim
First names (respectively) of rock singers Loggins and Messina.

Kenny and the Cadets
See **The Pendletones**

Kenny, Charles J.
Pen name used by author Erle Stanley Gardner.

Kenosha Kickers

Polka band that gives a ride to Kate McAllister (Catherine O'Hara) from Scranton to Chicago, in the film *Home Alone*.

Kensington General Hospital

San Francisco setting of the TV sitcom *House Calls*.

Kent Family Chronicles

Series of American historical novels by John Jakes:
> *The Bastard* (1974)
> *The Rebels* (1975)
> *The Seekers* (1975)
> *The Furies* (1976)
> *The Titans* (1976)
> *The Warriors* (1977)
> *The Lawless* (1978)
> *The Americans* (1980)

Kent, Grover

See **Supergrover**

Kent Road Tavern

Where a disguised King Richard (Ian Hunter) is first recognized upon his return to England, in the film *The Adventures of Robin Hood*.

Kent, Thomas

Alias used by Viola De Lesseps (Gwyneth Paltrow) while disguised as a male actor auditioning for the title character (Joseph Fiennes), in the film *Shakespeare in Love*.

"The Kentucky Colonel"

Nickname of baseball Hall of Famer Earle Combs.

Keogh, Captain Miles

See **Comanche**

Kerr

Middle name of English actor Laurence Olivier.

Kerry, Margaret

Model who posed for Disney animators to assist them in the creation of Tinker Bell in the film *Peter Pan*.

Kevin Joseph

Real first and middle names of actor Chuck Connors.

Key Caroline, Florida

Setting of the Stephen King short story "I Am the Doorway."

Keyes, Daniel

See **"Flowers for Algernon"**

key grip

Chief stagehand on a film set.

Key Mariah

Island setting of the TV series *Sweating Bullets*.

"Keystoner"

See **United States residents' nicknames**

KFLW

Employer of Los Angeles TV reporter Richard Thornburg (William Atherton) in the film *Die Hard*.

Khan, Abdullah Jaffa Bey

Real name of choreographer Robert Joffrey.

Khartoum

Thoroughbred racehorse whose head is left in the bed of his owner, movie producer Jack Woltz (John Marley), in the film *The Godfather*.

Khaury, Herbert

See **Larry Love, the Singing Canary**

Khmer Republic

Former name (1970–75) of Cambodia.

Kickapoo Joy Juice

Moonshine brewed by Lonesome Polecat and Hairless Joe in the comic strip *Li'l Abner*.

"The Kid"

Nickname of baseball Hall of Famer Ted Williams.

Nickname of Hall of Fame jockey Steve Cauthen.

Kid Crochet

Name under which Dino Crocetti (aka Dean Martin) boxed while in high school.

Kiddyland

Amusement park owned by Bud Flick and Lou Henry (Abbott and Costello) in the film *Dance with Me, Henry*.

KidRo Productions

Production company of talk-show host Rosie O'Donnell.

"The Kill"

Debut episode of the TV series *Peter Gunn*, which aired on September 22, 1958.

Kill Devil Hill

Kitty Hawk, North Carolina, site of the Wright brothers' first flight on December 17, 1903.

"Killer"

Nickname of singer Jerry Lee Lewis.

The Killer Angels

Novel by Michael Shaara that was the basis for the film Gettysburg.

Killyleagh, Baron

Title held by Prince Andrew of Great Britain.

Kilting

Allied code name for President Harry S Truman during World War II.

Kimila Ann

Real first and middle names of actress Kim Basinger.

Kim, Kazuo

Ukulele-playing cab driver (Poncie Ponce) who assists the detectives in the TV series Hawaiian Eye.

Kindred

Middle name of sci-fi author Philip K. Dick.

"Kiner's Korner"

Section of the left-field bleachers at Pittsburgh's Forbes Field where Pirate Hall of Famer Ralph Kiner hit many of his home runs.

"The King"

Nickname of actor Clark Gable.

Nickname of singer Elvis Presley.

King Edward Hotel

Home of the title character (Robert Blake) in the TV series Baretta.

"The Kingfish"

Nickname of Louisiana politician Huey Long.

Nickname of George Stevens (Freeman Gosden on radio, Tim Moore on TV), leader of the Mystic Knights of the Sea lodge in the radio and TV sitcom Amos 'n' Andy.

King Friday XIII

Puppet "ruler" in the children's TV series Mr. Rogers' Neighborhood.

King, Jack and the Jesters

Original name of singing group The Ink Spots.

King Jr., Leslie Lynch

Birth name of President Gerald Ford. His name was legally changed in 1935, after his divorced mother Dorothy Ayer Gardner King married paint salesman Gerald R. Ford.

King Lear daughters

The three daughters of the title character in the play by William Shakespeare:
  Goneril (the eldest)
  Regan, married to the Duke of Cornwall
  Cordelia (the youngest), married to the Duke of Albany

"The King of Angst"

Nickname of comedian Richard Lewis.

The King of Bartaria

Alternate title of the Gilbert and Sullivan comic opera The Gondoliers.

"The King of Broadway"

Nickname of songwriter George M. Cohan.

"The King of Comedy"

Nickname of director Mack Sennett.

"The King of Corn"

Nickname of bandleader Spike Jones.

"The King of Country Music"

Nickname of country singer Roy Acuff.

"The King of Swing"

Nickname of bandleader/clarinetist Benny Goodman.

"The King of the Cowboys"

Nickname of Western star Roy Rogers.

"King of the Mountain"

Debut episode of the TV series Kung Fu, which aired on October 14, 1972.

"The King of the One-Liners"

Nickname of comedian Henny Youngman.

"The King of Torts"

Nickname of attorney Melvin Belli.

"King Pong"

Nickname of Nolan Bushnell, founder of Atari, manufacturer of the first commercial video game, Pong, introduced in 1972.

Kingsbury
Middle name of newscaster Howard K. Smith.

King's College
Original name of Columbia University.

Kingsfield Jr., Professor Charles W.
Role for which John Houseman won a Best Supporting Actor Academy Award in the 1973 film *The Paper Chase*.

Kingsgate Films
Production company of actor Nick Nolte.

Kingsland, Arkansas
Birthplace of football coach Paul "Bear" Bryant and country singer Johnny Cash.

Kingsley
Middle name of author Norman Mailer.
The Kingsmen
Original name of country group The Statler Brothers. It was changed because of a pop group (of "Louie, Louie" fame) that had the same name.

King-Smith, Dick
See *The Sheep-Pig*

The King's Musketeer
See *Gypsy Lovers* and *The King's Musketeer*

Kings of Carolina
Original working title of the film *Something to Talk About*.

Kings of Queens
Fraternal lodge of Archie Bunker (Carroll O'Connor) in the TV sitcom *All in the Family*.

Kingston Falls
Setting of the film *Gremlins*.

Kingston Trio original members
Dave Guard, Nick Reynolds, and Bob Shane.

King, Tara
Partner of John Steed (Patrick Macnee) who succeeded Emma Peel (Diana Rigg) in the TV series *The Avengers*, portrayed by Linda Thorson.

King Timahoe
Pet Irish setter of President Richard Nixon.

King Tut
Pet dog of President Herbert Hoover.

Kintner, Alex
Raft-riding victim of the great white shark in the Steven Spielberg film *Jaws*, portrayed by Jeffrey Voorhees.

Kint, Roger "Verbal"
Role for which Kevin Spacey won a Best Supporting Actor Academy Award in the 1995 film *The Usual Suspects*.

KIPPERED HERRING
Words on the barrels in which the four stowaways (the Marx Brothers) hide, in the film *Monkey Business*.

Kirk Christiansen, Ole
Danish carpenter who invented Lego blocks circa 1949. They were first sold in the U.S. in 1961.

"The Kirkoff Case"
Debut episode of the TV series *The Rockford Files*, which aired on September 13, 1974.

Kirsebom
Last name of Swedish-born model Vendela.

Kirward Derby
Hat worn by Bullwinkle J. Moose that makes him intelligent, in the children's animated TV series *Rocky and His Friends*. The name is a spoonerism of TV host Durward Kirby.

"Kiss my grits!"
Catchphrase of Flo Castleberry (Polly Holliday) in the TV sitcom *Alice*.

Kiss (rock group) original members
Peter Kriss, Ace Frehley, Gene Simmons, and Paul Stanley.

Kit Kat Club
Berlin setting of the musical *Cabaret*.

KITT
See *Knight Industries Two Thousand*

"Kitten"
Jim Anderson's (Robert Young's) term of endearment for his younger daughter Kathy (Lauren Chapin), in the TV sitcom *Father Knows Best*.

Kitty
Name given by Anne Frank to her diary. Each of her diary's entries begins, "Dear Kitty."

Kitty Karry-All

Favorite doll of Cindy (Susan Olsen), in which she hides her allowance, in the TV sitcom *The Brady Bunch*.

Kiwi

U.S. Navy schooner that is the setting of the film and TV sitcom *The Wackiest Ship in the Army*.

Kix and Ronnie

First names (respectively) of country-music duo Brooks & Dunn.

KJCM

Radio station where Jack "The Nighthawk" Killian (Gary Cole) hosts an all-night call-in show, in the TV series *Midnight Caller*.

"Klaatu barada nikto"

Words spoken by Helen Benson (Patricia Neal) that stop the robot Gort (Lock Martin) from destroying the Earth, in the film *The Day the Earth Stood Still*.

KLAE Corporation

Employer of scientist Dr. Daniel Westin (David McCallum) in the TV series *The Invisible Man*.

Klass

Real last name of actor Gene Barry.

Klein

Real last name of film reviewer Judith Crist.

Real last name of singer/songwriter Carole King.

Klempner, John

See **A Letter to Five Wives**

Klinker, Effie

See **Bergen, Edgar, dummies of**

KLondike 5

See **555 (or KLondike 5)**

Klopstokia

Mythical nation that is the setting of the W. C. Fields film *Million Dollar Legs*.

KLOW

Portland, Oregon, radio station where Larry Alder (McLean Stevenson) works as a talk-show host, in the TV sitcom *Hello, Larry*.

kltpzyxm

Word that, when spoken by Superman nemesis Mr. Mxyzptlk, returns him to the Fifth Dimension. The word is "Mxyzptlk" spelled backward.

Knerr, Richard and Melin, Arthur "Spud"

Founders of the innovative toymaker WHAM-O, whose products have included the Frisbee, Superball, Hula Hoop and Hacky Sack. The company was named for its first product, the WHAM-O Slingshot, whose missile made that sound when it hit the target. Formerly owned by Mattel, WHAM-O became an independent company again in 1997.

Knickerbocker, Diedrich

Pen name used by author Washington Irving.

Knight

Maiden name of Emma Peel (Diana Rigg) in the TV series *The Avengers*.

A Knight at the Opera

1981 autobiography of Sir Rudolf Bing, former General Manager of the Metropolitan Opera in New York City.

Knight Industries Two Thousand

Full name of KITT, talking Pontiac Trans-Am driven by Michael Knight (David Hasselhoff) in the TV series *Knight Rider*. The voice of KITT was provided by actor William Daniels.

"Knight of the Phoenix"

Debut episode of the TV series *Knight Rider*, which aired on September 26, 1982.

Knights of the Scimitar

Fraternal lodge of Cliff Clavin (John Ratzenberger) in the TV sitcom *Cheers*.

Knights, William J.

See **Hill, Samuel E; Knights, William J.; and Nicholson, John H.**

"Knock Knock, Who's There"

Debut episode of the TV sitcom *Perfect Strangers*, which aired on March 25, 1986.

Knock Wood

1984 autobiography of actress Candice Bergen. Her father was ventriloquist Edgar Bergen.

Knothead and Splinter

Nephew and niece (respectively) of Woody Woodpecker.

"Know how"

Advertising slogan of Canon.

"Knowledge is good"

Motto of Faber College founder Emil Faber, in the film *National Lampoon's Animal House.*

"Knowledge that helps you think"

Advertising slogan of the *Encyclopedia Americana.*

Kohner, Kathy

Five-foot-tall, 95-pound California teen who inspired the 1957 novel *Gidget*, written by Frederick Kohner, Kathy's father.

Koko

Lowland gorilla that has been taught sign language by California psychologist Francine "Penny" Patterson since 1972. Today, Koko has a vocabulary of over 1,000 signs, understands about 2,000 words of spoken English, and has a "human" IQ in the 70–95 range.

"Kokomo" locales

This Beach Boys tune mentions these vacation spots (in order):

  Aruba
  Jamaica
  Bermuda
  Bahama
  Key Largo
  Montego
  Martinique
  Montserrat
  Port-au-Prince

Komet

Magazine that assigns freelance writer Peter Miller (Jon Voight) to track down World War II war criminal Eduard Roschmann (Maximilian Schell) in the film *The Odessa File.*

Komitet Gosudarstvennoi Bezopasnosti

Full name of Soviet secret service agency, the KGB. The name is Russian for "Committee for State Security."

konimeter

Instrument for measuring the amount of dust in the air.

Koninklijke Luchtvaart Maatschappij

What the letters in the name of Dutch airline KLM stand for, which is Dutch for "Royal Airline Company."

Konishiki

See **"Meat Bomb" and "Dump Truck"**

Konopka, Tadeus Wladyslaw

Real name of actor Ted Knight.

Kor

African city that is the setting of the H. Rider Haggard novel *She.*

KORN

Radio station in the TV series *Hee Haw.*

Kornblow, Ronald

See **Marx, Groucho, roles of**

Korova Milk Bar

Hangout of Alex (Malcolm McDowell) and his fellow Droogs in the film *A Clockwork Orange.*

Korzeniowski, Jozef Teodor Konrad Nalecz

Real name of novelist Joseph Conrad.

Kostyra

Maiden name of lifestyle guru Martha Stewart.

Kotkin

Real last name of magician David Copperfield.

Kotzin, Bernard

Real name of comedian Stubby Kaye.

Kovacs

Chimpanzee puppet on the children's TV show hosted by the title character (Robin Williams) in the film *Mrs. Doubtfire.*

Kovak, Sandra

Role for which Mary Astor won a Best Supporting Actress Academy Award in the 1941 film *The Great Lie.*

Kowalski, Stella

Role for which Kim Hunter won a Best Supporting Actress Academy Award in the 1951 film *A Streetcar Named Desire.*

KPPX

Radio station held hostage by heavy-metal rock group The Lone Rangers in the film *Airheads.*

Krabappel, Edna

Fourth-grade teacher of Bart Simpson in the animated TV sitcom *The Simpsons.*

Krämer

Real last name of author Erich Maria Remarque. Phonetically, "Remarque" is "Krämer" spelled backward.

Kramer, Joanna

Role for which Meryl Streep won a Best Supporting Actress Academy Award in the 1979 film *Kramer vs. Kramer*.

Kramer, Paul

Beverly Hills police officer slapped by Zsa Zsa Gabor on June 14, 1989, after he pulled over her Rolls-Royce Corniche for having expired license plates. Ms. Gabor, convicted of battery, was sentenced to three days in jail, 120 hours of community service, and paid $13,000 in court costs.

Kramer's Kandy Kitchen

Factory where Lucy Ricardo (Lucille Ball) and Ethel Mertz (Vivian Vance) once worked as chocolate wrappers, in the TV sitcom *I Love Lucy*.

Kramer, Ted

Role for which Dustin Hoffman won a Best Actor Academy Award in the 1979 film *Kramer vs. Kramer*.

Krampe

Real last name of actor Hugh O'Brian.

Krasner, Lee

Role for which Marcia Gay Harden won a Best Supporting Actress Academy Award in the 2000 film *Pollock*.

Krebs, Mary Tomlinson

Real name of actress Marjorie Main.

Kresge Jr., George Joseph

Real name of mentalist The Amazing Kreskin.

Kricfalusi, John

Creator of the animated TV series *The Ren & Stimpy Show*.

Kringle, Kris

Role for which Edmund Gwenn won a Best Supporting Actor Academy Award in the 1947 film *Miracle on 34th Street*.

Krustofsky, Herschel Schmoykel

Real name of Krusty the Clown in the animated TV sitcom *The Simpsons*.

Krypto

Pet dog of Superman.

Kubelsky, Benjamin

Real name of comedian Jack Benny.

"Ku-Ku"

See **"Dance of the Cuckoos"**

Kvack

Family duck in the comic strip *Hägar the Horrible*.

Kwan, Billy

Role for which Linda Hunt won a Best Supporting Actress Academy Award in the 1983 film *The Year of Living Dangerously*.

Kwik-E-Mart

Springfield convenience store in the TV sitcom *The Simpsons*.

Kwolek, Stephanie

DuPont chemist who in 1965 discovered the strong synthetic fiber Kevlar, whose many uses today include radial tires, bulletproof vests and firefighter suits.

Kwong Sang

Real first and middle names of actor Jackie Chan.

Kykuit

Pocantico Hills, New York, estate of John D. Rockefeller, completed in 1913. Its name is Dutch for "lookout."

Kyle, Selina

Real name of Batman adversary Catwoman.

KYOY

Employer of weatherman Harris K. Telemacher (Steve Martin) in the film *L.A. Story*.

Kyril I

The first Russian pope (Anthony Quinn), in the film *The Shoes of the Fisherman*.

Laa-Laa

See **Tinky Winky, Dipsy, Laa-Laa, and Po**

labanotation

Most popular system for notating choreography, introduced by Slovakian dance theorist Rudolf Laban in 1928.

La Belle Aurore

Paris nightclub owned by Rick Blaine (Humphrey Bogart) in the film *Casablanca*.

"Labor omnia vincit"

Motto of the American Federation of Labor, which is Latin for "Work conquers all."

Motto of the University of Illinois.

Lace

Secret Service code name for Jacqueline Kennedy.

La Cock

Real last name of game-show host Peter Marshall, and his sister, actress Joanne Dru.

La Coquette

Hot-air balloon that takes Passepartout (Cantinflas) and Phileas Fogg (David Niven) from Paris to southern Spain in the film *Around the World in 80 Days*.

Ladadog

Pet sheepdog of the Nash family in the TV sitcom *Please Don't Eat the Daisies*.

Laddie Boy

Pet Airedale of President Warren G. Harding.

Ladies' Day

Fashion magazine to which Esther Greenwood wins an internship, in the Sylvia Plath novel *The Bell Jar*.

Ladies Love Cool James

What the letters in the name of rap singer L. L. Cool J (James Todd Smith) stand for.

Ladrone Islands

Former name of the Mariana Islands.

Lady Byng Memorial Trophy

Awarded annually since 1925 to the NHL player "adjudged to have exhibited the best type of sportsmanship and gentlemanly conduct combined with a high standard of playing ability." It is named for the wife of former Canadian Governor General Baron Byng.

"Lady Day"

Nickname of blues singer Billie Holiday.

"The Lady in the Bottle"

Debut episode of the TV sitcom *I Dream of Jeannie*, which aired on September 18, 1965.

Lady Jane

Pet cat of Mr. Krook in the Charles Dickens novel *Bleak House*.

"Lady Madonna"

Theme song of the TV sitcom *Grace Under Fire*, performed by Aretha Franklin.

Lafayette

First name of sci-fi author L. Ron Hubbard.

Middle name of Captain Benjamin Sisko (Avery Brooks) in the TV series *Star Trek: Deep Space Nine*.

Lafayette College vs. Lehigh University

NCAA Division I's longest-running college football rivalry, with 136 games played through the 2000 season. This is 13 games more than the rivalry in second place, Princeton University vs. Yale University.

Lafayette National Park

Original name of Acadia National Park, the first national park east of the Mississippi River. It was given its present name in 1929.

La Femme, Churchy

Turtle friend of the title character in the comic strip *Pogo*.

Lagoon Islands

Former name of the Pacific island nation of Tuvalu.

Lai Choi San

Real name of the Dragon Lady in the comic strip *Terry and the Pirates*.

Laird, Peter

See **Teenage Mutant Ninja Turtles**

Lakeport

Home of the title characters in the Bobbsey Twins series of children's books.

"The Lake Shore Strangler"

Nickname of Charles Lee Ray (Brad Dourif), gunned-down criminal whose soul migrates to a doll named Chucky, in the film *Child's Play*.

Lake Wobegon, Minnesota

See **"Where all the women are strong, all the men are good-looking, and all the children are above average"**

Lakota Sioux, Cheyenne, and Arapaho

Native American tribes that opposed American troops in the Battle of the Little Bighorn, on June 25–26, 1876.

Lamar Hunt Trophy

Awarded annually to the American Football Conference champion. Lamar Hunt was a founder of the American Football League and longtime owner of the Kansas City Chiefs.

Lamarr, Hedley

Harvey Korman's role in the film *Blazing Saddles*.

Lamb and Company

Drug-factory employer of the title character's father in the Booth Tarkington novel *Alice Adams*.

Lamb Chop

See **Charley Horse, Lamb Chop, and Hush Puppy**

Lame Duck

Navy-Curtiss NC-4 Flying Boat that was the first aircraft to make a transatlantic flight, from Trepassey, Newfoundland to Lisbon, Portugal, May 16–27, 1919. The plane, with a crew of six, made numerous stops (landing on the ocean) en route.

Lamm, Herman K. "Baron"

See **Baron Lamm method**

La Motta, Jake

Role for which Robert De Niro won a Best Actor Academy Award in the 1980 film *Raging Bull*.

Lancaster

Middle name of author Ian Fleming.

Original name of Lincoln, Nebraska. The city took its present name when it was made capital of the state in 1867.

Lancaster Auto

Towing service operated by Eddie Sherman (Eddie Griffin) in the TV sitcom *Malcolm & Eddie*.

Lancaster Caramel Company

Successful business owned by Milton Hershey before he entered the chocolate business in 1894. He sold the caramel company in 1900 for $1,000,000 in order to concentrate on his new Hershey Chocolate Company.

Lance

See **Al, Lance, Lars, and Rölf**

Lancer

Secret Service code name for John F. Kennedy.

Lancing

Last name of Boy (Johnny Sheffield) in the Tarzan films.

Landis, Jerry

Stage name used by singer Paul Simon early in his career.

Landon, Margaret

See **Anna and the King of Siam**

Lane, Allan "Rocky"

Retired Western actor who voiced the title equine in the TV sitcom *Mister Ed*.

Lanford, Illinois

Setting of the TV sitcom *Roseanne*.

Langhorne, Irene

Wife of illustrator Charles Dana Gibson and the model for his "Gibson Girl" drawings.

Langley College

School attended by Blair Warner (Lisa Whelchel) in the TV sitcom *The Facts of Life*.

Langston, Murray

Real name of the "Unknown Comic" in the TV series *The Gong Show*. He disguised his identity by wearing a paper bag over his head.

Lanzoni

Last name of Italian model Fabio.

La Paloma

Ship that brings the title object from Hong Kong to San Francisco in the Dashiell Hammett novel *The Maltese Falcon*, and the film adaptation of the same name.

Lapidus, Herbert

Inventor of Odor Eaters shoe deodorizing pads in 1974.

Laputa

Land inhabited by scientific quacks in the Jonathan Swift novel *Gulliver's Travels*.

Lara

Pet dog of President James Buchanan.

Larch, Dr. Wilbur

Role for which Michael Caine won a Best Supporting Actor Academy Award in the 1999 film *The Cider House Rules*.

Largelamb, H. A.

Pen name used by inventor Alexander Graham Bell for articles published in *National Geographic*. The name is an anagram of "A. Graham Bell."

Larkin

Real last name of rock singer Joan Jett.

Larkin, John

See **Brown Beauty**

Larry

Pet German shepherd of Buddy Sorrell (Morey Amsterdam) in the TV sitcom *The Dick Van Dyke Show*.

See also **Vince and Larry**

Larry Love, the Singing Canary

Stage name used by Herbert Khaury before he became famous as Tiny Tim.

Lars

Deceased husband of Phyllis Lindstrom (Cloris Leachman) in the TV sitcom *The Mary Tyler Moore Show* and its spinoff *Phyllis*.

See also **Al, Lance, Lars, and Rölf**

La Salle Jr., Raskin, Pooley, and Crockett

Advertising-agency employer of the title character (Tony Randall) in the film *Will Success Spoil Rock Hunter?*

L-aspartyl L-phenylalanine methyl ester

Full chemical name of artificial sweetener aspartame, aka Nutrasweet.

The Lass That Loved a Sailor

Alternate title of the Gilbert and Sullivan comic opera H.M.S. *Pinafore*.

The Last Gasp

Greasewood City saloon in the film *My Little Chickadee*.

Last Honeymoon and Moonglow

Films starring Blanche Hudson (Joan Crawford) in the film *Whatever Happened to Baby Jane?*

"Last of the Red-Hot Mamas"

Nickname of singer Sophie Tucker.

Lathrop, Dorothy

See **Caldecott Medal**

Latigo, New Mexico

Setting of the TV Western series *Black Saddle*.

Latour, Father Jean Marie

Title character of the Willa Cather novel *Death Comes for the Archbishop*.

latrinophone

Musical instrument consisting of a toilet seat with strings, used by Spike Jones' orchestra.

La Trivia, Mayor

Neighbor of the title characters (Jim and Marion Jordan) in the radio and TV versions of the sitcom *Fibber McGee and Molly*, portrayed by Gale Gordon in the radio version and by Harold Peary on TV.

Latveria

Country ruled by Dr. Doom in the Marvel comics.

laughing jackass

Common name of the Australian kookaburra bird, for its distinctive cry.

"Laughing Water"

What the name "Minnehaha" means. Minnehaha is the love of the title character in the Henry Wadsworth Longfellow poem "The Song of Hiawatha."

Laugh-O-gram Films

First animation company of Walt Disney, in operation from 1922 to 1923.

"The Launching Pad"

Nickname of homer-friendly Atlanta-Fulton County Stadium, former home of the Atlanta Braves.

Laurania

Mythical Mediterranean country that is the setting of *Savrola*, the only novel written by Winston Churchill. The book was published in 1900.

Laurel and Hardy feature films

Pardon Us (1931)
Pack Up Your Troubles (1932)
The Devil's Brother (1933)
Sons of the Desert (1933)
Hollywood Party (1934)
Babes in Toyland (1934)
Bonnie Scotland (1935)
The Bohemian Girl (1936)
Our Relations (1936)
Way Out West (1937)
Pick a Star (1937)
Swiss Miss (1938)
Block-Heads (1938)
The Flying Deuces (1939)
A Chump at Oxford (1940)
Saps at Sea (1940)
Great Guns (1941)
A-Haunting We Will Go (1942)
Air Raid Wardens (1943)
Jitterbugs (1943)
The Dancing Masters (1943)
The Big Noise (1944)
The Bullfighters (1945)
Nothing But Trouble (1945)
Utopia, aka *Atoll K* (1950)

"Laurie"

See **Little Women title characters**

Lavoie, Roland Kent

Real name of pop singer Lobo.

Lawman

Biopic of Wyatt Earp starring Tom Mix (Bruce Willis), on which Earp (James Garner) serves as technical advisor, in the film *Sunset*.

Lawnfield

Home of President James A. Garfield in Mentor, Ohio.

Lawrence and *Niagara*

Successive flagships of Oliver Hazard Perry during the War of 1812's Battle of Lake Erie, where he defeated the English on September 10, 1813.

Lawrence, Captain James

See **Chesapeake**

Lawrence, Frances

Real name of the title character in the *Gidget* series of films and the TV sitcom of the same name.

Lawrence, Joseph

Missouri physician who invented Listerine in 1879, first used as a surgical antiseptic.

Lawrence Peter

Real first and middle names of baseball Hall of Famer Yogi Berra.

Lawrence, Richard

House painter who was the first attempted assassin of a U.S. president. On January 30, 1835, at the Capitol, he fired two pistols at President Andrew Jackson from a distance of only six feet. Both weapons misfired and Jackson was unhurt.

"The Law West of the Pecos"

Nickname of self-styled Western lawman Judge Roy Bean.

Lazy Bones

The first TV remote control, introduced by Zenith in 1950, which was connected to the set by a cable.

See also **Flashmatic**

Lazzaro

Real last name of actress Bernadette Peters.

LDL

See **low-density lipoprotein**

Leakin' Lena

Ship on which Beany travels in the children's animated TV series *Beany and Cecil*.

The Leaky Cauldron

Wizarding pub and boarding house in the Harry Potter series of books by J. K. Rowling.

"Leap Frog"

Theme song of bandleader Les Brown.

"Leapin' lizards!"

Favorite exclamation of the title character in the comic strip *Little Orphan Annie*.

"Learning to Do, Doing to Learn, Earning to Live, Living to Serve"

Motto of the Future Farmers of America.

Leather-Stocking Tales books

Series of five novels by James Fenimore Cooper featuring Natty Bumppo as the main character:

The Pioneers (1823)
The Last of the Mohicans (1826)
The Prairie (1827)
The Pathfinder (1840)
The Deerslayer (1841)

"leave luck to heaven"

What the name of game manufacturer Nintendo means in Japanese. Nintendo was founded in 1907 as a manufacturer of playing cards.

"Leave the driving to us"

Advertising slogan of Greyhound.

Lecomte, Benoit "Ben"

The first person to swim across the Atlantic Ocean. Starting from Hyannis, Massachusetts, on July 16, 1998, he reached Quiberon, France, on September 25, swimming a total of 3,736 nautical miles. A sailboat traveled with him, on which he rested frequently.

Lecter, Hannibal

Role for which Anthony Hopkins won a Best Actor Academy Award in the 1991 film The Silence of the Lambs.

The Ledger

Newspaper employer of the sportswriter title character (Dabney Coleman) in the TV sitcom The Slap Maxwell Story. His column is called Slap Shots.

Led Zeppelin original members

John Bonham, John Paul Jones, Jimmy Page, and Robert Plant.

Leek, Harold

Real name of actor Howard Keel.

"Lee's Fleas"

Nickname of the spectators who follow pro golfer Lee Trevino around the course. The rhyming name is patterned after "Arnie's Army," the followers of Arnold Palmer.

Leff, Pincus

Real name of comedian Pinky Lee.

Lefkosia

Alternate (Greek) name of Nicosia, Cyprus.

The Leftorium

Specialty store for left-handed people owned by Ned Flanders in the animated TV sitcom The Simpsons.

"Legacy"

Debut episode of the TV sitcom Wings, which aired on April 19, 1990.

"A Legend of Man's Hunger in His Youth"

Subtitle of the Thomas Wolfe novel Of Time and the River.

"Leges sine moribus vanae"

Motto of the University of Pennsylvania, which is Latin for "Laws are useless without morals."

Legion of Honor classes

French order of military and civil merit created by Napoleon in 1802. Admission requires either 20 years of peacetime civil achievement, or military bravery in wartime. The Legion's five classes, in descending order:

Grand cross
Grand officer
Commander
Officer
Knight

Leighton University

School attended by the title character (Penny Singleton) in the film Blondie Goes to College.

Leisure, David

See **Isuzu, Joe**

Leitch

Last name of pop singer/songwriter Donovan.

Real last name of actress Ione Skye, who is the daughter of Donovan.

Lektor

Decoding machine stolen from the Russian Embassy in Istanbul by James Bond (Sean Connery) in the film From Russia With Love.

Leland

Middle name of TV anchorman Walter Cronkite.

Leland College

School attended by Alex Keaton (Michael J. Fox) in the TV sitcom Family Ties.

Lemelson, Jerome H.

Professional inventor who created the Walkman, bar code technology, the camcorder, and many other innovative devices. At his death in 1997, his 500+ patents were the third-highest for any individual, behind only Thomas Edison and Polaroid founder Edwin Land.

Lemmon/Matthau films

The films in which Jack Lemmon and Walter Matthau appear together:

The Fortune Cookie (1966)
The Odd Couple (1968)
The Front Page (1974)
Buddy Buddy (1981)
JFK (1991)
Grumpy Old Men (1993)
Grumpier Old Men (1995)
The Grass Harp (1996)
Out to Sea (1997)
The Odd Couple II (1998)

Matthau had the title role in the film *Kotch* (1971), which was directed by Lemmon.

"Lemonade Lucy"

Nickname of Lucy Hayes, wife of U.S. president Rutherford B. Hayes, who did not serve alcoholic beverages in the White House.

Lemo Tomato Juice

Product for which Ginger Szabo (Tammy Lauren) is a radio spokesperson, in the TV series *Homefront*.

Lemuel

First name of the title character in the Jonathan Swift novel *Gulliver's Travels*.

"Lend a hand, care for the land!"

See **Woodsy Owl**

Leningrad

Former name (1924-91) of St. Petersburg, Russia.

Lennon Sisters members

Singing quartet (Dianne, Peggy, Kathy, and Janet) that made regular appearances on *The Lawrence Welk Show* from 1955 to 1968.

Leno, Jay, characters of

As portrayed by Leno on *The Tonight Show*:
Iron Jay (fitness expert)
Mr. Brain ("the smartest man in the universe")
Beyondo (psychic)

Lenox, Lady

See **Patience and Fortitude**

Lentulus Batiatus

Role for which Peter Ustinov won a Best Supporting Actor Academy Award in the 1960 film *Spartacus*.

Leo Astor and Leo Lenox

See **Patience and Fortitude**

Leon

Real first name of jazz cornetist Bix Beiderbecke.

Leon Allen

Real first and middle names of baseball Hall of Famer Goose Goslin.

Leonard

Middle name of actor Paul Newman.

First name of Dr. Gillespie (Raymond Massey), mentor of the title character (Richard Chamberlain) in the TV series *Dr. Kildare*.

See also **Marx Brothers' real names**

Leonardo

Pet cat of Pippo Poppolino (Bob Hope) in the film *Casanova's Big Night*.

Leonard Spencer

Middle names of British statesman Winston Churchill.

Leon Leonwood

First and middle names of catalog merchant L. L. Bean.

Leonov, Alexei

Russian cosmonaut who became the first man to take a spacewalk, outside the *Voskhod 2* spacecraft on March 18, 1965.

Léopoldville

Former name of Kinshasa, Zaire.

lepidopterist

Technical term for an expert in or collector of butterflies.

Lepofsky

Real last name of Ellery Queen co-creator Manfred Lee.

Lerner, George

Inventor of Mr. Potato Head, introduced by Hasbro in 1952.

Leroux, Gaston

French author of the novel *The Phantom of the Opera*, the basis of film productions and the Andrew Lloyd Webber musical of the same name.

Leroy

Real first name of the title character in the Encyclopedia Brown series of children's books by Donald J. Sobol.

Leroy Robert

Real first and middle names of Hall of Fame pitcher Satchel Paige. His nickname came from a former job as a baggage handler.

Leslie

Middle name of actor Errol Flynn.

Lester

Dummy of ventriloquist Willie Tyler, a regular on the TV series *Rowan and Martin's Laugh-In*.

Lester B. Pearson Trophy

Awarded annually since 1971 to the most outstanding NHL player, named for the former Canadian prime minister.

Letitia

Real first name of Buddy Lawrence (Kristy McNichol) in the TV series *Family*.

"Let's be careful out there"

Catchphrase of Sergeant Phil Esterhaus (Michael Conrad), as a reminder to officers at the end of roll call, in the TV series *Hill Street Blues*.

"Let's Dance"

Theme song of the Benny Goodman orchestra.

"Let's get out of here"

Line that is generally agreed to be most frequently spoken sentence in films. It is spoken twice in *Casablanca*, for example.

"Let's kick it up a notch!"

Catchphrase used by TV chef Emeril Lagasse when adding extra spice to his dishes.

"Lets you laugh at the weather"

Advertising slogan of London Fog.

Lettermen original members

Tony Butala, Bob Engemann, and Jim Pike.

A Letter to Five Wives

Novel by John Klempner that was the basis for the film *A Letter to Three Wives*.

"Let the Good Times In"

Demo song that gets the title characters a record contract, in the pilot episode of the TV sitcom *The Partridge Family*. The song was written by Carole Bayer Sager and Neil Sedaka.

"Let There Be Light"

Inscription on the libraries endowed by steel magnate/philanthropist Andrew Carnegie.

"Let Us Have Peace"

Inscription over Grant's Tomb in New York City.

"Let your fingers do the walking"

Advertising slogan of the Yellow Pages.

"Let your light shine"

Translation of the Greek motto of the University of Colorado.

leuconychia

Medical term for the white spots on fingernails caused by minor injury.

leukocytes

Medical term for white blood cells.

Leutze, Emanuel

Painter of *Washington Crossing the Delaware* in 1851.

Levine, Milton

Inventor of the Ant Farm in 1956.

Levitch, Joseph

Real name of comedian Jerry Lewis.

"Levittown"

Original working title of the Billy Joel tune "Allentown."

Levy

Real last name of songwriter Burton Lane.

Lewis, Al

Role for which George Burns won a Best Supporting Actor Academy Award in the 1975 film *The Sunshine Boys*.

Lewis/Martin films

See **Martin/Lewis films**

Lewis Robert

Real first and middle names of baseball Hall of Famer Hack Wilson.

Lewis, Tommy
Reserve Alabama running back in the 1954 Cotton Bowl, who leaped off the sidelines to tackle Rice running back Dicky Moegle, who was headed for an apparent touchdown. Moegle was awarded the touchdown by the officials.

Lexiko
Original name of Scrabble. The game was also called Criss-crosswords before it took its present name.

"Lex praesidium libertatis"
Motto of the Fraternal Order of Police, which is Latin for "Law is the safeguard of freedom."

Libby
Waitress on the cover of the Supertramp album *Breakfast in America*, according to her nametag.

The Liberator
Abolitionist newspaper founded by William Lloyd Garrison in 1831.

"The Liberator"
Nickname of Venezuelan statesman Simón Bolívar.

"Libertas et patria"
Motto of the Sons of the American Revolution, which is Latin for "Liberty and country."

Liberty
Pet golden retriever of President Gerald Ford.

"Liberty Bell March"
Theme song of the TV series *Monty Python's Flying Circus*, composed by John Philip Sousa.

"Liberty cabbage"
Term used by Americans during World War I for sauerkraut.

Liberty Coffee Shop
Employer of waitress Angie Falco Benson (Donna Pescow) in the TV sitcom *Angie*.

Liberty Enlightening the World
Actual name of the Statue of Liberty.

"Liberty, Intelligence, Our Nation's Safety"
Motto of the Lions Club.

"Liberty steaks"
Term used by Americans during World War I for hamburgers.

Libertyville, Pennsylvania
Setting of the Stephen King novel *Christine*.

Libra Parking Only
Street sign seen in the film *L.A. Story*.

librocubicularist
Term for a person who reads in bed, coined by author Christopher Morley in his novel *The Haunted Bookshop*.

Libya Hill
Hometown of George Webber in the Thomas Wolfe novel *You Can't Go Home Again*.

license-plate slogans, past and present
Continents (Africa, Europe, Asia, South America) and countries not listed have no known slogans on their license plates. This list excludes special issues such as environmental, athletic team, one-year commemoratives, etc.

UNITED STATES
Alabama: Heart of Dixie
Alaska: North to the Future; The Great Land; The Last Frontier
Arizona: Grand Canyon State
Arkansas: Opportunity Land; Land of Opportunity; The Natural State
California: The Golden State
Colorado: Colorful
Connecticut: Constitution State
Delaware: The First State
District of Columbia: Nation's Capital; A Capital City; Celebrate & Discover
Florida: Sunshine State
Georgia: Peach State; . . . On My Mind
Hawaii: Aloha; Aloha State
Idaho: Potatoes; Scenic; Vacation Wonderland; World Famous Potatoes; Famous Potatoes
Illinois: Land of Lincoln
Indiana: Heritage State; Hoosier State; Wander; Back Home Again; Hoosier Hospitality; Amber Waves of Grain; The Crossroads of America
Iowa: The Corn State
Kansas: The Wheat State; Midway USA
Kentucky: Bluegrass State
Louisiana: Sportsmen's Paradise; Sportsman's Paradise; Bayou State; LoUiSiAna
Maine: Vacationland
Maryland: Drive Carefully
Massachusetts: The Spirit of America
Michigan: Water Wonderland; Water Winter Wonderland; Great Lake State; Great Lakes
Minnesota: 10,000 Lakes; Explore
Mississippi: The Hospitality State

Missouri: Show-Me State

Montana: The Treasure State; Big Sky Country; Big Sky

Nebraska: The Beef State; Cornhusker State

Nevada: The Silver State

New Hampshire: Scenic; Photoscenic; Live Free or Die; First for Independence

New Jersey: Garden State

New Mexico: Sunshine State; The Land of Enchantment; Land of Enchantment

New York: The Empire State; Empire State

North Carolina: Drive Safely; First in Freedom; First in Flight

North Dakota: Peace Garden State; Discover the Spirit

Ohio: Seat Belts Fastened?; The Heart of It All!; Birthplace of Aviation

Oklahoma: Visit; Is OK!; OK!; Native America

Oregon: Pacific Wonderland

Pennsylvania: Keystone State; You've Got a Friend In; WWW.STATE.PA.US

Rhode Island: Discover; Ocean State

South Carolina: The Iodine State; The Iodine Products State; Smiling Faces, Beautiful Places

South Dakota: Great Faces, Great Places

Tennessee: Volunteer State; Sounds Good to Me

Texas: The Lone Star State

Utah: Center Scenic America; This Is the Place; Ski Utah!; Greatest Snow on Earth

Vermont: Green Mountains; Green Mountain State

Virginia: None

Washington: Evergreen State

West Virginia: Mountain State; Wild, Wonderful

Wisconsin: America's Dairyland

Wyoming: None (silhouette of a cowboy riding a bucking bronco)

UNITED STATES POSSESSIONS

American Samoa: Pago Pago Motu o Fiafiaga (Pago Pago Island of Paradise)

Guam: America's Day Begins In; Hafa Adai (Hello); Hub of the Pacific; Tano y Chamorro (Land of the Chamorros)

Panama Canal Zone: Funnel for World Commerce

Puerto Rico: Isla del Encanto (Island of Enchantment)

U.S. Virgin Islands: Tropical Playground; Vacation Adventure; American Paradise

CANADA

Alberta: Wild Rose Country

British Columbia: Beautiful

Manitoba: Sunny Manitoba, 100,000 Lakes; Friendly

New Brunswick: Picture Province

Newfoundland and Labrador: Canada's Happy Province; A World of Difference

Northwest Territories: Canada's Northland; Explore Canada's Arctic

Nova Scotia: Canada's Ocean Playground

Ontario: Keep It Beautiful; Yours to Discover

Prince Edward Island: Garden Province; The Place to Be . . . In; Seat Belts Save; Home of "Anne of Green Gables"; Birthplace of Confederation; Confederation Bridge

Quebec: La Belle Province (The Beautiful Province); Je Me Souviens (I remember)

Saskatchewan: Wheat Province; Home of the RCMP; Land of Living Skies

Yukon Territory: Land of the Midnight Sun; Home of the Klondike; The Klondike

CARIBBEAN

Aruba: Isla di Carnaval; One Happy Island

Bonaire: Divers Paradise

Curaçao: Bon Bini (Welcome)

Haiti: Perle des Antilles (Pearl of the Antilles)

Saba: Unspoiled Queen

St. Eustatius: The Golden Hook

St. Maarten: Friendly Island

CENTRAL AMERICA

Nicaragua: Libre (Free)

Panama: Paz y Justicia (Peace and Justice); Unidad Hacia el Futuro (Unity Toward the Future)

PACIFIC ISLANDS

Cook Islands: Kia Orana (Welcome)

Northern Mariana Islands: Hafa Adai (Hello)

Okinawa: Keystone of the Pacific

Palau: Charm of Micronesia

Yap: Island of Stone Money; Land of Stone Money

AUSTRALIA

Australian Capital Territory: Canberra, The Nation's Capital; Canberra, Heart of the Nation; Feel the Power of Canberra

New South Wales: The Premier State; The First State; Towards 2000

Northern Territory: Outback Australia; Nature Territory

Queensland: Sunshine State

South Australia: The Festival State

Tasmania: Holiday Isle

Victoria: Nuclear Free State; Garden State; On the Move

Western Australia: State of Excitement; The Golden State

"License to Steele"

Debut episode of the TV series *Remington Steele*, which aired on October 1, 1982.

Lichtenburg

Mythical country that is the setting of the musical *Call Me Madam*.

lickable wallpaper

Fruit-flavored creation of the title character (Gene Wilder) in the film *Willy Wonka and the Chocolate Factory*.

Lido

Real first name of automobile executive Lee Iacocca.

Liebowitz, Jon Stuart

Real name of TV host/comedian Jon Stewart.

Life Among the Lowly

Alternate title of the Harriet Beecher Stowe novel *Uncle Tom's Cabin*.

Life and Stuff

Original working title of the TV sitcom *Roseanne*.

Life as We Know It

Original working title of the TV sitcom *3rd Rock From The Sun*.

"Life at Plumfield with Jo's Boys"

Subtitle of the Louisa May Alcott novel *Little Men*.

Life in the Woods

Alternate title of the Henry David Thoreau book *Walden*.

"A Life in the Woods"

Subtitle of the Felix Salten novel *Bambi*.

Life Is Too Short

1991 autobiography of diminutive actor Mickey Rooney.

Life, The Game of, currency portraits

These faces (all mythical except for the highest two denominations) appear on the play money of the 1960 edition of the Milton Bradley board game:
    $500: Ransom A. Treasure
    $1,000: Basil O. Cash
    $5,000: Cyrus Bonanza
    $10,000: Hesperia Mint
    $20,000: G. I. Luvmoney
    $50,000: Milton Bradley
    $100,000: Art Linkletter Esq. (who endorsed the game)

Life with Mother Superior

Book by Jane Trahey that was the basis for the film *The Trouble with Angels*.

Life Without George

Book by Irene Kampen that was the basis for the TV sitcom *The Lucy Show*.

Lifshitz

Real last name of fashion designer Ralph Lauren.

"Light-Horse Harry"

Nickname of American Revolution hero Henry Lee, for his equestrian skill. He was the father of Civil War Confederate general Robert E. Lee.

"Lighthouse of the Mediterranean"

Nickname of Italian volcano Stromboli.

Lightstorm Entertainment

Production company of director James Cameron.

"The Light that never fails"

Advertising slogan of Metropolitan Life.

Lightyear, Buzz

Space ranger in the animated films *Toy Story* and *Toy Story II*, voiced by Tim Allen.

"Like Father, Like Daughter"

Debut episode of the TV sitcom *Taxi*, which aired on September 12, 1978.

Li'l Folks

Original name of the comic strip *Peanuts*.

Liliane Rudabet Gloria Elsveta

Real first and middle names of actress Leelee Sobieski.

Liliom

Work by Hungarian playwright Ferenc Molnár that was the basis for the Rodgers and Hammerstein musical *Carousel*.

Lillywhite

Middle name of Ed Norton (Art Carney) in the TV sitcom *The Honeymooners*.

Lime, Harry

Title character (Orson Welles) of the film *The Third Man*.

Lincoln-Douglas debate sites

Senatorial candidates Abraham Lincoln and Stephen Douglas visited these seven Illinois cities in their historic debates of 1858:

Ottawa: August 21
Freeport: August 27
Jonesboro: September 15
Charleston: September 18
Galesburg: October 7
Quincy: October 13
Alton: October 15

Lincoln International Airport

Setting of the Arthur Hailey novel *Airport* and the film adaptation of the same name.

Lincoln Prize

$50,000 award presented annually since 1991 by Gettysburg College for the best scholarly work on the Civil War.

Lindencroft

Bridgeport, Connecticut, mansion of showman P. T. Barnum, where he lived in the 1860s.

Lindenwald

Home of President Martin Van Buren in Kinderhook, New York.

Lindley

Real first name of bandleader Spike Jones.

Lindley Jr., Louis Bert

Real name of actor Slim Pickens.

Lindsay, Carmelita

See Mexican Spitfire films

Ling-Ling and Hsing-Hsing

Giant pandas received by the United States from the People's Republic of China in 1972, in exchange for a pair of muskoxen.

Lingvo Internacia

See Esperanto, Doktoro

Link

See Cuff and Link

Lin, Maya

Architect of the Vietnam Veterans Memorial in Washington, D.C., which opened in 1982. Her design, created while a graduate student at Yale University, was selected from over 1,400 submitted as part of a national competition.

"The Lion of Judah"

Nickname of Ethiopian emperor Haile Selassie.

"The Lion of Justice"

Nickname of King Henry I of Great Britain.

"The Lip"

Nickname of outspoken Hall of Fame baseball manager Leo Durocher.

Liparus

Supertanker of Karl Stromberg (Curt Jurgens) that captures English and American submarines in the James Bond film *The Spy Who Loved Me*.

Lipman, Hyman

Inventor of the pencil with attached eraser, patented in 1858.

Lisa Marie

Private jet of singer Elvis Presley, named for his daughter.

"Literary Capital of Alabama"

Nickname of Monroeville, Alabama, hometown of Harper Lee, author of *To Kill a Mockingbird*, as declared by the Alabama state legislature in 1997.

"literary piano"

Nickname of the first typewriter, invented by Christopher Sholes and patented in 1867.

Literary World

Magazine edited by Denis Burlap in the Aldous Huxley novel *Point Counter Point*.

"Littera Scripta Manet"

Motto of the National Archives in Washington, D.C., which is Latin for "The written word endures."

Little Beagle Junior

Pet dog of Senator Lyndon Johnson circa 1960. The initials of the dog's name, as his wife's (Lady Bird) and his daughters' (Lynda Bird and Luci Baines), were the same as the Senator's.

Little Ben

Favorite putter of pro golfer Ben Crenshaw.

Little Bend

Western town that orders Flower Belle Lee (Mae West) to leave, in the film *My Little Chickadee*.

Little Bend, Texas

Hometown of the title character (James Garner) in the TV Western series *Maverick*.

"little boots"
What the name of Roman emperor Caligula means in Latin.

Little Brother
Family dog in the animated film *Mulan.*

"little buddy"
The Skipper's (Alan Hale's) nickname for the title character (Bob Denver) in the TV sitcom *Gilligan's Island.*

"Little Caesar"
Nickname of Harlem Globetrotters founder Abe Saperstein, for his dictatorial demeanor.

"The Little Colonel"
Nickname of baseball Hall of Famer Pee Wee Reese.

"The Little Corporal"
Nickname of Napoleon.

"A little dab'll do ya"
Advertising slogan of Brylcreem hair cream.

Little Dipper School
Elementary school attended by Elroy Jetson (voiced by Daws Butler) in the children's animated TV sitcom *The Jetsons.*

"Little Ellick"
Nickname of Alexander Stephens, vice president of the Confederacy during the Civil War, who weighed less than 100 pounds.

"The Little Flower"
Nickname of New York City mayor Fiorello La Guardia. "Fiorello" is the Italian word for "little flower."

"The Little Giant"
Nickname of 19th-century statesman Stephen Douglas.

Little Hope, New Hampshire
Hometown of Suzanne Stone (Nicole Kidman) in the film *To Die For.*

Little Johnny Jones
1904 Broadway musical that introduced the George M. Cohan tunes "The Yankee Doodle Boy" and "Give My Regards to Broadway."

Little League Pledge
Recited by Little League baseball players before each game:

I trust in God. I love my country and will respect its laws. I will play fair and strive to win. But win or lose I will always do my best.

"Little Mac"
Nickname of Civil War Union general George McClellan.

"Little Miss Dynamite"
Nickname of singer Brenda Lee.

"Little Miss Poker Face"
Nickname of tennis pro Helen Wills Moody.

"Little Miss Sure Shot"
Nickname of sharpshooter Annie Oakley.

"Little Napoleon"
Nickname of Hall of Fame baseball manager John McGraw.

Little Nellie
Minicopter flown by James Bond (Sean Connery) in the film *You Only Live Twice.* It is equipped with heat-seeking air-to-air missiles, flame guns, rocket launchers, machine guns, smoke ejectors, and aerial mines.

Little Oil Drop
One-time cartoon mascot of Esso (Standard Oil of New Jersey).

"The little old winemaker"
See **Stossel, Ludwig**

Little People from Babyland General
Original name of Cabbage Patch Kids dolls.

"A little pig goes a long way"
Slogan used to promote the film *Babe.*

"Little Poison"
Nickname of baseball Hall of Famer Lloyd Waner.

"The Little Professor"
Nickname of bespectacled baseball player Dom DiMaggio, for his scholarly look.

Little Reata
Original name of the oil company owned by Jett Rink (James Dean) in the film *Giant.* He changes the name to Jetexas when threatened with legal action by Bick Benedict (Rock Hudson), owner of Reata Ranch.

Little Salem, Colorado
Hometown of the title character (Orson Welles) in the film *Citizen Kane*.

The Little School
Play that Jack Torrance wants to write at the Overlook Hotel, in the Stephen King novel *The Shining*.

Little Shortcake Fingers
Original name of Hostess Twinkies, coined by its inventor, James Dewar, in 1930.

"A little song, a little dance, a little seltzer down your pants"
Motto of Chuckles the Clown (Mark Gordon, Richard Schaal) in the TV sitcom *The Mary Tyler Moore Show*.

Little Tall, Maine
Setting of the Stephen King novel *Dolores Claiborne*.

Little Texas
Horse ridden by Theodore Roosevelt at the Spanish-American War's Battle of San Juan Hill on July 1, 1898.

The Little Theater off Times Square
New York City setting of the radio series *First Nighter*.

"The Little Three"
Nickname of this group of New England schools: Amherst College, Williams College, and Wesleyan University.

"Little Venice"
What the word "Venezuela" means in Spanish. The country was named in 1499 by Spanish explorers after seeing native villages perched on stilts.

Little White Dove
Love of the title character in the Johnny Preston tune "Running Bear."

Little Women title characters
The March sisters in the Louisa May Alcott novel:
Meg (the oldest): marries John Brooke
Jo: marries Professor Bhaer
Beth: dies of scarlet fever
Amy: marries "Laurie" (Theodore Lawrence)

Livi, Ivo
Real name of actor Yves Montand.

Living Island
Setting of the children's TV series *H. R. Pufnstuf*.

Livingston, Gentry and Mishkin
Ad-agency employer of Kip Wilson (Tom Hanks) and Henry Desmond (Peter Scolari) in the TV sitcom *Bosom Buddies*.

Lizzie Borden High
School that is the setting of the film *National Lampoon's Class Reunion*.

Lizzy
Curtis-Robin monoplane which Douglas "Wrong Way" Corrigan flew from Brooklyn, New York, to Dublin, Ireland, in July 1938.

Llanview
Suburban setting of the TV soap opera *One Life to Live*.

Llewellyn
Middle name of labor leader John L. Lewis.

Lloyd, Earl
First African-American to play in an NBA game, for the Washington Capitols on October 31, 1950.

LMW 28IF
License plate of the Volkswagen on the cover of the 1969 Beatles album *Abbey Road*, which helped fuel the false rumor that Paul McCartney was dead. "LMW" was supposed to have stood for "Linda McCartney Weeps" (Linda was Paul's wife), and "28IF" supposedly indicated that Paul would have been 28 years old had he lived.

Lobo Lounge
Where the title character is employed as a waitress in the TV sitcom *Roseanne*.

Locke/Eastwood films
See **Eastwood/Locke films**

Loco
Horse of Pancho (Leo Carrillo) in the TV series *The Cisco Kid*.

Loggins, Addie
Role for which Tatum O'Neal won a Best Supporting Actress Academy Award in the 1973 film *Paper Moon*.

Logo
Western town that is the setting of the film *High Plains Drifter*.

Lolly Willowes, or The Loving Huntsman
Novel by Sylvia Townsend Warner that was the first selection of the Book of the Month Club, in April 1926.

Loman, Willy
Title character of the Arthur Miller play *Death of a Salesman.*

Lombino, Salvatore
Real name of author Evan Hunter.

Lompoc State Bank
Employer of Egbert Sousé (W. C. Fields) in the film *The Bank Dick.*

Lon, Alice
See **"The Champagne Lady"**

"The Lone Eagle"
Nickname of aviator Charles Lindbergh.

Lonely Mountain
See **Smaug**

"Lonely Room"
Alternate title of "Theme from *The Apartment*," composed by Adolph Deutsch.

Lonely Street
Location of the title establishment in the Elvis Presley tune "Heartbreak Hotel."

The Lone Ranger introduction (TV series)
A fiery horse with the speed of light, a cloud of dust and a hearty "Hi-Yo, Silver!" The Lone Ranger! With his faithful Indian companion Tonto, the daring and resourceful masked rider of the plains led the fight for law and order in the early West. Return with us now to those thrilling days of yesteryear. The Lone Ranger rides again!

The Lone Rangers
See **KPPX**

"Lonesome George"
Nickname of comedian George Gobel.

Lonesome No More
Alternate title of the Kurt Vonnegut novel *Slapstick.*

Longabaugh, Harry
Real name of Western outlaw The Sundance Kid.

Longacre Square
Original name of New York City's Times Square. It was renamed for *The New York Times* when its offices relocated there in 1904.

The Longest Night
Film starring Jane Hudson (Bette Davis), but never released in the U.S., in the film *Whatever Happened to Baby Jane?*

Longmont, Virginia
Headquarters of governmental agency The Shop in the Stephen King novel *Firestarter.*

"long mountain"
What the name of Hawaiian volcano Mauna Loa means in Hawaiian.

Long Road Productions
Production company of actor Jean-Claude Van Damme.

Lonnie
Real first name of country singer Mel Tillis.

"The Look"
Nickname of actress Lauren Bacall.

"Look for the Silver Lining"
1920 Jerome Kern/Bud de Sylva tune that was adapted in the 1970s for the theme song of the International Ladies Garment Workers Union (ILGWU), "Look for the Union Label."

"Look Ma, no cavities!"
Advertising slogan of Crest toothpaste.

"Look sharp! Feel sharp! Be sharp!"
Advertising slogan of Gillette razor blades.

Loophole, J. Cheever
See **Marx, Groucho, roles of**

Looty
Pet Pekingese of Queen Victoria.

Lopez, Larry
Original name of Ricky Ricardo (Desi Arnaz) in the pilot episode of *I Love Lucy.*

Lorbrulgrud
Capital of Brobdingnag in the Jonathan Swift novel *Gulliver's Travels.*

Lord Ligonier

Ship that brings Kunta Kinte (LeVar Burton) to America in the TV miniseries *Roots*.

Lord Nelson

Family dog in the TV sitcom *The Doris Day Show*.

The Lord of the Rings

Fantasy-novel trilogy written by J. R. R. Tolkien:
    The Fellowship of the Ring (1954)
    The Two Towers (1955)
    The Return of the King (1956)
The Hobbit (1937) serves as an introduction to the trilogy, and *The Silmarillion* (published posthumously in 1977) is a prequel to all four previous books.

Lore

Evil brother of android Data in the TV series *Star Trek: The Next Generation*. Both characters are portrayed by Brent Spiner.

Lorene

See **Robert and Lorene**

Lorene, Alma

Role for which Donna Reed won a Best Supporting Actress Academy Award in the 1953 film *From Here to Eternity*.

Lorenzini

Real last name of *Pinocchio* author Carlo Collodi.

Lorne

Real first name of NHL Hall of Fame goalie Gump Worsley.

Los Angeles Sun

Newspaper employer of reporter Tim O'Hara (Bill Bixby) in the TV sitcom *My Favorite Martian*.

Los Angeles Tribune

Newspaper employer of the title character (Edward Asner) in the TV series *Lou Grant*.

Losantiville

Original name of Cincinnati, Ohio.

Lost Forest Game Preserve

Home of the title character in the comic strip *Mark Trail*.

Lost Moon

Book by astronaut James Lovell that was the basis for the film *Apollo 13*.

Loud, John

Inventor of the ballpoint pen, patented in 1888.

Louie

See **Huey, Dewey, and Louie**

Louie and Frankie

Talking lizards in TV commercials for Budweiser beer.

Louie's Sweet Shop

Local hangout in the Bowery Boys (aka Dead End Kids) series of films.

Louis

See **Arthur and Louis**

Louisa

German warship that captures Charlie Allnut (Humphrey Bogart) and Rose Sayer (Katharine Hepburn) in the film *The African Queen*.

Louise

Middle name of Ethel Mertz (Vivian Vance) in the TV sitcom *I Love Lucy*.

Unseen wife of Major Frank Burns (Larry Linville) in the TV sitcom *M*A*S*H*.

Unseen wife of Captain John McIntyre (Wayne Rogers) in the TV sitcom *M*A*S*H*.

"Louisiana Lightning"

Nickname of baseball pitcher Ron Guidry.

Louis Marshall

Real first and middle names of country singer/banjoist Grandpa Jones.

Lou's Cafe

Hill Valley, California, restaurant of 1955 where Marty McFly (Michael J. Fox) first meets his father (Crispin Glover) as a teenager, in the film *Back to the Future*.

Lou's Diner

Lunch hangout of Dagwood Bumstead in the comic strip *Blondie*.

Lou's Safari Club

Nightclub employer of cocktail waitress-turned-diplomat Sunny Davis (Goldie Hawn) in the film *Protocol*.

"Love and Marriage"

Theme song of the TV sitcom *Married . . . with Children*, performed by Frank Sinatra.

"Love and the Happy Days"

Segment of the TV series *Love, American Style* that was the basis for the TV sitcom *Happy Days*.

Love Bandit

First car of Richie Cunningham (Ron Howard), a 1952 red Ford convertible, in the TV sitcom *Happy Days*.

Love, Buddy

Ultra-cool alter ego of nerdy Julius Kelp (Jerry Lewis) in the 1963 version of the film *The Nutty Professor*. Buddy Love is also the name of Eddie Murphy's character in the 1996 version; his nerdy counterpart is named Sherman Klump.

The Love Bug (Herbie) films

The Love Bug (1969)
Herbie Rides Again (1974)
Herbie Goes to Monte Carlo (1977)
Herbie Goes Bananas (1980)

LoVecchio

Real last name of singer Frankie Laine.

"Lovee"

Instrumental theme of the TV game show *The Gong Show*.

"Love in Bloom"

Theme song of comedian Jack Benny.

Love Insurance

Novel by Earl Derr Biggers that was the basis for the Abbott and Costello film *One Night in the Tropics*.

"Love Is All Around"

Theme song of the TV sitcom *The Mary Tyler Moore Show*.

"Love Is Here to Stay"

Last tune composed by George Gershwin, for the 1938 film *The Goldwyn Follies*.

Lovelace, Eva

Role for which Katharine Hepburn won a Best Actress Academy Award in the 1933 film *Morning Glory*.

Loveless, Dr. Miguelito

Diminutive arch-nemesis of James T. West (Robert Conrad) in the TV series *The Wild Wild West*, portrayed by Michael Dunn.

Lovely

See **film awards, national**

"Love means never having to say you're sorry"

Line spoken by Jenny Barrett (Ali MacGraw) to her husband Oliver (Ryan O'Neal) in the film *Love Story*.

Line spoken by Judy Maxwell (Barbra Streisand) to Howard Bannister (Ryan O'Neal) at the end of the film *What's Up, Doc?*, which was released two years after O'Neal's appearance in *Love Story*. Bannister (O'Neal) replies, "That's the dumbest thing I ever heard."

"The Love Nest"

Theme song of radio and TV shows of George Burns and Gracie Allen.

"Lover Doll"

Rita Marlowe's (Jayne Mansfield's) nickname for the title character (Tony Randall) in the film *Will Success Spoil Rock Hunter?*

Love Spell Entertainment

Production company of actress Jennifer Love Hewitt.

"Love Train" locales

As mentioned in the O'Jays tune (in order):
England
Russia
China
Africa
Egypt
Israel

Lovin' Spoonful original members

Steve Boone, Joe Butler, John Sebastian, and Zal Yanovsky.

low-density lipoprotein

What "LDL," medical term for "bad" cholesterol, stands for.

Lowe, Edward

Inventor of Kitty Litter in 1947.

Löwenstein, László

Real name of actor Peter Lorre.

Lower Canada

Former name (1791–1841) of the province of Quebec, Canada.

Lowery Real Estate

Phoenix employer of Marion Crane (Janet Leigh) in the Alfred Hitchcock film *Psycho*.

Lowood

Boarding school attended by the title character of the Charlotte Brontë novel *Jane Eyre*.

"Low prices are just the beginning"

Advertising slogan of the Home Depot retail chain.

Lowry Air Force Base

Denver, Colorado site that housed the U.S. Air Force Academy from 1955 to 1958, when its current site in Colorado Springs was opened.

Lozupone

Maiden name of Carla Tortelli (Rhea Perlman) in the TV sitcom *Cheers*.

Lucas, Victoria

Pen name under which author Sylvia Plath originally published her novel *The Bell Jar*.

Luciani, Albino

Real name of Pope John Paul I, who served for 34 days in 1978.

Lucifer

First name of Pappy Yokum in the comic strip *Li'l Abner*.

Smug cat in the Disney animated film *Cinderella*.

Lucille

Gibson guitar of blues singer B. B. King.

Lucky

Pet dog of Ed Norton (Art Carney) in the TV sitcom *The Honeymooners*.

Family dog of the de Marcos (Michelle Pfeiffer, Alec Baldwin) in the film *Married to the Mob*.

Lucky Bag

Yearbook of the United States Naval Academy. "Lucky bag" is a nautical term for a ship's lost and found.

Lucky Charms original shapes

This General Mills children's cereal first appeared in 1964 with these shapes: pink hearts, yellow moons, orange stars, and green clovers.

Lucky Dan

Horse on which Doyle Lonnegan (Robert Shaw) mistakenly bets to win rather than to place, thus losing $500,000, in the film *The Sting*. He misinterprets the deliberately ambiguous telephone instruction "Place it on Lucky Dan."

Lucky Errand Bar and Grill

Pittsburgh establishment where James Leeds (William Hurt) worked as a bartender before becoming a speech teacher, in the film *Children of a Lesser God*.

The Lucky Liz

Aircraft that crashed in New Mexico on March 22, 1958, killing film producer Michael Todd, husband of actress Elizabeth Taylor.

Lucky Nugget

Saloon owned by Sam Trimble (Harry Guardino) in the film *The Adventures of Bullwhip Griffin*.

Lucrezia Borgia

Buffalo gun of Buffalo Bill Cody.

Ludlow, Maine

Setting of the Stephen King novel *Pet Sematary*.

Luellen, Lawrence

Inventor of the vending machine in 1908. The first vending machine dispensed water into a paper cup for a penny. The "Luellen Cup & Water Vendor" was the basis for what would eventually become the Dixie Cup company.

"Die Luft der Freiheit weht"

Motto of Stanford University, which is German for "The wind of freedom blows."

Lugosi, Bela

Role for which Martin Landau won a Best Supporting Actor Academy Award in the 1994 film *Ed Wood*.

Luke the Drifter

Pseudonym used by country singer Hank Williams.

Lula

Real first name of author (Lula) Carson McCullers.

Lulamae

Real first name of Holly Golightly (Audrey Hepburn) in the film *Breakfast at Tiffany's*.

"Lullaby of Birdland"

Theme song of jazz pianist George Shearing.

Lulu

Name of a gazelle described by author Isak Dinesen in her book *Out of Africa*.

Childhood pet dog of Ed Norton (Art Carney) in the TV sitcom *The Honeymooners*.

Lulubelle

Tank commanded by Sergeant Joe Gunn (Humphrey Bogart) in the film *Sahara*.

Lumberton

Setting of the film *Blue Velvet*.

Lum Ding's

Manhattan Chinese restaurant visited by Fran Kubelik and J. D. Sheldrake in the musical *Promises, Promises*.

Lumiere

Candlestick character (voiced by Jerry Orbach) in the Disney animated film *Beauty and the Beast*.

lunula

Scientific name for the small pale area at the base of fingernails.

Lusitania

Ancient Roman name for Portugal, for which the English ocean liner, sunk in 1915, was named.

Lutetia

Ancient Roman name for Paris, France.

Luther

Middle name of Colin Powell.

"Lux et lex"

Motto of the University of North Dakota, which is Latin for "Light and law."

"Lux et veritas"

Motto of Yale University, which is Latin for "Light and truth."

"Lux libertas"

Motto of the University of North Carolina, which is Latin for "Light and liberty."

"Lux sit"

Motto of the University of Washington, which is Latin for "Let there be light."

LV-246

Planet where the humans are wiped out, in the film *Aliens*.

Lycurgus, New York

Setting of the Theodore Dreiser novel *An American Tragedy*.

Lyle and Talbot

Bert's pet goldfish in the children's TV series *Sesame Street*.

Lyman

First name of author L. Frank Baum.

Lyman, William W.

Inventor of the familiar rotating-wheel mechanical can opener, introduced in 1870.

See also **Warner, Ezra J.**

Lynn

Real first name of Hall of Fame baseball pitcher (Lynn) Nolan Ryan.

First name of the title character (Christopher Hewett) in the TV sitcom *Mr. Belvedere*.

Lynn, Loretta

Role for which Sissy Spacek won a Best Actress Academy Award in the 1980 film *Coal Miner's Daughter*.

Lyon Estates

Neighborhood of Hill Valley, California, that is home to the McFly family of 1985 in the *Back to the Future* films.

Lyric

Secret Service code name for Caroline Kennedy.

"A Lyrical Drama in Four Acts"

Subtitle of the Percy Shelley poem *Prometheus Unbound*.

Lythion

Home planet of the title character (Jane Fonda) in the film *Barbarella*.

Ma and Pa Kettle films
Series starring Marjorie Main and Percy Kilbride as the title characters, following their successful appearance in the film *The Egg and I* (1947):
Ma and Pa Kettle (1949)
Ma and Pa Kettle Go to Town (1950)
Ma and Pa Kettle Back on the Farm (1951)
Ma and Pa Kettle at the Fair (1952)
Ma and Pa Kettle on Vacation (1953)
Ma and Pa Kettle at Home (1954)
Ma and Pa Kettle at Waikiki (1955)
The Kettles in the Ozarks (1956)*
The Kettles on Old Macdonald's Farm (1957)**
* Pa Kettle does not appear in this film
** Pa Kettle portrayed by Parker Fennelly

Macaroni
Pet pony of Caroline Kennedy while living in the White House. The pony was a gift from Vice President Lyndon Johnson.

Macavity Awards
Presented annually since 1987 by Mystery Readers International for outstanding mystery writing. They are named for the "mystery cat" in T. S. Eliot's *Old Possum's Book of Practical Cats*.

MacBride Aircraft
Employer of riveter Kay Walsh (Goldie Hawn) in the film *Swing Shift*.

Mac Carthy, Cormac
See "**Cormac Mac Carthy *fortis me fieri fecit*, A.D. 1446**"

MacCready, Paul
See **Gossamer Condor**

MacDonald, Anson
Pen name used by author Robert A. Heinlein.

MacDonald/Eddy films
The films in which Jeanette MacDonald and Nelson Eddy appear together:
Naughty Marietta (1935)
Rose-Marie (1936)
Maytime (1937)

Sweethearts (1938)
The Girl of the Golden West (1938)
New Moon (1940)
Bitter Sweet (1940)
I Married an Angel (1942)

Macdonald, Sir John Alexander
Scottish-born politician who served as the first prime minister of the Dominion of Canada from 1867 to 1873.

Macdougal
Pet frog of Madison High biology teacher Philip Boynton (Robert Rockwell) in the TV sitcom *Our Miss Brooks*.

Macedonia
Steamship commanded by Death Larsen in the Jack London novel *The Sea Wolf*.

Mace, Nancy Ruth
First woman to graduate from military college The Citadel, magna cum laude in business administration in 1999.

Mach 5
Car of the title character in the children's animated TV series *Speed Racer*.

Machine, Frankie
Title character of the Nelson Algren novel *The Man with the Golden Arm*, portrayed in the film adaptation of the same name by Frank Sinatra.

Macho Grande
Where Navy pilot Ted Stryker (Robert Hays) flies an ill-fated bombing mission, in the film *Airplane!*

Mackenzie
Laugh track machine used by many TV shows to provide canned laughter.

Mackintosh, Elizabeth
Real name of mystery writer Josephine Tey.

MacLeod, Connor
Title character (Christopher Lambert) of the film *Highlander*. In the TV-series adaptation of the same

name, the title character, Duncan MacLeod, is portrayed by Adrian Paul.

MacMillan Toy Company

Employer of Josh Baskin (Tom Hanks) in the film *Big*.

Macondo

Village that is the setting of the Gabriel García Márquez novel *One Hundred Years of Solitude*.

MacTavish, Craig

Last NHL player to be permitted to play without a helmet. The NHL mandated the wearing of helmets for the 1979–80 season, but NHL veterans who had not worn them previously were exempt. MacTavish retired in 1997, and was never seriously hurt.

Madame

Saucy senior-citizen puppet of ventriloquist Wayland Flowers.

Madame Ruth

Fortuneteller "with the gold-capped tooth" in the tune "Love Potion No. 9," performed most notably by The Clovers and The Searchers.

Madame X

RCA Victor's code name for the 45 RPM record, introduced in January 1949.

"Mad Dog"

Nickname of prison escapee Roy Earle (Humphrey Bogart) in the film *High Sierra*.

"Made from the best stuff of Earth"

Advertising slogan of Snapple beverages.

"Made it, Ma! Top of the world!"

Last words of gangster Cody Jarrett (James Cagney) in the film *White Heat*.

Madeleinegasse

Bohemian village that is the setting of the Franz Kafka novel *The Castle*.

Madguy Films

Production company of Madonna.

Madison

Name adopted by the mermaid (Daryl Hannah) after reading a Madison Avenue street sign, in the film *Splash*.

"The Mad Magpies"

Nickname of the title characters in the children's animated TV series *Heckle and Jeckle*, voiced by Frank Welker.

magazines' first issues

American Heritage: September 1949
Atlantic Monthly: November 1857
Boys' Life: March 1911
Business Week: September 7, 1929
Consumer Reports: May 1936
Cosmopolitan: March 1886
Discover: October 1980
Ebony: November 1945
Esquire: Autumn 1933
Field and Stream: August 1873
Fortune: February 1930
Games: September/October 1977
George: October/November 1995 (cover: Cindy Crawford)
Good Housekeeping: May 2, 1885
Gourmet: January 1941
Harper's: June 1850
Highlights for Children: June 1946
Jack and Jill: November 1938
Junior Scholastic: September 18, 1937
Ladies' Home Journal: December 1883
Life: November 23, 1936 (cover: Fort Peck Dam, Montana)
Look: January 1937
Mad: October/November 1952
McCall's: September 1897
The Nation: July 6, 1865
Modern Maturity: October/November 1958
Money: October 1972
Motor Trend: September 1949
Ms.: July 1972
National Geographic: October 1888
National Lampoon: April 1970
New York: April 8, 1968
The New Yorker: February 21, 1925
Newsweek: February 17, 1933
Omni: October 1978
People: March 4, 1974 (cover: Mia Farrow)
Playboy: December 1953 (cover: Marilyn Monroe)
Playgirl: January 1973
Popular Science: May 1872
Premiere: July/August 1987 (cover: Dan Aykroyd and Tom Hanks)
Psychology Today: May 1967
Reader's Digest: February 1922
Redbook: September 1903
Road and Track: June 1947
Rolling Stone: November 9, 1967 (cover: John Lennon)
Saturday Evening Post: August 5, 1821
Scientific American: August 28, 1845
Smithsonian: April 1970
Spin: May 1985 (cover: Madonna)

Sport: September 1946 (cover: Joe DiMaggio and Joe DiMaggio, Jr.)

The Sporting News: March 17, 1886

Sports Illustrated: August 16, 1954 (cover: Ed Mathews)

Sunset: May 1898

Time: March 3, 1923 (cover: Joseph G. Cannon, Republican congressman from Illinois)

TV Guide: April 3, 1953 (cover: Desiderio Alberto Arnaz IV, aka Desi Arnaz Jr., and Lucille Ball)

Us: May 3, 1977 (cover: Paul Newman)

Variety: December 16, 1905

Vogue: December 17, 1892

Woman's Day: October 7, 1937

Magee, Carl

Inventor of the parking meter, first used in 1935 in Oklahoma City, Oklahoma.

Maggie

Pet bulldog of author Truman Capote.

Maggio, Angelo

Role for which Frank Sinatra won a Best Supporting Actor Academy Award in the 1953 film *From Here to Eternity*.

Magic 8-Ball messages

THE 20 ANSWERS FOUND ON THE ICOSAHEDRON (20-SIDED FIGURE) INSIDE.

As I see it, yes.
Ask again later.
Better not tell you now.
Cannot predict now.
Concentrate and ask again.
Don't count on it.
It is certain.
It is decidedly so.
Most likely.
My reply is no.
My sources say no.
Outlook not so good.
Outlook good.
Reply hazy, try again.
Signs point to yes.
Very doubtful.
Without a doubt.
Yes.
Yes—definitely.
You may rely on it.

Magic Dunkers

Variety of Oreo cookies, introduced in 2000, that creates blue swirls of milk when dunked.

"The Magician of Iron"

Nickname of French engineer Alexandre Gustave Eiffel.

Magic in Mexico and *Witchcraft Around Us*

Books written by Sidney Redlitch in the John Van Druten play *Bell, Book and Candle*.

Magic Screen

Original name of Etch-a-Sketch.

"The magic that changes moods"

1940s advertising slogan for Wurlitzer jukeboxes.

magnesium sulfate

Chemical name of Epsom salt.

Magnetic Resonance Imaging

What the letters in the medical term "MRI" stand for.

"The Magnificent Bribe"

Debut episode of the TV series *Mr. Lucky*, which aired on October 24, 1959.

The Magnificent Seven title characters

Bernardo O'Reilly (Charles Bronson)
Chris Adams (Yul Brynner)
Chico (Horst Buchholz)
Britt (James Coburn)
Harry Luck (Brad Dexter)
Vin (Steve McQueen)
Lee (Robert Vaughn)

Bronson is the only actor to also portray one of the title characters of *The Dirty Dozen*.

The Magnificent Stranger

Original working title of the Clint Eastwood film *A Fistful of Dollars*.

Magnolio

Arabian stallion of George Washington while he was president of the United States.

Magpie and Stump

Tavern hangout of the law clerks in the Charles Dickens novel *The Life and Adventures of Nicholas Nickleby*.

Mag's Diversions

Original working title of the Charles Dickens novel *David Copperfield*.

Maguire, Sean

Role for which Robin Williams won a Best Supporting Actor Academy Award in the 1997 film *Good Will Hunting*.

"The Mahatma"

Nickname of Hall of Fame baseball executive Branch Rickey, most remembered for signing Jackie Robinson to his first major-league contract with the Brooklyn Dodgers.

Maher-shal-al-hash-baz

Son of Isaiah, whose name (at 18 letters) is the longest found in the King James Version of the Bible.

Mahon, Christy

Title character of the J. M. Synge play *The Playboy of the Western World.*

Mahoney, Breathless

Sultry singer (Madonna) in the film *Dick Tracy* (1990).

Maid of the Mist

Boat that gives tourists a close-up view of Niagara Falls.

"Maintain the right"

Motto of the Royal Canadian Mounted Police.

Maisie films

Starring Ann Sothern in the title role:
Maisie (1939)
Congo Maisie (1940)
Gold Rush Maisie (1940)
Maisie Was a Lady (1941)
Ringside Maisie (1941)
Maisie Gets Her Man (1942)
Swing Shift Maisie (1943)
Maisie Goes to Reno (1944)
Up Goes Maisie (1946)
Undercover Maisie (1947)

Maitland

Middle name of actor James Stewart.

Majestic-12

Secret government agency in the TV series *Dark Skies.*

Major Chord

New York City nightclub owned by Jimmy Doyle (Robert De Niro) in the film *New York, New York.*

"Make it so"

Catchphrase of Captain Jean-Luc Picard (Patrick Stewart) in the TV series *Star Trek: The Next Generation.*

Make Room! Make Room!

Novel by Harry Harrison that was the basis for the film *Soylent Green.*

"Making Our Dreams Come True"

Theme song of the TV sitcom *Laverne and Shirley,* performed by Cyndi Grecco.

Malamute Saloon

Setting of the Robert Service poem "The Shooting of Dan McGrew."

Maleficent

Wicked fairy in the Disney animated film *Sleeping Beauty.*

"male name" actresses

Listed below with notable films or TV series they have appeared in:
Drew Barrymore (real first name Andrew)
Glenn Close *(Fatal Attraction)*
Mel Harris *(thirtysomething)*
Cecil Hoffmann *(L.A. Law)*
James King *(Happy Campers)*
Michael Learned *(The Waltons)*
Carey Lowell *(Licence to Kill)*
Christopher Norris *(Trapper John, M.D.)*
Gene Tierney *(Laura)*
Sean Young *(No Way Out)*
In addition, Jerry Hall (model, ex-wife of Mick Jagger), Joey Heatherton (singer) and Stevie Nicks (singer) are female celebrities not primarily known for their acting.

Malice Domestic

See **Agatha Awards**

"Malihini Holiday"

Debut episode of the TV series *Hawaiian Eye,* which aired on October 7, 1959.

Mallahan

Middle name of novelist James M. Cain.

Mallory, George (1886–1924)

English mountaineer, who, when asked why he wanted to climb Mount Everest, replied "Because it is there."

Malloy, Terry

Role for which Marlon Brando won a Best Actor Academy Award in the 1954 film *On the Waterfront.*

Malone, James
Role for which Sean Connery won a Best Supporting Actor Academy Award in the 1987 film *The Untouchables.*

Malpaso Productions
Production company of actor/director Clint Eastwood.

Malsenior
Middle name of writer Alice Walker.

"Maluna ae o na lahui a pau ke ola ke kanaka"
Motto of the University of Hawaii, which is Hawaiian for "Above all nations is humanity."

Malvinas
Spanish name of the Falkland Islands.

Mama Magadini's Spicy Meat Balls
Product featured in the memorable 1970 "Mamma mia, that's a spicy meat ball" TV commercial-within-a-commercial for Alka-Seltzer.

Mamas & the Papas original members
"Mama" Cass Elliot, Denny Doherty, John Phillips, and Michelle Phillips.

"The Mama Who Came to Dinner"
Debut episode of the TV sitcom *Family Matters,* which aired on September 22, 1989.

Mamma Leoni's
Italian-restaurant birthplace of the title character in the comic strip *Garfield.*

Mammy
Role for which Hattie McDaniel won a Best Supporting Actress Academy Award in the 1939 film *Gone with the Wind.*

"A Man About the House"
Debut episode of the TV sitcom *Three's Company,* which aired on March 15, 1977.

"Man and His World"
Theme of Expo 67, the Montreal world's fair of 1967.

"The Manassa Mauler"
Nickname of boxer Jack Dempsey. Manassa, Colorado was Dempsey's birthplace.

La Manche
French name of the English Channel, which literally means "the sleeve."

Manderley
Cornwall estate that is the home of the title character in the Daphne du Maurier novel *Rebecca.*

Mandrake Falls, Vermont
Home of the title character (Gary Cooper) in the Frank Capra film *Mr. Deeds Goes to Town.*

Manfred
Oldest of the Marx Brothers, who died before his first birthday.

See also **Mighty Manfred the Wonder Dog**

The Man from Mars
Original working title of the Robert A. Heinlein novel *Stranger in a Strange Land.*

Mangel
Real last name of mime Marcel Marceau.

Manhattan Melodrama
Clark Gable film watched by bank robber John Dillinger at Chicago's Biograph Theatre on July 22, 1934, before being gunned down by FBI agents outside.

"Manhattan Melodrama"
See **"Bad in Every Man"**

Manicotti, Mrs.
Neighbor of the Kramdens in the TV sitcom *The Honeymooners,* portrayed by Zamah Cunningham.

"The Man in Black"
Nickname of country singer Johnny Cash.

"Man in the Space Age"
Theme of the Seattle World's Fair of 1962.

"A man may be down, but he's never out"
Slogan of the Salvation Army.

Manners
Butler in TV commercials for Kleenex napkins, portrayed by Dick Cutting.

Manny Award
Presented to inductees of the Nashville Songwriters Hall of Fame in Nashville, Tennessee. The name is short for "manuscript."

"Man of 10,000 Sound Effects"
Nickname of actor Michael Winslow, for his ability to mimic familiar sounds, most notably in the *Police Academy* series of films.

"Man of a Thousand Faces"
Nickname of actor Lon Chaney Sr.

"Man of a Thousand Voices"
Nickname of Mel Blanc, who provided the voices for most of the characters in Warner Bros. cartoons from the 1930s to the 1980s.

"A Man of Our Times"
Debut episode of the TV sitcom *Arli$$*, which aired on August 10, 1996.

"man of steel"
See **Dzugashvili**

"The Man of Steel"
Nickname of Superman.

"man of the forest"
What the word "orangutan" means in pidgin Malay.

Man of the House
1987 autobiography of former speaker of the House Tip O'Neill.

Manor Farm
Setting of the George Orwell novel *Animal Farm*.

Mansion House
Greasewood City hotel where Flower Belle Lee (Mae West) and Cuthbert J. Twillie (W. C. Fields) stay, in the film *My Little Chickadee*.

Manta III
Jake Bonner's (Steve Guttenberg's) boat in the film *Cocoon*.

Manuel
Role for which Spencer Tracy won a Best Actor Academy Award in the 1937 film *Captains Courageous*.

"The Man Who Was Death," "And All Through the House," and "Dig That Cat . . . He's Real Gone"
Debut episodes of the TV series *Tales from the Crypt*, which aired on June 10, 1989.

"Man, woman, birth, death, infinity"
Words spoken by Dr. Zorba (Sam Jaffe) at the beginning of each episode of the TV series *Ben Casey*.

"The Man You Love to Hate"
Nickname of actor Erich Von Stroheim, for his many villainous roles.

Manzini, Captain Bernard
Antique-car collector (Avery Schreiber) who is perpetually scheming to acquire Dave Crabtree's (Jerry Van Dyke's) 1928 Porter, in the TV sitcom *My Mother the Car*.

Mapother IV, Thomas Cruise
Real name of actor Tom Cruise.

Maquis Mouse
Speedboat that takes John Robie (Cary Grant) from Nice to Cannes, in the Alfred Hitchcock film *To Catch a Thief*.

Marbles
See **Snoopy's brothers and sisters**

Marbles, Jessica
Amateur sleuth (Elsa Lanchester) in the film *Murder By Death*. Her name is inspired by Dame Agatha Christie's Jane Marple.

Marcel
Pet monkey of Ross Geller (David Schwimmer) in the TV sitcom *Friends*.

Marching Along
1928 autobiography of march composer John Philip Sousa.

"The March King"
Nickname of composer John Philip Sousa.

"The March of Trivia"
Recurring segment on Fred Allen's radio show.

Mare Nostrum
Ancient Roman name of the Mediterranean Sea, which means "our sea."

Mare's Leg
Sawed-off rifle of bounty hunter Josh Randall (Steve McQueen) in the TV Western series *Wanted: Dead or Alive*.

Margalo
Bird friend of the title character in the E. B. White novel *Stuart Little*.

Margaret
Real first name of country singer (Margaret) LeAnn Rimes.

First name of the title character in the Oscar Wilde play *Lady Windermere's Fan*.

Maria de Lourdes Villiers

Real first and middle names of actress Mia Farrow.

Marie

Real first name of pop singer (Marie) Dionne Warwick.

Mariel Margaret

Real first and middle names of soccer star Mia Hamm.

Marilyn Pauline

Real first and middle names of actress Kim Novak.

Marina

Bridgeport, Connecticut, mansion of showman P. T. Barnum, where he lived from 1888 until his death in 1891.

Marion

Real first name of tennis pro Tony Trabert.

Middle name of Frank Burns (Larry Linville) in the TV sitcom *M*A*S*H*.

Marion Gordon

Real first and middle names of evangelist Pat Robertson.

Maris

Unseen wife of Niles Crane (David Hyde Pierce) in the TV sitcom *Frasier*.

Mark VII Ltd.

Production company of *Dragnet* star Jack Webb.

Market Security Bank & Trust

Manhattan employer of Sam Wheat (Patrick Swayze) in the film *Ghost*.

"The Marks Brothers"

Nickname of 1980s Miami Dolphins wide receivers Mark Clayton and Mark Duper, favorite targets of quarterback Dan Marino.

Marks, Johnny

See **May, Robert**

Marky

Cartoon boy in TV commercials for Maypo cereal, who utters the memorable line, "I want my Maypo!"

Marlais

Middle name of poet Dylan Thomas.

Marrener, Edythe

Real name of actress Susan Hayward.

Marriage: A Fraud and a Failure

Book, known as The Bachelor's Bible, written by Mortimer Brewster (Cary Grant) in the film *Arsenic and Old Lace*.

Marriage, Divorce and Selfhood

Book written by Jill Davis (Meryl Streep), ex-wife of Isaac Davis (Woody Allen), in the film *Manhattan*.

Marrix

Original family surname of the Marx Brothers. It was changed to Marx by their father Sam.

Mars and Murrie

What the letters in the name of M&Ms chocolate candies stand for. Forrest Mars and R. Bruce Murrie were the original partners in the M&Ms business.

Marsden

Last name of the lead singer of rock group Gerry and the Pacemakers.

Marsden, Julie

Role for which Bette Davis won a Best Actress Academy Award in the 1938 film *Jezebel*.

Marsden, Lucy

Title character of the Allan Gurganus novel *Oldest Living Confederate Widow Tells All*.

Marshal

Horse of Matt Dillon (James Arness) in the TV Western series *Gunsmoke*.

Marshall, Carly

Role for which Jessica Lange won a Best Actress Academy Award in the 1994 film *Blue Sky*.

Marshall High

School attended by the Thatcher children in the TV series *Life Goes On*.

Marston

Middle name of magazine publisher Hugh Hefner.

Marston, William Moulton

Creator of Wonder Woman, who first appeared in the December 1941 issue of *All Star Comics*. Marston was the inventor of the systolic blood-pressure test, which led to the creation of the polygraph.

Martha

Name of the last surviving passenger pigeon, who died in the Cincinnati Zoo on September 1, 1914.

Role for which Elizabeth Taylor won a Best Actress Academy Award in the 1966 film *Who's Afraid of Virginia Woolf?*

Pet sheepdog of former Beatle Paul McCartney.

Marthasville

Former name of Atlanta, Georgia.

Martin

Real first name of former Canadian prime minister (Martin) Brian Mulroney.

First name of the title character in the Sinclair Lewis novel *Arrowsmith.*

Former married name of Carol Brady (Florence Henderson) in the TV sitcom *The Brady Bunch.*

Martin, Dean

Dean of Grand Lakes College in the film *Back to School*, portrayed by Ned Beatty.

Martin/Lewis films

The films in which Dean Martin and Jerry Lewis appear together:
    My Friend Irma (1949)
    My Friend Irma Goes West (1950)
    At War with the Army (1950)
    That's My Boy (1951)
    Sailor Beware (1951)
    Jumping Jacks (1952)
    Road to Bali (1952)*
    The Stooge (1953)
    Scared Stiff (1953)
    The Caddy (1953)
    Money from Home (1953)
    Living It Up (1954)
    Three Ring Circus (1954)
    You're Never Too Young (1955)
    Artists and Models (1955)
    Pardners (1956)
    Hollywood or Bust (1956)
    * Martin and Lewis have cameo roles in this film

Martin, Luke

Role for which Jon Voight won a Best Actor Academy Award in the 1978 film *Coming Home.*

"The Martin Poster"

Debut episode of the TV Western series *Wanted: Dead or Alive*, which aired on September 6, 1958.

Marty Moose

See **Walley World**

Marvin

Real first name of playwright (Marvin) Neil Simon.

Last name of the title character (Pearl White) in the film serial *The Perils of Pauline* (1914).

Marvin Berry and the Starlighters

Band playing at the Enchantment Under the Sea Dance in the film *Back to the Future.* Marvin (Harry Waters Jr.) is the fictional cousin of rock singer Chuck Berry.

Marx Brothers' real names

    Chico: Leonard
    Groucho: Julius Henry
    Gummo: Milton
    Harpo: Adolph (changed to Arthur)
    Zeppo: Herbert

Marx, Groucho, roles of

Marx's humorous-sounding film-role names:
    Professor Quincy Adams Wagstaff: *Horse Feathers* (1932)
    Rufus T. Firefly: *Duck Soup* (1933)
    Otis B. Driftwood: *A Night at the Opera* (1935)
    Dr. Hugo Z. Hackenbush: *A Day at the Races* (1937)
    J. Cheever Loophole: *At the Circus* (1939)
    S. Quentin Quale: *Go West* (1940)
    Wolf J. Flywheel: *The Big Store* (1941)
    Ronald Kornblow: *A Night in Casablanca* (1946)
    Lionel Q. Deveraux: *Copacabana* (1947)
    Sam Grunion: *Love Happy* (1949)
    Emile J. Keck: *Double Dynamite* (1951)
    George Schmidlap: *Will Success Spoil Rock Hunter?* (1957)*
    * cameo role

Mary

Real first name of novelist (Mary) Flannery O'Connor.

Real first name of opera singer (Mary) Leontyne Price.

Real first name of actress (Mary) Debra Winger.

Mary Backstayge, Noble Wife

Soap opera featured in the comedy routines of Bob and Ray. The title was inspired by the radio soap opera *Mary Noble, Backstage Wife.*

Mary Elizabeth

Real first and middle names of actress Sissy Spacek.

Mary Jean

Real first and middle names of comedienne Lily Tomlin.

Mary Rose

Flagship of the navy of King Henry III. It has been restored and is today a tourist attraction at Portsmouth, England.

mascots

See **baseball mascots (major leagues); basketball mascots (NBA); football mascots (NFL); hockey mascots (NHL); Olympic mascots (Summer Games); Olympic mascots (Winter Games)**

Mason, Bonnie Jo

Stage name used by Cher early in her career.

Mason, Perry

See **Perry Mason book series**

Masquerade for Money

See **$20,000,000**

"The Master Blaster"

Nickname of bodybuilding guru Joe Weider.

Master of Ceremonies

Role for which Joel Grey won a Best Supporting Actor Academy Award in the 1972 film *Cabaret*.

"The Master of Disaster"

Nickname of heavyweight champion Apollo Creed (Carl Weathers) in the *Rocky* films.

"Master of the Universe"

See **Pierce & Pierce**

Masterson, Jill

See **Eaton, Shirley**

Mast, Jane

Pen name used by Mae West for some of her plays.

The Matadors

Original name of the pop group Smokey Robinson and The Miracles.

A Match Made in Space

Sci-fi novel written by George McFly (Crispin Glover) in the film *Back to the Future*.

The Matchmaker

Novel by Thornton Wilder that was the basis for the musical *Hello, Dolly!*

"Materna"

1882 religious song by Samuel Ward that with new lyrics by Katherine Lee Bates became "America the Beautiful."

Mathers, Marshall

Real name of rap star Eminem.

Mathieu, Henri Donat

Real name of fashion designer Yves St. Laurent.

Matisse

Family dog in the film *Down and Out in Beverly Hills*.

Matlock

Real first name of the title character (Lee Horsley) in the TV series *Matt Houston*.

Matowaka

Real name of Pocahontas.

"Matt Gets It"

Debut episode of the TV Western series *Gunsmoke*, which aired on September 10, 1955.

Matthau/Lemmon films

See **Lemmon/Matthau films**

Matt Helm films

Series starring Dean Martin as the title character:
The Silencers (1966)
Murderer's Row (1966)
The Ambushers (1968)
The Wrecking Crew (1969)

Matthew

Ship commanded by explorer John Cabot on his 1497 voyage to North America.

Matthews, Jeff

Real name of Moondoggie, boyfriend of the title character in the *Gidget* series of films, portrayed by James Darren.

Matty and Belle

Brother and sister mascots of Mattel.

Mauch Chunk

Seat of Carbon County, Pennsylvania, that in 1954 renamed itself Jim Thorpe, Pennsylvania, in honor of the sports legend.

Maurice

Real first name of Buddy Sorrell (Morey Amsterdam) in the TV sitcom *The Dick Van Dyke Show*.

Maurice Podoloff Trophy

Awarded annually since 1956 to the NBA's most valuable player, named for the first NBA commissioner.

Maurits Cornelius

First and middle names of Dutch graphic artist M. C. Escher.

Maverick

Code name for naval pilot Pete Mitchell (Tom Cruise) in the film *Top Gun*.

Max

Pet dog of Mike Roark (Tommy Lee Jones) in the film *Volcano*.

Pet dog of Prince Eric in the Disney animated film *The Little Mermaid*.

Pet dog of the title character in the Dr. Seuss children's book *How the Grinch Stole Christmas!*

Pet German shepherd of the title character (Lindsay Wagner) in the TV series *The Bionic Woman*.

Pet parrot of the Havelock family in the James Bond film *For Your Eyes Only*.

Maximus

Role for which Russell Crowe won a Best Actor Academy Award in the 2000 film *Gladiator*.

May

See **April, May, and June**

Maycomb, Alabama

Setting of the novel and film *To Kill a Mockingbird*.

"Mayday"

Nickname of Sam Malone (Ted Danson) during his former career as a Boston Red Sox pitcher, in the TV sitcom *Cheers*.

Mayfield

Setting of the TV sitcom *Leave It to Beaver*.

Mayflower 1

Pan Universe Airways' lunar spaceship in the film *Airplane II: The Sequel*.

May I have a large container of coffee?

Mnemonic for learning the first eight digits of pi (3.1415926), based on the lengths of the words.

Mayo, Jim

Pen name used by Western author Louis L'Amour early in his career.

"Mayonnaise"

Sergeant Emil Foley's (Louis Gossett, Jr.'s), nickname for Officer Candidate Zack Mayo (Richard Gere), in the film *An Officer and a Gentleman*.

"The Mayor of Rush Street"

Nickname of White Sox/Cubs broadcaster Harry Caray, for his frequenting of that street of Chicago nightclubs.

May, Robert

Advertising copywriter for Chicago department store Montgomery Ward who wrote the poem "Rudolph the Red-Nosed Reindeer" for a 1939 promotional brochure. The poem was set to music by Johnny Marks in 1947, and became a #1 hit for Gene Autry in 1949.

Mays, Carl

See **Chapman, Ray**

Maysville Pictures

Production company of actor George Clooney.

"May the Force be with you!"

Blessing of Obi-Wan Kenobi (Sir Alec Guinness) in the film *Star Wars*.

"May the good Lord take a liking to you"

Sign-off line of Roy Rogers in the children's TV series *The Roy Rogers Show*.

"May the Schwartz be with you!"

Blessing of Yogurt (Mel Brooks) in the film *Spaceballs*.

Mazaru

See **Mizaru, Mikazaru, and Mazaru**

Mazetta, Rose Marie

Real name of actress Rose Marie.

McBoing Boing, Gerald

Character created by Dr. Seuss who speaks in sound effects instead of words.

McBricker

Maiden name of Betty Rubble in the animated TV sitcom *The Flintstones*.

McCabe, Jason Lochinvar

Real name of The Fatman (William Conrad) in the TV series *Jake and the Fatman*.

McCall, Jack

See **dead man's hand**

McCall, Robert

Title character (Edward Woodward) in the TV series *The Equalizer*.

McCarthy, Charlie

See **Bergen, Edgar, dummies of**

McCarthy, Timothy

See **Delahanty, Thomas**

McClenny, Patsy

Real name of actress Morgan Fairchild.

McCormick, Kenny

Boy (voiced by Matt Stone) who is killed in most episodes of the animated TV series *South Park*.

McCoy's Restaurant and Bar

Where Cathy Hale (Faye Dunaway) meets CIA deputy chief Higgins (Cliff Robertson) in the film *Three Days of the Condor*.

McCulley, Johnston

Creator of Zorro. Zorro first appeared in the initial installment of the serialized novel *The Curse of Capistrano*, in the August 9, 1919, issue of the pulp magazine *All-Story Weekly*.

McCullough, J. F. and Alex

Founders of the Dairy Queen ice cream chain. The first Dairy Queen opened on June 22, 1940, in Joliet, Illinois.

McDonald, Belinda

Role for which Jane Wyman won a Best Actress Academy Award in the 1948 film *Johnny Belinda*.

McDougal's House of Horrors

Place from which Dracula (Bela Lugosi) and the Frankenstein monster (Glenn Strange) escape, in the film *Abbott and Costello Meet Frankenstein*.

McDowell's

Fast-food employer of Prince Akeem (Eddie Murphy) in the film *Coming to America*.

McElroy, William Omaha

Professor of Egyptology (Victor Buono) who, after a bump on the head, assumes the alter ego King Tut in the TV series *Batman*.

McFarlane, Todd

See **$3,005,000**

McFeely

Middle name of children's TV host Fred Rogers.

McGaffey, Ives

Inventor of the vacuum cleaner in 1869. He called it "The Whirlwind."

McGargle, Professor Eustace

See **Fields, W. C., roles/pen names of**

McGear, Mike

Stage name of rock singer Peter Michael McCartney, younger brother of former Beatle Paul McCartney. He changed his name soon after the Beatles became famous.

McGee, Charlie

Title character of the Stephen King novel *Firestarter*, portrayed in the film adaptation of the same name by Drew Barrymore.

McGillicuddy

Maiden name of Lucy Ricardo (Lucille Ball) in the TV sitcom *I Love Lucy*.

McGillicuddy, Cornelius

Real name of Hall of Fame baseball manager Connie Mack.

McGonigle's Carnival and Air Show

Employer of Blackie Benson and Heathcliff (Abbott and Costello) in the film *Keep 'Em Flying*.

McGrath, Ada

Role for which Holly Hunter won a Best Actress Academy Award in the 1993 film *The Piano*.

McGrath, Flora

Role for which Anna Paquin won a Best Supporting Actress Academy Award in the 1993 film *The Piano*.

McGruff

Canine detective created by the Advertising Council for commercials promoting crime prevention.

McKeeby, Dr. Byron H. and Wood, Nan

The two people depicted in the Grant Wood painting *American Gothic*. They are the artist's dentist and sister.

McKenna

Maiden name of Joanna Loudon (Mary Frann) in the TV series *Newhart*.

McKenzie, Father

Clergyman in the Beatles tune "Eleanor Rigby."

McKenzie, Spuds

Bull terrier in 1980s TV commercials for Bud Light beer.

McLaidlaw, Lina

Role for which Joan Fontaine won a Best Actress Academy Award in the 1941 film *Suspicion*.

McLamore, James and Edgerton, David

Founders of the Burger King fast-food chain. The first Burger King opened in 1954, in Miami, Florida.

McLean, Wilmer

Owner of the home in Appomattox Court House, Virginia, where Confederate General Robert E. Lee surrendered to Union General Ulysses S. Grant on April 9, 1865.

McLeish, Officer Steve

Role portrayed by Olympic decathlon champion Bruce Jenner in the TV series *CHiPs*, when Erik Estrada temporarily left the cast in a contract dispute.

McMann and Tate

Advertising-agency employer of Darrin Stephens (Dick York, Dick Sargent) in the TV sitcom *Bewitched*.

McManus, Declan Patrick

Real name of singer Elvis Costello.

McMath, Virginia Katherine

Real name of actress/dancer Ginger Rogers.

McMillan, Wellington

Millionaire banker that the title character imagines himself to be in a dream, in the James Thurber short story "The Secret Life of Walter Mitty."

McMurphy, Randle Patrick

Role for which Jack Nicholson won a Best Actor Academy Award in the 1975 film *One Flew Over the Cuckoo's Nest*.

McNamara, Frank and Schneider, Ralph

Founders of Diners Club, the first nationally accepted credit card, in 1950.

McNasty, Filthy

Bank robber accidentally apprehended by Egbert Sousé (W. C. Fields) in the film *The Bank Dick*.

McTammany Jr., John

Inventor of the player piano, patented in 1881.

McVicker, Joe

Inventor of Play-Doh, originally introduced in 1956 as a wallpaper cleaner.

Meadowbrook High

School attended by Andie Walsh (Molly Ringwald) in the film *Pretty in Pink*.

"Meal Ticket"

Nickname of Hall of Fame baseball pitcher Carl Hubbell.

The Mean Machine

Football team of convicts led by quarterback Paul Crewe (Burt Reynolds) in the film *The Longest Yard*.

Mearth

Son of the title characters (Robin Williams and Pam Dawber) in the TV sitcom *Mork and Mindy*, portrayed by Jonathan Winters.

"Meat Bomb" and "Dump Truck"

Affectionate nicknames of 600-pound Hawaii native Salevaa Atisanoe, aka Konishiki, the first non-Japanese *yokozuna* (grand champion) sumo wrestler.

Meathead

Pet bulldog of Harry Callahan (Clint Eastwood) in the film *Sudden Impact*.

"Meathead"

Archie Bunker's (Carroll O'Connor's) nickname for his son-in-law Mike Stivic (Rob Reiner) in the TV sitcom *All in the Family*.

"The Mechanical Man"

Nickname of baseball Hall of Famer Charlie Gehringer, for his quiet, methodical play.

mecometer

Instrument for measuring the length of a newborn infant.

"The 'Me' Decade"

Nickname of the 1970s, coined by author Tom Wolfe.

Medfield College of Technology

Setting of the Disney films *The Absent-Minded Professor*, the sequel *Son of Flubber*, the remake *Flubber*, and *The Misadventures of Merlin Jones*.

Media Monthly

Magazine employer of writer Lester Burnham (Kevin Spacey) in the film *American Beauty*.

medius

Scientific name for the middle finger.

medley relay

Olympic swimming event in which four different swimmers each go 100 meters, each using a different stroke, in this order: backstroke, breaststroke, butterfly, and freestyle.

Meeber

Last name of the title character in the Theodore Dreiser novel *Sister Carrie*.

Meeko

Raccoon friend of the title character in the Disney animated film *Pocahontas*.

Meetinghouse

Allied code name for Tokyo, Japan during World War II.

"Meet the Bunkers"

Debut episode of the TV sitcom *All in the Family*, which aired on January 12, 1971.

Meet the Press moderators

This NBC show, which debuted on November 6, 1947, is television's longest-running network series.
    Martha Rountree (1947–53)
    Ned Brooks (1953–65)
    Lawrence Spivak (1966–75)
    Bill Monroe (1975–84)
    Marvin Kalb (1984–87)
    Roger Mudd (co-moderator with Kalb, 1984–85)
    Chris Wallace (1987–88)
    Garrick Utley (1989–91)
    Tim Russert (1991–)

Mega-City One

Futuristic setting of the *Judge Dredd* comic books, and the film adaptation starring Sylvester Stallone in the title role.

The Megaphone

Trophy awarded to the winning team in the annual football game between Michigan State University and Penn State University.

Megopolis Zoo

Home of the title character (voiced by Don Adams) in the children's animated TV series *Tennessee Tuxedo and His Tales*.

"Melancholy Serenade"

Theme song of the TV series *The Jackie Gleason Show*, composed by Gleason.

Melange

The most valuable substance in the universe, a spice that lengthens life and is also needed for space travel, in the Frank Herbert novel *Dune*.

Melinda and Sue

Former girlfriends in the Neil Diamond tune "Solitary Man."

"Meliora"

Motto of the University of Rochester, which is Latin for "Always better."

Mellins

Brand of baby food on whose labels Humphrey Bogart appeared as an infant. The label's drawing was done by Bogart's mother, who was a commercial artist.

Mellish, Fielding

Woody Allen's role in the film *Bananas*.

The Mellow Tiger

Tavern in Castle Rock, Maine, in the Stephen King novel *Cujo*.

Melmac

Home planet of the title character (voiced by Paul Fusco) in the TV sitcom *ALF*.

Melmoth, Sebastian

Pen name used by writer Oscar Wilde.

"Melody in A Major"

Piece by Charles G. Dawes (Nobel Peace Prize winner and vice president under Calvin Coolidge) used for the Tommy Edwards tune "All in the Game."

Melville's Fine Sea Food

Restaurant located above the title establishment in the TV sitcom *Cheers*.

Memoirs of a Professional Cad

1960 autobiography of actor George Sanders, who specialized in scoundrel roles.

"Memphis Group"

What the initials stand for in the name of rock group Booker T. and the MGs.

The Men

Umbrella title of the three rotating TV adventure series *Assignment Vienna*, *The Delphi Bureau*, and *Jigsaw*.

Menches, Charles

Inventor of the ice cream cone in 1904, at the Louisiana Purchase Exposition in St. Louis, Missouri.

"Mens agitat molem"

Motto of the University of Oregon, which is Latin for "Mind moves the mass."

Mentzer, Josephine Esther

Birth name of cosmetics executive Estee Lauder.

Meow-Bow Animal Hospital

Where Macon Leary (William Hurt) boards his dog Edward, and first meets Muriel Pritchett (Geena Davis) in the film *The Accidental Tourist*.

Mercador, Ramón

Spanish-born assassin of exiled Russian Communist leader Leon Trotsky, near Mexico City on August 20, 1940.

Mercalli scale

See **modified Mercalli scale**

"The Merchant of Venom"

Nickname of insult comic Don Rickles.

Mercury spacecraft nicknames

The "7" in each name refers to the seven original Mercury astronauts:
Mercury 3 (1961, Alan Shepard): *Freedom 7*
Mercury 4 (1961, Virgil Grissom): *Liberty Bell 7*
Mercury 6 (1962, John Glenn): *Friendship 7*
Mercury 7 (1962, Scott Carpenter): *Aurora 7*
Mercury 8 (1962, Wally Schirra): *Sigma 7*
Mercury 9 (1963, Gordon Cooper): *Faith 7*

"Meridian"

Debut episode of the TV series *Naked City*, which aired on September 30, 1958.

Mérimée, Prosper

Author whose novella *Carmen* was the basis for the Georges Bizet opera of the same name.

Meriwether and William

First names (respectively) of explorers Lewis and Clark.

Merlin, Joseph

Belgian violinist who invented roller skates in 1759.

Mero, Rena

Real name of former WWF wrestler Sable.

"Merrily We Roll Along"

Instrumental theme of Warner Bros.' Merrie Melodies cartoons. The tune, cowritten by comedian Eddie Cantor, is different from the tune of the same name familiar to schoolchildren as "Mary Had a Little Lamb."

Merrin, Lankester

Title character of the William Peter Blatty novel *The Exorcist*, portrayed in the film adaptation of the same name by Max von Sydow.

"merry festival"

What "jai alai" means in the Basque language.

"The Merry-Go-Round Broke Down"

Instrumental theme of Warner Bros.' Looney Tunes cartoons.

"The Merry Madcap"

Nickname of 1930s heavyweight boxing champ Max Baer, for his comic antics in the ring.

The Merryman and His Maid

Alternate title of the Gilbert and Sullivan comic opera *The Yeoman of the Guard*.

"The Merry Monarch"

Nickname of King Charles II of England.

Merryweather

See **Flora, Fauna, and Merryweather**

Mersault

Title character of the Albert Camus novel *The Stranger*.

Mesa Grande, Arizona

Town near Fort Apache in the children's TV series *The Adventures of Rin Tin Tin*.

Mesalia, Ohio
Setting of the Kaufman and Hart play *The Man Who Came to Dinner.*

Meservey, Robert Preston
Real name of actor Robert Preston.

"Message from Beyond"
Debut episode of the TV series *Ironside*, which aired on September 14, 1967.

Messervy, Sir Miles
Real name of M, James Bond's boss, in the novels of Ian Fleming.

"A Metabiological Pentateuch"
Subtitle of the George Bernard Shaw play *Back to Methuselah.*

metacarpophalangeal joint
Medical term for a knuckle.

Metaluna
Planet that enlists American scientists to help repair its protective defense shield, in the film *This Island Earth.*

Meursault
Title character of the Jean-Paul Sartre novel *The Stranger.*

"Mexican Slayride"
Debut episode of the TV series *The A-Team*, which aired on January 23, 1983.

***Mexican Spitfire* films**
Series starring Lupe Velez in the title role of Carmelita Lindsay:
The Girl from Mexico (1939)
Mexican Spitfire (1939)
Mexican Spitfire Out West (1940)
Mexican Spitfire's Baby (1941)
Mexican Spitfire at Sea (1942)
Mexican Spitfire Sees a Ghost (1942)
Mexican Spitfire's Elephant (1942)
Mexican Spitfire's Blessed Event (1943)

Meyer's Lake
Favorite fishing spot of Andy Taylor (Andy Griffith) and his son Opie (Ronny Howard) in the TV sitcom *The Andy Griffith Show.*

Miami Sharks
Pro football team coached by Tony D'Amato (Al Pacino) in the film *Any Given Sunday.*

Miami Standard
Newspaper employer of Megan Carter (Sally Field) in the film *Absence of Malice.*

Michael
Middle name of entertainer/songwriter George M. Cohan.

Original first name of Martin Luther King Jr.

Real first name of the title character (Paul Hogan) in the *"Crocodile" Dundee* films.

Role for which John Mills won a Best Supporting Actor Academy Award in the 1970 film *Ryan's Daughter.*

See also **Fritz, Michael, Pierre, and José**

Michaela
First name of the title character (Jane Seymour) in the TV series *Dr. Quinn, Medicine Woman.*

Michael Phillip
Real first and middle names of Rolling Stones lead singer Mick Jagger.

Michael's Bar & Grill
Bronx restaurant hangout of the title character (Ernest Borgnine) in the film *Marty.*

Michaels, Dorothy
See **Southwest General**

Michael's Pub
New York City jazz club where Woody Allen often played clarinet on Monday nights, including March 29, 1978, when he won the Academy Award for Best Director for the film *Annie Hall.*

Michigan J. Frog
Cartoon mascot of the WB Network. He first appeared (unnamed) in the 1955 Warner Bros. cartoon "One Froggy Evening."

Michtom, Morris and Rose
Brooklyn, New York, toy-store owners who created the first teddy bear in 1903, which was the basis of their founding of the Ideal Toy company.

"The Mickey Farmer Case"
Debut episode of the TV series *Richard Diamond, Private Detective*, which aired on July 1, 1957.

***The Mickey Mouse Club* theme days**
As seen on the original 1955-59 series:
Monday: Fun with Music Day

Tuesday: Guest Star Day
Wednesday: Anything Can Happen Day
Thursday: Circus Day
Friday: Talent Round-Up Day

Micklewhite, Maurice

Real name of actor Michael Caine.

The Midas Touch

Play being written by Jeffrey Moss (Dean Martin) in the film *Bells Are Ringing*.

Mid-Atlantic Airlines

Account being handled by ad-agency art director Ted Kramer (Dustin Hoffman) in the film *Kramer vs. Kramer*.

Midge

On-air name of American-born World War II German propaganda broadcaster Mildred Elizabeth Gillars, known to American soldiers as Axis Sally. She was heard on the Radio Berlin program *Home Sweet Home*.

Midnight

Horse of Rowdy Yates (Clint Eastwood) in the TV series *Rawhide*.

Midnight Club

New York City nightspot where Ted Hanover (Fred Astaire), Jim Hardy (Bing Crosby), and Lila Dixon (Virginia Dale) perform, in the film *Holiday Inn*.

"The Midnight Idol"

Nickname of entertainer Wayne Newton.

"Midnight Plane to Houston"

Original title of the Gladys Knight and the Pips tune "Midnight Train to Georgia."

Midships

Yearbook of the U.S. Merchant Marine Academy.

A Midsummer Night's Dream

Orchestral suite by German composer Felix Mendelssohn whose "Wedding March" is the familiar music heard at the conclusion of wedding ceremonies.

Midvale, Illinois

Home of Linda Lee (Helen Slater) in the film *Supergirl* and the Superman comic books.

Midville

Setting of the comic strip *Dondi*.

Midville, Connecticut

Location of the title establishment in the film *Holiday Inn*.

Midwestern Airlines Flight 104

Plane that crashes into a Chicago bridge in the film *Hero*.

Midwest State

Setting of the film *She's Working Her Way Through College*.

The Midwich Cuckoos

Novel by John Wyndham that was the basis for the film *Village of the Damned* (1960).

Mighty Allen Art Players

Group that performed skits on Fred Allen's radio show, which presumably inspired the name of Johnny Carson's Mighty Carson Art Players on *The Tonight Show*.

Mighty Joe Young

Original name of rock group Stone Temple Pilots.

Mighty Manfred the Wonder Dog

Pet of the title character in the children's animated TV series *Tom Terrific*.

"Mighty Mo"

Nickname of World War II battleship U.S.S. *Missouri*.

"Mighty Mouth"

Nickname of speed-talking TV commercial spokesperson John Moschitta Jr., best known for his appearances for Federal Express. He has been clocked at 586 words per minute.

Mignon

Pet dog of Lisa Douglas (Eva Gabor) in the TV sitcom *Green Acres*.

"Mihi cura futuri"

Motto of Hunter College, which is Latin for "I care for the future."

Mikazaru

See **Mizaru, Mikazaru, and Mazaru**

Mike

Lion tamed by Hank Whirling (Victor Mature) in the film *The Big Circus*.

Mikey

See **Gilchrist, John**

Mikoyan, Artem and Gurevich, Mikhail

Russian aircraft engineers for whom the MiG fighter plane was named.

Milady Soap

Sponsor of the game show *Masquerade for Money* in the film *Champagne for Caesar*. Its advertising slogan: "The Soap That Sanctifies."

Milburn, New York

Setting of the Peter Straub novel *Ghost Story*.

Mildendo

Capital city of Lilliput in the Jonathan Swift novel *Gulliver's Travels*.

Mildred

Wife of Colonel Sherman Potter (Harry Morgan), whose picture is displayed on his desk, in the TV sitcom *M*A*S*H*. The photo is actually that of actress Spring Byington, with whom Morgan appeared in the TV sitcom *December Bride*.

Mildred Ella

Real first and middle names of athlete Babe Didrikson.

Mildred Kerr

Full name of Millie, pet springer spaniel of President George H. W. Bush.

Miles, Junior

Pen name used by Seagram CEO Edgar Bronfman Jr. for his songwriting. Miles is Bronfman's middle name.

Miles, Lotta

One-time mascot of Kelly-Springfield automobile tires.

Milestone Mo-Tel

The first motel in the United States, opened by Arthur Heineman in San Luis Obispo, California, in 1925.

Milfields Travel Agency

Where Gladys Aylward (Ingrid Bergman) books passage from London to China via the Trans-Siberian Railroad, in the film *The Inn of the Sixth Happiness*.

Milford Junction

English train station that is the setting of the film *Brief Encounter*.

"The Military Classic of the South"

See **Silver Shako**

"The milk chocolate melts in your mouth, not in your hand"

Advertising slogan of M&Ms.

"milk mustache" celebrities

Each of these actors and other celebrities has been featured, wearing a milk mustache, in print ads for the National Fluid Milk Processor Promotion Board from 1994 to 1998. Tag lines used in the ads: "What a surprise!" "Where's your mustache?" and "Got milk?" (Celebrities listed together appeared in the same ad.)

Lauren Bacall (actress)
Tyra Banks (model)
Tony Bennett (singer)
Yasmine Bleeth (actress)
Christie Brinkley (model)
Kevin Brown and Orel Hershiser (baseball pitchers; ad appeared before the 1997 World Series, with the line "Just a Reminder to Fill Your Pitchers with Milk.")
James Cameron (*Titanic* director; with the line "I Like to Float Big Chunks of Ice in Mine.")
Neve Campbell (actress)
Naomi Campbell (model)
Bill Clinton and Bob Dole (ad appeared the day before Election Day, 1996, with the line "Vote. Strengthen America's Backbone.")
David Copperfield (magician; levitating an upside-down glass of milk)
Bob Costas, Frank Gifford, and Al Michaels (sportscasters)
Billy Ray Cyrus (country singer)
Oscar De La Hoya (boxer)
Danny DeVito (actor) and Rhea Perlman (actress)
Hanson (rock group)
Iman (model)
Patrick Ewing (basketball player)
Brett Favre and Drew Bledsoe (quarterbacks; ad appeared before the 1997 Super Bowl, with the line, "This Sunday, Remember to Pass the Milk.")
Matthew Fox (actor)
Dennis Franz and Jimmy Smits (actors)
Daisy Fuentes (TV host)
Sarah Michelle Gellar (actress)
Ekaterina Gordeeva (figure skater)
Jeff Gordon (auto racer)
Amy Grant (singer)
Tony Hawk (skateboarder)
Joshua Jackson (actor)
Michael Johnson (Olympic runner)
Shirley Jones, Marion Ross, and Florence Henderson (sitcom moms)
Florence Griffith Joyner (track star)

Larry King (talk show host)
Nastassja Kinski (actress)
Lisa Kudrow and Jennifer Aniston (actresses)
Spike Lee (director)
Joan Lunden (talk show host)
Arie Luyendyk (auto racer)
Elle Macpherson (model)
Marilyn Monroe (actress; as part of an April Fool's Day 1998 fake news story about the discovery of a new Andy Warhol painting with a milk mustache)
Kate Moss (model)
Conan O'Brien (comedian/TV host)
LeAnn Rimes (country singer)
Cal Ripken Jr. (baseballer)
Joan Rivers (comedienne)
Dennis Rodman (basketball player)
Isabella Rossellini (actress)
Gabriela Sabatini (tennis pro)
Pete Sampras (tennis pro)
Paul Shaffer (talk-show band conductor/musician)
Lisa and Bart Simpson (TV cartoon characters)
Martha Stewart (lifestyle guru)
Jonathan Taylor Thomas (actor)
Ivana Trump (hotelier)
Eddie and Alex Van Halen (rock singers)
Vanna White (TV cohost)
Heather Whitestone (Miss America 1995)
Vanessa Williams (actress)
Amy Van Dyken (Olympic swimmer)
Kristi Yamaguchi (figure skater)
Steve Young (quarterback)
Billy Zane (actor; as The Phantom)

Millard Fillmore High

See **Monroe High**

Millar, Kenneth

Real name of whodunit author Ross Macdonald.

Millenios

Limited-edition version of Cheerios, sold in 1999 and 2000, that had 2s in addition to Os, thus could spell out "2000."

Millennial Church

Christian denomination whose members are commonly known as Shakers, for their practice of shaking during services.

Millennium Falcon

Spaceship of Han Solo (Harrison Ford) in the film *Star Wars*.

Miller

Middle name of novelist Ernest Hemingway.

Miller's Bakery

Only brand of cheesecake that Gloves Donahue (Humphrey Bogart) will eat, in the film *All Through The Night*. When offered a National cheesecake instead, he replies, "When I order cheesecake, I don't expect mucilage."

Millertown Bluff

Where Jim Stark (James Dean) and Buzz Gunderson (Corey Allen) engage in an ill-fated "chickie run" car race in the film *Rebel Without a Cause*.

Millie

See **Mildred Kerr**

Millsburg

Setting of the TV series *Window on Main Street*.

Mills, Robert

Architect who designed the Washington Monument in Washington, D.C. Its construction began in 1848, and it was dedicated in 1885.

Milton

Cartoon toaster in 1960s TV commercials for Kellogg's Pop-Tarts.

See also **Marx Brothers' real names**

Milwaukee Brewers

Original name of the Baltimore Orioles at their American League inception in 1901. The team moved to St. Louis in 1902 (where it was known as the Browns), and took its present name when it moved to Baltimore in 1954.

Minden

English ship on which Francis Scott Key was temporarily detained on the evening of September 13, 1814, in Baltimore harbor, where he wrote the lyrics of "The Star-Spangled Banner."

"A mind is a terrible thing to waste"

Advertising slogan of the United Negro College Fund.

Mind Over Matrimony

Working title of the latest book of Mortimer Brewster (Cary Grant) in the film *Arsenic and Old Lace*.

"Mind Your Business"

Motto on the first officially sanctioned U.S. coins, pennies that were minted in 1787.

Mineola Bank
First bank successfully robbed by the title characters (Faye Dunaway and Warren Beatty) in the film *Bonnie and Clyde*.

Miner, Jan
See **Salon East**

Minerva
Pet cat of Margaret Davis (Jane Morgan), landlord of the title character (Eve Arden) in the TV sitcom *Our Miss Brooks*.

See also **60 *Minutes* stopwatch brands**

Mines Field
Original name of Los Angeles International Airport.

Mingall de Bru y Deulofeo, Francisco de Asis Javier Cugat
Real name of Spanish bandleader Xavier Cugat.

Mingeborough, Massachusetts
Hometown of Tyrone Slothrop in the Thomas Pynchon novel *Gravity's Rainbow*.

Ming Tea
Rock band led by the title character (Mike Myers) in the *Austin Powers* films.

Mini-Me
Miniature cloned version of Dr. Evil (Mike Myers) in the film *Austin Powers: The Spy Who Shagged Me*, portrayed by Verne Troyer.

minimus
Scientific name for the smallest digit on the human hand and foot, aka the little toe and the pinkie.

Miniver, Kay
Role for which Greer Garson won a Best Actress Academy Award in the 1942 film *Mrs. Miniver*.

Minnesota State University
Setting of the TV sitcom *Coach*.

Minnesota Valley Canning Company
Original name of Green Giant.

"Minnie the Moocher"
Theme song of bandleader Cab Calloway.

minoxidil
Chemical name of the drug Rogaine.

Mintaka, Alnilam, and Alnitak
The three stars, from west to east, that make up Orion's Belt. Their names are the Arabic words for "belt," "string of pearls," and "girdle," respectively.

mintonette
Original name of the game of volleyball.

Minuteman Cafe
Restaurant run by Kirk Devane (Steven Kampmann) in the TV sitcom *Newhart*.

"A minute to learn . . . a lifetime to master"
Advertising slogan of the board game Othello.

"The Minute Waltz"
Nickname of Frédéric Chopin's waltz in D-flat major, Opus 64, Number 1. The nickname comes from *minute*, the French word for "small," not from the time it should take to perform.

Miracle Child
Horse ridden by Grace King (Julia Roberts) in the Nationals when she was 16 years old, in the film *Something to Talk About*.

"Miracle Cure"
Debut episode of the TV series *Diagnosis Murder*, which aired on October 29, 1993.

"Miracle of Coogan's Bluff"
Nickname given to the remarkable comeback of the 1951 New York Giants in winning the National League pennant. Coogan's Bluff is an area of Manhattan near the site of the Polo Grounds, the Giants' home stadium at that time.

"Mirage"
High-school nickname of singer Mariah Carey, because of all the classes she missed.

Mirage Enterprises
Production company of director Sydney Pollack.

Miranda Beach, Florida
Setting of the film *Body Heat*.

The Mirth Makers
Studio band led by Happy Kyne (Frank DeVol) in the TV series *Fernwood 2-Night*.

"Misha"
Nickname of ballet star Mikhail Baryshnikov.

"Missed it by that much!"

Catchphrase of the title character (Don Adams) in the TV sitcom *Get Smart*.

Missett, Judy Sheppard

Creator of the Jazzercise workout regimen.

missile experimental

See **"The Peacekeeper"**

"The Missing Body Mystery"

Debut episode of the TV series *Father Dowling Mysteries*, which aired on January 20, 1989.

"The Mission"

Theme song of NBC News, composed by John Williams.

Mission College

Setting of the Spike Lee film *School Daze*, which is based on Morehouse College, Lee's alma mater.

Missitucky

Mythical state that is the setting of the musical *Finian's Rainbow*.

Miss Kitty

Pet cat of Selina Kyle (Michelle Pfeiffer) in the film *Batman Returns*.

Missy

Mother of the title character's puppies in the film *Beethoven's 2nd*.

Mother of Snoopy in the comic strip *Peanuts*.

Mistake Out

Original name of Liquid Paper correction fluid.

The Mistakes of a Night

Alternate title of the Oliver Goldsmith play *She Stoops to Conquer*.

Misty Girl

Horse of Victoria Barkley (Barbara Stanwyck) in the TV Western series *The Big Valley*.

Misty Malarky Ying Yang

Pet Siamese cat of Amy Carter while she was living in the White House.

Mitch

Role for which Karl Malden won a Best Supporting Actor Academy Award in the 1951 film *A Streetcar Named Desire*.

Mitchell

Last name of the title character (Brandy) in the TV sitcom *Moesha*.

Mitchell, James Henry

Inventor of Fig Newtons, first sold by the Kennedy Biscuit Company in 1891.

Mizaru, Mikazaru, and Mazaru

The three monkeys of "See no evil, hear no evil, speak no evil" fame.

Mizzy, Vic

Composer of the theme songs for the TV sitcoms *The Addams Family* and *Green Acres*.

Mjolnir

In Norse mythology, the hammer of Thor.

"M'm! M'm! Good!"

Advertising slogan of Campbell's Soup.

Moana

Houseboat of the Bowden family (Jessica Lange, Nick Nolte, Juliette Lewis) in the film *Cape Fear* (1991).

Moby Dick

Pet goldfish of Rocky Balboa (Sylvester Stallone) in the film *Rocky*.

Moccasin

Allied code name for Wake Island during World War II.

Mockingbird Heights

Setting of the TV sitcom *The Munsters*.

The Modern Prometheus

Alternate title of the Mary Shelley novel *Frankenstein*.

modified Mercalli scale

Alternative to the Richter scale for measuring the intensity of earthquakes. Its 1–12 (I–XII) scale is based on the amount of damage caused, rather than the absolute intensity that is measured by the Richter scale. The original scale was devised by Italian geologist Giuseppe Mercalli in 1902; this modified scale was introduced by seismologist Charles F. Richter in 1956:

I   Barely felt
II   Felt by a small number of people
III Slightly felt indoors
IV   Felt indoors by many people
V   Felt by most people, very minor damage
VI   Felt by everyone, slight damage

VII Considerable damage in poorly constructed buildings

VIII Heavy damage in poorly constructed buildings

IX Considerable damage to well-constructed buildings

X Most buildings destroyed

XI Few buildings left standing

XII Total destruction

Modini

Real last name of actor Robert Stack.

Modugno, Domenico

See **"Nel Blu Dipinto Di Blu"**

Moegle, Dicky

See **Lewis, Tommy**

Mogwai

See **Gizmo**

Mohs scale

Relative scale for the hardness of minerals, developed by Austrian mineralogist Friedrich Mohs.

1 Talc
2 Gypsum
3 Calcite
4 Fluorite
5 Apatite
6 Orthoclase
7 Quartz
8 Topaz
9 Corundum
10 Diamond

Moira Angela

Middle names of Wendy Darling in the James M. Barrie novel *Peter Pan*.

Moldavia

European country where the wedding ceremony between Amanda Carrington (Catherine Oxenberg) and Prince Michael (Michael Praed) is interrupted by a terrorist attack, in the TV series *Dynasty*.

Molière Awards

French equivalent of America's Tony Awards for stage excellence, named for the French playwright.

Molina, Luis

Role for which William Hurt won a Best Actor Academy Award in the 1985 film *Kiss of the Spider Woman*.

Molly

See **Snoopy's brothers and sisters**

"Molly Brown"

Nickname of the *Gemini 3* spacecraft ridden by Virgil Grissom and John Young in 1965. Its "unsinkable" nickname was given by Grissom, whose Mercury spacecraft (*Liberty Bell 7* in 1961) sank upon reentry. This was the only Gemini spacecraft to have a nickname.

Monarch Theater

See **Footlight Frenzy**

Mona's House of Hair

Former employer of the title character (Delta Burke) in the TV sitcom *Delta*.

mondegreen

Term for a misheard word, phrase, or song lyric, coined by columnist Sylvia Wright, after mishearing words from the Scottish folk song "The Bonny Earl of Morray." She thought the lyric, "Oh, they have slain the Earl o' Morray and laid him on the green" was "Oh, they have slain the Earl o' Morray and Lady Mondegreen."

Monegasque

Term for a native of Monaco.

Money

See **Fame, Happiness, and Money**

Mongkut, King

Role for which Yul Brynner won a Best Actor Academy Award in the 1956 film *The King and I*.

Mongo

Planet ruled by Ming the Merciless in the Flash Gordon film serials.

Mongols

Nickname of Faber College's athletic teams in the film *National Lampoon's Animal House*.

Monkees members

Micky Dolenz, Davy Jones, Mike Nesmith, and Peter Tork.

Monkey Business

Yacht on which Democratic presidential candidate Gary Hart was photographed with model Donna Rice in 1987.

Monkey Planet

Novel by Pierre Boulle that was the basis for the film *Planet of the Apes*.

Monk's Cafe

Local hangout in the TV sitcom *Seinfeld*.

Mon Lei

50-foot Chinese junk owned by Robert L. Ripley, creator of the syndicated column *Believe It or Not!*

Monopoly spaces (American edition)

The spaces on the board (with the purchase cost, where applicable), moving counterclockwise from GO:

GO (collect $200 salary as you pass)
Mediterranean Avenue ($60)
Community Chest
Baltic Avenue ($60)
Income Tax (pay 10% or $200)
Reading Railroad ($200)
Oriental Avenue ($100)
Chance
Vermont Avenue ($100)
Connecticut Avenue ($120)
Jail
St. Charles Place ($140)
Electric Company ($150)
States Avenue ($140)
Virginia Avenue ($160)
Pennsylvania Railroad ($200)
St. James Place ($180)
Community Chest
Tennessee Avenue ($180)
New York Avenue ($200)
Free Parking
Kentucky Avenue ($220)
Chance
Indiana Avenue ($220)
Illinois Avenue ($240)
B&O Railroad ($200)
Atlantic Avenue ($260)
Ventnor Avenue ($260)
Water Works ($150)
Marvin Gardens ($280)
Go to Jail
Pacific Avenue ($300)
North Carolina Avenue ($300)
Community Chest
Pennsylvania Avenue ($320)
Short Line Railroad ($200)
Chance
Park Place ($350)
Luxury Tax (pay $75)
Boardwalk ($400)
GO

Monopoly spaces (British edition)

The spaces on the board (with the purchase cost, where applicable), moving counterclockwise from GO:

GO (collect £200 salary as you pass)
Old Kent Road (£60)
Community Chest
Whitechapel Road (£60)
Income Tax (pay £200)
Kings Cross Station (£200)
The Angel, Islington (£100)
Chance
Euston Road (£100)
Pentonville Road (£120)
Jail
Pall Mall (£140)
Electric Company (£150)
Whitehall (£140)
Northumberland Avenue (£160)
Marylebone Station (£200)
Bow Street (£180)
Community Chest
Marlborough Street (£180)
Vine Street (£200)
Free Parking
Strand (£220)
Chance
Fleet Street (£220)
Trafalgar Square (£240)
Fenchurch St. Station (£200)
Leicester Square (£260)
Coventry Street (£260)
Water Works (£150)
Piccadilly (£280)
Go to Jail
Regent Street (£300)
Oxford Street (£300)
Community Chest
Bond Street (£320)
Liverpool St. Station (£200)
Chance
Park Lane (£350)
Super Tax (pay £100)
Mayfair (£400)
GO

monopsony

Term in economics for a product with multiple manufacturers for which there is only one buyer, who can therefore control the price of the product. This is the inverse situation to that of a monopoly.

Monroe

Middle name of cartoonist Charles Schulz.

Monroe Elementary School

Topeka, Kansas, school attended by Linda Brown when the landmark civil-rights suit *Brown vs. Board of Education of Topeka* was initially filed in 1951.

Monroe High

Manhattan school that is the setting of the TV series *Head of the Class*. The school was later named Millard Fillmore High.

Monroe, Lyle

Pen name used by author Robert A. Heinlein.

Monroe, Montezuma

Jim Brown's football-coach role in the film *Any Given Sunday*.

Monroe, Rose Will

Riveter from Ypsilanti, Michigan, who was the model for the "Rosie the Riveter" posters of World War II that encouraged women to seek factory employment.

The Monster

Film playing at the drive-in during the opening credits of the animated TV sitcom *The Flintstones*.

"The Monster"

Nickname of 1960s Red Sox relief pitcher Dick Radatz, for his physique (6'5", 235 pounds) as well as his intimidating fastball.

Monster from Beneath the Sea

Original working title of the film *The Beast from 20,000 Fathoms*.

"Monsters of the Midway"

1940s nickname of the Chicago Bears. In the 1940s, they won the NFL championship four times and finished second four times.

The Monster That Devoured Cleveland

Film that Maynard G. Krebs (Bob Denver) often asks Dobie Gillis (Dwayne Hickman) to watch with him, in the TV sitcom *The Many Loves of Dobie Gillis*.

"Monster Twist"

Original title of the tune "Monster Mash," which was changed by songwriter Bobby "Boris" Pickett because of the popularity at that time of the dance called the "mashed potato."

Monstro

Whale that swallows Geppetto, Cleo, Figaro, and the title character in the Disney animated film *Pinocchio*.

Montalbán, Carlos

Portrayer of El Exigente, demanding coffee-bean buyer in TV commercials for Savarin coffee. He was the brother of actor Ricardo Montalbán.

Mont Cervin

French name for the Matterhorn, known in Italy as Monte Cervino.

Montegu, John (1718–1792)

Real name of the 4th Earl of Sandwich, for whom the sandwich is named. He had sliced meat and bread brought to him at gaming tables so he would not have to interrupt his play.

Montini, Giovanni Battista

Real name of Pope Paul VI, who served from 1963 to 1978.

Montpelier

Estate of President James Madison in Orange County, Virginia.

Montreal Tribune

Newspaper employer of crime reporter Victor Torres (Justin Louis) in the TV series *Urban Angel*.

Monty Python members

This comedy troupe was first seen on English television in the BBC series *Monty Python's Flying Circus* in 1969.

    Graham Chapman
    John Cleese
    Terry Gilliam
    Eric Idle
    Terry Jones
    Michael Palin

Terry Gilliam, an American, was the only non-Brit in the group.

Monumental Pictures

Film studio that is the setting of the film *Singin' in the Rain*.

Moo

Kingdom that is the setting of the comic strip *Alley Oop*.

Moody Blues original members

Graeme Edge, Denny Laine, Mike Pinder, Ray Thomas, and Clint Warwick.

Moody, King

First portrayer of clown Ronald McDonald in TV commercials for McDonald's. His previous best-known role had been as KAOS agent Starker in the TV sitcom *Get Smart*.

Mookie Blaylock

Former name of rock group Pearl Jam, for the NBA player. The group's first album, *Ten*, was named for Blaylock's uniform number.

Moon

Word in the title of all the songs heard in the film *An American Werewolf in London*, such as "Blue Moon," "Moondance," and "Bad Moon Rising."

Moonbase Alpha

Lunar research colony that is the setting of the TV series *Space: 1999*.

Moondoggie

See **Matthews, Jeff**

Moonglow

See **Last Honeymoon** and *Moonglow*

"Moonlight"

Nickname of Archibald Graham (Frank Whaley, Burt Lancaster) in the film *Field of Dreams*.

"Moonlight Serenade"

Theme song of bandleader Glenn Miller.

Moon, Marion

Maiden name of astronaut Buzz Aldrin's mother. Aldrin was the second man to walk on the moon.

"Moon Over Naples"

Original title of the tune "Spanish Eyes."

Moore

Middle name of Senator Edward Kennedy.

Moore and Prater

Last names (respectively) of singers Sam and Dave.

Moore, Ann

Former Peace Corps volunteer who created the Snugli infant carrier, patented in 1969. She got the idea from the traditional infant carriers she saw in Africa.

Moore, Mrs.

Role for which Peggy Ashcroft won a Best Supporting Actress Academy Award in the 1984 film *A Passage to India*.

Moore, Sara Jane

Woman who attempted to assassinate President Gerald Ford in San Francisco on September 22, 1975.

Moor's Indian Charity School

Original name of Dartmouth College.

Moose

Code name of David Caravaggio (Willem Dafoe) in the film *The English Patient*.

Mordor

Realm of evil Sauron the Great in J. R. R. Tolkien's *The Lord of the Rings* trilogy.

Moreno Reyes, Mario

Real name of Mexican-born entertainer Cantinflas.

Moreno, Wenceslao

Real name of ventriloquist Señor Wences.

More, Sir Thomas

Role for which Paul Scofield won a Best Actor Academy Award in the 1966 film *A Man for All Seasons*.

"More stars than there are in heaven"

Advertising slogan of MGM.

"The more you eat—the more you want"

Advertising slogan of Cracker Jack.

Morganfield, McKinley

Real name of blues singer Muddy Waters.

Morgan, Garrett A.

Inventor of the gas mask in 1912, which was originally called a "safety hood and smoke protector."

Morgan, Gwilym

Role for which Donald Crisp won a Best Supporting Actor Academy Award in the 1941 film *How Green Was My Valley*.

Morgan, Hank

Title character of the Mark Twain novel *A Connecticut Yankee in King Arthur's Court*.

Morgan, Julia

Architect who designed the San Simeon, California, estate of William Randolph Hearst.

Morgan, William G.

YMCA instructor in Holyoke, Massachusetts, who invented volleyball in 1895.

Morgenstern
Last name of the title character (Valerie Harper) in the TV sitcom *Rhoda*.

Morlocks
See **Eloi**

Morna
Real first name of singer (Morna) Anne Murray.

The Morning Express
Newspaper employer of photographer Casey (Richard Carlyle, Darren McGavin) in the TV series *Crime Photographer*.

Morning Post
Newspaper that is the setting of the film *The Front Page* (1931).

"The Morning Star of the Reformation"
Nickname of religious reformer John Wycliffe.

Morocco Mole
Sidekick of TV cartoon character Secret Squirrel.

Morovia
Grand duchy that is the homeland of Princess Charmein (Anna Maria Alberghetti) in the Jerry Lewis film *Cinderfella*.

Morrell, David
Author of the novel *First Blood*, upon which the film of the same name and the *Rambo* sequels were based.

Morris
Finicky cat in TV commercials for Nine Lives cat food.

Real first name of country singer Mac Davis.

Morrison, Herbert
Reporter for Chicago radio station WLS who gave the memorable eyewitness account of the explosion of the dirigible *Hindenburg*, at Lakehurst, New Jersey, on May 6, 1937.

Morrison, Jeanette Helen
Real name of actress Janet Leigh.

Morrison, Marion Michael
Real name of actor John Wayne.

Morrison, Walter Frederick
Inventor of the Frisbee, introduced by WHAM-O in 1957.

Morrison, William and Wharton, John
Tennessee candymakers who invented cotton candy (original name "Fairy Floss") in 1897.

Morris, Steveland Judkins
Real name of pop singer Stevie Wonder.

Morse, Theodore
See **"Come, Friends, Who Plough the Sea"**

Morton
Middle name of Tony Micelli (Tony Danza) in the TV sitcom *Who's The Boss?*

Morty
Moose in the opening credits of the TV series *Northern Exposure*.

Moschitta Jr., John
See **"Mighty Mouth"**

Mos Eisley
Tatooine spaceport city that is the setting of the cantina scene in the film *Star Wars*.

Moser, Emerson
Crayola senior crayon maker who retired in 1990 after 37 years of service. Upon his retirement he revealed that he was color-blind.

Moses, Daisy
Real name of Granny (Irene Ryan) in the TV sitcom *The Beverly Hillbillies*.

Moses Elkanah
First and middle names of the title character in the Saul Bellow novel *Herzog*.

Mosholu
Ship that brings young Vito Andolini (Oreste Baldini) to America in the film *The Godfather*.

Moss, Jerry
See **Alpert, Herb and Moss, Jerry**

Mossmoor Prison
Institution from which convicted bank robber Roy Earle (Humphrey Bogart) is released, at the beginning of the film *High Sierra*.

"The Most Trusted Name in Electronics"
Advertising slogan of RCA.

Mother
Shipboard computer in the film *Alien*.

"M-O-T-H-E-R (A Word That Means the World to Me)"

1915 tune by Theodore Morse and Howard Johnson that, in its two verses, explains what each letter in "mother" stands for.

FIRST VERSE

M "is for the million things she gave me"
O "means only that she's growing old"
T "is for the tears were shed to save me"
H "is for her heart of purest gold"
E "is for her eyes, with love-light shining"
R "means right, and right she'll always be"

SECOND VERSE

M "is for the mercy she possesses"
O "means that I owe her all I own"
T "is for her tender sweet caresses"
H "is for her hands that made a home"
E "means ev'rything she's done to help me"
R "means real and regular, you see"

Each verse ends, "Put them all together, they spell 'MOTHER', a word that means the world to me."

Mother Maybelle

Martin D45 acoustic guitar of rock singer/songwriter Stephen Stills, which he uses for all of his recordings. The guitar is named for country music legend Maybelle Carter.

"The Mother of Exiles"

Nickname of the Statue of Liberty.

"Mother of Mercy! Is this the end of Rico?"

Last words of gangster Cesare Enrico Bandello (Edward G. Robinson) in the film *Little Caesar*.

"Mother, please, I'd rather do it myself!"

Memorable complaint in a 1960s TV commercial for pain reliever Anacin.

Mother's

Bar where singer Edie Hart (Lola Albright), girlfriend of the title character (Craig Stevens) performs, in the TV series *Peter Gunn*.

Mötley Crüe original members

Tommy Lee, Mick Mars, Vince Neil, and Nikki Sixx.

Mott, Ma

Role for which Ethel Barrymore won a Best Supporting Actress Academy Award in the 1944 film *None But the Lonely Heart*.

The Mount

Home of novelist Edith Wharton in Lenox, Massachusetts.

"mountain of light"

What the name of the 106-carat Koh-i-noor Diamond means in Persian. It is currently part of the British Crown Jewels.

mountains, world's highest (by continent)

North America: Mount McKinley (Alaska, 20,320 feet)
South America: Mount Aconcagua (Argentina, 22,834 feet)
Europe: Mount Elbrus (Russia, 18,510 feet)
Asia: Mount Everest (Nepal/Tibet, 29,028 feet)
Africa: Mount Kilimanjaro (Tanzania, 19,340 feet)
Australia: Mount Kosciusko (New South Wales, 7,310 feet)
Antarctica: Vinson Massif (16,864 feet)

Mount Crumpit

Peak overlooking Whoville, where the title character takes his sleigh full of stolen Christmas presents, in the Dr. Seuss children's book *How the Grinch Stole Christmas!*

Mount Idy

Mythical hometown of comedian Charley Weaver (Cliff Arquette), which is populated with colorful characters such as Grandpa Ogg, Gomar Cool, and Wallace Swine.

Mount Knocknasheega

Domain of the leprechauns in the Disney film *Darby O'Gill and the Little People*.

Mount Lee

Location, within Griffith Park, of the famous Hollywood sign.

Mount Mazama

Volcano whose collapse about 7,700 years ago formed what is now Crater Lake, Oregon, which, at 1,932 feet, is the deepest lake in the United States.

Mount Wilshire

Active volcano formed in downtown Los Angeles in the film *Volcano*.

Mourning Becomes Electra trilogy

Series of plays by Eugene O'Neill, all published in 1931: *Homecoming*, *The Hunted* and *The Haunted*.

Mouseketeers, original

The 39 children who appeared at one time or another during the original 1955–59 run of the children's TV series *The Mickey Mouse Club*:

Nancy Abbate
Don Agrati (aka Don Grady, later of *My Three Sons*)
Sherry Alberoni
Sharon Baird
Billie Jean Beanblossom
Bobby Burgess
Lonnie Burr
Tommy Cole
Johnny Crawford (later of *The Rifleman*)
Dennis Day
Eileen Diamond
Dickie Dodd
Mary Espinosa
Bonnie Lynn Fields
Annette Funicello
Darlene Gillespie
Judy Harriet
Cheryl Holdridge
Linda Hughes
Dallas Johann
John Lee Johann
Bonni Lou Kern
Charley Laney
Larry Larsen
Cubby O'Brien
Karen Pendleton
Paul Petersen (later of *The Donna Reed Show*)
Lynn Ready
Mickey Rooney Jr. (son of Mickey Rooney)
Tim Rooney (son of Mickey Rooney)
Mary Lynn Sartori
Bronson Scott
Mike Smith
Jay-Jay Solari
Margene Storey
Ronnie Steiner
Mark Sutherland
Doreen Tracey
Don Underhill

THE TWO ADULT LEADERS ON THE SHOW:

Jimmie Dodd
Roy Williams, aka "The Big Mooseketeer" (who invented the mouse ears worn by everyone on the show)

"Moving In, Moving Out, Moving On"

Debut episode of the TV series *Sisters*, which aired on May 11, 1991.

The Moving Target

Novel by Ross Macdonald that was the basis for the film *Harper*.

"Movin' In"

Debut episode of the TV sitcom *Diff'rent Strokes*, which aired on November 3, 1978.

"Movin' on Up"

Theme song of the TV sitcom *The Jeffersons*.

"The MPH Line"

Nickname of the 1970s Chicago Blackhawks scoring line of Pit Martin, Jim Pappin, and Dennis Hull, for their speed, and the first letters in their respective last names.

"Mr. and Mrs. Swing"

Nickname of bandleader Red Norvo and his wife, singer Mildred Bailey.

Mr. B

Family pet rabbit in the comic strip *For Better or for Worse*.

"Mr. Basketball"

Nickname of basketball Hall of Fame player and coach Nat Holman.

"Mr. Big"

Debut episode of the TV sitcom *Get Smart*, which aired on September 18, 1965.

"Mr. Democrat"

Nickname of Texas congressman Sam Rayburn (1882–1961), who served for 17 years as Speaker of the House.

"Mr. Dynamite"

See **Brown, James, nicknames of**

"Mr. Excitement"

Nickname of soul singer Jackie Wilson.

"Mr. Guitar"

Nickname of country-music artist Chet Atkins.

"Mr. Longtail"

Nickname of Thoroughbred racehorse Whirlaway, winner of the Triple Crown in 1941.

Mr. Moto films

Detective series starring Peter Lorre in the title role (except for the 1965 film, which stars Henry Silva):

Think Fast, Mr. Moto (1937)

Thank You, Mr. Moto (1938)
Mr. Moto's Gamble (1938)
Mr. Moto Takes a Chance (1938)
Mysterious Mr. Moto (1938)
Mr. Moto's Last Warning (1939)
Mr. Moto in Danger Island (1939)
Mr. Moto Takes a Vacation (1939)
The Return of Mr. Moto (1965)

Mr. Mudd

Production company of actor John Malkovich.

"Mr. October"

Nickname of baseball player Reggie Jackson, for his World Series heroics.

"Mr. Please Please"

See **Brown, James, nicknames of**

"Mr. Republican"

Nickname of Ohio senator Robert Taft.

"Mr. Showmanship"

Nickname of pianist Liberace.

Mr. Smiley's

Fast-food employer of Lester Burnham (Kevin Spacey) after he quits his job as a magazine writer, in the film *American Beauty*.

Mr. Squid

Fast-food employer of assistant manager Ernie Floyd in the comic strip *The Piranha Club*.

Mr. Stay-Puft

Giant ghostly marshmallow in the film *Ghostbusters*.

"Mr. Teardrop"

Nickname of country singer Marty Robbins.

"Mr. Television"

Nickname of Milton Berle.

Mr. Trace, Keener Than Most Persons

Recurring whodunit featured in the comedy routines of Bob and Ray. The title was inspired by the radio series *Mr. Keen, Tracer of Lost Persons*.

"Mr. Warmth"

Nickname of insult comic Don Rickles.

Mudd, Samuel A.

Doctor who treated the broken leg of John Wilkes Booth on April 15, 1865, after Booth shot President Abraham Lincoln. Mudd was sentenced to life imprisonment, but was later pardoned by President Andrew Johnson.

"muddy confluence"

What the name of Kuala Lumpur, capital city of Malaysia, means in Malay.

Mudville

Setting and home team of the title character in the Ernest L. Thayer poem "Casey at the Bat." The poem first appeared, under the byline "Phin," in the *San Francisco Examiner* on June 3, 1888.

Mueller

Real last name of Pearl Jam vocalist Eddie Vedder.

Muffin

Pet cat of Earl and Opal in the comic strip *Pickles*.

Muffy

Pet dog of Laura Manion (Lee Remick) in the film *Anatomy of a Murder*.

Pet poodle of Barbara Stone (Bette Midler) in the film *Ruthless People*.

Muggle

Term for an ordinary person with no magical powers, in the Harry Potter series of books by J. K. Rowling.

Muggs, J. Fred

Male chimpanzee seen in the 1950s on the TV series *The Today Show*.

See also **Beebe, Phoebe B.**

Muhlenberg, Frederick Augustus Conrad

Lutheran minister from Pennsylvania who was the first to serve as Speaker of the House, from 1789 to 1791.

Muldoon, Oscar

Role for which Edmond O'Brien won a Best Supporting Actor Academy Award in the 1954 film *The Barefoot Contessa*.

Muldoon's Point

Local lovers' lane in the TV sitcom *The Partridge Family*.

Mules

High-school football team in the TV sitcom *Evening Shade*.

See also **Shermer High**

Mulford, Clarence E.

Creator of Western hero Hopalong Cassidy, who first appeared in the 1907 novel *Bar 20*.

Mullany, David

Inventor of the Wiffle Ball, introduced in 1953.

Muller, Kurt

Role for which Paul Lukas won a Best Actor Academy Award in the 1943 film *Watch on the Rhine*.

Multimixer

Milk-shake machine sold by Ray Kroc before he founded the McDonald's fast-food chain.

"Multis e gentibus vires"

Motto of Saskatchewan, Canada, which is Latin for "From many peoples, strength."

"Mum and Dad"

See **"Scotland Forever" and "Mum and Dad"**

Mumford Phys. Ed. Dept.

Words on the T-shirt worn by Axel Foley (Eddie Murphy) in the film *Beverly Hills Cop*.

Muncie College of Business Administration

Alma mater of Norville Barnes (Tim Robbins) in the film *The Hudsucker Proxy*.

Munday, Alex

See **Cook, Natalie; Sanders, Dylan; and Munday, Alex**

Mundy Lane Entertainment

Production company of actor Denzel Washington.

"Munit haec et altera vincit"

Motto of Nova Scotia, Canada, which is Latin for "One defends and the other conquers."

Munnerlyn

Middle name of novelist Margaret Mitchell.

"Munster Masquerade"

Debut episode of the TV sitcom *The Munsters*, which aired on September 24, 1964.

Muppet feature films

The Muppet Movie (1979)
The Great Muppet Caper (1981)
The Muppets Take Manhattan (1984)
The Muppet Christmas Carol (1992)
Muppet Treasure Island (1996)
Muppets from Space (1999)

The Muppet Movie cameo roles

These performers all make brief appearances in the film:

Edgar Bergen	Carol Kane
Milton Berle	Cloris Leachman
Mel Brooks	Steve Martin
James Coburn	Richard Pryor
Dom DeLuise	Telly Savalas
Elliott Gould	Orson Welles
Bob Hope	Paul Williams
Madeline Kahn	

Murat

Real first name of *Blondie* creator/cartoonist Chic Young.

Murder at Midnight

Radio show during which an actual murder is committed, in the Abbott and Costello film *Who Done It?*

"Murder by the Barrel"

Debut episode of the TV series *McMillan and Wife*, which aired on September 29, 1971.

"Murderers' Row"

Nickname of the 1927 New York Yankees, whose lineup included Hall of Famers Babe Ruth, Lou Gehrig, Tony Lazzeri, and Earle Combs.

The Murder Game

Longest-running thriller in Broadway history, written by Sidney Bruhl (Michael Caine) in the film *Deathtrap*.

Murder Most Fair

Last play written by Sidney Bruhl (Michael Caine) in the film *Deathtrap*.

The Murder of Gonzago

Play within the William Shakespeare play *Hamlet*.

"The Murder of Sherlock Holmes"

Debut episode of the TV series *Murder, She Wrote*, which aired on September 30, 1984.

Murdoch

Maiden name of Hope Steadman (Mel Harris) in the TV series *thirtysomething*.

Muriel

Real first name of actress Teresa Wright.

Murphy, Mrs.
Crime-solving cat of postmistress Mary Minot "Harry" Haristeen in the mystery novels of Rita Mae Brown.

Murray
Buchman family dog in the TV sitcom *Mad About You*.

Real last name of actress Jean Stapleton.

Murray of Fala Hill
Full name of Fala, pet Scottie of President Franklin D. Roosevelt.

Murrie, R. Bruce
See **Mars and Murrie**

muselet
Technical term for the wire that holds a Champagne cork in place.

Muses
In Greek mythology, the nine daughters of Zeus and Mnemosyne who preside over the arts, listed below with their specialties:
Calliope (epic poetry)
Clio (history)
Erato (lyric poetry)
Euterpe (music)
Melpomene (tragedy)
Polyhymnia (religious music)
Terpsichore (dance)
Thalia (comedy)
Urania (astronomy)

museums, unusual
A sampling of American museums devoted to unusual topics, and where to find them:
Bad Art: Dedham, Massachusetts
Angels: Beloit, Wisconsin
Asphalt: Rohnert Park, California
Baking: Manhattan, Kansas
Bananas: Auburn, Washington
Barbed Wire: Lacrosse, Kansas
Bathroom Fixtures: Worcester, Massachusetts
Fasteners: Julian, California
Gourds: Angier, North Carolina
Mustard: Mount Horeb, Wisconsin
Pez Dispensers: Burlingame, California
Sand: Freeport, Maine
Sandpaper: Two Harbors, Minnesota
Sewing Machines: Arlington, Texas
Snowmobiles: Sayner, Wisconsin
SPAM: Austin, Minnesota
Superman: Metropolis, Illinois
Surfing: Santa Cruz, California
Telephones: Leslie, Georgia
Thermometers: Onset, Massachusetts
UFOs: Roswell, New Mexico
Vacuum Cleaners: North Canton, Ohio
Voodoo: New Orleans, Louisiana
Whiskey History: Bardstown, Kentucky
Wooden Nickels: San Antonio, Texas

Musical Knights
Band led by Horace Heidt.

Musical Stages
1975 autobiography of Broadway songwriter Richard Rodgers.

Music, Lorenzo
Voice of the unseen doorman Carlton in the TV sitcom *Rhoda*.

Muskies
Original nickname of the Minnesota franchise during the 1967–1968 inaugural season of the American Basketball Association.

mustard yellow
Color of the belt awarded to the World Hot Dog Eating Champion at the annual contest at Nathan's Famous in Coney Island, New York.

The Mutants of 2051 A.D.
Film made by Bob and Doug McKenzie (Rick Moranis and Dave Thomas) in the film *Strange Brew*.

Mutki
Pet dog of Anna Bronski (Anne Bancroft) in the Mel Brooks film *To Be or Not to Be*.

Mutt Cutts
Employer of dog groomer Harry Dunne (Jeff Daniels) in the film *Dumb and Dumber*.

My Answer
Syndicated newspaper column of evangelist Billy Graham, in which he answers letters from his readers.

My Backyard
Original name of rock group Lynyrd Skynyrd. The group's better-known name is derived from Leonard Skinner, a high-school gym teacher who disliked long hair.

My Brother Paul

Book by Theodore Dreiser that was the basis for the biopic *My Gal Sal*, about songwriter Paul Dresser, Dreiser's brother.

My Day

Syndicated newspaper column written by Eleanor Roosevelt from 1935 to 1962.

"My Favorite Martin"

Debut episode of the TV sitcom *My Favorite Martian*, which aired on September 29, 1963.

"My Life"

Theme song of the TV sitcom *Bosom Buddies*, performed by Billy Joel.

My Life and Fortunes

1963 autobiography of oil tycoon J. Paul Getty.

My Life Is in Your Hands

1928 autobiography of comedian Eddie Cantor.

"My mother thanks you, my father thanks you, my sister thanks you, and I thank you."

Line used by Broadway performer/songwriter George M. Cohan at the end of a show, to acknowledge applause.

"My Old New England Home"

Original title of the 1903 Richard Gerard/Harry Armstrong tune "Sweet Adeline." The title character of the tune had been named "Rosalie," but was changed in honor of opera star Adelina Patti.

myopia

Medical term for nearsightedness.

Mypos

Mythical Mediterranean island that is the homeland of Balki Bartokomous (Bronson Pinchot) in the TV sitcom *Perfect Strangers*.

My Posse Don't Do Homework

Book by Louanne Johnson that was the basis for the film *Dangerous Minds*.

Myra Ellen

Real first and middle names of rock singer Tori Amos.

Myron

Dog of Dick and Dora Charleston (David Niven and Maggie Smith) in the film *Murder by Death*.

Real first name of telejournalist Mike Wallace.

Myrtle

Family pet goat in the TV series *The Waltons*.

"My Shawl"

Theme song of the Xavier Cugat orchestra.

Myshkin, Prince Lef

Title character of the Fyodor Dostoevsky novel *The Idiot*.

Mystery Machine

Car driven by Shaggy and his high-school friends in the children's animated TV series *Scooby-Doo, Where Are You?*

Mystery Readers International

See **Macavity Awards**

Mystery Writers of America

See **Edgar Allan Poe Awards**

Mystic Knights of the Sea

Fraternal lodge in the radio and TV sitcom *Amos 'n' Andy*.

Mythopoeic Fantasy Awards

Presented annually since 1971 by the Mythopoeic Society, for adult and children's fantasy works.

"My Time Is Your Time"

Theme song of singer Rudy Vallee.

"My True Story" characters

This tune by The Jive Five concerns the love triangle of Sue, Earl and Lorraine.

My Turn at Bat

1969 autobiography of baseball Hall of Famer Ted Williams.

"My Twilight Dream"

Theme song of pianist Eddy Duchin.

My Wicked Wicked Ways

1959 autobiography of actor Errol Flynn.

"My Wild Beautiful Bird"

Subtitle of the Chuck Jackson tune "Any Day Now."

Naboombu

Legendary island where Eglantine Price (Angela Lansbury) finds a magic spell that helps England win World War II, in the Disney film *Bedknobs and Broomsticks*.

Nadsat

Language spoken by the teens in the Anthony Burgess novel *A Clockwork Orange*. It is a mixture of English and Russian.

Nail, Kathleen Sue

Real name of actress Kate Capshaw.

Naitauba

Fiji island once owned by actor Raymond Burr.

Nakatomi Plaza

40-story Los Angeles skyscraper that is the setting of the film *Die Hard*.

Nana

Darling family sheepdog in the James M. Barrie novel *Peter Pan*.

Nancy Drew films

Series starring Bonita Granville in the title role:
   Nancy Drew, Detective (1938)
   Nancy Drew—Reporter (1939)
   Nancy Drew—Troubleshooter (1939)
   Nancy Drew and the Hidden Staircase (1939)

Nanny and Nanko

Pet goats of presidential son Tad Lincoln.

"The Nanny Named Fran"

Theme song of the sitcom *The Nanny*, performed by Ann Hampton Callaway.

"Nanny Will Do"

Debut episode of the TV sitcom *Nanny and the Professor*, which aired on January 21, 1970.

Napaloni, Benzino

Jack Oakie's role in the film *The Great Dictator*, which is a spoof of Benito Mussolini.

Napier, Jack

Real name of the Joker (Jack Nicholson) in the film *Batman*.

Napoleon

Secret Service code name for singer Frank Sinatra.

"The Napoleon of Crime"

Sherlock Holmes' nickname for his archenemy, Professor James Moriarty, in the stories of Sir Arthur Conan Doyle.

Napolitano, Anne

Role for which Mercedes Ruehl won a Best Supporting Actress Academy Award in the 1991 film *The Fisher King*.

Naps

See **Blues**

Narcissus

Shuttlecraft of the spaceship *Nostromo* in the film *Alien*.

Boat of the title character (Minerva Urecal) in the TV series *The Adventures of Tugboat Annie*.

nares

Medical term for the nostrils.

"A Narrative of Adventures in the South Seas"

Subtitle of the Herman Melville novel *Omoo*.

Nascimento, Edson Arantes do

Real name of soccer great Pelé.

Nash, Carter

Real identity of the title character in the TV sitcom *Captain Nice*, portrayed by William Daniels. Nash is a police chemist who accidentally discovers a potion that transforms him into the inept superhero.

Nash, Clarence "Ducky" (1904–1985)

Longtime voice of Donald Duck in Disney cartoons.

Nasier, Alcofribas

Pen name used by François Rabelais for his novel *Gargantua and Pantagruel*, which is an anagram of his real name.

nasion

Technical term for the space between the eyebrows.

Nastily Exhausting Wizarding Tests

See **N.E.W.T.s**

"Nasty"

Nickname of Romanian tennis pro Ilie Nastase, for his on-court behavior.

"The Nasty Boys"

Nickname of the Cincinnati Reds relief pitching staff of Rob Dibble, Norm Charlton, and Randy Myers in its World Series-winning year of 1990.

Nathalie

Real first name of actress Tippi Hedren.

Nathan, Daniel

Real name of Ellery Queen co-creator Frederic Dannay.

National Association of W Lovers

Group that Bert is a member of, in the children's TV series *Sesame Street*.

National cheesecake

See **Miller's Bakery**

National Indian Knitting Enterprises

Manufacturing company (makers of bikes, roller skates, skateboards, jogging suits, and shoes) owned by Sam Birdwater (Chief Dan George) in the film *Americathon*. The company's logo is NIKE.

National Organization of Men Against Amazonian Masterhood

See **NO MA'AM**

National Paper

Employer of paper-bag wrapper Paula Pokrifki (Debra Winger) in the film *An Officer and a Gentleman*.

National Register

Tabloid employer of Jack McGee (Jack Colvin), who is pursuing the title character (Bill Bixby/Lou Ferrigno) in the TV series *The Incredible Hulk*.

National Union Life and Limb Insurance Company

Original name of Metropolitan Life at its founding in 1863.

natrium

Former name for sodium, from which its chemical symbol Na is derived.

Nat's Bar

Favorite watering hole of Don Birnam (Ray Milland) in the film *The Lost Weekend*.

"Natty"

Comedienne Gracie Allen's nickname for her husband, comedian George Burns. His real name was Nathan Birnbaum.

Naugatuck, Nell

English maid (Hermione Baddeley) who replaced Florida Evans (Esther Rolle) in the TV sitcom *Maude*.

Navigator Islands

Former name of Samoa.

Nazerman, Sol

Title character (Rod Steiger) in the film *The Pawnbroker*.

NBA commissioners

> 1949–63: Maurice Podoloff
> 1963–75: Walter Kennedy
> 1975–84: Larry O'Brien
> 1984–present: David Stern

NBC Blue Network

Original name of the American Broadcasting Company (ABC).

NCC-1701

Registration number of the starship U.S.S. *Enterprise* in the TV series *Star Trek*.

Neal, Patricia

Real name of actress/author Fannie Flagg, who changed it because of the actress of the same name.

"Near You"

Theme song of comedian Milton Berle.

Nebula Awards

Presented annually since 1965 by the Science Fiction and Fantasy Writers of America for outstanding writing.

Nederlander, Ned

See **Bottoms, Dusty; Day, Lucky; and Nederlander, Ned**

"negotiable order of withdrawal"

What the letters in "NOW account" stand for.

Neil

Pet St. Bernard of the Kerbys (Anne Jeffreys and Robert Sterling) in the TV sitcom *Topper*.

"Neither snow, nor rain, nor heat, nor gloom of night stays these couriers from the swift completion of their appointed rounds"

Inscription on the main post office building in New York City. It is adapted from a passage written by Greek historian Herodotus in the fifth century B.C., praising Persian messengers.

"Nel Blu Dipinto Di Blu"

Original Italian title of the Domenico Modugno tune "Volare," first recipient of Grammy awards for Song of the Year and Record of the Year, in 1958. The original title means "In the blue, the picture of blue."

Nelle

Real first name of author (Nelle) Harper Lee.

Nellie

Horse of TV cartoon character Quick Draw McGraw.

Nelson, Benjamin Earl

Real name of singer Ben E. King.

Nelson, Christian K.

Iowan who invented the Eskimo Pie in 1921.

Nelson, Prince Rogers

Full birth name of pop singer Prince.

Nelson, Sophie

Role for which Anne Baxter won a Best Supporting Actress Academy Award in the 1946 film *The Razor's Edge*.

Nemo's

Restaurant hangout in the TV sitcom *Everybody Loves Raymond*.

nephometer

Instrument for measuring the amount of cloud cover in the sky.

nephoscope

Instrument for measuring velocity and direction of movement of clouds.

nerd

Word coined by Dr. Seuss, first used in his 1950 children's book *If I Ran the Zoo*.

Nermal

Feline nemesis of the title character in the comic strip *Garfield*.

Nero

Pet cat of Laura Holt (Stephanie Zimbalist) in the TV series *Remington Steele*.

Netherfield Park

London home of eligible bachelor Mr. Bingley in the Jane Austen novel *Pride and Prejudice*.

Network 23

Television station on which the computer-generated title character (Matt Frewer) is seen, in the TV series *Max Headroom*.

Neuman, Alfred E.

See **"What, me worry?"**

Neustadter, Arnold

Inventor of the Rolodex rotary card file circa 1946.

Nevada Club

See **The Ronelles**

"Never give a saga an even break!"

Slogan used to promote the Mel Brooks film *Blazing Saddles*.

Neverland

California estate of pop singer Michael Jackson.

"Never underestimate the power of a woman"

Advertising slogan of *Ladies' Home Journal*.

New Amsterdam

Former name of New York City, which was renamed in 1664 after its takeover by Great Britain.

Newbery Medal

Awarded annually by the American Library Association for the most distinguished contribution to American literature for children. Named for 18th-century English bookseller John Newbery, it was first awarded to Hendrik Willem Van Loon in 1922 for *The Story of Mankind*.

Newbold Revel

Warwickshire estate of author Sir Thomas Malory.

The New Bulletin

Newspaper employer of *Odds and Ends* columnist Ann Mitchell (Barbara Stanwyck) in the Frank Capra film *Meet John Doe*.

New Carthage

Setting of the Edward Albee play *Who's Afraid of Virginia Woolf?*

New City, California
Setting of the TV sitcom *The People's Choice*.

"The New Colossus"
Poem by Emma Lazarus that is inscribed at the base of the Statue of Liberty.

Newcomers
Extraterrestrials who coexist with humans in the film and TV series *Alien Nation*.

New Congress Club
Honolulu soldiers' hangout in the film *From Here to Eternity*.

Newell Convers
First and middle names of artist N. C. Wyeth.

Newel, Sylvester
Real name of Pardner (Clint Eastwood) in the film *Paint Your Wagon*.

New Essex, North Carolina
Setting of the film *Cape Fear* (1991).

"new flower"
What the name of Addis Ababa, capital of Ethiopia, means in Amharic (the official language of Ethiopia).

New Grenada
Former name of the South American nation Colombia.

New Hebrides
Former name of the Pacific island nation of Vanuatu.

New Holland
Former name of Australia, given by Dutch explorer Abel Tasman circa 1642.

"The New Housekeeper"
Debut episode of the TV sitcom *The Andy Griffith Show*, which aired on October 3, 1960.

"A New Life"
Debut episode of the TV series *JAG*, which aired on September 23, 1995.

"The New Man"
Debut episode of the TV series *Tales From the Darkside*, which aired on September 30, 1984.

Newman, Christopher
Title character of the Henry James novel *The American*.

Newman, Paul, "H" films of
The 14 feature films of actor Paul Newman whose titles have a word beginning with the letter H:
The Helen Morgan Story (1957)
The Long Hot Summer (1958)
The Left Handed Gun (1958)
Cat on a Hot Tin Roof (1958)
The Hustler (1961)
Hemingway's Adventures of a Young Man (1962)
Hud (1963)
Harper (1966)
Hombre (1967)
Cool Hand Luke (1967)
The Secret War of Harry Frigg (1968)
Sitting Bull's History Lesson, aka *Buffalo Bill and the Indians* (1976)
Harry and Son (1984)
The Hudsucker Proxy (1994)

Newman, Stan
Pseudonym used by Dick Clark for the early rap-style record "Jenkins' Band," produced for Cameo Records circa 1960. (Thanks to Dick Clark for this information.)

Newman/Woodward films
See **Woodward/Newman films**

New North Hospital
Setting of the TV series *The Interns*.

The New Pilgrim's Progress
Alternate title of the Mark Twain novel *The Innocents Abroad*.

New Place
Home of William Shakespeare at Stratford-upon-Avon, England.

Newport, Christopher
See **Sarah Constant, Goodspeed, and Discovery**

New Prospect, Oklahoma
Setting of the TV series *Hec Ramsey*.

"news"
What the name of Russian newspaper *Izvestia* means in Russian.

Newspeak
Language spoken in the George Orwell novel *1984*.

Newsview

Magazine employer of Donald Hollinger (Ted Bessell), boyfriend of Ann Marie (Marlo Thomas) in the TV sitcom *That Girl*.

New Switzerland

Name given by Mr. Robinson (John Mills) to the island where his family is shipwrecked, in the Disney film *Swiss Family Robinson*.

Newton

Real first name of novelist (Newton) Booth Tarkington.

Pet basset hound of Ol' Lonely (Gordon Jump), the repairman in ads for Maytag appliances. The dog is named for Maytag's headquarters in Newton, Iowa.

Newtowne

Original name of Cambridge, Massachusetts.

N.E.W.T.s

High-level examinations at Hogwarts, in the Harry Potter series of books by J. K. Rowling. The letters stand for "Nastily Exhausting Wizarding Tests."

The New Yardbirds

Original name of rock group Led Zeppelin.

New York Banner

Newspaper employer of architecture critic Ellsworth Toohey in the Ayn Rand novel *The Fountainhead*.

New York Chronicle

Newspaper employer of Martin Lane (William Schallert) in the TV sitcom *The Patty Duke Show*.

New York City Municipal Orphanage

Setting of the musical *Annie*.

New York Curb Market Association

Original name of the American Stock Exchange.

The New York Deli

Eatery run by Remo and Jean DaVinci (Jay Thomas and Gina Hecht) in the TV sitcom *Mork and Mindy*.

New York Eagle

Newspaper employer of the title character (Richard Widmark, Carleton Young, Staats Cotsworth) in the radio series *Front Page Farrell*.

New York Evening Chronicle

Newspaper employer of city editor-turned-college student James Gannon (Clark Gable) in the film *Teacher's Pet*.

New York Herald

Newspaper employer of sportswriter Oscar Madison (Jack Klugman) in the TV sitcom *The Odd Couple*.

New York Knights

Major-league baseball team for which Roy Hobbs (Robert Redford) hits a dramatic home run in the film *The Natural*.

New York Loons

Baseball team inherited by the title feline in the H. Allen Smith novel *Rhubarb*.

New York Mail

Former newspaper employer of Peter Warne (Clark Gable) in the Frank Capra film *It Happened One Night*.

"New York Sack Exchange"

Nickname of the 1980s New York Jets defensive line of Mark Gastineau, Joe Klecko, Marty Lyons, and Abdul Salaam.

New York Sentinel

New York Times-like newspaper in the film *The Paper*. The paper's motto is "All the News in the World."

New York Stories sections

1984 film consisting of three shorter films:
"Life Lessons" (directed by Martin Scorsese)
"Life Without Zoe" (directed by Francis Ford Coppola)
"Oedipus Wrecks" (directed by Woody Allen)
Publicity slogan for the film: "One City. Three Stories Tall."

New York Sun

Newspaper whose offices are the setting of the film *The Paper*. The paper's motto is "It shines for all."

Newspaper employer of columnist Mike Logan (Ted Danson) in the TV sitcom *Ink*.

New York Wrecking Company

Business owned by Joe Gerard (David Groh), husband of the title character (Valerie Harper) in the TV sitcom *Rhoda*.

"The next best thing to being there"

Advertising slogan of AT&T for Long Distance calling.

"The next best thing to your good cooking"

Advertising slogan of Swanson TV dinners.

NFL presidents/commissioners

The NFL's chief executive held the title of President until the term of Elmer Layden, when the title was changed to Commissioner.

1920: Jim Thorpe
1921–39: Joe Carr
1939–41: Carl Storck
1941–46: Elmer Layden
1946–59: Bert Bell
1960–89: Pete Rozelle
1989–present: Paul Tagliabue

Nguyen Tat Thanh

Real name of Vietnamese revolutionary Ho Chi Minh.

NHL presidents/commissioners

The NHL's chief executive held the title of President until the term of Gary Bettman, when the title was changed to Commissioner.

1917–43: Frank Calder
1943–46: Mervyn "Red" Dutton
1946–77: Clarence Campbell
1977–92: John A. Ziegler, Jr.
1992–93: Gil Stein
1993–present: Gary Bettman

Niagara

See **Lawrence** and *Niagara*

Nicholas

Real first name of poet (Nicholas) Vachel Lindsay.

Nicholas, Captain Samuel

First commandant of the U.S. Marine Corps, appointed by Continental Congress president John Hancock in 1775.

Nichols, Darrell and Darrell

Law firm in *The Lawyers* segment of the TV series *The Bold Ones*.

Nichols, Julie

Role for which Jessica Lange won a Best Supporting Actress Academy Award in the 1982 film *Tootsie*.

Nicholson, Colonel

Role for which Sir Alec Guinness won a Best Actor Academy Award in the 1957 film *The Bridge on the River Kwai*.

Nicholson, John H.

See **Hill, Samuel E; Knights, William J.; and Nicholson, John H.**

Nick

Role for which Christopher Walken won a Best Supporting Actor Academy Award in the 1978 film *The Deer Hunter*.

Nick Nack

Diminutive servant of Scaramanga (Christopher Lee) in the James Bond film *The Man with the Golden Gun*, portrayed by Hervé Villechaize.

Nicolo Perfume

Employer of Lise Bouvier (Leslie Caron) in the film *An American in Paris*.

Nidetch, Jean

Creator of the Weight Watchers diet program in 1963. Her company was sold to H. J. Heinz for $72,000,000 in 1978.

Nielli, Marie

Real name of French fashion designer Nina Ricci.

"Night Bus"

Short story by Samuel Hopkins Adams that was the basis for the Frank Capra film *It Happened One Night*.

"The Nighthawk"

See **KJCM**

Nightmare

Horse of Casper the Friendly Ghost.

"Nightmare"

Theme song of bandleader Artie Shaw.

Nightmare on Elm Street films

A Nightmare on Elm Street (1984)
A Nightmare on Elm Street Part 2: Freddy's Revenge (1985)
A Nightmare on Elm Street 3: Dream Warriors (1987)
A Nightmare on Elm Street 4: The Dream Master (1988)
A Nightmare on Elm Street 5: The Dream Child (1989)
Freddy's Dead: The Final Nightmare (1991)
New Nightmare (1994)

Night of Love

Perfume tried out by Edna May Benstrom (Madge Blake) in the film *An American in Paris*.

"The Night of the Inferno"

Debut episode of the TV series *The Wild Wild West*, which aired on September 17, 1965.

Night of the Living Dead **films**

Night of the Living Dead (1968)
Dawn of the Dead (1979)
Day of the Dead (1985)
Night of the Living Dead (1990)

Nightshade, Dudley

Nemesis of the title character in the children's animated TV series *Crusader Rabbit*, voiced by Russ Coughlan.

Nights of Cabiria

Federico Fellini film that was the basis for the musical *Sweet Charity*.

"The Nighttime, Sniffling, Sneezing, Coughing, Achy, Stuffy Head, Fever So You Can Rest Medicine"

Advertising slogan for Vicks NyQuil.

"Night Train"

Nickname of pro football Hall of Fame defensive back Dick Lane.

"Night with Daddy G"

Instrumental tune by the Church Street Five to which Gary U.S. Bonds added lyrics, becoming "Quarter to Three," which reached #1 on the U.S. *Billboard* pop chart in 1961.

Nigma, Edward

Real name of Batman adversary The Riddler.

Nigro

Real last name of pop singer/songwriter Laura Nyro.

"Nil sine magno labore"

Motto of Brooklyn College, which is Latin for "Nothing without great effort."

Nimbus 2000

First broomstick of the title character in the Harry Potter series of books by J. K. Rowling.

Nina

Name that caricaturist Al Hirschfeld has been hiding in his drawings since the birth of his daughter Nina in 1945.

Nine Sisters

Record album where Sonny Malone (Michael Beck) first sees a picture of Kira (Olivia Newton-John) in the film *Xanadu*.

Nip and Tuck

Pet canaries of President Calvin Coolidge.

Nippon Electric Company

What the letters in the name of Japanese computer manufacturer NEC stand for.

"Nisi dominus frustra"

Motto of Edinburgh, Scotland, which is Latin for "Expect the Lord in vain."

Nissan, George

Inventor of the trampoline circa 1936.

Nixon, Marni

Performer best known for dubbing the singing voices of Deborah Kerr in the *The King and I* (1956), Natalie Wood in *West Side Story,* and Audrey Hepburn in *My Fair Lady*. She was formerly married to film composer Ernest Gold and is the mother of pop musician/composer Andrew Gold.

Nkima

Pet chimp of Tarzan in the stories of Edgar Rice Burroughs.

Noah, Dr.

Villainous alter ego of Jimmy Bond (Woody Allen), nephew of Sir James Bond (David Niven) in the film *Casino Royale.*

Noel

Real first name of singer (Noel) Paul Stookey (of Peter, Paul, and Mary).

Pet pig of Suzanne Sugarbaker (Delta Burke) in the TV sitcom *Designing Women.*

Noid

One-time cartoon mascot of Domino's Pizza.

"Nola"

Theme song of bandleader Vincent Lopez.

Nolan, Gypo

Role for which Victor McLaglen won a Best Actor Academy Award in the 1935 film *The Informer.*

Nolan, Johnny

Role for which James Dunn won a Best Supporting Actor Academy Award in the 1945 film *A Tree Grows in Brooklyn.*

Nolan, Philip

Title character of the Edward Everett Hale short story "The Man Without a Country."

NO MA'AM

Acronym for the National Organization of Men Against Amazonian Masterhood, whose members include Al Bundy (Ed O'Neill), in the TV sitcom *Married . . . with Children.*

"No más, no más"

Memorable words (Spanish for "No more, no more") spoken by boxer Roberto Duran to end his welterweight title bout with Sugar Ray Leonard on November 25, 1980.

"No matter what shape your stomach is in"

Advertising slogan of Alka-Seltzer.

"Non"

Only word (French for "no") spoken in the Mel Brooks film *Silent Movie,* spoken by mime Marcel Marceau.

No Name City, California

Setting of the film *Paint Your Wagon.*

"No-Name Defense"

Nickname of the largely unheralded members of the Miami Dolphins defensive unit of the early 1970s.

No Name Hat Factory

See **Batterson**

"Non sibi sed suis"

Motto of Tulane University, which is Latin for "Not for oneself, but for one's people."

Nool, Jungle of

Home of the title character in the Dr. Seuss children's book *Horton Hears a Who!*

Noonan, Fred

Navigator who accompanied Amelia Earhart on her ill-fated attempt to fly around the world in 1937.

Noo Noo

Vacuum cleaner that cleans up after the title characters in the children's TV series *Teletubbies.*

no plan like yours to study history wisely

Mnemonic learned by English schoolchildren for the names of the royal houses of Great Britain: Normandy, Planagenet, Lancaster, York, Tudor, Stuart, Hanover, and Windsor.

Norbert

Pet Norwegian ridgeback dragon of Rubeus Hagrid, in the Harry Potter series of books by J. K. Rowling.

Normal, Abby

Former owner of the brain taken by Igor (Marty Feldman) for the title character's (Gene Wilder's) experiment, in the Mel Brooks film *Young Frankenstein.*

Norman

Real first name of pro football quarterback Boomer Esiason.

Middle name of basketball Hall of Famer Wilt Chamberlain.

Newborn calf delivered by Mitch Robbins (Billy Crystal) in the film *City Slickers.*

Normandie Hotel

Manhattan home of Nick and Nora Charles in the Dashiell Hammett novel *The Thin Man.*

Norman Eugene

Real first and middle names of actor Clint Walker.

Norman, Sarah

Role for which Marlee Matlin won a Best Actress Academy Award in the 1986 film *Children of a Lesser God.*

Norns

The goddesses of fate in Norse mythology, comparable to the Fates of Greek mythology:

    Urd (goddess of the past)
    Verdandi (goddess of the present)
    Skuld (goddess of the future)

Norris, Josephine

Role for which Olivia de Havilland won a Best Actress Academy Award in the 1946 film *To Each His Own.*

Norris, Mrs.

Pet cat of Argos Filch, Hogwarts caretaker in the Harry Potter series of books by J. K. Rowling.

North Dallas Bulls

Pro football team of receiver Phillip Elliott (Nick Nolte) and quarterback Seth Maxwell (Mac Davis) in the film *North Dallas Forty.*

Northern Rhodesia

Former name of the African nation Zambia.

North Fork

Rival boys' ranch of the Triple R in the "Adventures of Spin and Marty" segment of the children's TV series *The Mickey Mouse Club.*

North Fork, New Mexico

Setting of the TV Western series *The Rifleman*.

North Manual Trades High

School that is the setting of the Ed McBain novel *The Blackboard Jungle*.

Northridge Junior College

School attended by Ryan and Tiffany Malloy (Kevin Connolly and Nikki Cox) in the TV sitcom *Unhappily Ever After*.

The North Star

Abolitionist newspaper founded by Frederick Douglass in 1847.

Northumberland

Wrecked ship from which children Emmeline and Dick are washed ashore a remote island, in the Henry de Vere Stacpoole novel *The Blue Lagoon*.

Norvell

Middle name of comedian Oliver Hardy.

Norway, Nevil Shute

Real name of English novelist Nevil Shute.

Norway Productions

Production company of *Star Trek* creator Gene Roddenberry.

Norwich, Vermont

Setting of the TV sitcom *Newhart*.

Norwood

Last name of pop singer Brandy.

Nostradamus

Real first name of bailiff Bull Shannon (Richard Moll) in the TV sitcom *Night Court*.

Nostromo

Spaceship setting of the film *Alien*.

notaphilist

Technical term for a collector of bank notes or paper currency.

"Nothing in moderation"

Epitaph of comedian Ernie Kovacs.

Nothing Lasts Forever

Original title of the Roderick Thorp novel *Die Hard*, which the basis for the film of the same name. The book was renamed for its second edition.

"Nothing says lovin' like something from the oven"

Advertising slogan of Pillsbury.

"Nothing's Gonna Stop Me Now"

Theme song of the TV sitcom *Perfect Strangers*, performed by David Pomeranz.

"NOT JUST ANOTHER STATE"

Motto on the flag of the state that includes Springfield, setting of the TV sitcom *The Simpsons*. The state has been left deliberately unidentified on the series.

Not the Cosbys

Original working title of the TV sitcom *Married . . . with Children*.

Not Tonight, Josephine!

Original working title of the film *Some Like It Hot*.

"Not unto ourselves alone are we born"

Motto of Willamette University.

Nova

Original name of *Omni* magazine, which was changed for legal reasons before publication of the first issue in 1978.

Novak, Joseph

Pen name used by author Jerzy Kosinski early in his career.

Nova Robotics

Manufacturer of robot Number 5 (voiced by Tim Blaney) in the film *Short Circuit*.

novels, authors' first

Louisa May Alcott: *The Inheritance* (1849)
L. Frank Baum: *Father Goose* (1899)
Saul Bellow: *Dangling Man* (1944)
Pearl S. Buck: *East Wind, West Wind* (1930)
Edgar Rice Burroughs: *Tarzan of the Apes* (1914)
Albert Camus: *The Stranger* (1942)
Truman Capote: *Other Voices, Other Rooms* (1948)
Barbara Cartland: *Jigsaw* (1925)
Willa Cather: *Alexander's Bridge* (1912)
Raymond Chandler: *The Big Sleep* (1939)
John Cheever: *The Wapshot Chronicle* (1957)
Dame Agatha Christie: *The Mysterious Affair at Styles* (1920)
Tom Clancy: *The Hunt for Red October* (1984)
Mary Higgins Clark: *Where Are the Children?* (1975)
James Fenimore Cooper: *Precaution* (1820)

Len Deighton: *The Ipcress File* (1962)
Philip K. Dick: *Solar Lottery* (1955)
Charles Dickens: *The Pickwick Papers* (1836–37)
E. L. Doctorow: *Welcome to Hard Times* (1960)
John Dos Passos: *One Man's Initiation—1917* (1920)
Theodore Dreiser: *Sister Carrie* (1900)
William Faulkner: *Soldier's Pay* (1926)
Edna Ferber: *Dawn O'Hara* (1911)
F. Scott Fitzgerald: *This Side of Paradise* (1920)
E. M. Forster: *Where Angels Fear to Tread* (1905)
Zane Grey: *Betty Zane* (1904)
John Grisham: *A Time to Kill* (1988)
Dashiell Hammett: *Red Harvest* (1929)
Nathaniel Hawthorne: *Fanshawe* (1828)
Robert A. Heinlein: *Rocket Ship Galileo* (1947)
Ernest Hemingway: *The Sun Also Rises* (1926)
John Hersey: *A Bell for Adano* 1944)
Aldous Huxley: *Crome Yellow* (1921)
John Irving: *Setting Free the Bears* (1969)
Henry James: *Watch and Ward* (1871)
James Joyce: *A Portrait of the Artist as a Young Man* (1916)
Faye Kellerman: *Ritual Bath* (1986)
Jack Kerouac: *The Town and the City* (1950)
Stephen King: *Carrie* (1974)
Ira Levin: *A Kiss Before Dying* (1953)
Sinclair Lewis: *Hike and the Aeroplane* (1912)
Jack London: *The Son of the Wolf* (1900)
Carson McCullers: *The Heart Is a Lonely Hunter* (1940)
Norman Mailer: *The Naked and the Dead* (1948)
Bernard Malamud: *The Natural* (1952)
Thomas Mann: *Buddenbrooks* (1901)
Somerset Maugham: *Lisa of Lambeth* (1897)
Larry McMurtry: *Horseman, Pass By* (1961)
Herman Melville: *Typee* (1846)
Flannery O'Connor: *Wise Blood* (1952)
John O'Hara: *Appointment in Samarra* (1934)
Thomas Pynchon: *V* (1963)
Anne Rice: *Interview With the Vampire* (1976)
Philip Roth: *Letting Go* (1962)
Sidney Sheldon: *The Naked Face* (1970)
John Steinbeck: *Cup of Gold* (1929)
William Styron: *Lie Down in Darkness* (1951)
Booth Tarkington: *The Gentleman From Indiana* (1899)
Mark Twain: *The Gilded Age* (1873)
John Updike: *The Poorhouse Fair* (1959)
Gore Vidal: *Williwaw* (1946)
Kurt Vonnegut: *Player Piano* (1960)
Robert Penn Warren: *Night Rider* (1939)
Evelyn Waugh: *Decline and Fall* (1928)
Edith Wharton: *The Valley of Decision* (1902)
Thornton Wilder: *Cabala* (1926)

"A Novel Without a Hero"

Subtitle of the William Makepeace Thackeray novel *Vanity Fair*.

"Novus ordo seclorum"

Latin phrase on the reverse of the Great Seal of the United States, which is on the back of a $1 bill. It means "A new order of the ages."

Nowicki, Janet Lynn

Real name of figure skater Janet Lynn.

"Now what's all this crud about no movie tonight?"

Last line of the film *Mister Roberts*, spoken by Ensign Pulver (Jack Lemmon).

'N Sync (pop group) members

Lance Bass, J. C. Chasez, Joey Fatone, Chris Kirkpatrick, and Justin Timberlake.

Nuclear Man

Foe of the title character (Christopher Reeve) in the film *Superman IV: The Quest for Peace*, portrayed by Mark Pillow.

Nudgy

The first pinball machine with flippers (originally called "nudge levers"), introduced by Bally in October 1947.

"Nuke"

Nickname of pitcher Ebby Calvin LaLoosh (Tim Robbins) in the film *Bull Durham*.

Number 6

Patrick McGoohan's title role in the TV series *The Prisoner*.

"Numen lumen"

Motto of the University of Wisconsin, which is Latin for "God, our light."

numerical groups

Terms for a group of various numbers of persons or things.

    1: monad, unit
    2: duad, duo
    3: triad, trio
    4: tetrad, quartet
    5: pentad, quintet
    6: hexad, sextet
    7: heptad, septet

8: ogdoad, octet
9: ennead, nonet
10: decad
11: hendecad
1,000: chiliad
10,000: myriad

Nunzio

See **Stinky and Nunzio**

Nutmeg

Last name of the family that owns the title feline in the comic strip *Heathcliff*.

"Nutmegger"

See **United States residents' nicknames**

"Nuts!"

Memorable reply of General Anthony McAuliffe to a German surrender ultimatum at Bastogne, Belgium, during the Battle of the Bulge in December 1944.

Nuxhall, Joe

See **15 years, 10 months, 11 days**

NY152

E-mail name of Joe Fox (Tom Hanks) in the film *You've Got Mail*.

Nyasaland

Former name of the African nation Malawi.

Nynuk

Original name of pop group New Kids on the Block.

Oakdale, Illinois

Setting of the TV soap opera *As the World Turns*.

Oak Hill

Estate of President James Monroe in Loudoun County, Virginia.

Oasis Hotel

Las Vegas setting of the TV sitcom *Blansky's Beauties*.

Oat Meal, Nebraska

See **Dead Man's Fang, Arizona; Oat Meal, Nebraska; and Coyoteville, New Mexico**

"Ob-La-Di, Ob-La-Da"

Theme song of the TV series *Life Goes On*, performed by series star Patti LuPone and the cast.

O'Boogie, Dr. Winston

Pseudonym used by former Beatle John Lennon as the guitarist on Elton John's recording of the tune "Lucy in the Sky with Diamonds."

O'Brien, Howard Allen

Birth name of novelist Anne Rice. (Her parents wanted a son.)

O'Brien, Mary

Real name of pop singer Dusty Springfield.

O'Brien, Mathers and Clark

Wall Street law firm that hires Alex Keaton (Michael J. Fox) in the final episode of the TV sitcom *Family Ties*.

obverse

Technical term for the ("heads") side of a coin that has the principal design. The opposite ("tails") side is called the "reverse."

O'Casey, Michael Francis

Real name of Bub (William Frawley) in the TV sitcom *My Three Sons*.

"occupation" surnames

Common surnames whose original meanings were occupations:

Ackerman: plowman
Barker: leather tanner
Baxter: baker
Brewster: brewer
Carter: wagon driver
Chandler: candle maker
Clark: clerk
Cohen: priest
Collier: coal miner
Conner: inspector
Cooper: barrelmaker
Currier: curer of hides
Dyker: stonemason
Faber: artisan
Fletcher: arrow maker
Fowler: bird hunter
Fuller: cleaner of cloth goods
Granger: farmer
Hacker: woodcutter
Harper: minstrel
Hayward: fence inspector
Hooper: maker of barrel hoops
Kaufman: merchant
Keeler: bargeman
Lederer: leather maker
Marshall: horse doctor
Mercer: cloth merchant
Pitman: coal miner
Sawyer: sawer of timber into boards
Schneider: tailor
Tinker: traveling salesman
Travers: collector of bridge tolls
Tucker: cleaner of cloth goods
Webster: weaver
Wainwright: wagon maker
Wechsler: moneychanger

Oceania

Empire ruled by Big Brother in the George Orwell novel *Nineteen Eighty-Four*.

Ocean Pictures

Production company of director Harold Ramis.

Ockleman, Constance Frances Marie

Real name of actress Veronica Lake.

O'Connor

Maiden name of Elaine Nardo (Marilu Henner) in the TV sitcom *Taxi*.

Octagon House

Washington, D.C., residence of President James Madison following the burning of the White House by English troops in 1814.

Octavius, Dr. Otto

Real identity of Spider-Man archenemy Doctor Octopus.

octothorp

Technical term for the symbol "#," aka "number sign" or "pound sign."

The Odd Couple introduction

These words were spoken before the opening credits of the TV sitcom version of the Neil Simon play:

On November 13th, Felix Unger was asked to remove himself from his place of residence. That request came from his wife. Deep down he knew she was right, but he also knew that someday he would return to her. With nowhere else to go, he appeared at the home of his childhood friend, Oscar Madison. Sometime earlier, Madison's wife had thrown him out, requesting that he never return. Can two divorced men share an apartment without driving each other crazy?

Odds and Ends

See **The New Bulletin**

Odell, Clinton

Creator of Burma-Shave, America's first brushless shaving cream, introduced in 1925.

"Ode on Intimations of Immortality"

Poem by William Wordsworth that was the source for the title of the film *Splendor in the Grass*.

Odie

Canine nemesis of the title character in the comic strip *Garfield*.

Odie Colognie

Skunk advisor of the title character in the children's animated TV series *King Leonardo and His Short Subjects*.

Odorama

Aromatic device used for the first time for the 1981 film *Polyester*. It consisted of scratch-and-sniff cards handed to audience members, which were to be used at specific moments in the film.

See also **Smell-O-Vision**

O'Dowd, George Alan

Real name of rock singer Boy George.

Odyssey 100

The first home video game system, introduced by Magnavox in 1972.

Of a Certain Age

Broadway play starring Elise Eliot (Goldie Hawn) in the film *The First Wives Club*.

"Of all the gin joints in all the towns in all the world, she walks into mine."

Memorable line spoken by Rick Blaine (Humphrey Bogart) in the film *Casablanca*.

O'Fearna, Sean Aloysius

Real name of director John Ford.

O'Ferrall

Last name of the title character in the George du Maurier novel *Trilby*.

Offal Court

London home of Tom Canty in the Mark Twain novel *The Prince and the Pauper*.

Office of Scientific Intelligence (OSI)

Government organization that creates the bionic implants for Steve Austin (Lee Majors) in the TV series *The Six Million Dollar Man*.

The Off-Islanders

Novel by Nathaniel Benchley that was the basis for the film *The Russians Are Coming! The Russians Are Coming!*

Of Man and the Unconscious

Book manuscript being read by Richard Sherman (Tom Ewell) in the film *The Seven Year Itch*.

Ogg, Grandpa

See **Mount Idy**

Oggilby, Og

Boyfriend of Myrtle Sousé (Una Merkel) in the film *The Bank Dick*, portrayed by Grady Sutton. Myrtle's father Egbert (W. C. Fields) says that the name "sounds like a bubble in a bathtub."

Ogilvy, Gavin

Pen name used by author James M. Barrie.

O'Hara, Kimball

Full name of the title character in the Rudyard Kipling novel *Kim*.

O'Hara, Scarlett

Role for which Vivien Leigh won a Best Actress Academy Award in the 1939 film *Gone with the Wind*.

Oh, God! films

Series of films starring George Burns in the title role:
Oh, God! (1977)
Oh, God! Book II (1980)
Oh, God! You Devil (1984)

"Oh if a man tried to take his time on Earth, and prove before he died what one man's life could be worth, I wonder what would happen to this world"

Epitaph of singer/songwriter Harry Chapin, which is the conclusion of his song "I Wonder What Would Happen in This World."

Ohlsson, Greta

Role for which Ingrid Bergman won a Best Supporting Actress Academy Award in the 1974 film *Murder on the Orient Express*.

"Oh no, it wasn't the airplanes. It was beauty killed the beast."

Memorable last line of the film *King Kong* (1933), spoken by movie producer Carl Denham (Robert Armstrong), who brought the title character to New York.

Ohtar

Middle Eastern country where cocktail waitress-turned-diplomat Sunny Davis (Goldie Hawn) is sent, in the film *Protocol*.

Oil Can Harry

Feline nemesis of cartoon superhero Mighty Mouse.

OK Oil

Company that purchases the Clampetts' land in Bug Tussle, in the TV sitcom *The Beverly Hillbillies*.

Okon, Thomas

Boy in a memorable 1979 TV commercial, who offers football player "Mean Joe" Greene a Coca-Cola, and receives a jersey from Greene in return.

Okrent, Daniel

Time, Inc., editor-at-large and baseball-book author who invented Rotisserie League Baseball in 1979.

Olaf

See **Snoopy's brothers and sisters**

O-Lan

Role for which Luise Rainer won a Best Actress Academy Award in the 1937 film *The Good Earth*.

Ol' Bullet

Dog of Snuffy Smith in the comic strip *Barney Google and Snuffy Smith*.

"Old Aches and Pains"

Nickname of baseball Hall of Famer Luke Appling, for his frequent injuries.

"old beanpole"

Prince Eric's nickname for his manservant Grimsby, in the Disney animated film *The Little Mermaid*.

Old Blue

Pet bloodhound of Will Stockdale (Sammy Jackson) in the TV sitcom *No Time for Sergeants*.

"Old Brains"

Nickname of Civil War Union general Henry Halleck.

Old Brass Spittoon

Trophy awarded to the winning team in the annual football game between Michigan State University and the University of Indiana.

Oldcastle, Sir John

15th-century leader of the Lollards, upon which William Shakespeare based his character Falstaff.

"Old Creepy"

Nickname of Canadian-born gangster Alvin Karpis, the only man ever arrested by FBI director J. Edgar Hoover. Karpis served over 26 years in Alcatraz (1936–1962), more than any other inmate.

"The Old Detective's Pupil"

See **Coryell, John Russell**

Old Dollar

Horse of John Bernard Books (John Wayne) in the film *The Shootist*.

"The Oldest Star in Pictures"

Advertising slogan of the film production company Pathé Brothers, best-known for its newsreels and crowing-rooster mascot.

Old Friends
Original working title of the film *As Good As It Gets.*

"Old Fuss and Feathers"
Nickname of 19th-century general Winfield Scott.

"Old Hoss"
Nickname of Hall of Fame baseball pitcher Charles Gardner Radbourn.

Old Ike
Ram of President Woodrow Wilson, one of the herd of sheep that kept the White House lawns cropped during World War I.

Old Ironsides
Strong cologne that Paul Manning (Walter Matthau) wears in the film *A Guide for the Married Man.*

"The Old Lady of Threadneedle Street"
Nickname of the Bank of England.

"Old Lead Bottom"
Nickname of Captain Binghamton (Joe Flynn) in the TV sitcom *McHale's Navy.*

"The Old Maestro"
Nickname of bandleader Ben Bernie.

"Old Man Eloquent"
Nickname of John Quincy Adams, coined while he was a congressman from Massachusetts, after his term as U.S. president.

The Old Man of Lochnagor
Children's book written by Prince Charles of Great Britain.

"Old Noll"
Nickname of English statesman Oliver Cromwell.

The Old Oaken Bucket
Trophy awarded to the winning team in the annual football game between Purdue University and the University of Indiana.

Old Possum's Book of Practical Cats
Book by T. S. Eliot that was the basis for the Andrew Lloyd Webber musical *Cats.*

"The Old Professor"
Nickname of Hall of Fame baseball manager Casey Stengel.

"The Old Ranger"
*See **Death Valley Days** hosts*

"Old Salamander"
Nickname of Civil War Union admiral David Farragut.

Oldstyle, Jonathan
Pen name used by author Washington Irving.

"The Old Trail"
Theme song of the radio and TV Western series *Gunsmoke.*

"Old Vic"
Nickname of London's Royal Victorian Theatre. It was called the Royal Coburg Theatre when it first opened in 1818.

Old Whiskers
Pet goat of President Benjamin Harrison.

Old Whitey
Horse of President Zachary Taylor.

Oleander Arms
Apartment complex where Esther Blodgett (Judy Garland) lives, in the film *A Star Is Born* (1954).

O'Leary, Cheeri
First mascot of Cheerios, introduced in 1942.

O'Leary, Molly
Role for which Alice Brady won a Best Supporting Actress Academy Award in the 1937 film *In Old Chicago.*

"Ole Miss"
Nickname of the University of Mississippi.

"The Ole Mongoose"
Nickname of 1950s light-heavyweight boxing champ Archie Moore.

Olive
Real first name of singer (Olive) Marie Osmond.

Oliver
First name of Daddy Warbucks in the comic strip *Little Orphan Annie.*

Oliver Air Force Base
Setting of the TV sitcom *No Time for Sergeants.*

"Oliver Buys a Farm"
Debut episode of the TV sitcom *Green Acres*, which aired on September 15, 1965.

olive sizes

Listed below with the count ranges per kilogram:
- Bullet (351–380)
- Fine (321–350)
- Brilliant (291–320)
- Superior (261–290)
- Large (231–260)
- Extra Large (201–230)
- Jumbo (181–200)
- Extra Jumbo (161–180)
- Giant (141–160)
- Colossal (121–140)
- Super Colossal (111–120)
- Mammoth (101–110)
- Super Mammoth (91–100)

Olivier Awards

English equivalent of America's Tony Awards for stage excellence, named for English actor Laurence Olivier.

"Ol' Lonely"

See **White, Jesse**

O Lost

Original working title of the Thomas Wolfe novel *Look Homeward, Angel.*

Olsen, Scott and Brennan

Brothers who invented Rollerblades in 1980.

Olson, Mrs.

See **Christine, Virginia**

Olson, Sara Jane

Alias used by former Symbionese Liberation Army (SLA) member Kathleen Ann Soliah, when apprehended by federal authorities in June 1999, after 24 years as a fugitive. She was wanted for a murder committed during a 1974 SLA bank robbery.

Olsson

Last name of Swedish-born actress/singer Ann-Margret.

Ol' Yellow Eyes Is Back

1991 album of pop standards recorded by actor Brent Spiner, who portrayed Data in the TV series *Star Trek: The Next Generation.* The album's title, inspired by the title of the 1973 Frank Sinatra album *Ol' Blue Eyes Is Back,* refers to the color of Spiner's eyes in his *Star Trek* role. Backup vocals on one tune, "It's a Sin to Tell a Lie," are provided by "The Sunspots," four of Spiner's *Star Trek* costars: LeVar Burton, Michael Dorn, Jonathan Frakes, and Patrick Stewart.

Olympia

Flagship of Commodore George Dewey's U.S. Asiatic Squadron, which defeated the Spanish fleet at the Spanish-American War's Battle of Manila Bay on May 1, 1898.

Olympic mascots (Summer Games)

- 1972 (Munich): Waldi, a dachshund
- 1976 (Montreal): Amik, a beaver
- 1980 (Moscow): Misha, a bear
- 1984 (Los Angeles): Sam, an eagle
- 1988 (Seoul): Hodori, a tiger cub
- 1992 (Barcelona): Cobi, a mountain sheepdog with human shape
- 1996 (Atlanta): Izzy, a biologically unidentifiable cartoon character (Izzy is short for "Whatizit")
- 2000 (Sydney): Syd, a platypus; Millie, an echidna; and Olly, a kookaburra

Olympic mascots (Winter Games)

- 1976 (Innsbruck): Schneemandl, a Tyrolean snowman
- 1980 (Lake Placid): Roni, a raccoon
- 1984 (Sarajevo): Vucko, a wolf
- 1988 (Calgary): Hidy and Howdy, bears
- 1992 (Albertville): Magique, an animated Savoyard star
- 1994 (Lillehammer): Haakon and Kristin, Norwegian folk-character children
- 1998 (Nagano): Sukki, Nokki, Lekki, and Tsukki the Snowlets (baby owls)

Olympics national abbreviations

Afghanistan: AFG
Albania: ALB
Algeria: ALG
American Samoa: ASA
Andorra: AND
Angola: ANG
Antigua and Barbuda: ANT
Argentina: ARG
Armenia: ARM
Aruba: ARU
Australia: AUS
Austria: AUT
Azerbaijan: AZE
Bahamas: BAH
Bahrain: BRN
Bangladesh: BAN
Barbados: BAR
Belarus: BLR
Belgium: BEL
Belize: BIZ
Benin: BEN

Bermuda: BER
Bhutan: BHU
Bolivia: BOL
Bosnia and Herzegovina: BIH
Botswana: BOT
Brazil: BRA
British Virgin Islands: IVB
Brunei: BRU
Bulgaria: BUL
Burkina Faso: BUR
Burundi: BDI
Cambodia: CAM
Cameroon: CMR
Canada: CAN
Cape Verde: CPV
Cayman Islands: CAY
Central African Republic: CAF
Chad: CHA
Chile: CHI
Chinese Taipei: TPE
Colombia: COL
Comoros: COM
Congo: CGO
Cook Islands: COK
Costa Rica: CRC
Croatia: CRO
Cuba: CUB
Cyprus: CYP
Czech Republic: CZE
Democratic Republic
  of the Congo: COD
Denmark: DEN
Djibouti: DJI
Dominica: DMA
Dominican Republic: DOM
Ecuador: ECU
Egypt: EGY
El Salvador: ESA
Equatorial Guinea: GEQ
Eritrea: ERI
Estonia: EST
Ethiopia: ETH
Federated States of Micronesia: FSM
Fiji: FIJ
Finland: FIN
France: FRA
Gabon: GAB
Gambia: GAM
Georgia: GEO
Germany: GER
Ghana: GHA
Great Britain: GBR
Greece: GRE
Grenada: GRN
Guam: GUM

Guatemala: GUA
Guinea: GUI
Guinea-Bissau: GBS
Guyana: GUY
Haiti: HAI
Honduras: HON
Hong Kong: HKG
Hungary: HUN
Iceland: ISL
India: IND
Indonesia: INA
Iran: IRI
Iraq: IRQ
Ireland: IRL
Israel: ISR
Italy: ITA
Ivory Coast: CIV
Jamaica: JAM
Japan: JPN
Jordan: JOR
Kazakhstan: KAZ
Kenya: KEN
Korea: KOR
Kuwait: KUW
Kyrgyzstan: KGZ
Laos: LAO
Latvia: LAT
Lebanon: LIB
Lesotho: LES
Liberia: LBR
Libya: LBA
Liechtenstein: LIE
Lithuania: LTU
Luxembourg: LUX
Macedonia: MKD
Madagascar: MAD
Malawi: MAW
Malaysia: MAS
Maldives: MDV
Mali: MLI
Malta: MLT
Mauritania: MTN
Mauritius: MRI
Mexico: MEX
Moldova: MDA
Monaco: MON
Mongolia: MGL
Morocco: MAR
Mozambique: MOZ
Myanmar: MYA
Namibia: NAM
Nauru: NRU
Nepal: NEP
Netherlands: NED
Netherlands Antilles: AHO

New Zealand: NZL
Nicaragua: NCA
Niger: NIG
Nigeria: NGR
Norway: NOR
Oman: OMA
Pakistan: PAK
Palau: PLW
Palestine: PLE
Panama: PAN
Papua New Guinea: PNG
Paraguay: PAR
People's Republic of China: CHN
Peru: PER
Philippines: PHI
Poland: POL
Portugal: POR
Puerto Rico: PUR
Qatar: QAT
Romania: ROM
Russian Federation: RUS
Nicaragua: NCA
Niger: NIG
Nigeria: NGR
Norway: NOR
Oman: OMA
Pakistan: PAK
Palau: PLW
Palestine: PLE
Panama: PAN
Papua New Guinea: PNG
Paraguay: PAR
People's Republic of China: CHN
Peru: PER
Philippines: PHI
Poland: POL
Portugal: POR
Puerto Rico: PUR
Qatar: QAT
Romania: ROM
Russian Federation: RUS
Rwanda: RWA
Saint Kitts and Nevis: SKN
Saint Lucia: LCA
Saint Vincent and the Grenadines: VIN
San Marino: SMR
São Tomé and Principe: STP
Saudi Arabia: KSA
Senegal: SEN
Seychelles: SEY
Sierra Leone: SLE
Singapore: SIN
Slovakia: SVK
Slovenia: SLO
Solomon Islands: SOL

Somalia: SOM
South Africa: RSA
South Korea: KDR
Spain: ESP
Sri Lanka: SRI
Sudan: SUD
Suriname: SUR
Swaziland: SWZ
Sweden: SWE
Switzerland: SUI
Syria: SYR
Tajikistan: TJK
Tanzania: TAN
Thailand: THA
Togo: TOG
Tonga: TGA
Trinidad and Tobago: TRI
Tunisia: TUN
Turkey: TUR
Turkmenistan: TKM
Uganda: UGA
Ukraine: UKR
United Arab Emirates: UAE
United States of America: USA
Uruguay: URU
Uzbekistan: UZB
Vanuatu: VAN
Venezuela: VEN
Vietnam: VIE
Virgin Islands: ISV
Western Samoa: SAM
Yemen: YEM
Yugoslavia: YUG
Zambia: ZAM
Zimbabwe: ZIM

Olympics presidents

See **International Olympic Committee presidents**

O'Malley, Father Chuck

Role for which Bing Crosby won a Best Actor Academy Award in the 1944 film *Going My Way*.

Omega Beta Zeta

Sorority of Cici Cooper (Sarah Michelle Gellar) in the film *Scream 2*.

Omen films

The Omen (1976)
Damien: Omen II (1978)
The Final Conflict (1981)

Omidyar, Pierre

Founder of Internet auction site eBay in 1995.

"Omigosh!"

Favorite exclamation of Dagwood Bumstead in the comic strip *Blondie*.

Omni

Time-travel device of Phineas Bogg (Jon-Erik Hexum) in the TV series *Voyagers*.

Omni Consumer Products

Powerful corporation that controls Delta City and the lives of its residents in TV's *Robocop—The Series*.

"Omphale's Spinning Wheel"

Instrumental theme of the radio series *The Shadow*, composed by Camille Saint-Saëns.

omphaloskepsis

Mystic contemplation of one's navel.

On-Broadway

Syndicated newspaper column of Walter Winchell.

The Once and Future King series

Group of novels based on Arthurian legend by T. H. White. (The novels were the basis for the Lerner and Loewe musical *Camelot*.)

The Sword in the Stone (1938)
The Queen of Air and Darkness (1939)
The Ill-Made Knight (1940)
The Candle in the Wind (1958)

White also wrote what he intended to be the fifth book in the series, *The Book of Merlyn*, which was published posthumously in 1977.

"Once Upon a Time in the City of New York"

Debut episode of the TV series *Beauty and the Beast*, which aired on September 25, 1987.

Ondaatje, Michael

Author of the novel *The English Patient*, upon which the film of the same name was based.

"One Armed Bandits"

Debut episode of the TV series *The Dukes of Hazzard*, which aired on January 26, 1979.

"One City. Three Stories Tall"

See *New York Stories* sections

One-Eyed Bart

Western villain portrayed by Mr. Potato Head in the film *Toy Story*.

"One Froggy Evening"

See **Michigan J. Frog**

The One Hundred Guinea Cup

Original name of the America's Cup yachting trophy.

O'Neill, Rose

Cartoonist who created the Kewpie doll in 1909.

"One morning I shot an elephant in my pajamas. How he got in my pajamas I don't know."

Memorable line spoken by Captain Jeffrey T. Spaulding (Groucho Marx) in the film *Animal Crackers*.

"One O'Clock Jump"

Theme song of jazz bandleader/pianist Count Basie.

"One ringie dingie, two ringie dingies . . ."

Catchphrase of Lily Tomlin's telephone-operator character Ernestine.

"One Riot, One Ranger"

Debut episode of the TV series *Walker, Texas Ranger*, which aired on April 21, 1993.

One-Two-One Club

Singles support group attended by the title character (Judd Hirsch) in the TV sitcom *Dear John*.

"Only Nixon could go to China"

Old Vulcan proverb, as stated by Mr. Spock (Leonard Nimoy) in the film *Star Trek VI: The Undiscovered Country*.

"On the Blue Water: A Gulf Stream Letter"

Ernest Hemingway short story, first published in the April 1936 issue of *Esquire* magazine, that was the basis for his novel *The Old Man and the Sea*.

On the Other Hand

1989 autobiography of actress Fay Wray. The title refers to her role in the film *King Kong* (1933), where the title character held her in his hand.

"On the Pulse of Morning"

Poem read by Maya Angelou at the inauguration of President Bill Clinton on January 20, 1993, which was written by Angelou for the occasion.

onychocryptosis

Medical term for an ingrown toenail.

"Ooh! Ooh!"

All-purpose exclamation of Officer Gunther Toody (Joe E. Ross) in the TV sitcom *Car 54, Where Are You?*

Oompa-Loompas

Diminutive candymaking employees of the title character (Gene Wilder) in the film *Willy Wonka and the Chocolate Factory*.

"The Oomph Girl"

Nickname of actress Ann Sheridan.

Ooqueah

See **Egingwah, Ooqueah, Ootah, and Seegloo**

Ooragnak

Indian tribe of Chief Thunderthud (Bill Lecornec) in the children's TV series *Howdy Doody*. ("Ooragnak" is "kangaroo" spelled backward.)

Ootah

See **Egingwah, Ooqueah, Ootah, and Seegloo**

Opel, Robert

Advertising executive who streaked past David Niven during the Academy Awards telecast in April 1974.

"Open Channel D"

Phrase used by U.N.C.L.E. agents to initiate audio communications, in the TV series *The Man from U.N.C.L.E.*

Open Kettle

See **Rosenberg, William**

"Open me first!"

Advertising slogan of Kodak cameras during the Christmas season.

"openness"

What the word "glasnost" means in Russian.

Operation Barbarossa

German code name for the invasion of Russia during World War II.

Operation Coronet

See **Operation Olympic and Operation Coronet**

Operation Crossroads

Military code name for the atomic bomb tests at Bikini atoll in 1946.

Operation Detachment

Code name for the Allied invasion of Iwo Jima in 1945.

Operation Experiment

Code name for the Arctic atomic bomb explosion that releases the title character in the film *The Beast from 20,000 Fathoms*.

Operation Grand Slam

Code name for the plan of the title character (Gert Frobe) to break into Fort Knox, in the James Bond film *Goldfinger*.

Operation Olympic and Operation Coronet

Code names for the proposed Allied invasions of the Japanese islands of Kyushu (November 1945) and Honshu (March 1946), respectively, during World War II. They were never carried out, due to the Japanese surrender in August 1945.

Operation Overlord

Allied code name for the D-Day invasion during World War II.

Operation, playing pieces in

Removing these 12 (mostly plastic) pieces from a caricature of a body is the object of this game:

Adam's apple (apple)
Anklebone connected to the knee bone (rubber band)
Bread basket (bread slice)
Broken heart
Butterflies in stomach (butterfly)
Charlie horse (horse)
Funny bone
Spare ribs
Water on the knee (pail)
Wish bone
Wrenched ankle (wrench)
Writer's cramp (pencil)

Operation Sea Lion

German code name for the planned invasion of England during World War II.

Operation Thunderbolt

Code name for the Israeli commando rescue of the airplane passengers held hostage at Entebbe, Uganda, on July 4, 1976.

Operation Torch

Code name for the Allied landing in North Africa during World War II, which began on November 8, 1942.

Operation Trove

Code name for James Bond's (Roger Moore's) mission to stop the sale of counterfeit Fabergé eggs, in the film *Octopussy*.

Operation Undertow

Code name for James Bond's (Roger Moore's) mission to recover a ballistic-missile launch system, in the film *For Your Eyes Only*.

Operation Urgent Fury

Code name for the U.S. invasion of Grenada, which began on October 25, 1983.

Operation Vittles

Code name for the 1948–49 Berlin Airlift, which supplied the city with food and fuel when land access was blocked by the Russians.

Operation Z

Japanese code name for the attack on Pearl Harbor during World War II.

Operation Zapata

CIA code name for the Bay of Pigs invasion of April 1961.

O. P. Henley Textile Mill

Employer of Norma Rae Webster (Sally Field) in the film *Norma Rae*.

Optimism

Alternate title of the Voltaire novel *Candide*.

"The Oracle of Omaha"

Nickname of investment guru Warren Buffett, whose headquarters are in Omaha, Nebraska.

"The Orange Crush"

Nickname of the late 1970s powerful defensive unit of the Denver Broncos.

Orange Glorious

Manhattan juice-bar employer of Steve Laird (Dean Martin) and Seymour (Jerry Lewis) in the film *My Friend Irma*.

Orange Grove, California

Town near Camp Fremont in the TV sitcom *The Phil Silvers Show* aka *You'll Never Get Rich*.

Orange, Max

Pen name used by author Joseph Heller as a writer for the TV sitcom *McHale's Navy*.

Orbit High

School attended by Judy Jetson in the children's animated TV sitcom *The Jetsons*.

Orca

Boat of Quint (Robert Shaw) in the Steven Spielberg film *Jaws*.

"Ordinary Girl"

Theme song of the TV sitcom *Clueless*, performed by China Forbes.

Ordinary Wizarding Levels

See **O.W.L.s**

O'Reed, Margaret

Real name of actress Martha Raye.

Orefice, Guido

Role for which Roberto Benigni won a Best Actor Academy Award in the 1998 film *La Vita è Bella*.

Orenthal James

First and middle names of pro football Hall of Famer O. J. Simpson.

Organized Crime Bureau

Employer of undercover agent Vinnie Terranova (Ken Wahl) in the TV series *Wiseguy*.

"Oriental Blues"

Instrumental theme of the TV series *The Ernie Kovacs Show*.

Orion

Cat of Gentle Rosenberg (Mike Nussbaum) whose collar holds a gem containing the Arquillian Galaxy, in the film *Men in Black*.

Orly County, Georgia

Setting of the TV sitcom *Lobo*, aka *The Misadventures of Sheriff Lobo*.

Orowitz, Eugene Maurice

Real name of actor Michael Landon.

Orphan Ann

On-air name of American-born World War II Japanese propaganda broadcaster Iva Ikoku Toguri, known to American soldiers as Tokyo Rose. She was heard on the Radio Tokyo program *Zero Hour*.

Orr

Real last name of pop singer Sheena Easton.

Orr, Mary

See **"The Wisdom of Eve"**

Orteig Prize

$25,000 offered in 1919 by hotel owner Raymond B. Orteig for the first nonstop flight between Paris and New York. The prize was claimed by Charles Lindbergh after his historic flight of May 1927.

Orthodox

Allied code name for the Aleutian Islands during World War II.

Orville

First name of Sergeant Snorkel in the comic strip *Beetle Bailey*.

Orvon

Real first name of Gene Autry.

Osborne Industries

Employer of maintenance supervisor Harry Grafton (Phil Silvers) in the TV sitcom *The New Phil Silvers Show*.

Oscar

Pet lizard of Opie Taylor (Ronny Howard) in the TV sitcom *The Andy Griffith Show*.

Oscar Hammerstein Theater

New York City theater, built in 1927, that housed the TV variety series *The Ed Sullivan Show*. The theater, aka CBS Studio 50, was renamed the Ed Sullivan Theater in 1967, and today is host to David Letterman's late-night show.

Osceola, Chief

See **Renegade**

Oscillation Overthruster

Device in the title character's (Peter Weller's) Jet Car, that enables him to travel to the title location, in the film *The Adventures of Buckaroo Banzai Across the Eighth Dimension*.

O'Shea, Sugarpuss

Barbara Stanwyck's role in the film *Ball of Fire*.

OSI

See **Office of Scientific Intelligence (OSI)**

Oslin, George P.

Western Union executive who invented the singing telegram in 1933.

Osmond family

The singing children of George and Olive Osmond, listed below from oldest to youngest:

Alan
Wayne
Merrill
Jay
Donny
Marie
Jimmy

"O Sole Mio"

Italian tune whose melody was the basis for the Elvis Presley tune "It's Now or Never."

Osterberg, James

Real name of punk-rock singer Iggy Pop.

Oswald, Lee Harvey

Accused assassin of President John F. Kennedy in Dallas, Texas on November 22, 1963. Oswald was killed by nightclub owner Jack Ruby in a Dallas police station two days later.

"Oswald Means Order"

Mayoral-campaign slogan of Oswald Cobblepot, aka The Penguin (Danny DeVito), in the film *Batman Returns*.

Otaheite

Former name of Tahiti.

Otis Day and the Knights

See **Dexter Lake Club**

Otis Dewey

Real first and middle names of country singer Slim Whitman.

Otto

Inflatable autopilot in the film *Airplane!*

First name of the title character (Don Rickles) in the TV sitcom *C.P.O. Sharkey*.

Original name of the title character in the comic strip *Little Orphan Annie*, which creator Harold Gray changed before the strip's first publication in 1924.

Hound dog in the Disney animated film *Robin Hood*.

Otto's Auto Orphanage

See **Bronco's Auto Repairs and Otto's Auto Orphanage**

Ottumwa, Iowa

Hometown of Radar O'Reilly (Gary Burghoff) in the TV sitcom *M*A*S*H*.

Our American Cousin

Play that President Abraham Lincoln was watching at Ford's Theater in Washington, D.C., when he was shot by John Wilkes Booth on April 14, 1865.

Our Changing Times

Newspaper column written by Donald Jarvess (John Hodiak) in the film *Battleground*.

"Our Very First Show"

Debut episode of the TV sitcom *Full House*, which aired on September 22, 1987.

OUTATIME

California license plate of Dr. Emmett L. Brown's (Christopher Lloyd's) De Lorean time machine in the film *Back to the Future*.

"Outwit, outplay, outlast"

Motto of the TV game show *Survivor*.

Overacker

Last name of Baby LeRoy, infant nemesis of W. C. Fields in the films *Tillie and Gus*, *It's a Gift*, and *The Old-Fashioned Way*.

Overbrook Entertainment

Production company of actor Will Smith, named for his Philadelphia high school. Overbrook High is also the alma mater of basketball Hall of Famer Wilt Chamberlain.

"Over hill, over dale, our love will never fail"

Inscription on the wedding ring of Major Margaret Houlihan (Loretta Swit) in the TV sitcom *M*A*S*H*.

Overlook Hotel

Rocky Mountain setting of the Stephen King novel *The Shining*.

"Overture to The Flying Dutchman"

Instrumental theme of the children's TV series *Captain Video and His Video Rangers*, composed by Richard Wagner.

Owens, Dana

Real name of rap singer Queen Latifah.

Owlie Skywarn

Cartoon owl mascot of the National Weather Service and the Federal Emergency Management Agency (aka FEMA).

O.W.L.s

Standard-level examinations at Hogwarts, in the Harry Potter series of books by J. K. Rowling. The letters stand for "Ordinary Wizarding Levels."

"Own it all"

Advertising slogan for the board game Monopoly.

Oyl, Castor

Brother of Olive Oyl in the Popeye cartoons.

Oyl, Cole and Nana

Father and mother (respectively) of Olive Oyl in the Popeye cartoons.

Oyster Island

Former name of New York Harbor's Ellis Island. It was also known as Gibbet Island before taking its current name.

Oz book series

The 14 books in the series written by L. Frank Baum:
The Wizard of Oz (1900)
The Land of Oz (1904)
Ozma of Oz (1907)
Dorothy and the Wizard in Oz (1908)
The Road to Oz (1909)
The Emerald City of Oz (1910)
The Patchwork Girl of Oz (1913)
Tik-Tok of Oz (1914)
The Scarecrow of Oz (1915)
Rinkitink in Oz (1916)
The Lost Princess of Oz (1917)
The Tin Woodman of Oz (1918)
The Magic of Oz (1919)
Glinda of Oz (1920)

Ozcot

Hollywood, California, home of author L. Frank Baum from 1910 until his death in 1919.

Ozersky, Philip

Washington University research scientist who caught the 70th home-run ball of 1998 hit by Mark McGwire on September 27th at St. Louis' Busch Stadium.

See also **$3,005,000**

Oznowicz

Real last name of puppeteer/director Frank Oz.

Pabst, Karl K.
Engineer who designed the Jeep in 1940.

"Pace ac bello merita"
Motto of the Federal Emergency Management Agency (aka FEMA), which is Latin for "Service in peace and war."

Pacelli, Eugenio Maria Giuseppe Giovanni
Real name of Pope Pius XII, who served from 1939 to 1958.

Pacer, Ranger, Corsair, and Citation
The four models of Edsel automobiles when first introduced by the Ford Motor Company for the 1958 model year. The Edsel station wagons were called Bermuda, Roundup, and Villager.

Pacific Aero Products Company
Original name of Boeing.

Pacific All-Risk Insurance Company
Employer of Walter Neff (Fred MacMurray) in the film *Double Indemnity*.

P.A.G.A.N.
Acronym for People Against Good and Normalcy, a radical group led by Reverend Jonathan Whirley (Christopher Plummer) in the film *Dragnet* (1987).

Page Milk Company
Sponsor of a 1946 show on Tulsa radio station KTUL that featured singer Clara Ann Fowler. The company changed her name to Patti Page, which the singer has used ever since.

Page, Mistress
See **Ford, Mistress and Page, Mistress**

Pahoo-Ka-Ta-Wah
Pawnee Indian sidekick (X. Brands) of the title character (Jock Mahoney) in the TV Western series *Yancy Derringer*. His name means "wolf that stands in water."

Paige
Middle name of actor Matt Damon.

Painted Valley
Home of Western hero Red Ryder.

"Paint It Black"
Theme song of the TV series *Tour of Duty*, performed by the Rolling Stones.

Pajeau, Charles
Inventor of Tinkertoy in 1914.

Pal
Male stunt dog who was the first collie to portray Lassie on screen, in the film *Lassie Come Home*.

Palace Ballroom
Employer of the singer of the Rodgers and Hart tune "Ten Cents a Dance," according to the introductory verse.

Palais Royal Orchestra
See **Aeolian Concert Hall**

Paleologus, Faith
Role for which Gale Sondergaard won a Best Supporting Actress Academy Award in the 1936 film *Anthony Adverse*.

Pallazzo, Enrico
Opera singer impersonated by Lt. Frank Drebin (Leslie Nielsen) in the film *The Naked Gun: From the Files of Police Squad!*

"Palmam qui meruit ferat"
Motto of the University of Southern California, aka USC, which is Latin for "Let whoever earns the palm bear it."

Palmer, Vera Jane
Real name of actress Jayne Mansfield.

Palmer, Violet
See **Kantner, Dee and Palmer, Violet**

"Palms of Glory"
Debut episode of the TV Western series *The Big Valley*, which aired on September 15, 1965.

Palmyra

Nassau, Bahamas estate of Emilio Largo (Adolfo Celi) in the James Bond film *Thunderball.*

Palomas Downs

Racetrack where Lilly Dillon (Anjelica Huston) bets heavily on a longshot to lower the odds for her bookmaker employer, in the film *The Grifters.*

Palomino Club

Favorite watering hole of Colt Seavers (Lee Majors) in the TV series *The Fall Guy.*

Pamela

See **Jerry and Pamela**

Pamela Lyndon

First and middle names of author P. L. Travers.

Panayiotou, Georgios Kyriacos

Real name of pop singer George Michael.

Pandaemonium

Capital of the underworld in the John Milton epic poem *Paradise Lost.*

Pandora Theater

Where Nick (Robert Prosky) gives young Danny Madigan (Austin O'Brien) a magic ticket that allows him to enter the movie screen, in the film *Last Action Hero.*

P&P Chair Company

Asheboro, North Carolina, manufacturer of the rocking chair used by President John F. Kennedy in the White House.

Pansy

Margaret Mitchell's original first name for Scarlett O'Hara in her novel *Gone With the Wind.*

Pan Universe Airways

See **Mayflower 1**

"Papa"

Nickname of composer Joseph Haydn.

Nickname of author Ernest Hemingway.

"Papa Bear"

Nickname of pro football pioneer George Halas.

"Papa Doc"

Nickname of Haitian physician/dictator François Duvalier.

Papathanassiou, Evangelos

Real name of Greek-born pop keyboardist/composer Vangelis.

Paper, Little Jackie

Friend of the title character in the Peter, Paul, and Mary tune "Puff the Magic Dragon."

"Pappy's Lambs"

Nickname of the 214th Squadron nurses, in the TV series *Black Sheep Squadron.*

"Paradise by the Dashboard Light"

Million-selling 1978 Meat Loaf tune that includes a play-by-play excerpt of baseball broadcaster Phil Rizzuto. Rizzuto was awarded a Gold Record along with Meat Loaf for the recording.

Paradise Cove Trailer Colony

Malibu Beach home of the title character (James Garner) in the TV series *The Rockford Files.*

Paradise Island

Birthplace of superheroine Wonder Woman.

Paradise Road

Site of the climactic drag race between John Milner (Paul LeMat) and Bob Falfa (Harrison Ford) in the film *American Graffiti.*

Paradis Loest

Advertising agency taken over by Annie Paradis (Diane Keaton) from her husband Aaron (Stephen Collins) in the film *The First Wives Club.*

Pard

Pet dog of Roy Earle (Humphrey Bogart) in the film *High Sierra.*

The Parish Boy's Progress

Alternate title of the Charles Dickens novel *Oliver Twist.*

"Park Avenue Beat"

Instrumental theme of the TV series *Perry Mason.*

Park Central Hotel

Employer of bellhop Jose Jimenez (Bill Dana) in the TV sitcom *The Bill Dana Show.*

Parker, Peter

Secret identity of comic-book hero Spider-Man, portrayed by Nicholas Hammond on TV.

Parker, Robert Leroy

Real name of Western outlaw Butch Cassidy.

Parker, Sean

See **Fanning, Shawn and Parker, Sean**

Parkview Hotel

Where Rick Gassko (Tom Hanks) has his title bash in the film *Bachelor Party*.

Parkway Productions

Production company of director Penny Marshall.

Park, Willie

Winner of the first British Open golf tournament, held at Prestwick Club in Ayrshire, Scotland, in 1860.

Parkyakarkis

Greek food-stand owner on radio's *Eddie Cantor Show*, portrayed by Harry Einstein, who was the father of actor Albert Brooks. (The younger Brooks' real name is Albert Einstein.)

parotitis

Medical term for the mumps.

Parrish, Homer

Role for which Harold Russell won a Best Supporting Actor Academy Award in the 1946 film *The Best Years of Our Lives*.

Parrotheads

What fans of country singer Jimmy Buffett call themselves.

Parsons, Bill

Credited singer of the tune "The All-American Boy," though it was actually performed by Bobby Bare.

"Parva sub ingenti"

Motto of Prince Edward Island, Canada, which is Latin for "The small under the protection of the great."

Pasha

Pet Yorkshire terrier of President Richard Nixon.

Pass, John and Stow, John

Philadelphia craftsmen who cast the Liberty Bell in 1753.

Passkey

Secret Service code name for Gerald Ford.

pasta names

The English translation of the names of Italian pasta varieties:

    cannelloni: little tubes
    fettuccine: little ribbons
    linguine: little tongues
    manicotti: pipes
    mostaccioli: little mustaches
    ravioli: little turnips
    rigatoni: little stripes
    spaghetti: strings
    tortellini: little fritters
    vermicelli: little worms

Pasteur, Louis

Role for which Paul Muni won a Best Actor Academy Award in the 1936 film *The Story of Louis Pasteur*.

patella

Medical term for the kneecap.

"The Pathfinder"

Nickname of Western explorer John C. Fremont.

Patience and Fortitude

The marble lions (Patience is at left) that have "guarded" the entrance to the main branch of the New York Public Library since its dedication in May 1911. Sculpted by Edward Clark Potter, the lions were named by New York mayor Fiorello La Guardia in the 1930s. The lions had formerly been called Leo Astor and Leo Lenox (after library founders John Jacob Astor and James Lenox), as well as Lord Astor and Lady Lenox.

"A patient waiter is no loser"

Message successfully transmitted via Morse code in the first public demonstration of the telegraph, at Morristown, New Jersey on January 6, 1838. Samuel Morse received the message, which was sent by his colleague and financial backer Alfred Vail. Vail, who was the actual inventor of Morse code, received the more well-known message "What hath God wrought?" sent by Morse from Washington, D.C., to Baltimore on May 24, 1844.

Patio Diet Cola

Original name of Diet Pepsi when first introduced in the 1960s.

Patna

Steamer on which the title character serves in the Joseph Conrad novel *Lord Jim*.

Patrick

Pet Irish wolfhound of President Herbert Hoover.

"Patrol Torpedo"

What "PT" in "PT boat" stands for.

"Patron Saint of the Gentleman's 'C' "

See **Walden, Thaddeus Eli**

PATSY Awards

Presented annually by the American Humane Association for film and TV performances of animals, from 1951 to 1978, and 1983 to 1986. PATSY stands for "Performing Animal Top Star of the Year." Winners were selected by a poll of entertainment editors, writers and critics.

Patterson, Francine "Penny"

See **Koko**

Patton Jr., General George S.

Role for which George C. Scott won a Best Actor Academy Award in the 1970 film *Patton*.

"Pauci fideles"

Motto of the U.S. Air Force Academy at Colorado Springs, Colorado. It is Latin for "The few, the faithful."

Paul

Real first name of artist (Paul) Jackson Pollock.

Paul Bunyan's Axe

Trophy awarded to the winning team in the annual football game between the University of Minnesota and the University of Wisconsin.

Pauline Wayne

Cow of President William Howard Taft that grazed on the White House grounds.

Paul Revere, Valentine, and Epitaph

Racehorses being touted by the trio of singers of the Frank Loesser tune "Fugue for Tinhorns" in the musical *Guys and Dolls*.

"The pause that refreshes"

Advertising slogan of Coca-Cola.

Pavano, Carl

Montreal Expos pitcher who gave up the 70th (and final) home run of 1998 hit by St. Louis Cardinal Mark McGwire, on September 27th at Busch Stadium.

Pavel

First name of Ensign Chekov (Walter Koenig) in the TV series *Star Trek*.

Pavor Manor

Ancestral home of Clare Quilty in the Vladimir Nabokov novel *Lolita*.

Pax

German shepherd guide dog of the title character (James Franciscus) in the TV series *Longstreet*.

"Pax et lux"

Motto of Tufts University, which is Latin for "Peace and light."

Pazuzu

Demon (voiced by Mercedes McCambridge) that possesses Regan MacNeil (Linda Blair) in the film *The Exorcist*.

PC's Limited

Original name of Dell Computer Corporation, when started by Michael Dell in his college dorm room in 1984.

Peabody

See **Edwards and Peabody**

"Peace"

Sign-off line of *The Today Show* host Dave Garroway.

Peace and Quiet

Original working title of the Marx Brothers film *A Day at the Races*.

"Peace! Bread! Land!"

Slogan of the Bolsheviks at the time of the Russian Revolution.

Peacefield

Home of President John Adams in Quincy, Massachusetts. It was later the home of his son, President John Quincy Adams.

"Peace is our profession"

Motto of the U.S. Strategic Command, formerly known as the Strategic Air Command.

"The Peacekeeper"

Nickname of the MX missile, an American ICBM. MX stands for "missile experimental."

The Peace Pipe

Trophy awarded to the winning team in the annual football game between the University of Toledo and Bowling Green University.

"Peace Through Understanding"

Theme of the 1964–65 New York World's Fair.

Peachum, Polly

Person mentioned in the original lyrics of the Kurt Weill/Marc Blitzstein tune "Mack the Knife" that Bobby Darin replaces with "Lotte Lenya" (wife of Weill) in his 1959 recording.

Peak XV

Former name of Mount Everest, before it was known to be the world's highest mountain. It was named for Sir George Everest, former surveyor general of India, in 1865.

Peake

See **Chessie and Peake**

Peanut Gallery

Bleacher audience of children in the children's TV series *Howdy Doody*.

Pearl

Real first name of author (Pearl) Zane Grey.

Pearl Harbor Memorial Highway

Portion of Interstate 10 that runs through Arizona. It was renamed on December 7, 1995, in honor of the ill-fated battleship U.S.S. *Arizona*.

"Pearl of the Antilles"

Nickname of Cuba.

"Pearl of the Atlantic"

Nickname of the Portuguese island of Madeira, located off the coast of Morocco.

Pearls Before Swine

Alternate title of the Kurt Vonnegut novel *God Bless You, Mr. Rosewater*.

Pearl Street Productions

Production company of actors Matt Damon and Ben Affleck.

Peay, Benjamin Franklin

Real name of pop singer Brook Benton.

Peck, Harry Thurston

Editor of the trade journal *The Bookman*, who in 1895 introduced the first bestseller list for books in his publication.

Peck, Templeton

Real name of "Face" (Dirk Benedict) in the TV series *The A-Team*.

Pecos

Horse of Wrangler Jane (Melody Patterson) in the TV sitcom *F Troop*.

Pedro

See **Johnny**

Peebles' Pet Shop

Residence of the title character (voiced by Allan Melvin) in the children's animated TV series *Magilla Gorilla*.

"The Peek-a-boo Girl"

Nickname of actress Veronica Lake, for her hairdo that covered one eye.

"A Peep at Polynesian Life"

Subtitle of the Herman Melville novel *Typee*.

Peepeye, Pipeye, Poopeye, and Pupeye

Nephews of Popeye in the animated cartoons.

peerage, ranks of English

The usually hereditary titles granted by the King or Queen of England, upon the recommendation of the Prime Minister, listed below from highest to lowest. The terms for the wives of each (or women granted the title in their own right) are listed in parentheses:

Duke (duchess)
Marquess/marquis (marchioness)
Earl (countess)
Viscount (viscountess)
Baron (baroness)

The Peer and the Peri

Alternate title of the Gilbert and Sullivan comic opera *Iolanthe*.

Pegasus

Thoroughbred racehorse owned by Max Zorin (Christopher Walken) in the James Bond film *A View to a Kill*.

Pelham Grenville

First and middle names of English-born writer P. G. Wodehouse.

"pelican"

What the name of San Francisco Bay island Alcatraz means in Spanish.

Pelican Falls, Vermont

Hometown of Nancy Peterson (Janet Leigh) in the film *Two Tickets to Broadway*.

Peller, Clara

See **"Where's the beef?"**

Pelli, Cesar

Argentine-born architect who designed the 1,483-foot Petronas Towers in Kuala Lumpur, Malaysia, completed in 1998.

Pemberton, John Stith

Atlanta pharmacist who invented Coca-Cola in 1886.

Pencey Prep

Pennsylvania school that Holden Caulfield flunks out of, in the J. D. Salinger novel *The Catcher in the Rye.*

Pendant Publishing

Employer of Elaine Benes (Julia Louis-Dreyfus) in the TV sitcom *Seinfeld.*

The Pendletones

Original name of the pop group The Beach Boys. It was later called Kenny and the Cadets, then Carl and the Passions, before adopting its best-known name.

Pendleton University

Where Dick Solomon (John Lithgow) teaches physics in the TV sitcom *3rd Rock From The Sun.*

Pendragon

Last name of legendary English ruler King Arthur.

Penelope

Real first name of the title character (Soleil Moon Frye) in the TV sitcom *Punky Brewster.*

Penfold Hearts

Brand of golf ball used by James Bond (Sean Connery) in his game with the title character (Gert Frobe) in the film *Goldfinger.* Goldfinger's ball is a Slazenger.

"The Penguin"

Nickname of baseball player Ron Cey, for his short legs.

Pennebaker Productions

Production company of actor Marlon Brando. Pennebaker was his mother's maiden name.

Penniman, Richard Wayne

Real name of rock singer Little Richard.

"Penny Black"

Nickname of the world's first postage stamp, issued by Great Britain in 1840 and depicting Queen Victoria.

Pennyworth

Last name of Alfred, butler of Bruce Wayne in the Batman comics.

Penrod Pooch

Janitor alter ego of the title character in the children's animated TV series *Hong Kong Phooey,* voiced by Scatman Crothers.

Pensione Bertolini

Inn in Florence, Italy, that is the setting of the E. M. Forster novel *A Room with a View.*

The Pension Grillparzer

Book written by the title character in the John Irving novel *The World According to Garp.* Irving later wrote a short story with the same title.

PENSYLVANIA

How the word "Pennsylvania" is misspelled on the Liberty Bell.

The Pentateuch

Collective name of the first five books of the Bible: Genesis, Exodus, Leviticus, Numbers, and Deuteronomy.

Pentimento

Book by Lillian Hellman that was the basis for the film *Julia.*

People Against Good and Normalcy

See **P.A.G.A.N.**

People Like Us

Original working title of the film *Philadelphia.*

People Magazine

Employer of investigative correspondent Jeff Dillon (Tony Franciosa) in the TV series *The Name of the Game.* The series ended in 1971, three years before the debut of Time Inc.'s *People* magazine.

People magazine's Sexiest Man Alive

Awarded by the magazine annually since 1985 (except 1994):

1985	Mel Gibson
1986	Mark Harmon
1987	Harry Hamlin
1988	John F. Kennedy Jr.
1989	Sean Connery
1990	Tom Cruise
1991	Patrick Swayze
1992	Nick Nolte
1993	Richard Gere and Cindy Crawford (Sexiest Couple)

1995 Brad Pitt
1996 Denzel Washington
1997 George Clooney
1998 Harrison Ford
1999 Richard Gere
2000 Brad Pitt

"people's car"

What the name of automaker Volkswagen means in German.

People's Messenger

Newspaper edited by Hovstad in the Henrik Ibsen play *An Enemy of the People.*

Pepperinge Eye

English village that is the setting of the Disney film *Bedknobs and Broomsticks.*

Peppy

Cartoon owl mascot of Wise potato chips.

Pepsi and milk

Favorite drink of Laverne De Fazio (Penny Marshall) in the TV sitcom *Laverne and Shirley.*

Pequod

Whaler that is the setting of the Herman Melville novel *Moby-Dick.*

Percevel

Middle name of illustrator Norman Rockwell.

perchloroethylene

Solvent used in dry cleaning, known as "perc" for short.

Perelmuth, Jacob Pincus

Real name of opera star Jan Peerce.

"The Perfect Fool"

Nickname of comedian Ed Wynn.

Perfection

Desert hamlet attacked by giant earthworms in the film *Tremors.*

Perfectly Frank

1992 Tony Bennett album, in which Bennett performs tunes made famous by Frank Sinatra, including "Night and Day," "The Lady Is a Tramp," and "One for My Baby."

"The Perfect Song"

See **"Angel's Serenade"**

Performing Animal Top Star of the Year

See **PATSY Awards**

Perisphere

See **Trylon and Perisphere**

Peritas

Pet greyhound of Alexander the Great.

Perkins, Edwin

Hastings, Nebraska, chemist who invented Kool-Aid in 1927. The original seven flavors were: Cherry, Grape, Lemon-Lime, Orange, Raspberry, Root Beer, and Strawberry.

Perkins, Frances

First woman to serve in the U.S. Cabinet, as Franklin D. Roosevelt's secretary of labor from 1933 to 1945.

Permalia

Margaret Mitchell's original name for Melanie in her novel *Gone With the Wind.*

Perma One

Space-station setting of the TV sitcom *Quark.*

Perrin, Vic

Speaker of the introduction to the TV series *The Outer Limits.*

Perry, Audrey Faith

Real name of country singer Faith Hill.

Perry, (Mary) Antoinette

Actress and director for whom the Tony Awards are named.

Perry Mason book series

The 82 full-length Perry Mason novels written by Erle Stanley Gardner, with their original publication dates:

The Case of the Velvet Claws (1933)
The Case of the Sulky Girl (1933)
The Case of the Lucky Legs (1934)
The Case of the Howling Dog (1934)
The Case of the Curious Bride (1934)
The Case of the Counterfeit Eye (1935)
The Case of the Caretaker's Cat (1935)
The Case of the Sleepwalker's Niece (1936)
The Case of the Stuttering Bishop (1936)
The Case of the Dangerous Dowager (1937)
The Case of the Lame Canary (1937)
The Case of the Substitute Face (1938)
The Case of the Shoplifter's Shoe (1938)

The Case of the Perjured Parrot (1939)
The Case of the Rolling Bones (1939)
The Case of the Baited Hook (1940)
The Case of the Silent Partner (1940)
The Case of the Haunted Husband (1941)
The Case of the Empty Tin (1941)
The Case of the Drowning Duck (1942)
The Case of the Careless Kitten (1942)
The Case of the Buried Clock (1943)
The Case of the Drowsy Mosquito (1943)
The Case of the Crooked Candle (1944)
The Case of the Black-Eyed Blonde (1944)
The Case of the Golddigger's Purse (1945)
The Case of the Half-Wakened Wife (1945)
The Case of the Borrowed Brunette (1946)
The Case of the Fandancer's Horse (1947)
The Case of the Lazy Lover (1947)
The Case of the Lonely Heiress (1948)
The Case of the Vagabond Virgin (1948)
The Case of the Dubious Bridegroom (1949)
The Case of the Cautious Coquette (1949)
The Case of the Negligent Nymph (1950)
The Case of the One-Eyed Witness (1950)
The Case of the Fiery Fingers (1951)
The Case of the Angry Mourner (1951)
The Case of the Moth-Eaten Mink (1952)
The Case of the Grinning Gorilla (1952)
The Case of the Hesitant Hostess (1953)
The Case of the Green-Eyed Sister (1953)
The Case of the Fugitive Nurse (1954)
The Case of the Runaway Corpse (1954)
The Case of the Restless Redhead (1954)
The Case of the Glamorous Ghost (1955)
The Case of the Sun Bather's Diary (1955)
The Case of the Nervous Accomplice (1955)
The Case of the Terrified Typist (1956)
The Case of the Demure Defendant (1956)
The Case of the Gilded Lily (1956)
The Case of the Lucky Loser (1957)
The Case of the Screaming Woman (1957)
The Case of the Daring Decoy (1957)
The Case of the Long-Legged Models (1958)
The Case of the Foot-Loose Doll (1958)
The Case of the Calendar Girl (1958)
The Case of the Deadly Toy (1959)
The Case of the Mythical Monkeys (1959)
The Case of the Singing Skirt (1959)
The Case of the Waylaid Wolf (1960)
The Case of the Duplicate Daughter (1960)
The Case of the Shapely Shadow (1960)
The Case of the Spurious Spinster (1961)
The Case of the Bigamous Spouse (1961)
The Case of the Reluctant Model (1962)
The Case of the Blonde Bonanza (1962)
The Case of the Ice-Cold Hands (1962)

The Case of the Mischievous Doll (1963)
The Case of the Stepdaughter's Secret (1963)
The Case of the Amorous Aunt (1963)
The Case of the Daring Divorcee (1964)
The Case of the Phantom Fortune (1964)
The Case of the Horrified Heirs (1964)
The Case of the Troubled Trustee (1965)
The Case of the Beautiful Beggar (1965)
The Case of the Worried Waitress (1966)
The Case of the Queenly Contestant (1967)
The Case of the Careless Cupid (1968)
The Case of the Fabulous Fake (1969)
The Case of the Fenced-In Woman (1972)
The Case of the Postponed Murder (1973)

Perry, Stephen
English rubber manufacturer who invented rubber bands, patented in 1845.

The Persecution and Assassination of Jean-Paul Marat as Performed by the Inmates of the Asylum of Charenton Under the Direction of the Marquis de Sade
Full name of the Peter Weiss play known as *Marat/Sade* for short.

Perske, Betty Joan
Real name of actress Lauren Bacall.

"Persons attempting to find a motive in this narrative will be prosecuted; persons attempting to find a moral in it will be banished; persons attempting to find a plot in it will be shot."
Notice at the beginning of the Mark Twain novel *The Adventures of Huckleberry Finn*.

Persons in Need of Supervision
See **P.I.N.S.**

"Perstare et praestare"
Motto of New York University, which is Latin for "To persevere and to excel."

pertussis
Medical term for whooping cough.

Peschkowsky
Real last name of director Mike Nichols.

Peshkov, Aleksey Maksimovich
Real name of author Maxim Gorki.

Peshtigo, Wisconsin
Town destroyed by a fire started on October 8, 1871—the same day as the Chicago Fire.

Pete

Mongrel dog (aka Petey) in the *Our Gang* series of film shorts, aka *The Little Rascals*.

Peter and the Wolf characters/instruments

This symphonic fairy tale for narrator and orchestra was written by composer Sergei Prokofiev in 1936, to teach the instruments of the orchestra to children. The characters below are represented by the indicated instruments in the piece:

Bird: flute
Duck: oboe
Cat: clarinet
Grandfather: bassoon
Wolf: French horns
Peter: strings
Rifle shots of the hunters: kettledrum and bass drum

The Peter Principle

"In a hierarchy, every employee tends to rise to his level of incompetence." This was introduced in the 1969 book of the same name cowritten by Canadian sociologist Laurence J. Peter.

Peters, Jane Alice

Real name of actress Carole Lombard.

Peterson, Roger

Pilot of the Beechcraft Bonanza that crashed after takeoff from Clear Lake, Iowa, on February 3, 1959, killing pop singers Buddy Holly, Ritchie Valens, and J. P. Richardson (aka The Big Bopper).

Pete's Super Submarines

See **DeLuca, Fred and Buck, Peter**

Petey Petit

Pet papillon dog of actress Glenn Close.

Petrograd

Former name (1914–24) of St. Petersburg, Russia.

Petty, Marsh & Company

Investment-firm employer of Tess McGill (Melanie Griffith) in the film *Working Girl*.

Petunia

Girlfriend of cartoon character Porky Pig.

"Peyo"

See **Culliford, Pierre "Peyo"**

pfefferminz

See **Haas III, Eduard**

Phantom

White horse of the title character (Guy Williams) in the TV series *Zorro*.

"The Phantom"

Nickname of jewel thief Sir Charles Litton (David Niven) in the film *The Pink Panther*.

Pharaoh, New York

Home of Annie Laird (Demi Moore) in the film *The Juror*.

Pharaohs

Gang that kidnaps Curt (Richard Dreyfuss) in the film *American Graffiti*.

Phelps Department Store

Setting of the Marx Brothers film *The Big Store*.

Philadelphia

Former name (until 635 A.D.) of Amman, Jordan.

Philip Francis

First and middle names of Captain Queeg in the Herman Wouk novel *The Caine Mutiny*, portrayed in the film version of the same name by Humphrey Bogart.

Philippan

Sword of Marc Antony.

Philip St. John Basil

Real first and middle names of actor Basil Rathbone.

phillumenist

Technical term for a collector of matchbook covers or matchboxes.

philographer

Technical term for a collector of autographs.

"Philosophy, the guide of life"

Greek translation of the words represented by the initials of Phi Beta Kappa, the first fraternity. Phi Beta Kappa was founded in 1776 at the College of William and Mary.

Philo Vance films

Series featuring the fictional detective created by novelist S. S. Van Dine. The films are listed below with the portrayer of Vance:

Canary Murder Case (1929) (William Powell)

The Greene Murder Case (1929) (William Powell)
Bishop Murder Case (1930) (Basil Rathbone)
Benson Murder Case (1930) (William Powell)
The Kennel Murder Case (1933) (William Powell)
The Dragon Murder Case (1934) (Warren William)
Casino Murder Case (1935) (Paul Lukas)
The Garden Murder Case (1936) (Edmund Lowe)
The Scarab Murder Case (1936) (Wilfrid Hyde-White)
Night of Mystery (1937) (Grant Richards)
The Gracie Allen Murder Case (1939) (Warren William)
Calling Philo Vance (1940) (James Stephenson)
Philo Vance Returns (1947) (William Wright)
Philo Vance's Gamble (1947) (Alan Curtis)
Philo Vance's Secret Mission (1947) (Alan Curtis)

Phil's

Bar hangout of *F.Y.I.* staff members in the TV sitcom *Murphy Brown.*

philtrum

Scientific name for the indentation above the upper lip.

Philtrum Press

Book-publishing company owned by author Stephen King.

Phin

See **Mudville**

Phineas Taylor

First and middle names of showman P. T. Barnum.

Phippsboro Bulletin

Small-town newspaper run by Robert Major (Robert Sterling) in the TV sitcom *Ichabod and Me.*

"Phi Slamma Jamma"

Nickname of the University of Houston basketball teams of the early 1980s that included future NBA stars Hakeem Olajuwon and Clyde Drexler.

phobias, common

Some of the most frequently seen terms for abnormal fears:
acrophobia: heights
aerophobia: drafts
agoraphobia: open spaces, crowds, public places
aichmophobia: needles
ailurophobia: cats
algophobia: pain
ambulophobia: walking
androphobia: men
Anglophobia: England, English culture
aphenphosmphobia: being touched
apiphobia: bees
arachibutyrophobia: peanut butter sticking to the roof of one's mouth
arachnophobia: spiders
astraphobia: thunder and lightning
atychiphobia: failure
aurophobia: gold
automysophobia: getting dirty
aviophobia: flying
batrachophobia: frogs
bibliophobia: books
catoptrophobia: mirrors
chionophobia: snow
choreophobia: dancing
claustrophobia: enclosed places
cremnophobia: precipices
cyberphobia: working with computers
cynophobia: dogs
dendrophobia: trees
didaskaleinophobia: going to school
ecophobia: home
entomophobia: insects
ergophobia: work
erythrophobia: red, blushing
Francophobia: France, French culture
gamophobia: marriage
gephyrophobia: crossing bridges
glossophobia: speaking in public
gynephobia: women
heliophobia: the Sun
hemophobia: blood
herpetophobia: reptiles
hippophobia: horses
hydrophobia: water
iatrophobia: doctors
ichthyophobia: fish
lalophobia: speaking
logophobia: words
lyssophobia: going insane
monophobia: being alone
musophobia: mice
mysophobia: dirt
neophobia: new things
nosophobia: disease
nyctophobia: darkness
ochlophobia: crowds
odontophobia: dentists
ombrophobia: rain
ophidiophobia: snakes
ornithophobia: birds
panophobia: everything
pathophobia: disease

peccatophobia: sinning
philemaphobia: kissing
phobophobia: one's own fears
photophobia: light
pogonophobia: beards
psychrophobia: cold
pyrophobia: fire
sesquipedalophobia: long words
Sinophobia: Chinese, Chinese culture
sitophobia: food
spectrophobia: ghosts
taphephobia: being buried alive
thalassophobia: the sea
thanatophobia: dying
toxiphobia: being poisoned
traumatophobia: injury
triskaidekaphobia: the number 13
xenophobia: strangers, foreigners
zoophobia: animals

Phoenician Films

Production company of actress Tia Carrere.

Phoenix Foundation

Think-tank employer of the title character (Richard Dean Anderson) in the TV series *MacGyver*.

phonetic punctuation

Memorable routine of comedic pianist Victor Borge, where he read a passage from a book, making humorous sounds for punctuation marks.

Phyllis Dorothy

First and middle names of mystery novelist P. D. James.

Pianosa

Italian island that is the setting of the Joseph Heller novel *Catch-22*.

pianos, sizes of grand

Listed below by overall length:
5'8": Baby grand
5'10": Living Room grand
6': Professional grand
6'4": Drawing Room grand
6'8": Parlour grand
7'4": Half Concert grand
8'11" or longer: Concert grand

Picariello

Real last name of pop singer Freddy "Boom Boom" Cannon.

Picayune Intelligence

Frostbite Falls, Minnesota, newspaper in the children's TV series *Rocky and His Friends*.

Picayune Intelligencer

Lompoc, California, newspaper in the film *The Bank Dick*.

Pickax City, Michigan

Setting of the "Cat Who" mysteries of Lilian Jackson Braun.

Pickersgill, Mary Young

Designer and maker of the 15-star, 15-stripe American flag that was flying over Fort McHenry in Baltimore harbor on September 13, 1814, when Francis Scott Key wrote the words to "The Star-Spangled Banner."

Pickfair

Beverly Hills mansion built in 1920 by married acting couple Douglas Fairbanks and Mary Pickford.

"pick me up"

What the name of the dessert tiramisu means in Italian.

"pie"

What the word "pizza" means in Italian.

"piecrust promise"

Something "easily made, easily broken," according to the title character (Julie Andrews) of the Disney film *Mary Poppins*.

Piedmont High

School attended by young genius T. J. Henderson (Tahj Mowry) in the TV sitcom *Smart Guy*.

Piedmont, New Mexico

Small town where the title virus is unleashed in the film *The Andromeda Strain*.

Pierce & Pierce

Wall Street employer of self-styled "Master of the Universe" Sherman McCoy in the Tom Wolfe novel *The Bonfire of the Vanities*.

Pierce, Mildred

Title role for which Joan Crawford won the 1945 Best Actress Academy Award.

Pierino Roland

Real first and middle names of singer Perry Como.

Pierre

See **Fritz, Michael, Pierre, and José**

A Pig in a Poke

Game show on which the Griswold family (Chevy Chase, Beverly D'Angelo, Dana Hill, Jason Lively) wins a trip, in the film *National Lampoon's European Vacation*.

"Pigpen"

Nickname of Grateful Dead organ and harmonica player Ron McKernan.

Pig's Eye

Original name of St. Paul, Minnesota. It was the nickname of fur trapper Pierre Parrant, one of the first settlers.

The Pig Stand

The first drive-in restaurant, also the first restaurant to employ carhops. It was opened by Royce Hailey in Dallas, Texas in 1921.

Pilar

Role for which Katina Paxinou won a Best Supporting Actress Academy Award in the 1943 film *For Whom the Bell Tolls*.

Pilgrim and Alert

Ships on which Richard Henry Dana served, as recounted in his book *Two Years Before the Mast*.

Pilgrims

See **Americans**

Pilletti, Marty

Role for which Ernest Borgnine won a Best Actor Academy Award in the 1955 film *Marty*.

Pinafore

Secret Service code name for Betty Ford.

"pine-eye"

What the word "Pinocchio" means in Italian.

Pine Ridge, Arkansas

Setting of the radio sitcom *Lum and Abner*. Waters, Arkansas, changed its name to Pine Ridge in 1936, in honor of the show.

Pine Valley, Pennsylvania

Setting of the TV soap opera *All My Children*.

Ping

Alter ego of the title character (voiced by Ming-Na, singing voice by Lea Salonga) while disguised as a male soldier, in the Disney animated film *Mulan*.

The Pinheads

Rock band of Marty McFly (Michael J. Fox) in the film *Back to the Future*, which plays "The Power of Love" at an audition. One of the judges is Huey Lewis, whose group (Huey Lewis and the News) performs the song on the film's soundtrack.

"Pinkie"

Adam Bonner's (Spencer Tracy's) pet name for his wife Amanda (Katharine Hepburn) in the film *Adam's Rib*.

Pink Ladies

Betty Rizzo's (Stockard Channing's) gang in the film *Grease*.

"The Pink Palace"

Nickname of the Beverly Hills Hotel.

"Pink Palace of the Pacific"

Nickname of the Royal Hawaiian Hotel in Honolulu.

Pink Panther films

PETER SELLERS AS INSPECTOR CLOUSEAU

The Pink Panther (1964)
A Shot in the Dark (1964)
The Return of the Pink Panther (1975)
The Pink Panther Strikes Again (1976)
Revenge of the Pink Panther (1978)
Trail of the Pink Panther (1982)

OTHERS AS INSPECTOR CLOUSEAU

Inspector Clouseau (1968): Alan Arkin
Curse of the Pink Panther (1983): Ted Wass
Son of the Pink Panther (1993): Roberto Benigni
   (as Jacques Clouseau, Jr.)

Pinky

See **Inky, Blinky, Pinky, and Clyde**

"Pinky"

Amanda Bonner's (Katharine Hepburn's) pet name for her husband Adam (Spencer Tracy) in the film *Adam's Rib*.

Pin Pals

Homer Simpson's bowling team in the animated TV sitcom *The Simpsons*.

P.I.N.S.

Acronym for Persons in Need of Supervision, the five foster children overseen by Phil Fish (Abe Vigoda) and his wife Bernice (Florence Stanley) in the TV sitcom *Fish*.

Pinzón, Martin Alonzo and Vicente Yañez

Brothers who captained the *Pinta* and *Niña* (respectively), the ships that accompanied Christopher Columbus (captaining the *Santa Maria*) on his first voyage to the New World in 1492.

Pipe Dream

See **Chain Reaction and Pipe Dream**

Pipeye

See **Peepeye, Pipeye, Poopeye, and Pupeye**

Pippet

Black dog attacked by the great white shark in the Steven Spielberg film *Jaws*.

pips

Technical term for the spots on dice, dominoes and playing cards.

Pirates

Original nickname of the Pittsburgh Steelers at their NFL inception in 1933. The team took its present name in 1941.

Pirrip Jr., Phillip

Real name of Pip, central character in the Charles Dickens novel *Great Expectations*.

"Pistol Pete"

Nickname of basketball player Pete Maravich.

Nickname of tennis pro Pete Sampras.

Pitching and Wooing

1973 autobiography of baseball pitcher and notable ladies' man Bo Belinsky.

The Pits

Bar owned by flashy police informant Huggy Bear (Antonio Fargas) in the TV series *Starsky and Hutch*.

"Pitter Patter Petrie"

Nickname of Rob Petrie (Dick Van Dyke) as an amateur boxer in the Army, in the TV sitcom *The Dick Van Dyke Show*.

Pixel

Feline title character in the Robert A. Heinlein novel *The Cat Who Walks Through Walls*.

Pixie

Horse of Tagg Oakley (Jimmie Hawkins) in the TV Western series *Annie Oakley*.

Pixie and Dixie

See **"I hate meeces to pieces!"**

Pizza Bowl

Milwaukee pizzeria/bowling alley owned by Frank De Fazio (Phil Foster) in the TV sitcom *Laverne and Shirley*.

Placerville, Maine

Setting of the Richard Bachman (Stephen King) novel *Rage*.

planchette

Device on legs that spells out messages on a Ouija board.

Planet of the Apes films

Planet of the Apes (1968)
Beneath the Planet of the Apes (1970)
Escape From the Planet of the Apes (1971)
Conquest of the Planet of the Apes (1972)
Battle for the Planet of the Apes (1973)

plangonologist

Technical term for a collector of dolls.

"Plastics"

Memorable word of career advice given to Benjamin Braddock (Dustin Hoffman) by family friend Mr. Maguire (Walter Brooke) in the film *The Graduate*.

plastron

Scientific name for the lower (ventral) shell of a turtle or tortoise.

Platinum Palace

Record store where Danny McGuire (Gene Kelly) meets Sonny Malone (Michael Beck) in the film *Xanadu*.

Plattville, Indiana

Setting of the Booth Tarkington novel *The Gentleman from Indiana*.

The Player cameo roles

These people all appear as themselves in this 1992 film directed by Robert Altman, which satirizes the film industry:

Steve Allen	Buck Henry
Richard Anderson	Anjelica Huston
Rene Auberjonois	Kathy Ireland
Harry Belafonte	Sally Kellerman
Shari Belafonte	Sally Kirkland
Karen Black	Jack Lemmon
Gary Busey	Andie MacDowell
Robert Carradine	Marlee Matlin
Charles Champlin	Malcolm McDowell
Cher	Jayne Meadows
James Coburn	Martin Mull
Cathy Lee Crosby	Nick Nolte
John Cusack	Alexandra Powers
Paul Dooley	Bert Remsen
Peter Falk	Burt Reynolds
Felicia Farr	Julia Roberts
Louise Fletcher	Mimi Rogers
Dennis Franz	Jill St. John
Teri Garr	Susan Sarandon
Leeza Gibbons	Rod Steiger
Althea Gibson	Lily Tomlin
Scott Glenn	Robert Wagner
Jeff Goldblum	Ray Walston
Elliott Gould	Bruce Willis
Joel Grey	

Play-Tone Records

See **The Wonders**

"play well"

English translation of the Danish words *"leg godt,"* from which the name of construction-toy manufacturer LEGO is derived.

Pleasant Island

Former name of the Pacific island nation of Nauru.

Please Stand By

Original working title of the TV series *The Outer Limits.*

Pleasure Island

Amusement park where the title character and his friends are transformed into donkeys, in the Disney animated film *Pinocchio.*

Plimpton, James Leonard

Massachusetts inventor of four-wheel roller skates in 1863. Previous skates had three wheels in a row, which made turning extremely difficult.

"Plop plop, fizz fizz, oh, what a relief it is"

Advertising slogan of Alka-Seltzer.

plumbum

Latin name for lead, from which its chemical symbol Pb is derived.

Plummer, Ed

See **Johnson, Sherwood "Shakey" and Plummer, Ed**

Plunkett, Roy J.

DuPont chemist who discovered Teflon in 1938.

Pluto

Title feline of the Edgar Allan Poe short story "The Black Cat."

Pluto Platter

Original name of the Frisbee.

pluviometer

Scientific name for a rain gauge.

Po

See **Tinky Winky, Dipsy, Laa-Laa, and Po**

poetical feet

The groups of syllables that make up a unit of verse:
anapest: two unaccented syllables, one accented
dactyl: one accented, two unaccented
iamb: one unaccented, one accented
pyrrhic: two unaccented
spondee: two accented
trochee: one accented, one unaccented

"The Poet of the Piano"

Nickname of pianist/bandleader Carmen Cavallaro.

Pogo

Original name of rock group Poco, which changed its name to avoid legal difficulties with the comic strip *Pogo.*

Poindexter, Buster

Stage name used by actor David Johansen for his "saloon singer" persona.

Pointer Sisters members

Pop-soul quartet consisting of sisters Anita, Bonnie, June, and Ruth.

Poison Zoomack

Nemesis of the title character in the children's TV series *Rootie Kazootie.*

poker hands and odds

Listed below from highest to lowest, with the odds against being dealt each hand in a five-card game:

Royal flush (649,740 to 1)
Straight flush (72,193 to 1)
Four of a kind (4,165 to 1)
Full house (694 to 1)
Flush (509 to 1)
Straight (255 to 1)
Three of a kind (47 to 1)
Two pair (21 to 1)
One pair (2.4 to 1)
No pair (2 to 1)

The Poker Night

Original working title of the Tennessee Williams play *A Streetcar Named Desire*.

Pokey

Pet basset hound of Porky (Donald Keeler) in the 1950s version of the TV series *Lassie*.

Polar Burger

See **Frosty Palace**

Polaris

Yearbook of the U.S. Air Force Academy.

Spaceship setting of the children's TV series *Tom Corbett, Space Cadet*.

Polfuss, Lester William

Real name of guitarist Les Paul.

Police Academy films

Police Academy (1984)
Police Academy 2: Their First Assignment (1985)
Police Academy 3: Back in Training (1986)
Police Academy 4: Citizens on Patrol (1987)
Police Academy 5: Assignment Miami Beach (1988)
Police Academy 6: City Under Siege (1989)
Police Academy VII: Mission to Moscow (1994)

The Police, original members

Stewart Copeland, Henri Padovani, and Sting.

police radio codes

These are similar to CB radio codes (listed separately):

10-0	Caution
10-1	Signal weak
10-2	Signal good
10-3	Stop transmitting
10-4	Message received
10-5	Relay
10-6	Busy
10-7	Out of service
10-8	In service
10-9	Repeat
10-10	Fight in progress
10-11	Animal problem
10-12	Stand by
10-13	Report conditions
10-14	Prowler report
10-15	Civil disturbance
10-16	Domestic problem
10-17	Meet complainant
10-18	Urgent
10-19	Go to station
10-20	Location
10-21	Phone __
10-22	Disregard
10-23	Arrived at scene
10-24	Assignment complete
10-25	Report to __
10-26	Detaining suspect
10-27	Driver's license information
10-28	Vehicle registration information
10-29	Check for wants/warrants
10-30	Unauthorized use of radio
10-31	Crime in progress
10-32	Person with gun
10-33	Emergency, stand by
10-34	Riot
10-35	Major crime alert
10-36	Correct time
10-37	Investigate suspicious vehicle
10-38	Stop suspicious vehicle
10-39	Use lights and siren
10-40	Respond quietly
10-41	Beginning shift
10-42	Ending shift
10-43	Information
10-44	Permission to leave
10-45	Dead animal
10-46	Assist motorist
10-47	Emergency road repair
10-48	Traffic control
10-49	Traffic signal out
10-50	Traffic accident
10-51	Request tow truck
10-52	Request ambulance
10-53	Roadway blocked
10-54	Livestock on roadway
10-55	Intoxicated driver
10-56	Intoxicated pedestrian
10-57	Hit-and-run accident
10-58	Direct traffic
10-59	Escort
10-60	Squad in vicinity

10-61 Personnel in vicinity
10-62 Reply to message
10-63 Prepare to copy
10-64 Local message
10-65 Network message
10-66 Cancel message
10-67 Clear for network message
10-68 Dispatch information
10-69 Message received
10-70 Fire alarm
10-71 Advise of nature of fire
10-72 Report progress on fire
10-73 Smoke report
10-74 Negative
10-75 In contact with __
10-76 En route to __
10-77 E.T.A.
10-78 Request assistance
10-79 Notify coroner
10-80 Pursuit in progress
10-81 Breathalyzer report
10-82 Reserve lodgings
10-83 School crossing detail
10-84 E.T.A.
10-85 Arrival delayed
10-86 Operator on duty
10-87 Pick up
10-88 Advise of telephone number
10-89 Bomb threat
10-90 Bank alarm
10-91 Pick up subject
10-92 Illegally parked vehicle
10-93 Blockage
10-94 Drag racing
10-95 Subject in custody
10-96 Detain subject
10-97 Test signal
10-98 Escaped prisoner
10-99 Wanted or stolen

Polidor

Sister sub of the *Seaview* in the TV series *Voyage to the Bottom of the Sea.*

The Polka

Bar owned by Minnie, title character of the Giacomo Puccini opera *The Girl of the Golden West.*

"Polka Dot"

First-grade nickname of Martha Livingston (Jane Fonda) in the film *Agnes of God.*

Polka Dottie

Girlfriend of the title character in the children's TV series *Rootie Kazootie.*

Poll

Pet parrot of President Andrew Jackson.

pollex

Medical term for the thumb.

Polley, Eugene

See **Flashmatic**

Pollock, Major

Role for which David Niven won a Best Actor Academy Award in the 1958 film *Separate Tables.*

Polly Pigtails

Original name of *YM* magazine. It was later called *Calling All Girls* and *Young Miss* before taking its present name, which now stands for "Young and Modern."

polymethyl methacrylate

Chemical name of Lucite and Plexiglas.

Polynesia

Pet parrot of the title character in the Doctor Dolittle series of children's novels by Hugh Lofting.

polytetrafluoroethylene

Chemical name of Teflon.

polyvinyl acetate

Synthetic plastic that is the main ingredient in the chewing gums manufactured today.

Pom

See **Alexander, Flora, and Pom**

Pommard 1934

Brand and vintage of wine bottles that conceal uranium ore in the Alfred Hitchcock film *Notorious.*

Pong

See **"King Pong"**

Pongo

Pet dog of the title character (Cary Elwes) in the Mel Brooks film *Robin Hood: Men in Tights.*

Pontiac Greeting Card Company

Company for whom Maxwell Smart (Don Adams) has a "front" sales job, in the TV sitcom *Get Smart.*

Pontipee

Last name of the brothers in the musical *Seven Brides for Seven Brothers.*

Poochie

Pet dog of the title character in the comic strip *Nancy*.

Pookie

Lion puppet in the children's TV series *The Soupy Sales Show*.

Pooky

Teddy bear of the title character in the comic strip *Garfield*.

pool-ball colors

See **billiard-ball colors**

poona

Original name of badminton, as played in India in the 19th century.

Poopeye

See **Peepeye, Pipeye, Poopeye, and Pupeye**

"Poopsie"

Zelda Gilroy's (Sheila James') term of endearment for the title character (Dwayne Hickman) in the TV sitcom *The Many Loves of Dobie Gillis*.

"Poosh 'em Up"

Nickname of baseball Hall of Famer Tony Lazzeri, for his ability to advance baserunners.

Pop!

See **Snap!, Crackle!, and Pop!**

Pope, John Russell

Architect who designed the Jefferson Memorial in Washington, D.C., dedicated in 1943.

Popes Creek Plantation

Virginia birthplace of George Washington in 1732.

"Popeye"

See **Doyle, James "Popeye"**

Pop Jenks' Sugar Bowl

Favorite hangout of the title character in the comic strip *Harold Teen*.

Poplawski, Stephen J.

Inventor of the kitchen blender in 1922.

"Popo"

Nickname of advice columnist Abigail Van Buren, aka Dear Abby.

Poppert, Ruth

Role for which Cloris Leachman won a Best Supporting Actress Academy Award in the 1971 film *The Last Picture Show*.

Poppin' Fresh

Name of the Pillsbury Doughboy.

Poppins, Mary

Title role for which Julie Andrews won the 1964 Best Actress Academy Award.

Poppolino, Pippo

Bob Hope's role in the film *Casanova's Big Night*.

"Pops"

Nickname of baseball Hall of Famer Willie Stargell.

Nickname of bandleader Paul Whiteman.

Pop's Choklit Shoppe

Teen hangout in Archie comics.

"Population: Zero"

Debut episode of the TV series *The Six Million Dollar Man*, which aired on January 18, 1974.

Poquelin, Jean-Baptiste

Real name of French playwright Molière.

"Porcupine"

Moe Howard's affectionate nickname for Larry Fine (because of his unusual hairdo) in the Three Stooges shorts.

Porkchop

Pet dog of the title character (voiced by Billy West) in the animated TV series *Doug*.

Pork Corners, Iowa

Hometown of Sergeant Snorkel in the comic strip *Beetle Bailey*.

"Porky's Duck Hunt"

1937 Warner Bros. cartoon that is the debut appearance of Daffy Duck.

***Porky's* films**

Porky's (1981)
Porky's II: The Next Day (1983)
Porky's Revenge (1985)

Port Charles

Setting of the TV soap opera *General Hospital*.

Porter

Last name of the title couple (Harry Morgan and Cara Williams) in the TV sitcom *Pete and Gladys*.

Porthos

See **Aramis, Athos, and Porthos**

Portsmouth Spartans

Original name of the Detroit Lions at their NFL inception in 1930. The team took its present name when it moved from Portsmouth, Ohio, to Detroit in 1934.

"The Portuguese"

Poet Robert Browning's nickname for his wife Elizabeth Barrett Browning, hence the title of the latter's poetry collection *Sonnets from the Portuguese*.

Portuguese East Africa

Former name of the African nation Mozambique.

Portuguese Guinea

Former name of the African nation Guinea-Bissau.

Portuguese West Africa

Former name of the African nation Angola.

Port Washington, Wisconsin

Setting of the TV sitcom *Step by Step*.

"positive crankcase ventilation"

What "PCV" in "PCV valve" stands for.

positronic ray

Weapon invented by Durand Durand (Milo O'Shea) in the film *Barbarella*.

postal rate changes, U.S.

History of the effective dates for rate changes in the cost of a first-class letter:
July 1, 1863: 3 cents
October 1, 1863: 2 cents
November 3, 1917: 3 cents (war emergency rate)
July 1, 1919: 2 cents
July 6, 1932: 3 cents
August 1, 1958: 4 cents
January 7, 1963: 5 cents
January 7, 1968: 6 cents
May 16, 1971: 8 cents
March 2, 1974: 10 cents
December 31, 1975: 13 cents
May 29, 1978: 15 cents
March 22, 1981: 18 cents
November 1, 1981: 20 cents
February 17, 1985: 22 cents
April 3, 1988: 25 cents
February 3, 1991: 29 cents
January 1, 1995: 32 cents
January 1, 1999: 33 cents
January 7, 2001: 34 cents
Prior to 1863, letter rates were based in part on the distance traveled.

Posture Foundation

What the "PF" stands for in the name of PF Flyers sneakers.

Potowatomie

Indian tribe of Tonto, sidekick of The Lone Ranger.

Potter

Maiden name of Ethel Mertz (Vivian Vance) in the TV sitcom *I Love Lucy*.

Potter, Edward Clark

See **Patience and Fortitude**

Pottersville

Name of Bedford Falls in the "alternate reality" of the film *It's a Wonderful Life*.

Potts, Isaac

Owner of the house rented by General George Washington for his headquarters at Valley Forge, Pennsylvania, during the encampment of the Continental Army in the winter of 1777–78.

Potts, Marvin

Advertising agency art director who created the smiling frosted pitcher design for Kool-Aid in 1954. He was inspired by the patterns that his son traced on a frosty windowpane.

Pottstown, Illinois

Where Ed O'Brien (Gene Kelly) and Denny Ryan (Frank Sinatra) perform the title tune in a vaudeville act, in the film *Take Me Out to the Ball Game*.

Pottsylvania

Home of Boris Badenov and Natasha Fatale in the children's TV series *Rocky and His Friends*.

pourvoir hydrogene

French term, meaning "power of hydrogen," from which "pH" is derived; pH measures the concentration of hydrogen ions in a solution, on a 0-14 scale.

Powdered Toast

Favorite snack of the title characters in the animated TV series *The Ren & Stimpy Show*.

The Power of Environment

Book written by psychology professor Peter Boyd (Ronald Reagan) in the film *Bedtime for Bonzo*.

"The Power of Music"

Alternate title of the John Dryden poem "Alexander's Feast."

Powers, Francis Gary

See **Abel, Rudolf**

Practical Handbook of Bee Culture

Book written by Sherlock Holmes in retirement, as cited in the Sir Arthur Conan Doyle story *His Last Bow*.

"Prae omnia fraternitas"

Motto of the Friars Club, which is Latin for "Before all things, brotherhood."

"Prairie Provinces"

Nickname of the Canadian provinces of Manitoba, Saskatchewan, and Alberta.

Prairie Stop, Indiana

Rural locale where Roger Thornhill (Cary Grant) is shot at by a cropdusting airplane, in the Alfred Hitchcock film *North by Northwest*.

Pran, Dith

Role for which Haing S. Ngor won a Best Supporting Actor Academy Award in the 1984 film *The Killing Fields*.

Prater

See **Moore and Prater**

Pratt, Anthony

English inventor of the board game Clue in 1944.

Pratt, William Henry

Real name of actor Boris Karloff.

Prax, Prairie of

Setting of the Dr. Seuss children's story *The Zax*.

"Prayer"

See **"Bad in Every Man"**

The Preacher

Alternate name of Ecclesiastes, a book of the Bible.

Precious Pupp

Conniving pet dog of Granny Sweet in the children's animated TV series *The Atom Ant Show*.

"precision"

What the name of electronics manufacturer Seiko means in Japanese.

"The Prefab Four"

Nickname of the "manufactured" rock group the Monkees, inspired by the "Fab Four" nickname of the Beatles.

Preis, Alfred

Designer of the U.S.S. *Arizona* Memorial in Pearl Harbor, Hawaii. It was opened to the public in 1962.

Prejean, Sister Helen

Role for which Susan Sarandon won a Best Actress Academy Award in the 1995 film *Dead Man Walking*.

Prendergast

Real last name of English film composer John Barry.

Prendergast Tool & Die

Employer of Archie Bunker (Carroll O'Connor) in the TV sitcom *All in the Family*.

"Prescription for Death"

Debut episode of the TV series *Law & Order*, which aired on September 13, 1990.

"The present time"

What the name of Seoul-based industrial company Hyundai means in Korean.

The Preservation of Favoured Races in the Struggle for Life

Alternate title of the Charles Darwin book *On the Origin of Species by Means of Natural Selection*.

presidents in films, fictional

Memorable portrayals of fictional U.S. presidents. They are listed below alphabetically by performer, character name (if any), film, and year:

Mason Adams: *The Final Conflict* (1981)
Eddie Albert: *Dreamscape* (1984)
Alan Alda: *Canadian Bacon* (1995)
Dan Aykroyd (William Haney): *My Fellow Americans* (1996)
Jim Backus: *Slapstick (of Another Kind)* (1984)
Ed Begley: *The Monitors* (1969)
Richard Belzer: *Species II* (1998)
Jeff Bridges (Jackson Evans): *The Contender* (2000)
Lloyd Bridges (Thomas "Tug" Benson): *Hot Shots! Part Deux* (1993)
Ronny Cox (Jack Neil): *Murder at 1600* (1997)

Robert Culp: *The Pelican Brief* (1993)

Michael Douglas (Andrew Shepherd): *The American President* (1995)

Andrew Duggan (President Trent): *In Like Flint* (1967)

Charles Durning (David Stevens): *Twilight's Last Gleaming* (1977)

Henry Fonda: *Fail-Safe* (1964)

Henry Fonda: *Meteor* (1979)

Harrison Ford (James Marshall): *Air Force One* (1997)

James Franciscus (James Cassidy): *The Greek Tycoon* (1978)

Morgan Freeman (Tom Beck): *Deep Impact* (1998)

James Garner (Matt Douglas): *My Fellow Americans* (1996)

George Gobel: *Rabbit Test* (1978)

Gene Hackman (Alan Richmond): *Absolute Power* (1997)

Hal Holbrook (Adam Scott): *The Kidnapping of the President* (1980)

Harvey Korman: *Jingle All the Way* (1996)

Jack Lemmon (Russell P. Kramer): *My Fellow Americans* (1996)

Fredric March (Jordan Lyman): *Seven Days in May* (1964)

E. G. Marshall: *Superman II* (1980)

Kevin Kline (Bill Mitchell): *Dave* (1993)

Bob Newhart (Manfred Link): *First Family* (1980)

Jack Nicholson (James Dale): *Mars Attacks!* (1996)

Gregory Peck: *Amazing Grace and Chuck* (1987)

Donald Pleasence: *Escape from New York* (1981)

Bill Pullman (Thomas J. Whitmore): *Independence Day* (1996)

John Ritter (Chet Roosevelt): *Americathon* (1979)

Tim Robbins: *Austin Powers: The Spy Who Shagged Me* (1999)

Cliff Robertson: *Escape From L.A.* (1996)

Roy Scheider (President Carlson): *Executive Target* (1997)

Roy Scheider (Robert Baker): *The Peacekeeper* (1997)

Roy Scheider (Jack Cahill): *Chain of Command* (2000)

Franchot Tone: *Advise & Consent* (1962)

Jack Warden ("Bobby"): *Being There* (1979)

William Windom: *Escape From the Planet of the Apes* (1971)

Presley, Elvis, #1 tunes of

These 18 tunes all reached #1 on the U.S. *Billboard* pop chart:

"Heartbreak Hotel" (1956)

"I Want You, I Need You, I Love You" (1956)

"Hound Dog" (1956)

"Don't Be Cruel" (1956)

"Love Me Tender" (1956)

"Too Much" (1957)

"All Shook Up" (1957)

"(Let Me Be Your) Teddy Bear" (1957)

"Jailhouse Rock" (1957)

"Don't" (1958)

"Hard Headed Woman" (1958)

"A Big Hunk O' Love" (1959)

"Stuck on You" (1960)

"It's Now or Never" (1960)

"Are You Lonesome To-night" (1960)

"Surrender" (1961)

"Good Luck Charm" (1962)

"Suspicious Minds" (1969)

Presley, Elvis, feature films of

Love Me Tender (1956)

Loving You (1957)

Jailhouse Rock (1957)

King Creole (1958)

G.I. Blues (1960)

Flaming Star (1960)

Wild in the Country (1961)

Blue Hawaii (1961)

Follow That Dream (1962)

Kid Galahad (1962)

Girls! Girls! Girls! (1962)

It Happened at the World's Fair (1963)

Fun in Acapulco (1963)

Kissin' Cousins (1964)

Viva Las Vegas (1964)

Roustabout (1964)

Girl Happy (1965)

Tickle Me (1965)

Harum Scarum (1965)

Frankie and Johnny (1966)

Paradise, Hawaiian Style (1966)

Spinout (1966)

Easy Come, Easy Go (1967)

Double Trouble (1967)

Clambake (1967)

Stay Away, Joe (1968)

Speedway (1968)

Live a Little, Love a Little (1968)

Charro! (1969)

The Trouble with Girls (1969)

Change of Habit (1969)

Presley, Jesse Garon

Twin brother of Elvis Presley, who died at birth.

Pressure Point

Original working title of the James Bond film *The World Is Not Enough.*

Preston and Logan

Last names of the title characters (Alex Winter and Keanu Reeves, respectively) in the *Bill and Ted's . . .* films.

Preston, Terry

Stage name once used by country singer Ferlin Husky.

"A Pretty Girl Is Like a Melody"

Irving Berlin tune composed for *Ziegfeld Follies of 1919*, used thereafter as the theme song for each edition of the Ziegfeld Follies.

Pretty Lady

Broadway-bound musical that is the focus of the musical *42nd Street*.

Charter boat operated by Jake Hanson (Grant Show) in the TV series *Melrose Place*.

Prettywillie, Elmer

See **Fields, W. C., roles/pen names of**

Pretzel

Original name of the game Twister.

Pet dog of bar owner Dinty Moore in the comic strip *Bringing Up Father*.

Priddy High

School attended by Tiffany and Ryan Malloy (Nikki Cox and Kevin Connolly) in the TV sitcom *Unhappily Ever After*.

The Pride

Flagship of French privateer Jean Lafitte.

Pride Rock

Home of Mufasa and family in the Disney animated film *The Lion King*.

Pridwin

Shield of legendary British monarch King Arthur.

"Prime Time"

Self-styled nickname of baseball/football player Deion Sanders.

The Primettes

Original name of pop group The Supremes.

Primrose, Charles

Real name of the title character in the Oliver Goldsmith novel *The Vicar of Wakefield*.

"Primrose Lane"

Theme song of the TV series *The Smith Family*, performed by Mike Minor.

Prince Charles, titles of

Prince Charles of Great Britain holds all of the titles listed below:
- Prince of Wales
- Duke of Cornwall
- Duke of Rothesay
- Earl of Carrick
- Lord of Renfrew
- Lord of the Isles
- Prince and Great Steward of Scotland
- Earl of Chester

Prince, Diana

Secret identity of superheroine Wonder Woman.

"The Prince of Destruction"

Nickname of Tartar conqueror Tamerlane.

"Prince of Humbugs"

Nickname of showman P. T. Barnum.

"The Prince of Players"

Nickname of 19th-century actor Edwin Booth.

"Princes of the Universe"

Theme song of the TV series *Highlander*, performed by Queen.

Princes of Wales

The title "Prince of Wales" has been bestowed to the eldest son of English reigning monarchs since 1301. Prince Charles is the 21st to hold the title, which is an appointment rather than a birthright. The list below includes the date that the title was bestowed, holders of the title, their father or mother, and their fate:

- **1301** Edward (son of Edward I): became King Edward II in 1307
- **1343** Edward (son of Edward III): died in 1376
- **1376** Richard (son of Edward, Prince of Wales): became King Richard II in 1377
- **1399** Henry (son of Henry IV): became King Henry V in 1413
- **1454** Edward (son of Henry VI): died in 1471
- **1471** Edward (son of Edward IV): became King Edward V in 1483
- **1483** Edward (son of Richard III): died in 1484
- **1489** Arthur (son of Henry VII): died in 1502
- **1504** Henry (son of Henry VII): became King Henry VIII in 1509
- **1610** Henry (son of James I): died in 1612
- **1616** Charles (son of James I): became King Charles I in 1625

1638 Charles (son of Charles I): became King Charles II in 1649

1688 James (son of James II): forfeited title when James II abdicated in 1688

1714 George (son of George I): became King George II in 1727

1729 Frederick (son of George II): died in 1751

1751 George (son of Frederick, Prince of Wales): became King George III in 1760

1762 George (son of George III): became King George IV in 1820

1841 Albert Edward (son of Victoria): became King Edward VII in 1901

1901 George (son of Edward VII): became King George V in 1910

1910 Edward (son of George V): became King Edward VIII in 1936

1958 Charles (son of Elizabeth II)

"Princess"

Jim Anderson's (Robert Young's) term of endearment for his older daughter Betty (Elinor Donahue), in the TV sitcom *Father Knows Best*.

Princess Aurora

Title character of the Disney animated film *Sleeping Beauty*, voiced by Mary Costa.

"Princess O'Hara"

Short story by Ramon Runyon that was the basis for the Abbott and Costello film *It Ain't Hay*.

Princip, Gavrilo

Serbian student who assassinated Austrian archduke Franz Ferdinand in Sarajevo on June 28, 1914, which precipitated the start of World War I.

Prisoners of Love

Musical produced by inmates Max Bialystock (Zero Mostel) and Leo Bloom (Gene Wilder) in the Mel Brooks film *The Producers*.

Pritchett, Muriel

Role for which Geena Davis won a Best Supporting Actress Academy Award in the 1988 film *The Accidental Tourist*.

Pritzker Prize

Awarded annually since 1979 by the Hyatt Foundation for lifetime achievement in architecture. The Pritzker family owns the Hyatt hotel chain.

Prizzi, Maerose

Role for which Anjelica Huston won a Best Supporting Actress Academy Award in the 1985 film *Prizzi's Honor*.

"Proclaim liberty throughout the land unto all the inhabitants thereof"

Inscription on the Liberty Bell. It is a quotation from Leviticus 25:10 (King James Version).

Procrastinator of the Year award

Presented by the Procrastinators Club of America, not surprisingly, on an irregular basis.

1957 An ecdysiast, "For putting things off"

1964 Comedian Jack Benny, for never getting around to turning 40

1965 Murray Rappaport, for breaking the world's record for an overdue library book

1969 Dean Martin and Jerry Lewis, "Comedy Team of the Year" (more than 10 years after they split up)

1972 Elmer T. Klassen, U.S. Postmaster General, for late delivery of mail

1982 *Arizona Republic* (newspaper), for printing a September 31st edition

1988 Illinois-Central Railroad, for a train that left the station in 1903 and has yet to arrive

1991 Seafood Shanty Restaurants, for eliminating early-bird specials

1992 U.S. Congress, for tardiness in adopting a Federal budget

1995 Congressman Tom DeLay, for having such a nice name

1995 Walter Birckhead, who worked at the Melrose Diner for 50 years, starting at the age of 40

1999 "To be announced"

"Pro ecclesia, pro Texana"

Motto of Baylor University, which is Latin for "For Church, for Texas."

Professor Tigwissel's Burglar Alarm

The first comic strip to appear in a newspaper, in the *New York Graphic*, on September 11, 1875.

Profiles in Courage subjects

John F. Kennedy's Pulitzer Prize-winning 1956 book profiles these eight Americans who took politically risky positions:

John Quincy Adams
Thomas Hart Benton
Sam Houston
Lucius Quintus Cincinnatus Lamar
George Norris
Edmund G. Ross
Robert Taft
Daniel Webster

Profound Anger

Rock band of Chip Flagston in the comic strip *Hi and Lois*.

"Progress is our most important product"

Advertising slogan of General Electric.

"Pro humanitate"

Motto of Wake Forest University, which is Latin for "For humanity."

Project Main Strike

Code name of Max Zorin's (Christopher Walken's) plan to flood and destroy Silicon Valley in the James Bond film *A View to a Kill*.

Project Tic Toc

Secret time-travel experiment headquartered beneath the Arizona desert in the TV series *The Time Tunnel*.

propylene glycol

Chemical name of antifreeze.

"Pro scientia et sapentia"

Motto of the University of Mississippi, which is Latin for "For science and wisdom."

"Prosperity is just around the corner"

Slogan of Herbert Hoover and the Republican party in the presidential campaign of 1932.

"protected bay"

What "Honolulu" means in Hawaiian.

Protector

Spaceship in the mythical 1970s TV series *Galaxy Quest*, in the film of the same name.

"The Protectors"

Debut episode of the TV series *T. J. Hooker*, which aired on March 13, 1982.

Proteus

Nuclear submarine that is miniaturized for a trip through a human body in the film *Fantastic Voyage*.

See also **Valentine and Proteus**

Proton Energy Pill

Secret weapon of cartoon superhero Roger Ramjet, which gives him the power of 20 atom bombs for 20 seconds.

Proudfoot, Epiphany

Lisa Bonet's role in the film *Angel Heart*.

Prozorov, Olga, Masha, and Irina

Title characters of the Anton Chekhov play *Three Sisters*.

Prudence Prim

Pet collie of President Calvin Coolidge.

Prufrock Productions

Production company of actress Meg Ryan.

pruritus

Medical term for itching.

Psyche at Nature's Mirror

Logo of White Rock beverages.

Psycho-Neurotic Institute for the Very, Very Nervous

California asylum run by Dr. Richard H. Thorndyke (Mel Brooks) in the film *High Anxiety*.

PT 73

Boat commanded by the title character (Ernest Borgnine) in the TV sitcom *McHale's Navy*.

P. T. Barnum's Monster Classical and Geological Hippodrome

Original name of New York City's first Madison Square Garden, which opened in 1874. Several other arenas at a succession of different Manhattan locations have also been called "Madison Square Garden."

Pubert

Infant son of Morticia and Gomez Addams (Anjelica Huston and Raul Julia), born with a full mustache, in the film *Addams Family Values*.

"Puberty Love"

Song that causes the title menaces to return to normal size, in the film *Attack of the Killer Tomatoes!*

Publius

Pen name used for the 1787–88 publication of the *Federalist Papers*, designed to build support for the ratification of the U.S. Constitution in New York state. Its articles were written by Alexander Hamilton, John Jay, and Thomas Jefferson.

Puck-Man

See **Iwatani, Toru**

Puddleby-on-the-Marsh

English home of the title character in the Doctor Dolittle series of children's novels by Hugh Lofting.

"Pudge"
Nickname of Hall of Fame baseball catcher Carlton Fisk.

Pudgy
Pet dog of the title character in Betty Boop cartoons.

Puerto Barrio, Mexico
Setting of the Tennessee Williams play *The Night of the Iguana*.

Puff
Pet cat of Dick and Jane in the memorable elementary school readers.

"Puff Daddy" (or "Puffy")
Nickname of rap artist Sean Combs.

"Puffin' Billy"
Instrumental theme of the children's TV series *Captain Kangaroo*.

Puffington, Podine
See **Bergen, Edgar, dummies of**

Puffy
Obnoxious pet dog of Magda (Lin Shaye), next-door neighbor of the title character (Cameron Diaz) in the film *There's Something About Mary*.

Pulau Tiga
Uninhabited island off the coast of Borneo that was the setting of the initial run of TV game show *Survivor*.

"The Pulse of Paradise"
Slogan of the *Honolulu Star-Bulletin*.

Pulver, Ensign Frank
Role for which Jack Lemmon won a Best Supporting Actor Academy Award in the 1955 film *Mister Roberts*.

Pumbaa
Warthog friend (voiced by Ernie Sabella) of the title character (voiced by Matthew Broderick) in the Disney animated film *The Lion King*.

Punch Productions
Production company of actor Dustin Hoffman.

Punchy
Diminutive cartoon character in an aloha shirt, in TV commercials for Hawaiian Punch.

Punxsutawney Phil
Groundhog that makes the long-range weather forecast at Punxsutawney, Pennsylvania, each Groundhog Day (February 2). According to folklore, if he sees his shadow, there will be six more weeks of winter. If not, there will be an early spring.

Pupeye
See **Peepeye, Pipeye, Poopeye, and Pupeye**

Pupkin, Rupert
Comedian-wannabe portrayed by Robert De Niro in the film *The King of Comedy*.

Purcell, Andy "Champ"
Role for which Wallace Beery won a Best Actor Academy Award in the 1931 film *The Champ*.

Purebred, Sweet Polly
Girlfriend of cartoon superhero Underdog, voiced by Norma McMillan.

"A Pure Woman Faithfully Presented"
Subtitle of the Thomas Hardy novel *Tess of the d'Urbervilles*.

Puritans
See **Americans**

The Purple Onion
San Francisco nightclub where many famous performers made their debut, including Phyllis Diller, The Kingston Trio, and the Smothers Brothers.

"Purple People Eaters"
Nickname of the late 1960s–70s defensive front four of the Minnesota Vikings: Carl Eller, Gary Larsen, Jim Marshall, and Alan Page.

Pushinka
Pet dog of Caroline Kennedy while living in the White House. The dog was a gift from Soviet leader Nikita Khrushchev.

Pushmi-Pullyu
African beast with two full bodies facing in opposite directions, in the Hugh Lofting children's novel *The Story of Doctor Dolittle*.

"Put a tiger in your tank"
Advertising slogan of Esso.

"Put Love in the White House"
Campaign slogan of presidential candidate John P. Wintergreen in the George and Ira Gershwin musical *Of Thee I Sing*.

Putnam's Landing, New York

Setting of the film *Rally 'Round the Flag, Boys!*

Pyewacket

Siamese-cat familiar of witch Gillian Holroyd (Kim Novak) in the film *Bell, Book and Candle*.

Pyramid Corners, Oklahoma

Setting of the TV sitcom *The Torkelsons*.

pyramidion

Technical term for the small pyramid at the apex of an obelisk, such as the Washington Monument in Washington, D.C.

Pyramus and Thisbe

Play within the William Shakespeare play *A Midsummer Night's Dream*.

"Quad Cities"

Nickname of the neighboring cities of Rock Island, Illinois; Moline, Illinois; Davenport, Iowa; and Bettendorf, Iowa.

quadrivium

Term used during the Middle Ages for the higher division of the seven liberal arts, comprising arithmetic, geometry, astronomy, and music.

See also **trivium**

"Quaecumque sunt vera"

Motto of Northwestern University, which is Latin for "Whatsoever things are true."

"Quaerite primo regnum Dei"

Motto of Newfoundland, Canada, which is Latin for "Seek ye first the kingdom of God."

Quaffle

Red ball used for scoring in Quidditch, in the Harry Potter series of books by J. K. Rowling.

Quahog, Rhode Island

Setting of the animated TV sitcom *Family Guy*.

Quake City, California

Setting of the Disney film *The Apple Dumpling Gang*.

Quale, S. Quentin

See **Marx, Groucho, roles of**

"The quality goes in before the name goes on"

Advertising slogan of Zenith televisions.

"Quality Is Job 1"

Advertising slogan of the Ford Motor Company.

Quality Value Convenience

What the initials of the name of cable TV shopping channel QVC stand for.

Quant, Mary

English fashion designer who created the miniskirt circa 1964.

Quantum Computer Services

Original name of America Online.

Quarles

Pen name used by Edgar Allan Poe for the publication of his poem "The Raven" in the February 1845 issue of *The American Review*.

The Quarrymen

Original name of the Beatles. They were later called Johnny and the Moondogs, then The Silver Beetles, before adopting their best-known name.

"The Quasar of Rock"

Nickname of singer Little Richard.

"quatrains"

What the word "Rubáiyát" means in Persian.

Queen Alexandra and Murray

"Lost" 38th play of William Shakespeare, according to the 2,000 Year Old Man, in the comedy routines of Mel Brooks and Carl Reiner.

Queen Anne's Revenge

Flagship of pirate Blackbeard (real name Edward Teach), which sank off the coast of North Carolina in 1718.

Queen Conch

Fishing boat of Harry Morgan (Humphrey Bogart) in the film *To Have and Have Not*.

Queenie

Pet dog of the title character in the comic strip *Dondi*.

"The Queen of Country Music"

Nickname of country singer Kitty Wells.

"The Queen of Crime"

Nickname of author Dame Agatha Christie.

Queen of Diamonds

Playing card that, when seen by the hypnotically programmed Raymond Shaw (Laurence Harvey), turns him into an assassin, in the film *The Manchurian Candidate*.

"The Queen of Disco"
Nickname of singer Donna Summer.

"The Queen of Roads"
Nickname of the Appian Way, the ancient Roman road from Rome to Brundisium.

"The Queen of Soul"
Nickname of singer Aretha Franklin.

"The Queen of the Adriatic"
Nickname of Venice, Italy.

"The Queen of the Blues"
Nickname of singer Dinah Washington.

Queen of the Night
Film starring Rachel Marron (Whitney Houston) in the film *The Bodyguard*.

"The Queen of the Screamers"
Nickname of 1940s horror-film actress Evelyn Ankers, for her memorable on-screen skill.

"The Queen of the West"
Nickname of Western star Dale Evans.

Queen (rock group) original members
John Deacon, Brian May, Freddie Mercury, and Roger Taylor.

Queen's College
Original name of Rutgers University.

Queensland and Northern Territory Air Service
Original name of Australian airline QANTAS when it began operations in 1922.

"Quentin's Theme"
Theme song of the TV soap opera *Dark Shadows*, performed by The Charles Randolph Grean Sounde.

"The Quest"
Subtitle of the *Man of La Mancha* tune "The Impossible Dream."

Questel, Mae
See **Bluebelle, Aunt**

"The quicker picker upper"
Advertising slogan of Bounty paper towels.

Quidditch
See **7**

Quiet Woman Inn
Establishment owned by Damon Wildeve in the Thomas Hardy novel *The Return of the Native*.

Quigley
Real last name of actress Jane Alexander.

Quince Productions
Production company of actor Edward Asner.

Quincy
First name of myopic cartoon character Mr. Magoo, voiced by Jim Backus.

Pet dog of Luther Van Dam (Jerry Van Dyke) in the TV sitcom *Coach*.

Pet iguana of Jason Fox in the comic strip *Fox Trot*.

Quinlan
Middle name of sportscaster Bob Costas.

quintal
Metric measure of weight equal to 100 kilograms, or about 220.5 pounds.

Quintilis
Former name of the month of July, which was renamed for Julius Caesar in 44 B.C.

Quinton
First name of the title character (Ernest Borgnine) in the TV sitcom *McHale's Navy*.

Quixano, Alonso
Real name of the title character in the Miguel de Cervantes novel *Don Quixote de la Mancha*.

Quixote
Middle name of evil Dr. Miguelito Loveless (Michael Dunn) in the TV series *The Wild Wild West*.

Quonsett, Ada
Role for which Helen Hayes won a Best Supporting Actress Academy Award in the 1970 film *Airport*.

Rabbi mysteries

Series of novels written by Harry Kemelman featuring Rabbi David Small:

Friday the Rabbi Slept Late (1964)
Saturday the Rabbi Went Hungry (1966)
Sunday the Rabbi Stayed Home (1969)
Monday the Rabbi Took Off (1972)
Tuesday the Rabbi Saw Red (1974)
Wednesday the Rabbi Got Wet (1976)
Thursday the Rabbi Walked Out (1978)
Someday the Rabbi Will Leave (1985)
One Fine Day the Rabbi Bought a Cross (1987)
The Day the Rabbi Resigned (1992)
That Day the Rabbi Left Town (1996)

Rabbit tetralogy

Series of four books by John Updike with Harry "Rabbit" Angstrom as the main character:

Rabbit, Run (1960)
Rabbit Redux (1971)
Rabbit Is Rich (1981)
Rabbit at Rest (1990)

The last two books were each awarded a Pulitzer Prize. Updike's 2000 book *Licks of Love* includes the novella *Rabbit Remembered*, a postscript to the series.

Rabinovitch, Emanuel

Real name of painter/photographer Man Ray.

Rabinowitz, Jakie (aka Robin, Jack)

Title character (Al Jolson) of the film *The Jazz Singer* (1927).

Rachel

Ship that rescues Ishmael, sole survivor of the *Pequod*, in the Herman Melville novel *Moby-Dick*.

Rachel and Robin

Twin daughters of Julie and Gabe Kotter (Marcia Strassman and Gabe Kaplan) in the TV sitcom *Welcome Back, Kotter*.

Rachel's Place

Chicago diner hangout in the TV sitcom *Family Matters*.

"Racing With the Moon"

Theme song of singer Vaughn Monroe.

Radar

Teddy bear of Big Bird on the children's TV series *Sesame Street*. It is named for the *M*A*S*H* character who owned a teddy bear.

Radd, Norin

Real name of comics superhero Silver Surfer.

Radio Center Drug Store

Where Chuck Larkin and Mervyn Milgrim (Abbott and Costello) work as soda jerks, in the film *Who Done It?*

radio detecting and ranging

What the word "radar" is an acronym for.

Radio Keith Orpheum

What the letters in the name of film production company RKO stood for. RKO was formed in 1928 in a merger between the film studios of RCA (Radio Corporation of America) and the Keith-Albee-Orpheum theater chain.

radio phonetic alphabet

These words are used in two-way radio communication to transmit letters of the alphabet:

A	Alpha	N	November
B	Bravo	O	Oscar
C	Charlie	P	Papa
D	Delta	Q	Quebec
E	Echo	R	Romeo
F	Foxtrot	S	Sierra
G	Golf	T	Tango
H	Hotel	U	Uniform
I	India	V	Victor
J	Juliet	W	Whiskey
K	Kilo	X	X-ray
L	Lima	Y	Yankee
M	Mike	Z	Zulu

Raffles

Chimpanzee that accurately predicts which TV shows will earn high ratings, in the Disney film *The Barefoot Executive*.

Rafter
Horse of Paladin (Richard Boone) in the TV series *Have Gun Will Travel.*

Ragsdale, Harold
Real name of singer Ray Stevens.

Rainbow
Secret Service code name for Nancy Reagan.

Rainbow Division
Nickname of the 42nd Division of the Allied Expeditionary Force during World War I and the 42nd Infantry Division during World War II, because of the geographic and ethnic diversity of the units.

Rainbow Hill
Rehab center in the Tennessee Williams play *Cat on a Hot Tin Roof.*

Rainbow Warrior
Flagship of international environmental activist group Greenpeace.

Rain, Douglas
Actor who provided the voice of HAL in the film *2001: A Space Odyssey.*

The Raindrops
Stage name used by songwriters Ellie Greenwich and Jeff Barry for their recording of the tune "The Kind of Boy You Can't Forget."

Raisin Puffs
Favorite cereal of Balki Bartokomous (Bronson Pinchot) in the TV sitcom *Perfect Strangers.*

Rajah
Pet tiger of Princess Jasmine in the Disney animated film *Aladdin.*

Ralf
Talking computer of Richie Adler (Matthew Laborteaux) in the TV series *Whiz Kids.*

RALPH
Organization of fans of the TV sitcom *The Honeymooners.* The letters stand for "Royal Association for the Longevity and Preservation of the Honeymooners."

Ralphie
Buffalo mascot of the University of Colorado.

Ramblers
See **Catholics**

The Ramblin' Yodeler
Stage name used by rock-music pioneer Bill Haley early in his career.

Ramistella
Real last name of singer/songwriter Johnny Rivers.

"Ramon"
Debut episode of the TV sitcom *Barney Miller,* which aired on January 23, 1975.

Ramón Raquello and his Orchestra
See **Hotel Park Plaza**

Rampart Hospital
Los Angeles setting of the TV series *Emergency.*

Rampling, Anne
Pen name used by author Anne Rice.

Ranch Breakfast
Cereal made by Ampco Industries that is endorsed by Sonny Steele (Robert Redford) in the film *The Electric Horseman.*

Randall
Real first name of country singer Hank Williams Jr.

Last name of the title character in the Kate Douglas Wiggin novel *Rebecca of Sunnybrook Farm.*

Rand, Benjamin
Role for which Melvyn Douglas won a Best Supporting Actor Academy Award in the 1979 film *Being There.*

R&B Toys
Employer of salesman Scott Calvin (Tim Allen) in the Disney film *The Santa Clause.*

Ranft
Real last name of actor George Raft.

Ranger
Pet dog of Radar O'Reilly (Gary Burghoff) in the TV sitcom *M*A*S*H.*

See also **Pacer, Ranger, Corsair, and Citation**

Rangers
See **Rydell High**

Rankin, Jeanette
Republican from Montana who in 1916 became the first woman to be elected to Congress. A lifetime pacifist, she was the only member of Congress to vote against U.S. entry into World War II.

"Rapid Robert"

Nickname of Hall of Fame baseball pitcher Bob Feller, for his blazing fastball.

Rapp

Last name of the lead singer of rock group Danny and the Juniors.

"Rapper's Delight"

1979 Sugarhill Gang tune that was the first rap record to appear on the U.S. Top 40 *Billboard* pop chart.

"Rapture" cars

Cars mentioned in the Blondie tune (in order): Cadillacs, Lincolns, Mercurys, and Subarus.

rasceta

Scientific name for the creases of skin on the inside surface of the wrist.

Rasmussen

Original family surname of Clinton attorney general Janet Reno. It was changed to Reno by her father Henry.

Rasputin and the Empress (1932)

Only film in which siblings John, Lionel, and Ethel Barrymore appear together.

Rastus

Chef on boxes of Cream of Wheat cereal.

Ratched, Nurse Mildred

Role for which Louise Fletcher won a Best Actress Academy Award in the 1975 film *One Flew Over the Cuckoo's Nest*.

Rate a Record

Segment of the TV series *American Bandstand* where audience members evaluate a new record on a scale from 35 to 98, often based on it having "a good beat" and being able to "dance to it."

"rat's mouth"

What the name of Boca Raton, Florida, means in Spanish.

The Rattlesnakes

Original name of pop group The Bee Gees. They were later called Wee Johnny Hays and the Bluecats before adopting their best-known name.

Raveloe

Setting of the George Eliot novel *Silas Marner*.

Raven

Code name of fighter pilot Jimmy Wilder (Harry Connick Jr.) in the film *Independence Day*.

Ravenclaw

See **Gryffindor House**

Ravenscroft, Thurl

Voice of Tony the Tiger in TV commercials for Kellogg's Frosted Flakes.

Ravish

Perfume for which murder victim Lisa Convy (Terri Welles) was a spokesmodel in the film *Looker*. The perfume's slogan: "It fulfills your deepest desires."

Rawhide

Secret Service code name for Ronald Reagan.

Rawhide

Racing boat of Scott Hayward (Elvis Presley) in the film *Clambake*.

Rawlins, Horace

Winner of the first U.S. Open golf tournament, held at Rhode Island's Newport Golf Club in 1895.

Ray, Anthony

Real name of rap artist Sir Mix-a-Lot.

Raymond, Henry J. and Jones, George

Founders of *The New York Times*, whose first issue was published on September 18, 1851.

Raytown

Midwestern setting of the TV sitcom *Mama's Family*.

Razor

Horse of Lucas McCain (Chuck Connors) in the TV Western series *The Rifleman*.

"Reach out and touch someone"

Advertising slogan of AT&T.

"Read my lips: No new taxes"

Slogan of Republican candidate George H. W. Bush in the 1988 presidential campaign.

"The Real Deal"

Nickname of 1990s heavyweight boxing champ Evander Holyfield.

Real Estate, Captain

Role portrayed by Watergate felon G. Gordon Liddy in the TV series *Miami Vice*.

Réard, Louis

French fashion designer who created the bikini, introduced July 5, 1946.

Rebecca

Middle name of country singer Dolly Parton.

Pet raccoon of President Calvin Coolidge.

"rebuilding"

What the word "perestroika" means in Russian.

Reckless

Family dog in the TV series *The Waltons*.

Red

Pet dog of Roger Spelding (Fred Clark) in the film *Visit to a Small Planet*.

"Red"

Nickname of oil-well firefighter Paul N. Adair, who inspired the John Wayne film *The Hellfighters*, on which Adair served as technical advisor.

Red Alert

See *Two Hours to Doom*

Red Auerbach Trophy

Awarded annually since 1963 to the NBA's coach of the year, renamed in 1967 for the former Boston Celtics coach.

Red Crescent

Name for the Red Cross in Islamic countries.

Reddy Kilowatt

Cartoon mascot for over 200 electric utilities worldwide from the 1920s to the 1970s.

Red Hour Films

Production company of actor Ben Stiller.

Red Lantern Award

Prize given to the last musher to cross the finish line in the annual Iditarod Trail Sled Dog Race.

Rednow, Eivets

Pseudonym used by Stevie Wonder for his recording of the tune "Alfie," which is "Stevie Wonder" spelled backwards.

Redoutable

French flagship from which an unknown sniper shot and killed English admiral Lord Nelson in 1805.

"The Red River Shootout"

See **The Golden Hat**

The Red Rooster

Restaurant visited by Schwartz, Flick, and the gang after the junior prom in the Jean Shepherd story "Wanda Hickey's Night of Golden Memories."

Red Rover

Coach horse of Jess Birdwell (Gary Cooper) in the film *Friendly Persuasion*.

Red Ryder Carbine Action Two-Hundred Shot Lighting Loader Range Model Air Rifle

Christmas present received by Ralphie Parker (Peter Billingsley) in the film *A Christmas Story*.

"red stick"

What "Baton Rouge" means in French. The city was named for a red post that marked a boundary between Indian tribes.

Red Strokes Entertainment

Film production company of country singer Garth Brooks.

Red Tab Device

Tag attached to the right back pockets of Levi's that has the brand name printed on it.

Red Triangle Circus

Former employer of The Penguin's (Danny DeVito's) henchmen in the film *Batman Returns*.

Reduco Obesity Slayer

Product in a newspaper ad whose "Before" and "After" photos serve as the cameo appearance of director Alfred Hitchcock in the film *Lifeboat*.

Red Vineyard at Arles

Only painting sold by artist Vincent van Gogh during his lifetime.

Redwood

Original name of rock group Three Dog Night.

reeding

Technical term for the narrow vertical grooves around the edge of certain coins, including U.S. dimes, quarters, and half dollars.

Rees-Jones, Trevor

Bodyguard of Princess Diana who was the only survivor of the Paris auto crash of August 31, 1997, that killed Diana, her friend Dodi Fayed, and chauffeur Henri Paul.

Reference and User Services Assocation
See **Dartmouth Medal**

"Reflections"
Theme song of the TV series *China Beach*, performed by Diana Ross and the Supremes.

Reform Club
London starting and ending point for the journey of Phileas Fogg (David Niven) in the film *Around the World in 80 Days*.

"The Refrigerator"
Nickname of 6'2", 335-pound pro footballer William Perry.

The Regal Beagle
Neighborhood pub hangout in the TV sitcom *Three's Company*.

Regal Order of the Golden Door to Good Fellowship
Fraternal lodge of Sheriff Andy Taylor (Andy Griffith) in the TV sitcom *The Andy Griffith Show*.

Regan
Middle name of comedian Eddie Murphy.

Reginald
First name of Jeeves, English valet in the short stories and novels of P. G. Wodehouse.

Reginald Carey
Real first and middle names of actor Rex Harrison.

"The regulars are out!"
What Paul Revere really shouted during his famous night ride of April 18, 1775, not "The British are coming!" Colonial Americans of that time still considered themselves British subjects, thus Revere would not have referred to the King's soldiers as "British."

Reichardt, Patricia
Real name of Peppermint Patty in the comic strip *Peanuts*.

Reid, Britt
Secret identity of the title character in the radio and TV series *The Green Hornet*.

Reimers, Edwin "Ed"
TV spokesperson for Allstate Insurance from 1957 to 1979.

Reiner, Max
Pen name used by author Taylor Caldwell.

Reiniger, Robert
Real name of songwriter Meredith Willson.

"Relief is just a swallow away"
Advertising slogan of Alka-Seltzer.

"The Reluctant Stowaway"
Debut episode of the TV series *Lost in Space*, which aired on September 15, 1965.

"Remembering You"
Closing theme of the TV sitcom *All in the Family*.

Remembrance of Things Past
Novel in seven parts by Marcel Proust:
    Swann's Way (1913)
    Within a Budding Grove (1919)
    The Guermantes Way (1920)
    Cities of the Plain (1921)
    The Captive (1923)
    The Sweet Cheat Gone (1925)
    Time Regained (1927)

R.E.M. original members
Bill Berry, Peter Buck, Mike Mills, and Michael Stipe.

Remulac
Home planet of the Coneheads in the TV series *Saturday Night Live*. When asked about their origin, they claim to be from France.

"Rendezvous with Yesterday"
Debut episode of the TV series *The Time Tunnel*, which aired on September 9, 1966.

Renegade
Horse of Chief Osceola, mascot of the Florida State University Seminoles.

Renfrew
Maiden name of Shirley Partridge (Shirley Jones) in the TV sitcom *The Partridge Family*.

Renfro, Bryan
See **Berwick, Ray and Renfro, Bryan**

The Reno Brothers
Original working title of Elvis Presley's first film, *Love Me Tender*.

"The Reno Rocket"
Nickname of cyclist Greg LeMond.

Reprise Records

Company created by Frank Sinatra to produce his recordings.

"Requiem for a Son"

Debut episode of the TV series *Barnaby Jones*, which aired on January 28, 1973.

"Rerun"

Nickname of Freddie Stubbs (Fred Berry) in the TV sitcom *What's Happening!!*, for all the classes he has repeated.

Resolution and *Adventure*

Ships commanded by Captain James Cook on his second circumnavigation of the globe in 1772–75.

"Respect"

Debut episode of the TV sitcom *Murphy Brown*, which aired on November 14, 1988.

"Respice, adspice, prospice"

Motto of City College of New York, which is Latin for "Look to the past, look to the present, look to the future."

Resurrection Athletic Club

Converted Philadelphia church where Rocky Balboa (Sylvester Stallone) wins a boxing match, at the start of the film *Rocky*.

Retsyn

See **Chlorophyll and Retsyn**

Rettoni

Real last name of gymnast Mary Lou Retton.

Return to Love Canal

Play written by Jeff Slater (Bill Murray) in the film *Tootsie*.

Reuben Award

Presented annually since 1946 by the National Cartoonists Society to the Cartoonist of The Year. Named for Rube Goldberg, first president of the Society.

  1946 Milton Caniff (*Steve Canyon*)
  1947 Al Capp (*Li'l Abner*)
  1948 Chic Young (*Blondie*)
  1949 Alex Raymond (*Rip Kirby*)
  1950 Roy Crane (*Buz Sawyer*)
  1951 Walt Kelly (*Pogo*)
  1952 Hank Ketcham (*Dennis the Menace*)
  1953 Mort Walker (*Beetle Bailey*)
  1954 Willard Mullin (Sports)

  1955 Charles Schulz (*Peanuts*)
  1956 Herbert L. Block aka Herblock (Editorial)
  1957 Hal Foster (*Prince Valiant*)
  1958 Frank King (*Gasoline Alley*)
  1959 Chester Gould (*Dick Tracy*)
  1960 Ronald Searle (Advertising and Illustration)
  1961 Bill Mauldin (Editorial)
  1962 Dik Browne (*Hi & Lois*)
  1963 Fred Lasswell (*Barney Google and Snuffy Smith*)
  1964 Charles Schulz (*Peanuts*)
  1965 Leonard Starr (*On Stage*)
  1966 Otto Soglow (*The Little King*)
  1967 Rube Goldberg (Humor in Sculpture)
  1968 Pat Oliphant (Editorial)
  1968 Johnny Hart (*B.C.* and *The Wizard of Id*)
  1969 Walter Berndt (*Smitty*)
  1970 Alfred Andriola (*Kerry Drake*)
  1971 Milton Caniff (*Steve Canyon*)
  1972 Pat Oliphant (Editorial)
  1973 Dik Browne (*Hägar the Horrible*)
  1974 Dick Moores (*Gasoline Alley*)
  1975 Bob Dunn (*They'll Do It Every Time*)
  1976 Ernie Bushmiller (*Nancy*)
  1977 Chester Gould (*Dick Tracy*)
  1978 Jeff MacNelly (Editorial)
  1979 Jeff MacNelly (*Shoe*)
  1980 Charles Saxon (Advertising)
  1981 Mell Lazarus (*Miss Peach* and *Momma*)
  1982 Bil Keane (*Family Circus*)
  1983 Arnold Roth (Advertising)
  1984 Brant Parker (*The Wizard of Id*)
  1985 Lynn Johnston (*For Better or for Worse*)
  1986 Bill Watterson (*Calvin and Hobbes*)
  1987 Mort Drucker (*Mad* magazine)
  1988 Bill Watterson (*Calvin and Hobbes*)
  1989 Jim Davis (*Garfield*)
  1990 Gary Larson (*The Far Side*)
  1991 Mike Peters (*Mother Goose & Grimm*)
  1992 Cathy Guisewite (*Cathy*)
  1993 Jim Borgman (Editorial)
  1994 Gary Larson (*The Far Side*)
  1995 Garry Trudeau (*Doonesbury*)
  1996 Sergio Aragones (*Mad Magazine*)
  1997 Scott Adams (*Dilbert*)
  1998 Will Eisner (*The Spirit*)
  1999 Patrick McDonnell (*Mutts*)

Revelation Motors

Auto company headed by the title character of the Sinclair Lewis novel *Dodsworth*.

Revelations Entertainment

Production company of actor Morgan Freeman.

"Revenge"

Debut episode of the TV sitcom *Clarissa Explains It All*, which aired on March 23, 1991.

Revenue Cutter School of Instruction

Former name of the U.S. Coast Guard Academy.

Revenue Marine

Original name of the seagoing service that would eventually become the U.S. Coast Guard. Founded in 1790 to guard the coastline against smugglers, it took its present name in 1915 when it merged with the U.S. Lifesaving Service.

reverse

See **obverse**

Rex

Horse of the title character (Richard Simmons) in the children's TV series *Sergeant Preston of the Yukon*.

Pet King Charles spaniel of President Ronald Reagan.

Family dog in the TV sitcom *The Life of Riley*.

Reynolds, Dr. Thomas

Real name of the title character (Jon Hall) in the TV series *Ramar of the Jungle*.

Reynolds, Joshua

Inventor of mood rings, a 1975 fad, that changed color based on the body temperature of the wearer.

Rheaume, Manon

First woman to play in a regular-season professional hockey game, as a goalie for the International Hockey League's Atlanta Knights on December 13, 1992.

rhinoplasty

Medical term for plastic surgery of the nose, aka a "nose job."

rhinorrhea

Medical term for a runny nose.

Rhode Island College

Original name of Brown University.

Rhys-Jones, Sophie

See **Earl of Wessex**

"Rhythm on the Reservation"

See **105**

rhytidectomy

Medical term for a face lift, which is from the Greek for "wrinkle removal."

Rice, Donna

See **Monkey Business**

Richard

First name of Mr. Blackwell, creator of the annual "worst-dressed list" since 1960.

Real first name of Chip Douglas (Stanley Livingston) in the TV sitcom *My Three Sons*.

Richard Alonzo

Real first and middle names of tennis great Pancho Gonzales.

Richard Bernard

Real first and middle names of comedian Red Skelton.

Richardson, Jiles Perry

Real name of rock singer The Big Bopper.

Richmond Reed

Real first and middle names of actor John Carradine.

Rich, Robert

Pen name used by blacklisted scriptwriter Dalton Trumbo for his Oscar-winning screenplay of the 1956 film *The Brave One*.

Richter, Charles F.

See **modified Mercalli scale**

Richthofen, Manfred von

Real name of World War I German aviator The Red Baron. The nickname was derived from his red Fokker airplane.

Rich Uncle Pennybags

Cartoon mascot of the board game Monopoly.

Rick's Café Americain

Nightclub owned by Rick Blaine (Humphrey Bogart) in the film *Casablanca*.

Ridarelli

Real last name of singer Bobby Rydell.

Riddle

Middle name of labor leader Jimmy Hoffa, last seen at a Bloomfield Hills, Michigan, restaurant on July 30, 1975.

Riddles, Libby

First woman to win the Iditarod Trail Sled Dog Race, in 1985.

Ridgemont, New York

Setting of the TV sitcom *Please Don't Eat the Daisies*.

Rid-O-Rat

Rat poison that Violet Newstead (Lily Tomlin) mistakenly adds to the coffee of her boss Franklin Hart (Dabney Coleman) in the film *9 to 5*. The Rid-O-Rat box resembles a nearby box of Skinny and Sweet, an artificial sweetener.

Rienzi

Morgan horse of Civil War Union general Philip Sheridan.

Riff Raff

Hunchback henchman (Richard O'Brien) of Dr. Frank-N-Furter (Tim Curry) in the film *The Rocky Horror Picture Show*.

Riff's Bar

Local watering hole in the TV sitcom *Mad About You*.

Rigel

See **Aldebaran, Altair, Antares, and Rigel**

Riggs, Lynn

See **Green Grow the Lilacs**

Rights-of-Man

English merchant ship from which the title character is pressed into military service in the Herman Melville novel *Billy Budd*.

Riley

Real first name of blues singer B. B. King.

"Ring around the collar"

Catchphrase in TV commercials for Wisk detergent.

Ring cycle

See **Wagner's *Ring* cycle**

Ringgold Wilmer

Real first and middle names of writer Ring Lardner.

Ringling brothers

Family of circus entrepreneurs:
    Albert (1852–1916)
    August (1854–1907)
    Otto (1858–1911)
    Alfred (1861–1919)
    Charles (1863–1926)
    John (1866–1936)
    Henry (1869–1918)

Ringo

Horse of Josh Randall (Steve McQueen) in the TV series *Wanted: Dead or Alive*.

The Rinky Dinks

Pseudonym used by Bobby Darin for his recording of the tune "Early in the Morning." Darin performed all the vocal tracks of the "group."

Río Bravo (or Río Bravo del Norte)

What natives of Mexico call the Rio Grande.

Rios, Tere

See **The Fifteenth Pelican**

Ripper, General Jack D.

Sterling Hayden's role in the film *Dr. Strangelove*.

The Rippers

Rock band led by Jesse (John Stamos) in the TV sitcom *Full House*.

"Rippling Rhythm"

Nickname of the music style of Shep Fields and his orchestra.

Rising Sun

Favorite horse of singer Elvis Presley.

"rising sun"

What the name of Japanese electronics manufacturer Hitachi means in Japanese.

RITA Awards

Presented annually since 1997 by the Romance Writers of America for excellence in the romance genre.

Ritchie, John Simon

Real name of punk-rock singer Sid Vicious.

Ritt's Groceries

Texas store robbed by Clyde Barrow (Warren Beatty) to impress Bonnie Parker (Faye Dunaway), in the film *Bonnie and Clyde*.

Ritty, James

Dayton, Ohio, native who invented the cash register, patented in 1879.

River Bend, Missouri

See **General Pershing Veterans Administration Hospital**

Riverboro, Maine

Setting of the Kate Douglas Wiggin novel *Rebecca of Sunnybrook Farm.*

River City, Iowa

Setting of the musical *The Music Man.* It is based on Mason City, Iowa, hometown of Meredith Willson, the musical's author and composer, where the film version premiered in 1962.

Riverdale

Hometown of Archie Andrews and the gang in Archie comics.

River Gulch, Arkansas

Hometown of Cherie (Marilyn Monroe) in the film *Bus Stop.*

River Heights

Home of the title character in the Nancy Drew series of children's books.

"river horse"

What the word "hippopotamus" means in Greek.

River Queen

See **Bill Bassler's Revenge and Hearts of Gold**

River Run, Ohio

Setting of the TV series *Homefront.*

Riverside, Iowa

Town that has proclaimed itself to be the future birthplace of *Star Trek* captain James T. Kirk (William Shatner).

Riverside, John

Pen name used by author Robert A. Heinlein.

rivers of major U.S. cities and state capitals

(State capitals not listed are not located on a river.)
  Albany, New York: Hudson
  Albuquerque, New Mexico: Rio Grande
  Annapolis, Maryland: Severn
  Augusta, Maine: Kennebec
  Austin, Texas: Colorado
  Baltimore, Maryland: Patapsco
  Baton Rouge, Louisiana: Mississippi
  Bismarck, North Dakota: Missouri
  Boise, Idaho: Boise
  Boston, Massachusetts: Charles, Mystic

Charleston, West Virginia: Elk, Kanawha
Chicago, Illinois: Chicago
Cheyenne, Wyoming: Crow Creek
Cincinnati, Ohio: Ohio
Cleveland, Ohio: Cuyahoga
Colorado Springs, Colorado: Monument Creek, Fountain Creek
Columbia, South Carolina: Congaree
Columbus, Ohio: Scioto
Concord, New Hampshire: Merrimack
Dallas, Texas: Trinity
Denver, Colorado: South Platte
Des Moines, Iowa: Des Moines, Raccoon
Detroit, Michigan: Detroit
El Paso, Texas: Rio Grande
Fort Worth, Texas: Trinity
Frankfort, Kentucky: Kentucky
Harrisburg, Pennsylvania: Susquehanna
Hartford, Connecticut: Connecticut
Indianapolis, Indiana: White
Jackson, Mississippi: Pearl
Jacksonville, Florida: St. Johns
Jefferson City, Missouri: Missouri
Kansas City, Missouri: Missouri
Lansing, Michigan: Grand, Red Cedar
Little Rock, Arkansas: Arkansas
Memphis, Tennessee: Mississippi
Miami, Florida: Miami
Milwaukee, Wisconsin: Milwaukee, Menomonee, Kinnickinnic
Minneapolis, Minnesota: Mississippi
Montgomery, Alabama: Alabama
Montpelier, Vermont: Winooski
Nashville, Tennessee: Cumberland
New York, New York: Hudson, East, Harlem
Oklahoma City, Oklahoma: North Canadian
Omaha, Nebraska: Missouri
Philadelphia, Pennsylvania: Delaware, Schuylkill
Phoenix, Arizona: Salt
Pierre, South Dakota: Missouri
Pittsburgh, Pennsylvania: Allegheny, Monongahela, Ohio
Portland, Oregon: Willamette
Providence, Rhode Island: Providence
Richmond, Virginia: James
Sacramento, California: Sacramento
Salem, Oregon: Willamette
Salt Lake City, Utah: Jordan
San Antonio, Texas: San Antonio
San Jose, California: Coyote, Guadalupe
Springfield, Illinois: Sangamon
St. Louis, Missouri: Mississippi
St. Paul, Minnesota: Mississippi
Topeka, Kansas: Kansas

Trenton, New Jersey: Delaware
Tucson, Arizona: Santa Cruz
Tulsa, Oklahoma: Arkansas
Washington, D.C.: Potomac, Anacostia

rivers of major world cities

Alexandria, Egypt: Nile
Amsterdam, Netherlands: Amstel
Baghdad, Iraq: Tigris
Bangkok, Thailand: Chao Phraya
Belgrade, Yugoslavia: Danube, Sava
Berlin, Germany: Spree, Havel
Bogotá, Colombia: Bogotá
Brussels, Belgium: Senne
Budapest, Hungary: Danube
Buenos Aires, Argentina: Río de la Plata
Cairo, Egypt: Nile
Calcutta, India: Hugli
Damascus, Syria: Barada
Delhi, India: Yamuna
Dublin, Ireland: Liffey
Ho Chi Minh City, Vietnam: Saigon
Hong Kong, China: Pearl
Jakarta, Indonesia: Liwung
Kiev, Ukraine: Dnieper
Lisbon, Portugal: Tagus
Lima, Peru: Rímac
London, England: Thames
Madrid, Spain: Manzanares
Melbourne, Australia: Yarra
Montreal, Canada: St. Lawrence
Moscow, Russia: Moskva
Paris, France: Seine
Prague, Czech Republic: Moldau
Rome, Italy: Tiber
Saint Petersburg, Russia: Neva
Santiago, Chile: Mapocho
São Paulo, Brazil: Tietê
Seoul, South Korea: Han
Shanghai, China: Huangpu
Tokyo, Japan: Sumida
Vienna, Austria: Danube
Warsaw, Poland: Vistula
Zagreb, Croatia: Sava
Zürich, Switzerland: Limmat, Sihl

R.M.S. *Mongolia*

Ship that takes Passepartout (Cantinflas) and Phileas Fogg (David Niven) from Suez to Bombay in the film *Around the World in 80 Days*.

Roach

Pet dog of Annie Paradis (Diane Keaton) in the film *The First Wives Club*.

roadeo

Competition for drivers of large vehicles, such as trucks, buses, and snowplows, which tests safety and driving skills.

Road films

Series starring Bing Crosby and Bob Hope:
 Road to Singapore (1940)
 Road to Zanzibar (1941)
 Road to Morocco (1942)
 Road to Utopia (1945)
 Road to Rio (1947)
 Road to Bali (1952)
 The Road to Hong Kong (1962)

"The Roadrunner"

Nickname of speedy NHL Hall of Famer Yvan Cournoyer.

Road to Montezuma

Original working title of the Abbott and Costello film *Pardon My Sarong*.

Roadway Bus Company

Employer of Florida Evans (Esther Rolle) in the TV sitcom *Good Times*.

Robard

Middle name of industrialist Howard Hughes.

Robert

First name of the title character (Bob Crane) in the TV sitcom *Hogan's Heroes*.

Robert and Lorene

First names (respectively) of mime team Shields and Yarnell.

Robert Craig

Real first and middle names of daredevil Evel Knievel.

Robert F. Kennedy Junior High

School attended by Kevin Arnold (Fred Savage) in the TV sitcom *The Wonder Years*.

Robert, General Henry Martyn

U.S. Army engineering officer who published his first edition of *Robert's Rules of Order* in 1876.

Robert Moses

Real first and middle names of Hall of Fame baseball pitcher Lefty Grove.

Roberts

Maiden name of former English prime minister Margaret Thatcher.

Roberts, Barbara Millicent

Full name of Barbie.

Roberts, Gilroy

Designer of the obverse ("heads") of the Kennedy half dollar, minted since 1964.

Robertson, Anna Mary

Birth name of painter Grandma Moses.

Robertson, Morgan

See *The Wreck of the Titan*

Roberts, Xavier

Creator of Cabbage Patch Kids dolls, circa 1977.

Robin

See **Rachel and Robin**

Robin Hood

Term in archery for driving the tip of an arrow into the end of another arrow already in the target. This was a legendary skill of Robin Hood.

Robin, Jack

See **Rabinowitz, Jakie (aka Robin, Jack)**

Robin's Nest

Hawaiian estate of Robin Masters (unseen, but voiced by Orson Welles) in the TV series *Magnum, p.i.*

Robinson

First name of the title character (Wally Cox) in the TV sitcom *Mr. Peepers.*

Robinson-Danforth Commission Company

Original name of Ralston Purina.

Robinson, Frank M.

See *The Tower* and *The Glass Inferno*

Robinson, Ray Charles

Real name of singer Ray Charles. He changed his name to avoid confusion with boxer Sugar Ray Robinson.

Robot Kenwood Chef

The first modern-day food processor, invented by Kenneth Wood and introduced in 1947.

Rob Roy

Pet collie of President Calvin Coolidge.

Robusti, Jacopo

Real name of Italian Renaissance painter Tintoretto.

Rochester Royals

Original name of the Sacramento Kings at their NBA inception in 1948.

Rocinante

Horse of the title character in the Miguel de Cervantes novel *Don Quixote de la Mancha.*

"The Rock"

Nickname of San Francisco Bay island Alcatraz, site of the former federal prison that is now a tourist attraction.

Nickname of Philippine island Corregidor.

Rock and Roll Hall of Fame charter members

The first-year performer inductees of 1986:
    Chuck Berry
    James Brown
    Ray Charles
    Sam Cooke
    Fats Domino
    Everly Brothers
    Buddy Holly
    Jerry Lee Lewis
    Elvis Presley
    Little Richard

"Rock and Roll Heaven" subjects

This Righteous Brothers "tribute" tune mentions the first names of these music legends (in order):
    Jimi (Hendrix)
    Jim (Morrison)
    Janis (Joplin)
    Jimmy (Croce)
    Otis (Redding)
    Bobby (Darin)

Rockatansky

Last name of the title character (Mel Gibson) in the *Mad Max* films.

Rockdale High

School attended by Tony Rivers (Michael Landon) in the film *I Was a Teen-age Werewolf.*

"Rocket"

Nickname of baseball pitcher Roger Clemens.

Nickname of Australian tennis great Rod Laver.

Nickname of NHL Hall of Famer Maurice Richard.

Rocket Records

Company created by Elton John to produce his recordings.

Rockford Peaches

Team in the All-American Girls' Professional Baseball League managed by Jimmy Dugan (Tom Hanks) whose team members include catcher Dottie Hinson (Geena Davis), center fielder Mae Mordabito (Madonna), and third baseman Doris Murphy (Rosie O'Donnell), in the film *A League of Their Own*.

"The Rock of Chicamauga"

Nickname of Civil War Confederate general George Thomas.

Rock Ridge

Setting of the Mel Brooks film *Blazing Saddles*.

Rocks and Halo

Pet Akitas of baseball star Cal Ripken Jr.

rocks, classifications of

Listed below with examples of each:
   magma: molten rock (lava)
   igneous: formed from magma (granite, pumice, basalt)
   sedimentary: formed from the remains of other rocks (sandstone, shale, limestone)
   metamorphic: formed from other rocks by heat and/or pressure (mica, slate, marble)

Rock Throw, West Virginia

Hometown of Jennifer Marlowe (Loni Anderson) in the TV sitcom *WKRP in Cincinnati*.

Rockwell High

School attended by Jane Burnham (Thora Burch) in the film *American Beauty*. The school's athletic teams are the Spartans.

Rockwell, Rick

See **Conger, Darva and Rockwell, Rick**

Rocky

Role for which Gig Young won a Best Supporting Actor Academy Award in the 1969 film *They Shoot Horses, Don't They?*

"Rocky Dies Yellow: Killer Coward at End"

Newspaper headline at the conclusion of the film *Angels with Dirty Faces*, referring to the execution of convicted murderer William "Rocky" Sullivan (James Cagney). He decides to feign fear, to help deter young people from violence.

Rodent, Chuck

How the destructive gopher is billed in the closing credits of the film *Caddyshack*.

Roderick Andrew

Real first and middle names of actor Roddy McDowall.

Roderick David

Real first and middle names of rock singer Rod Stewart.

Rodman Wanamaker Trophy

Presented annually to the winner of the PGA Championship golf tournament. It is named for the department-store magnate who cofounded the PGA.

Rodriguez, Francisco

Real name of Chico (Freddie Prinze) in the TV sitcom *Chico and the Man*.

Rodriguez, Javier

Role for which Benicio Del Toro won a Best Supporting Actor Academy Award in the 2000 film *Traffic*.

Rogers

Real last name of playwright Sam Shepard.

Rogers/Astaire films

See **Astaire/Rogers films**

Rogers, Thomas D.

Designer of the reverse ("tails") of the Sacagawea dollar, minted since 2000.

Roland

Real first name of jazz trumpeter Bunny Berrigan.

roleo

Term for a logrolling tournament.

Rölf

See **Al, Lance, Lars, and Rölf**

Rolfe, Hans

Role for which Maximilian Schell won a Best Actor Academy Award in the 1961 film *Judgment at Nuremberg*.

Rolihlahla

Middle name of Nelson Mandela, which is slang in the Xhosa language for "troublemaker." The name has the literal meaning "pulling the branch of a tree."

Rolling Stones original members

Mick Jagger, Brian Jones, Keith Richards, Charlie Watts, and Bill Wyman.

"Rollin' Stone"

1948 tune by Muddy Waters that inspired the name of rock group The Rolling Stones.

The Romance of Monte Beni

Alternate title of the Nathaniel Hawthorne novel *The Marble Faun.*

Romance Writers of America

See **RITA Awards**

Les Romanesques

Play by Edmond Rostand that was the basis for the musical *The Fantasticks.*

Romanoff, Noodles and Hyde, Jacqueline

Nemeses of cartoon superhero Roger Ramjet.

The Romantic Egoist

Original working title of the F. Scott Fitzgerald novel *This Side of Paradise.*

"Romantic Improvisations"

Debut episode of the TV sitcom *Mad About You,* which aired on September 23, 1992.

Romeo

Pet cat of romance novelist Joan Wilder (Kathleen Turner) in the film *Romancing the Stone.*

Romeo and Ethel, the Pirate's Daughter

Original title of the play that would become *Romeo and Juliet,* in the film *Shakespeare in Love.*

Rome, seven hills of

Rome, Italy, is built on these seven hills: Aventine, Caelian, Capitoline, Esquiline, Palatine, Quirinal, and Viminal.

Rome, Wisconsin

Setting of the TV series *Picket Fences.*

Ronald

Real first name of actor Christopher Walken.

Ronald Reagan Hospital

See **"We cure people the old fashioned way"**

Roncalli, Angelo Giuseppe

Real name of Pope John XXIII, who served from 1958 to 1963.

The Ronelles

Singing trio led by Deloris Van Cartier (Whoopi Goldberg), performing at Reno's Nevada Club, in the film *Sister Act.*

Ronnie

See **Kix and Ronnie**

Ronzoni

Middle name of singer Luther Vandross. His mother gave him this name because Ronzoni pasta was the only thing she could eat when she was pregnant with him.

"Room Enough for Two"

Theme song of the TV sitcom *My Sister Sam,* performed by Kim Carnes.

Rooney/Garland films

See **Garland/Rooney films**

Roosevelt

184-foot ship of Robert Peary, specially constructed for his polar explorations.

"rope-a-dope"

Strategy often employed by boxer Muhammad Ali, where he rested against the ropes in a defensive position, absorbing his opponents' punches until they tired out.

Roquelaire, A. N.

Pen name used by author Anne Rice.

Rosalie

See **"My Old New England Home"**

Rosalie Anderson

Real first and middle names of actress Andie MacDowell.

Rosa's Cantina

Where Felina performs, in the Marty Robbins tune "El Paso."

Roscoe

Middle name of journalist Edward R. Murrow.

Pet dog of Earl and Opal in the comic strip *Pickles.*

Roscoe and DeSoto

Pet Dobermans of Sykes (voiced by Robert Loggia) in the Disney animated film *Oliver & Company*.

Rosebud

Middle name of Ritchie Petrie (Larry Matthews) in the TV sitcom *The Dick Van Dyke Show*.

"Rosebud"

Dying word of Charles Foster Kane (Orson Welles) in the film *Citizen Kane*, which was the name of his childhood sled.

Roseburg High

Alma mater of Mary Richards (Mary Tyler Moore) in the TV sitcom *The Mary Tyler Moore Show*.

"A Rose for Lotta"

Debut episode of the TV Western series *Bonanza*, which aired on September 12, 1959.

Rosemond

Middle name of actress Elizabeth Taylor.

Rosenbaum, Alisa

Real name of novelist Ayn Rand.

Rosenbaum, Borge

Real name of comedic pianist Victor Borge.

Rosenberg, Leonard

Real name of actor Tony Randall.

Rosenberg, William

Founder of the Dunkin' Donuts restaurant chain. His first shop, originally called "Open Kettle," opened in Quincy, Massachusetts in 1948.

Rosenblatt Stadium

Omaha, Nebraska, site of the annual College World Series since 1964. The stadium is known locally as "The Blatt."

Rosenthal, Joe

See **5**

Rosenvold, Norway

Setting of the Henrik Ibsen play *Ghosts*.

Roseville, Kansas

Town near Fort Baxter in the TV sitcom *The Phil Silvers Show*, aka *You'll Never Get Rich*.

Rosie

Waitress in TV commercials for Bounty paper towels, portrayed by Nancy Walker.

Rosie

Name of the magazine formerly known as *McCall's*, as of the May, 2001 issue, the result of a partnership with TV talk show host Rosie O'Donnell.

Ross' Landing

Original name of Chattanooga, Tennessee.

Rossum's Universal Robots

What the letters in the title of the Karel Čapek play *R.U.R.* stand for.

Rostron, Arthur Henry

Captain of the *Carpathia*, the ship that rescued the 705 survivors of the R.M.S. *Titanic* on April 15, 1912. Rostron received the Medal of Honor from President Taft for the rescue.

Roth Kane and Donovan

Ad-agency employer of art director Ted Kramer (Dustin Hoffman) in the film *Kramer vs. Kramer*.

"Rough Housing"

Debut episode of the TV sitcom *The Facts of Life*, which aired on August 24, 1979.

Roundabout

Original name of British rock group Deep Purple.

Roundup

See **Pacer, Ranger, Corsair, and Citation**

"Round up the usual suspects"

Memorable line spoken by Captain Louis Renault (Claude Rains) in the film *Casablanca*.

Roussimoff

Last name of French-born pro wrestler Andre the Giant.

Route 66, major cities on

Route 66 was one of America's major east-west highways from the 1940s to the 1960s.
  Chicago, Illinois
  St. Louis, Missouri
  Springfield, Missouri
  Tulsa, Oklahoma
  Oklahoma City, Oklahoma
  Amarillo, Texas
  Albuquerque, New Mexico
  Flagstaff, Arizona
  Los Angeles, California

Rover

Family pet peacock in the TV series *The Waltons*.

See also **Snoopy's brothers and sisters**

Rowan Oak

Oxford, Mississippi, home of author William Faulkner, where he did most of his writing.

rowel

Technical term for the small, multipointed wheel attached to the spurs of cowboy boots.

Rowe, Lisa

Role for which Angelina Jolie won a Best Supporting Actress Academy Award in the 1999 film *Girl, Interrupted*.

Rowena

Middle name of the title character in the Kate Douglas Wiggin novel *Rebecca of Sunnybrook Farm*.

Rowland Hussey

First and middle names of retail-chain founder R. H. Macy.

Rowlands, John

Real name of English journalist/explorer Henry Morton Stanley.

Royal Association for the Longevity and Preservation of the Honeymooners

See **RALPH**

Royal Coburg Theatre

See **"Old Vic"**

"Royal Flush"

Debut episode of the TV sitcom *The Monkees*, which aired on September 12, 1966.

Royal Rube Award

Presented annually to the nation's top "sprint" greyhound by the National Greyhound Association. It is named for an star greyhound of the 1930s.

RR Diner

Eatery owned by Norma Jennings (Peggy Lipton) in the TV series *Twin Peaks*.

R. S. Owens & Company

Chicago manufacturer that has produced the statuettes presented at the annual Academy Awards ceremonies since 1982.

rubeola

Medical term for the measles.

Rubessa

Real last name of game-show host Gene Rayburn.

Ruby

Pet cat of Susanna Kaysen (Winona Ryder) in the film *Girl, Interrupted*.

Ruby, Jack

See **Oswald, Lee Harvey**

Rudolph V, King

Title character of the Anthony Hope novel *The Prisoner of Zenda*.

Rudolph, Vernon Carver

Founder of the Krispy Creme donut store chain. The first Krispy Kreme store opened in 1937 in Winston-Salem, North Carolina.

Rueckheim, F. W. and Louis

Creators of Cracker Jack, introduced at the 1893 Columbian Exposition in Chicago, Illinois.

Ruff

Pet dog of the title character in the comic strip *Dennis the Menace*.

Rufus

Pet poodle of Winston Churchill.

Rufus Parnell

Real first and middle names of auto racer Parnelli Jones.

"Rumble in the Jungle"

Nickname of the heavyweight championship fight between George Foreman and Muhammad Ali in Kinshasa, Zaire on October 30, 1974. Ali won by a knockout in the eighth round.

Rum Runner

Boat owned by Michael Gallagher (Paul Newman) in the film *Absence of Malice*.

"Runaway"

Theme song of the TV series *Crime Story*, performed by Del Shannon.

Ruppert Mundys

Baseball team that is the focus of Philip Roth's *The Great American Novel*.

Ruritania

Country ruled by King Rudolf in the Anthony Hope novel *The Prisoner of Zenda*.

Rushville Center

Setting of the radio soap opera *Ma Perkins*.

Russell Bros. Circus

Troupe on whose caravan Barry Kane (Robert Cummings) and Pat Martin (Priscilla Lane) hitch a ride while on the run from police, in the Alfred Hitchcock film *Saboteur*.

Russell, Majors and Waddell

Leavenworth, Kansas, freight company that owned and operated the Pony Express from April 1860 to October 1861.

Rusty Barnacle

Seafood restaurant frequented by the title family in the animated TV sitcom *The Simpsons*.

Ruth

Mule of deputy Festus Haggen (Ken Curtis) in the TV Western series *Gunsmoke*.

Ruth Elizabeth

Real first and middle names of actress Bette Davis.

Rutland College

Rival of Medfield College of Technology in the Disney film *The Absent-Minded Professor*.

Ryan Airlines

San Diego company that built *The Spirit of St. Louis*, the airplane piloted by Charles Lindbergh on his historic solo flight across the Atlantic in May 1927. The plane's name is derived from the home of Lindbergh's financial backers.

Rydell High

School that is the setting of the musical *Grease*. Its football team is the Rangers.

Ryder, Jonathan

Pen name used by author Robert Ludlum.

Ryman Auditorium

Nashville setting of the country-music radio series *Grand Ole Opry* from 1942 to 1974.

S

Full middle name of President Harry S Truman, in honor of both his paternal grandfather Anderson Shippe Truman and his maternal grandfather Solomon Young.

Saarinen, Eero

See **Jefferson National Expansion Monument**

sabaac

Card game in which Lando Calrissian (Billy Dee Williams) lost the spaceship *Millennium Falcon* to Han Solo (Harrison Ford), as recounted in the film *The Empire Strikes Back*.

Sacchi, Robert

Humphrey Bogart look-alike who portrays the title character in the film *The Man with Bogart's Face*, and has portrayed Bogart in numerous appearances on TV.

Sacco, Lugee

Real name of falsetto singer Lou Christie.

Sack of Suds

Convenience-store murder scene in the film *My Cousin Vinny*.

Sackrider

Middle name of artist Frederic Remington.

Sacramento Register

Newspaper employer of Tom Bradford (Dick Van Patten) in the TV sitcom *Eight Is Enough*.

The Sacred Cow

Presidential plane of Franklin D. Roosevelt.

"Sacred Emily"

Poem by Gertrude Stein that contains the line "Rose is a rose is a rose is a rose."

Sacred Stars of the Milky Way

Fraternal lodge of Vic Gook (Art Van Harvey) in the radio sitcom *Vic and Sade*. Vic serves as Grand Exalted Big Dipper in the Drowsy Venus Chapter.

The Saddlemen

See **The Down Homers**

"safety hood and smoke protector"

See **Morgan, Garrett A.**

Saffir-Simpson scale

Scale used to measure the intensity of hurricanes, based on their wind speed:
  Category 1: 74–95 miles per hour
  Category 2: 96–110 miles per hour
  Category 3: 111–130 miles per hour
  Category 4: 131–155 miles per hour
  Category 5: greater than 155 miles per hour
A hurricane is considered "major" if it is Category 3 or higher.

Sagamore Hill

Home of President Theodore Roosevelt in Oyster Bay, New York.

"The Saga of an American Family"

Subtitle of the Alex Haley book *Roots*.

Sailor

Horse of Spin Evans (Tim Considine) in the "Adventures of Spin and Marty" segment of the children's TV series *The Mickey Mouse Club*.

Saint-Aubin, Horace de

Pen name used by author Honoré de Balzac.

The Saint films

Series based on the character created by British author Leslie Charteris, listed below with the portrayer of Simon Templar, the title character:
  The Saint in New York (1938): Louis Hayward
  The Saint Strikes Back (1939): George Sanders
  The Saint in London (1939): George Sanders
  The Saint's Double Trouble (1940): George Sanders
  The Saint Takes Over (1940): George Sanders
  The Saint in Palm Springs (1941): George Sanders
  The Saint's Vacation (1941): Hugh Sinclair
  The Saint Meets the Tiger (1943): Hugh Sinclair
  The Saint's Girl Friday (1954): Louis Hayward
  The Saint (1997): Val Kilmer

Salem

Midwestern setting of the TV soap opera *Days of Our Lives*.

Pet black cat of the title character (Melissa Joan Hart) in the TV sitcom *Sabrina, the Teenage Witch*, voiced by Nick Bakay.

Salem House

School attended by the title character of the Charles Dickens novel *David Copperfield*.

Salieri, Antonio

Role for which F. Murray Abraham won a Best Actor Academy Award in the 1984 film *Amadeus*.

"Salinas Jackpot"

Debut episode of the TV series *Cannon*, which aired on September 14, 1971.

Salinas Valley

Original working title of the John Steinbeck novel *East of Eden*.

Salomey

Yokum family pig in the comic strip *Li'l Abner*.

Salon East

Beauty parlor that is the setting of the Palmolive dishwashing liquid commercials featuring Madge the manicurist (Jan Miner).

Sal Stewart and His Serenaders

USO orchestra in the film *1941*.

Salty

Pet cat of the title character (Lea Thompson) in the TV sitcom *Caroline in the City*.

"Salus populi"

Motto of the University of Missouri, which is Latin for "The welfare of the people."

Sam

Cartoon toucan on boxes of Kellogg's Froot Loops cereal.

Samantha

Pet goose of the Birdwells (Dorothy McGuire, Gary Cooper) in the film *Friendly Persuasion*.

Sam's American Choice

"Premium" house brand of the Wal-Mart retail chain.

Samson

Horse of Prince Phillip in the Disney animated film *Cinderella*.

Sam the Lion

Role for which Ben Johnson won a Best Supporting Actor in the 1971 film *The Last Picture Show*.

Samuel

Real first name of author (Samuel) Dashiell Hammett.

Samuel Joel

Real first and middle names of actor Zero Mostel.

Samuels, Marie

Phony name used by Marion Crane (Janet Leigh) when checking into the Bates Motel, in the Alfred Hitchcock film *Psycho*.

Samuelson, Ralph

18-year-old who invented water skis in 1922. They were first used on Lake Pepin, Minnesota.

Sanders, Dylan

See **Cook, Natalie; Sanders, Dylan; and Munday, Alex**

Sanderson, Ben

Role for which Nicolas Cage won a Best Actor Academy Award in the 1995 film *Leaving Las Vegas*.

Sandhurst

Location of the British Royal Military Academy, the counterpart to West Point.

Sandpiper Air

Commuter air service operated by Joe and Brian Hackett (Timothy Daly and Steven Weber) in the TV sitcom *Wings*.

Sandrock, New Mexico

Setting of the film *The Harvey Girls*.

Sandwich Islands

Former name of the Hawaiian Islands.

Sanford, John Elroy

Real name of comedian Redd Foxx.

"The San Francisco Treat"

Advertising slogan of Rice-A-Roni.

Sani-Towel

First paper towel manufactured in the United States, introduced by Scott Paper in 1907.

San Jobel

Prison where Alexander Mundy (Robert Wagner) served time before becoming a government operative, in the TV series *It Takes a Thief*.

San Marcos

South American country where Howard Cosell broadcasts a live presidential assassination on *Wide World of Sports*, in the Woody Allen film *Bananas*. At the end of the broadcast, Cosell says, "You've heard it with your own eyes."

Caribbean island that is the setting of the Abbott and Costello film *One Night in the Tropics*.

San Marino, California

Setting of the film *Father of the Bride* (1991) and the 1995 sequel.

San Miguel, Mexico

Setting of the Clint Eastwood film *A Fistful of Dollars*.

San Monique

Caribbean island ruled by Dr. Kananga (Yaphet Kotto) in the James Bond film *Live and Let Die*.

San Pablo

Gunboat on which Jake Holman (Steve McQueen) is stationed in the film *The Sand Pebbles*. The title of the film comes from the crew's nickname for the vessel.

San Pueblo, California

Setting of the TV sitcom *The Partridge Family*.

San Remo

Setting of the TV series *Petrocelli*.

Santa Carla, California

Setting of the film *The Lost Boys*.

Santa Mira, California

Setting of the film *Invasion of the Body Snatchers* (1956).

Santana Pictures

Production company of actor Humphrey Bogart.

Santa Rosita State Park

See **The Big W**

Santa Royale, California

Home of the title character in the comic strip *Mary Worth*.

Santa's reindeer

In the order introduced by Clement Moore in his poem "A Visit From St. Nicholas." It was first published in the *Troy Sentinel* (a New York newspaper) on December 23, 1823.

> Dasher
> Dancer
> Prancer
> Vixen
> Comet
> Cupid
> Donder
> Blitzen

Santa Teresa, California

Setting of the "Alphabet" mystery novels of Sue Grafton.

Santiago

Title character of the Ernest Hemingway novel *The Old Man and the Sea*.

Santo Poco

Mexican village that is the setting of the film *¡Three Amigos!*

"Sappy Bullfighters"

See **190**

Saraceni, Eugenio

Real name of golf great Gene Sarazen.

Sarah Constant, Goodspeed, and *Discovery*

The three ships, under the command of Christopher Newport, that brought the first settlers to Jamestown, Virginia, in May 1607. (The *Goodspeed* is referred to as the *Godspeed* in some sources.)

Sarah Siddons Award

Prize given to Eve Harrington (Anne Baxter) in the film *All About Eve*. Although this was not a real award when the film was released in 1950, the film was the impetus for the creation of a real Sarah Siddons Society, which has bestowed a real Sarah Siddons Award annually since 1951.

Sarek

Vulcan father of Mr. Spock (Leonard Nimoy) in the TV series *Star Trek*, portrayed by Mark Lenard.

Sarkhan

Asian nation that is the setting of the film *The Ugly American*.

Sassy

See **Homeward Bound: The Incredible Journey** animals

Satan's Alley

Musical that is the Broadway debut of dancer Tony Manero (John Travolta) in the film *Staying Alive*.

"satchel mouth"

What "Satchmo," nickname of jazz trumpeter Louis Armstrong, is short for.

"Saturday Night Massacre"

Nickname given to the political events of October 20, 1973. On this day, President Richard Nixon ordered Attorney General Elliot Richardson to fire Watergate special prosecutor Archibald Cox. Richardson resigned rather than comply. Richardson's deputy, William Ruckelshaus, also refused to fire Cox and also resigned. Cox was eventually dismissed by Solicitor General Robert Bork.

Saturn Films

Production company of actor Nicolas Cage.

Saunders, Caleb

Pen name used by author Robert A. Heinlein.

Saunders, Clarence

Founder of the Piggly Wiggly grocery chain. The first Piggly Wiggly opened on September 6, 1916 at 79 Jefferson Street in Memphis, Tennessee.

Saunders, Richard

Pen name used by Benjamin Franklin for the publication of his *Poor Richard's Almanack*.

See also Duc de Duras

"Sausage King of Chicago"

See Froman, Abe

"Sauviter in modo, fortiter in re"

Motto of Dwight D. Eisenhower, which is Latin for "Gently in manner, strongly in deed."

The Savage Secret

See Treasures of Lust and The Savage Secret

"Savage Sunday"

Debut episode of the TV series *Starsky and Hutch*, which aired on September 10, 1975.

Save-A-Soul Mission

Organization led by Sarah Brown in the Frank Loesser musical *Guys and Dolls*.

"Save Me"

Original theme song of the TV series *Baywatch*, performed by Peter Cetera. "I'm Always Here" (performed by Jim Jamison) and "Current of Love" (performed by series star David Hasselhoff) were subsequently used.

"Save the Planet"

Slogan of the Hard Rock Cafe.

Savoyards

What devoted fans of the comic operas of Gilbert and Sullivan call themselves. The name comes from London's Savoy Theatre, built in 1881 to perform Gilbert and Sullivan operas.

Savoy Big Five

Basketball team organized by Abe Saperstein in 1926, the precursor of the Harlem Globetrotters.

Savoy Special

Bat used by Roy Hobbs (Robert Redford) to hit the climactic home run in the film *The Natural*, after Wonderboy, his favorite bat, is broken.

The Saxons

Original name of rock group The Bay City Rollers.

"Say kids! What time is it?"

Opening line of the children's TV series *Howdy Doody*, to which the appropriate response is "It's Howdy Doody time!"

Scannon

Newfoundland dog that accompanied Lewis and Clark on their 1804–06 expedition.

scapula

Medical term for the shoulder blade.

Scar

Horse of Vint Bonner (John Payne) in the TV Western series *Restless Gun*.

The Scarlet Lady

Racing boat of J. J. Jamison (Bill Bixby) in the film *Clambake*.

Scatter

Pet chimpanzee of singer Elvis Presley.

Schaper, Herb

Letter carrier who invented the game Cootie in 1948. He whittled the wooden pieces of the prototype.

Scher

Real last name of actress Estelle Getty.

Schiller, August

Role for which Emil Jannings won a Best Actor Academy Award in the 1927 film *Wings*.

Schlachta
Real last name of actor Dennis Franz.

Schlag, Felix
Designer of the Jefferson nickel, minted since 1938.

Schlegel, Margaret
Role for which Emma Thompson won a Best Actress Academy Award in the 1992 film *Howards End*.

Schlesinger, Bruno Walter
Real name of conductor Bruno Walter.

Schleswig-Holstein-Sonderburg-Glücksburg, Philippos
Birth name of Prince Philip of Great Britain.

Schmidlap, George
See **Marx, Groucho, roles of**

Schmidt
Real last name of *Howdy Doody* host "Buffalo Bob" Smith.

Schmidt, Gottfried
Inventor of the automatic pinspotter used in bowling.

Schneider, Leonard Alfred
Real name of comedian Lenny Bruce.

Schneider, Ralph
See **McNamara, Frank and Schneider, Ralph**

Schneider, Wilhelm
Inventor of the merry-go-round, patented in 1871.

"Schnozzola"
Nickname of comedian Jimmy Durante.

Schofield
Last name of the title character in the Booth Tarkington novel *Penrod*.

"The Schoolmaster"
Nickname of Marko Ramius, captain of the title vessel in the Tom Clancy novel *The Hunt for Red October*.

Schotzli
Susan Evers' (Hayley Mills') horse in the Disney film *The Parent Trap* (1961).

Schrift, Shirley
Real name of actress Shelley Winters.

Schultz, Charmaine
Full name of Schultzy (Ann B. Davis) in the TV sitcom *The Bob Cummings Show*.

Schumacher, Louise
Role for which Beatrice Straight won a Best Supporting Actress Academy Award in the 1976 film *Network*.

Schuyler
Real first name of the title character (Kirby Grant) in the children's TV series *Sky King*.

Schwartz, Bernard
Real name of actor Tony Curtis.

Schwartz, Jeremiah
Real name of comic actor Andy Devine.

Schwenk
Middle name of lyricist Sir William Gilbert of Gilbert and Sullivan fame.

Scicolone, Sofia Villani
Real name of actress Sophia Loren.

Science Fiction and Fantasy Writers of America
See **Nebula Awards**

Science Fiction Theater
Favorite TV show of George McFly (Crispin Glover) in the film *Back to the Future*.

Science Frontiers
Company owned by alien sympathizer Nathan Bates (Lane Smith) in the TV series *V*.

the science of culture
Name given to the science of anthropology by its founder, Edward Burnett Tylor.

"Scientiae cedit mare"
Motto of the U.S. Coast Guard Academy in New London, Connecticut. It is Latin for "The sea yields to science."

Scientifically Treated Petroleum
What the letters of the name of gasoline additive STP stand for. The letters originally stood for "Studebaker Test Products."

sclerometer
Instrument for measuring the hardness of minerals.

Scobie, Reverend Jonathan
Baptist minister who invented the rickshaw while visiting Japan in 1869.

Scoggins, Jerry

Singer of the theme song of the TV sitcom *The Beverly Hillbillies*.

Scoop VII

Satellite whose return to Earth brings with it the title virus, in the film *The Andromeda Strain*.

Scope: The Show-Book of the World

Original working title of *Life* magazine.

Scoreboard

Secret Service code name for Dwight D. Eisenhower.

"Scorpio"

Nickname of the serial killer (Andy Robinson) in the film *Dirty Harry*.

Scortia, Thomas N.

See **The Tower** and **The Glass Inferno**

"Scotland Forever" and "Mum and Dad"

Phrases tattooed on the right forearm of actor Sean Connery.

Scott, Diana

Role for which Julie Christie won a Best Actress Academy Award in the 1965 film *Darling*.

Scott Frost

See **Triple Crown races (harness-racing trotters)**

"The Scottish play"

What stage performers and crew call the William Shakespeare play *Macbeth*. The speaking of the name of the play is supposed to bring bad luck.

Scott, Tommy

Stage name used by Thomas Jones Woodward early in his career, before changing his name to Tom Jones.

"The Scourge of God"

Nickname of Attila the Hun.

"Scourge of the West"

Nickname of Captain Wilton Parmenter (Ken Berry) in the TV sitcom *F Troop*.

"Scout"

Nickname of Jean Louise Finch in the Harper Lee novel *To Kill a Mockingbird*.

Scoville units

A measure of the "hotness" of peppers. Some sample Scoville-unit measurements:

Bell peppers: 0

Jalapeño peppers: 2,500–5,000
Habanero peppers (the hottest of all peppers): 200,000–300,000
Pure capsaicin (the "hot" ingredient in peppers): 16,000,000

Scragg

Maiden name of Daisy Mae Yokum in the comic strip *Li'l Abner*.

Scraps

Pet dog of Joey (Rossie Harris) in the film *Airplane!*

Screaming Eagles

Minnesota State University football team coached by Hayden Fox (Craig T. Nelson) in the TV sitcom *Coach*.

Nickname of the U.S. Army's 101st Airborne Division.

Screaming Mimi

Pink helicopter of Nick Ryder (Joe Penny) in the TV series *Riptide*.

Screen Actors Guild presidents

1933	Ralph Morgan
1933–35	Eddie Cantor
1935–38	Robert Montgomery
1939–40	Ralph Morgan
1940–42	Edward Arnold
1942–44	James Cagney
1944–46	George Murphy
1946–47	Robert Montgomery
1947–52	Ronald Reagan
1952–57	Walter Pidgeon
1957–58	Leon Ames
1958–59	Howard Keel
1959–60	Ronald Reagan
1960–63	George Chandler
1963–65	Dana Andrews
1965–71	Charlton Heston
1971–73	John Gavin
1973–75	Dennis Weaver
1975–79	Kathleen Nolan
1979–81	William Schallert
1981–85	Edward Asner
1985–88	Patty Duke
1988–95	Harry Gordon
1995–99	Richard Masur
1999–present	William Daniels

scripophilist

Technical term for a collector of old stock and bond certificates for their aesthetics and/or rarity (rather than intrinsic value).

Scruffy

Family dog in the TV sitcom *The Ghost and Mrs. Muir*.

Scrumdidilyumptious

Extra-long chocolate bar manufactured by the title character (Gene Wilder) of the film *Willy Wonka and the Chocolate Factory*.

scrumpdillyishus

Adjective describing the ice cream at Dairy Queen in 1970s TV commercials.

Scrumptious, Truly

Sally Ann Howes' role in the film *Chitty Chitty Bang Bang*.

Scud

Mean pet dog of bully Sid (voiced by Erik von Detten) in the film *Toy Story*.

Scuttle

Bumbling seagull in the Disney animated film *The Little Mermaid*, voiced by Buddy Hackett.

Seaborn Legend

Ocean-liner setting of the film *Speed 2: Cruise Control*.

Seabreeze Point

San Francisco lovers' lane in the Disney film *The Love Bug*.

Seacliff Children's Home

Where the title character saves a child from a fire, in the film *Mighty Joe Young* (1949).

The Sea-Cook

Original title of the Robert Louis Stevenson novel *Treasure Island*.

Seadog

Pet dog of Cap'n Crunch in TV commercials for the cereal of the same name.

Sea Dragons

Elite Marine task force led by Lieutenant Colonel Bill Kelly (James Brolin) in the TV series *Pensacola: Wings of Gold*.

Seafood

Yacht of Al Czervik (Rodney Dangerfield) in the film *Caddyshack*.

"The Sea-Green Incorruptible"

Nickname of French Revolution leader Robespierre.

Sea Haven

Hometown of the title character (Jim Carrey) in the film *The Truman Show*.

Seaman, Elizabeth Cochrane

Real name of *New York World* reporter Nellie Bly, best-known for her 1889 trip around the world, in emulation of Phileas Fogg in Jules Verne's novel *Around the World in Eighty Days*. She completed her trip in 72 days, 6 hours, 11 minutes, and 14 seconds.

Searcher

Starship on which the title character (Gil Gerard) serves, in the TV series *Buck Rogers in the 25th Century*.

"Searchin' My Soul"

Theme song of the TV series *Ally McBeal*, performed by Vonda Shepard.

Searchlight

Secret Service code name for Richard Nixon.

SeaRiver Mediterranean

Current name of the oil tanker originally called the *Exxon Valdez*, which spilled 11 million gallons of oil into Alaska's Prince William Sound in March 1989. The tanker had been renamed the *Exxon Mediterranean* in 1990 before receiving its current name.

Sea Shadows Inn

Setting of the film *Same Time, Next Year*.

"Seattle"

Theme song of the TV series *Here Come the Brides*, performed by Perry Como.

Seattle Pilots

Original name of the Milwaukee Brewers at their American League inception in 1969. The team took its present name when it moved to Milwaukee in 1970, and switched to the National League in 1998.

Seavers, Colt

Title character (Lee Majors) of the TV series *The Fall Guy*.

SSRN Seaview

Atomic submarine commanded by Admiral Harriman Nelson (Richard Basehart) in the TV series *Voyage to the Bottom of the Sea*.

Sebastian

Everett family rooster in the TV sitcom *Nanny and the Professor*.

"Second Hand Furniture Dealer"
Occupation of gangster Al Capone, according to his business cards.

"The second most dangerous man in London"
How Sherlock Holmes describes Colonel Sebastian Moran, assistant to Professor Moriarty, in the Sir Arthur Conan Doyle short story "The Adventure of the Empty House."

The Second World War
The six volumes of the epic work by Winston Churchill:
> *The Gathering Storm* (1948)
> *Their Finest Hour* (1949)
> *The Grand Alliance* (1950)
> *The Hinge of Fate* (1950)
> *Closing the Ring* (1951)
> *Triumph and Tragedy* (1953)

"The Secret of the Silent Hills"
Instrumental theme of the 1950s version of the children's TV series *Lassie*.

Secret Order of Beavers
Fraternal lodge of Dwayne Schneider (Pat Harrington Jr.) in the TV sitcom *One Day at a Time*.

Section One
Secret government anti-terrorist organization for which the title character (Peta Wilson) works as a covert agent, in the TV series *La Femme Nikita*.

Security Concepts, Inc.
Company that creates a law-enforcement cyborg from the body of slain officer Alex Murphy (Peter Weller) in the film *RoboCop*.

Sedges, John
Pen name used by author Pearl S. Buck.

"See a different game"
Advertising slogan of *The Sporting News*.

See, Allan
Real name of actor Gavin MacLeod.

Seeberger, Charles D.
Inventor of the escalator circa 1900.

Seegloo
See **Egingwah, Ooqueah, Ootah, and Seegloo**

"Seems Like Old Times"
Theme song of Arthur Godfrey's radio shows.

"Seer of Seers"
Nickname of weather prognosticator Punxsutawney Phil of Groundhog Day fame.

Sefton
Role for which William Holden won a Best Actor Academy Award in the 1953 film *Stalag 17*.

Seiki Kogaku Kenkyusho
Original name of Canon, which is Japanese for "Precision Optical Research Laboratory."

Sekulovich, Mladen
Real name of actor Karl Malden.

Selby Flats, California
See **Five Points; Springfield**

self-contained underwater breathing apparatus
What the word "scuba" is an acronym for.

Self Portrait
1963 autobiography of painter/photographer Man Ray.

Selkirk, Alexander
Marooned Scottish sailor who was the inspiration for the Daniel Defoe novel *Robinson Crusoe*.

Selma
Miniature computer of Captain Darien Lambert (Dale Midkiff) in the TV series *Time Trax*, voiced by Elizabeth Alexander.

selvage
Technical term for the excess margin around a sheet of stamps.

Selwyn, Art
Role for which Don Ameche won a Best Supporting Actor Academy Award in the 1985 film *Cocoon*.

Seminole-Ritz
Florida hotel where Sweet Sue and Her Society Syncopators are booked, in the film *Some Like It Hot*.

"Semper eadem"
Motto of Queen Elizabeth I of England, which is Latin for "Ever the same."

"Semper fidelis"
Motto of the U.S. Marine Corps, which is Latin for "Always faithful."

"Semper paratus"

Motto of the U.S. Coast Guard, which is Latin for "Always prepared."

"The Senior Service"

Nickname of the British Royal Navy.

Señor Pizza

Employer of delivery boy Randy Bodek (Patrick Dempsey) in the film *Loverboy.*

"The Sentimental Gentleman of Swing"

Nickname of bandleader Tommy Dorsey.

Serbs, Croats, and Slovenes, Kingdom of the

Former name (1918–29) of Yugoslavia.

Serrated Edge

See *Inner Urges, Human Instinct, Animal Nature,* **and** *Serrated Edge*

"Service Above Self"

Motto of Rotary International.

Service Games

What the name of video game manufacturer Sega is an acronym for.

Seton, Elizabeth Ann

First native-born American to be canonized, in 1975. She founded the Sisters of Charity in 1813, the first American religious society.

Seven Beauties

1976 Italian film for which director Lina Wertmuller became the first woman to be nominated for a Best Director Academy Award.

seven deadly sins

Avarice, envy, gluttony, lust, pride, sloth, and wrath.

Seven Dwarfs

As seen in the Disney animated film *Snow White and the Seven Dwarfs*:
Bashful
Doc (the leader, and the only one wearing glasses)
Dopey (the only one without a beard, the only one with blue eyes, and the only one who never speaks)
Grumpy
Happy (the only one without thin, dark eyebrows; his are white and bushy)
Sleepy
Sneezy
They are all brothers, and are all diamond miners.

"The Seven Mules"

Nickname of the 1920s offensive line of the Notre Dame football team, which blocked for the Four Horsemen:
Joe Bach (tackle)
Chuck Collins (end)
Ed Huntsinger (end)
Noble Kizer (guard)
Rip Miller (tackle)
John Weibel (guard)
Adam Walsh (center)

See also **"The Four Horsemen"**

The Seven Pillars of Wisdom

Book by T. E. Lawrence that was the basis for the film *Lawrence of Arabia.*

"The Seven Sisters"

Nickname of this group of women's colleges:
Barnard College
Bryn Mawr College
Mount Holyoke College
Radcliffe College (now co-ed)
Smith College
Wellesley College
Vassar College (now co-ed)

Nickname of this group of women's magazines:
Better Homes & Gardens
Family Circle
Good Housekeeping
Ladies' Home Journal
McCall's
Redbook
Woman's Day

Seven Wonders of the Ancient World

Pyramids of Giza
Hanging Gardens of Babylon
Mausoleum of Halicarnassus
Temple of Artemis at Ephesus
Colossus of Rhodes
Pharos (lighthouse) of Alexandria
Statue of Zeus at Olympia

Severson

Real last name of rock singer Eddie Vedder.

Sexiest Man Alive

See ***People*** **magazine's Sexiest Man Alive**

Sextant

Allied code name for the "Big Three" (Franklin D. Roosevelt, Winston Churchill, Chiang Kai-shek) conference at Cairo, Egypt, in November 1943.

Sextilis

Former name of the month of August, which was renamed for Augustus Caesar in 8 B.C.

Seymour

Middle name of English composer Sir Arthur Sullivan of Gilbert and Sullivan fame.

Middle name of actress Jane Fonda.

Sgt. Pepper's Lonely Hearts Club Band cover subjects

In addition to the four Beatles, the faces of each of these singers, actors, and other celebrities can be seen on the cover of this 1967 album:

Fred Astaire (dancer/actor)
Aubrey Beardsley (illustrator)
Marlon Brando (actor)
Bobby Breen (singer)
Lenny Bruce (comedian)
William Burroughs (author)
Lewis Carroll (author)
Stephen Crane (author)
Aleister Crowley (poet)
Tony Curtis (actor)
Marlene Dietrich (actress)
Dion (singer)
Diana Dors (actress)
Bob Dylan (singer)
Albert Einstein (scientist)
W. C. Fields (comedian)
Huntz Hall (actor)
Oliver Hardy (comedian)
Aldous Huxley (author)
C. G. Jung (psychologist)
Stan Laurel (comedian)
T. E. Lawrence (aka Lawrence of Arabia)
Sonny Liston (boxer)
Dr. David Livingstone (missionary/explorer)
Karl Marx (philosopher)
Tom Mix (actor)
Marilyn Monroe (actress)
Sir Robert Peel (statesman)
Edgar Allan Poe (author)
Tyrone Power (actor)
George Bernard Shaw (playwright)
Terry Southern (author)
Karlheinz Stockhausen (composer)
Stu Sutcliffe (former Beatle)
Shirley Temple (actress/stateswoman)
Dylan Thomas (poet)
Johnny Weissmuller (athlete/actor)
H. G. Wells (author)
Mae West (actress)
Oscar Wilde (author/playwright)

Shadow

See **Homeward Bound: The Incredible Journey** animals

"Shadow"

Nickname of fire expert Donald Rimgale (Robert De Niro) in the film *Backdraft*.

Shadowfax

Horse of wizard Gandalf in J. R. R. Tolkien's *The Lord of the Rings* trilogy.

Shady Rest Hotel

Establishment run by Kate Bradley (Bea Benaderet) in the TV sitcom *Petticoat Junction*.

Shaft films

Starring Richard Roundtree in the 1970s films, and Samuel L. Jackson in the 2000 remake:

Shaft (1971)
Shaft's Big Score! (1972)
Shaft in Africa (1973)
Shaft (2000)

Shagwell, Felicity

Heather Graham's role in the film *Austin Powers: The Spy Who Shagged Me*.

Shakespeare, common expressions from

All of these common expressions originated from the plays of William Shakespeare, listed below with their source:

All the world's a stage (*As You Like It*; II, vii, 139)
Brevity is the soul of wit (*Hamlet*; II, ii, 90)
Come full circle (*King Lear*; V, iii, 176)
The course of true love never did run smooth (*A Midsummer-Night's Dream*; I, i, 134)
Eaten out of house and home (*King Henry IV, Part II*; II, i, 82)
Every mother's son (*A Midsummer-Night's Dream*; I, ii, 81)
Foregone conclusion (*Othello*; III, iii, 429)
Forever and a day (*As You Like It*; IV, i, 151)
Good riddance (*Troilus and Cressida*; II, i, 130)
Murder most foul (*Hamlet*; I, v, 27)
Neither a borrower, nor a lender be (*Hamlet*; I, iii, 75)
One fell swoop (*Macbeth*; IV, iii, 219)
Parting is such sweet sorrow (*Romeo and Juliet*; II, ii, 184)
Pomp and circumstance (*Othello*; III, iii, 354)
The play's the thing (*Hamlet*; II, ii, 641)
Pound of flesh (*The Merchant of Venice*; IV, i, 307)
Primrose path (*Hamlet*; I, 3, 50)
Quiet as a lamb (*King John*; IV, i, 80)
Salad days (*Antony and Cleopatra*; I, v, 73)

Seen better days (*As You Like It;* II, vii, 120)

Sink or swim (*King Henry IV, Part I;* I, iii, 194)

Something is rotten in the state of Denmark (*Hamlet;* I, iv, 90)

Star-cross'd lovers (*Romeo and Juliet;* Prologue, 6)

Too much of a good thing (*As You Like It;* IV, i, 124)

Tower of strength (*King Richard III;* V, iii, 12)

Uneasy lies the head that wears a crown (*King Henry IV, Part II;* III, i, 31)

Westward-ho! (*Twelfth Night;* III, i. 148)

What's done is done (*Macbeth;* III, ii, 12)

What's in a name? (*Romeo and Juliet;* II, ii, 43)

With bated breath (*The Merchant of Venice;* I, 3, 125)

Shakespeare opening lines

Notable opening lines from the plays of William Shakespeare, listed below with the speaker of the line:

ANTONY AND CLEOPATRA

"Nay, but this dotage of our general's / O'erflows the measure." [*Philo*]

THE COMEDY OF ERRORS

"Proceed, Solinus, to procure my fall / And by the doom of death end woes and all." [*Aegeon*]

HAMLET

"Who's there?" [*Bernardo*]

JULIUS CAESAR

"Home! home, you idle creatures, get you home!" [*Flavius*]

KING HENRY IV, PART II

"Open your ears; for which of you will stop / The vent of hearing when loud Rumour speaks?" [*Rumour, the Presenter*]

KING HENRY V

"O for a Muse of fire, that would ascend / The brightest heaven of invention, / A kingdom for a stage, princes to act / And monarchs to behold the swelling scene!" [*Chorus*]

KING HENRY VI, PART I

"Hung be the heavens with black, yield day to night!" [*Duke of Bedford*]

KING HENRY VIII

"I come no more to make you laugh: things now / That bear a weighty and a serious brow, / Sad, high, and working, full of state and woe, / Such noble scenes as draw the eye to flow, / We now present." [*From the Prologue*]

KING LEAR

"I thought the King had more affected the Duke of Albany than Cornwall." [*Earl of Kent*]

MACBETH

"When shall we three meet again / In thunder, lightning, or in rain?" [*First Witch*]

THE MERRY WIVES OF WINDSOR

"Sir Hugh, persuade me not; I will make a Star-chamber matter of it; if he were twenty Sir John Falstaffs, he shall not abuse Robert Shallow, Esquire." [*Justice Shallow*]

A MIDSUMMER'S NIGHT DREAM

"Now, fair Hippolyta, our nuptial hour / Draws on apace; four happy days bring in / Another moon" [*Theseus, Duke of Athens*]

OTHELLO

"Tush! never tell me; I take it much unkindly / That thou, Iago, who hast had my purse / As if the strings were thine, shouldst know of this." [*Roderigo*]

PERICLES, PRINCE OF TYRE

"To sing a song that old was sung, / From ashes ancient Gower is come; / Assuming man's infirmities, / To glad your ear, and please your eyes." [*Gower*]

RICHARD III

"Now is the winter of our discontent / Made glorious summer by this sun of York; / And all the clouds that lour'd upon our house / In the deep bosom of the ocean buried." [*Richard, Duke of Gloucester*]

ROMEO AND JULIET

"Two households, both alike in dignity, / In fair Verona, where we lay our scene, / From ancient grudge break to new mutiny, / Where civil blood makes civil hands unclean." [*Chorus*]

THE TAMING OF THE SHREW

"I'll pheeze you, in faith." [*Christopher Sly*]

THE TEMPEST

"Boatswain!" [*Ship-Master*]

TITUS ANDRONICUS

"Noble patricians, patrons of my right, / Defend the justice of my cause with arms, / And, countrymen, my loving followers, / Plead my successive title with your swords." [*Saturninus*]

TROILUS AND CRESSIDA

"In Troy, there lies the scene." [*From the Prologue*]

TWELFTH NIGHT

"If music be the food of love, play on" [*Orsino, Duke of Illyria*]

THE WINTER'S TALE

"If you shall chance, Camillo, to visit Bohemia, on the like occasion whereon my services are now on foot, you shall see, as I have said, great difference betwixt our Bohemia and your Sicilia." [*Archidamus*]

Shalhoub, Michel

Real name of actor Omar Sharif.

Shamforoff

Original family surname of author Irwin Shaw, which was changed by his parents.

Shamley Productions

Production company of director Alfred Hitchcock.

Shamrock

Name of five yachts owned by tea magnate Sir Thomas Lipton, with which he unsuccessfully competed for the America's Cup. His last try was in 1930.

Shane, Bo

Stage name used by actress Bo Derek before she married actor John Derek.

Shangri-la

Original name of presidential retreat Camp David, as dubbed by Franklin D. Roosevelt in 1942. It was given its present name by Dwight D. Eisenhower in 1953, for his grandson.

Sharks

See **Jets and Sharks**

Sharpie

Parrot in 1950s TV commercials for Gillette razor blades.

"The Sharpshooter"

Debut episode of the TV Western series *The Rifleman*, which aired on September 30, 1958.

Shazam

Magic word that changes Billy Batson into Captain Marvel. The letters in "Shazam" stand for:
The wisdom of Solomon
The strength of Hercules
The stamina of Atlas
The power of Zeus
The courage of Achilles
The speed of Mercury

"Shazbot!"

Orkan expletive used by Mork (Robin Williams) in the TV sitcom *Mork and Mindy*.

Shears, Billy

Name under which Ringo Starr sings the Beatles tune "With a Little Help from My Friends," on the album *Sgt. Pepper's Lonely Hearts Club Band*.

Sheep, Meryl

Thespian Muppet in the children's TV series *Sesame Street*.

The Sheep-Pig

Novel by Dick King-Smith that was the basis for the film *Babe*.

"She Fell Among Thieves"

Debut episode of the TV series *Mystery!*, which aired on February 5, 1980.

Sheffield, Dr. Washington Wentworth

Connecticut dentist who invented the toothpaste tube in 1892.

Sheindlin

Last name of the retired New York Family Court judge who presides in the TV series *Judge Judy*.

Shekles Jr., Gail

Real name of actor Craig Stevens.

Shelby

Real first name of country singer/actor Sheb Wooley.

Sheldon, William H.

See **body types**

Sheleen, Kid/Strawn, Tim

Roles for which Lee Marvin won a Best Actor Academy Award in the 1965 film *Cat Ballou*. (Marvin played a dual role in the film.)

Shelley, Norman

English actor who impersonated English prime minister Winston Churchill for the BBC radio broadcast of Churchill's famous "Dunkirk" speech on June 6, 1940. Churchill had delivered the address to Parliament earlier that day, but was too busy to make the broadcast.

Shelob

Giant spider encountered by Frodo Baggins in J. R. R. Tolkien's *The Lord of the Rings* trilogy.

Shelton Jackson

Real first and middle names of director Spike Lee.

Shep

Pet elephant of the title character in the children's animated TV series *George of the Jungle*, and the film adaptation of the same name.

Shepard, Kristin

Sister-in-law of J. R. Ewing (Larry Hagman) in the TV series *Dallas*, portrayed by Mary Crosby. She was revealed to be the answer to the question "Who shot J. R.?" in the November 21, 1980 episode of the series. The question had been a worldwide obsession since the previous March 21, when the episode in which J. R. was shot was first aired.

Shere Khan

Tiger in Rudyard Kipling's *The Jungle Book*.

Sheridan College

Employer of psychology professor Peter Boyd (Ronald Reagan) in the film *Bedtime for Bonzo*.

Sheridan Falls

Setting of the radio sitcom *My Favorite Husband*.

Sherlock Holmes novels

The four full-length Sherlock Holmes novels written by Sir Arthur Conan Doyle, with the dates they were first published in book form:

A Study in Scarlet (1888)
The Sign of Four (1890)
The Hound of the Baskervilles (1902)
The Valley of Fear (1915)

Sherlock Holmes (Rathbone/Bruce) films

Films in which Basil Rathbone and Nigel Bruce appear together as Holmes and Dr. Watson:

The Hound of the Baskervilles (1939)
The Adventures of Sherlock Holmes (1939)
Sherlock Holmes and the Voice of Terror (1942)
Sherlock Holmes and the Secret Weapon (1942)
Sherlock Holmes in Washington (1943)
Sherlock Holmes Faces Death (1943)
Sherlock Holmes and the Spider Woman (1944)
The Scarlet Claw (1944)
The Pearl of Death (1944)
The House of Fear (1945)
The Woman in Green (1945)
Pursuit to Algiers (1945)
Terror by Night (1946)
Dressed to Kill (1946)

Sherlock Holmes short stories

The Sherlock Holmes short stories written by Sir Arthur Conan Doyle, listed below with the book collection in which they first appeared:

THE ADVENTURES OF SHERLOCK HOLMES (1892)

"A Scandal in Bohemia"
"The Red-Headed League"
"A Case of Identity"
"The Boscombe Valley Mystery"
"The Five Orange Pips"
"The Man with the Twisted Lip"
"The Adventure of the Blue Carbuncle"
"The Adventure of the Speckled Band"
"The Adventure of the Engineer's Thumb"
"The Adventure of the Noble Bachelor"
"The Adventure of the Beryl Coronet"
"The Adventure of the Copper Beeches"

THE MEMOIRS OF SHERLOCK HOLMES (1894)

"Silver Blaze"
"The Stock-broker's Clerk"
"The Yellow Face"
"The *Gloria Scott*"
"The Musgrave Ritual"
"The Reigate Puzzle"
"The Crooked Man"
"The Resident Patient"
"The Greek Interpreter"
"The Naval Treaty"
"The Final Problem"

THE RETURN OF SHERLOCK HOLMES (1905)

"The Adventure of the Empty House"
"The Adventure of the Norwood Builder"
"The Adventure of the Dancing Men"
"The Adventure of the Solitary Cyclist"
"The Adventure of the Priory School"
"The Adventure of Black Peter"
"The Adventure of Charles Augustus Milverton"
"The Adventure of the Six Napoleons"
"The Adventure of the Three Students"
"The Adventure of the Golden Pince-Nez"
"The Adventure of the Missing Three-Quarter"
"The Adventure of the Abbey Grange"
"The Adventure of the Second Stain"

HIS LAST BOW (1917)

"The Adventure of Wisteria Lodge"
"The Adventure of the Cardboard Box"
"The Adventure of the Red Circle"
"The Adventure of the Bruce-Partington Plans"
"The Adventure of the Dying Detective"
"The Disappearance of Lady Frances Carfax"
"The Adventure of the Devil's Foot"
"His Last Bow"

THE CASE BOOK OF SHERLOCK HOLMES (1927)

"The Adventure of the Illustrious Client"
"The Adventure of the Blanched Soldier"
"The Adventure of the Mazarin Stone"
"The Adventure of the Three Gables"

"The Adventure of the Sussex Vampire"
"The Adventure of the Three Garridebs"
"The Problem of Thor Bridge"
"The Adventure of the Creeping Man"
"The Adventure of the Lion's Mane"
"The Adventure of the Veiled Lodger"
"The Adventure of Shoscombe Old Place"
"The Adventure of the Retired Colourman"

Shermer High

Illinois school that is the setting of the film *The Breakfast Club*.

Illinois school attended by Wyatt Donnelly (Ilan Mitchell-Smith) and Gary Wallace (Anthony Michael Hall) in the film *Weird Science*. The school's athletic teams are the Mules.

Sherwood Forest Plantation

Estate of President John Tyler near Williamsburg, Virginia.

Sherwood Forrest

Married name of *F.Y.I.* reporter Corky (Faith Ford) in the TV sitcom *Murphy Brown*.

Shields, James

Mexican War general who is the only man to have represented three different states in the U.S. Senate: Illinois (1849-1855), Minnesota (1858-1859) and Missouri (1879).

Shiloh Ranch

Setting of the TV Western series *The Virginian*.

Shimerda

Last name of the title character in the Willa Cather novel *My Ántonia*.

Shinbone

Setting of the film *The Man Who Shot Liberty Valance*.

Shinn, Eulalie Mackecknie

Wife of George Shinn, mayor of River City, Iowa, in the musical *The Music Man*.

"Shipwreck"

Nickname of Hollywood stuntman Alvin Kelly, who became nationally famous in the 1920s for his feats of flagpole sitting. He spent 49 days atop a flagpole at Atlantic City, New Jersey's Steel Pier in 1930.

Shlabotnik, Joe

Favorite baseball player of Charlie Brown in the comic strip *Peanuts*.

Shoelace Productions

Production company of actress Julia Roberts.

Shoeless Joe

Novel by W. P. Kinsella that was the basis for the film *Field of Dreams*.

Shoemaker-Levy 9

Comet that crashed on the planet Jupiter in July 1994.

Shoemaker, P. Martin

Full name of the title bird in the comic strip *Shoe*.

Shoe Shine Boy

Secret identity of cartoon superhero Underdog, voiced by Wally Cox.

Sholes, Christopher

See **"literary piano"**

Shooters

Bar/poolroom hangout in the TV series *Melrose Place*.

The Shop

See **Longmont, Virginia**

The Shop Around the Corner

Neighborhood bookstore owned by Kathleen Kelly (Meg Ryan) in the film *You've Got Mail*. The name of the store is the same as the 1940 film that inspired *You've Got Mail*.

Shopgirl

E-mail name of Kathleen Kelly (Meg Ryan) in the film *You've Got Mail*.

Shopton

Setting of the Tom Swift series of children's novels.

Shores Hotel

Miami establishment where Scott Hayward (Elvis Presley) and Tom Wilson (Will Hutchins) stay, in the film *Clambake*.

"Shortcake"

Fonzie's (Henry Winkler's) nickname for Joanie Cunningham (Erin Moran) in the TV sitcom *Happy Days*.

"short shirt"

What the name of the English clipper ship *Cutty Sark* means in Scottish. The name comes from a garment worn by a character in the Robert Burns poem "Tam o'Shanter." Originally launched in 1869, the ship, now fully restored, is a tourist attraction in Greenwich, England.

The Short-Timers

Novel by Gustav Hasford that was the basis for the film *Full Metal Jacket*.

Shotz Brewery

Milwaukee employer of the title characters (Penny Marshall and Cindy Williams) in the TV sitcom *Laverne and Shirley*.

Shoumatoff, Elizabeth

Russian-born artist for whom President Franklin Delano Roosevelt was sitting for a watercolor portrait at Warm Springs, Georgia, on April 12, 1945, when he suffered his fatal stroke.

Showcase Studios

New York City rehearsal hall where dancer Paula McFadden (Marsha Mason) trains in the film *The Goodbye Girl*.

"Show me the money!"

See **14**

Shrewsbury

Middle name of humorist Irvin S. Cobb.

Shrublands

Rehab center where James Bond (Sean Connery) stays in the films *Thunderball* and *Never Say Never Again*.

Shugart, Alan

IBM researcher who invented the floppy disk in 1971.

Shuster, Joe

See **Siegel, Jerry and Shuster, Joe**

Shuster University

College attended by Clark Kent (John Haymes Newton, Gerard Christopher) in the TV series *Superboy*. It is named for Superman co-creator Joe Shuster.

S.I.A.

Government-agency employer of former jewel thief Alexander Mundy (Robert Wagner) in the TV series *It Takes a Thief*.

Si and Am

Siamese cats in the Disney animated film *Lady and the Tramp*.

Siciliano, Angelo

Real name of bodybuilding guru Charles Atlas.

"The Sick Boy and the Sitter"

Debut episode of the TV sitcom *The Dick Van Dyke Show*, which aired on October 3, 1961.

"Sicut patribus sit Deus nobis"

Motto of Boston, Massachusetts, which is Latin for "God be with us, as He was with our fathers."

Sid

Pet cat of the title character in the comic strip *Ziggy*.

Sidekicks

Athletic-shoe manufacturing company owned by George Banks (Steve Martin) in the film *Father of the Bride* (1991).

Sidewinder, Colorado

Setting of the Stephen King novel *Misery*.

Sidney

Real first name of playwright Paddy Chayefsky.

Sidney Joseph

First and middle names of humorist S. J. Perelman.

Sid's Pizza Parlor

Favorite hangout of the title character (Scott Baio) in the TV sitcom *Charles in Charge*, which is owned by his mother Lillian (Ellen Travolta). It was renamed the Yesterday Cafe after it was remodeled into a diner.

Siebert, Muriel

First woman to purchase a seat on the New York Stock Exchange, in 1967.

Siegel, Jerry and Shuster, Joe

Cleveland teenagers who created Superman in 1933. Superman first appeared in the January 1933 issue of their self-published fanzine *Science Fiction*, five years before Superman's comic-book debut in *Action Comics #1* (June 1938).

Siegl, Zev

See **Baldwin, Jerry; Bowker, Gordon; and Siegl, Zev**

Siemens, Werner von

German inventor of the electric elevator in 1880.

Sigmund

See **Jackson 5 members**

Silberman, Jerome

Real name of actor Gene Wilder.

sildenafil citrate

Chemical name of the drug Viagra.

"Silly little ass!"

Catchphrase of Tinker Bell in the James M. Barrie novel *Peter Pan*.

"Silly Scandals"

See **105**

"The Silly Song"

First instrumental theme used for the TV game show *Hollywood Squares*.

The Silver Beetles

See **The Quarrymen**

Silver Buffalo Award

Presented by the Boy Scouts of America annually since 1926 for distinguished service to youth.

Silver Creek, Colorado

Mining-town birthplace of the title character (Dorothy Lowell, Vivian Smolen) in the radio soap opera *Our Gal Sunday*, as mentioned in each show's opening.

Silver Dart

Jet aircraft of the title character (Richard Webb) in the children's TV series *Captain Midnight*.

"Silver Fox"

Theme song of the TV talk show *Donahue*.

"The Silver Fox"

Nickname of country singer Charlie Rich.

Nickname of former First Lady Barbara Bush.

Silver Shako

Trophy awarded to the winning team in the annual football game between Virginia Military Institute and The Citadel, known as "The Military Classic of the South." A shako is a type of military hat.

Silver Slipper

Nightclub employer of chorus girl Sally Lee (Eleanor Powell) in the film *Broadway Melody of 1938*.

Silver Sow Award

Trophy given to Les Nessman (Richard Sanders) for his hog reports, in the TV sitcom *WKRP in Cincinnati*.

Silverstone

Estate of John Beresford Tipton (unseen, but voiced by Paul Frees), title character of the TV series *The Millionaire*.

simethicone

Active ingredient in many antacids.

Simian Films

Production company of actors Hugh Grant and Elizabeth Hurley.

Simijian, Luther

Inventor of the automated teller machine (ATM).

Simmons, Toni

Role for which Goldie Hawn won a Best Supporting Actress Academy Award in the 1969 film *Cactus Flower*.

Simmons, Veta Louise

Role for which Josephine Hull won a Best Supporting Actress Academy Award in the 1950 film *Harvey*.

Simon

Middle name of playwright George S. Kaufman.

Simone

Family dog in the TV sitcom *The Partridge Family*.

"Si monumentum requiris, circumspice"

Epitaph on the memorial to architect Sir Christopher Wren at London's St. Paul's Cathedral, which he designed. It is Latin for "If you seek his monument, look around you."

Simpson, Arthur

Role for which Peter Ustinov won a Best Supporting Actor Academy Award in the 1964 film *Topkapi*.

Simpsonville

Midwestern setting of the radio soap opera *Young Widder Brown*.

Sims, Gordon

Real name of Venus Flytrap (Tim Reid) in the TV sitcom *WKRP in Cincinnati*.

Sinatra, Frank, wives of

Nancy Barbato (married 1939, divorced 1951)
Ava Gardner (married 1951, divorced 1957)
Mia Farrow (married 1966, divorced 1968)
Barbara Marx (married 1976)

Sinclair, Helen

Role for which Dianne Wiest won a Best Supporting Actress Academy Award in the 1994 film *Bullets Over Broadway*.

Sinestro

Archenemy of comics superhero The Green Lantern.

"Sinful Caesar sipped his snifter, seized his knees, and sneezed"

Diction-practice phrase for Don Lockwood (Gene Kelly) in the film *Singin' in the Rain*.

singers in films, unlikely

Warren Beatty and Dustin Hoffman "That's Amore" and "Strangers in the Night" in *Ishtar*

Candice Bergen "Better Than Ever" in *Starting Over*

Ingrid Bergman "The Children's Marching Song" in *The Inn of the Sixth Happiness*

Irving Berlin "Oh, How I Hate to Get Up in the Morning" in *This Is the Army*

Shirley Booth "I'm in the Mood for Love" in *About Mrs. Leslie*

Ernest Borgnine "The Best Things in Life Are Free" in *The Best Things in Life Are Free*

Marlon Brando "Luck Be a Lady" in *Guys and Dolls*

Mel Brooks and Anne Bancroft "Sweet Georgia Brown" (sung in Polish) in *To Be or Not to Be*

Yul Brynner "Mad About the Boy" in *The Magic Christian*

Sean Connery "Pretty Irish Girl" in *Darby O'Gill and the Little People*

Billy Crystal and Meg Ryan "Surrey with the Fringe on Top" in *When Harry Met Sally . . .*

Bette Davis "I've Written a Letter to Daddy" in *Whatever Happened to Baby Jane?*

Robert De Niro "Blue Moon" in *New York, New York*

Kirk Douglas "Pretty Little Girl in the Yellow Dress" in *The Last Sunset*

Charles Durning "Mary's a Grand Old Name" in *Tootsie*

Clint Eastwood "I Talk to the Trees" and "Gold Fever" in *Paint Your Wagon*

Henry Fonda "Red River Valley" in *The Grapes of Wrath*

Clark Gable "Puttin' on the Ritz" in *Idiot's Delight*

Jackie Gleason "Call Me Irresponsible" in *Papa's Delicate Condition*

Oliver Hardy "Honolulu Baby" in *Sons of the Desert*

Audrey Hepburn "La Vie en Rose" in *Sabrina*

Diane Keaton "Seems Like Old Times" in *Annie Hall*

Sophia Loren "Bing! Bang! Bong!" in *Houseboat*

Lee Marvin "The First Thing You Know" and "Wand'rin' Star" in *Paint Your Wagon*

Peter O'Toole "The Impossible Dream" in *Man of La Mancha*

Jason Robards "Bye Bye Blackbird" in *Melvin and Howard*

Will Rogers "When the Blue of the Night Meets the Gold of the Day" in *Doubting Thomas*

Sylvester Stallone "Too Close to Paradise" in *Paradise Alley*

Spencer Tracy "Don't Cry Little Fish" in *Captains Courageous*

Gene Wilder and Peter Boyle "Puttin' on the Ritz" in *Young Frankenstein*

"The Singing Cowboy"

Nickname of Gene Autry.

"The Singing Ranger"

Nickname of country singer Hank Snow.

singultus

Medical term for a hiccup.

Sinking Spring Farm

Kentucky birthplace of President Abraham Lincoln in 1809.

Sinnock, John R.

Designer of the Roosevelt dime (minted since 1946) and the Franklin half dollar (minted 1948-63).

"Sins of the Past"

Debut episode of the TV series *Xena: Warrior Princess*, which aired in September 1995.

sins, seven deadly

See **seven deadly sins**

Siple, Paul

Polar explorer who originated the wind chill factor circa 1940.

Sir Barton

See **Triple Crown races (Thoroughbred horse racing)**

Sirhan, Sirhan Bishara

Clerk who shot New York senator and presidential candidate Robert F. Kennedy at the Ambassador Hotel in Los Angeles, California on June 5, 1968. Kennedy died the next day.

Sirin, Vladimir

Pen name used by author Vladimir Nabokov early in his career.

Sister Mary Clarence

Name given to Deloris Van Cartier (Whoopi Goldberg) while masquerading as a nun at St. Katherine's convent, in the film *Sister Act*.

Sister Sledge members

Pop singing quartet consisting of sisters Debra, Joni, Kathy, and Kim.

sitcom settings, real-life

Alice: Phoenix, Arizona
All in the Family: New York City (Queens)
Amos 'n' Andy: New York City (Manhattan)
Barney Miller: New York City (Manhattan)
The Beverly Hillbillies: Beverly Hills, California
Bewitched: Westport, Connecticut
The Bob Newhart Show: Chicago, Illinois
Cheers: Boston, Massachusetts
Caroline in the City: New York City (Manhattan)
Chico and the Man: East Los Angeles, California
The Cosby Show: New York City (Brooklyn)
Designing Women: Atlanta, Georgia
Dharma & Greg: San Francisco, California
The Dick Van Dyke Show: New Rochelle, New York
Diff'rent Strokes: New York City (Manhattan)
The Drew Carey Show: Cleveland, Ohio
Empty Nest: Miami, Florida
Family Ties: Columbus, Ohio
Frasier: Seattle, Washington
Friends: New York City (Manhattan)
Full House: San Francisco, California
The Goldbergs: New York City (Bronx)
The Golden Girls: Miami, Florida
Good Times: Chicago, Illinois
Growing Pains: Huntington, New York
Happy Days: Milwaukee, Wisconsin
Head of the Class: New York City (Manhattan)
Home Improvement: Detroit, Michigan
The Honeymooners: New York City (Brooklyn)
I Dream of Jeannie: Cocoa Beach, Florida
I Love Lucy: New York City (Manhattan)
The Jeffersons: New York City (Manhattan)
Just Shoot Me: New York City (Manhattan)
Kate & Allie: New York City (Manhattan)
Laverne and Shirley: Milwaukee, Wisconsin; Burbank, California
Mad About You: New York City (Manhattan)
Malcolm & Eddie: Kansas City, Missouri
Mama: San Francisco, California
Martin: Detroit, Michigan

The Mary Tyler Moore Show: Minneapolis, Minnesota
M*A*S*H: Uijongbu, South Korea
Maude: Tuckahoe, New York
Mork and Mindy: Boulder, Colorado
Mr. Belvedere: Beaver Falls, Pennsylvania
Murphy Brown: Washington, D.C.
My Favorite Martian: Los Angeles, California
My Little Margie: New York City (Manhattan)
The Nanny: New York City (Manhattan)
Night Court: New York City (Manhattan)
The Odd Couple: New York City (Manhattan)
One Day at a Time: Indianapolis, Indiana
The Patty Duke Show: New York City (Brooklyn)
Perfect Strangers: Chicago, Illinois
Rhoda: New York City (Manhattan)
Sanford and Son: Los Angeles, California
Seinfeld: New York City (Manhattan)
Spin City: New York City (Manhattan)
Taxi: New York City (Manhattan)
That Girl: New York City (Manhattan)
That's My Mama: Washington, D.C.
Three's Company: Santa Monica, California
Too Close for Comfort: San Francisco, California
Welcome Back Kotter: New York City (Brooklyn)
Who's the Boss?: Fairfield, Connecticut
Will & Grace: New York City (Manhattan)
Wings: Nantucket, Massachusetts

"Sit on it!"

Dismissive exclamation frequently used by Fonzie (Henry Winkler) in the TV sitcom *Happy Days*.

"Les Six"

Group of French composers who became popular soon after World War I:
Georges Auric
Louis Durey
Arthur Honegger
Darius Milhaud
Francis Poulenc
Germaine Tailleferre

Six Chix contributors

This innovative comic strip, which debuted in January 2000, features the work of these six different cartoonists, each of whom appears on a specific day of the week:
Isabella Bannerman (Monday)
Margaret Shulock (Tuesday)
Rina Piccolo (Wednesday)
Ann Telnaes (Thursday)
Kathryn LeMieux (Friday)
Stephanie Piro (Saturday)
The six take turns on the Sunday strip.

Six Flags Over Texas flags

Arlington, Texas, amusement park, the first in the Six Flags chain, which opened in 1961. It is named for the six national flags that have flown over Texas:

Spain
France
Mexico
Republic of Texas (the current Texas state flag)
Confederate States of America
United States

Sixth Man Award

Presented annually since 1983 to the NBA's best nonstarting player.

"The Skaters"

1882 instrumental tune (aka "Skaters Waltz") by French composer Emile Waldteufel that is the most frequently played piece of music at ice skating rinks.

"Skeeter"

Nickname of Olympic track star Wilma Rudolph.

The Skeleton in the Cupboard

Alternate title of the Somerset Maugham novel *Cakes and Ale.*

"Skid"

Nickname of Mark McCormick (Daniel Hugh-Kelly), former auto racer turned crime fighter in the TV series *Hardcastle and McCormick.*

Skikne, Larushka Mischa

Real name of actor Laurence Harvey.

"skill"

What "kung fu" means in Chinese.

Skinner, Leonard

See **My Backyard**

Skinny and Sweet

See **Rid-O-Rat**

ski-trail symbols

Beginner: green circle
Intermediate: blue square
Advanced: black diamond
Expert: double black diamond

"SKNXX-X!"

Sound of Dagwood's snoring in the comic strip *Blondie.*

Skull and Bones members

Notable former members of Yale University's ultra-secret society, which has only 15 members at any one time:

George H. W. Bush (president)
George W. Bush (president)
W. Averell Harriman (statesman)
Henry Luce (cofounder of *Time* magazine)
Archibald MacLeish (poet)
Potter Stewart (Supreme Court justice)
William Howard Taft (president)
Robert Taft (senator)

Skull Island

Where the title beast is found in the film *King Kong* (1933).

Skynet

Supercomputer waging war against humanity in the film *Terminator 2: Judgment Day.*

Skypad Apartments

Home of the title family in the children's animated TV sitcom *The Jetsons.*

Skyrocket

Palomino horse of Marty Markham (David Stollery) in the "Adventures of Spin and Marty" segment of the children's TV series *The Mickey Mouse Club.*

Skywalker, Anakin

Former identity of Darth Vader in the *Star Wars* series of films. He is the father of Luke Skywalker (Mark Hamill) and Princess Leia Organa (Carrie Fisher).

Slade, Frank

Role for which Al Pacino won a Best Actor Academy Award in the 1992 film *Scent of a Woman.*

Slaghoople

Maiden name of Wilma Flintstone in the animated TV sitcom *The Flintstones.*

"Slammin' Sammy"

Nickname of golf great Sam Snead.

Nickname of baseball player Sammy Sosa.

Slap Shots

See **The Ledger**

The Slave of Duty

Alternate title of the Gilbert and Sullivan comic opera *The Pirates of Penzance.*

Sledge, Mac
Role for which Robert Duvall won a Best Actor Academy Award in the 1983 film *Tender Mercies*.

"Sleep"
Theme song of bandleader Fred Waring's Pennsylvanians.

Sleep-Tite Pajama Factory
Setting of the musical *The Pajama Game*.

Sleet, Al
"Hippy dippy weatherman" character created by comedian George Carlin.

Sleipnir
In Greek mythology, the eight-legged horse of Odin.

Slescynski, Gertrude
Real name of Eve Harrington (Anne Baxter) in the film *All About Eve*.

Slice, Candy
Punk-rocker character of Gilda Radner in the TV series *Saturday Night Live*.

Slick Air
Charter airline owned by Sally "Slick" Monroe (Shannon Tweed) in the TV series *Fly by Night*.

Slightly Read Bookshop
Setting of the radio soap opera *Life Can Be Beautiful*.

"Slim"
Harry Morgan's (Humphrey Bogart's) nickname for Marie Browning (Lauren Bacall) in the film *To Have and Have Not*.

"Slinging Sammy"
Nickname of pro football Hall of Fame quarterback Sammy Baugh.

Sloper, Catherine
Role for which Olivia de Havilland won a Best Actress Academy Award in the 1949 film *The Heiress*.

slud
Past tense of the verb "slide," as used by sportscaster and baseball Hall of Famer Dizzy Dean.

Slye, Leonard Franklin
See **Weston, Dick**

Slytherin
See **Gryffindor House**

"small"
What the word "piccolo" means in Italian.

Small-Fawcett, Nigel
Inept English diplomat who attempts to aid James Bond (Sean Connery) in the film *Never Say Never Again*. He is portrayed by Rowan Atkinson, who later became famous as Mr. Bean.

"The Smartest Horse in the Movies"
Nickname of Trigger, golden palomino of Western star Roy Rogers.

Smart Shop
Phoenix lingerie shop patronized by Laura Manion (Lee Remick) in the film *Anatomy of a Murder*.

The Smasher's Mail
See ***The Hatchet, The Home Defender,*** **and** ***The Smasher's Mail***

Smaug
Dragon living in Lonely Mountain, whose stolen treasure is recovered by Bilbo Baggins in the J. R. R. Tolkien novel *The Hobbit*.

S.M.C. Cartage Company
Chicago building at 2122 N. Clark Street whose garage was the setting of the St. Valentine's Day Massacre on February 14, 1929.

Smellie, William
Editor of the first edition of the *Encyclopaedia Britannica*, first published in Edinburgh, Scotland, in 1768.

Smell-O-Vision
Film process that released odors into a movie theater at appropriate moments of a film. It was first used in the 1960 film *A Scent of Mystery*.

See also **Odorama**

Smerdyakov
See **Dmitri, Ivan, Alyosha, and Smerdyakov**

"Smile and Show Your Dimple"
Original title of the Irving Berlin tune "Easter Parade."

"Smile, Darn Ya, Smile"
Theme song of radio comedian Fred Allen.

Smilex
Deadly chemical used by The Joker (Jack Nicholson) in the film *Batman*.

Smiley

Baxter family dog in the comic strip *Hazel*.

See also **Happy, Walter, and Smiley**

Smiley, Guy

Game-show host in the children's TV series *Sesame Street*. Shows he has hosted include *To Tell a Face*, *Beat the Time*, and *The Triangle Is Right*.

Smith

Last name of Sluggo in the comic strip *Nancy*.

Middle name of General George Patton.

Real last name of telejournalist Linda Ellerbee.

Smith, Al

See **Bagby Jr., Jim and Smith, Al**

Smith & Wells Engraving Co.

San Francisco firm that prints Paladin's (Richard Boone's) business cards, in the TV Western series *Have Gun Will Travel*.

Smith, Burl

Real name of Gopher (Fred Grandy) in the TV sitcom *The Love Boat*.

Smith, C. Harold

See **Binney, Edwin and Smith, C. Harold**

Smithee, Alan (or Allen)

Pseudonym created by the Directors Guild of America for directors who want their name taken off the credits of a film.

Smithfield

Original name of Olympia, Washington.

Smith, Gladys Louise

Real name of actress Mary Pickford.

Smith, Hamilton E.

Inventor of the first mechanical (hand-cranked) washing machine circa 1858.

Smith, Harold Jay

Real name of actor Jay Silverheels.

Smith, Homer

Role for which Sidney Poitier won a Best Actor Academy Award in the 1963 film *Lilies of the Field*.

Smith, Horton

Winner of the first Masters golf tournament, held at the Augusta National Golf Club in 1934.

Smith, James Todd

Real name of rap singer L. L. Cool J.

Smith, Johnston

Pen name used by author Stephen Crane.

Smith Jr., Walker

Real name of 1950s middleweight boxing champ Sugar Ray Robinson.

Smithline

Real last name of fashion designer Adele Simpson.

Smith, Maria Ann

Australian orchardist who in 1868 developed the Granny Smith apple named for her.

Smith, Robert

Real name of deejay Wolfman Jack.

Smith, Rosamond

Pen name used by author Joyce Carol Oates for her mystery novels.

Smith, Samuel Francis

Massachusetts seminary student who in 1831 wrote the lyrics to the tune "America," for which he used the music of the British national anthem "God Save the King (Queen)."

Smith's Weekly

New York magazine employer of writer Philip Green in the Laura Z. Hobson novel *Gentleman's Agreement*.

Smith, Thorne

See Topper **feature films**

Smith, Valentine Michael

Title character of the Robert A. Heinlein novel *Stranger in a Strange Land*.

Smoke

Palomino of film cowboy Dick Foran.

"Smoke Rings"

Theme song of Glen Gray and the Casa Loma Orchestra.

Smokers

Pirate gang led by Deacon (Dennis Hopper) in the film *Waterworld*.

Smokey

Blue Tick coon hound mascot of the University of Tennessee.

"Smokin' Joe"
Nickname of 1970s heavyweight boxing champion Joe Frazier.

"The Snake"
Nickname of NFL quarterback Ken Stabler.

"The Snake Pit"
Nickname of Grace Hall, collegiate wrestling arena at Lehigh University, for its loud and intimidating spectators.

Snake's End
Setting of the film *The Villain.*

Snap!, Crackle!, and Pop!
Cartoon characters seen on boxes of Kellogg's Rice Krispies cereal since the 1930s. They can be distinguished by their different headgear:
  Snap!: baker's hat
  Crackle!: red-striped stocking cap
  Pop!: military hat

Snare, Richie
Pseudonym used by former Beatle Ringo Starr as the drummer on the Harry Nilsson album *Son of Schmilsson.*

Snellen, Hermann
Dutch ophthalmologist who in 1862 invented the familiar eye chart and test of visual acuity named for him.

Snerd, Mortimer
See **Bergen, Edgar, dummies of**

Snert
Family dog in the comic strip *Hägar the Horrible.*

Snoopington, J. Pinkerton
Bank examiner (Franklin Pangborn) in the film *The Bank Dick.*

Snoopy's brothers and sisters
As seen in the comic strip *Peanuts.*

BROTHERS
Andy
Marbles
Rover
Olaf
Spike

SISTERS
Belle
Molly

Snopes trilogy
Series of novels by William Faulkner chronicling the Snopes family.
  The Hamlet (1940)
  The Town (1957)
  The Mansion (1959)

snorkasaurus
See **Dino**

Snow
Family dog in the TV series *The Monroes.*

"snowfall"
What the word "Nevada" means in Spanish.

Snowflake
Dolphin mascot of the Miami Dolphins that is recovered by the title character (Jim Carrey) in the film *Ace Ventura, Pet Detective.*

Snowlets
See **Olympic mascots (Winter Games)**

Snuffles
Tracking dog of cartoon lawman Quick Draw McGraw.

Soapsuds
Favorite horse of humorist Will Rogers.

"The Soap That Sanctifies"
See **Milady Soap**

"The Sobbin' Women"
Short story by Stephen Vincent Benét that was the basis for the musical *Seven Brides for Seven Brothers.*

Sobol, Donald J.
See **Idaville**

Société Anonyme Belge d'Exploitation de la Navigation Aérienne
What the name of Belgian airline Sabena is an acronym for, which is French for "Joint-stock company for the exploitation of aerial navigation."

Society for the Preservation and Encouragement of Barbershop Quartet Singing in America
See **S.P.E.B.S.Q.S.A.**

"The Society Party"
Debut episode of the TV sitcom *Laverne and Shirley,* which aired on January 27, 1976.

"Sock it to me!"
Catchphrase of Judy Carne on the TV series *Rowan and Martin's Laugh-In*.

Socks
Pet cat of President Bill Clinton.

"Socks"
Chuck Browning's (Peter Fonda's) nickname for Tracy Ballard (Blythe Danner) in the film *Futureworld*.

Socrates
Middle name of Greek shipping magnate Aristotle Onassis.

sodium hypochlorite
Active ingredient in household bleach.

sodium lauryl sulfate
Foaming agent used in toothpaste.

Soft Warehouse
Original name of the CompUSA computer-store chain.

"soft way"
What the word "judo" means in Chinese.

Sogo
City of evil in the film *Barbarella*.

Sojourner
Vehicle that explored the surface of Mars, brought there in the spacecraft *Pathfinder*, which landed on July 4, 1997.

Solex Agitator
High-tech device that converts solar radiation into electricity, recovered by James Bond (Roger Moore) in the film *The Man with the Golden Gun*.

Solitaire
Girlfriend of Dr. Kananga (Yaphet Kotto) in the James Bond film *Live and Let Die*, portrayed by Jane Seymour.

Sol-leks and Dave
Sled-dog companions of Buck in the Jack London novel *The Call of the Wild*.

Solness, Halvard
Title character of the Henrik Ibsen play *The Master Builder*.

Solomon
Real last name of jazz flutist Herbie Mann.

Solomon, Aubrey
Original name of Israeli statesman Abba Eban.

"So Long, Patrick Henry"
Debut episode of the TV series *I Spy*, which aired on September 15, 1965.

"So Long, Samoa"
Original title of the Cole Porter tune "Farewell, Amanda," introduced by David Wayne in the film *Adam's Rib*.

"So long until tomorrow"
Sign-off line of CBS radio broadcaster Lowell Thomas.

Soma
Drug that causes forgetfulness, in the Aldous Huxley novel *Brave New World*.

somatypes
See **body types**

"Someday I'll Find You"
Appropriate theme song of the radio series *Mr. Keen, Tracer of Lost Persons*.

"Some of These Days"
Theme song of singer Sophie Tucker.

"Someone is going to pay"
Slogan used to promote the film *Ransom*.

Somersets
See **Americans**

Somers Islands
Former name of Bermuda.

Something's Got to Give
Film that Marilyn Monroe was working on at the time of her death.

"Something special in the air"
Advertising slogan of American Airlines.

Something That Happened
Original title of the John Steinbeck novel *Of Mice and Men*.

"Somethin's Cookin'"
Cartoon that the title character (voiced by Charles Fleischer) and Baby Herman (voiced by Lou Hirsch)

are working on, at the start of the film *Who Framed Roger Rabbit*.

Sometimes I Wonder

1965 autobiography of songwriter Hoagy Carmichael. The title is the first three words of Carmichael's best-known tune, "Star Dust."

"Sometimes you feel like a nut, sometimes you don't"

Advertising slogan of Peter Paul candy bars Mounds and Almond Joy.

"Somewhere in the Night"

Theme song of the TV series *Naked City*.

Sommers, Jaime

Title character (Lindsay Wagner) in the TV series *The Bionic Woman*.

somnambulism

Medical term for sleepwalking.

The Songbird

Cessna airplane piloted by the title character (Kirby Grant) in the children's TV series *Sky King*.

"Songbird of the South"

Nickname of singer Kate Smith.

"Song of the High Seas"

Instrumental theme of the TV documentary *Victory at Sea*, composed by Richard Rodgers.

Sonja

Girlfriend of the title feline in the comic strip *Heathcliff*.

Sonny

Cartoon cuckoo in TV commercials for Cocoa Puffs cereal.

Son of Adam

Book by Sir Denis Forman that was the basis for the film *My Life So Far*.

"Sooner"

See **United States residents' nicknames**

Sophie

Horse of Colonel Sherman T. Potter (Harry Morgan) in the TV sitcom *M*A*S*H*.

The Sorrow and the Pity

Film seen by Alvy Singer (Woody Allen) and the title character (Diane Keaton) in the film *Annie Hall*.

"Sorry about that, Chief!"

Catchphrase of the title character (Don Adams) in the TV sitcom *Get Smart*.

"Sorry, we're closed"

Final line in the final episode of the TV sitcom *Cheers*, spoken by Sam Malone (Ted Danson). The episode aired on May 20, 1993.

SOTHPAW

Pennsylvania license plate of lefthander Rocky Balboa's (Sylvester Stallone's) Lamborghini sports car in the film *Rocky IV*.

Soubirous, Bernadette

Role for which Jennifer Jones won a Best Actress Academy Award in the 1943 film *The Song of Bernadette*.

"Soul Brother Number One"

See **Brown, James, nicknames of**

"The Soul of the American Outdoors"

Slogan of *Field and Stream* magazine.

"Soulsville, U.S.A."

Subtitle of the Wilson Pickett tune "634-5789."

Soundabout

Original name of the Sony Walkman when first introduced in 1979.

"The Sound Heard 'Round the World"

Advertising slogan of Panasonic soon after its products were introduced in the U.S. in the early 1960s.

sound navigation and ranging

What the word "sonar" is an acronym for.

Sound of Music

Original name of the Best Buy retail chain.

The Sound of Music children

The seven children of Captain Georg von Trapp (from oldest to youngest): Liesl, Friedrich, Louisa, Kurt, Brigitta, Marta, and Gretl.

The Sources of the Susquehanna

Alternate title of the James Fenimore Cooper novel *The Pioneers*.

Sousé, Egbert

See **Fields, W. C., roles/pen names of**

"The Southbound Bus"

Debut episode of the TV series *Touched by an Angel*, which aired on September 21, 1994.

Southdale

The first enclosed, climate-controlled shopping mall, which opened in Edina, Minnesota, in 1956.

Southern Cross

New York City restaurant run by Amanda Shelton (Sarah Michelle Gellar) in the film *Simply Irresistible*.

The Southern Cross

San Angelo, Texas, ranch owned by Clayton Farlow (Howard Keel) in the TV series *Dallas*.

Southern Made Doughnuts

Only product for which Elvis Presley ever did a TV commercial. He sang the product's jingle during an appearance on the local program *Louisiana Hayride* in Shreveport, Louisiana, on November 6, 1954.

Southport, North Carolina

Setting of the film *I Know What You Did Last Summer*.

South Sea

Vasco Nuñez de Balboa's name for the Pacific Ocean, which in 1513 he became the first European to see.

Southwest General

TV soap opera on which Michael Dorsey/Dorothy Michaels (Dustin Hoffman) gets the role of Emily Kimberly, in the film *Tootsie*.

Sovereign Grand Inspector General

See **33**

"So we beat on, boats against the current, borne back ceaselessly into the past"

Epitaph of author F. Scott Fitzgerald, which is the last line of his novel *The Great Gatsby*.

Spacely's Space Sprockets

Employer of George Jetson (voiced by George O'Hanlon) in the children's animated TV sitcom *The Jetsons*.

"Spaceman"

Nickname of eccentric baseball pitcher Bill Lee.

Space Sucker

Favorite video game of Arnold Jackson (Gary Coleman) in the TV sitcom *Diff'rent Strokes*.

Space Transporter

Teleportation device developed by Lex Luthor (Lyle Talbot) in the 1950 movie serial *Atom Man vs. Super-*

man, at least 15 years before Gene Roddenberry "invented" the transporter for the TV series *Star Trek*.

"Spaghetti Western" trilogy

Nickname of this group of three films starring Clint Eastwood, directed by Sergio Leone:
   A Fistful of Dollars (1964)
   For a Few Dollars More (1965)
   The Good, the Bad, and the Ugly (1966)

Spalding, Edna

Role for which Sally Field won a Best Actress Academy Award in the 1984 film *Places in the Heart*.

Spanish Main

Former name of the Caribbean Sea, as the route of Spanish treasure galleons.

Sparkling Springs Lake

Setting of the Marx Brothers film *A Day at the Races*. It calls itself "America's foremost summer resort."

Sparkplug

Horse of Barney Google in the comic strip *Barney Google and Snuffy Smith*.

Sparky

Dog brought back to life by the title character (John Travolta) in the film *Michael*.

Horse of Pee-wee Herman (Paul Reubens) in the film *Big Top Pee-wee*.

Original name of Alka-Seltzer mascot Speedy.

"Sparky"

Childhood nickname of cartoonist Charles Schulz.

Sparrowhawk

Code name that Joseph Turner (Robert Redford) gives to Cathy Hale (Faye Dunaway) for her meeting with CIA deputy chief Higgins (Cliff Robertson) in the film *Three Days of the Condor*.

SPARs

Members of the U.S. Women's Coast Guard Reserve during World War II, derived from the Coast Guard motto, *"Semper paratus."*

Sparta, Mississippi

Setting of the film and TV series *In the Heat of the Night*.

Spartans

See **Rockwell High**

S.P.E.B.S.Q.S.A.

Abbreviation for the Society for the Preservation and Encouragement of Barbershop Quartet Singing in America. The organization, founded in 1938, is headquartered in Kenosha, Wisconsin.

Special Executive for Counter-Terrorism, Revenge and Extortion

Full name of SPECTRE, evil organization in the James Bond films.

Speckter, Martin K.

See interrobang

Speedee

1950s cartoon mascot (with a hamburger-bun head) of McDonald's.

"Speedo"

Nickname of Earl Carroll, lead singer of The Cadillacs and the inspiration for their tune "Speedo."

Speedwell

Ship that was to accompany the *Mayflower* on its voyage to America in 1620. It was left behind in England because it was leaking badly and could not be repaired.

Speedy

Pet dog of the title character in the TV sitcom *The Drew Carey Show*.

Speedy Service Window Washing Company

Employer of Ted Higgins and Homer Hinchcliffe (Abbott and Costello) in the film *The Noose Hangs High*.

spelunker

Technical term for a recreational explorer of caves.

Spelvin, George

Pseudonym frequently used by theater performers who don't want their real names listed, often because their name already appears elsewhere in the credits.

"Spem reduxit"

Motto of New Brunswick, Canada, which is Latin for "Hope restored."

Spenlow and Jorkins

Law firm where the title character works as a trainee in the Charles Dickens novel *David Copperfield*.

S. Peter Pryor Junior College

School attended by Dobie Gillis (Dwayne Hickman) and Maynard G. Krebs (Bob Denver) in the TV sitcom *The Many Loves of Dobie Gillis*.

Sphere

Middle name of jazz pianist Thelonious Monk.

sphygmomanometer

Technical term for the device that measures blood pressure. The word is derived from the Latin word for "pulse."

Spice Girls original members

- Victoria Adams (Posh Spice)
- Melanie Brown (Scary Spice)
- Emma Bunton (Baby Spice)
- Melanie Chisholm (Sporty Spice)
- Geri Halliwell (Ginger Spice)

Spider

Original first name of the title character in the comic strip *Beetle Bailey*.

"Spider"

Nickname of tennis great Althea Gibson, for her long arms and legs.

"Spiderman"

Nickname of baseball star Nomar Garciaparra.

Spidermonkey Island

Tropical destination of the title character in the Hugh Lofting children's novel *The Story of Doctor Dolittle*.

Spiegel Grove

Home of President Rutherford B. Hayes in Fremont, Ohio.

Spike

See Snoopy's brothers and sisters

Spilsbury, John

English printer who became the first retailer of jigsaw puzzles in 1762.

Spindrift

Spaceship in the TV series *Land of the Giants*.

Spingarn Medal

Awarded annually since 1915 by the NAACP for outstanding achievement. It is named for Joel Elias Spingarn, NAACP board chairman when the award was originated.

Spinney, Caroll

Actor inside the Big Bird costume in the children's TV series *Sesame Street*.

Spirit Dance Entertainment

Production company of actor Forest Whitaker.

The Spirit of Bataan

Personal airplane of General Douglas MacArthur during World War II.

The Spirit of Ecstasy

Hood ornament on Rolls-Royce automobiles, commissioned in 1910 and designed by sculptor Charles Sykes. It was originally called *The Spirit of Speed*.

"The Splendid Splinter"

Nickname of baseball Hall of Famer Ted Williams.

"*Splendor sine occasu*"

Motto of British Columbia, Canada, which is Latin for "Splendor without diminishment."

Splinter

See **Knothead and Splinter**

Spocks, Pandora

Portrayer of Serena, mischievous cousin of Samantha Stephens (Elizabeth Montgomery) in the TV sitcom *Bewitched*, according to the credits. Serena is actually portrayed by Ms. Montgomery.

Spoken Sanskrit

Book written by Colonel Pickering in the Lerner and Loewe musical *My Fair Lady*.

sporran

Fur pouch suspended from a belt that is often worn with a kilt by Scottish men.

Sport

Horse of Adam Cartwright (Pernell Roberts) in the TV Western series *Bonanza*.

Pet dog of Betty and Bob (Claudette Colbert and Fred MacMurray) in the film *The Egg and I*.

The Sportlight

Syndicated newspaper column of sportswriter Grantland Rice.

"Sporto"

John Bender's (Judd Nelson's) nickname for Andrew Clark (Emilio Estevez) in the film *The Breakfast Club*.

Sports Cars Illustrated

Original name of *Car and Driver* magazine when first published in 1955. It took its present name in 1962.

Sports Management International

Employer of the title character (Tom Cruise) at the start of the film *Jerry Maguire*.

Spot

Pet dog of Dick and Jane in the memorable elementary school readers.

Striped pet cat of Data (Brent Spiner) in the TV series *Star Trek: The Next Generation*.

Spot Fetcher Bush

Pet English springer spaniel of President George W. Bush. She is the daughter of Millie, pet dog of Bush's parents.

Spouter Inn

New Bedford, Massachusetts, establishment where Ishmael first meets Queequeg, in the Herman Melville novel *Moby-Dick*.

Spring Creek, Dakota Territory

Setting of the O. E. Rölvaag novel *Giants in the Earth*.

Springfield

Setting of the TV sitcom *Father Knows Best*.

Setting of the TV soap opera *The Guiding Light* since 1966. Previously, the series had been set in Selby Flats, California.

Setting of the animated TV sitcom *The Simpsons*.

Springfield, Jebediah Obadiah Zachariah Jedediah

Founder of Springfield in the animated TV sitcom *The Simpsons*.

Springtime

Secret Service code name for Mamie Eisenhower.

Springtime for Hitler

Broadway musical produced by Max Bialystock (Zero Mostel) and Leo Bloom (Gene Wilder) in the Mel Brooks film *The Producers*.

Springwood

Hyde Park, New York, home of President Franklin D. Roosevelt.

Springwood, Ohio

Setting of the *Nightmare on Elm Street* series of films.

Spritzer, Sidney
Audience heckler in the 1966–67 edition of *The Milton Berle Show*, portrayed by Irving Benson.

Spunky
Pet dog of Fonzie (Henry Winkler) in the TV sitcom *Happy Days*.

Spur Awards
Presented annually since 1953 by the Western Writers of America for distinguished writing about the American West.

Spy Magazine
Tabloid that covers the society wedding of Tracy Lord (Katharine Hepburn and Grace Kelly, respectively) in the film *The Philadelphia Story* and its musical remake *High Society*.

The Spy Who Laughed at Danger
Film for which the title character (Burt Reynolds) works as a stunt man, in the film *Hooper*.

"Squash Capital of the South"
See **Grady, South Carolina**

The Squeaking Door
Original name of the radio series *Inner Sanctum*.

"Squeaky"
Nickname of Lynette Fromme, who attempted to assassinate President Gerald Ford in Sacramento on September 5, 1975.

Squiggman, Andrew
Real name of Squiggy (David L. Lander) in the TV sitcom *Laverne and Shirley*.

"The Squire"
Nickname of golf great Gene Sarazen, for his elegant style.

S.S. American
Setting of the Cole Porter musical *Anything Goes*.

S.S. Americus
Setting of the famous "stateroom scene" in the Marx Brothers film *A Night at the Opera*.

S.S. General Grant
Ship that takes Passepartout (Cantinflas) and Phileas Fogg (David Niven) from Yokohama to San Francisco in the film *Around the World in 80 Days*.

S.S. Guppy
Ship commanded by the title character in TV commercials for Cap'n Crunch cereal.

S.S. Minnow
Ship whose "three-hour tour" maroons its seven passengers and crew in the TV sitcom *Gilligan's Island*.

S.S. Ocean Queen
Setting of the TV sitcom *Oh! Susanna*, aka *The Gale Storm Show*.

S.S. Rangoon
Ship that takes Passepartout (Cantinflas) and Phileas Fogg (David Niven) from Bombay to Hong Kong in the film *Around the World in 80 Days*.

S.S. Ultima
Ship on which Sam and Fran travel to Europe in the Sinclair Lewis novel *Dodsworth*.

S.S. Viking
Ship attacked by giant ants in the film *Them!*

Stab
Film based on the book *The Woodsboro Murders* by Gale Weathers (Courteney Cox), in the film *Scream 2*.

Novel written by Charlie Prince (George Wendt) in the film *Dreamscape*.

Stafford, Indiana
Hometown of Richard Kimble (David Janssen) in the original TV series *The Fugitive*.

Stage Show
Musical variety series hosted by Tommy and Jimmy Dorsey, on which Elvis Presley made his network TV debut on January 28, 1956.

"Stage to Lordsburg"
Short story by Ernest Haycox that was the basis for both versions of the film *Stagecoach*.

Stag Party
Original working title of *Playboy* magazine.

Stahr, Monroe
Title character of the F. Scott Fitzgerald novel *The Last Tycoon*.

Stainer
Real last name of actor Leslie Howard.

"The Stakeout"
Debut episode of the TV series *Seinfeld*, which aired on May 31, 1990.

Stalag 13
See **Hammelburg**

Stalingrad
Former name (1925–61) of Volgograd, Russia.

Stallard, Tracy
Boston Red Sox pitcher who gave up the record 61st home run of 1961 hit by New York Yankee Roger Maris, on October 1st at Yankee Stadium.

Stan
Unseen husband of Karen Walker (Megan Mullally) in the TV sitcom *Will & Grace*.

"Stand"
Theme song of the TV sitcom *Get a Life* performed by R.E.M.

Standard Oil components
The major components of Standard Oil of New Jersey, after it was broken up by order of the U.S. Supreme Court in 1911:
Amoco: Standard Oil of Indiana
Chevron: Standard Oil of California
Esso (later Exxon): Standard Oil of New Jersey
Mobil: Standard Oil of New York
Sohio: Standard Oil of Ohio

Standish Arms
Home of Clark Kent (George Reeves) in the children's TV series *The Adventures of Superman*.

Stanford University Network
What the name of computer manufacturer Sun Microsystems originally stood for. It was founded in 1982 by a group of Stanford students and alumni.

Stanley
Real first name of singer Bobby Vinton.

Stanley, George
See **Gibbons, Cedric**

stannum
Latin name for tin, from which its chemical symbol Sn is derived.

Stanton Institute of Architecture
School from which Howard Roark is expelled in the Ayn Rand novel *The Fountainhead*.

Stanton, Schuyler
Pen name used by author L. Frank Baum.

Starbuck, Bill
Title character (Burt Lancaster) of the film *The Rainmaker* (1956).

Stardom
Original name of *Seventeen* magazine when first published in 1942. It took its present name in 1944.

Stardust
Horse of the title character (Gene Barry) in the TV series *Bat Masterson*.

Stardust Ballroom
Where the title character (Ernest Borgnine) first meets Clara Snyder (Betsy Blair) in the film *Marty*.

Star Gazer
Horse that Dubonnet competes against in the film *Broadway Melody of 1938*.

Stark, Abe
See **"Hit sign, win suit"**

Starkey, Richard
Real name of Beatles drummer Ringo Starr.

Starkfield, Massachusetts
Setting of the Edith Wharton novel *Ethan Frome*.

Stark, Willie
Role for which Broderick Crawford won a Best Actor Academy Award in the 1949 film *All the King's Men*.

Starlight
Secret Service code name for Pat Nixon.

Starling, Clarice
Role for which Jodie Foster won a Best Actress Academy Award in the 1991 film *The Silence of the Lambs*.

Star of Hope
Waterford crystal geodesic sphere dropped from New York City's One Times Square to usher in the year 2000.

The Star of Rhodesia
423-carat diamond owned by Lady Margaret Carstairs (Mary Forbes) that Sherlock Holmes (Basil Rathbone) is hired to protect, in the film *Terror by Night*.

"The Stars and Bars"

Nickname of the flag of the Confederate States of America.

"The Star-Spangled Banner"

First music video shown on VH-1 on its January 1, 1985 premiere broadcast, performed by Marvin Gaye.

Starting Gate

Jazz club frequented by the title character (Ron Leibman) in the TV series *Kaz*.

Star Trek films

Star Trek: The Motion Picture (1979)
Star Trek II: The Wrath of Khan (1982)
Star Trek III: The Search for Spock (1984)
Star Trek IV: The Voyage Home (1986)
Star Trek V: The Final Frontier (1989)
Star Trek VI: The Undiscovered Country (1991)
Star Trek: Generations (1994)
Star Trek: First Contact (1996)
Star Trek: Insurrection (1998)

State Fair Omaha

Words on the hot-air balloon in which the title character (Frank Morgan) leaves the Emerald City, in the film *The Wizard of Oz*.

state residents' nicknames

See **United States residents' nicknames**

Statler and Waldorf

Balcony hecklers in the children's TV series *The Muppet Show*, voiced by Richard Hunt and Jim Henson (respectively).

Statler Brothers original members

Phil Balsley, Lew DeWitt, Don Reid, and Harold Reid.

Statue of Freedom

19½-foot tall statue that stands atop the U.S. Capitol in Washington, D.C. It was designed by Thomas Crawford and installed on December 2, 1863.

Statue of the Three Servicemen

Bronze sculpture by Frederick Hart added to the Vietnam Veterans Memorial in Washington, D.C., in 1984.

The Statutory Duel

Alternate title of the Gilbert and Sullivan comic opera *The Grand Duke*.

Stay-Put Lipstick

Product for which the ad-agency title character (Tony Randall) lines up Rita Marlowe (Jayne Mansfield) as a commercial spokesperson in the film *Will Success Spoil Rock Hunter?*

St. Catherine Labouré Hospital

See **Cape Cod Casualty Company, Inc.**

St. Charlotte's Orphanage

Los Angeles establishment where Vincent Benedict (Danny DeVito) was raised, in the film *Twins*.

St. Clare, Evangeline

Full name of Little Eva in the Harriet Beecher Stowe novel *Uncle Tom's Cabin*.

St. Clete's School for Wayward Girls

School attended by Carla Tortelli (Rhea Perlman) in the TV sitcom *Cheers*.

St. Cloud's Orphanage

Where Homer Wells (Tobey Maguire) is raised, in the film *The Cider House Rules*.

St. Dominic's

Church that is the setting of the film *Going My Way*.

Steagles

1943 NFL team formed from the combined ranks of the Pittsburgh Steelers and Philadelphia Eagles, due to the manpower shortage caused by World War II.

Steamboat Geyser

World's tallest active geyser, in Yellowstone National Park, Wyoming. It produces water-vapor plumes up to 500 feet high.

Stearns and Harrington

Former law-firm employer of Frank Galvin (Paul Newman) in the film *The Verdict*.

"The Steel Curtain"

Nickname of the 1970s defensive unit of the Pittsburgh Steelers, led by "Mean Joe" Greene, L. C. Greenwood, Ernie Holmes, and Dwight White.

Steele, Johnnie

Owner of the title vehicle in the tune "In My Merry Oldsmobile."

Steeltown, USA

Setting of the Marc Blitzstein musical *The Cradle Will Rock*.

Steinitz, William
Austrian who was the first world chess champion, holding the title from 1866 to 1894.

Stein, Julius Kerwin
Real name of songwriter Jule Styne.

Steinmetz, Tennessee
Buddy Hackett's role in the film *The Love Bug*.

Stephanie
Real first name of singer Natalie Cole.

Real first name of rock singer Stevie Nicks.

Stephen
Real first name of president (Stephen) Grover Cleveland.

Stephen Hero
Original working title of the James Joyce novel *A Portrait of the Artist As a Young Man*.

Stephens, James
*See **The Crock of Gold***

Stephenson, Al
Role for which Fredric March won a Best Actor Academy Award in the 1946 film *The Best Years of Our Lives*.

Steps in Time
1959 autobiography of screen dancer Fred Astaire.

Stern, Kessler, Goldstein and Krumpnick
Law-firm employer of Helen Tasker (Jamie Lee Curtis) in the film *True Lies*.

Stern, Richard Martin
*See **The Tower** and **The Glass Inferno***

sternum
Medical term for the breastbone.

Stetson, Lee
Real name of secret agent Scarecrow (Bruce Boxleitner) in the TV series *Scarecrow and Mrs. King*.

"Steve"
Marie Browning's (Lauren Bacall's) nickname for Harry Morgan (Humphrey Bogart) in the film *To Have and Have Not*.

Stevenson Aircraft
Company where the title character is employed as a riveter in the radio and 1949–50 (Jackie Gleason) TV version of the sitcom *The Life of Riley*. For the 1953–58 TV version starring William Bendix, the name was changed to Cunningham Aircraft.

Stevenson Burton
Full first and middle names of the title character in the comic strip *Steve Canyon*.

Stevens, Ruby
Real name of actress Barbara Stanwyck.

Stevens, Yvette Marie
Real name of pop singer Chaka Khan.

St. Evrémonde
Real last name of Charles Darnay in the Charles Dickens novel *A Tale of Two Cities*.

Stewart Aircraft Works
Los Angeles employer of Barry Kane (Robert Cummings) in the Alfred Hitchcock film *Saboteur*.

Stewart/Hitchcock films
*See **Hitchcock/Stewart films***

Stewart, Rollen
Spectator who has appeared at many major sporting events displaying a sign reading "John 3:16."

St. Gregory Hotel
San Francisco setting of the TV series *Hotel*. The series' opening credits use the exterior of San Francisco's Fairmont Hotel.

St. Helen of the Blessed Shroud Orphanage
Where the title characters (Dan Aykroyd and John Belushi) are raised, in the film *The Blues Brothers*.

stibium
Latin name for antimony, from which its chemical symbol Sb is derived.

Stiles
Last name of the title character (Bruce Davison) in the film *Willard*.

"Stinkerbell"
Teddy Reed's (Sela Ward's) nickname for her sister Frankie (Julianne Phillips) in the TV series *Sisters*.

Stinkie
See **The Ghostly Trio**

Stinky and Nunzio
Pet dogs of Dharma (Jenna Elfman) in the TV sitcom *Dharma & Greg*.

St. Katherine's
See **Sister Mary Clarence**

St. Louis Browns
See **Milwaukee Brewers**

St. Louis Wolves
Team name on the uniform of Dexter Broadhurst (Bud Abbott) in the Abbott and Costello film *The Naughty Nineties*, while they are performing their famous "Who's on First?" routine.

St. Martins, Pennsylvania
Hometown of Billy Wyatt (Mark Harmon) in the film *Stealing Home*.

St. Mary Mead
English village home of Dame Agatha Christie sleuth Miss Jane Marple.

stock-ticker symbols, one-letter
As of this writing, the three letters of the alphabet unassigned to stock-ticker symbols are I, M, and V. I and M are being reserved by the New York Stock Exchange for Intel and Microsoft, respectively, in the hope that these companies will someday trade on the NYSE.
- A Agilent Technologies (telecommunications spinoff of Hewlett-Packard)
- B Barnes Group (auto and airplane parts)
- C Citigroup (formerly Citibank)
- D Dominion Resources (Virginia power company)
- E ENI (Italian energy company)
- F Ford Motor Company
- G Gillette
- H Harcourt General (book publishing)
- J Jackpot Enterprises (gaming machines)
- K Kellogg
- L Liberty Financial (asset management)
- N Inco (mining)
- O Realty Income Corporation (real estate)
- P Phillips Petroleum
- Q Qwest Communications (telecommunications)
- R Ryder System (truck leasing)
- S Sears Roebuck
- T AT&T
- U U.S. Airways
- W Westvaco (paper products)
- X USX (U.S. Steel)
- Y Alleghany Corporation (insurance, mining)
- Z Venator (retailing, formerly Woolworth)

Stockton
Middle name of "gonzo journalist" Hunter S. Thompson.

St. Olaf, Minnesota
Hometown of Rose Nylund (Betty White) in the TV sitcom *The Golden Girls*.

A Stone for Danny Fisher
Novel by Harold Robbins that was the basis for the Elvis Presley film *King Creole*.

Stone, Marvin
Manufacturer of paper cigarette holders who invented the drinking straw in 1888.

Stone, Matt
See **McCormick, Kenny**

Stoner, Harry
Role for which Jack Lemmon won a Best Actor Academy Award in the 1973 film *Save the Tiger*.

Stone, Sheriff John
Constable who takes away the first mate, in the Beach Boys tune "Sloop John B."

Stony Hill
Farm setting of the Arthur Miller play *After the Fall*.

Stookey
See **Yarrow, Stookey, and Travers**

"the stool pigeon"
Original name for the "tilt" device in a pinball machine.

"Storm Cloud Cantata"
Orchestral piece by Arthur Benjamin performed during the climactic Albert Hall scene of the Alfred Hitchcock film *The Man Who Knew Too Much* (1956). The piece was written for Hitchcock's original 1934 version of the film.

Stormy
Pet St. Bernard of the title character (Betty White) in the TV sitcom *Life With Elizabeth*.

"A Story of the Buried Life"

Subtitle of the Thomas Wolfe novel *Look Homeward, Angel*.

"A Story of the Grand Banks"

Subtitle of the Rudyard Kipling novel *Captains Courageous*.

"A Story of Wall-street"

Subtitle of the Herman Melville short story "Bartleby the Scrivener."

"The Storyteller"

Nickname of country singer Tom T. Hall.

Stossel, Ludwig

Portrayer of the "little old winemaker" in TV commercials for Italian Swiss Colony wine.

Stotz, Carl E.

Founder of Little League baseball. The first Little League game was played in Williamsport, Pennsylvania, on June 6, 1939.

Stovall, Major Harvey

Role for which Dean Jagger won a Best Supporting Actor Academy Award in the 1949 film *Twelve O'Clock High*.

Stow, John

See **Pass, John and Stow, John**

St. Patricks

See **Arenas**

St. Petersburg, Missouri

Setting of the Mark Twain novel *The Adventures of Tom Sawyer*. The town is modeled after Twain's hometown of Hannibal, Missouri.

Strange

Middle name of Robert McNamara, Secretary of Defense under President John F. Kennedy.

"Strange Things Are Happening"

Theme song (aka "The Ho-Ho Song") of the TV comedy/variety series *The Red Buttons Show*.

"Strange Things Happen"

Subtitle of the Dickey Lee tune "Laurie."

Strate

Last name of the title character (Sonny Shroyer) in the TV sitcom *Enos*.

Stratfield Saye

Hampshire, England, home of the Duke of Wellington, purchased for him in 1817 by Parliament after his victory at the Battle of Waterloo.

Stratford Inn

Establishment owned by Joanna and Dick Loudon (Mary Frann and Bob Newhart) in the TV sitcom *Newhart*.

"Stratocruiser"

See **Boeing passenger planes**

"Stratoliner"

See **Boeing passenger planes**

Stratton, Charles Sherwood

Real name of the diminutive General Tom Thumb, the first major attraction promoted by P. T. Barnum, beginning in 1842.

Strausser

Real last name of playwright Tom Stoppard.

Strawberry Fields

Triangular section of New York City's Central Park dedicated to the memory of former Beatle John Lennon.

Strawn, Tim

See **Sheleen, Kid/Strawn, Tim**

Streaky

Pet cat of Supergirl in the Superman comics.

"The Streetbeater"

Theme song of the TV sitcom *Sanford and Son*, composed by Quincy Jones.

Streeter, Edward

Author of the novel *Father of the Bride*, which was the basis for the films of the same name.

Stretch

See **The Ghostly Trio**

"Stretch"

Nickname of baseball Hall of Fame first baseman Willie McCovey, for his ability to field errant throws with one foot on the base.

Strickland Propane

Employer of Hank Hill (voiced by Mike Judge) in the animated TV sitcom *King of the Hill*.

Strickler, David

Pharmacist from Latrobe, Pennsylvania, who invented the banana split in 1904.

stridulation

Technical term for the shrill sound made by crickets and other animals by rubbing together parts of the body.

Stripes epilogue

In which the main characters appear on the covers of these (real and mythical) publications:
  Louise Cooper (Sean Young): *Road Life*
  Sergeant Hulka (Warren Oates): *Springfield Daily Examiner*
  Dewey Oxberger (John Candy): *Tiger Beat*
  Stella (P. J. Soles): *Penthouse*
  Captain Stillman (John Larroquette): *Nome News*
  John Winger (Bill Murray): *Newsworld*
  Russell Ziskey (Harold Ramis): *Guts*

Strite, Charles

Inventor of the pop-up toaster, patented in 1919.

Strong, Arnold

Stage name used by actor Arnold Schwarzenegger for his first film, 1969's *Hercules in New York*. The film was rereleased in 1970 as a comedy under the title *Hercules Goes Bananas*.

"Stronger than dirt"

Advertising slogan of Ajax laundry detergent.

Stroud, Robert

Title character (Burt Lancaster) of the film *Birdman of Alcatraz*.

St. Swithin's Teaching Hospital

London setting of the TV sitcom *Doctor in the House*.

Stuart and Clyde

Last names (respectively) of English pop duo Chad and Jeremy.

Studebaker Test Products

See **Scientifically Treated Petroleum**

Students Wildly Indignant About Nearly Everything

See **S.W.I.N.E.**

"Studiis et rebus honestis"

Motto of the University of Vermont, which is Latin for "For things and studies that are honest."

Studlendgehawn

Real last name of actress Goldie Hawn.

Studs Lonigan trilogy

Series of novels by James T. Farrell:
  Young Lonigan: A Boyhood in Chicago Streets (1932)
  The Young Manhood of Studs Lonigan (1934)
  Judgment Day (1935)

"A Study of Provincial Life"

Subtitle of the George Eliot novel *Middlemarch*.

Stupendous Man

Calvin's imaginary superhero in the comic strip *Calvin and Hobbes*.

Stuyvesant Museum of Natural History

Employer of paleontologist Dr. David Huxley (Cary Grant) in the film *Bringing Up Baby*.

"Stuzzicadenti"

Childhood nickname of actress Sophia Loren. The word is Italian for "toothpick."

St. Vitus' Dance

Boat residence of Sonny Crockett (Don Johnson) in the TV series *Miami Vice*.

Styx original members

John Curulewski, Dennis DeYoung, Chuck Panozzo, John Panozzo, and James Young.

Substitutiary Locomotion

Spell being perfected by Eglantine Price (Angela Lansbury) that brings inanimate objects to life, in the Disney film *Bedknobs and Broomsticks*.

Sudan

Circus lion found in the title character's (Paul Reubens') house in the film *Big Top Pee-wee*.

Sue

See **Melinda and Sue**

"Sufferin' succotash!"

All-purpose exclamation of cartoon character Sylvester J. Pussycat.

"Sugar Babe"

Luke McCoy's (Richard Crenna's) term of endearment for his wife Kate (Kathy Nolan) in the TV sitcom *The Real McCoys*.

"Sugar Blues"

Theme song of bandleader Clyde McCoy.

"Suicide Is Painless"

Theme song of the film and TV sitcom *M*A*S*H*.

"Suicide Sal"

Nickname of infamous bank robber Bonnie Parker.

suit of lights

Traditional costume worn by matadors and bandilleros in bullfighting. In the original Spanish, it is called *traje de luces*.

"Sulfur Island"

What the name of Pacific island Iwo Jima means in Japanese.

Sullivan, Annie

Role for which Anne Bancroft won a Best Actress Academy Award in the 1962 film *The Miracle Worker*.

Sullivan Award

Presented annually since 1930 by the Amateur Athletic Union (AAU) to the outstanding amateur athlete in the United States. It is named for James E. Sullivan, founder and past president of the AAU.

Sullivan, John Florence

Real name of radio comedian Fred Allen.

Sultana

Steamboat that exploded and sank on the Mississippi River near Memphis, Tennessee, on April 27, 1865. 1,547 people were killed, including many Union soldiers returning home from the Civil War.

Summerfield

Setting of the radio sitcom *The Great Gildersleeve*.

The Summer of the Shark

Original working title of the Peter Benchley novel *Jaws*.

The Sun Also Sets

TV soap opera that is the focus of the film *Soapdish*.

"Sun-Down Poem"

Original title of the Walt Whitman poem "Crossing Brooklyn Ferry."

Sunk Creek Ranch

Setting of the Owen Wister novel *The Virginian*.

"The Sun King"

Nickname of King Louis XIV of France.

Sunnydale, California

Setting of the TV series *Buffy the Vampire Slayer*.

"Sunny Jim"

Nickname of baseball Hall of Famer Jim Bottomley.

Sunny Shores Villa

St. Petersburg, Florida, retirement home that is the setting of the film *Cocoon*.

Sunnyside

Tarrytown, New York, home of author Washington Irving.

Sun Princess

Ocean-liner setting of the TV sitcom *Love Boat: The Next Wave*.

Sunrise, Colorado

Setting of the TV series *Bus Stop*.

Sunshine Cab Company

Employer of Alex Rieger (Judd Hirsch), Louie De Palma (Danny DeVito), and Elaine Nardo (Marilu Henner) in the TV series *Taxi*.

The Sunspots

See **Ol' Yellow Eyes Is Back**

"Suos cultores scientia coronat"

Motto of Syracuse University, which is Latin for "Knowledge crowns those who seek her."

Superbas

See **Bridegrooms**

Supergrover

Superhero in the children's TV series *Sesame Street*. His secret identity is Grover Kent, ace doorknob salesman for Acme, Inc.

Superman, The Adventures of opening

The introduction of the 1950s children's TV series:
    The Adventures of Superman! Faster than a speeding bullet. More powerful than a locomotive. Able to leap tall buildings at a single bound. Look . . . up in the sky. It's a bird . . . it's a plane . . . it's Superman! Yes, it's Superman. Strange visitor from another planet who came to Earth with powers and abilities far beyond those of mortal men. Superman, who can change the course of mighty rivers, bend steel in his bare

hands. And who, disguised as Clark Kent, mild-mannered reporter for a great metropolitan newspaper, fights a never-ending battle for truth, justice, and the American way.

SuperMex

Nickname of pro golfer Lee Trevino.

Supman, Milton

Real name of comedian Soupy Sales.

Supremes original members

Florence Ballard, Diana Ross, and Mary Wilson.

Surf and Sand Playhouse

Cape Cod setting of the Rodgers and Hart musical *Babes in Arms*.

Surf Ballroom

Clear Lake, Iowa, nightspot where singers Buddy Holly, The Big Bopper, and Ritchie Valens gave their last performances on February 2, 1959, the day before their fatal plane crash.

"Surfin' Safari" locales

This Beach Boys tune mentions these surfing-beach locations (in order):
Huntington
Malibu
Rincon
Laguna
Cerro Azul
Doheny
Hawaii
Peru

Surprise Party

"Ticket" on which comedienne Gracie Allen ran a tongue-in-cheek campaign for president of the United States in 1940. One of her campaign slogans was "Down with common sense."

"Surrender Dorothy"

Message written across the sky with black smoke by the Wicked Witch of the West (Margaret Hamilton) in the film *The Wizard of Oz*.

Surrey

Middle name of silent-screen Western star William S. Hart.

"survey says . . ."

Catchphrase of the hosts of the TV game show *Family Feud*, first used by Richard Dawson.

Susan

Real first name of actress Sigourney Weaver.

Susan

Original working title of the Jane Austen novel *Northanger Abbey*.

Susan B. Anthony Hotel

Women-only New York City residence that is the setting of the TV sitcom *Bosom Buddies*.

Susan Elinor

Real first and middle names of Scarlett O'Hara's sister Suellen, in the Margaret Mitchell novel *Gone With the Wind*.

Susan Eloise

First and middle names of novelist S. E. Hinton.

Susan Ker

Real first and middle names of actress Tuesday Weld.

Susanswerphone

Telephone answering service that is the setting of the musical *Bells Are Ringing*.

Sutcliffe, Stu

Bass guitarist of the Beatles who left the group in April 1961 to become a painter.

Sutton Place

Surrey, England estate purchased by oil magnate J. Paul Getty in 1959, in which he installed a pay phone for the use of his guests.

Svenska Aeroplan AB

What the letters of automaker Saab stand for, which is Swedish for "Swedish Airplane, Ltd." The company was founded in 1937 as a military aircraft manufacturer.

Swahn, Oscar

*See **64 years, 258 days***

"The Swamp"

Nickname of Gainesville's Ben Hill Griffin Stadium, home of the University of Florida Gators football team, because "only the Gators come out alive."

Nickname of the surgeon's quarters in the TV sitcom *M*A*S*H*.

"The Swamp Fox"

Nickname of Revolutionary War general Francis Marion.

Swan Song Records
Company created by Led Zeppelin to produce its recordings.

Sweathogs
Students in the remedial class taught by the title character (Gabe Kaplan) in the TV sitcom *Welcome Back, Kotter*. The main Sweathogs are:
Vinnie Barbarino (John Travolta)
Juan Epstein (Robert Hegyes)
Freddie "Boom Boom" Washington (Lawrence Hilton-Jacobs)
Arnold Horshack (Ron Palillo)

"Sweden"
What the word "Suède" means in French, from which the name of the fabric is derived.

"The Swedish Nightingale"
Nickname of singer Jenny Lind.

Sweeney, Charles
See **Bock's Car**

Sweet Apple, Ohio
Setting of the musical *Bye Bye Birdie*.

"Sweet babboo"
Sally Brown's term of endearment for Linus Van Pelt in the comic strip *Peanuts*.

"Sweet Baby James"
Nickname of singer James Taylor.

"The sweetest music this side of heaven"
Slogan of Guy Lombardo and the Royal Canadians.

"Sweet Georgia Brown"
Theme song of the Harlem Globetrotters, played during their elaborate warm-up drills.

Sweethaven
Setting of the film *Popeye*.

Sweet Home Farm
Kentucky setting of the Toni Morrison novel *Beloved*.

"Sweet Little Sixteen" locales
This Chuck Berry tune mentions these locations (in order):
Boston
Pittsburgh, Pa.
Texas
Frisco Bay
St. Louis
New Orleans

"Sweetness"
Nickname of pro football Hall of Famer Walter Payton.

"The sweet science"
Nickname of the sport of boxing.

The Sweet Sioux Tomahawk
Trophy awarded to the winning team in the annual football game between Northwestern University and the University of Illinois.

"Sweet Soul Music" subjects
This Arthur Conley "tribute" tune mentions these soul singers (in order):
Lou Rawls
Sam and Dave
Wilson Pickett
Otis Redding
James Brown

Sweet Sue and Her Society Syncopators
See **Seminole-Ritz**

Sweetwater, Arizona
Setting of the TV series *Bret Maverick*.

Swenson
Last name of the title character (Gena Rowlands) in the film *Gloria*.

"Swifty"
Nickname of Hollywood agent Irving Lazar.

S.W.I.N.E.
Abbreviation for the Students Wildly Indignant About Nearly Everything, a radical group in the comic strip *Li'l Abner* in the 1960s.

Swinetrek
See **Hogthrob, Captain Link**

Swine, Wallace
See **Mount Idy**

SWINGER
License plate of the title character's (Mike Myers) red Jaguar XKE in the film *Austin Powers: International Man of Mystery*.

"Swinging on a Star"
Epitaph of songwriter James Van Heusen, who wrote the tune of the same name.

Theme song of the TV sitcom *Out of This World*.

"A Swinging Safari"
First instrumental theme used by the TV game show *The Match Game*, composed by Bert Kaempfert.

"The Switchman"
Debut episode of the TV series *The Sentinel*, which aired on March 20, 1996.

Swithen, John
Pen name used by author Stephen King.

Switzer, Carl
Real name of Alfalfa, child actor in the *Our Gang* film shorts, aka *The Little Rascals*.

Swoosh
Logo of shoe manufacturer Nike.

Swoyer, Ann Myrtle
Real name of actress Nancy Walker.

Sycamore Springs
Hometown of Nick Charles (William Powell) in the *Thin Man* series of films.

Sydenstricker
Middle name of author Pearl S. Buck. Her full maiden name was Pearl Comfort Sydenstricker.

Sykes, Charles
See *The Spirit of Ecstasy*

Sylvania
Country at war with Freedonia in the Marx Brothers film *Duck Soup*.

Symbionese Liberation Army
See **Cinque**

Symbol
Allied code name for the January 1943 conference at Casablanca, Morocco attended by Franklin D. Roosevelt and Winston Churchill.

symphony nicknames
"1905": Shostakovich's #11
"1917": Shostakovich's #12
"The Age of Anxiety": Bernstein's #2
"Afternoon": Haydn's #7
"Alleluia": Haydn's #30
"Antarctica": Vaughan Williams' #7
"Apocalyptic": Bruckner's #7
"Babi-Yar": Shostakovich's #13
"Bear": Haydn's #82
"Chase": Haydn's #73

"Choral": Beethoven's #9
"Classical": Prokofiev's #1
"Clock": Haydn's #101
"Dance": Copland's #1
"Dante": Liszt (unnumbered)
"Drum Roll": Haydn's #103
"Eroica": Beethoven's #3
"Evening": Haydn's #8
"Farewell": Haydn's #45
"Faust": Liszt (unnumbered)
"Fire": Haydn's #59
"First of May": Shostakovich's #3
"The Great": Schubert's #9
"Haffner": Mozart's #35
"Hen": Haydn's #83
"Horn Signal": Haydn's #31
"Imperial": Haydn's #53
"Italian": Mendelssohn's #4
"Jeremiah": Bernstein's #1
"Jupiter": Mozart's #41
"Lamentation": Haydn's #26
"Laudon": Haydn's #69
"Leningrad": Shostakovich's #7
"Linz": Mozart's #36
"Little Russian": Tchaikovsky's #2
"London": Vaughan Williams' #2
"London Symphonies": Haydn's #93–104
"Maria Theresa": Haydn's #48
"Mercury": Haydn's #43
"Military": Haydn's #100
"Miracle": Haydn's #96
"Morning": Haydn's #6
"(From the) New World": Dvořák's #9
"Nordic": Hanson's #1
"October": Shostakovich's #2
"Oxford": Haydn's #92
"Paris": Mozart's #31
"Paris Symphonies": Haydn's #82–87
"Passion": Haydn's #49
"Pastoral": Beethoven's #6, Milhaud's #2, Vaughan Williams' #3
"Philosopher": Haydn's #22
"Polish": Tchaikovsky's #3
"Prague": Mozart's #38
"Pathétique": Tchaikovsky's #6
"Queen": Haydn's #85
"Reformation": Mendelssohn's #5
"Requiem": Hanson's #4
"Resurrection": Mahler's #2
"Rhenish": Schumann's #3
"Romantic": Bruckner's #4, Hanson's #2
"Schoolmaster": Haydn's #55
"Scottish": Mendelssohn's #3
"Sea": Hanson's #7, Vaughan Williams' #1
"Serenade": Milhaud's #3

"Short": Copland's #2
"Spring": Milhaud's #1, Schumann's #1
"Surprise": Haydn's #94
"Symphony of a Thousand": Mahler's #8
"Toy": Haydn (unnumbered)
"Tragic": Haydn's #44, Schubert's #4
"Unfinished": Schubert's #8
"Wagner": Bruckner's #3
"Winter Daydreams": Tchaikovsky's #1

"Syncopated City"

Original title of the George and Ira Gershwin tune "Fascinating Rhythm."

Syncopated Money

Music/business-news radio show hosted by Alex P. Keaton (Michael J. Fox) while at Leland College, in the TV sitcom *Family Ties*.

Synpave Rebound Ace

Hard tennis-court surface used at the Australian Open and other pro tournaments.

Syracuse Nationals

Original name of the Philadelphia 76ers at their NBA inception in 1949. The team took its present name when it moved to Philadelphia in 1963.

Szathmary

Real last name of comedian Bill Dana.

Szemanski

Real last name of the Shubert family of theatrical producers.

T

T-1000
Improved cyborg model in the film *Terminator 2: Judgment Day*, portrayed by Robert Patrick.

Tabei, Junko
First woman to reach the summit of Mount Everest, on May 16, 1975.

Taft Hotel
See **Gladstone, Mr.**

Tait College
Setting of the Broadway musical *Good News*.

"Take it easy, but take it"
Sign-off line of author Studs Terkel on his radio broadcasts.

Takes On Productions
Production company of actress Tracey Ullman.

Talbot
See **Lyle and Talbot; Tiger and Talbot**

"The Talented Husband"
U.S. debut episode of the TV series *The Saint*, which aired on October 4, 1962.

"A Tale of Acadie"
Subtitle of the Henry Wadsworth Longfellow narrative poem *Evangeline*.

"A Tale of the Christ"
Subtitle of the Lew Wallace novel *Ben-Hur*.

"A Tale of the Great Dismal Swamp"
Subtitle of the Harriet Beecher Stowe novel *Dred*.

"A Tale of the Seaboard"
Subtitle of the Joseph Conrad novel *Nostromo*.

Taliaferro
Middle name of educator Booker T. Washington.

Taliesin
Residence of architect Frank Lloyd Wright, built in 1911 in Spring Green, Wisconsin. It was named for

a poet from Welsh mythology, whose name means "shining brow" in English.

Taliesin West
Scottsdale, Arizona winter home and workshop of architect Frank Lloyd Wright, which was designed by him.

Talkartoons
First cartoons of pioneer animator Max Fleischer, which marked the debut of Fleischer creation Betty Boop circa 1930.

Talking It Over
Syndicated newspaper column of Hillary Rodham Clinton.

Tall, Dark and Gruesome
1977 autobiography of horror-film star Christopher Lee.

Tamba
Chimpanzee sidekick of the title character (Johnny Weissmuller) in the children's TV series *Jungle Jim*.

Tana Supreme
Brand of gasoline sold at Grace's Diner in the film *Bus Stop*.

Tango
Horse of Captain Christopher Pike (Jeffrey Hunter) in the TV series *Star Trek*.

Tania
Name taken by Patricia Hearst as a member of the Symbionese Liberation Army, the radical group that kidnapped her in 1974.

Tanner III, Edward Everett
Real name of Patrick Dennis, author of the novel *Auntie Mame*.

Tao House
Home of playwright Eugene O'Neill in Danville, California.

Taprobane
Ancient Roman name for Sri Lanka.

Taratupa

Pacific island setting of the TV sitcom *McHale's Navy*.

TARDIS

Acronym for "Time and Relative Dimension in Space," the time-and-space-travel machine of the title character in the British TV series *Dr. Who*.

Target

Horse of the title character (Gail Davis) in the TV Western series *Annie Oakley*.

"Tar Heel"

See **United States residents' nicknames**

Tarker's Mills, Maine

Setting of the Stephen King novel *Cycle of the Werewolf*.

Tarnmoor, Salvator R.

Pen name used by author Herman Melville.

tarot cards

MAJOR ARCANA (22)

The Chariot
Death
The Devil
The Emperor
The Empress
The Fool
The Hanged Man
The Hermit
The Hierophant (interpreter of sacred mysteries)
The High Priestess
Judgement [sic]
Justice
The Lovers
The Magician
The Moon
The Star
Strength
The Sun
Temperance
The Tower
Wheel of Fortune
The World

CUPS (14)

Ace, 2 through 10, Page, Knight, Queen, King

PENTACLES (14)

Ace, 2 through 10, Page, Knight, Queen, King

SWORDS (14)

Ace, 2 through 10, Page, Knight, Queen, King

WANDS (14)

Ace, 2 through 10, Page, Knight, Queen, King

"Tar Paper Stomp"

Original title of the tune "In the Mood."

Tarpley, Brenda Mae

Real name of pop singer Brenda Lee.

"Tarzan"

Nickname of Olympic pole-vault star Don Bragg.

Tarzan/Weissmuller films

Tarzan films starring Johnny Weissmuller in the title role:
Tarzan the Ape Man (1932)
Tarzan and His Mate (1934)
Tarzan Escapes (1936)
Tarzan Finds a Son! (1939)
Tarzan's Secret Treasure (1941)
Tarzan's New York Adventure (1942)
Tarzan Triumphs (1943)
Tarzan's Desert Mystery (1943)
Tarzan and the Amazons (1945)
Tarzan and the Leopard Woman (1946)
Tarzan and the Huntress (1947)
Tarzan and the Mermaids (1948)

Tashmore Lake, Maine

Setting of the Stephen King novella *Secret Window, Secret Garden*.

"Tastes great, less filling"

Advertising slogan of Miller Lite beer.

Tatis, Fernando

St. Louis Cardinal who became the first major leaguer to hit two grand-slam home runs in one inning, on April 23, 1999.

Tatooine

Planet on which Luke Skywalker (Mark Hamill) grew up, in the *Star Wars* films.

tauromachy

Technical term for bullfighting.

Taylor, Brother

Preacher in the Bobbie Gentry tune "Ode to Billie Joe."

Taylor/Burton films

The films in which Elizabeth Taylor and Richard Burton appear together:
Cleopatra (1963)
The V.I.P.s (1963)
The Sandpiper (1965)
Who's Afraid of Virginia Woolf? (1966)
The Taming of the Shrew (1967)

Doctor Faustus (1967)
The Comedians (1967)
Boom! (1968)
Anne of the Thousand Days (1969)*
Hammersmith Is Out (1972)
Under Milk Wood (1973)
* Taylor has a cameo role in this film

Taylor, Elizabeth, husbands of

Nicky Hilton (married 1950, divorced 1951)
Michael Wilding (married 1952, divorced 1957)
Michael Todd (married 1957, died 1958)
Eddie Fisher (married 1959, divorced 1964)
Richard Burton (married 1964, divorced 1974)
Richard Burton (married 1975, divorced 1976)
John Warner (married 1976, divorced 1982)
Larry Fortensky (married 1991, divorced 1996)

T-Birds

Danny Zuko's (John Travolta's) gang in the film *Grease.*

TCB

Letters on the gold pendant worn by Elvis Presley, which stand for "Taking care of business."

Tea Biscuit

Racehorse unwittingly stolen by Grover Mockridge and Wilbur Hoolihan (Abbott and Costello) in the film *It Ain't Hay.*

Teach, Edward

See **Queen Anne's Revenge**

Teatro Alla Scala

Full name of La Scala opera house in Milan, Italy, which means "theater at the stairway."

Technical Hierarchy for the Removal of Undesirables and the Subjugation of Humanity

Full name of THRUSH, evil organization in the TV series *The Man from U.N.C.L.E.*

Tech Noir

Disco that is the scene of a shootout in the film *The Terminator.*

Techtronics

Satellite-manufacturing company owned by Willard Whyte (Jimmy Dean) in the James Bond film *Diamonds Are Forever.*

Tee Hee

"Right hand" man of Mr. Big (Yaphet Kotto) in the James Bond film *Live and Let Die*, portrayed by Julian Harris. He has a mechanical substitute for his right hand, which he lost to a crocodile.

Teena, Brandon/Brandon, Teena

Role for which Hilary Swank won a Best Actress Academy Award (as a girl masquerading as a boy) in the 1999 film *Boys Don't Cry.*

Teenage Mutant Ninja Turtles

Quartet of pizza-loving comic-book heroes named for Italian Renaissance artists, created by Kevin Eastman and Peter Laird in 1983. They debuted on syndicated television in 1987.
Donatello
Leonardo
Michaelangelo (spelled differently from Michelangelo the artist)
Raphael

teeth of mammals

The normal number of teeth of a representative selection of adult mammals:

0	echidna, platypus
6	elephant (including the two tusks, which are actually elongated incisors)
16	muskrat
18	walrus
20	beaver, aardvark
22	groundhog, prairie dog, squirrel
28	rabbit
30	"big cats" (lion, tiger)
32	chimpanzee, giraffe, human
34	elk, mink, skunk
36	otter
42	canines (dog, fox, wolf)
40	raccoon
42	bear
44	pig

"The Teeth of the Barracuda"

Debut episode of the TV series *The Mod Squad*, which aired on September 24, 1968.

Teichman

Real last name of dance instructor Arthur Murray.

Tejada

Real last name of actress Raquel Welch.

See also **Wong Airline**

Tektel Systems

Washington, D.C., "front" employer of federal agent Harry Tasker (Arnold Schwarzenegger) in the film *True Lies.*

Telegrafnoye Agentsvo Sovietskavo Soyuza

What the acronym of former Soviet news agency TASS stands for, which is Russian for "Telegraph Agency of the Soviet Union."

Telemovies

The first pay TV service, launched in Bartlesville, Oklahoma, in October 1957. It offered 11 hours of first-run movies for $9.50 per month. A similar service had been previously tested in Palm Springs, California, in 1953.

The Telephone Trophy

Trophy awarded to the winning team in the annual football game between Iowa State University and the University of Missouri.

Telestrator

Electronic device used by TV sportscasters to draw directly over the action when showing an instant replay.

Teletouch Drive

Innovative automatic transmission gearshift of the Edsel automobile, which consisted of push buttons at the center of the steering wheel.

Tell Me Darling

Play starring Neely O'Hara (Patty Duke) in the film *Valley of the Dolls*.

"Tell Me What You FEEL" "Tell Me What You WANT"

Book written by psychiatrist Isaac Sobol (Bill Macy), father of psychiatrist Ben Sobol (Billy Crystal) in the film *analyze this*.

"Tell ya what I'm gonna do!"

Catchphrase of pitchman/comedian Sid Stone on *Texaco Star Theater*, aka *The Milton Berle Show*.

Tempered Blade

Novel by Monte Barrett that was the basis for the TV Western series *The Adventures of Jim Bowie*.

Templar, Simon

See The Saint films

Templeton

Rat friend of the title character in the E. B. White children's book *Charlotte's Web*.

Tempo

Secret Service code name for Laura Bush.

Temptations original members

Elbridge Bryant, Melvin Franklin, Eddie Kendricks, Otis Williams, and Paul Williams.

Tennenbaum

Real last name of author Irving Stone.

"The Tennessee Plowboy"

Nickname of country singer Eddy Arnold.

"The Tenth Satire of Juvenal Imitated"

Subtitle of the Samuel Johnson poem "The Vanity of Human Wishes."

"tentmaker"

What the word "Khayyám" means in Persian.

Terence

Real first name of actor Steve McQueen.

Terence Hanbury

First and middle names of writer T. H. White.

Tereshkova, Valentina

Russian cosmonaut who was the first woman in space. Her *Vostok 6* spacecraft, launched on June 16, 1963, completed 48 Earth orbits before landing on June 19.

Terminal

Allied code name for the "Big Three" (Harry S Truman, Winston Churchill/Clement Attlee, Joseph Stalin) conference at Potsdam, Germany, in 1945.

"The Terminator"

Nickname of baseball relief pitcher Jeff Reardon.

Terminus

Planet that is home to the Encyclopedia Foundation in Isaac Asimov's *Foundation Trilogy*.

"Termite Terrace"

Nickname of the group of buildings that housed the animation unit of Warner Bros. from 1935 to 1955.

Terra V

Spaceship commanded by Buzz Corry (Ed Kemmer) in the children's TV series *Space Patrol*.

"Terras irradient"

Motto of Amherst College, which is Latin for "Let them illuminate the earth."

Terrytown

Home of cartoon superhero Mighty Mouse.

Terwillinger College

Alma mater of the title character in the Sinclair Lewis novel *Elmer Gantry*.

terylene

See **Dickson, J. T. and Winfield, John R.**

Teschmacher, Eve

Girlfriend of Lex Luthor (Gene Hackman) in the film *Superman*, portrayed by Valerie Perrine.

Tess

What they call "the rain" in the Lerner and Loewe tune "They Call the Wind Maria."

Testorf, Helga

Subject of the "Helga pictures," a series of over 200 pencil drawings, watercolors and works in tempera created by Andrew Wyeth from 1971 to 1985.

Tet

Pet dog of Stringfellow Hawke (Jan-Michael Vincent) in the TV series *Airwolf*.

Tetch, Jervis

Real name of Batman adversary The Mad Hatter.

Tetiaroa

1,600-acre atoll near Tahiti owned by actor Marlon Brando.

"The Teutonic Titwillow"

Nickname of Lili Von Shtupp (Madeline Kahn) in the film *Blazing Saddles*.

Texas Theater

Dallas theater outside which Lee Harvey Oswald was arrested on November 22, 1963, for the assassination of President John F. Kennedy.

"The Texas Troubadour"

Nickname of country singer Ernest Tubb.

Thaddeus

First name of the Chief of CONTROL (Edward Platt) in the TV sitcom *Get Smart*. His last name is never revealed.

"Thank heaven for"

Epitaph of songwriter Frederick Loewe, who wrote the tune "Thank Heaven for Little Girls."

"Thanks"

Word printed on the back of the guitar of country singer Ernest Tubb, which he would flip over after a song to acknowledge applause.

"Thanks for the Memory"

Oscar-winning song that became the theme of Bob Hope. It was introduced by Hope and Shirley Ross in the film *The Big Broadcast of 1938*, Hope's feature film debut.

"Thanks to you, it works"

Advertising slogan of the United Way.

"Thank you for your support"

Closing line of the folksy 1980s TV commercials for Bartles & Jaymes wine coolers.

"That's a joke, son!"

Catchphrase of Senator Beauregard Claghorn (Kenny Delmar) on Fred Allen's radio show. Claghorn was the inspiration for the Warner Bros. cartoon character Foghorn Leghorn, who used the same catchphrase.

"That's all folks"

Epitaph of cartoon voicemaster Mel Blanc.

"That's Rich!"

Advertising slogan for Nestle's 100 Grand candy bar.

"That's right, you're wrong!"

Catchphrase of Kay Kyser in the radio game show *Kay Kyser's Kollege of Musical Knowledge*. He used the phrase to indicate a "correct" response to a true-false question, where contestants were required to give the wrong answer. If a contestant gave the "wrong" correct answer, Kyser said, "That's wrong, you're right!"

Thayer, Ethel

Role for which Katharine Hepburn won a Best Actress Academy Award in the 1981 film *On Golden Pond*.

Thayer Jr., Norman

Role for which Henry Fonda won a Best Actor Academy Award in the 1981 film *On Golden Pond*.

Thelma

Real first name of actress Butterfly McQueen.

Real first name of Trixie Norton (Joyce Randolph) in the TV sitcom *The Honeymooners*.

thenar

Medical term for the fleshy masses of muscle at the base of the thumb and the outer side of the palm of the hand.

"Then Came You"

Theme song of the TV sitcom *Webster*.

Theopolis, Dr.
Talking computer in the TV series *Buck Rogers in the 25th Century*.

There and Back Again
Alternate title of the J. R. R. Tolkien novel *The Hobbit*.

"There's a New Girl in Town"
Theme song of the TV sitcom *Alice*, performed by series star Linda Lavin.

Thérèse
First name of Madame Defarge in the Charles Dickens novel *A Tale of Two Cities*.

These Friends of Mine
Original title of the TV sitcom *Ellen*.

"They finished their job—let's finish ours!"
Slogan used to promote the sale of U.S. Victory Bonds after World War II.

"They make money the old-fashioned way . . . they earn it"
Advertising slogan of investment firm Smith Barney, spoken in TV commercials by John Houseman and Leo McKern.

Thibault, Jacques-Anatole-François
Real name of author Anatole France.

"A Thief Is a Thief"
Debut episode of the TV series *It Takes a Thief*, which aired on January 9, 1968.

"The Thief of Bad Gags"
Nickname of comedian Milton Berle, because of his reputation for using other comedians' material.

"Think God"
Slogan created by Tracy (Louanne) for the title character (George Burns) in the film *Oh, God! Book II*.

"Thinking of You"
Theme song of bandleader Kay Kyser.

"Think of it as money"
Advertising slogan of Bank Americard.

Thin Man films
Series based on the Dashiell Hammett novel *The Thin Man*, starring William Powell and Myrna Loy as Nick and Nora Charles:
The Thin Man (1934)
After the Thin Man (1936)
Another Thin Man (1939)
Shadow of the Thin Man (1941)
The Thin Man Goes Home (1944)
Song of the Thin Man (1947)

"This Bird Has Flown"
Subtitle of the Beatles tune "Norwegian Wood."

"This Can't Be Yogurt!!"
See **Hickingbotham, Frank D.**

"This . . . is London"
Opening line of Edward R. Murrow's memorable CBS broadcasts during World War II.

"This is not goodbye, this is just good night"
Sign-off line of pioneer rock-and-roll deejay Alan Freed.

"This time, it's REALLY REALLY personal"
Slogan for the 2015 film *Jaws 19*, playing at a Hill Valley theater in the film *Back to the Future Part II*. The *Jaws* film is directed by Max Spielberg, real-life son of Steven Spielberg.

"This we'll defend"
Motto of the U.S. Army.

Thode, Earl
Winner of the first pro rodeo All-Around Champion Cowboy competition in 1929.

Thomas
Real first name of President (Thomas) Woodrow Wilson.

Thomas, Bigger
Title character of the Richard Wright novel *Native Son*.

Thomas, Elton
Pen name used by actor Douglas Fairbanks Sr. for the film scripts he wrote.

Thomas Hewitt Edward
First and middle names of the title character (Robert Loggia) in the TV series *T. H. E. Cat*.

Thomas Jefferson
See **Harrison**

Thomas Jonathan
Real first and middle names of Civil War Confederate general Stonewall Jackson.

Thomas Lanier

Real first and middle names of playwright Tennessee Williams.

Thompson, Ernest

Author of the play *On Golden Pond*, upon which the film of the same name was based.

Thompson seedless

Variety of grapes used for producing raisins.

Thorkelson

Real last name of singer Peter Tork of the Monkees.

Thornapple, Brutus P.

Title character of the comic strip *The Born Loser*.

Thornfield

English estate where the title character is employed as a governess, in the Charlotte Brontë novel *Jane Eyre*.

Thorn, Trooper

Name used by Sean Thornton (John Wayne) as a professional boxer, in the film *The Quiet Man*.

Thorp, Roderick

See Nothing Lasts Forever

"Those Were the Days"

Opening theme song of the TV sitcom *All in the Family*, performed by series stars Carroll O'Connor and Jean Stapleton.

Those Who Care

Soap opera in which Dick Preston (Dick Van Dyke) stars as Dr. Brad Fairmont, in the TV sitcom *The New Dick Van Dyke Show*.

"Three Bells to Perdido"

Debut episode of the TV Western series *Have Gun Will Travel*, which aired on September 14, 1957.

"three diamonds"

What the name of Japanese conglomerate Mitsubishi means in Japanese. The company's logo consists of three diamonds.

Three Oaks Medical Center

Employer of the title character (Alan Bunce, Carl Frank, Charles Irving, Sandy Becker) in the radio soap opera *Young Dr. Malone*.

"three oceans"

What the name of electronics company Sanyo means in Japanese.

"three stars"

What the name of Seoul-based electronics company Samsung means in Korean.

"Three Stars Will Shine Tonight"

Theme song of the TV series *Dr. Kildare*.

Three Stooges' real names

> Moe Howard: Moses Horwitz
> Larry Fine: Louis Feinberg
> Curly Howard: Jerome Lester Horwitz
> Shemp Howard: Samuel Horwitz
> Joe Besser: Jerome Besser
> Joe DeRita: Joseph Wardell

The Three Tenors

Collective name of opera stars José Carreras, Plácido Domingo, and Luciano Pavarotti, for the recordings and tours they have done together.

Three Thousand

Original working title of the film *Pretty Woman*.

Thrift, Jane Angelica

Real name of Wrangler Jane (Melody Patterson) in the TV sitcom *F Troop*.

"Thrilla in Manila"

Nickname of the heavyweight championship fight between Muhammad Ali and Joe Frazier in Manila on October 1, 1975. Ali won by TKO in the 14th round.

Throttlebottom, Alexander

Vice president of the United States in the George and Ira Gershwin musical *Of Thee I Sing*.

THRUSH

See **Technical Hierarchy for the Removal of Undesirables and the Subjugation of Humanity**

Thrushcross Grange

Farm rented by Mr. Lockwood from Heathcliff in the Emily Brontë novel *Wuthering Heights*.

Thule

Kingdom of which the title character is the lost heir, in the comic strip *Prince Valiant*.

Thumper

Rabbit friend of the title character in the Disney animated film *Bambi*.

See also **Bambi and Thumper**

Thunderhead

Boys' camp near the girls' Camp Inch in the Disney film *The Parent Trap* (1961).

The Thundering Herd

Band led by Woody Herman.

"The Thundering Herd"

Nickname of investment firm Merrill Lynch.

Thurlowe

Middle name of Ensign Frank Pulver (Jack Lemmon) in the film *Mister Roberts*.

Thurlowe, Kate

Role for which Jo Van Fleet won a Best Supporting Actress Academy Award in the 1955 film *East of Eden*.

Thursday, Philadelphia

Shirley Temple's role in the film *Fort Apache*.

THX 138

License plate of the yellow Deuce Coupe owned by John Milner (Paul LeMat) in the film *American Graffiti*, the second film directed by George Lucas. The first film directed by Lucas was *THX 1138*.

Tibbets, Paul

See Enola Gay

Tiberius

Middle name of Captain James T. Kirk (William Shatner) in *Star Trek*.

Middle name of Woodrow "Woody" Boyd (Woody Harrelson) in the TV series *Cheers*.

tibia

Medical term for the shinbone.

ticker-tape parade honorees

Over 150 ticker-tape parades have been held in Manhattan's "Canyon of Heroes" on lower Broadway since 1886. This list omits certain honorees (such as some foreign heads of state) whose names would be unfamiliar to most people today:

October 29, 1886 Dedication of the Statue of Liberty

April 29, 1889 Centenary of the inauguration of George Washington

September 30, 1899 Return from Manila of Admiral George Dewey

June 18, 1910 Return from African safari of Theodore Roosevelt

September 8, 1919 General John J. Pershing, commander of the American Expeditionary Force

November 18, 1919 Edward, Prince of Wales (later known as the Duke of Windsor)

October 28, 1921 Ferdinand Foch, marshal of France

October 5, 1923 David Lloyd George, British prime minister

August 6, 1924 American Olympic athletes

June 23, 1926 flight of Richard E. Byrd and Floyd Bennett over the North Pole

July 2, 1926 Bobby Jones, winner of the British Open golf tournament

August 27, 1926 Gertrude Ederle, first woman to swim across the English Channel

June 13, 1927 Solo transatlantic flight of Charles Lindbergh

July 18, 1927 Transatlantic flight of Richard E. Byrd and the crew of the *America*

August 22, 1928 American Olympic athletes

July 6, 1928 Amelia Earhart, aviator

July 18, 1930 Expedition to Antarctica by Richard E. Byrd

July 2, 1930 Bobby Jones, winner of the British Open golf tournament

July 2, 1931 Flight around the world of Wiley Post and Harold Gatty

October 22, 1931 Pierre Laval, premier of France

June 20, 1932 Transatlantic flight of Amelia Earhart

July 26, 1933 Flight around the world in eight days by Wiley Post

July 15, 1938 Flight around the world in three days by Howard Hughes

August 5, 1938 Flight from New York City to Ireland by Douglas "Wrong Way" Corrigan

June 19, 1945 General Dwight D. Eisenhower, commander of the Allied Expeditionary Force

August 27, 1945 General Charles de Gaulle of France

September 14, 1945 General Jonathan Wainwright, hero of Corregidor

October 9, 1945 Fleet Admiral Chester Nimitz

October 27, 1945 President Harry S Truman

December 14, 1945 Fleet Admiral William S. Halsey

March 15, 1946 British prime minister Winston Churchill

March 19, 1948 Eamon de Valera, prime minister of Ireland

August 19, 1949 Connie Mack, 50th year as manager of the Philadelphia Athletics baseball team

October 17, 1949 Jawaharlal Nehru, prime minister of India

April 20, 1951 General Douglas MacArthur

May 9, 1951 David Ben-Gurion, prime minister of Israel

July 7, 1952 American Olympic athletes

July 21, 1953 Ben Hogan, winner of the British Open golf tournament

June 1, 1954 Haile Selassie, emperor of Ethiopia

August 2, 1954 Syngman Rhee, president of South Korea

September 27, 1954 New York Giants, winners of the National League pennant

May 23, 1956 Sukarno, president of Indonesia

May 13, 1957 Ngo Dinh Diem, president of South Vietnam

July 11, 1957 Althea Gibson, winner of the Wimbledon women's singles championship

October 21, 1957 Queen Elizabeth II of the United Kingdom

May 20, 1958 Van Cliburn, winner of the Moscow International Tchaikovsky Piano Competition

February 10, 1959 Willy Brandt, mayor of West Berlin

May 29, 1959 King Baudouin of Belgium

September 11, 1959 Princess Beatrix of the Netherlands

March 9, 1960 Carol Heiss, Winter Olympics figure skating champion

April 26, 1960 Charles de Gaulle, president of France

October 19, 1960 John F. Kennedy, Democratic presidential nominee

November 2, 1960 President Dwight D. Eisenhower and vice president Richard Nixon

April 10, 1961 New York Yankees, winners of the American League pennant

March 1, 1962 John Glenn, first American to orbit the Earth

April 9, 1962 New York Yankees, winners of the 1961 World Series

April 12, 1962 New York Mets' entry into the National League

April 16, 1962 The Shah of Iran and Empress Farah

June 5, 1962 M. Scott Carpenter, second American to orbit the Earth

June 8, 1962 Archbishop Makarios of Cyprus

May 22, 1963 L. Gordon Cooper, astronaut

October 4, 1963 Haile Selassie, emperor of Ethiopia

March 29, 1965 Virgil I. Grissom and John Young, *Gemini 3* astronauts

May 19, 1965 Chung Hee Park, president of South Korea

January 10, 1969 Frank Borman, William Anders and James Lovell, *Apollo 8* astronauts

August 13, 1969 Buzz Aldrin, Neil Armstrong and Michael Collins, *Apollo 11* astronauts

October 20, 1969 New York Mets, winners of the World Series

October 19, 1978 New York Yankees, winners of the World Series

October 3, 1979 Pope John Paul II

January 30, 1981 The American hostages released from Iran

August 15, 1984 American Olympic medalists

May 7, 1985 Vietnam War veterans

October 28, 1986 New York Mets, winners of the World Series

June 20, 1990 Nelson Mandela of South Africa

June 10, 1991 Persian Gulf War veterans

June 25, 1991 Korean War veterans

June 17, 1994 New York Rangers, winners of the Stanley Cup

October 29, 1996 New York Yankees, winners of the World Series

October 17, 1998 Sammy Sosa, baseball player

October 23, 1998 New York Yankees, winners of the World Series

November 16, 1998 John Glenn, U.S. senator and space-shuttle astronaut

October 29, 1999 New York Yankees, winners of the World Series

October 30, 2000 New York Yankees, winners of the World Series

ticker-tape parades, multiple honorees

SEVEN (1)

New York Yankees (1961, 1962, 1978, 1996, 1998, 1999, 2000)

THREE (2)

Richard E. Byrd (1926, 1927, 1930)
New York Mets (1962, 1969, 1986)

TWO (7)

Charles de Gaulle (1945, 1960)
Amelia Earhart (1928, 1932)
Dwight D. Eisenhower (1945, 1960)
John Glenn (1962, 1998)
Haile Selassie (1954, 1963)
Bobby Jones (1926, 1930)
Wiley Post (1931, 1933)

Tick-Licker

Favorite rifle of Daniel Boone.

Tide Rips

Yearbook of the U.S. Coast Guard Academy.

Tidwell, Rod

Role for which Cuba Gooding Jr. won a Best Supporting Actor Academy Award in the 1996 film *Jerry Maguire*.

"The ties that bind the lives of our people in one indissoluble union are perpetuated in the archives of our government, and to their custody this building is dedicated"

Inscription over the entrance of the National Archives in Washington, D.C.

Tiger

Family sheepdog in the TV sitcom *The Brady Bunch*.

Family sheepdog in the TV sitcom *The Patty Duke Show*.

See also **Blackie, Bounder, and Tiger**

"The Tiger"

Nickname of World War I–era French prime minister Georges Clemenceau.

Tiger and Talbot

Pet dogs of Sir Ector (voiced by Sebastian Cabot) in the Disney animated film *The Sword in the Stone*.

Tiki

Yacht captained by Adam Troy (Gardner McKay) in the TV series *Adventures in Paradise*.

Tilbury Town

Setting of the Edward Arlington Robinson poems "Richard Cory" and "Miniver Cheevy."

Tilley, Eustace

Foppish cartoon character often on the cover of *The New Yorker* magazine.

Timber Hill, Montana

Hometown of Bo Decker (Don Murray) in the film *Bus Stop*.

Timberwolf

Secret Service code name for George H. W. Bush.

"Time and Relative Dimension in Space"

See **TARDIS**

time intervals

horal: hourly
semidiurnal: twice a day
diurnal: daily
triweekly: three times a week (or every three weeks)
semiweekly: twice a week
biweekly: twice a week (or every two weeks)
weekly: once a week
semimonthly: twice a month
bimonthly: twice a month (or every two months)
monthly: once a month
trimonthly, quarterly: every three months
semiannual, semiyearly: twice a year
biannual: twice a year (or every two years)
annual: once a year
biennial: every two years
triennial: every three years
quadrennial: every four years
quinquennial: every five years
sexennial: every six years
septennial: every seven years
octennial: every eight years
novennial: every nine years
decennial: every ten years
undecennial: every 11 years
duodecennial: every 12 years
quindecennial: every 15 years
vicennial: every 20 years
tricennial: every 30 years
semicentennial: every 50 years
centennial: every 100 years
sesquicentennial: every 150 years
bicentennial: every 200 years
tricentennial: every 300 years
quadricentennial: every 400 years
quincentennial: every 500 years
millennial: every 1,000 years
bimillennial: every 2,000 years

Time magazine's Man/Person of the Year

1927 Charles Lindbergh
1928 Walter P. Chrysler
1929 Owen Young (industrialist/diplomat)
1930 Mahatma Gandhi
1931 Pierre Laval
1932 Franklin D. Roosevelt
1933 Hugh Johnson (National Recovery Administration)
1934 Franklin D. Roosevelt
1935 Haile Selassie
1936 Wallis Warfield Simpson
1937 General and Mme. Chiang Kai-shek
1938 Adolf Hitler
1939 Joseph Stalin
1940 Winston Churchill
1941 Franklin D. Roosevelt
1942 Joseph Stalin
1943 George C. Marshall
1944 Dwight D. Eisenhower
1945 Harry S Truman
1946 James F. Byrnes

1947 George C. Marshall
1948 Harry S Truman
1949 Winston Churchill
1950 The American Fighting Man
1951 Mohammed Mossadegh (Premier of Iran)
1952 Queen Elizabeth II
1953 Konrad Adenauer
1954 John Foster Dulles
1955 Harlow Curtice (president of General Motors)
1956 Hungarian Freedom Fighter
1957 Nikita Khrushchev
1958 Charles de Gaulle
1959 Dwight D. Eisenhower
1960 15 American scientists: George Beadle (geneticist); Charles Draper (engineer); John Enders (virologist); Donald Glaser (physicist); Joshua Lederberg (biologist); Willard Libby (chemist); Linus Pauling (chemist); Edward Purcell (physicist); I. I. Rabi (physicist); Emilio Segre (physicist); William Shockley (physicist); Edward Teller (physicist); Charles Townes (physicist); James Van Allen (physicist); Robert Woodward (chemist)
1961 John F. Kennedy
1962 Pope John XXIII
1963 Martin Luther King, Jr.
1964 Lyndon Johnson
1965 William Westmoreland
1966 Man and woman, 25 years old and younger
1967 Lyndon Johnson
1968 William Anders, Frank Borman, and James Lovell
1969 Middle Americans
1970 Willy Brandt
1971 Richard Nixon
1972 Richard Nixon and Henry Kissinger
1973 John Sirica
1974 King Faisal
1975 12 American women: Susan Brownmiller (author); Kathleen Byerly (naval officer); Alison Cheek (priest); Jill Ker Conway (college president); Betty Ford (first lady); Ella Grasso (Governor of Connecticut); Carla Hills (HUD Secretary); Barbara Jordan (Texas congresswoman); Billie Jean King (athlete); Susie Sharp (North Carolina jurist); Carol Sutton (newspaper editor); Addie Wyatt (labor leader)
1976 Jimmy Carter
1977 Anwar Sadat
1978 Deng Xiaoping
1979 Ayatollah Khomeini
1980 Ronald Reagan

1981 Lech Walesa
1982 The Computer
1983 Ronald Reagan and Yuri Andropov
1984 Peter Ueberroth
1985 Deng Xiaoping
1986 Corazon Aquino
1987 Mikhail Gorbachev
1988 Endangered Earth
1989 Mikhail Gorbachev (named Man of the Decade)
1990 George H. W. Bush
1991 Ted Turner
1992 Bill Clinton
1993 The Peacemakers: Yitzhak Rabin, Yasser Arafat; F. W. de Klerk; Nelson Mandela
1994 Pope John Paul II
1995 Newt Gingrich
1996 Dr. David Ho (AIDS researcher)
1997 Andy Grove (Intel CEO)
1998 Bill Clinton and Kenneth Starr
1999 Jeffrey Bezos (Amazon.com CEO)
2000 George W. Bush

Time magazine's Man/Person of the Year, multiple winners

THREE (1)
Franklin D. Roosevelt (1932, 1934, 1941)

Two (11)
Winston Churchill (1940, 1949)
Bill Clinton (1992, 1998)
Deng Xiaoping (1978, 1985)
Dwight D. Eisenhower (1944, 1959)
Mikhail Gorbachev (1987, 1989)
Lyndon Johnson (1964, 1967)
George C. Marshall (1943, 1947)
Richard Nixon (1971, 1972)
Ronald Reagan (1980, 1983)
Joseph Stalin (1939, 1942)
Harry S Truman (1945, 1948)

"Time to re-tire"
Advertising slogan of Fisk auto tires.

Timon
Meerkat friend (voiced by Nathan Lane) of the title character (voiced by Matthew Broderick) in the Disney animated film *The Lion King*.

Timothy Q. Mouse
Friend of the title character in the Disney animated film *Dumbo*.

tinea pedis
Medical term for athlete's foot.

Tineff

Albert Einstein's sailboat, which he used circa 1938 at his summer home in Long Island, New York. The name is a Yiddish word meaning "worthless."

Tinka Tonka

Indian tribe of Princess Summerfall Winterspring (Judy Tyler) in the children's TV series *Howdy Doody*.

Tinky Winky, Dipsy, Laa-Laa, and Po

Title characters of the children's TV series *Teletubbies*.

"The Tin Star"

Short story by John W. Cunningham that was the basis for the film *High Noon*.

TIPC Network

Original name of computer retailer Gateway.

"Tippecanoe and Tyler too"

Slogan of Whig candidate William Henry Harrison in the presidential campaign of 1840.

Tippy

"Wonder dog" in the comedy routines of Bob and Ray.

Tipton Grange

Home of Dorothea and Celia Brooke in the George Eliot novel *Middlemarch*.

Tirtoff, Romain de

Real name of Art Deco artist Erté.

Titans

Original nickname of the New York Jets at their AFL inception in 1960. The team took its present name in 1963.

tittle

Term for the dot on an i, in an umlaut, or in other printed characters.

"Tivoli Melody"

Original title of the Lawrence Welk tune "Calcutta," which reached #1 on the U.S. *Billboard* pop chart in 1961.

TM-Bar Ranch

Home of Tom Mix in his Western radio series.

T negative

Blood type of Mr. Spock (Leonard Nimoy) in the TV series *Star Trek*.

"To Alexander Woollcott, for reasons that are nobody's business"

Dedication line of the Kaufman and Hart play *The Man Who Came to Dinner*. The title character of the play, Sheridan Whiteside, is based on Woollcott.

"To Anacreon in Heaven"

English drinking song that was used by Francis Scott Key as the melody for "The Star-Spangled Banner."

"The Toastmaster General"

Nickname of entertainer George Jessel, for his many appearances as a banquet master of ceremonies.

Toast of the Town

Original name of the TV variety series *The Ed Sullivan Show* when it debuted on June 20, 1948. Guest stars on the first show included the comedy team of Dean Martin and Jerry Lewis, singing fireman John Kokoman, pianist Eugene List, dancer Kathryn Lee, songwriters Rodgers and Hammerstein, comedian Lee Goodman, fight referee Ruby Goldstein, and the dancing troupe The Toastettes.

To Be or Not to Bop

1979 autobiography of bebop jazz trumpeter Dizzy Gillespie.

Tobias, Sarah

Role for which Jodie Foster won a Best Actress Academy Award in the 1988 film *The Accused*.

Tobias Vincent

Real first and middle names of actor Tobey Maguire.

Toby

Childhood pet dog of Jo Harding (Helen Hunt) in the film *Twister*.

Today's World

Magazine employer of Doris Martin (Doris Day) in the TV sitcom *The Doris Day Show*.

"The Toe of the Boot"

Nickname of the Calabria region of Italy.

"Together Through the Years"

Theme song of the TV sitcom *The Hogan Family*, performed by Roberta Flack.

Toguri, Iva Ikoku

See **Orphan Ann**

Tokyo Denkikagaku Kogyo

What the letters in the name of Japanese electronics manufacturer TDK stand for, which is Japanese for "Tokyo Electronic Science Production."

Tokyo Tsushin Denki

Original name of the Sony Corporation.

"To learn, to search, to serve"

Motto of the State University of New York.

"To Make the Best Better"

Motto of the 4-H Club.

Tomaling

Maiden name of actress Susan Sarandon, whose former husband was actor Chris Sarandon.

Tom and Jerry

Stage name used by Simon and Garfunkel early in their careers.

Tomania

Country ruled by Adenoid Hynkel (Charlie Chaplin) in the film *The Great Dictator*.

Tomasi, Rollo

Name created by Ed Exley (Guy Pearce) for the unknown murderer of his father, in the film *L.A. Confidential*.

Tombaugh, Clyde

Astronomer who discovered the planet Pluto in 1930.

Tomkins Corners

Home of the title character (Shirley Bell, Janice Gilbert) in the children's radio series *Little Orphan Annie*.

Tom Landry Middle School

School attended by Bobby Hill (voiced by Pamela Segall) in the animated TV sitcom *King of the Hill*.

Tommy

Boyfriend of the title character in the Ray Peterson tune "Tell Laura I Love Her."

Tomorrow

Magazine employer of Tom Corbett (Bill Bixby) in the TV sitcom *The Courtship of Eddie's Father*.

Tabloid newspaper owned by Elliot Carver (Jonathan Pryce) in the James Bond film *Tomorrow Never Dies*.

Tomorrow Is Another Day

Original working title of the Margaret Mitchell novel *Gone With the Wind*.

Tompkins, Samuel Yewell

Real name of actor Tom Ewell.

Tom Swift book series

The Tom Swift character was conceived by Edward Stratemeyer, whose company contracted with various authors to write the individual books. The original series consists of these 40 novels:

Tom Swift and His Motor Cycle (1910)
Tom Swift and His Motor Boat (1910)
Tom Swift and His Airship (1910)
Tom Swift and His Submarine Boat (1910)
Tom Swift and His Electric Runabout (1910)
Tom Swift and His Wireless Message (1911)
Tom Swift Among the Diamond Makers (1911)
Tom Swift in the Caves of Ice (1911)
Tom Swift and His Sky Racer (1911)
Tom Swift and His Electric Rifle (1911)
Tom Swift in the City of Gold (1912)
Tom Swift and His Air Glider (1912)
Tom Swift in Captivity (1912)
Tom Swift and His Wizard Camera (1912)
Tom Swift and His Great Search Light (1912)
Tom Swift and His Giant Cannon (1913)
Tom Swift and His Photo Telephone (1914)
Tom Swift and His Aerial Warship (1915)
Tom Swift and His Big Tunnel (1916)
Tom Swift in the Land of Wonders (1917)
Tom Swift and His War Tank (1918)
Tom Swift and His Air Scout (1919)
Tom Swift and His Undersea Search (1920)
Tom Swift Among the Fire Fighters (1921)
Tom Swift and His Electric Locomotive (1922)
Tom Swift and His Flying Boat (1923)
Tom Swift and His Great Oil Gusher (1924)
Tom Swift and His Chest of Secrets (1925)
Tom Swift and His Airline Express (1926)
Tom Swift Circling the Globe (1927)
Tom Swift and His Talking Pictures (1928)
Tom Swift and His House on Wheels (1929)
Tom Swift and His Big Dirigible (1930)
Tom Swift and His Sky Train (1931)
Tom Swift and His Giant Magnet (1932)
Tom Swift and His Television Detector (1933)
Tom Swift and His Ocean Airport (1934)
Tom Swift and His Planet Stone (1935)
Tom Swift and His Giant Telescope (1939)
Tom Swift and His Magnetic Silencer (1941)

An additional 33 novels in the series were published between 1954 and 1971, with a more contemporary sci-fi orientation for baby boomers, as the "New Tom Swift Jr. Adventures:"

Tom Swift and His Flying Lab (1954)
Tom Swift and His Jetmarine (1954)
Tom Swift and His Rocket Ship (1954)

Tom Swift and His Giant Robot (1954)
Tom Swift and His Atomic Earth Blaster (1954)
Tom Swift and His Outpost in Space (1955)
Tom Swift and His Diving Seacopter (1956)
Tom Swift in the Caves of Nuclear Fire (1956)
Tom Swift on the Phantom Satellite (1956)
Tom Swift and His Ultrasonic Cycloplane (1957)
Tom Swift and His Deep-Sea Hydrodome (1958)
Tom Swift in the Race to the Moon (1958)
Tom Swift and His Space Solartron (1958)
Tom Swift and His Electronic Retroscope (1959)
Tom Swift and His Spectromarine Selector (1960)
Tom Swift and the Cosmic Astronauts (1960)
Tom Swift and the Visitor from Planet X (1961)
Tom Swift and the Electronic Hydrolung (1961)
Tom Swift and His Triphibian Atomicar (1962)
Tom Swift and His Megascope Space Prober (1962)
Tom Swift and the Asteroid Pirates (1963)
Tom Swift and His Repelatron Skyway (1963)
Tom Swift and His Aquatomic Tracker (1964)
Tom Swift and His 3-D Telejector (1964)
Tom Swift and His Polar-Ray Dynasphere (1965)
Tom Swift and His Sonic Boom Trap (1965)
Tom Swift and His Subocean Geotron (1966)
Tom Swift and the Mystery Comet (1966)
Tom Swift and the Captive Planetoid (1967)
Tom Swift and His G-Force Inverter (1968)
Tom Swift and His Dyna-4 Capsule (1969)
Tom Swift and His Cosmotron Express (1970)
Tom Swift and the Galaxy Ghosts (1971)

Tom Thumb

First American-built locomotive, created by Peter Cooper in 1830.

Tom Thumb golf

See **Carter, Garnet**

Tonite! At the Capri Lounge

1976 album featuring Mary Kay Place in character as country singer Loretta Haggers from the TV sitcom *Mary Hartman, Mary Hartman.*

Tony

First name of the title character (Robert Blake) in the TV series *Baretta.*

"Toodles!"

Parting word of the title character (Sally Field) in the TV sitcom *Gidget.*

Too Hot to Handle

Title used for the Ian Fleming novel *Moonraker* when first published in paperback form in the United States in 1957.

"A tool for modern times"

Slogan used in 1970s TV commercials for the IBM personal computer, which featured Charlie Chaplin's "Little Tramp" character. (*Modern Times* was Chaplin's last silent film.)

Tool Time

Cable TV show hosted by Tim Taylor (Tim Allen) in the TV sitcom *Home Improvement.*

Toonces

Car-driving feline puppet in the TV series *Saturday Night Live.*

Too-Too

Pet owl of the title character in the Doctor Dolittle series of children's novels by Hugh Lofting.

Toot Sweets

Candy whistles invented by Caractacus Potts (Dick Van Dyke) in the film *Chitty Chitty Bang Bang.*

Topper feature films

Series based on characters created by author Thorne Smith, starring Roland Young in the title role:
Topper (1937)
Topper Takes a Trip (1939)
Topper Returns (1941)

Top Story

Tabloid TV show for which Gale Weathers (Courteney Cox) is a correspondent, in the film *Scream.*

Toriano

See **Jackson 5 members**

Tornado

Black horse of the title character (Guy Williams) in the TV series *Zorro.*

"The Tornado"

Nickname of baseball pitcher Hideo Nomo, for his twisting windup.

Torquay

Resort town in Devon, England that is the setting of the TV sitcom *Fawlty Towers.*

Torrence

See **Berry and Torrence**

Torresola, Griselio

See **Collazo, Oscar and Torresola, Griselio**

"tortoises"

What the name of the Galápagos Islands means in Spanish.

torus

Term in geometry for a donut shape.

To Serve and Protect

See ***In & Out* Academy Award nominees**

totalizers

Digital readouts that display the gallons and the amount of purchase on a gasoline pump.

"To teach, to serve, and to inquire into the nature of things"

Motto of the University of Georgia.

To Tell a Face

See **Smiley, Guy**

"To the Pure"

Debut episode of the TV series *Ben Casey*, which aired on October 2, 1961.

The Tower* and *The Glass Inferno

The two novels by Richard Martin Stern, and Thomas N. Scortia & Frank M. Robinson (respectively) that were the basis of the film *The Towering Inferno*.

Towle, P. J.

Minnesota grocer who created Log Cabin syrup in 1887. It was named in honor of Abraham Lincoln, and its original tin was in the shape of Lincoln's boyhood home.

Town of Passion

Favorite soap opera of Laura Petrie (Mary Tyler Moore) in the TV sitcom *The Dick Van Dyke Show*.

The Town of Titipu

Alternate title of the Gilbert and Sullivan comic opera *The Mikado*.

Townsend Investigations

Employer of the title characters in the TV series *Charlie's Angels*.

"The Toy Parade"

Instrumental theme of the TV sitcom *Leave It to Beaver*.

Trachsel, Steve

Chicago Cubs pitcher who gave up the record-breaking 62nd home run of 1998 hit by St. Louis Cardinal Mark McGwire, on September 8th at Busch Stadium.

Tracy/Hepburn films

See **Hepburn/Tracy films**

Trader

Pet dog of the title character (Johnny Weissmuller) in the children's TV series *Jungle Jim*.

Trahey, Jane

See ***Life with Mother Superior***

traje de luces

See **suit of lights**

"The Tra La La Song"

Theme song of the children's TV series *The Banana Splits*.

Tralfamadore

Planet that Billy Pilgrim is kidnapped to, in the Kurt Vonnegut novel *Slaughterhouse-Five*.

Tranquility

Secret Service code name for Barbara Bush.

Trans American Flight 209

Setting of the film *Airplane!*

Trans-Global Enterprises

Business "front" of CIA agent Vince Ricardo (Peter Falk) in the film *The In-Laws*.

Trask Engineering

Employer of Henry Mitchell (Herbert Anderson) in the TV sitcom *Dennis the Menace*.

Trask Industries

Employer of Tess McGill (Melanie Griffith) in the film *Working Girl*.

The Travel Book Co.

London bookstore owned by William Thacker (Hugh Grant) in the film *Notting Hill*.

"Travelin' Man" locales

Places mentioned in the Ricky Nelson tune where he has a girlfriend waiting for him: Mexico, Alaska, Berlin, Hong Kong, and Waikiki.

Travers

See **Yarrow, Stookey, and Travers**

Trax

Record-store employer of Andie Walsh (Molly Ringwald) in the film *Pretty in Pink*.

Traynor, John "Jay"

Original lead singer of the pop group Jay and the Americans, who left after the group's first hit, "She Cried." He was succeeded by Jay Black (real name David Blatt).

Traywick

Real last name of country singer Randy Travis.

The Treasure House

Residence of the title character (Bob Keeshan) in the children's TV series *Captain Kangaroo*.

Treasures of Lust and *The Savage Secret*

Romance novels written by Joan Wilder (Kathleen Turner) in the film *Romancing the Stone*.

treaties, major war-ending

Seven Years' War (aka French and Indian War): Treaty of Paris (1763)
American Revolution: Treaty of Paris (1783)
War of 1812: Treaty of Ghent (1814)
Mexican War: Treaty of Guadalupe Hidalgo (1848)
Crimean War: Treaty of Paris (1856)
Franco-Prussian War: Treaty of Frankfurt (1871)
Spanish-American War: Treaty of Paris (1898)
Boer War: Treaty of Vereeniging (1902)
Russo-Japanese War: Treaty of Portsmouth (1905)
World War I: Treaty of Versailles (1919)

The Tree and the Blossom

Original title of the Grace Metalious novel *Peyton Place*.

Treemonisha

1911 ragtime opera composed by Scott Joplin.

Treetops Tattler Tribune

Newspaper edited by the title bird of the comic strip *Shoe*.

Tremaine, Lady

Wicked stepmother of the title character in the Disney animated film *Cinderella*.

Treneer, Maurice

Miles Laboratories chemist who created Alka-Seltzer, introduced in 1931.

Tresch, Samuel Arthur

Title character (George C. Scott) of the TV sitcom *Mr. President*.

Trevor

Pet toad of Neville Longbottom in the Harry Potter series of books by J. K. Rowling.

Triana

Yacht of marine archaeologist/English agent Timothy Havelock (Jack Hedley) in the James Bond film *For Your Eyes Only*.

The Triangle Is Right

See **Smiley, Guy**

triathlon components

A 1.5-kilometer run, followed by a 40-kilometer bike race, followed by a 10-kilometer run. The Triathlon World Championship has been held annually since 1989.

"Tribal Rites of the New Saturday Night"

Article by Nik Cohn, appearing in the June 7, 1976, issue of *New York* magazine, that was the basis for the film *Saturday Night Live*.

Tribeca Productions

Production company of actor Robert De Niro.

Tri-Cities Blackhawks

Original name of the Atlanta Hawks at their NBA inception in 1949. The team played its home games in Moline, Illinois; Rock Island, Illinois; and Davenport, Iowa.

Trinidad

See **Victoria**

trinitrotoluene

Full chemical name of explosive compound TNT.

Trinity

Code name for the site at Alamogordo, New Mexico where the first atomic bomb was detonated on July 16, 1945.

Trinity College

Former name of Duke University.

Trip

Role for which Denzel Washington won a Best Supporting Actor Academy Award in the 1989 film *Glory*.

triple bagel

Term in tennis for a straight-set shutout match of 6-0, 6-0, 6-0.

Triple Crown races (harness-racing pacers)

The races that currently make up the pacers' Triple Crown, listed below with their locations:
- Cane Pace (Freehold Raceway, Freehold, New Jersey)
- Little Brown Jug (Country Fairgrounds, Delaware, Ohio)
- Messenger Stake (Ladbroke at the Meadows, Meadow Lands, Pennsylvania)

The first horse to win all three races in a single year was Adios Butler in 1959.

Triple Crown races (harness-racing trotters)

The races that currently make up the trotters' Triple Crown, listed below with their locations:
- Yonkers Trot (Yonkers Raceway, Yonkers, New York)
- Hambletonian (The Meadowlands, East Rutherford, New Jersey)
- Kentucky Futurity (Red Mile Harness Track, Lexington, Kentucky)

The first horse to win all three races in a single year was Scott Frost in 1955.

Triple Crown races (Thoroughbred horse racing)

- Kentucky Derby: Churchill Downs, Louisville, Kentucky (first Saturday in May)
- Preakness Stakes: Pimlico Race Course, Baltimore, Maryland (two weeks after Kentucky Derby)
- Belmont Stakes: Belmont Park, Elmont, New York (three weeks after Preakness Stakes)

The first horse to win all three races in a single year was Sir Barton in 1919.

Triple Crown winners (baseball)

The players who led their league in batting average, home runs, and RBIs in the same season:

NATIONAL LEAGUE

Heinie Zimmerman (1912)
Rogers Hornsby (1922, 1925)
Chuck Klein (1933)
Joe Medwick (1937)

AMERICAN LEAGUE

Nap Lajoie (1901)
Ty Cobb (1909)
Jimmie Foxx (1933)
Lou Gehrig (1934)
Ted Williams (1942, 1947)
Mickey Mantle (1956)
Frank Robinson (1966)
Carl Yastrzemski (1967)

Triple Crown winners (harness-racing pacers)

Horses that have won the Cane Pace, Little Brown Jug, and Messenger Stakes in the same year:
Adios Butler (1959)
Bret Hanover (1965)
Romeo Hanover (1966)
Rum Customer (1968)
Most Happy Fella (1970)
Niatross (1980)
Ralph Hanover (1983)
Western Dreamer (1997)
Blissful Hall (1999)

Triple Crown winners (harness-racing trotters)

Horses that have won the Yonkers Trot, Hambletonian, and Kentucky Futurity in the same year:
Scott Frost (1955)
Speedy Scot (1963)
Ayres (1964)
Nevele Pride (1968)
Lindy's Pride (1969)
Super Bowl (1972)

Triple Crown winners (Thoroughbred horseracing)

Horses that won the Kentucky Derby, Preakness Stakes, and Belmont Stakes in the same year:
Sir Barton (1919)
Gallant Fox (1930)
Omaha (1935)
War Admiral (1937)
Whirlaway (1941)
Count Fleet (1943)
Assault (1946)
Citation (1948)
Secretariat (1973)
Seattle Slew (1977)
Affirmed (1978)

Triple Lindy

Trick dive performed by Thornton Melon (Rodney Dangerfield) during an intercollegiate competition in the film *Back to School*.

Triple R Ranch

Boys' summer camp setting of the "Adventures of Spin and Marty" segment of the children's TV series *The Mickey Mouse Club*.

Triple X

Code name of KGB agent Major Anya Amasova (Barbara Bach) in the James Bond film *The Spy Who Loved Me*.

Trivia

1966 quiz book by Edwin Goodgold and Dan Carlinsky, that was the first to use the word "trivia" in the title.

"A trivial comedy for serious people"

Subtitle of the Oscar Wilde play *The Importance of Being Earnest*.

trivium

Term used during the Middle Ages for the lower division of the seven liberal arts, comprising grammar, rhetoric, and logic.

See also **quadrivium**

Tromaville, New Jersey

Setting of the *Toxic Avenger* series of films.

Trooper

White horse of R.O.T.C. commander Douglas C. Neidermeyer (Mark Metcalf) in the film *National Lampoon's Animal House*.

"The Troubadour"

English translation of the title of the Giuseppe Verdi opera *Il trovatore*.

Troyal

Real first name of country singer (Troyal) Garth Brooks.

Troyer, Verne

See **Mini-Me**

Truax, Ariel

Ann-Margret's role in the film *Grumpy Old Men*.

Truck Shackley and the Texas Critters

Puppet band in the TV musical variety series *Barbara Mandrell and the Mandrell Sisters*.

True Blue Productions

Production company of actress Kirstie Alley.

Trueheart, Tess

Wife of comic-strip detective Dick Tracy.

True Love

Sailboat of C. K. Dexter Haven (Cary Grant and Bing Crosby, respectively) in the film *The Philadelphia Story* and its musical remake *High Society*.

Truly, Lovable

Cartoon letter carrier in 1960s TV commercials for Post Alpha Bits cereal.

Truman and Adler

Last names of the title characters (Eric McCormack and Debra Messing, respectively) in the TV sitcom *Will & Grace*.

Truman, Harry S.

Sheriff (Michael Ontkean) who assists FBI agent Dale Cooper (Kyle MacLachlan) investigate the murder of Laura Palmer (Sheryl Lee) in the TV series *Twin Peaks*.

Trump

Satire magazine started in 1957 by Hugh Hefner to compete with *Mad*. It lasted for only two issues.

Truscott-Jones, Reginald Alfred

Real name of actor Ray Milland.

"Trust your car to the man who wears the star"

Advertising slogan of Texaco.

"Trusty Scout"

What the words "Kemo Sabe" mean, according to Tonto (Jay Silverheels) in the 1949 premiere episode of the TV series *The Lone Ranger*.

"truth"

What the name of Russian newspaper *Pravda* means in Russian.

Trylon and Perisphere

Theme structures of the 1939–40 New York World's Fair. The Trylon was a 700-foot high three-sided obelisk; the Perisphere was a hollow globe 200 feet in diameter.

Trzcinski, Edmund

See **0**

Tsaritsyn

Former name (until 1925) of Volgograd, Russia.

"TSOP (The Sound of Philadelphia)"

Instrumental theme of the TV series *Soul Train*.

Tuck

See **Nip and Tuck**

Tudbury's

Department store frequented by the title character of the comic strip *Blondie*.

Tudor Hall

Family home near Baltimore, Maryland, of English actor Junius Brutus Booth, and the childhood home of Booth's son, Lincoln assassin John Wilkes Booth.

Tukey, John Wilder

Princeton University mathematical statistician who is credited with coining the computer terms "software" and "bit" (short for "binary digit").

Tumbler

Secret Service code name for George W. Bush.

"Tuna"

Nickname of NFL coach Bill Parcells.

Tuna Fish Music

Music publishing company of songwriter Laura Nyro.

Tun Tavern

Boston inn that is considered the birthplace of the U.S. Marine Corps. The Continental Congress resolution creating the Marines was approved there on November 10, 1775.

Tupper, Earl

See **Wonder Bowl**

Turbo Man

Hot-selling action figure sought by Howard Langston (Arnold Schwarzenegger) for his son's Christmas present, in the film *Jingle All the Way*.

"Turk"

Nickname of NHL player Derek Sanderson.

Turk and Duke

Pet Great Danes of the title family in the Disney film *Swiss Family Robinson*.

"Turkish"

What the word "turquoise" means in French.

The Turnabouts

Vocal group that backs up Merrilee Rush on her tune "Angel of the Morning."

Turner, Robert

Winner of the first All-American Soap Box Derby in 1934.

Turnipseed, Donald

Driver of the 1946 Ford that was hit in the September 30, 1955, collision near Cholame, California, that killed actor James Dean in his Porsche Spyder.

Tusitala

Samoans' name for author Robert Louis Stevenson, which means "teller of tales." Stevenson lived on a Samoan estate named Vailima from 1889 until his death in 1894.

Tuttle

Last name of Elmo, Dagwood's bratty young neighbor in the comic strip *Blondie*.

Tuvim

Real last name of actress Judy Holliday.

TW4

Former name of rock group Styx.

Twelve Oaks

Ashley family plantation in the Margaret Mitchell novel *Gone With the Wind*.

Twicker, Hickory

Jack Haley's "Kansas" role in the film *The Wizard of Oz*.

Twiki

Robot in the TV series *Buck Rogers in the 25th Century*, portrayed by Felix Silla and voiced by Mel Blanc.

Twilight

Original title of the William Faulkner novel *The Sound and the Fury*.

The Twilights

Vocal group that backs up Phil Phillips on his tune "Sea of Love."

The Twilight Zone openings

These three openings were spoken by host Rod Serling at various times during the show's 1959–1965 run:

> There is a fifth dimension, beyond which that is known to man. It is a dimension as vast as space, and as timeless as infinity. It is the middle ground between light and shadow, between science and superstition. And it lies between the pit of man's fears and the summit of his knowledge. This is the dimension of imagination. It is an area which we call The Twilight Zone.

> You're traveling to another dimension. A dimension not only of sight and sound, but of mind. A journey into a wondrous land whose boundaries are that of imagination. There's a signpost up ahead. Your next stop: The Twilight Zone.

> You unlock this door with the key of imagination. Beyond it is another dimension. A dimension of sound, a dimension of sight, a

dimension of mind. You're moving into a land of both shadow and substance, of things and ideas. You've just crossed over into The Twilight Zone.

Twillie, Cuthbert J.
See **Fields, W. C., roles/pen names of**

"Twinkles"
Mike Brady's (Robert Reed's) term of endearment for his wife Carol (Florence Henderson) in the TV sitcom *The Brady Bunch*.

"Twinkle Star"
Original name of the Herb Alpert/Tijuana Brass tune "The Lonely Bull."

Twin Oaks
California diner that is the setting of the 1946 and 1981 versions of the film *The Postman Always Rings Twice*.

Twitty
See **Conway and Twitty**

Twitty City
Hendersonville, Tennessee theme park of country singer Conway Twitty, which opened in 1982. It is called Trinity Music City today.

Two Hours to Doom
Novel (aka *Red Alert*) by Peter George that was the basis for the film *Dr. Strangelove*.

"Two on a Raft"
Debut episode of the TV sitcom *Gilligan's Island*, which aired on September 26, 1964.

Two Socks
Wolf companion of Lieutenant John Dunbar (Kevin Costner) in the film *Dances with Wolves*.

Two Thousand Maniacs!
1964 horror film that inspired the name of rock group 10,000 Maniacs.

Tyler
Maiden name of Carol Brady (Florence Henderson) in the TV sitcom *The Brady Bunch*.

Tylor, Edward Burnett
See **the science of culture**

tympanic membrane
Medical term for the eardrum.

Tyre
Middle name of golf great Bobby Jones.

U2 members

Adam Clayton, David "The Edge" Evans, Paul "Bono" Hewson, and Larry Mullen Jr.

Ubangi-Shari

Former name of the Central African Republic.

Udall, Melvin

Role for which Jack Nicholson won a Best Actor Academy Award in the 1997 film *As Good As It Gets*.

"Ue o Muite Aruko"

Original Japanese title of the Kyu Sakamoto tune "Sukiyaki," which translates as "I Look Up When I Walk."

Uga

Bulldog mascot of the University of Georgia.

Uhler

Middle name of actor Jack Lemmon.

Ulanga

River traveled by missionary Rose Sayer (Katharine Hepburn) and boat captain Charlie Allnut (Humphrey Bogart) in the film *The African Queen*.

ullage

Term in winemaking for the unfilled space in a bottle or barrel.

"The ultimate driving machine"

Advertising slogan of BMW automobiles.

Ulysses

Pet raccoon of Ben Calhoun (Dale Robertson) in the TV Western series *The Iron Horse*.

umbilicus

Medical term for the navel.

Unadulterated Food Products

Original name of the Snapple company.

Uncas

Title character of the James Fenimore Cooper novel *The Last of the Mohicans*.

Uncle Luigi's Good Time Bar and Pizza Parlor

San Francisco restaurant destroyed by Tony Carlson (Chevy Chase) when he drives his car through its front window, in the film *Foul Play*.

"Uncle Miltie"

Nickname of comedian Milton Berle.

"Uncommon Valor Was a Common Virtue"

Inscription at the base of the U.S. Marine Corps War Memorial, aka the Iwo Jima Memorial, at Arlington National Cemetery.

Undershaft

Last name of the title character in the George Bernard Shaw play *Major Barbara*.

Unfinished Arizona

Furniture-store chain owned by Nathan Arizona (Trey Wilson) in the film *Raising Arizona*.

Unica

Brand of lock on the wine-cellar door of the Rio de Janeiro mansion of Alex Sebastian (Claude Rains) in the Alfred Hitchcock film *Notorious*.

Uniform Resource Locator

What the letters in "URL," the term for an Internet address, stand for.

Union Street

Book by Pat Barker that was the basis for the film *Stanley & Iris*.

The Unisphere

12-story stainless steel globe built by U.S. Steel as the symbol of the 1964–65 New York World's Fair, still standing today in Flushing Meadow Park.

UNIT

U.S. counterintelligence team for which Thomas Remington Sloane III (Robert Conrad) is the top agent, in the TV series *A Man Called Sloane*.

United Arab Emirates sheikdoms

Seven sheikdoms in the Middle East that became a single independent state in 1971:

Abu Dhabi
Ajman
Dubai
Fujairah
Ras al-Khaimah
Sharjah
Umm al-Qaiwain

United Artists founders

Production company founded in 1919 by Charlie Chaplin, D. W. Griffith, Douglas Fairbanks Sr., and Mary Pickford (Fairbanks' wife). The company was sold to MGM in 1981.

United Broadcasting Company

Employer of Tom Rath in the Sloan Wilson novel *The Man in the Gray Flannel Suit.*

United Business Company

Original name of H&R Block.

United Community Funds and Councils of America

See **Community Chests and Councils of America**

United Galaxy Sanitation Patrol

Employer of Adam Quark (Richard Benjamin) in the TV sitcom *Quark.*

United Nations official languages

Arabic, Chinese, English, French, Russian, and Spanish.

United Nations secretaries-general

Listed below with their native countries and terms of office:

1946–52: Trygve Lie (Norway)
1953–61: Dag Hammarskjöld (Sweden)
1961–71: U Thant (Burma, now known as Myanmar)
1972–81: Kurt Waldheim (Austria)
1982–91: Javier Pérez de Cuellar (Peru)
1992–96: Boutros Boutros-Ghali (Egypt)
1997–present: Kofi Atta Annan (Ghana)

American diplomat Alger Hiss (who later ran afoul of the House Un-American Activities Committee and California congressman Richard Nixon) served as secretary-general at the U.N. founding conference at San Francisco in 1945, and is sometimes considered to be the first U.N. secretary-general.

United Network Command for Law and Enforcement

Full name of U.N.C.L.E. in the TV series *The Man from U.N.C.L.E.*

United Society of Believers in Christ's Second Appearing

Official name of the Shakers sect.

United States flag, stars and stripes on

Each star on the American flag represents a state of the Union. Since 1795, new stars have been added as new states have been admitted.

13 stars: 1777 – 1795 (original 13 colonies)
15 stars: 1795 – 1818 (Vermont, Kentucky)
20 stars: 1818 – July 3, 1819 (Tennessee, Ohio, Louisiana, Indiana, Mississippi)
21 stars: July 4, 1819 – July 3, 1820 (Illinois)
23 stars: July 4, 1820 – July 3, 1822 (Alabama, Maine)
24 stars: July 4, 1822 – July 3, 1836 (Missouri)
25 stars: July 4, 1836 – July 3, 1837 (Arkansas)
26 stars: July 4, 1837 – July 3, 1845 (Michigan)
27 stars: July 4, 1845 – July 3, 1846 (Florida)
28 stars: July 4, 1846 – July 3, 1847 (Texas)
29 stars: July 4, 1847 – July 3, 1848 (Iowa)
30 stars: July 4, 1848 – July 3, 1851 (Wisconsin)
31 stars: July 4, 1851 – July 3, 1858 (California)
32 stars: July 4, 1858 – July 3, 1859 (Minnesota)
33 stars: July 4, 1859 – July 3, 1861 (Oregon)
34 stars: July 4, 1861 – July 3, 1863 (Kansas)
35 stars: July 4, 1863 – July 3, 1865 (West Virginia)
36 stars: July 4, 1865 – July 3, 1867 (Nevada)
37 stars: July 4, 1867 – July 3, 1877 (Nebraska)
38 stars: July 4, 1877 – July 3, 1890 (Colorado)
43 stars: July 4, 1890 – July 3, 1891 (North Dakota, South Dakota, Montana, Washington, Idaho)
44 stars: July 4, 1891 – July 3, 1896 (Wyoming)
45 stars: July 4, 1896 – July 3, 1908 (Utah)
46 stars: July 4, 1908 – July 3, 1912 (Oklahoma)
48 stars: July 4, 1912 – July 3, 1959 (New Mexico, Arizona)
49 stars: July 4, 1959 – July 3, 1960 (Alaska)
50 stars: July 4, 1960 – present (Hawaii)

At first, each stripe on the American flag represented a state of the Union. In 1818, this was changed back by Congress to the fixed number of 13, to represent the original 13 colonies.

13 stripes: 1777–1795
15 stripes: 1795–1818 (Vermont, Kentucky)
13 stripes: 1818–present

United States national capitals

The cities that have served as capitals of the United States (by definition, where Congress has met), from the First Continental Congress to the present:

September 1774 to December 1776: Philadelphia, Pennsylvania

December 1776 to March 1777: Baltimore, Maryland

March 1777 to September 1777: Philadelphia, Pennsylvania

September 1777: Lancaster, Pennsylvania

September 1777 to July 1778: York, Pennsylvania

July 1778 to June 1783: Philadelphia, Pennsylvania

June 1783 to November 1783: Trenton, New Jersey

November 1783 to January 1785: Annapolis, Maryland

January 1785 to July 1790: New York, New York

July 1790 to October 1800: Philadelphia, Pennsylvania

October 1800 to present: Washington, D.C.

United States residents' nicknames

THE 50 STATES

Alabama: Alabaman, Alabamian
Alaska: Alaskan
Arizona: Arizona, Arizonan
Arkansas: Arkansan (ar-KAN-zin)
California: Californian
Connecticut: Nutmegger
Delaware: Delawarean (del-a-WARE-ee-an)
Florida: Floridian, Floridan
Georgia: Georgian
Hawaii: Hawaiian
Idaho: Idahoan
Illinois: Illinoisan, Illinoian, Illinoisian
Indiana: Indianan, Indianian, Hoosier
Iowa: Iowan, Hawkeye
Kansas: Kansan, Jayhawker
Kentucky: Kentuckian
Louisiana: Louisianan, Louisianian
Maine: Mainer, down-easter
Maryland: Marylander
Massachusetts: Bay Stater
Michigan: Michigander, Michiganite, Wolverine
Minnesota: Minnesotan
Mississippi: Mississippian
Missouri: Missourian
Montana: Montanan
Nebraska: Nebraskan, Cornhusker
Nevada: Nevadan, Nevadian
New Hampshire: New Hampshirite, New Hampshireman
New Jersey: New Jerseyan, New Jerseyite

New Mexico: New Mexican
New York: New Yorker
North Carolina: North Carolinian, Tar Heel
North Dakota: North Dakotan
Ohio: Ohioan, Buckeye
Oklahoma: Oklahoman, Sooner
Oregon: Oregonian
Pennsylvania: Pennsylvanian, Keystoner
Rhode Island: Rhode Islander
South Carolina: South Carolinian
South Dakota: South Dakotan
Tennessee: Tennesseean, Volunteer
Texas: Texan
Utah: Utahan, Utahn
Vermont: Vermonter
Virginia: Virginian
Washington (and Washington, D.C.): Washingtonian
West Virginia: West Virginian
Wisconsin: Wisconsinite, Badger
Wyoming: Wyomingite

U.S. TERRITORIES

Guam: Guamanian
Puerto Rico: Puerto Rican, *puertoriqueño*
Virgin Islands: Virgin Islander

United World News

Employer of foreign correspondent Steve Martin (Raymond Burr) in the film *Godzilla, King of the Monsters.*

Universal Exports (London) Ltd.

"Front" company for the British Secret Service in the James Bond films.

University of New York

School attended by Felicity Porter (Keri Russell) in the TV series *Felicity.*

University of Southern North Dakota at Hoople

"School" where Peter Schickele (aka P. D. Q. Bach) teaches.

university team nicknames

See **college team nicknames**

The Unknown Comic

See **Langston, Murray**

"Untersee"

What "U" in "U-boat" stands for, which is German for "undersea."

Up in the Air

Original working title of the Abbott and Costello film *Keep 'Em Flying*.

Upper Georgetown High

Washington, D.C., school attended by the title character (Jonathan Ward) in the TV series *The New Adventures of Beans Baxter*.

Upper Volta

Former name of the African nation Burkina Faso.

Upsidaisium

Antigravity metal found in the mine inherited by Bullwinkle, in the children's animated TV series *Rocky and His Friends*.

Uptodate

Tabloid TV show for which Gale Weathers (Courteney Cox) is a correspondent, in the film *Scream 2*.

Upton Machine Company

Original name of appliance manufacturer Whirlpool.

"Urbs in horto"

Motto of Chicago, Illinois, which is Latin for "A city in a garden."

Urian

Pet wolfhound of English queen Anne Boleyn, who was beheaded along with her.

Urich, Robert, TV series of

As of this writing, Urich has starred in 14 TV series, more than any other actor.
Bob & Carol & Ted & Alice (1973)
S.W.A.T. (1975–76)
Soap (1977–81)
Tabitha (1977–78)
Vega$ (1978–81)
Gavilan (1982)
Spenser: For Hire (1985–88)
American Dreamer (1990–91)
National Geographic Explorer (1991–94)
Crossroads (1992)
It Had to Be You (1993)
The Lazarus Man (1996)
Vital Signs (1997)
Love Boat: The Next Wave (1998–99)

Urick

Real last name of the pop quartet The Ames Brothers: Ed, Gene, Joe, and Vic.

Urquelle, Stefan

Suave alter ego of nerdy Steve Urkel (Jaleel White) in the TV sitcom *Family Matters*.

U.S.A. series

Trilogy of historical novels by John Dos Passos, which cover the period from 1900 to the 1930s:
The 42nd Parallel (1930)
1919 (1932)
The Big Money (1936)

U.S.S. *Alaska*

Ship being launched at the Brooklyn Navy Yard, that Barry Kane (Robert Cummings) prevents the destruction of, in the Alfred Hitchcock film *Saboteur*.

U.S.S. *Appleby*

Navy destroyer that is the setting of the TV sitcom *Ensign O'Toole*.

U.S.S. *Cygnus*

Spaceship of Dr. Hans Reinhardt (Maximilian Schell) in the Disney film *The Black Hole*.

U.S.S. *Dallas*

Submarine captained by Bart Mancuso in the Tom Clancy novel *The Hunt for Red October*.

U.S.S. *Defiant*

Starship assigned to the title space station in the TV series *Star Trek: Deep Space Nine*.

U.S.S. *Despatch*

The first presidential yacht, used by Rutherford B. Hayes, James A. Garfield, Grover Cleveland, and Benjamin Harrison.

U.S.S. *Hartford*

Flagship of Civil War Union admiral David Farragut at the battles of New Orleans (April 1862) and Mobile Bay (August 1864).

U.S.S. *Mayflower*

Presidential yacht used by Theodore Roosevelt, William Howard Taft, Warren G. Harding, and Calvin Coolidge.

U.S.S. *Memphis*

Navy cruiser that brought Charles Lindbergh back from Europe after his pioneering solo flight across the Atlantic. The ship arrived in the U.S. on June 11, 1927.

U.S.S. *Montana*

Nuclear submarine that sinks under mysterious circumstances, in the film *The Abyss*.

U.S.S. *Palomino*

Spaceship that is the setting of the Disney film *The Black Hole*.

U.S.S. *Reluctant*

Cargo ship that is the setting of the play and film *Mister Roberts*.

U.S.S. *Scorpion*

Nuclear submarine that sank southwest of the Azores on May 22, 1968, with 99 people aboard.

U.S.S. *Sea Tiger*

Submarine that is setting of the film and TV series *Operation Petticoat*.

U.S.S. *Thresher*

Nuclear submarine that sank off the coast of New England on April 10, 1963, with 129 people aboard.

U.S.S. *Triton*

First submarine to circumnavigate the Earth while submerged, completing the voyage in 83 days, 9 hours, and 54 minutes in 1960.

U.S.S. *Williamsburg*

Presidential yacht used by Harry S Truman.

"Ut incepit fidelis, sic permanet"

Motto of Ontario, Canada, which is Latin for "Loyal she began, so she remains."

"Ut prosim"

Motto of Virginia Tech, which is Latin for "That I may serve."

"Utraque unum"

Motto of Georgetown University, which is Latin for "Unity from diversity."

Utzon, Jorn

Danish-born architect who designed the Sydney Opera House, which opened in 1973.

V-8, juices in

The name of V-8 comes from the eight vegetable juices it contains: beet, carrot, celery, lettuce, parsley, spinach, tomato, and watercress.

"The vacation of the future today!"

See **Delos**

"The Vagabond Lover"

Nickname of singer Rudy Vallee.

Vail, Alfred

See **"A patient waiter is no loser"**

Vailima

See **Tusitala**

Val Barker Cup

Award presented to the outstanding boxer at each summer Olympics. It is named for the first general secretary of the International Amateur Boxing Association.

Valentine

See **Paul Revere, Valentine, and Epitaph**

Valentine and Proteus

Title characters of the William Shakespeare play *Two Gentlemen of Verona*.

Valentine, Charity Hope

Title character of the musical play *Sweet Charity*, portrayed by Shirley MacLaine in the film adaptation of the same name.

Valentine Patrick William

Middle names of comedian/TV host/songwriter/author Steve Allen.

Valerie

Real first name of country singer June Carter Cash.

Valkenvania, New Jersey

Setting of the film *Nothing but Trouble*.

Valkyries

In Norse mythology, the choosers of the slain who are worthy of a place in Valhalla. Their names, as they appear in Richard Wagner's *Der Ring des Nibelungen*:

Brünnhilde
Gerhilde
Grimgerde
Helmwige
Ortlinde
Rossweisse
Schwertleite
Siegrune
Waltraute

Valley Falls High

School attended by the title character in the Chip Hilton series of children's novels by Clair Bee.

Valley Forge

Spaceship home of botanist Freeman Lowell (Bruce Dern) in the film *Silent Running*.

"The Vamp"

Nickname of silent-screen actress Theda Bara, for her vampirish screen persona.

Recurring segment in the TV comedy/variety series *The Sonny and Cher Comedy Hour* where Cher portrays famous women in history.

Van Brunt, Abraham

Real name of Brom Bones, rival of Ichabod Crane in the Washington Irving short story "The Legend of Sleepy Hollow."

Van Cortland

Real last name of rock singer David Crosby.

Van Daan, Mrs.

Role for which Shelley Winters won a Best Supporting Actress Academy Award in the 1959 film *The Diary of Anne Frank*.

Vanderbilt, Harold Stirling

Descendant of Cornelius Vanderbilt who invented contract bridge in 1925. He was also a skilled yachtsman, a three-time winner of America's Cup (1930, 1934, 1937).

Vanderpool

See **Baker and Vanderpool**

Van Diemen's Land

Former name of Tasmania, given by explorer Abel Tasman in honor of the governor of the Dutch East Indies who commissioned Tasman's voyage.

Van Dyne, Edith

Pen name used by author L. Frank Baum.

Van Halen original members

Michael Anthony, David Lee Roth, Alex Van Halen, and Eddie Van Halen. Sammy Hagar succeeded Roth as lead vocalist in 1985.

Van Hossmere, Muzzy

Carol Channing's role in the film *Thoroughly Modern Millie*.

vanity card

Television term for the end-of-show credit for the personal production company that created the program. Well-known examples include the hammering hands of Jack Webb in *Dragnet*, and the meowing kitten in series produced by Mary Tyler Moore's MTM.

Van Kannel, Theophilus

Inventor of the revolving door in 1888.

van Kuijk, Andreas Cornelis

Real name of Colonel Tom Parker, manager of Elvis Presley.

Van Varenberg

Real last name of actor Jean-Claude Van Damme.

Van Winkle, Robert

Real name of rap artist Vanilla Ice.

Van Wormer, John

Inventor of the milk carton, patented in 1915.

Vare Trophy

Annual award given by the LPGA to the pro with the lowest scoring average. It is named for 1920s amateur golf star Glenna Collett Vare.

The Variatones

Original name of the pop group The Four Seasons. They were later called The Four Lovers before adopting their best-known name.

varicella

Medical term for chickenpox.

variometer

Instrument used in airplanes and hot-air ballooning to measure the rate of ascent and descent.

varnas

The traditional social classes of Hindu India:
Brahman (priests)
Kshatriya (nobles, warriors)
Vaisya (merchants, farmers)
Sudra (artisans, laborers)

Varney Speed Lines

Original name of Continental Airlines.

"The Varsity Sport of the Mind"

Slogan used for College Bowl competitions.

Vaselino, Rhubarb

Stan Laurel's toreador role in the 1922 silent film *Mud and Sand*. The role and film were parodies of the Rudolph Valentino silent film of the same year, *Blood and Sand*.

"vast wasteland"

Memorable phrase used by FCC chairman Newton Minow to describe television, in a speech to the National Association of Broadcasters on May 9, 1961.

Vaughn, Yvonne

Real name of country singer Donna Fargo.

"The Vaulting Vicar"

Nickname of Olympic pole-vault star Bob Richards, who is an ordained minister.

V-E Day

May 8, 1945, the day on which the Allies celebrated victory in Europe in World War II.

Veen, Adelaida

Full name of the title character in the Vladimir Nabokov novel *Ada*.

Vega

Star system that beams back to Earth the television transmissions of the opening ceremonies of the 1936 Berlin Summer Olympic Games, in the film *Contact*.

vegetarians, types of

Listed below by the degree of exclusion of animal products from the diet:

Semi-vegetarian: eats dairy products, eggs, fish and chicken

Pesco-vegetarian: eats dairy products, eggs and fish

Lacto-ovo-vegetarian (or ovo-lacto-vegetarian): eats dairy products and eggs

Lacto-vegetarian: eats dairy products

Ovo-vegetarian: eats eggs

Vegan: eats no animal products of any kind

Velardi, Arizona

Setting of the TV Western series *Johnny Ringo*.

Vella La Cava

Solomon Islands setting of the TV series *Baa Baa Black Sheep*.

Velline

Real last name of pop singer Bobby Vee.

"Velut arbor aevo"

Motto of the University of Toronto, which is Latin for "As a tree with the passage of time."

Velvet Apple Music

Music publishing company of country singer Dolly Parton.

"The Velvet Fog"

Nickname of singer Mel Tormé.

Ventiports

Name given to the holes in the left and right front fenders of Buick automobiles. They first appeared in the 1949 model year.

Venture

Ship that brings the title beast to New York in the film *King Kong* (1933).

Vera

Unseen wife of Norm Peterson (George Wendt) in the TV sitcom *Cheers*.

Vera

Title vessel in the Katherine Anne Porter novel *Ship of Fools*.

"Verbal"

See **Kint, Roger "Verbal"**

Verdell

Pet dog of Simon Bishop (Greg Kinnear) in the film *As Good As It Gets*.

The Verdict Is Yours

TV series on which Jim McKay portrayed a court reporter from 1957 to 1960, before beginning his long stint as host of *ABC's Wide World of Sports* in 1961.

Vergeltungswaffe

What the initial letter in the World War II weapons V-1 (pilotless aircraft bomb) and V-2 (ballistic missile bomb) stood for, which is German for "retaliation weapon."

"Veritas"

Motto of Harvard University, which is Latin for "Truth."

"Veritas et virtus"

Motto of the University of Pittsburgh, which is Latin for "Truth and virtue."

"Veritas, unitas, caritas"

Motto of Villanova University, which is Latin for "Truth, unity, love."

"Veritas vos liberabit"

Motto of Johns Hopkins University, which is Latin for "The truth will set you free."

Verloc, Adolf

Title character of the Joseph Conrad novel *The Secret Agent*.

Vermilion Sea

Former name of the Gulf of California.

"Vermont's Finest"

Slogan for Ben & Jerry's ice cream, which was adopted when it was discovered that there were no other ice cream manufacturers in Vermont.

Vermont Today

TV talk show hosted by Dick Loudon (Bob Newhart) in the TV sitcom *Newhart*.

Vermouth, Apollo C.

Pseudonym used on a number of occasions (as singer and producer) by former Beatle Paul McCartney.

Verne

See **Jules and Verne**

Vernet

Middle name of actor Lloyd Bridges.

Vernon

Real first name of Hall of Fame baseball pitcher Lefty Gomez.

Verplanck, New York

Setting of the film *Drowning Mona.*

The Versatiles

Original name of pop group The 5th Dimension.

"Very interesting!"

Catchphrase of Arte Johnson's German soldier character in the TV series *Rowan and Martin's Laugh-In.*

Very Superior Old Pale

What the letters "V.S.O.P.," found on bottles of premium cognac, stand for.

Veto

Pet dog of President James A. Garfield.

vexillophile

Technical term for a collector of flags.

Vezina Trophy

Awarded annually since 1927 to the NHL's best goaltender, named for former Montreal Canadiens goalie Georges Vezina.

Via Lactea

Ancient Roman name for the Milky Way, which in Latin means "Milky Way."

"Viam sapientiae monstrabo tibi"

Motto of DePaul University, which is Latin for "I will show you the way of wisdom."

vibrissae

Scientific name for the whiskers of a feline.

Vic

Horse of George Armstrong Custer at the Battle of the Little Bighorn on June 25–26, 1876.

Vice President of Public Relations and Terror

Title of KAOS agent Konrad Siegfried (Bernie Kopell) in the TV sitcom *Get Smart.*

Victor

First name of the title character in the Mary Shelley novel *Frankenstein.*

Horse of Dan Reid, nephew of The Lone Ranger.

Victor Company of Japan

What the initials of consumer electronics company JVC stand for. The company was founded in 1927 as a manufacturer of phonographs and phonograph records.

Victoria

Secret Service code name for Lady Bird Johnson.

Victoria

First ship to circumnavigate the Earth. It left Spain on September 20, 1519, one of three ships under the command of Ferdinand Magellan. (The other two ships, *Concepción* and *Trinidad,* did not complete the voyage.) It returned to Spain on September 8, 1522, under the command of Juan Sebastian del Cano. (Magellan was killed in the Philippines on April 27, 1521.)

Victoria Davey

Real first and middle names of actress Tori Spelling.

Victor, Wyoming

Amtrak stop where Nell Porter (Blair Brown) and Ernie Souchak (John Belushi) get married in the film *Continental Divide.*

The Victory Bell

Trophy awarded to the winning team in the annual football game between Duke University and the University of North Carolina.

Trophy awarded to the winning team in the annual football game between U.C.L.A. and U.S.C.

Victory, Missouri

Setting of the TV sitcom *Grace Under Fire.*

Video Home System

What the letters in VCR format VHS stand for.

"Video Killed the Radio Star"

First music video shown on MTV on its August 1, 1981 premiere broadcast, performed by The Buggles.

Village People costumes

Members of this campy vocal group wear these costumes: biker, construction worker, cowboy, Indian, policeman, and soldier.

Villager

See **Pacer, Ranger, Corsair, and Citation**

The Village Virus

Original working title of the Sinclair Lewis novel *Main Street.*

Villa Mauresque

French Riviera home of author W. Somerset Maugham.

Vince and Larry

Crash-test dummies in TV commercials for the National Highway Traffic Safety Administration, promoting the use of seat belts.

"Vince aut morire"

Motto of the Minutemen soldiers in the American Revolution, which is Latin for "Conquer or die."

Vince Lombardi Trophy

Presented each year to the winning team in the Super Bowl, named for the Green Bay Packers coach who won the first two Super Bowls in 1967-68. The sterling-silver trophy is manufactured by Tiffany's.

Vincent

The "Beast" title character (Ron Perlman) of the TV series *Beauty and the Beast*.

Vincent Edward

Real first and middle names of baseball/football player Bo Jackson.

"Vinegar Joe"

Nickname of World War II general Joseph Stilwell.

Vinomori, Blavdak

Minor character in the Vladimir Nabokov novel *King, Queen, Knave*, whose name is an anagram of the author's.

Vinton, Will

See **California Raisins**

Violet

Pet pig of actor Boris Karloff.

Viper Three

Novel by Walter Wager that was the basis for the film *Twilight's Last Gleaming*.

Virgil, Texas

Setting of the film *True Stories*.

Virginia Elizabeth

Real first and middle names of actress Geena Davis.

Virtue Rewarded

Alternate title of the Samuel Richardson novel *Pamela*.

virtues, cardinal

The seven qualities of good in human conduct, which combine the four virtues of Plato with the three Christian virtues.

PLATONIC VIRTUES

Justice
Fortitude
Prudence
Temperance

CHRISTIAN VIRTUES

Faith
Hope
Charity

"The Virus"

Nickname of Cyrus Grissom (John Malkovich), who masterminds the plane hijacking in the film *Con Air*.

Viscuso, Sal

Voice of the camp announcer in the TV sitcom *M*A*S*H*. He portrayed Father Timothy Flotsky in the TV sitcom *Soap*.

VISOR

Electronic device that allows Geordi La Forge (LeVar Burton) to see, in the TV series *Star Trek: The Next Generation*. It is an acronym for "Visual Instrument and Sensory Organ Replacement."

"Vita, dulcedo, spes"

Motto of the University of Notre Dame, which is Latin for "Life, sweetness, hope."

"Vital Organic"

What "VO" stands for in the name of Alberto VO5 hair dressing, which is made with five organic emollients.

Vitameatavegamin

Liquid tonic that Lucy Ricardo (Lucille Ball) was once a spokesperson for, in the TV sitcom *I Love Lucy*.

vitamin names and deficiencies

Vitamins' chemical names, with diseases caused by a deficiency of the vitamins:

A   (retinol): night blindness
B_1 (thiamine): beriberi
B_2 (riboflavin)
B_3 (niacin, nicotinic acid): pellagra
B_6 (pyridoxine)
B_9 (folic acid)
B_{12} (cobalamin, cyanocobalamin)
C   (ascorbic acid): scurvy

D_1 (lumisterol and calciferol): rickets
E   (tocopherol)
K_1 (phylloquinone)

Vito, Mona Lisa

Role for which Marisa Tomei won a Best Supporting Actress Academy Award in the 1992 film *My Cousin Vinny*.

V-J Day

August 15, 1945, the day on which Japan accepted Allied surrender terms, ending World War II.

"Vogue," celebrities in

As mentioned in the Madonna tune (in order):
   Greta Garbo
   (Marilyn) Monroe
   (Marlene) Dietrich
   (Joe) DiMaggio
   Marlon Brando
   Jimmy (James) Dean
   Grace Kelly
   Jean Harlow
   Gene Kelly
   Fred Astaire
   Ginger Rogers
   Rita Hayworth
   Lauren (Bacall)
   Katharine (Hepburn)
   Lana (Turner)
   Bette Davis

"The Voice"

Nickname of singer Frank Sinatra.

Volney

Name of the original MGM lion mascot. He lived in Memphis' Overton Park Zoo and died in 1944.

Voltafiore

Italian town that is the setting of the final season of the TV sitcom *McHale's Navy*.

Volunteer

Secret Service code name for Lyndon Johnson.

"Volunteer"

See **United States residents' nicknames**

von Backwards, Countess

Girlfriend of The Count in the children's TV series *Sesame Street*. She has a penchant for counting in reverse order.

von Bulow, Claus

Role for which Jeremy Irons won a Best Actor Academy Award for the 1990 film *Reversal of Fortune*.

Vondervotteimittiss

Dutch borough that is the setting of the Edgar Allan Poe short story "The Peril in the Belfry."

Von Schlef, Contessa Lisl

Girlfriend of Columbo (Topol) in the James Bond film *For Your Eyes Only*, portrayed by Cassandra Harris, wife of subsequent screen 007 Pierce Brosnan.

Vosca

Childhood pet cat of actress Natalie Wood.

"Vote yourself a farm"

Slogan of the Republican party in the presidential campaign of 1860, offering Western land to anyone who would settle on it. This promise was fulfilled with the passage of the Homestead Act in 1862.

Vox

Stage surname used by U2 lead singer Bono for the group's first album, *Boy*.

"Vox clamantis in deserto"

Motto of Dartmouth College, which is Latin for "The voice of one crying in the wilderness."

Voyager

Experimental lightweight airplane flown by Dick Rutan and Jeana Yeager on the first nonstop around-the-world flight without refueling, December 14–23, 1986. The 24,986-mile flight began and ended at California's Andrews Air Force Base.

Voyage to Space

Film watched by Joe Buck (Jon Voight) at a movie theater in an early scene of the film *Midnight Cowboy*.

"The Vulcan Affair"

Debut episode of the TV series *The Man From U.N.C.L.E.*, which aired on September 22, 1964.

Vulcania

South Seas island hideaway of Captain Nemo (James Mason) in the Disney film *20,000 Leagues Under the Sea*.

Vulcanite Optical Instrument Company

Original name of Bausch & Lomb.

Vulgaria

Country visited by Caractacus Potts (Dick Van Dyke) in the film *Chitty Chitty Bang Bang*.

Vulture

English ship on which Benedict Arnold fled to England in 1780.

Homemade spaceship used by Harry Broderick (Andy Griffith) in the TV series *Salvage 1*.

WABAC Machine
Device (pronounced "WAY-back") used by Mr. Peabody and his pet boy Sherman to travel through time in the "Peabody's Improbable History" segment of the children's animated TV series *Rocky and His Friends*.

Wabasha, Minnesota
Setting (pronounced "WAW-buh-shaw") of the *Grumpy Old Men* films.

Wack
Pet duck of the title character in the comic strip *Ziggy*.

Wade, Benjamin Franklin
Ohio senator, who, as president pro tem of the Senate, would have become President of the United States if Andrew Johnson had been found guilty at his 1868 impeachment trial.

Waffles
Pet dachshund of Mary Wilke (Diane Keaton) in the film *Manhattan*.

Wager, Walter
See 58 Minutes; Viper Three

Waggles
Pet dog of B. J. Hunnicutt (Mike Farrell) in the TV sitcom *M*A*S*H*.

The Wagner Company
Employer of Willy Loman in the Tennessee Williams play *Death of a Salesman*.

Wagner, George Raymond
Real name of 1950s pro wrestler Gorgeous George.

Wagner's *Ring* cycle
Four musical dramas composed by Richard Wagner, whose original/Anglicized titles and premiere dates are listed below:
Das Rheingold (The Rhine Gold): 1869
Die Walküre (The Valkyrie): 1870
Siegfried: 1876
Götterdämmerung (Twilight of the Gods): 1876

Wagstaff
Middle name of TV host/producer Dick Clark.

Wagstaff, Professor Quincy Adams
See Marx, Groucho, roles of

Wait for Baby
See But Millions

Wait, Pearl B.
Carpenter and cough-medicine manufacturer from LeRoy, New York, who invented Jell-O in 1897. The four flavors originally sold were: Lemon, Orange, Raspberry, and Strawberry.

Wakefield, Ruth
Inventor of chocolate chip cookies circa 1930, at her Toll House Inn in Whitman, Massachusetts.

"Wake up America, it's time to stump the experts"
Opening line of the radio game show *Information, Please!* The line was preceded by the crowing of a rooster.

"Wake up wonderful!"
Advertising slogan of Simmons Beautyrest mattresses.

"Wake up your liver bile"
Advertising slogan of Carter's Little Liver Pills.

Wakita, Oklahoma
Town destroyed by a tornado in the film *Twister*.

Waldemere
Bridgeport, Connecticut, mansion of showman P. T. Barnum, where he lived from 1868 to 1888.

Walden, Thaddeus Eli
Harvard dropout who founded Walden College in the comic strip *Doonesbury*. His nickname is "The Patron Saint of the Gentleman's 'C'."

Waldo
Family dog in the TV sitcom *Nanny and the Professor*.

Waldorf

See **Statler and Waldorf**

Waldteufel, Emile

See **"The Skaters"**

Walkabout Creek, Northern Territory

Australian setting of the film *"Crocodile" Dundee.*

Walker

Middle name of President George W. Bush.

Last name of the title character in the rock opera *Tommy.*

Last name of the title character in the Jim Croce tune "You Don't Mess Around with Jim."

Walker, Edward Craven

English inventor of the Lava Lamp, first sold in 1963. Its moving patterns are a mixture of oil and water heated by a light bulb at the bottom.

Walker, Mary Edwards

Only woman to receive the Medal of Honor. Walker, one of the first female physicians in the United States, was a surgeon for the Union army during the Civil War.

Walking Piano

Device on which Mac MacMillan (Robert Loggia) and Josh Baskin (Tom Hanks) play duets (by dancing on the device's huge keys) in the film *Big.* They play "Heart and Soul" and "Chopsticks" at Manhattan's F. A. O. Schwarz toy store.

"Walking the Floor Over You"

Theme song of country singer Ernest Tubb.

"Walk with You"

Theme song of the TV series *Touched by an Angel,* performed by series costar Della Reese.

Wallace and McQuade

Advertising agency headed by Angela Bower (Judith Light) in the TV sitcom *Who's the Boss?*

Wallacetown, Florida

Location of the title establishment in the film *Porky's.*

Waller

See **Asher and Waller**

Walley World

Los Angeles, California, amusement park that is the Griswold family's destination in the film *National Lampoon's Vacation.* Walley World's mascot is Marty Moose.

Wallop, John Douglass

See **The Year the Yankees Lost the Pennant**

"The walls of Jericho"

What Peter Warne (Clark Gable) calls the blanket hanging on a rope that separates his motel-room bed from that of Ellie Andrews (Claudette Colbert), in the Frank Capra film *It Happened One Night.*

Wally's Filling Station

Mayberry employer of Gomer Pyle (Jim Nabors) in the TV sitcom *The Andy Griffith Show.*

Walnut Grove, Minnesota

Initial setting of the TV series *Little House on the Prairie.*

Walrus

Pirate ship commanded by Captain Flint in the Robert Louis Stevenson novel *Treasure Island.*

"The Walrus"

Nickname of pro golfer Craig Stadler, for his handlebar mustache.

Walter

Real first name of Radar O'Reilly (Gary Burghoff) in the TV sitcom *M*A*S*H.*

Real first name of (Walter) Bruce Willis.

Middle name of Maynard G. Krebs (Bob Denver) in the TV sitcom *The Many Loves of Dobie Gillis.*

Pet Pomeranian dog of Suzanne Stone (Nicole Kidman) in the film *To Die For.*

See **Happy, Walter, and Smiley**

Walter James Vincent

Real first and middle names of Hall of Fame baseball shortstop Rabbit Maranville.

Walter Lanier

Real first and middle names of baseball broadcaster Red Barber.

Walter Marty

Real first and middle names of astronaut Wally Schirra.

Walter Payton Award

Annual trophy given to the outstanding player in Division I-AA college football.

Walter Wellesley

Real first and middle names of sportswriter Red Smith.

Walton

Middle name of director George Lucas.

Walton, Frederick

Inventor of linoleum in 1863.

"Walt sent me"

Password at the Ink and Paint Club, in the film *Who Framed Roger Rabbit*.

waltzes in popular music

These tunes are all written in waltz (three-quarter) time:

"After the Ball" (1892)
"Always" (1925)
"America," aka "God Save the King (Queen)" (c. 1619)
"Annie's Song" (1974)
"Delilah" (1969)
"I Feel Pretty" (1957)
"In My Merry Oldsmobile" (1905)
"In the Good Old Summertime" (1902)
"Let Me Call You Sweetheart" (1910)
"Meet Me in St. Louis, Louis" (1904)
"Moon River" (1961)
"My Favorite Things" (1959)
"Oh, What a Beautiful Mornin'" (1943)
"The Sidewalks of New York" (1894)
"Some Day My Prince Will Come" (1937)
"Sunrise Sunset" (1964)
"Take Me Out to the Ball Game" (1908)
"Time in a Bottle" (1973)
"True Love" (1956)
"Try to Remember" (1960)
"What's New, Pussycat?" (1965)
"When Irish Eyes Are Smiling" (1912)

"The Waltz King"

Nickname of composer Johann Strauss Jr.

"Waltz through washday"

Advertising slogan of Maytag washers and dryers.

Wandrous, Gloria

Role for which Elizabeth Taylor won a Best Actress Academy Award in the 1960 film *Butterfield 8*.

Wang, Sidney

Sleuth (Peter Sellers) in the film *Murder by Death*. His name is inspired by Earl Derr Biggers' Charlie Chan.

Wanker

Maiden name of Peg Bundy (Katey Sagal) in the TV sitcom *Married . . . with Children*.

"Wanna buy a duck?"

Catchphrase of radio comedian Joe Penner.

The War Cry

Weekly newspaper of the Salvation Army.

Ward, Arthur Sarsfield

Real name of author Sax Rohmer, creator of Chinese master criminal Fu Manchu.

Wardell, Joseph

See **Three Stooges' real names**

Ward, Samuel

See **"Materna"**

Ward, Seth

Real name of country singer Jimmy Dean.

Warhead

Original working title of the James Bond film *Never Say Never Again*.

The Warlocks

Original name of rock group The Grateful Dead.

Warne, Peter

Role for which Clark Gable won a Best Actor Academy Award in the 1934 film *It Happened One Night*.

Warner, Ezra J.

Inventor of the first can opener, a rather unwieldy combination bayonet and scythe, patented in 1858.

See also **Lyman, William W.**

Warner, Sylvia Townsend

See **Lolly Willowes, or The Loving Huntsman**

"War of the Silver Kings"

Debut episode of the TV Western series *Maverick*, which aired on September 22, 1957.

Warren

Real first name of Potsie Weber (Anson Williams) in the TV sitcom *Happy Days*.

The Warriors

Original working title of the film *Kelly's Heroes*.

"Wart"

Nickname of young (future king) Arthur (voiced by Rickie Sorensen) in the Disney animated film *The Sword in the Stone.*

Wash and Brush Up Co.

Emerald City establishment where Dorothy (Judy Garland), the Tin Man (Jack Haley), the Cowardly Lion (Bert Lahr), and the Scarecrow (Ray Bolger) get spruced up before meeting the title character (Frank Morgan), in the film *The Wizard of Oz.*

Washington Herald

Employer of investigative reporter Gray Grantham (Denzel Washington) in the film *The Pelican Brief.*

Washington Merry-Go-Round

Syndicated political column of Drew Pearson.

Washington Times-Herald

Newspaper for which Jacqueline Bouvier worked as Inquiring Photographer before her marriage to John F. Kennedy.

Washkansky, Louis

South African grocer who received the world's first human heart transplant, performed by Dr. Christiaan Barnard on December 3, 1967. Washkansky lived for 18 days after the transplant.

"The Waste Land" sections

Poem by T. S. Eliot consisting of these five parts:
"The Burial of the Dead"
"A Game of Chess"
"The Fire Sermon"
"Death by Water"
"What the Thunder Said"

Watch the Skies

Original working title of the Steven Spielberg film *Close Encounters of the Third Kind.*

"Water Displacement"

What "WD" stands for in the name of WD-40 spray lubricant. It was originally developed for the aerospace industry, to prevent rust and corrosion of metal.

The Water Is Wide

Book by Pat Conroy that was the basis for the film *Conrack.*

Waterkeyn, André

See **The Atomium**

"waterless place"

What the word "Gobi" means in Mongolian.

Waterloo

Original name of Austin, Texas. It was renamed in honor of pioneer Stephen Austin when it became capital of the Republic of Texas in 1839.

Waters, Arkansas

See **Pine Ridge, Arkansas**

Waterton Publishing Company

Employer of fact checker Herman Brooks (William Ragsdale) in the TV sitcom *Herman's Head.*

Wathahuck

Indian name of legendary athlete Jim Thorpe. A member of the Sac and Fox tribes, his Indian name means "bright path."

Watkins, Chrissie

First victim of the shark in the film *Jaws,* portrayed by Susan Backlinie. She spoofs this role in the opening scene of the film *1941.* Both films were directed by Steven Spielberg.

Watts, Mrs.

Role for which Geraldine Page won a Best Actress Academy Award in the 1985 film *The Trip to Bountiful.*

Wavekrest

Research ship of Milton Krest (Anthony Zerbe) in the James Bond film *Licence to Kill.*

Waverly

Maiden name of Helen Kimble (Diane Brewster), slain wife of the title character (David Janssen) in the original TV series *The Fugitive.*

Wax: Or the Discovery of Television Among the Bees

First full-length film made available for Internet viewing, on May 23, 1993.

Waybury Inn

Actual establishment (in East Middlebury, Vermont) seen in the opening credits of the TV sitcom *Newhart.*

Wayne, John, singers in films of

These performers (with one or more U.S. *Billboard* top-40 tunes to their credit) are listed below with the John Wayne film(s) in which they appeared:
Paul Anka (*The Longest Day*)

Ann-Margret (*The Train Robbers*)
Frankie Avalon (*The Alamo*)
Pat Boone (*The Greatest Story Ever Told*)
Walter Brennan (*Red River, Rio Bravo* and five
    others)
Red Buttons (*Hatari, The Longest Day*)
Glen Campbell (*True Grit*)
Johnny Crawford (*El Dorado*)
Bing Crosby (*Cancel My Reservation*)*
Fabian (*North to Alaska*)
Phil Harris (*The High and the Mighty*)
Tab Hunter (*The Sea Chase*)
Dean Martin (*Rio Bravo, The Sons of Katie Elder*)
Sal Mineo (*The Longest Day, The Greatest Story
    Ever Told*)
Ricky Nelson (*Rio Bravo*)
Fess Parker (*Island in the Sky*)
Debbie Reynolds (*How the West Was Won*)
Tommy Sands (*The Longest Day*)
Frank Sinatra (*Cast a Giant Shadow*)
Bobby Vinton (*Big Jake, The Train Robbers*)
* Wayne and Crosby make cameo appearances
    in this film

Waynesboro, Ohio

Setting of the Helen Hooven Santmyer novel . . . *And
Ladies of the Club.*

Wayneville, Iowa

Hometown of Homer Simpson in the Nathanael
West novel *The Day of the Locust.*

WBFL

Buffalo, New York TV station that is the setting of
the TV sitcom *Buffalo Bill.*

WBJX

TV station employer of sportscaster George Pa-
padapolis (Alex Karras) in the TV sitcom *Webster.*

WD-40

Code name of secret agent Dick Steele (Leslie
Nielsen) in the film *Spy Hard.*

"We Are the World" participants

This *Billboard* #1 song was recorded as a fundraiser
on January 18, 1985 at Los Angeles' A&M Studios,
after the Grammy Award ceremonies.

Michael Boddicker
Lindsey Buckingham
Kim Carnes
Ray Charles
Paulinho da Costa
Bob Dylan
Bob Geldof

Daryl Hall
James Ingram
Jackie Jackson
La Toya Jackson
Marlon Jackson
Michael Jackson
Randy Jackson
Tito Jackson
Al Jarreau
Waylon Jennings
Billy Joel
Louis Johnson
Quincy Jones
Cyndi Lauper
Huey Lewis and the News
Kenny Loggins
Bette Midler
Willie Nelson
John Oates
Michael Omartian
Jeffrey Osborne
Steve Perry
Greg Phillinganes
The Pointer Sisters
Lionel Richie
John Robinson
Smokey Robinson
Kenny Rogers
Diana Ross
Sheila E.
Paul Simon
Bruce Springsteen
Tina Turner
Dionne Warwick
Stevie Wonder

Wear Well Shoes

Employer of salesman Lenny Markowitz (Adam
Arkin) in the TV sitcom *Busting Loose.*

Weary Willie

Clown character portrayed by Emmett Kelly.

Weatherwax, Rudd

Original trainer of the title character in the children's TV series *Lassie*, who was succeeded by his
son Bob.

Weaver

Worker ant in the animated film *Antz*, voiced by
Sylvester Stallone.

"The Weaver of Raveloe"

Subtitle of the George Eliot novel *Silas Marner.*

Webb, Brenda Gail
Real name of singer Crystal Gayle.

Webb, Charles
Author of the novel *The Graduate*, upon which the film of the same name is based.

Webb, J. L.
Name on the sample cards in ads for the Discover card.

"We bring good things to life"
Advertising slogan of General Electric.

Webster, Dan'l
Title amphibian in the Mark Twain short story "The Celebrated Jumping Frog of Calaveras County."

Webster Groves, Missouri
Setting of the TV series *Lucas Tanner*.

Webster, Jean
See Daddy Long Legs

Webster, Norma Rae
See **Wilson, Norma Rae/Webster, Norma Rae**

"We build excitement"
Advertising slogan of Pontiac automobiles.

"We Can Remember It for You Wholesale"
Short story by sci-fi author Philip K. Dick that was the basis for the film *Total Recall*.

"We cure people the old fashioned way"
Motto of Ronald Reagan Hospital, from which Ted Stryker (Robert Hays) escapes, in the film *Airplane II: The Sequel*.

"We deliver for you"
Advertising slogan of the United States Postal Service.

"We do it all for you"
Advertising slogan of McDonald's.

"We don't just bark . . . we bite"
Motto of Guard Dog Security, employer of guards Frank Dooley (John Candy) and Norman Kane (Eugene Levy) in the film *Armed and Dangerous*.

"We Do Our Part"
Slogan on signs and decals given to participants in the New Deal era's National Recovery Administration, aka NRA.

Weebo
Flying robot assistant of Professor Phil Brainard (Robin Williams) in the film *Flubber*.

Weed, Steven
California teacher who was the fiancé of Patricia Hearst at the time of her kidnapping on February 5, 1974.

Wee Johnny Hays and the Bluecats
See **The Rattlesnakes**

Weekend at Party Pier
Film in which The Wonders perform, in the film *that thing you do!*

Weemawee High
School that is the setting of the TV sitcom *Square Pegs*.

Weeping Water, Nebraska
Hometown of Matthew Harrison Brady in the Lawrence and Lee play *Inherit the Wind*.

Weertz, Louis
Real name of pianist Roger Williams.

"Weezy"
George Jefferson's (Sherman Hemsley's) nickname for his wife Louise (Isabel Sanford) in the TV sitcom *The Jeffersons*.

"We have two billion people in our waiting room"
Slogan once used by Doctors Without Borders, an international medical relief agency.

Weinstein, Nathan Wallenstein
Real name of novelist Nathanael West.

Weiss, Ehrich
Real name of magician Harry Houdini.

Weiss Jr., Carl Austin
Physician who assassinated Louisiana senator Huey Long on September 10, 1935.

Welch, Dr. Thomas Bramwell
Physician and dentist from Vineland, New Jersey, who in 1869 became the first to successfully pasteurize Concord grape juice, for use as an "unfermented sacramental wine" by the parishioners of his church. Today, Welch's is the world's leading manufacturer of grape juices, jams, and jellies.

"Welcome to the Hellmouth"

Debut episode of the TV series *Buffy: The Vampire Slayer*, which aired on March 10, 1997.

Welker, Frank

See **"The Mad Magpies"**

"Well, excuuuse me!"

Catchphrase used by Steve Martin in his comedy routines.

"Well I'll be a blue-nosed gopher!"

Catchphrase of ranch hand Ollie (Dennis Moore) in the "Adventures of Spin and Marty" segment of the children's TV series *The Mickey Mouse Club*.

"Well, I'll be a dirty bird!"

Catchphrase of TV comedian George Gobel.

The Wellingtons

Group that performs the theme song of the TV sitcom *Gilligan's Island*.

"We'll leave the light on for you"

Slogan of the Motel 6 chain, spoken in radio commercials by Tom Bodett.

"We'll Meet Again"

Tune that plays over the closing scenes of nuclear detonation in the film *Dr. Strangelove*, performed by Vera Lynn.

"We love you, baby"

Message embossed in Braille on the back of the Paul McCartney and Wings album *Red Rose Speedway*. The message was intended for pop singer Stevie Wonder.

Welton Academy

Prep-school setting of the film *Dead Poets Society*.

"We Never Fail to Do What's Right"

Motto of the Rescue Aid Society in the Disney animated film *The Rescuers*.

"We Never Sleep"

Slogan of Pinkerton's detective agency.

Wentworth

Maiden name of Lovey Howell (Natalie Schafer) in the TV sitcom *Gilligan's Island*.

Wentworth Place

London home of poet John Keats.

Wentworth scale

Scale used in geology to measure the size of loose rocks, based on their diameter (listed below in millimeters):

Boulder: greater than 256 (10 inches)
Cobble: 64–256
Pebble: 4–64
Granule: 2–4
Sand: $\frac{1}{16}$–2
Silt: $\frac{1}{256}$–$\frac{1}{16}$
Clay: less than $\frac{1}{256}$

We're Here

Fishing schooner owned by Disko Troop in the Rudyard Kipling novel *Captains Courageous*.

"We're in touch, so you be in touch"

Sign-off line of Hugh Downs in the TV series *20/20*.

"We're not worthy! We're not worthy!"

How Wayne Campbell (Mike Myers) and Garth Algar (Dana Carvey) greet rock star Alice Cooper in the film *Wayne's World*.

Werthan, Daisy

Role for which Jessica Tandy won a Best Actress Academy Award in the 1989 film *Driving Miss Daisy*.

"We Shield Millions"

What the call letters of Nashville's *Grand Ole Opry* radio station WSM originally stood for. This was the advertising slogan of the National Life and Accident Company, the station's original owner.

Wesley

Middle name of *Star Trek* creator Gene Roddenberry, for whom the *Star Trek: The Next Generation* character Wesley Crusher (Wil Wheaton) was named.

Wesley, Arthur

Birth name of English war hero the Duke of Wellington.

Wessex

Mythical English county that is the setting of the novels of Thomas Hardy.

Westbridge High

School attended by the title character (Melissa Joan Hart) in the TV sitcom *Sabrina, the Teenage Witch*.

Westdale High

School attended by the Brady children in the TV sitcom *The Brady Bunch*.

West Egg, New York

Long Island home of Nick Carraway and Jay Gatsby in the F. Scott Fitzgerald novel *The Great Gatsby*.

Westerburg High

Setting of the film *Heathers*.

Western Biological Laboratory

Salinas, California, company owned by Doc in the John Steinbeck novel *Cannery Row*.

Western State University

Setting of the TV sitcom *Hank*.

Western University

Los Angeles school that is the setting of the film *Blue Chips*.

Western Writers of America

See **Spur Awards**

Westfield Academy

Military prep-school setting of the TV sitcom *McKeever and the Colonel*.

Westland

Home of President Grover Cleveland in Princeton, New Jersey.

Westmacott, Mary

Pen name used by Dame Agatha Christie for six romance novels.

Westminster Abbey, famous people buried at

POETS/WRITERS

Robert Browning
Geoffrey Chaucer
Charles Dickens
John Dryden
Thomas Hardy
Samuel Johnson
Rudyard Kipling
John Masefield
Richard Sheridan
Edmund Spenser
Alfred Lord Tennyson

OTHERS

Charles Darwin (naturalist)
David Garrick (Shakespearean actor)
George Frideric Handel (composer)
David Livingstone (missionary/explorer)
Sir Isaac Newton (physicist/mathematician)
Laurence Olivier (actor)
Ernest Rutherford (physicist)

See also **17**

Westminster College

School in Fulton, Missouri, where on March 5, 1946, former English prime minister Winston Churchill gave the speech that introduced the phrase "iron curtain."

Weston, Dick

Stage name used by Cincinnati-born Leonard Franklin Slye before changing his name to Roy Rogers.

Weston, Stanley

Creator of the G.I. Joe action figure in 1965.

West, Otto

Role for which Kevin Kline won a Best Supporting Actor Academy Award in the 1988 film *A Fish Called Wanda*.

Westover, Charles

Real name of pop singer Del Shannon.

Wet

1979 "theme" album by Barbra Streisand, whose song titles all contain a reference to water:
    "Wet"
    "Kiss Me in the Rain"
    "I Ain't Gonna Cry Tonight"
    "Niagara"
    "On Rainy Afternoons"
    "Come Rain or Come Shine"
    "After the Rain"
    "Splish Splash"
    "No More Tears (Enough Is Enough)" (duet with
        Donna Summer)

"The Wet Bandits"

Self-styled nickname of bungling burglars Marv (Daniel Stern) and Harry (Joe Pesci) in the film *Home Alone*.

"We try harder"

Advertising slogan of Avis Rent-a-Car.

"We will sell no wine before its time"

Advertising slogan of Paul Masson wines, spoken in TV commercials by Orson Welles.

WFDR-TV

Washington, D.C., employer of the title fowl in the comic strip *Mallard Fillmore*.

WGEO

Washington, D.C., radio station that is the setting of the TV sitcom *FM*.

Wharton, John

See **Morrison, William and Wharton, John**

"What a dump!"

Memorable line spoken by Rose Moline (Bette Davis) in the film *Beyond the Forest*.

"What? And Get Out of Show Business?"

Debut episode of the TV sitcom *The Partridge Family*, which aired on September 25, 1970.

"What a revoltin' development this is!"

Catchphrase of the title character (Lionel Stander, Jackie Gleason, William Bendix) in the radio and TV versions of the sitcom *The Life of Riley*.

"What a surprise!"

See **"milk mustache" celebrities**

"What a Wonderful World"

Original theme song of the TV sitcom *Family Matters*, performed by Louis Armstrong. After the first season, "As Days Go By" was used.

"What becomes a Legend most?" celebrities

Each of these actors, singers, and other celebrities was featured in the 1968–1979 print-ad campaign for Blackglama minks. Each subject's remuneration was a mink coat, custom-designed if requested.

    Lauren Bacall
    Pearl Bailey
    Carol Burnett
    Maria Callas
    Carol Channing
    Claudette Colbert
    Joan Crawford
    Bette Davis
    Marlene Dietrich
    Faye Dunaway
    Joan Fontaine
    Dame Margot Fonteyn (ballet dancer)
    Judy Garland
    Paulette Goddard
    Martha Graham (choreographer)
    Helen Hayes
    Rita Hayworth
    Lillian Hellman (playwright)
    Lena Horne
    Ruby Keeler

    Suzy Knickerbocker (columnist)
    Angela Lansbury
    Peggy Lee
    Shirley MacLaine
    Mary Martin
    Melina Mercouri
    Ethel Merman
    Liza Minnelli
    Rudolf Nureyev (ballet dancer)
    Leontyne Price
    Diana Ross
    Rosalind Russell
    Renata Scotto
    Barbara Stanwyck
    Beverly Sills
    Barbra Streisand
    Liv Ullmann
    Diana Vreeland (fashion-magazine editor)
    Raquel Welch

"Whatever you desire"

See **Fleur-de-Lis**

"What hath God wrought?"

See **"A patient waiter is no loser"**

Whatizit

See **Olympic mascots (Summer Games)**

"What, me worry?"

Catchphrase of *Mad* magazine mascot Alfred E. Neuman.

"What mighty contests rise from trivial things"

Quote by poet Alexander Pope that appears on the box of the original Genus Edition of the board game Trivial Pursuit.

What's It All About?

1992 autobiography of actor Michael Caine. The title song of the film *Alfie*, which starred Caine, includes the book's title in its lyrics.

"What's My Crime?"

Favorite TV show of Horace and Jasper Badun, in the Disney animated film *101 Dalmatians*.

What You Will

Alternate title of the William Shakespeare play *Twelfth Night*.

Wheatland

Estate of President James Buchanan near Lancaster, Pennsylvania.

Wheeler, Schuyler

Inventor of the electric fan in 1882.

The Wheel Spins

Novel by Ethel Lina White that was the basis for the Alfred Hitchcock film *The Lady Vanishes*.

"When it absolutely, positively, has to be there overnight"

Advertising slogan of Federal Express.

"When it rains, it pours"

Advertising slogan of Morton Salt.

"When It's Sleepy Time Down South"

Theme song of trumpeter Louis Armstrong.

"When lift plus thrust is greater than load plus drag"

How Sister Bertrille (Sally Field) explains her ability to fly, in the TV sitcom *The Flying Nun*.

"When the Blue of the Night Meets the Gold of the Day"

Theme song of singer Bing Crosby.

"When the Moon Comes Over the Mountain"

Theme song of singer Kate Smith.

"When We're Singin'"

Original theme song of the TV sitcom *The Partridge Family*. For the third season, new lyrics were written for the song, which became the new theme, "Come On, Get Happy."

"When you care enough to send the very best"

Advertising slogan of Hallmark Cards.

"When you're slapped, you'll take it and like it!"

Memorable line spoken by Sam Spade (Humphrey Bogart) to Joel Cairo (Peter Lorre) in the film *The Maltese Falcon*.

"Where all the women are strong, all the men are good-looking, and all the children are above average"

Garrison Keillor's description of Lake Wobegon, Minnesota, on his radio series *A Prairie Home Companion*.

"Where do you want to go today?"

Advertising slogan of Microsoft.

"Where Everybody Knows Your Name"

Theme song of the TV sitcom *Cheers*, performed by Gary Portnoy.

"Where Is Everybody?"

First episode of the TV series *The Twilight Zone*, which aired on October 2, 1959.

"Where research is the key to tomorrow"

Advertising slogan of 3M.

"Where Smiles Never End"

Advertising slogan of Ringling Brothers and Barnum & Bailey circus.

"Where's the beef?"

Advertising slogan of Burger King, spoken by octogenarian Clara Peller in memorable 1980s TV commercials.

Where's the Rest of Me?

1965 autobiography of actor Ronald Reagan. The title comes from a line he spoke in the film *Kings Row*.

"Where's your mustache?"

See **"milk mustache" celebrities**

"Where the elite meet to eat"

Slogan of the title establishment in the radio sitcom *Duffy's Tavern*.

"Where were you in '62?"

Slogan used to promote the film *American Graffiti*.

Whiplash, Snidely

Cartoon character nemesis of Mountie Dudley Do-Right, voiced by Hans Conried.

"Whiplash Willie"

See **Gingrich, William H. "Whiplash Willie"**

"Whipped Cream"

Theme song of the TV game show *The Dating Game*, performed by Herb Alpert and the Tijuana Brass.

"Whipper"

Nickname of Judge Jennifer Cone (Dyan Cannon) in the TV series *Ally McBeal*.

Whipple, Mr.

See **Wilson, Dick**

Whipsnade, Larson E.

See **Fields, W. C., roles/pen names of**

"The Whirlwind"
See **McGaffey, Ives**

Whiskers
Cartoon cat (voiced by Danny DeVito) that works for the LAPD in the film *Last Action Hero*.

Whiskey
Horse of Cactus Jack Slade (Kirk Douglas) in the film *The Villain*.

"Whistling Bells"
Theme song of the TV sitcom *Our Miss Brooks*.

"The White Angel"
Nickname of World War II war criminal Christian Szell (Laurence Olivier) in the film *Marathon Man*.

White, Carietta
Full name of the title character in the Stephen King novel *Carrie*, portrayed in the film adaptation of the same name by Sissy Spacek.

White, Ethel Lina
See **The Wheel Spins**

White, Eve
See **Eve (Eve White/Eve Black/Jane)**

White Fang and Black Tooth
Canine characters in the children's TV series *The Soupy Sales Show*.

White Flash
Horse of film cowboy Tex Ritter.

Whitehead, Commander
British naval officer in print ads and TV commercials for Schweppes beverages since the 1950s.

Whitehouse, Glen
Role for which James Coburn won a Best Supporting Actor Academy Award in the 1998 film *Affliction*.

White, Jesse
Actor who portrayed "Ol' Lonely," the Maytag Repairman in TV commercials from 1967 to 1989. He was succeeded by actor Gordon Jump.

Whiteley's
London shop where the gown worn at Ascot by Eliza Doolittle is bought, in the Lerner and Loewe musical *My Fair Lady*.

"white mountain"
What the name of extinct Hawaiian volcano Mauna Kea means in Hawaiian.

White Nose
Family cat in the Happy Hollisters series of children's books.

White O'Mornin'
Ancestral home bought by Sean Thornton (John Wayne) in the film *The Quiet Man*.

Whiteside, Sheridan
See **"To Alexander Woollcott, for reasons that are nobody's business"**

White Surrey
Horse of King Richard III of Great Britain.

White Way Hotel
New York City setting of the Marx Brothers film *Room Service*.

"Whither are you going?"
What the Latin title of the Henryk Sienkiewicz novel *Quo Vadis?* means in English.

Whittier
Last name of the title character in the Eleanor Hodgman Porter novel *Pollyanna*.

"Whiz Kids"
Nickname of the 1950 Philadelphia Phillies, who won the National League pennant with a starting lineup all under 30 years old.

"Who could ask for anything more?"
Phrase used in three songs of George and Ira Gershwin:
"I Got Rhythm" (1930, written for the Broadway musical *Girl Crazy*)
"I'm About to Be a Mother" (1931, written for the Broadway musical *Of Thee I Sing*)
"Nice Work If You Can Get It" (1937, written for the film *A Damsel in Distress*)

"Whoever you are—I have always depended on the kindness of strangers"
Memorable line spoken by Blanche Dubois in the Tennessee Williams play *A Streetcar Named Desire*.

"Who Killed Holly Howard?"
Debut episode of the TV series *Burke's Law*, which aired on September 20, 1963.

"Who Needs Wings to Fly?"

Theme song of the TV sitcom *The Flying Nun*.

The Who, original members

Roger Daltrey, John Entwistle, Keith Moon, and Pete Townshend.

"Who's for Swordfish?"

Debut episode of the TV sitcom *Car 54, Where Are You?*, which aired on September 17, 1961.

"Who shot J. R.?"

See **Shepard, Kristin**

"Who's on First?" team

In the order mentioned in the Abbott and Costello film *The Naughty Nineties*:

Who: first base
What: second base
I Don't Know: third base
Why: left field
Because: center field
Tomorrow: pitcher
Today: catcher
I Don't Care: shortstop

No right fielder is mentioned in the routine.

"Who the hell was Regis Philbin?"

Trivia question in the 1978 book *The Great 1960s Quiz*, published 11 years before the premiere of *Live with Regis and Kathie Lee*, and 21 years before the American premiere of *Who Wants to Be a Millionaire*. The answer to the question, Philbin's principal claim to fame at that time, was "Joey Bishop's sidekick on his [1967–69] late night show."

Who-ville

Setting of the Dr. Seuss children's book *How the Grinch Stole Christmas!*

"Who Wants to Be a Millionaire?"

Cole Porter tune introduced by Frank Sinatra and Celeste Holm in the 1956 film *High Society*, 43 years before the U.S. premiere of the TV game show of the same name.

Who Wants to Be a Millionaire, The Album

2000 "theme" CD, whose tunes "capture the spirit" of the game show of the same name. Tunes and performers are listed below:

"I Want to Be a Millionaire" (Jack and Jenna)
"Money (That's What I Want)" (Barrett Strong)
"For the Love of Money" (The O'Jays)
"Telephone Line" (ELO)
"Goldfinger" (Shirley Bassey)
"Call Me" (Blondie)
"When the Going Gets Tough, the Tough Get Going" (Billy Ocean)
"You Got It" (Roy Orbison)
"Operator" (Manhattan Transfer)
"Diamonds Are a Girl's Best Friend" (T-Bone Burnett)
"Pennies from Heaven" (Regis Philbin)

"Why me? Why is it always me?"

Catchphrase of Captain Binghampton (Joe Flynn) in the TV sitcom *McHale's Navy*.

Wian, Bob

Founder of the Big Boy restaurant chain. The first Big Boy (previously known as Bob's Pantry), opened in 1937 in Glendale, California.

"The Wicked Wasp of Twickenham"

Nickname of poet Alexander Pope.

Widows and Orphans Friendly Society

Original name of Prudential Insurance.

Wigglesworth, Bunny

Foppish brother of the title character in the film *Zorro, the Gay Blade*. Both roles were played by George Hamilton.

Wigglesworth, Professor Waldo

Fox sidekick of cartoon frog Hoppity Hooper, voiced by Hans Conried.

Wight

Real last name of author/veterinarian James Herriot.

Wilbur

Real first name of pro football Hall of Fame coach Weeb Ewbank.

Pig friend of the title spider in the E. B. White children's novel *Charlotte's Web*.

Wildbank

Home of composer John Philip Sousa in Sands Point, New York.

"Wild Bill"

Nickname of William Donovan, director of the Office of Strategic Services (OSS), the World War II intelligence agency that was the predecessor of the Central Intelligence Agency.

"The Wild Bull of the Pampas"

Nickname of Argentine boxer Luis Firpo.

Wildcountry

See **Young Country**

Wildfire

Favorite horse of Godfrey Cass in the George Eliot novel *Silas Marner*.

"A Wild Hare"

1940 Warner Bros. cartoon in which Bugs Bunny first says "What's up, Doc?"

"Wild Thing"

Nickname of Cleveland Indian pitcher Ricky Vaughn (Charlie Sheen) in the films *Major League* and *Major League II*.

Wiles, Andrew

Princeton University mathematician who proved in 1993 what had been the most famous unsolved problem in mathematics, Fermat's Last Theorem.

Wiley

Last name of the title character (Bill Murray) in the film *What About Bob?*

Wilfred Bailey

Real first and middle names of actor Bill Bixby.

Wilhelm

Real first name of composer (Wilhelm) Richard Wagner.

First name of Colonel Klink (Werner Klemperer) in the TV sitcom *Hogan's Heroes*.

Middle name of Clark Griswold (Chevy Chase) in the National Lampoon "Vacation" series of films.

See also **Jacob and Wilhelm**

Wilkes, Annie

Role for which Kathy Bates won a Best Actress Academy Award for the 1990 film *Misery*.

Will a jolly man make a jolly visitor?

Mnemonic for the last names of the first eight U.S. presidents: Washington, Adams, Jefferson, Madison, Monroe, (John Quincy) Adams, Jackson, and Van Buren.

Willard

Real first name of actor Will Smith.

Willard, Archibald

Ohio artist who painted *Yankee Doodle*, commonly known as *The Spirit of '76*, for Philadelphia's Centennial Exposition of 1876.

William

Real first name of jazz bandleader/pianist Count Basie.

Real first name of actor (William) Clark Gable.

First name of author W. Somerset Maugham.

Real first name of actor (William) Claude Rains.

Real first name of director (William) Oliver Stone.

Middle name of TV host Johnny Carson.

See also **Meriwether and William**

William Alexander

Real first and middle names of comedian Bud Abbott.

William Arthur Philip Louis

Full name of Prince William of Great Britain, elder son of Prince Charles and Princess Diana.

William Bradley

Real first and middle names of actor Brad Pitt.

William Christopher

First and middle names of composer W. C. Handy.

William Edward Burghardt

First and middle names of civil-rights leader W. E. B. Du Bois.

William Frederick

Real first and middle names of Buffalo Bill Cody.

William Harrison

Real first and middle names of boxer Jack Dempsey.

William Randolph

Real first and middle names of jazz drummer Cozy Cole.

William Royce

Real first and middle names of rock singer Boz Scaggs.

Williamson Music Company

Music publishing company founded in 1943 by Rodgers and Hammerstein. It is so named because the fathers of Richard Rodgers and Oscar Hammerstein II were both named William.

Willie

Hansen family dog in the TV series *Mama*.

Willie and Joe

Infantrymen who regularly appeared in the *Stars and Stripes* cartoons of Bill Mauldin during World War II.

Willow, Maine

Setting of the Stephen King short story "Rainy Season."

Willows, Wisconsin

Hometown of Barbie, where she attends Willows High School.

Wills, Frank

Security guard who discovered the break-in at Democratic National Committee headquarters at Washington, D.C.'s Watergate Hotel on June 17, 1972.

"The Willy Moran Story"

Debut episode of the TV Western series *Wagon Train*, which aired on September 18, 1957.

"Will You Ever Win?"

Subtitle of the Fleetwood Mac tune "Rhiannon."

Wilma

Real first name of Deanie Loomis (Natalie Wood) in the film *Splendor in the Grass*.

Wilshire Memorial Hospital

Medical center where Dr. Michael Mancini (Thomas Calabro) serves his residency in the TV series *Melrose Place*.

Wilson

Name given by marooned Chuck Noland (Tom Hanks) to a volleyball that washes ashore, in the film *Cast Away*.

Wilson, Charles Kemmons

Founder of the Holiday Inn motel chain, which he named for the 1942 Bing Crosby/Fred Astaire film of the same name. The first Holiday Inn opened in 1952 in Memphis, Tennessee.

Wilson, Dick

Actor who has portrayed grocer Mr. Whipple in TV commercials for Charmin bathroom tissue since 1964.

Wilson, John

Real name of author Anthony Burgess.

Wilson, Norma Rae/Webster, Norma Rae

Role for which Sally Field won a Best Actress Academy Award in the 1979 film *Norma Rae*. (Field's character got married during the film.)

Wilson, Wilson

Neighbor of the Taylor family in the TV sitcom *Home Improvement*, portrayed by Earl Hindman.

"Window Shopping"

Instrumental theme of the TV game show *The Price Is Right* while Bill Cullen was host.

Windrip, Berzelius "Buzz"

President of the United States who becomes a dictator, in the Sinclair Lewis novel *It Can't Happen Here*.

Windsor College

Ohio school attended by Sidney Prescott (Neve Campbell) in the film *Scream 2*.

Winfield, John R.

See **Dickson, J. T. and Winfield, John R.**

Winfred-Louder

Cleveland department-store employer of the title character in the TV sitcom *The Drew Carey Show*.

Wing

Real last name of rock singer Grace Slick of Jefferson Airplane.

"The Wings of Man"

Advertising slogan of Eastern Airlines.

Wings Over the World

Pacifist organization seeking to found a new order based on technology, in the film *Things to Come*.

Winifred

Real first name of actress Jacqueline Bisset.

Winkel, Dietrich

Musician who invented the metronome in 1812.

Winnie Mae

Lockheed Vega monoplane of aviator Wiley Post, in which he made the first solo flight around the world on July 15–22, 1933.

Winslow, Phil and Dottie

Owners of the title canine, a Great Dane, in the comic strip *Marmaduke*.

Winston Conrad

Real first and middle names of game-show host Wink Martindale.

Winterbottom, Augustus

See **Fields, W. C., roles/pen names of**

Winter River, Connecticut

Setting of the film *Beetlejuice*.

"A Winter's Idyll"

Subtitle of the John Greenleaf Whittier poem "Snow-Bound."

Winters, Katy

1960s TV spokesperson for Secret deodorant.

"Wire Paladin San Francisco"

Words below the title phrase on the business card of Paladin (Richard Boone) in the TV Western series *Have Gun Will Travel*.

"The Wisdom of Eve"

Short story by Mary Orr that was the basis for the film *All About Eve*.

Wisdom of the Heart

Play starring Elise McKenna (Jane Seymour) in the film *Somewhere in Time*.

Wishbone, Johnny

Alias used by Axel Foley (Eddie Murphy) posing as a psychic from St. Croix, in the film *Beverly Hills Cop II*.

Wistful Vista

Setting of the radio sitcom *Fibber McGee and Molly*. The McGees (Jim and Marian Jordan) lived at 79 Wistful Vista in the town of Wistful Vista.

Witchcraft Around Us

See **Magic in Mexico** and **Witchcraft Around Us**

"The Witch of Wall Street"

Nickname of notoriously frugal Hetty Green (1834–1916), believed at one time to be the richest woman in the United States.

The Witch's Curse

Alternate title of the Gilbert and Sullivan comic opera *Ruddigore*.

"With a Little Help from My Friends"

Theme song of the TV sitcom *The Wonder Years*, performed by Joe Cocker.

"The Wizard of Oz"

Nickname of baseball player Ozzie Smith, for his defensive acrobatics.

"The Wizard of the North"

Nickname of author Sir Walter Scott.

"The Wizard of Westwood"

Nickname of former UCLA basketball coach John Wooden.

WJM

Minneapolis TV station that is the setting of the TV sitcom *The Mary Tyler Moore Show*. The call letters are derived from the initials of station owner Wild Jack Monroe (Slim Pickens).

Wladek

Real first name of pro wrestler Killer Kowalski.

WNYX

New York City radio station that is the setting of the TV sitcom *Newsradio*.

Wo Fat

Underworld crime boss and arch-nemesis of Steve McGarrett (Jack Lord) in the TV series *Hawaii Five-O*, portrayed by Khigh Dhiegh.

Wofford, Chloe Anthony

Birth name of novelist Toni Morrison.

Woganowski, Dom

Real name of Woogie (Chris Elliott), former boyfriend of the title character (Cameron Diaz) in the film *There's Something About Mary*.

Wojtyla, Karol

Real name of Pope John Paul II.

Wolf

Pet dog of the title character in Washington Irving short story "Rip Van Winkle."

Pet German shepherd of Eddie Haskell (Ken Osmond) in the TV sitcom *Leave It to Beaver*.

Wolf and Gnasher

Pet dogs of Heathcliff in the Emily Brontë novel *Wuthering Heights*.

Wolf-Beiderman

Comet on a collision course with Earth in the film *Deep Impact*.

Wolf City, Wyoming

Setting of the film *Cat Ballou*.

Wolfgang

Middle name of werewolf Eddie Munster (Butch Patrick) in the TV sitcom *The Munsters*.

Wolfinger, Ambrose

See **Fields, W. C., roles/pen names of**

"The Wolf of Wall Street"

Nickname of Thurston Howell III (Jim Backus) in the TV sitcom *Gilligan's Island*.

wolfram

Alternate name for tungsten, from which its chemical symbol W is derived.

Wollstonecraft

Middle name of author Mary Shelley.

"Wolverine"

See **United States residents' nicknames**

Wolves

Baseball team of Ed O'Brien (Gene Kelly) and Denny Ryan (Frank Sinatra) in the film *Take Me Out to the Ball Game*.

"The Woman"

How Sherlock Holmes refers to Irene Adler, the only woman who ever bested him, in the Arthur Conan Doyle short story "A Scandal in Bohemia."

"Woman Haters"

See **190**

"Woman is fickle"

English translation of *"La donna è mobile,"* title of the Giuseppe Verdi aria from the opera *Rigoletto*.

"A woman never forgets the man who remembers"

1950s advertising slogan for Whitman's chocolates.

Wonder Bowl

Original name of the first Tupperware product sold by Earl Tupper in 1947.

Wonderboy

Favorite bat of Roy Hobbs in the Bernard Malamud novel *The Natural*, and the film version of the same name, where Hobbs is portrayed by Robert Redford.

"The Wonderful One-Hoss Shay"

Alternate title of the Oliver Wendell Holmes poem "The Deacon's Masterpiece."

"Wonderful Season of Love"

See **"For Those Who Are Young"**

The Wonders

Rock quartet managed by Play-Tone Records executive Mr. White (Tom Hanks), in the film *that thing you do!*

The Wonder Who

Pseudonym used by The Four Seasons for their recording of "Don't Think Twice."

WonderWorld

Amusement park owned by Uncle Dave (Alan Young) in the film *Beverly Hills Cop III*.

"The Wonder Years"

Ages 1 through 12, according to ads for Wonder Bread.

Wong Airline

Carrier that flies CIA agent Vince Ricardo (Peter Falk) and dentist Sheldon Kornpett (Alan Arkin) to the Latin American nation of Tejada, in the film *The In-Laws*.

Wood, Anne and Davenport, Andrew

Creators of the children's TV series *Teletubbies*, which debuted on the BBC Two network on March 31, 1997.

Woodard, Lynette

The first woman to play for the Harlem Globetrotters, from 1985 to 1987.

Woodhouse

Last name of the title character of the Jane Austen novel *Emma*.

Woodhouse, Andrew John

Title character of the film *Rosemary's Baby*.

Wood, Kenneth

See **Robot Kenwood Chef**

Wood, Nan

See **McKeeby, Dr. Byron H. and Wood, Nan**

Woods and Wildlife

Magazine employer of the title character in the comic strip *Mark Trail*.

Woodsboro, California

Setting of the *Scream* series of films.

The Woodsboro Murders
See **Stab**

Woods, Ilene
Voice of the title character in the Disney animated film *Cinderella*.

Woodstock
Bird friend of Snoopy in the comic strip *Peanuts*.

Woodstock '69 performers
The acts that appeared on the main stage of the Woodstock Music and Arts Fair, at Bethel, New York, on August 15–17, 1969.

AUGUST 15
Richie Havens
Country Joe McDonald
John Sebastian
Incredible String Band
Bert Sommer
Sweetwater
Tim Hardin
Ravi Shankar
Melanie
Arlo Guthrie
Joan Baez

AUGUST 16
Quill
Keef Hartley
Santana
Mountain
Canned Heat
Grateful Dead
Creedence Clearwater Revival
Janis Joplin
Sly and the Family Stone
The Who
Jefferson Airplane

AUGUST 17
Joe Cocker
Country Joe and the Fish
Ten Years After
The Band
Blood, Sweat and Tears
Johnny Winter
Crosby, Stills, Nash and Young
Paul Butterfield Blues Band
Sha Na Na
Jimi Hendrix

Woodsy Owl
"Pollution prevention bird" cartoon mascot of the U.S. Forest Service since the 1970s, whose slogans have included "Give a hoot, don't pollute!" and "Lend a hand, care for the land!"

Woodward
Real first name of cowboy singer Tex Ritter.

Woodward/Newman films
The films in which Joanne Woodward and Paul Newman appear together:
> *Rally 'Round the Flag, Boys!* (1958)
> *The Long, Hot Summer* (1958)
> *From the Terrace* (1960)
> *Paris Blues* (1961)
> *A New Kind of Love* (1963)
> *Winning* (1969)
> *WUSA* (1970)
> *The Drowning Pool* (1975)
> *Harry and Son* (1984)
> *Mr. & Mrs. Bridge* (1990)

Woodward, Thomas Jones
See **Scott, Tommy**

Woody
Old station wagon ridden by the title characters (Michael Cole, Clarence Williams III, Peggy Lipton) in the TV series *The Mod Squad*.

Toy hero in the animated films *Toy Story* and *Toy Story II*, voiced by Tom Hanks.

Woofer
Pet dog of Winky Dink in the children's TV series *Winky Dink and You*.

Woof-Woof
Werewolf doll of Eddie Munster (Butch Patrick) in the TV sitcom *The Munsters*.

"Wool Hat"
Nickname of Michael Nesmith of the Monkees, who often wore one.

Woolworth
Term in bowling for a 5-10 split.

W.O.P.R.
War Operations Planning Research computer at NORAD headquarters in the film *WarGames*.

Workman
Allied code name for Iwo Jima during World War II.

"Works for me!"

Catchphrase of the title character (Fred Dryer) in the TV series *Hunter*.

The World According to Bensenhaver

Book written by the title character in the John Irving novel *The World According to Garp*.

A World for Two

Film for which Vicki Lester (Judy Garland) wins an Academy Award, in the film *A Star Is Born* (1954).

World Illustrated

Magazine employer of reporter/photographer Shirley Logan (Shirley MacLaine) in the TV sitcom *Shirley's World*.

"The world is not enough"

Motto of the Bond family, identified by heraldry expert Sir Hilary Bray (George Baker) in the James Bond film *On Her Majesty's Secret Service*.

"The World On Time"

Advertising slogan of Federal Express.

The World Set Free

1914 sci-fi novel by H. G. Wells in which he coined the term "atomic bomb" for a weapon of great power. It is made from a substance called Carolinum.

"The World's Largest Outdoor Cocktail Party"

Nickname of the tailgate party held each year before the University of Florida/University of Georgia football game.

"World's Largest" roadside attractions

A sampling of many such self-proclaimed man-made giants throughout the United States:
   Alligator: Christmas, Florida (200 feet long)
   Baseball bat: Louisville, Kentucky (120 feet high, 68,000 pounds)
   Cherry pie: George, Washington (!) (containing 400 pounds of cherries, baked every July 4th)
   Chest of drawers: High Point, North Carolina (32 feet high)
   Chicken: Marietta, Georgia (55 feet high)
   Crow: Belgrade, Michigan (18 feet high)
   Crystal ball: Westerville, Ohio (700 pounds)
   Cuckoo clock: Wilmot, Ohio (23.5 feet high)
   Dixie Cup: Lexington, Kentucky (9 feet high, 1,360-gallon capacity)
   Fire hydrant: Beaumont, Texas (24 feet high)
   Globe: Yarmouth, Maine (41 feet in diameter)
   Harp (playable): Santa Fe, New Mexico (13 feet high)
   Horse: Grand Rapids, Michigan (28 feet long, 24 feet high, 27,000 pounds)
   Icosahedron (solid figure with 20 faces): Lexington, Massachusetts (15 feet high)
   Kaleidoscope: Mt. Tremper, New York (60 feet high)
   Ketchup bottle: Collinsville, Illinois (170 feet high)
   Office chair: Anniston, Alabama (33 feet high)
   Porch swing: Hebron, Nebraska (32 feet long)
   Potato chip: Blackfoot, Idaho (25 inches by 14 inches)
   Rubber stamp: Cleveland, Ohio (48 feet long; it reads "FREE")
   Stove: Detroit, Michigan (25 feet high)
   Strawberry: Strawberry Point, Iowa (12 feet high)
   Teapot: Chester, West Virginia (14 feet high)
   Thermometer: Baker, California—"Gateway to Death Valley" (134 feet high, in honor of the 134-degree temperature recorded in Death Valley in 1913)
   Weather vane: White Lake, Michigan (48 feet high)

"World's Largest Store"

What the call letters of Chicago radio and TV station WLS originally stood for, in reference to Sears Roebuck, its former owner.

"The World's Most Perfectly Developed Man"

Nickname of bodybuilder Charles Atlas.

"The World's Worst Juggler"

Nickname of vaudevillian Freddy James, who later became radio comedian Fred Allen.

World Theater

See **Fitzgerald Theater**

"The World Turned Upside Down"

Tune to which English and Hessian troops departed on October 19, 1781, after their surrender to General George Washington at the Battle of Yorktown.

World War II

Snoopy's archenemy, the cat next door, in the comic strip *Peanuts*.

Worldwide Pants, Inc.

Production company of TV talk host David Letterman.

World Wide Wicket Company

Employer of up-and-comer J. Pierrepont Finch in the Frank Loesser musical *How to Succeed in Business Without Really Trying*.

Worrell

See Ernest **feature films**

Wossamotta U.

College attended by Rocky and Bullwinkle in the children's animated TV series *Rocky and His Friends*.

Would, Holli

Cartoon character that becomes human in the film *Cool World*, portrayed by Kim Basinger.

Would I Lie to You?

Original working title of the film *Tootsie*.

"Would you believe . . . ?"

Catchphrase of the title character (Don Adams) in the TV sitcom *Get Smart*.

WPIG

Rival radio station in the TV sitcom *WKRP in Cincinnati*.

Wragby Hall

Chatterley family estate in the D. H. Lawrence novel *Lady Chatterley's Lover*.

"Wrecking"

Nickname of Paul Crewe (Burt Reynolds) in the film *The Longest Yard*.

The Wreck of the Titan

1898 novelette by Morgan Robertson (original title *Futility*) that is eerily prophetic of the 1912 sinking of the R.M.S. *Titanic*. The English-built, "practically unsinkable" *Titan* was "the largest craft afloat," had insufficient lifeboat capacity, and sank after ramming into an iceberg during a transatlantic voyage. Robertson also wrote the war-themed short story "Beyond the Spectrum," which has similarly eerie parallels to World War II (Japanese bombing Hawaii, etc.). These two works are often cited by believers in psychic phenomena as proof that it is possible to predict the future.

Wretched, Colorado

Setting of the TV sitcom *Pistols 'n' Petticoats*.

Wright, Frank

See **Allen, Roy**

Wright, James

General Electric engineer who accidently invented Silly Putty in 1943, while searching for a new kind of synthetic rubber. Silly Putty's principal ingredients are boric acid and silicone oil.

Wright, John Lloyd

Son of architect Frank Lloyd Wright who invented Lincoln Logs circa 1916.

Wrightsville

Town invaded by the Black Rebels motorcycle club in the film *The Wild One*.

Wright, Sylvia

See **mondegreen**

Wright, Willard Huntington

Real name of mystery writer S. S. Van Dine.

"Write if you get work"

Sign-off line of Ray Goulding of Bob and Ray radio fame.

See also **"Hang by your thumbs"**

"Wrong Way"

Nickname of college football player Roy Riegels, who, at the 1929 Rose Bowl, ran over 70 yards in the wrong direction after recovering a fumble.

See also **Lizzy**

Wuetherich, Rolf

Passenger in actor James Dean's Porsche Spyder on September 30, 1955, who was badly injured but survived the crash that killed Dean. Wuetherich was Dean's auto-race mechanic.

Wyatt, Wheeler, Hellerman, Tetlo and Brown

Former law-firm employer of Andrew Beckett (Tom Hanks) in the film *Philadelphia*.

Wyld Stallyns

Garage band of the title characters (Alex Winter and Keanu Reeves, respectively) in the *Bill and Ted's . . .* films.

WYN

Boston television station that is the setting of the TV sitcom *Goodnight, Beantown*.

Wynant, Clyde

Title character of the Dashiell Hammett novel *The Thin Man*, portrayed in the film adaptation of the same name by Edward Ellis. He is a missing inventor sought by Nick and Nora Charles.

Wyndham, John

*See **The Midwich Cuckoos***

Wynne, Arthur

Inventor of the crossword puzzle, which first appeared in the *New York World* on December 21, 1913.

Wystan Hugh

First and middle names of poet W. H. Auden.

WZAZ

TV station in TV sitcom *Fernwood 2-Night*, on which the talk show of the same name is broadcast.

WZUP

Detroit radio station where Martin Payne (Martin Lawrence) works as a talk-show host, in the TV sitcom *Martin*.

"X-22"

Debut episode of the TV series *Matt Houston*, which aired on September 26, 1982.

Xanadu

49,000-acre Florida estate of Charles Foster Kane (Orson Welles) in the film *Citizen Kane*.

Xanthos

See **Balios and Xanthos**

XERB

Wolfman Jack's radio station in the film *American Graffiti*.

X-Y Position Indicator for a Display System

Original name of the computer mouse.

"Yakety Sax"

Instrumental theme of the TV series *The Benny Hill Show*, performed by Boots Randolph.

Yakhoob, Muzyad

Real name of entertainer Danny Thomas.

Yamasaki, Minoru

Architect who designed the twin towers of New York City's World Trade Center, completed in 1973.

"The Yankee Clipper"

Nickname of baseball Hall of Famer Joe DiMaggio.

yap.com

Employer of news correspondent Roland Hedley in the comic strip *Doonesbury*.

Yardbirds original members

Chris Dreja, Jim McCarty, Keith Relf, Paul Samwell-Smith, and Anthony Topham. Eric Clapton succeeded Topham in 1963, before the group's first album.

Yarmy

Real last name of comedian Don Adams.

Yarrow, Stookey, and Travers

Last names (respectively) of singers Peter, Paul, and Mary.

Yasgur, Max

Bethel, New York, farmer on whose land the Woodstock Music and Arts Fair was held on August 15–17, 1969.

"Yeah, that's the ticket!"

Catchphrase of perpetual liar Tommy Flanagan (Jon Lovitz) in the TV series *Saturday Night Live*.

The Year the Yankees Lost the Pennant

Novel by John Douglass Wallop that was the basis for the musical *Damn Yankees*.

Yeary II, Harvey Lee

Real name of actor Lee Majors.

Yelberton Abraham

First and middle names of pro football Hall of Fame quarterback Y. A. Tittle.

Yellowstone Springs, Montana

Where Arlo Guthrie briefly attends college, in the film *Alice's Restaurant*.

Yen Sid

Name of the sorcerer in the "Sorcerer's Apprentice" segment of the Disney animated film *Fantasia*. Yen Sid is "Disney" spelled backward.

Yeobright, Clym

Title character of the Thomas Hardy novel *The Return of the Native*.

Yes original members

Jon Anderson, Peter Banks, Bill Bruford, Tony Kaye, and Chris Squire.

Yesterday Cafe
See **Sid's Pizza Parlor**

Yezo

Former name of the Japanese island of Hokkaido.

"The Yiddish Mark Twain"

Nickname of author Shalom Aleichem.

Yin

Real last name of novelist Leslie Charteris.

"Yip"

Nickname of lyricist E. Y. Harburg, best known for his collaboration with songwriter Harold Arlen on the score of *The Wizard of Oz*.

YKK
See **Yoshida Kogyo Kabushikikaisha**

Yoknapatawpha County, Mississippi

Setting of most of the novels of William Faulkner, which he modeled on Lafayette County, Mississippi, where he lived most of his life.

See also **Jefferson, Mississippi**

"Yoo-hoo, Mrs. Bloom!"

Words often spoken by Molly Goldberg (Gertrude Berg) to her neighbor across the courtyard (Olga Fabian) in the TV sitcom *The Goldbergs*.

Yooks

See **Bitsy Big-Boy Boomeroo**

York, Alvin C.

Role for which Gary Cooper won a Best Actor Academy Award in the 1941 film *Sergeant York*.

York, Duke of

Title held by Prince Andrew of Great Britain.

Yorktown Productions

Production company of director Norman Jewison.

Yoshida Kogyo Kabushikikaisha

What the letters "YKK," found on the pull tabs of many zippers, stand for. It is Japanese for "Yoshida Industries Limited," the world's largest manufacturer of zippers.

"You ain't heard nothin' yet!"

Catchphrase of singer Al Jolson.

You and Your Emotions

Call-in radio show that Jonah Baldwin (Ross Malinger) phones to help his father Sam (Tom Hanks) find a wife, in the film *Sleepless in Seattle*.

You Asked for It

Title used for the Ian Fleming novel *Casino Royale* when first published in paperback form in the United States in 1955.

"You deserve a break today"

Advertising slogan of McDonald's.

"You do it, we print it"

Motto of the *Fernwood-Courier Press* in the TV sitcom *Mary Hartman, Mary Hartman*.

"You don't have to read it all, but it's nice to know it's all there"

Advertising slogan of *The New York Times*.

"You hockey puck!"

All-purpose put-down used by insult comic Don Rickles.

"You know how to whistle, don't you, Steve? You just put your lips together and blow."

Memorable line spoken by Marie Browning (Lauren Bacall) to Harry Morgan (Humphrey Bogart) in the film *To Have and Have Not*.

"You'll believe a man can fly"

Slogan used to promote the film *Superman*.

"You Look at Me"

Theme song of the TV sitcom *Joanie Loves Chachi*, performed by Erin Moran and Scott Baio, the show's stars.

"You . . . look . . . mahvelous!"

Catchphrase of comedian Billy Crystal's character Fernando.

"You May Be Right"

Theme song of the TV sitcom *Dave's World*, performed by Southside Johnny.

"Young and Modern"

See **Polly Pigtails**

Young Country

Original name of the country-music group Alabama. It was later called Wildcountry before adopting its best-known name.

Young Miss

See **Polly Pigtails**

"You press the button and we do the rest"

Advertising slogan used for the first Kodak camera in 1888. It was the first camera to use roll film, which was returned to the company for developing. The camera cost $25; the roll held 100 pictures.

"You rang?"

Catchphrase of beatnik Maynard G. Krebs (Bob Denver) in the TV sitcom *The Many Loves of Dobie Gillis*.

Catchphrase of butler Lurch (Ted Cassidy) in the TV sitcom *The Addams Family*.

"You're All the World to Me"

Tune by Burton Lane and Alan Jay Lerner that is heard while Tom Bowen (Fred Astaire) dances on the ceiling, in the film *Royal Wedding*.

"You're My Greatest Love"

Theme song of the TV sitcom *The Honeymooners*, composed by Jackie Gleason.

"Your Feet's Too Big"

Appropriate theme song of the TV sitcom *Harry and the Hendersons* (Harry being a Bigfoot), performed by Leon Redbone.

Your Money or Your Life

English TV game show being watched by Kevin's (Craig Warnock's) parents at the beginning of the film *Time Bandits*.

"Yowsah, Yowsah, Yowsah"

Subtitle of the Chic tune "Dance, Dance, Dance."

Ytterby

Village in Sweden for which four rare-earth elements discovered there were named: erbium, terbium, ytterbium and yttrium.

Yuengling

Oldest brewery in the United States, founded in 1829 in Pottsville, Pennsylvania, and still located there.

Yuki

Pet mongrel dog of President Lyndon Johnson. The dog was found at a Texas gas station by Johnson's daughter Luci.

Yule Jr., Joe

Real name of actor Mickey Rooney.

YUM

Stock-ticker symbol of TRICON Global Restaurants, operator of the Kentucky Fried Chicken, Pizza Hut, and Taco Bell chains.

Yuri

First name of the title character in the Boris Pasternak novel *Doctor Zhivago*, portrayed in the film adaptation of the same name by Omar Sharif.

Z-4195
Neurotic ant hero in the animated film *Antz*, voiced by Woody Allen.

Zachary, Tom
Washington Senators pitcher who gave up the record-breaking 60th home run of 1927 hit by New York Yankee Babe Ruth, on September 30th at Yankee Stadium.

Zamba
Lion in 1960s TV commercials for the Dreyfus Fund.

Zamenhof, Ludwig Lejzer
See **Esperanto, Doktoro**

Zametkin
Middle name of author Laura Z. Hobson.

Zamunda
African homeland of Prince Akeem (Eddie Murphy) in the film *Coming to America*.

Zangara, Giuseppe
Bricklayer who attempted to assassinate president-elect Franklin D. Roosevelt in Miami, Florida, on February 15, 1933. Zangara's shots killed Chicago mayor Anton Cermak and wounded five others.

Zap
See **Zip and Zap**

Zap-Em
Exterminating business run by Edgar (Vincent D'Onofrio) in the film *Men in Black*.

Zapruder, Abraham
Dallas manufacturer of ladies' dresses who shot the famous 478-frame film of the assassination of President John F. Kennedy on November 22, 1963, using an eight-millimeter Bell and Howell movie camera.

Zawistowska, Sophie
Role for which Meryl Streep won a Best Actress Academy Award in the 1982 film *Sophie's Choice*.

Zebra 3
Code name for David Starsky's (Paul Michael Glaser's) 1974 red Ford Torino in the TV series *Starsky and Hutch*.

Zeiger
Real last name of talk-show host Larry King.

"Zeke from Cabin Creek"
Nickname of NBA Hall of Famer Jerry West while a student at West Virginia University.

Zelle, Margaretha Geertruida
Real name of World War I spy Mata Hari.

Zelnicek
Maiden name of hotelier Ivana Trump.

Zena
Girlfriend of Bazooka Joe in the comics included with Bazooka bubble gum.

Zener cards
See **25**

Zenith
Mythical Midwestern city that is the setting of the Sinclair Lewis novel *Babbitt*, and the hometown of the title character in the Lewis novel *Dodsworth*.

Zenith International Studios
Company that buys the film rights for the first novel of Hubbell Gardner (Robert Redford) in the film *The Way We Were*.

Zenker, Arnold
CBS executive who substituted for Walter Cronkite on the *CBS Evening News* during a 1967 strike of AFTRA (American Federation of Television and Radio Artists).

Zephir
Monkey friend of Babar in the series of children's books by Jean and Laurent de Brunhoff.

zerberts

Cliff Huxtable's (Bill Cosby's) word for the kisses he gives his daughter Rudy (Keshia Knight Pulliam), in the TV sitcom *The Cosby Show*.

Zero

Pet dog of the title character in the comic strip *Little Annie Rooney*.

Liquid computer in the film *Rollerball*.

"Zero Hour"

See **Orphan Ann**

Zetox

Home planet of The Great Gazoo (voiced by Harvey Korman) in the animated TV sitcom *The Flintstones*.

Zeus and Apollo

Doberman pinschers that guard Robin Masters' Hawaii estate in the TV series *Magnum, p.i.*

Ziggy

Supercomputer in the TV series *Quantum Leap*.

Zimmerman

Real last name of singer/songwriter Bob Dylan.

Real last name of singer Ethel Merman.

Zimmer, Norma

See **"The Champagne Lady"**

Zion High German Reformed Church

Building in Allentown, Pennsylvania, where the Liberty Bell was stored during the American Revolution.

Zip

Family dog in the Happy Hollisters series of children's books.

Zip and Zap

Nephews of Disney cartoon chipmunks Chip and Dale.

ZIP codes, consecutive-digit

    12345 Schenectady, New York
    23456 Virginia Beach, Virginia
    45678 Scottown, Ohio

ZIP codes, single-number

    22222 Arlington, Virginia
    44444 Newton Falls, Ohio
    55555 Young America, Minnesota

"The Zipper"

369-foot electronic billboard encircling One Times Square in New York City that has displayed news headlines since 1928.

Zog I

Last king of Albania, who ruled from 1928 to 1939.

Zoll, Dr. Paul M.

Massachusetts cardiologist who invented the pacemaker in 1952.

Zonal Organization World Intelligence Espionage

See **Z.O.W.I.E.**

Zone Improvement Plan

What the "zip" in ZIP code stands for. It was introduced by the U.S. Postal Service in 1963.

Zonko's

Wizard joke shop at Hogsmeade, in the Harry Potter series of books by author J. K. Rowling.

"Zot!"

Sound of a thunderbolt in the comic strip *B.C.*

Z.O.W.I.E.

Acronym for Zonal Organization World Intelligence Espionage, employer of secret agent Derek Flint (James Coburn) in the film *Our Man Flint*.

zucchetto

Skullcap of various colors worn by Roman Catholic clergymen:
    Priests: black
    Bishops: violet
    Cardinals: red
    The Pope: white

Zuck, Alexandra

Real name of actress Sandra Dee.

Zuckerman

Real last name of actor/screenwriter Buck Henry.

Zuckerman trilogy

Group of novels written by Philip Roth:
    The Ghostwriter (1979)
    Zuckerman Unbound (1981)
    The Anatomy Lesson (1983)
Zuckerman Bound (1985) contains all three of the books in the trilogy.

Zyra

Planet orbiting the star that is approaching Earth in the film *When Worlds Collide*, to which a single Earth spaceship brings the surviving group that will start a new society.

ZZ Top members

Frank Beard, Billy Gibbons, and Dusty Hill.

ZZZ

Last entry in the *Random House Webster's Unabridged Dictionary, Second Edition*, defined as "the sound of a person snoring."

Zzzzzip, Zelmo

Last name in the Manhattan telephone directory.

INDEX

Angel Heart Proudfoot, Epiphany

"Angel of the Morning" The Turnabouts

Angelou, Maya "On the Pulse of Morning"

angels angels, hierarchy of; museums, unusual

Angels in the Outfield (1951) Joe

Angels with Dirty Faces Bogart/Cagney films; El Toro Club; Everwrite Fountain Pen Co.; "Rocky Dies Yellow: Killer Coward at End"

Angie "Different Worlds"; Liberty Coffee Shop

Angola Portuguese West Africa

Anheuser-Busch Bavarian Brewery; BUD; business partners

Animal Crackers After the Hunt; Edgar; "Hooray for Captain Spaulding"; Hungerdunger, Hungerdunger, Hungerdunger, Hungerdunger and McCormick; "One morning I shot an elephant in my pajamas. How he got in my pajamas I don't know."

Animal Farm "All animals are equal, but some animals are more equal than others"; Manor Farm

Animal House, National Lampoon's Animal House, National Lampoon's epilogue; *Daily Faberian*; Deathmobile; Delta Tau Chi; Dexter Lake Club; Emily Dickinson College; Faber College; "Knowledge is good"; Mongols; Trooper

animals "animal" adjectives

Animals, The Alan Price Combo

animals in films PATSY Awards

animals, mythical animals, mythical multipart

Animaniacs Buttons

Aniston, Jennifer "milk mustache" celebrities

Anka, Paul Wayne, John, singers in films of

Ankara, Turkey Angora

Ankers, Evelyn "The Queen of the Screamers"

Anna Christie "Garbo talks!"; "Gimme a whiskey, ginger ale on the side. And don't be stingy, baby."

Anna Karenina first lines of famous works

Annan, Kofi Atta United Nations secretaries-general

Anne of Cleaves Henry VIII, six wives of

Anne of the Thousand Days Taylor/Burton films

Anne, Queen 17

Annie New York City Municipal Orphanage

Annie Hall, Anhedonia; *Denial of Death*; Hall, Annie; Michael's Pub; singers in films, unlikely; *The Sorrow and the Pity*

Annie Oakley Diablo; Forest; Pixie; Target

"Annie's Song" waltzes in popular music

"Anniversary Song" *The Danube Waves*

Ann-Margret Dezire, Jezebel; Olsson; Truax, Ariel; Wayne, John, singers in films of

Ann Sothern Show, The Bartley House Hotel

Another Thin Man "Dream Butcher"; *Thin Man* films

Another World Bay City

ant "animal" adjectives

antacids simethicone

Ant, Adam born and died on the same date; Goddard, Stuart Leslie

Antarctic Circle 66 degrees, 32 minutes

anteater "animal" adjectives

antelope "animal" adjectives

Ant Farm Levine, Milton

Anthony Adverse Paleologus, Faith

Anthony, Susan B. Brownell

anthropology the science of culture

antibiotics "Celebrate the Century" subjects

antifreeze propylene glycol

antimony stibium

Anton, Susan "The Bakersfield Flash"

Antony and Cleopatra Shakespeare opening lines

Antz Azteca; Bala, Princess; Weaver; Z-4195

"Any Day Now" "My Wild Beautiful Bird"

Any Given Sunday Miami Sharks; Monroe, Montezuma

Anything but Love Chicago Weekly

Anything Goes S.S. American

"Anything Goes" Club Obi Wan

Any Which Way You Can Beddoe, Philo; Black Widows; Bonnie; Clyde; Eastwood/Locke films

AOL Time Warner Castle Rock Entertainment

Apartment, The Academy Award winning directors, multiple; Consolidated Life of New York; "Lonely Room"

ape "animal" adjectives

Apocalypse Now Heart of Darkness

Apollo 11 "Here men from the planet Earth first set foot upon the moon. July 1969 A.D. We came in peace for all mankind."

Apollo 13 "Ex luna, scientia"; Lost Moon

Apollo, Project Apollo mission module nicknames

Appian Way "The Queen of Roads"

Apple Dumpling Gang, The Quake City, California

Apple, Fiona 90

Appleseed, Johnny Chapman, John

Appling, Luke "Old Aches and Pains"

Appointment in Samarra novels, authors' first

Appointment with Murder The Falcon films

Appomattox Court House, Virginia, McLean, Wilmer

Aquino, Corazon *Time* magazine's Man/Person of the Year

Arabic alphabet 28

Arachnophobia Canaima, California

Arafat, Yasser *Time* magazine's Man/Person of the Year

Aragones, Sergio Reuben Award

Arcaro, Eddie born and died on the same date; George

archery 9; fletching; Robin Hood

Archie comics Forsythe Pendleton; Hot Dog; Pop's Choklit Shoppe; Riverdale

Archies Dante, Ron

architecture Pritzker Prize

Arctic Circle 66 degrees, 32 minutes

Arden, Elizabeth Graham, Florence Nightingale

Arden, Eve "Face the Music with Me"; Minerva

area codes 86; 321; 792; area codes, North American

"Are You Lonesome To-night" Presley, Elvis, #1 tunes of

Argus 100

Ariosto "the immortal four of Italy"

arithmetic 2,520; quadrivium

Arizona "Four Corners" states

Arizona Republic Procrastinator of the Year award

Arkansas, University of The Golden Boot

Arkin, Alan *Pink Panther* films; Wong Airline

Arlen, Harold Arluck, Hyman; died on the same date

Arlington National Cemetery Arlington National Cemetery, famous people buried in

ArliŞŞ "A Man of Our Times"

Arliss, George Disraeli, Benjamin

armadillo "animal" adjectives

diamond "4 C's"; 58; 3,106 carats
Diamond, Neil Melinda and Sue
Diamond Rio Diamond Rio members
Diamonds Are Forever Bambi and Thumper; Case, Tiffany; James Bond films/actors; James Bond film songs/singers; Techtronics
Diana, Princess Emanuel, David and Elizabeth; Rees-Jones, Trevor
diapers, disposable Donovan, Marion
Diary of Anne Frank, The Academy Award winning actors, multiple; Van Daan, Mrs.
Diaz, Cameron Cook, Natalie; Sanders, Dylan; and Munday, Alex; Puffy; Woganowski, Dom
Dibble, Rob "The Nasty Boys"
dice 7; 21; pips
Dick and Jane Puff; Spot
Dickens, Charles 114; Amy; Belle Sauvage Inn; Black Lion Inn; Blue Boar Inn; Boz; Bull's-eye; Cross Keys Inn; Dawkins, John; Diogenes; Dotheboys Hall; *Eatanswill Gazette* and *Eatanswill Independent*; first lines of famous works; Gad's Hill Place; George and Vulture Inn; Grip; Harmon, John; "It is a far, far better thing that I do, than I have ever done; it is a far, far better rest that I go to than I have ever known."; Jip; John Huffam; Lady Jane; Magpie and Stump; *Mag's Diversions*; novels, authors' first; *The Parish Boy's Progress*; Pirrip Jr., Phillip; Salem House; Spenlow and Jorkins; St. Evrémonde; Thérèse; Westminster Abbey, famous people buried at
Dick, Philip K. *Do Androids Dream of Electric Sheep?*; Kindred; novels, authors' first; "We Can Remember It for You Wholesale"
Dick Powell's Zane Grey Theater 26
Dick Tracy Reuben Award
Dick Tracy **(film)** Academy Award songs; Caprice, Big Boy; Mahoney, Breathless
Dick Van Dyke Show, The The Alan Brady Show; Camp Crowder; Fiona; *Head of the Family*; Henderson, Mr.; Larry; Maurice; "Pitter Patter Petrie"; Rosebud; "The Sick Boy and the Sitter"; sitcom settings, real-life; *Town of Passion*
Dickey, James Cahulawassee River
Dickinson, Angie Brown, Angeline
Dickinson, Emily 7
dictionary, unabridged ZZZ
Diddley, Bo Bates, Otha Ellas
Didrikson, Babe Mildred Ella
Die Hard $640,000,000; KFLW; Nakatomi Plaza; *Nothing Lasts Forever*
Die Hard 2 58 Minutes; Highland Lake Community Church
Die Hard with a Vengeance Chester A. Arthur Elementary School
Diem, Ngo Dinh ticker-tape parade honorees
Dietrich, Marlene *Around the World in 80 Days* cameo roles; "Hot Voodoo"; *Sgt. Pepper's Lonely Hearts Club Band* cover subjects; "Vogue," celebrities in; "What becomes a Legend most?" celebrities
Diff'rent Strokes 45 Minutes from Harlem; "Movin' In"; sitcom settings, real-life; Space Sucker
Dilbert Catbert; Reuben Award
Diller, Phyllis Driver; *Hello, Dolly!* title-role portrayers; The Purple Onion

Dillinger, John Baron Lamm method; *Manhattan Melodrama*
Dillon, Matt *In & Out* Academy Award nominees
DiMaggio, Dom "The Little Professor"
DiMaggio, Joe Bagby Jr., Jim and Smith, Al; died on the same date; magazines' first issues; "Vogue," celebrities in; "The Yankee Clipper"
dime 118; Sinnock, John R.
Diner directors' first feature films; Fells Point Diner
Diners Club McNamara, Frank and Schneider, Ralph
diner slang, numerical
Dinesen, Isak Lulu
Ding Dong School Horwich, Dr. Frances; "I'm Your School Bell"
Dinosaurs 60,000,003 B.C.
Dion The Del Satins; DiMucci; *Sgt. Pepper's Lonely Hearts Club Band* cover subjects
director pseudonyms Smithee, Alan (or Allen)
directors directors' first feature films; directors' last feature films
Dire Straits Dire Straits original members
Dirty Dancing Academy Award songs; Kellerman's Mountain House
Dirty Dozen, The *The Magnificent Seven* title characters
Dirty Harry 2211; "Scorpio"
Discover magazines' first issues
Discover card Webb, J. L.
discus 1 kilogram; 2 kilograms
Disney cartoons Hee, T.
Disney comic books Gearloose, Gyro
Disney Corporation cast members
Disneyland Disneyland, original areas of; Fritz, Michael, Pierre, and José
Disney, Walt 64; Elias; Harvard University, notable honorary degree recipients; Laugh-O-gram Films
Disraeli Disraeli, Benjamin
distress signal CQD
Divine Lady, The Academy Award winning directors, multiple
diving 3 meters; 10 meters
Divorcée, The Jerry
Dixie composer biopics (popular)
"Dixie" Emmett, Daniel Decatur
Dixie Chicks Dixie Chicks original members
Dixie Cup Luellen, Lawrence; "World's Largest" roadside attractions
Djibouti French Somaliland
Dmytryk, Edward "The Hollywood Ten"
Dobie Gillis, The Many Loves of Benevolent Order of the Bison; Central City; Charlie Wong's Ice Cream Parlor; Endicott Building; Gillis, Davey; The Good Conduct Medal; *The Monster That Devoured Cleveland*; "Poopsie"; S. Peter Pryor Junior College; Walter; "You rang?"
Doc Bogert, Joe
Doc Hollywood Grady, South Carolina
Doctor Dolittle Chee-Chee; Dab-Dab; Gub-Gub; Jip; Polynesia; Puddleby-on-the-Marsh; Too-Too
Doctor Dolittle **(film)** Academy Award songs
Doctor Dolittle, The Story of Pushmi-Pullyu; Spidermonkey Island
Doctor Faustus 24 years
Doctor Faustus **(film)** Taylor/Burton films